PROFESSIONAL LEGA

PROFESSIONAL LEGAL ETHICS

Critical Interrogations

DONALD NICOLSON

and

JULIAN WEBB

OXFORD

UNIVERSITY PRESS

OXFORD

UNIVERSITY PRESS

Great Clarendon Street, Oxford OX2 6DP

Oxford University Press is a department of the University of Oxford.
It furthers the University's objective of excellence in research, scholarship,
and education by publishing worldwide in

Oxford New York

Athens Auckland Bangkok Bogotá Buenos Aires Calcutta
Cape Town Chennai Dar es Salaam Delhi Florence Hong Kong Istanbul
Karachi Kuala Lumpur Madrid Melbourne Mexico City Mumbai
Nairobi Paris São Paulo Singapore Taipei Tokyo Toronto Warsaw

with associated companies in Berlin Ibadan

Oxford is a registered trade mark of Oxford University Press
in the UK and in certain other countries

Published in the United States
by Oxford University Press Inc., New York

British Library Cataloguing in Publication Data

Data available

Library of Congress Cataloging in Publication Data
Nicolson, Donald.
Professional legal ethics : critical interrogations / Donald Nicolson and Julian Webb.
p. cm.
Includes bibliographical references and index.
1. Legal ethics—Great Britain. 2. Legal ethics. I. Webb, Julian S. II. Title.
KD479.N53 1999
174′.3′0941—dc21
99-048741
ISBN 0-19-876471-5

1 3 5 7 9 10 8 6 4 2

Typeset in Garamond
by Best-Set Typesetters Ltd., Hong Kong
Printed in Great Britain
on acid-free paper by
Biddles Ltd., Guildford and King's Lynn

Dedication

To Pat and Colin Nicolson, and the memory of Sidney Webb.

Preface

When we told people that we were writing a book on professional legal ethics, one of two reactions were commonplace, either: 'that should be a short book' or even more predictably: 'isn't that an oxymoron?' Both reactions in their own way explain exactly why we felt it was important to write this book, and neither prediction has turned out to be true.

While we have not retracted from a position which is ultimately critical of current professional norms and institutions in England and Wales, we found that the arguments for the current norms and values, although often little developed or articulated in the Anglo-Welsh context, were not easily dismissed. Consequently, the book grew beyond its projected length, even though we have deliberately selected only what we consider to be the main philosophical debates within professional legal ethics. Here we found that it was not true to say that the legal professional is solely concerned with upholding its self-interest and totally unconcerned about the ethics of lawyer behaviour. It is true that the dominant conception of the lawyer's role is one which resembles the 'hired gun' of popular perception, but, as we found, there are *prima facie* persuasive justifications for this role and in many cases much value in the idea that clients can depend on zealous partisans prepared to go to the wall to protect their interests. Nor is such a role, as presently constructed, totally devoid of ethical limits. At the same time, however, we argue that these justifications and ethical limits, and professional legal ethics as a whole are so based on a formalistic approach to ethics and the values of liberalism that they act to anaesthetize the moral conscience of lawyers. Thus institutionally, and perhaps even personally, they are likely to be predisposed to disregard any harm caused by legal representation to opponents, the general public, the environment, and even their clients. In this way, the profession as a whole is prevented from fulfilling whatever potential it might have as an instrument of justice and protector of those in need in society.

We have sought to state the law and practice as at 31 May 1999. Unfortunately this meant that we have been unable to take account of Andy Boon and Jenny Levin's book, *The Ethics and Conduct of Lawyers in England and Wales*, and the 1999 edition of the *Law Society's Guide to the Professional Conduct of Solicitors*, which were published, respectively just before and after we had submitted our final manuscript. Given that our primary concern has been with the philosophy and principle underlying codified professional ethics, as far as we can ascertain, neither work requires changes to our core arguments.

We have, of course, accumulated a number of debts in the process of writing this book, most particularly to Aileen McHarg, without whose valuable and constructive criticism it would have been much the poorer. We would also like to thank Alan Paterson who, as Convenor of the Practice, Professions and Ethics section of SPTL gave us a forum to test some of our ideas and shared with us his own insights into lawyers' ethics, to Leslie Sheinman for his comments on a number of chapters, to Rachel Nee who cheerfully went beyond the call of duty in providing secretarial assistance and to Amir Ghaffari, Alisdair Murray, Olivia van der Werff, and Juliet Williams for research assistance. In addition, Donald Nicolson would like to thank his Law Department for granting him a year's sabbatical to write this book.

Finally, while writing responsibility for Chapters 4 and 10 were jointly shared, Chapters 1–2 and 6–9 were written by Donald Nicolson and Chapters 3 and 5 by Julian Webb. All the ideas in this book were, however, very much the product of a joint enterprise and healthy debate.

DONALD NICOLSON
JULIAN WEBB

Contents

1

Introduction

> [T]he practice of law, in its nature the noblest and most beneficial to mankind, is in its abuse an abasement of the most sordid kind.
>
> Lord Bolingbroke[1]

> Ethics? I thought that was a county North of London.
>
> Senior City Solicitor[2]

1. LAWYERS AND JUSTICE

The prevailing rhetoric of law, albeit not necessarily the practice, has always been one of justice. There is never an appeal to law without an (at least legitimatory) appeal to justice.[3] As key actors in the legal system, lawyers are particularly well placed to promote justice and hence serve society. To a considerable extent the quality of law and the legal process is in their hands, not only and most obviously lawyers elevated to the bench, but also the thousands of independent practitioners, and those employed by businesses, state institutions, and advice organisations. How they behave is crucial for the way the law develops, for the experience of those who come into contact with the legal process and for the ability of law to uphold its claim to be an instrument of justice. Indeed, while many enter the legal profession as a means to social status and wealth, if university application forms are to be believed, at least some lawyers embark on their legal careers with the aim of upholding justice and helping the needy. Similarly, the image of lawyers as fearless protectors of the weak and upholders of equality is one which can be found in the profession's own legitimatory rhetoric.[4]

Yet despite legal and professional rhetoric, and the commendable aspirations of some legal neophytes, British lawyers have, since at least Shakespearean times, attracted the sort of vitriol normally reserved for society's worst deviants,[5] as the constant proliferation of anti-lawyer jokes testifies.[6] As we shall see throughout this book, lawyers frequently act in immoral and unjust ways with significant harmful consequences for clients, their opponents, the general public, the environment and even

---

[1] Quoted by Hutchinson 1998, p.169. [2] Comment made at symposium on ethics in 1998.
[3] See Douzinas and Warrington 1994, esp ch.4. [4] See Ch.7, section 2.1.
[5] See Dick the Butcher in *Henry VI, Part II*, Act IV Scene ii: 'The first thing we do, let's kill all the lawyers'. See also eg the scorn heaped on lawyers by Dickens (*Bleak House*, as well as the character of Jaggers in *Great Expectations*) and Trollope (*The Three Clerks, Phineas Redux*); Pannick 1992, pp.128–9.
[6] Mostly from America: see eg http://www.wwlia.org/jokes.htm; http://www.scroom.com/humour/ /lawyer.html, but see also White and Jenks 1991.

for the moral integrity of lawyers themselves. Moreover, most of the bright-eyed crusaders for justice who enter the profession are likely to end up as cynical[7] legal technicians concerned only with making money and solving what they consider to be technical legal problems using technical skills.

The argument of this book is that an important reason for this gap between the rhetorical justifications for law and the legal profession, on the one hand, and the reality of legal practice, on the other, lies in the current state of the profession's ethics. Certainly, there are—as we shall see[8]—significant institutional and ideological pressures preventing lawyers from upholding the rhetoric surrounding law and legal professionalism. Nevertheless, we shall argue that lawyers' ethics are so dominated by the influences of formalism and liberalism that they are discouraged from developing and displaying the type of ethical character and values which would enable them to uphold the rhetoric of justice and hence their claim to be an ethical profession.

By formalism, we mean an approach to social knowledge and action which emerged from the Enlightenment's emphasis on logical rationality and scientific methodology. It seeks to reduce social behaviour to the mechanical application of categorical rules, without consideration of context, consequence, or the substantive merits of the behaviour in question. There are, for example, formalistic approaches to knowledge, adjudication, and, most importantly for our purposes, ethics. Whilst having similar Enlightenment origins, liberalism is more narrowly an approach to social ordering which argues, essentially, that human flourishing is best achieved by allowing individuals maximum freedom to pursue their goals, restricted only by minimal rules of the game designed to prevent (illegitimate) harm to others and supported only by a minimal state responsible for upholding these rules.

The idea that liberalism and formalism combine to ensure that law imposes and legitimates a socio-economic status which favours some at the expense of others is by no means new. This can be seen from Critical Legal Studies scholars' explicit criticism of what they call liberal legalism,[9] and more implicitly in other critical theories, such as marxism, feminism, and postmodernism. However, in Britain at least, this critique has yet to be extended to the behaviour of legal practitioners, notwithstanding their centrality to law's operation and development. Although earlier eras have seen widespread public criticism of lawyers,[10] legal academics have, ironically, been much more concerned with the ethics of other professions, in particular the medical profession, than their own.

For some this lack of academic interest can be attributed to the lack of a 'defining cultural moment' such as the Watergate scandal which prompted an extensive and continuing examination of American lawyers' ethical standards or the Nuremberg tribunals which had a similar effect as regards medical ethics.[11] Also relevant is the

[7] See Stivers 1994 for the argument that cynicism is more generally becoming a dominant response to the existing social order.
[8] Ch.3.   [9] Also sometimes called legal liberalism: see further Ch.7, section 3.2.2.
[10] See Mellinkoff 1973.   [11] Morgan 1995, p.208.

traditional distinction between 'academic' and 'vocational' issues in legal education,[12] which has led academic lawyers to concentrate on law's content and ignore the apparently less intellectually challenging issues relating to legal practice. However, far more important, in our view, has been the dominance of legal formalism and the black-letter approach to the study and teaching of law which has ensured that questions of the morality and justice of law, and the ethics of its practitioners, have largely been banished from the legal academy.[13] Although an interest in issues of legal justice was rediscovered in the late 1960s, influenced *inter alia* by student radicalism and the feminist movement, and while it did lead to some evidence of lawyer behaviour being uncovered, it was more concerned with law as a system, law's social context and the gap between law in the books and law in action than with the way in which individual practitioners resolve ethical dilemmas.[14]

Thus until a decade ago discussion of professional legal ethics in the United Kingdom was confined to a few guides to professional legal ethics and what was quaintly but revealingly called professional etiquette written by professional insiders,[15] as well as brief expositions of prevailing ethical norms in 'how to' books on legal practice.[16] Perhaps motivated by the belief that strict control of entry to the profession ensured that all lawyers were made of the 'right stuff' and hence could be counted on to act honourably and with probity—in other words, as gentlemen— little need was seen for discussion of or instruction in ethics.[17]

By contrast, the 1990s, and particularly its latter half, has seen the sudden growth of interest in lawyers' ethics, evidenced by academic articles,[18] collections of essays,[19] a textbook,[20] a special edition of a journal,[21] and the launch of another dedicated to the subject.[22] Moreover, a handful of universities have responded to the Lord Chancellor's Advisory Committee's call for a greater focus on ethics throughout legal education[23] by establishing undergraduate ethics courses. For some,[24] the interest in professional legal ethics has emerged from the growing academic interest in legal skills and clinical legal education. For others,[25] the interest stems more from the widespread 'ethical turn' which characterises postmodernist approaches to social critique[26] and has come to influence legal theory more broadly. Events such as the end

---

[12] Sheinman 1997, p.140. [13] See further Ch.3, section 6.

[14] See eg Baldwin and McConville 1977; Genn 1987; Davis 1994; McConville *et al* 1994; Neale and Smart 1997. But cf Boon 1995; McConville 1998, which address ethical issues more directly.

[15] Lund 1960; Boulton 1975.

[16] See eg Hilbery 1959; Napley 1991, ch.2; du Cann 1993, ch.2; Sherr 1993, *passim*.

[17] See eg Thornton 1995, pp.55–6 (regarding the Bar) and for examples of this discourse, see Ch.6, section 2.1.

[18] Including Tur 1992a; 1992b; and 1994; O'Dair 1997; Jackson 1997; Blake and Ashworth 1998; Ipp 1998; McConville 1998; Nicolson and Webb 1999.

[19] Cranston (ed.) 1995; Parker and Sampford (eds.) 1995; Economides (ed.) 1998. However, while published in this country the latter two collections draw heavily on international contributions.

[20] Boon and Levin 1999.

[21] Vol. 4, nos. 1/2 of *International Journal of the Legal Profession* (1997).

[22] *Legal Ethics*, launched in 1998. [23] ACLEC 1996, paras. 1.19–1.20.

[24] See eg Maughan and Webb 1995, ch.4; Webb 1996; Boon 1996; Brayne *et al* 1998.

[25] See Nicolson 1994 and 1997. [26] See Ch.2, section 7.1.

of the Cold War have brought about a realisation that there are no large-scale or certain answers to world problems. The feminist slogan 'the personal is political' has come to characterise theory in general and manifests itself in the growing interest in issues like medical ethics, animal rights and, by the same token, professional legal ethics. Indeed, it would seem that a concern with ethics is 'a defining stigmata of the closing decades of the century',[27] reflected in the recent concern with standards in public life, which has been generated by political scandals, the impropriety of financial institutions, recently revealed miscarriages of justice, and by widespread fears over environmental and food safety issues. Nevertheless, whatever the exact causes for the recent interest in professional legal ethics, it is clear that the profession will no longer be able to escape the critical gaze of the academic community.

2. DEFINING PROFESSIONAL LEGAL ETHICS

Thus far we have spoken as if the phrase 'professional legal ethics' has one meaning, whereas in fact it has at least two. This flows from an ambiguity in the term 'ethics' itself.[28] In one sense, it is used to denote the branch of philosophical study concerned with morality, moral problems, and moral judgements, including issues of justice. Alternatively, it can refer descriptively to the norms held by individuals, groups, or institutions in responding to moral issues. In both uses we see a more or less circular reference to the notion of morality. Thus one might define ethics as involving (the study of) norms relating to how one should behave, or, in terms of the broader Greek tradition, how one should live,[29] from a moral, rather than pragmatic or aesthetic perspective. Certainly, many writers attempt to distinguish the terms 'ethics' and 'morality' and their derivatives 'ethical' and 'moral' in terms of etymology,[30] application[31] or even authenticity.[32] However, their conclusions are so contradictory that we feel justified in using the terms interchangeably. We will, however, speak of 'professional legal ethics'[33] rather than 'professional legal morality' given that it

---

[27] Morgan 1995, p.204. [28] See Singer 1991, p.v; Bauman 1995, pp.10–11.

[29] See Ch.2, esp section 5.

[30] Thus 'ethics' is said to derive from the Greek *ethike*, used to denote the science of character (Hutchinson 1998, p.119) or possibly also *ethos* meaning the pondering of the 'abode of man' (Douzinas and Warrington 1994, p.86, quoting Heidigger), whereas 'morality' stems from the Latin *mores* which suggests the prevailing norms in particular communities: Williams 1985, p.6.

[31] Thus flowing from the etymology it is sometimes said that the former applies to the norms of individuals and the latter to commonly held norms; whereas others argue for the opposite association: eg Hazard 1978, p.1; Koniak 1996.

[32] Thus some ethicists see 'morality' as a bastardisation of 'real ethics' (eg Williams 1985, esp p.6 and ch.10) while others (eg Bauman 1993, 1995) argue that 'ethics' is a bastardisation of 'real morality', both referring to the impact of Enlightenment theory on individuals' moral/ethical character or conscience— see further Ch.2, esp sections 5 and 7.

[33] We have used this term rather than the wider 'legal ethics' because the latter suggests the study of all questions of morality and justice in relation to law, the legal system and its actors rather than merely discussion of the ethical issues facing practising lawyers. Nevertheless, it must be noted that 'legal ethics'

denotes both lawyers' ethics as a topic or study and their formally or informally adopted norms.[34]

As a topic of philosophical study, professional legal ethics falls under the sub-category of 'applied' or 'practical ethics'. Instead of examining, justifying, and criticising the content, source and status of general ethical norms as an abstract exercise, applied ethics looks at how such norms may be applied to, require modification in, or even be irrelevant or harmful to practical, real-life moral issues such as abortion, nuclear weapons, animal welfare, and so on. In the cases of professionals like lawyers, such dilemmas can involve decisions which face individual practitioners, such as whether they should override instructions in order to uphold clients' best interests, whether they should pursue immoral client goals or use immoral tactics to achieve client ends, or whether they should breach client confidentiality in order to prevent great harm to others or the environment. Issues such as these are usually termed 'micro-ethical' issues. Equally important, however, are a number of 'macro-ethical' issues[35] which confront lawyers as a collectivity, such as whether and how best to lay down formal rules of ethical behaviour, how to ensure effective and equal access to legal services, the accountability of the profession to the public it serves, and so on.

3. AIMS, METHODS, AND ARGUMENTS

In looking at both macro- and micro-issues of professional legal ethics, our main aim will be one of critique and reconstruction. Obviously, however, these normative tasks require first a description of extant professional legal ethics norms. There are two possible ways of performing this task. The first, which particularly applies to micro-ethical issues, is to observe lawyers in action or to interview them about how they have resolved actual ethical dilemmas in the past or would resolve hypothetical dilemmas. This empirical approach is extremely important both because actual lawyer behaviour is unlikely to match formal ethical norms exactly and because there will always be ethical issues not covered by such norms.

Unfortunately, however, there is currently very little hard evidence as to the actual behavioural norms of British lawyers. As we have already seen,[36] a number of empirical studies have unearthed important information as to lawyer behaviour. However,

---

and 'professional legal ethics' do not occupy hermetically sealed spheres. As we shall see throughout this book, questions of how lawyers should and do resolve ethical dilemmas they face in practice are crucially affected by questions of the ethics of law, the legal system, and access to justice, and the answers to be found in law, jurisprudential theory, and general academic discourse.

[34] cf Sheinman 1997, p.142, who confines 'professional ethics' to guides to behaviour which are not externally imposed on lawyers but 'arise out of its own efforts'.

[35] Our use of these terms follows Edel 1986, pp.322–3; O'Dair 1997, p.312. cf Morgan 1995, p.212, making the finer distinction between macro-ethical issues as involving relationships between groups, and individuals and groups, and 'meso'-ethical issues as involving 'bureaucratic, administrative and other management decision making tasks, particularly with allocations of resource'.

[36] At n.14.

they have dealt only with isolated areas of practice and only with ethical issues indirectly. Consequently, they provide an inadequate basis for reaching general conclusions about lawyer norms. Although we might have sought to fill this gap, in our view, wide-ranging empirical research will be far more effective if it is preceded by the sort of conceptual critique engaged in throughout this book. Such critique may help in the choice of areas to be investigated and the shaping of the investigative goals.[37] Consequently, while we will refer to existing empirical evidence where relevant, in evaluating the current state of professional legal ethics, we will largely base our critique on norms the inclusion of which we have inferred from a combination of written sources and social influences. Albeit somewhat speculative, our approach may at least encourage others to provide detailed evidence refuting our conclusions.

The first and more formal source we will draw on is the wide variety of written discourses on professional legal ethics, which are likely to influence lawyer behaviour. Given their role as the basis of professional discipline and education, the most important of these are the Law Society's *Guide to the Professional Conduct of Solicitors*[38] (henceforth the LSG) and the Bar's *Code of Conduct of the Bar of England and Wales*[39] (henceforth the CCB). While not law themselves,[40] these 'codes'[41] are based on and restate various statutes and regulations, common law principles on tort, contract, agency, fiduciary and adjectival law, and decisions of the courts acting in their supervisory capacity over the profession, as well as the norms promulgated by the professions themselves in the exercise of their regulatory powers. Other written discourses likely to influence lawyers, albeit lacking the same formal status, include isolated judicial *obiter dicta* on issues of professional ethics, pedagogical manuals on professional conduct,[42] 'how to' guides to legal practice,[43] and the rare discussions of ethics in professional journals like the *Law Society's Gazette*, *New Law Journal*, or *Counsel*.

The second main influence on lawyers' norms are those ethical values which they learn throughout their personal and professional lives and which either reinforce or conflict with written discourse on professional legal ethics. All lawyers are exposed to general ethical theories which are at play in society, as well as prevailing ideologies about politics, economics, gender, race, etc.—the dominant versions of which

[37] Indeed, on the basis of our study we would suggest that empirical studies could look at the extent to which lawyers refuse to pursue immoral ends or use immoral means (cf Chs.6–8) and the extent to which confidentiality rules do in fact discourage the revealing of client secrets (cf Ch.9, esp section 4.2).

[38] London, The Law Society, 7th edn., 1996.

[39] London, The Bar Council, 1990, as amended.

[40] Para 1.03, LSG. There is no equivalent statement in the CCB, though its status is essentially the same. See further Cranston 1995, pp.3–4.

[41] Unlike the CCB, the LSG does not constitute a code in the strict sense of the word, but is rather a collection of the rules emanating from the sources discussed above. On the other hand, given that these norms are collected in one document and are likely to be seen by solicitors as authoritative, they will tend to operate very much like a code and thus can be loosely described as such (but cf Sheinman 1997, p.143).

[42] See Inns of Court School of Law 1997; Silverman 1997.   [43] See at n.16.

are by and large compatible with liberalism. On entry to law school, prospective lawyers are exposed to the values contained within law's content as well as to various assumptions about the lawyer's proper role. Again, these draw heavily on both liberalism and formalism. Finally, all of the above influences are continually built upon through the processes of socialisation flowing from the customs and etiquette of lawyering, various institutional and social pressures and the more formal messages emanating from the codes and the way in which they are enforced.

Consequently, Chapters 3 to 5 outline the philosophical, sociological, and regulatory contexts to professional legal ethics which influence the way that lawyers are likely to apply the various written norms governing the micro-ethical dilemmas discussed later. However, these chapters are not purely descriptive. It also examines a number of macro-ethical issues arising from the sociological and regulatory contexts. In particular, it asks whether these contexts could be reformed to better ensure the development and maintenance of high ethical standards, both for lawyers as a collectivity and in addressing micro-ethical dilemmas. In so doing, we will draw upon a range of influences from philosophy, sociology and social theory, public law theories of regulation, and developmental psychology.

However, whereas the literature relevant to Chapters 3 to 5 is either largely generic to Common Law jurisdictions or has been relatively well-developed in the British context, the academic neglect of professional legal ethics means that there is little by way of a home-grown literature to draw upon in discussing issues of micro-ethics. Consequently, in Chapters 5 to 9 we have relied rather heavily on the literature of other jurisdictions, most notably the United States, where ethical debates have raged for far longer and in more detail than elsewhere. However, as Luban—one of the main contributors to this debate—has pointed out, such borrowing needs to be undertaken with caution.[44] While there is no doubt that ethical issues in this country are very similar to those in the United States and other common law jurisdictions, it is clearly also possible that the answers supplied there reflect local conditions.[45] We have not, therefore, adopted a truly comparative approach and made detailed comparisons with the formally adopted norms of other jurisdictions. Moreover, even analysing the codes in jurisdictions with similar institutional backgrounds would consume far too much space and time for what is needed at this early stage of the professional legal ethics debate. For similar pragmatic reasons, we have confined our attention to the ethics of lawyers who practise in England and Wales, rather than also including those in Scotland and Northern Ireland.[46]

Space constraints have also dissuaded us from attempting to deal with every macro- and micro-issue of professional legal ethics in England and Wales. This would only have produced a 'Cook's Tour' involving superficial discussion and polemic rather than the detailed critique required by the fact that the justifications for the

---

[44] Luban 1996, p.3.
[45] Such as the existence of a constitutional right to legal representation: see Ch.7, n.99.
[46] For discussions of Scottish professional legal ethics, see eg Phillips 1990; Paterson 1997.

current rules and the underlying conception of the lawyer's proper role are *prima facie* plausible. Consequently, we have chosen to concentrate on four important micro-ethical issues: the meaning and extent of autonomy in the lawyer–client relationship, the pursuit of immoral client ends, the use of immoral means to client ends, and client confidentiality.

No doubt many—most notably, practitioners themselves—would not necessarily regard these as the most important ethical dilemmas. Certainly on a day to day basis lawyers are more worried about conflicts of interest and client accounts, as well as a whole host of other more prosaic concerns,[47] while client complaints relate primarily to matters of diligence such as tardiness or negligence and the charging of excessive fees.[48] These issues are clearly important and often technically problematic for practitioners. However, the problem here is not the existence of the relevant duties—clearly lawyers should be honest, diligent and avoid conflicts of interests.[49] Instead, the difficulties relate to how best to ensure that they uphold these duties. By contrast, the four issues we shall deal with involve duties which are highly contested both in relation to their justification and limits. Moreover, each in their own way goes to the core of the lawyer's *raison d'être*—the effective representation of client interests. Finally and most importantly, the current resolution of each of these four issues provides the best illustrations of what we regard as the main problem with professional legal ethics. This is the extent to which it is influenced by formalism and liberalism and the impact this has in anaesthetising lawyers' moral consciences and allowing, if not encouraging, lawyers to cause harm to clients, third parties, the general public, and the environment.[50]

In developing this critique, we will draw upon a wide variety of critical ethical theories (communitarian, feminist, and postmodernist) and jurisprudential theories (marxist, feminist, and postmodernist). And in moving from critique to reform, we will adopt what we shall describe as a contextual approach.[51] Our approach is contextual in three ways. First, as we have already argued, professional legal ethics needs to be understood in its philosophical, sociological, and regulatory contexts. Secondly, we shall argue that formalism and liberalism largely ignore the real-life situations in which lawyers and other ethical agents operate. In this way, they mask and reinforce the power relations at play both in one-to-one relationships and in society at large. Thirdly, flowing from this, we shall develop an approach to professional legal ethics which requires consideration of the various contexts central to legal work and the

[47] See Crawley and Brammall 1995, pp.107–9; Austen *et al* 1998, pp.17–19.

[48] Lewis 1996; Christensen *et al* 1999, p.49.

[49] The exclusion of conflicts of interest as a discrete topic can also be justified on the conceptual ground that they are only problematic because they lead to an undermining of the primary duties of loyalty, diligence, and confidentiality, which are owed to clients.

[50] We have deliberately referred to both the interests of the general public *and* the environment because of our belief that the two do not overlap—animals in particular have interests of their own which extend beyond their use to humans.

[51] For slightly different but less developed contextual approaches, see Wilkins 1990, pp.515ff; Hutchinson 1998; Simon 1998.

various factors relevant in different contexts. In line with our general approach to ethics, this is aimed not so much at providing lawyers with clear-cut solutions to ethical dilemmas but at encouraging them to confront the ethical dimension to legal practice.

Indeed, while we will offer a wide variety of suggestions for reform to current professional legal ethics, the main aim of the book is as much to raise awareness of the importance of this nascent topic as it is to encourage specific changes. By raising awareness, we hope to help engender higher ethical standards on the part of lawyers. Influenced by postmodernist approaches to ethics,[52] we do not think that there is one correct version of 'high ethical standards'. Moreover, influenced by the much earlier tradition of virtue ethics, we think that of equal importance to the content of formal ethical norms is the question of lawyers' character and in particular their commitment to take moral responsibility for their actions *inter alia* by deciding for themselves how they should respond to ethical issues. Consequently, as the first step in achieving our aim, we wish to initiate debate about the rules and roles currently adopted in written discourses on professional legal ethics in the hope that these will be critically evaluated by lawyers throughout their legal careers, from law school to retirement. As Tur has persuasively argued, the life of law is 'necessarily, an adventure in applied ethics'.[53] By making lawyers more conscious of this fact and by exposing to critical interrogation current norms, we hope to lay the foundations for transcending the ironic but nonetheless cynical approach to ethics exemplified by the London solicitor quoted at the beginning of this chapter. Equally, we hope to help realise the possibility held out by Lord Bolingbroke that the practice of law can be both noble and beneficial to society.[54]

---

[52] See Ch.2, section 7.   [53] Tur 1992b, p.223; and 1994, p.83.
[54] cf also Sampford 1998, p.50.

2

The Philosophical Context: Theoretical Approaches to the Content and Status of Ethics

> It is not a trivial question, Socrates said: what we are talking about is how one should live . . . The aims of moral philosophy . . . are bound up with the fate of Socrates' question, even if it is not true that philosophy, itself, can reasonably hope to answer it.
>
> Bernard Williams[1]

1. INTRODUCTION

All action, whether of a personal or institutional nature, takes place against a background of explicitly or implicitly held ideas. When lawyers lay down their professional norms and when they resolve moral dilemmas not governed by these norms, they do so in terms of ethical ideas that are generally at large in society. These ideas can, in turn, be traced back to various secular and religious thinkers who for centuries have sought to influence morality by reflective thought and argumentation. Although most people do not experience their ethical values in terms of the sort of well thought-out theories proposed by philosophers, nevertheless theoretical ideas usually filter through to ordinary citizens indirectly through a complex process of social dissemination involving the family, schools, universities, the media, etc., in terms of which those who have direct contact with ethical theory may influence the values of the general population.[2]

As we shall see,[3] the nature of legal education means that lawyers are largely in the same position as ordinary citizens as regards their exposure to explicit ethical theorising. However, they also have a more specific, albeit still indirect, exposure to ethical ideas through the values and approaches to ethics contained in substantive legal doctrines and their professional norms, both of which are laid down by institutional actors under the direct or indirect influence of prevailing ethical theories. These values and approaches, as we noted in the last chapter and shall see throughout this book, are most influenced by liberalism and formalism, but also draw upon other theoretical approaches such as that of utilitarianism.

Consequently, we have two main aims in this chapter. The first is to provide an understanding of the philosophical ideas to which lawyers may directly or indirectly be exposed. The second is to examine the theoretical alternatives to these ideas as a basis for criticising and rethinking the current state of professional legal ethics. Ful-

---

[1] Williams 1985, p.1.   [2] See eg Fox and DeMarco 1986.   [3] Ch.3, section 6.

filling these aims may, however, perform a number of subsidiary functions. First, we will gain a useful language to discuss the ethical issues raised throughout this book. Second, it may improve debate over professional legal ethics in that theoretical discussion of ethics is said to bring 'clarity, critical analysis and ingrained habits of careful evaluation of argument'.[4] Finally, by exposing prospective and qualified practitioners, and even academics, to the wide range of ethical debates and approaches, we hope to ignite an interest in ethics that will be carried through into their professional and even personal lives. It is not naively assumed that exposure to ethical theory will necessarily make one more moral. Nevertheless, such exposure might light the spark that leads particular individuals to re-examine their lives and actions. Even those with an existing interest in philosophical ethics may be inspired, as indeed we have been, by the less familiar ethical ideas contained in this chapter.

2. THE SCOPE OF PHILOSOPHICAL ETHICS

The ethical theories we will discuss involve the philosophical questions of what ethical values people *ought* to have and why, rather than the empirical question of what values they actually possess. This is not totally to deny the relevance of what may be called ethical sociology or anthropology. The fact that people do not, will not or cannot[5] adopt a particular approach to ethics provides progressively more persuasive reasons for rejecting that approach. On the other hand, as the dominance of anti-semitism in Nazi Germany illustrates, the mere fact that particular views are widely held clearly does not establish their normative claim. Consequently, our focus will be primarily on the persuasiveness of the various approaches to morality considered from a philosophical perspective.

Apart from applied ethics, the philosophical study of ethics covers two main topics. 'Normative' or 'substantive' ethics involves the 'first-order' inquiry as to the content of ethical theories. It addresses the question of how, in general, we should behave or, put more grandly by Socrates, how we should live.[6] In surveying the answers provided by the major competing moral theories, we shall not look at the specific norms they offer. For one thing, many, such as 'do not kill' or 'be charitable', are less relevant to professional legal ethics. Moreover, at this level of generality, most Western philosophers tend to develop similar lists of norms despite the different ethical traditions.[7] This is because the content of ethical theories does not stray too far from ethics as practised in society and most Westerners have been socialised into adopting relatively similar ethical norms. Consequently, instead of listing the specific norms found in Western[8] ethical philosophy, we will concentrate

---

[4] Almond 1995, p.2.   [5] cf Flanagan 1991, esp ch.2.

[6] Plato's *Republic* 352D, cited in Williams 1985, p.1.

[7] cf MacIntyre 1985, ch.4 regarding Kant, Hume, and Kierkegaard.

[8] We have not ignored non-Western traditions because we regard them as inferior, but because they have had little impact on ethical practice in the UK. In any case, many of the concerns and approaches of Eastern ethics mirror those in the West: see Singer 1991, Part II *passim*.

on five ethical *traditions* or *approaches*, which differ in the way that they prioritise
and resolve conflicts between the norms which they largely share. Of these deontology, consequentialism and virtue ethics are often described as the classical ethical
traditions, while the ethics of care—associated with feminism—and the ethics of
alterity—associated with postmodernism—represent two more recent developments.
We have chosen these approaches because they have either had an important influence over current professional legal ethics or because they provide the most significant alternatives for rethinking the current position. We have concentrated on secular
ethical traditions because the above ethical theories already bear the trace of Judaeo-
Christian ethics[9] and because religious ethics are unlikely to be widely adopted in
an increasingly secular and pluralist society.

The second major concern of philosophical ethics is known as 'meta-ethics'. It
involves theories not *of*, but *about*, ethics and is concerned with various 'second-
order' questions about the status of normative ethical theories. The most important
of these is why we should follow particular ethical approaches. This in turn raises
the question of the source of ethics. In broad terms, there can be said to be two
opposing meta-ethical approaches, with a continuum of variations between them.
At one extreme is moral realism, which holds that ethical norms have an objective
existence that can be discovered and described in the same way as other aspects of
the 'real' world. At the other extreme[10] are moral sceptics who claim that moral
norms exist only as personal opinions of individual moral agents—what can be called
ethical subjectivism[11]—or, at most, the shared values of particular communities—
usually called ethical relativism.

Normative ethics is obviously of great importance to professional legal ethics given
that applied ethics attempts to resolve specific ethical issues by applying and tailor-
ing general theories on how to live to particular areas of living. Meta-ethics is equally
important, albeit less obviously so, for at least two reasons.

First, the meta-ethical foundations of particular normative ethical theories may
affect their ability to command adherence. Although conceptually separate issues, in
practical terms the content and status of ethics are significantly interconnected. For
example, if one believes that ethics are derived from universally applicable reason,
one is more likely to adopt Kantian ethics as the answer to how one ought to live[12]
than if one believes ethics are objectively based on human nature or that ethics
cannot be objectively derived. At the same time, it must be noted that adoption
of a particular normative theory does not logically entail adherence to its meta-
ethical foundation. One can, for instance, adopt Kant's requirement that ethical

---

[9] See section 3.2, below regarding Kant and cp the similarities between Christian (Preston 1991) and
postmodernist ethics (section 7.4, below).

[10] But see also amoralism or nihilism, discussed below in section 7.3.

[11] Also called 'personalism' (Leff 1979; Fishkin 1984, esp at pp.20–1) or 'decisionism' (Cornell 1985,
p.300).

[12] See section 3.2, below.

norms should be universally applicable without accepting that ethical norms in fact do apply universally across different individuals and communities or are based on universal human reason. Equally, adoption of a particular meta-ethical position does not entail acceptance of any normative theory with which it is commonly associated.

The second reason for looking at meta-ethics is because of the alleged political implications of adopting particular approaches. For example, postmodernists argue that moral realism acts as a smokescreen for some to impose their views on others, while realists argue that the adoption of moral scepticism leads to amorality and quiescence in the face of immorality and injustice.

It is thus necessary to look at both normative and meta-ethical issues. We shall do so by first examining the normative approaches of deontology, consequentialism, virtue ethics and feminist ethics. In doing so, we shall note in passing their meta-ethical foundations in order to enable us to properly examine the debate between realism and scepticism when discussing postmodernism.

3. DEONTOLOGICAL ETHICS

3.1 Introduction

In containing the most important source of ethical formalism and political liberalism, it is the ethical theory known as deontology that has had the greatest influence on professional legal ethics.[13] Deontological theories are formulated in terms of duties (or rules, principles, or rights) which prohibit certain behaviour, such as killing or lying, or which require certain behaviour, such as honesty, according to its supposed intrinsic qualities, rather than its consequences. The deontological approach can best be understood through a comparison with its main rival, consequentialism.[14] The latter defines moral behaviour as that which promotes or maximises favoured non-moral values or goals, such as happiness, wealth creation, self-fulfilment, etc. What makes an action morally right or wrong is not its intrinsic qualities, but the total amount of good or bad (however that is defined) produced. The difference between deontology and consequentialism is often said to be that the former concentrates on 'the right', holding that one can define what is morally right prior to defining what is the good life, whereas for consequentialists what is regarded as right flows from prior definitions of 'the good'. A deontologist may regard behaviour as right no matter how harmful its consequences, whereas a consequentialist would never separate what is right from what is good.

---

[13] As indeed on most professional codes: see Harris 1994.
[14] Sometimes also called teleological.

3.2 Kant's Ethics[15]

While deontology has a relatively long history in both secular and religious thought, its modern influence is largely down to the seventeenth century philosopher Kant,[16] who provides the starting point for our discussion.

Kant is arguably the most important ethical philosopher of the modern era. As regards the specific norms he favours, Kant's ideas were not particularly novel for his time, largely reflecting his Lutheran background. However, he provided these ideas with a gloss which stresses the centrality of human freedom, dignity and equality and which has crucially influenced the development of Western human rights and liberal theory.

Kant believed that to act morally is to act out of conscious acceptance of one's duties, rather than prudence or natural inclination. Moreover, morality presupposes autonomy (literally self-legislation): we must lay down our duties for ourselves rather than have them imposed 'heteronomously' by secular or religious authorities. However, this did not lead Kant to a subjectivist meta-ethics. Instead, he believed that universal and objective moral duties could be derived from reason. Drawing on his important work on epistemology,[17] Kant argued that moral principles are like those of mathematics and logic. Their existence cannot be proved in the same way as material matter, yet they are true because we constantly act upon them as if they are true: they are 'necessary truths'. According to Kant there are certain moral principles which are true in an *a priori* and self-evident sense and which are knowable by all rational persons.

These principles are to be found in what he calls the 'Categorical Imperative'. Unlike 'hypothetical imperatives', which require certain behaviour as a condition to achieve something else (for example, particular skills or states like happiness), the Categorical Imperative is obeyed because its obligations are regarded as required for their own sake. Instead of taking the form of 'you ought to do X if you want Y', the Categorical Imperative simply states, 'You ought to do X'.

Although Kant spoke of the Categorical Imperative as the single test of morality, in fact he provided different formulations of it. The first important formulation lays down the required form of moral obligations and is sometimes called the Formulation of the Universal Law or the Principle of Universality. It states that self-legislating individuals can only set standards for themselves if they can, without self-contradiction, will that all others would act in the same way. For instance, the maxim

---

[15] The following discussion draws primarily on MacIntyre 1967, ch.14, Raphael 1994, ch.6; Williams 1985, ch.4; O'Neill 1991.

[16] Kant's ideas fit within the main deontological approach, known as rule-deontology. By contrast, the now largely defunct 'act-deontology' holds that the uniqueness of every ethical situation requires that moral decisions should be made according to each individual's conscience, intuition, or faith, etc., rather than by following binding moral rules—see Frankena 1963, pp.21–3; Beauchamp 1982, pp.115–6; an approach which has similarities to existentialist (see Warnock 1970) and postmodernist ethics (see section 7, below).

[17] ie the study of whether and how we can know things.

'keep promises only when convenient' breaches the Categorical Imperative in that if everyone acted in the same way the practice of promise-keeping would break down. Consequently, the individual must require promise-keeping in all circumstances (as must everyone else). Using similar reasoning, Kant assumes—but does not show— that many other standards of conventional morality, such as the prohibitions against murder, lying and suicide, satisfy the Categorical Imperative. However, unlike 'perfect' duties involving negative prohibitions, which hold for all persons in all circumstances, Kant accepts that duties of a positive nature, such as the duty to help others, impose only 'imperfect' obligations. This is because they cannot be universalised without willing away essential means to one's own ends. In this way, Kant made respectable the essential distinctions between harming and helping, and between acts and omissions, which allows liberalism to move away from the more demanding Christian ethic of helping the needy. Kant only requires limited beneficence. We are not required to help all persons all the time, but merely prohibited from adopting a policy of never helping the needy. Nevertheless, his universalisation principle is commendable in removing the possibility of exempting some from the demands placed upon others. At the same time, it is largely formal and no more than a side-constraint, albeit an important one, on morality. The universalisation principle is equally compatible with non-moral or even immoral maxims, such as 'always eat mussels on Mondays' or 'persecute all those who hold false religious beliefs'.[18]

Consequently, Kant's second formulation of the Categorical Imperative—the so-called 'Formula of the End in Itself'[19]—requires that we treat others 'not simply as a means but always at the same time as an end'. This clearly relates to the content rather than the form of ethics and has been described as a 'highly articulated version of a demand for respect for persons'.[20] More specifically, the second formulation prohibits us from preventing others from exercising their autonomy. We can use people as means to our ends, but we cannot treat them as *mere* means to our ends by preventing them from choosing whether or not to help us with our ends.[21] Consequently, we are also obliged—albeit only imperfectly—to help others exercise their own autonomy.

For his time, Kant's ethics were profoundly liberatory. By accepting that everyone has equal capacity to legislate their own morality, Kant freed individuals from the moral authority of the church and state, and from an ethics which ties them into their social function. His emphasis on equality, autonomy and human dignity provided the ethical counterpart to the growing influence of liberalism in the political domain. However, as *the* philosopher of liberal individualism, Kant has naturally attracted censure from a wide variety of critics, as we shall see. Yet, even on its own terms, his theory contains serious flaws.[22]

---

[18] MacIntyre 1985, p.46.   [19] O'Neill 1991, p.178.   [20] ibid.
[21] eg slavery is prohibited, but salaried domestic service allowed: cf Raphael 1994, pp.56–7.
[22] In addition to the references cited in n.15, see Frankena 1963, pp.26–7; MacIntyre 1985, esp pp.45–6.

First, Kant is rather mysterious about how his various formulations of the Categorical Imperative derive from reason. Why are these and only these formulations self-evidently true? Kant seems to argue that this truth stems from the desire by rational people to avoid logical self-contradiction. Even accepting for now[23] the desirability of basing ethics on reason, at a technical level it can be argued that Kant's ethics lack internal coherence. For example, many of the maxims he assumes are derivable from the universality principle are not nearly as persuasive as the only worked through example of promise-keeping. Moreover, some have questioned whether the Categorical Imperative's second formulation flows from the first. It has been argued that one can without self-contradiction adopt the maxim, 'Let everyone but me be treated as a means to an end'.[24]

More importantly, Kant's ethical system has been criticised as being too abstract to provide much guidance to moral actors. Apart from the Categorical Imperative's minimal side-constraints, individuals must develop their own moral principles. Moreover, the absolute nature of Kant's ethical principles—the fact that obedience is required in all circumstances and irrespective of the consequences—can lead to plainly counter-intuitive conclusions, such as that one cannot lie to save lives. Finally, Kant offers no way of resolving conflicting obligations. Two types of conflict may arise. Inter-obligation conflicts involve two or more obligations, such as the duty not to lie versus the duty not to kill, whereas intra-obligation conflicts involve situations where a particular obligation can be regarded as equally leading to more than one outcome, such as where the driver of a runaway lorry has no option but to kill one person rather than another. In such situations, moral actors must presumably make an unguided choice, in which case the attempt to provide a monistic (or more accurately dualistic) test for ethics fails. This failure is particularly problematic in that it is precisely where obligations conflict that the most important ethical dilemmas arise and where ethical theory would be most useful.

3.3 Contemporary Deontology[25]

Subsequent deontological theories have attempted to solve the problems of indeterminacy, counter-intuitiveness and conflicting obligations in various ways. We shall look at two of the most prominent attempts.[26]

Contemporary deontologists such as Fried[27] and Donegan[28] ground their theories

---

[23] But see section 3.4, below.   [24] MacIntyre 1985, p.46.

[25] This term is taken from Davis 1991, upon whom this section is primarily based.

[26] A third approach side-steps the problem of conflicting deontological duties by rejecting the idea of absolute moral duties based on one supreme test in favour of an 'ethic of prima facie duties'—duties that we should follow all things being equal and which compete with each other on an equal footing, requiring us to balance them against each other in order to decide which should take precedence. This approach, made famous by Ross (1930, ch.2), has not found favour with most other deontologists because of its radical indeterminacy and, at least for some, because its meta-ethical foundations are based on intuitionism (see further section 7.2). See generally, Frankena 1963, pp.23–5; Harman 1977, pp.119–23; Beauchamp 1982, pp.124–8; Dancy 1991a.

[27] Fried 1978.   [28] Donegan 1977.

in the fundamental principle that we show respect for all rational persons. However, in an attempt to eradicate the problems with Kant's similar theory, the duties derived from this principle are reduced in scope. Thus, respect for persons is held to always prevent one from causing harm to others, but never to help relieve harm, making it wrong, for example, to harm one person in order to save five threatened by some natural disaster. In classic ethical terms, this may be said to distinguish, respectively, a duty of 'non-maleficence' from one of 'beneficence'. In addition, deontological duties are narrowly confined to an agent's intended actions and decisions, rather than to the full range of unforeseen or even foreseen, but undesired, consequences that may flow from their actions or decisions. These ideas are sometimes formulated as the 'doctrine of double effect', which limits moral responsibility to harm which is intended as an end or necessary means to an end, but excludes harm which moral agents 'merely cause or fail to prevent' as a side-effect of the pursuit of intended ends.[29] For example, while soldiers cannot seek directly to kill civilians, they are not morally prohibited from bombing legitimate military targets because of the possibility of civilian casualties. Finally, both Fried and Donegan accept that the absolute nature of deontological duties may yield in catastrophic situations. For instance, one person may be killed to save a whole nation.

None of these moves is, however, entirely persuasive. Because it is extremely difficult if not impossible to coherently distinguish catastrophic from non-catastrophic situations, the possibility is created of the absolute nature of deontological constraints being eroded, if not surreptitiously avoided, by an expansion of its ambit. Moreover, no guidance is given as to how one is to act in those extreme situations where normal deontological duties are no longer binding. This suggests that either one's account of ethical duties must engage with their consequences, or the model is likely to fail.

The double effect doctrine fares somewhat better. It has proved useful, albeit not uncontroversial, in certain contexts, such as distinguishing palliative care from mercy-killing, and is at least implicitly reflected in certain rules of professional legal ethics.[30] However, its value is limited. The fact that less moral blame usually attaches to foreseen, as opposed to intentional, harm does not mean that the former is never blameworthy. Indeed, one can envisage situations where the foreseen by-products of actions attract greater moral obliquity than intended harm, such as where great civilian loss results from destroying insignificant military targets. The doctrine does not enable one to weigh the likelihood of foreseen harm against the value of the intended benefit. Nor does it consider whether or not, or how easily, any foreseen harmful by-product of moral action can be avoided, or regard as relevant the fact that actors, while not directly desiring harmful by-products, anticipate them with 'ghoulish relish'.[31] Moreover, it is extremely difficult, if not impossible, to consistently distinguish intended means to ends from merely foreseen consequences.

Ultimately, the doctrine does little more than uphold the already existing distinction between causing harm and not preventing harm. For example, lying

---

[29] See Wright 1994–5, p.812ff.   [30] See Ch.8 at n.142.   [31] Wright 1994–5, p.816.

is wrong because it is aimed at deception, but merely failing to disclose the truth is not condemned because it is not necessarily so aimed. But even this traditional distinction is unpersuasive. In some situations, such as where one may save many lives by lying, the failure to prevent harm may reflect far greater immorality than the breach of deontological duties.

However, possibly the greatest problem with contemporary deontology lies in its source and overall character. Like Kant, Fried and Donegan fail to justify convincingly why ethics should ultimately be based on respect for persons, rather than some other principle. Equally, they fail to establish persuasively that respect for persons requires individuals to refrain from lying but allows them to withhold the truth, or prohibits stealing by the poor but allows the rich to ignore their needs. Clearly the consequences and motives for withholding the truth may be far worse than for lying, whereas respect for persons and their freedom is meaningless without means to survive. To be convincing, contemporary deontologists need to provide a more persuasive case as to why certain actions are on their list of obligations and why others are omitted. They would also be rather more convincing if there was more internal agreement about their lists' contents.

But even if the above criticisms were met, Fried and Donegan can be criticised for encouraging a legalistic and highly minimalist approach to ethics. Moral agents are only expected to be concerned with the strict letter of rules rather than their spirit, let alone the possibility that morality might require them to go beyond existing duties. As long as their rules are not knowingly breached, deontologists can rest easy that they do no wrong, especially as inadvertent or even foreseen but unwanted rule-breaking is excluded from moral censure.[32] After a few minimal duties are complied with, individuals are allowed maximum freedom to pursue self-interest. This clearly provides an ethical foundation for political libertarianism and laissez-faire economic theories. Yet an approach which allows (albeit does not compel) individuals idly to stand back and allow babies to drown, accident victims to bleed to death and the poor to starve is hardly one to attract the support of more humane liberals, let alone the opponents of liberalism—marxists, feminists, postmodernists and the like.

3.4 Gewirth's Principle of Generic Consistency[33]

The most impressive attempt at a rule-deontological ethical theory is that of Gewirth, who returns to the challenge of establishing a rationally based monistic test of morality. Like Kant, Gewirth argues that all moral agents must, on pain of self-contradiction, accept his 'supreme moral principle'. His argument contains three stages.

The first involves the idea that individuals only qualify as moral agents if they can control their own actions and pursue their own purposes. In terms of the 'generic

---

[32] cf Barry 1979, p.643: 'a good man cannot be defined as one who obeys certain minimum standards of duty. Victorian novels and biographies are thickly populated with self-righteous prigs who never did anything wrong . . . but still managed to make life hell for everyone around them.'
[33] See eg Gewirth 1978 and 1996.

features of action', moral agents require and hence value both freedom—the ability to make unforced choices and control one's actions—and certain goods which constitute their well-being. These goods are categorised hierarchically. Most important are the basic goods, such as life and physical integrity, which are necessary to achieve any purpose at all. Second in the hierarchy are non-subtractive goods, such as the right not to be lied to or defamed, which are necessary to maintain agents' general level of purpose fulfilment in the sense that without them they would be less able to achieve their purposes. Lowest in the hierarchy are 'additive goods', such as self-esteem, self-respect, knowledge and wealth and peace, which enable agents to increase their level of well-being over and above basic levels. The next step in Gewirth's argument is his contention that moral agents do not simply desire freedom and well-being; they regard themselves as having 'generic rights'[34] to them. To deny this right to the necessary conditions of their action would be to deny their status as moral agents. Finally, Gewirth argues that moral agents must rationally recognise that all others have equal rights to freedom and well-being in that one cannot logically claim rights that one denies to others. This gives rise to the awkwardly termed 'Principle of Generic Consistency' (PGC), which states: 'Act in accord with the generic rights of your recipients[35] as well as yourself.'

Gewirth's theory clearly constitutes an improvement on its rivals. Instead of simply assuming the existence of axiomatic moral principles, he sets out premises, which are themselves rationally derived from allegedly incontrovertible features of life, from which he purports to logically deduce his principles. By setting out a hierarchy of goods, ranked according to different categories as well as within these categories, and by exploring how these goods interrelate with the generic rights to freedom, Gewirth's PGC provides a means to resolve conflicts between moral duties. It also avoids the formalistic and abstract nature of other deontological approaches in paying due regard to context and the concrete situations in which moral agents find themselves. Thus the necessary goods are not defined in absolute terms, but depend on what is necessary for action in particular social conditions. Finally, by stressing that moral agents are not just required to refrain from interfering with the rights of others, but must also take reasonable steps to support their vindication,[36] Gewirth goes beyond the narrowness of other deontological theories.

However, his theory is not without its flaws.[37] Inevitably, for such an ambitious attempt at 'grand theorising', one can raise minor quibbles about its details.[38] Perhaps equally inevitable, but more serious is the fact that certain core concepts and much of the PGC's details are left indeterminate and, at times, downright ambiguous. For instance, Gewirth is rather vague as to the content of the various goods

---

[34] They are 'generic' because they flow from the 'generic features of agency'.

[35] ie those people whom your actions and omissions affect.

[36] His positive duties are, however, more limited than negative duties (see eg Gewirth 1976, p.136).

[37] For an overview, see eg Regis 1984; Williams 1985, p.56ff; Wyschogrod 1990, pp.69–72, and for an attempt to meet these criticisms, see Beyleveld 1991.

[38] eg animal welfarists might criticise his privileging humans over animals, while his argument that Christian Scientists act involuntarily when they refuse blood transfusions (Gewirth 1976, pp.262–3) is patronising.

necessary for action. And while he does provide a fairly plausible scheme for resolving inter-obligation conflicts, he says little about intra-obligation conflicts, other than that family members may be favoured over others. However, even if these flaws were to be rectified, there remain stringent criticisms of his general framework for moral decision-making.

Thus, his claim to rationality and reliance on rights is highly controversial. It has been argued that, even if freedom and well-being are necessary for action, it does not logically follow that moral agents must claim these as 'rights'. The idea of rights adds nothing to Gewirth's theory. Indeed, rights are not an inherent part of moral discourse, but arose relatively late in moral history.[39] Following Bentham, many regard the idea that rights are anything other than human constructions laid down by state institutions as 'nonsense upon stilts'.[40] For many critical theorists, rights are inherently problematic.[41] They can be said to be individualistic in encouraging self-interest and competitiveness,[42] undermining community solidarity and helping to divide and buy off oppressed groups. To constitute individuals as right bearers is to alienate them from themselves.[43] Instead of seeing individuals as being constituted by their own powers and characteristics, they are treated as owning these powers and characteristics. And then when mediated in terms of rights, the individual's relation to others is constructed as one of subject to object. Even if group rights are developed in recognition of the fact that equality of individual rights simply upholds the dominance of those with greater power, it can be argued that rights talk presupposes and ultimately fosters individualism and with it the continued dominance of the powerful.

Equally problematic is Gewirth's conclusion that moral agents must acknowledge the equal rights of others. It may be morally praiseworthy to do so. For those who are or are likely to be dependent on others, it may indeed be prudent to do so. But for those with sufficient power and resources not to need anyone's help, it may well be rational to refuse to recognise the claims of others. In other words, Gewirth fails adequately to justify the move from prudence or self-interest to morality.

Nor does he persuasively establish that the specific goods and specific resolutions of conflict between goods are rationally required by the necessary conditions of action. For instance, why is confidence as to the general possibility of attaining one's goods a basic good? Is it really necessary that one is protected against promise breaking, lying or defamation in order to be able to act purposively? It would undoubtedly make effective action considerably more difficult, but if one knows in advance never to trust others, effective action is not impossible. As regards the detailed working out of Gewirth's theory, there frequently seems to be no necessary logical relation to his basic ideas. Why, for instance, must police officers and military per-

---

[39] Gewirth deals with this point at pp.98–102, but unconvincingly: see eg MacIntyre 1985, p.67.
[40] Quoted eg in Moore 1982, p.1069.
[41] See eg Campbell 1988; Smart 1989, ch.7; Kingdom 1991, but cf the ambivalence within Critical Legal Studies, discussed by Price 1985, pp.273–5.
[42] Gewirth recognises, but seems unperturbed by this: 1978, p.95.   [43] See Lacey 1996, p.147.

sonnel, but no others, endanger their lives to rescue others? On occasions such as these, Gewirth simply seems to be giving his personal view unhindered by the need for rational justification.

However, even if Gewirth is able to construct a rationally coherent moral scheme based on the necessary conditions for action, one can ask why this should be the relevant starting point. Why not start somewhere else like love or the needs of others?[44] Moreover, one can question whether logical rationality should be a primary value in ethics. Rationality may make ethical theories more understandable and easier to evaluate, but not necessarily more moral.[45] Gewirth's theory is intellectually impressive, but it may fail to inspire moral behaviour. According to a long line of thinkers, reason cannot move one to act morally. Reason, Hume argued, cannot tell us what actions are moral; it can only tell us what actions are prudent.[46] Instead, we are moved to act by passion, by sentiments and by feelings of approval or disapproval. More fundamentally, as we shall see, many argue that the sort of morality which is derived from reason tends to be austere and misses much of what makes us human, such as empathy, love, pity and compassion.

4. CONSEQUENTIALISM[47]

4.1 Introduction

Our analysis of Kant, Fried and Donegan, and of Gewirth's responses, shows that deontologists are forced to recognise that morality is connected to conceptions of the social good, and the context and consequences of human behaviour. In this way, deontology moves closer to consequentialism. However, when one looks at consequentialism we see the opposite journey: consequentialists are forced to adopt certain positions similar to those of deontologists.

As we have seen, consequentialists define right behaviour as that which ensures the greatest amount of whatever is regarded as good. This, it is argued, gives consequentialism the advantage of simplicity. By avoiding having to define separately what is good and what is right, consequentialism avoids having to stipulate when and justify why 'right' behaviour has to be followed when in conflict with 'the good'. Similarly, most consequentialist theories involve a relatively simple manner of resolving moral dilemmas—one must do whatever ensures the greatest amount of good. Consequentialism is also claimed to be more honest than its competitors. While all theories contain conceptions of the good, even if only implicitly, and whereas deontologists are also often forced to refer to consequences when resolving conflicting duties, only consequentialism explicitly justifies its conceptions of the good rather than sneaking them in through the back door. Finally, a theory that identifies certain things as good and then requires their promotion seems more logical than one which

---

[44] See sections 6 and 7, below.   [45] Leff 1979, pp.1238–9.
[46] See Beauchamp 1982, p.350.   [47] See generally Pettit 1991.

admits, even if implicitly, that certain things are good, but then does not require their promotion. For instance, it seems perverse for deontologists to value the sanctity of life, but then require moral agents to avoid lying rather than save lives.

When it comes to their content, a wide variety of goods might form the basis of consequentialist theories. However, by far the most well-known and influential consequentialist theory is utilitarianism.[48] Because it has so thoroughly dominated consequentialism—and indeed ethics in general in particular historical contexts—we will concentrate largely on exploring its merits and demerits, both as a theory in its own right and as an example of consequentialism. However, there is another form of consequentialism which has attracted sufficient support to justify brief evaluation. This is the theory of egoism.

4.2 Egoism[49]

Egoism argues that moral agents should pursue their own self-interest, desires and sense of happiness. For a theory that appears to conflate morality with prudence and selfishness, egoism has attracted a surprising amount of support and can even be argued to underlie various aspects of professional legal ethics.[50] At the same time, however, its supporters have struggled to justify why the pursuit of self-interest deserves to be called a moral theory at all.

One approach argues that people are naturally motivated to pursue self-interest. Three objections can be directed at this 'psychological egoism'. One is the response to all moral arguments that rely on some allegedly natural state to justify moral propositions. This was most famously raised by Hume who tentatively asked whether one can ever infer moral conclusions from the existence of factual propositions.[51] Despite doubts about the nature of Hume's objection,[52] the point remains valid that one cannot persuasively argue that people should act in particular ways simply because they in fact do so, without attempting to show why such actions are morally valuable.

In any event, as a second problem, egoism ignores the fact that at least some people frequently act against self-interest solely in order to benefit others. It is no answer to say that they remain egoists because they were actually doing what they wanted, because then psychological egoism becomes the rather lame argument that we always do what we want—be it selfish or altruistic. Alternatively, egoists might argue that altruism is not a natural human response but stems from false socialisation. However, this raises the final problem with psychological egoism and indeed all forms of argument from nature. In reality, humans never exist in a state of nature completely unaf-

---

[48] Indeed, many conflate consequentialism and utilitarianism: Williams 1985, p.16.
[49] See Frankena 1963, pp.19–21; Harman 1977, ch.12; Beauchamp 1982, pp.56–66; Williams 1985, pp.11–13; Baier 1991.
[50] See Ch.4, section 3.3; Ch.6, sections 2.3 and 3.3; Ch.9, section 3.
[51] See Atkinson 1992, pp.876–7.
[52] See eg Pigden 1991, pp.423–5, and see further Atkinson ibid.

fected by their social background. From the moment of birth, social influences shape human psychology. Arguments from nature thus contain enormous potential for normative claims to be smuggled in under the guise of empirical description.

A *prima facie* more plausible attempt to justify egoism relies on Adam Smith's famous argument that the universal pursuit of self-interest will lead to a general increase in social well-being as if guided by some 'hidden hand'. If empirically supported, this might indeed provide a powerful argument for egoism. However, there is no clear empirical evidence showing that the unrestrained pursuit of self-interest benefits everyone economically or in any other way.[53] Given that the interests of individuals are often in conflict, the free market and other spheres of human activity where self-interest is allowed to go unrestrained usually end up as an opportunity for the rich and powerful to benefit themselves at the expense of the poor and powerless.

A final attempt to justify egoism argues that it is self-evidently rational for persons to pursue their self-interest and, consequently, if rational, then it must be ethical. The immediate response to this is to point out that societies made up of ethical egoists would involve incessant conflict. Whereas one might think that the whole purpose of morality involved the reduction and resolution of inter-personal conflicts, ethical egoism seems to foster and justify these conflicts.

One[54] common answer to this takes us into the type of social contract theory[55] associated with Hobbes and Locke, whereby people are said to agree to certain limits on the pursuit of self-interest in the form of moral and/or legal rules, not because they feel that these limits are morally required, but because they are in their rational long-term interest. The problem here is that we cannot guarantee that self-interested individuals will obey rules simply because they might further their long-term interests. It is also doubtful whether any society has managed to produce moral or legal rules that are in everyone's equal interest—long-term or otherwise.

More specifically, there are well-recognised problems with social contractarianism. There has never been a social contract as envisaged by ethical egoism. Nor does it help to argue that people would have agreed to such a contract if offered the opportunity. No one is likely to feel bound to something that they *might* have agreed to but did not in fact do so, especially if it limits their self-interest. Moreover, the plausibility of arguing that moral and legal rules flow from agreements between rational persons, whether real or hypothetical, is substantially undercut by the fact that they do not seem to promote everyone's interests equally. Attempts, most famously by Rawls,[56] to rescue the social contractarian tradition by hypothesising some ideal situation whereby inequalities are unable to effect the contract reached have been more successful,[57] but significantly have emerged from the deontological rather than the consequentialist tradition.

Ultimately, however, ethical egoism is faced with the persuasive argument that

---

[53] Galbraith 1992, ch.8; Hutton 1995, ch.7.
[54] See also the utilitarian argument at section 4.3, below.   [55] See generally Kymlicka 1991.
[56] Rawls 1971.   [57] But cf nn.163–8 *passim*, below.

intuitively, whether due to nature or—as is more likely—nurture, most people are unlikely to support an ethic which may justify the worst sorts of immorality simply because its perpetrator was motivated by 'natural' or 'rational' self-interest. Even if there are rules agreed to by all egoists limiting self-interest, situations involving interpersonal conflict will always arise which the rules do not cover and where pursuit of self-interest will presumably be allowed, if not encouraged. It is for just such reasons that the more altruistically flavoured theory of utilitarianism has dominated consequentialism.

4.3 Utilitarianism[58]

4.3.1 *Utilitarianism Defined and Defended*

The classical utilitarianism of Bentham, Mill, and Sidgwick famously holds that moral actors must strive to increase the general level of social happiness. As we shall see, subsequent utilitarians have moved away from this narrow, hedonistic, definition of the good to include other social goals and values. What has been retained, however, is the idea that right action is that which promotes or, as the term utilitarianism suggests, is useful to social welfare.

A number of advantages can be claimed for utilitarianism. Apart from its simplicity, both in working like a mathematical calculation whereby the net utility over disutility of one action can be weighed against the net utility over disutility of all alternatives[59] and providing a simple method of resolving conflicts between different moral considerations, utilitarianism has an intuitive appeal. Increasing happiness or other forms of welfare seems to be an obvious and reasonable aim for a moral theory. Indeed, moral theories might seem pointless unless they are useful to some social goal.[60] Utilitarianism also appears to reflect common sense notions of morality. Unlike egoism, it recognises that morality cannot simply be about pursuing self-interest. Equally, it avoids the problems of absolutist deontological duties. For instance, it may explain why we lie or break promises in order to prevent harm to others. Furthermore, by requiring people to promote the general good, utilitarianism remedies egoism's failure to respect others and deontology's failure to take seriously the promotion of social goods. At the same time, it is said to retain important liberal notions of equality and respect for persons. This is because welfare is to be judged impartially from the perspective of Mill's 'disinterested and benevolent spectator'[61] and because according to Bentham, in making the utilitarian calculation, 'everybody [is] to count for one, nobody for more than one'.[62]

But while utilitarianism has these advantages over egoism and most forms of deon-

---

[58] The following discussion is based primarily upon Frankena 1963, pp.29–35; Williams 1972, pp.96–112; Mackie 1977, ch.6; Beauchamp 1982, ch.8; Simmonds 1986, ch.1; MacIntyre 1967, pp.232–44; Goodin 1991; Raphael 1994, ch.4.

[59] See eg Bentham's use of seven dimensions to his 'hedonic calculus'.

[60] See Goodin 1991, p.241: 'promoting things that are good in themselves, without being good *for* anyone, is not what ethics is principally about'.

[61] See Beauchamp 1982, p.77.   [62] ibid, p.80.

tology, it suffers from disagreements as to the content of the principle of utility and why it should be followed. In attempting to justify why we ought to maximise happiness—defined as the presence of pleasure and the absence of pain—and no other social good, most[63] hedonic (or hedonistic) utilitarians argue that humans are naturally driven by pleasures and pain. But, leaving aside the doubts as to whether we can ever identify the content of human nature and assuming that humans are motivated by happiness thus defined, utilitarians still need to explain why it is moral to promote everyone's pleasure and reduce their pain. One response is that rational people would realise that maximisation of their own pleasure requires social co-operation and that altruism best ensures this co-operation. But even if this does logically follow, which is doubtful, this line of argumentation falls foul of Hume's criticism of reason as a source of morality. According to Hume, just as each individual wants pleasure and to avoid pain, so through sympathy we tend to want the same for others. It is because of this human faculty that we disapprove of acts like murder and approve of actions such as charity which give others pleasure.

This view is perhaps more plausible than its rationalist rival, yet it still fails to provide a persuasive justification for utilitarian morality. One problem is that Hume and the utilitarians who follow him accepted that humans have only a limited propensity towards sympathy and altruism. Indeed, they believed that law was needed to ensure that people acted as sympathetic and altruistic utilitarians. More fundamentally, and somewhat ironically, this explanation fails to avoid Hume's 'no ought from is' question. Even if people do want each other's happiness, it still needs to be shown that this is a good worth pursuing. This has yet to be done persuasively.

In fact, classical utilitarianism has largely been abandoned, both because of its meta-ethical problems and its hedonistic standard. Most people are not simply pleasure seekers. They are also capable of self-sacrifice and devotion to goals other than increasing pleasure or reducing pain, such as knowledge, friendship, and art. While many things may be regarded as social goods, hedonic utilitarianism fails to establish why happiness should be singled out as the most important or all-inclusive social good. Moreover, by conjuring up images of frivolous, self-centred hedonists, classical utilitarianism suggests a rather impoverished notion of morality. Finally, it suggests that the pleasure which some derive from harmful acts can count and, indeed, that sadism may be moral if it outweighs the victim's pain even by a marginal amount.

Consequently, later utilitarians have either sought a new unitary test of utility or abandoned a monistic standard altogether. Thus self-styled 'ideal utilitarians' argued that social goods such as knowledge, beauty, courage, health, and love have intrinsic value over and above any pleasure or happiness they may generate and that right action is that which promotes the greatest amount of a plurality of intrinsic goods. Preference utilitarians, on the other hand, formulated a monistic test capable of

---

[63] But see also Sidgwick's reliance on intuition and our common sense moral convictions: eg Schneewind 1991, p.153 and cf contra the fact that other intuitionists come up with social goods other than happiness: see eg Finnis 1980.

including everyone's view of the good by requiring behaviour which maximises everyone's opportunity to satisfy their desires, whatever these might be. Finally, welfare utilitarians require the promotion of people's long-term, objective interests, rather than their short-term, subjective preferences.

However, none of these approaches provides a completely persuasive substitute for hedonic utilitarianism. For one thing, very little is provided by way of meta-ethical justification other than an unconvincing reliance on intuition or implicit references to liberal values. Moreover, each alternative version has its own problems. Ideal utilitarianism comes close to 'embracing an aesthetic ideal, regardless of whether or not that is good for any living being',[64] thus moving far from utilitarianism's original idea of social usefulness, and also runs the risk of elitism. Welfare utilitarianism faces similar paternalistic problems because it requires some people to decide for others what is in their interests. Preference utilitarianism avoids these problems and retains Bentham and Mill's liberal intentions only to reduce morality to a question of consumer demand and free market economics writ large.[65] In endorsing no moral standards other than what people want, it is, for example, compatible with racist preferences, suggesting that if enough people want segregated neighbourhoods, their desires must be satisfied, no matter how otherwise immoral.

4.3.2 *Criticisms of Utilitarianism*[66]

The problems with utilitarianism go beyond its failure to provide a convincing test of utility and meta-ethical basis.[67] Despite its claim to simplicity,[68] it is commonly criticised for being unworkable. Measuring the value of social goods is far from unproblematic. Measuring their objective value can result in some imposing their values on others, whereas it is practically impossible to measure their subjective value to individuals. And even if goods could be measured, it is extremely difficult to make comparisons across persons and across goods. How does one weigh one person's pleasure in watching sport against another's pleasure in drinking beer, obtaining an education or engaging in charity work?[69] How does one weigh the pleasure sadists obtain from hurting others against the pain of their victims?[70] Arguably, utility is simply a 'pseudo-concept available for a variety of ideological uses'.[71] Furthermore, because they are more easily quantifiable, utilitarianism is likely to give precedence to goods of a material nature, rather than those like love, friendship, or artistic expression, thus encouraging societies in which materialistic values and cost–benefit calculations reign supreme.

---

[64] Goodin 1991, p.243.

[65] The link between utilitarianism (not just in its preference utilitarianism form) and certain neo-liberal economic theory is not difficult to see.

[66] This section is also intended to illustrate many of the criticisms that can be levelled at consequentialism in general.

[67] In addition to the problems discussed below, utilitarianism contains a number of areas of uncertainty: see eg Mackie 1977, pp.126–7.

[68] Which in any event is only of limited value if utilitarianism is not otherwise useful: Williams 1972, p.100 and 1985, p.106.

[69] cf MacIntyre 1985, p.64.   [70] cf Simmonds 1986, pp.20–1.   [71] MacIntyre 1985, p.64.

On the other hand, even some critics of utilitarianism accept that, while we cannot measure and compare utility with exact precision, we can and regularly do make rough and ready utilitarian-type calculations.[72] Moreover, what is important is not that we achieve, but that we strive for maximum accuracy. In response, it is argued that requiring people to be incessant moral calculators is overly demanding. Utilitarianism is also criticised for expecting excessive self-sacrifice. For instance, it will always be to the greater good for us to drop what we are doing and devote our lives to ending world poverty.[73] Unattainable moral standards, it is argued, might result in their being ignored altogether. Alternatively, the person who tries to live like a utilitarian 'moral saint'[74] might end up devoid of those non-moral aspects of human life which give it value—the pursuit of knowledge, companionship, hobbies, etc.

Utilitarianism is also criticised for leading to counter-intuitive results. Like all consequentialist theories, in being solely forward-looking, utilitarianism struggles to explain why, for example, people should keep promises. Promise-keeping might be useful in facilitating social co-operation, but this would not condemn the secret breaking of promises. Nor can utilitarianism explain why, for instance, a promise to perform a particular action tips the balance against an alternative action having equivalent or even lesser utility. Similarly, utilitarianism seems to suggest that, if utility requires the overriding of deontological duties, then the required action is simply morally justified. By contrast, virtue ethicists note that the morally virtuous would still feel regret at breaking one of these duties and may be under a duty to make reparations.[75] Utilitarianism is also said to be counter-intuitive in not allowing our personal relationships with others to weigh in the utilitarian calculus, even if the scales are evenly balanced.

Even more damaging are allegations that utilitarianism shows insufficient respect for equality and liberty. It is criticised for being concerned only with welfare maximisation, not with its egalitarian distribution over society.[76] Utilitarianism seems to favour societies where a few have large amounts of welfare, while most people have little, if this would ensure a greater aggregate amount of welfare than more egalitarian distributions. Consequently, it is argued that the principle of equality needs to be supplemented by a principle of justice.[77]

Even more problematic is the suggestion that utilitarianism leaves no behaviour unthinkable: murder, rape, and torture may all be demanded by the principle of utility. Utilitarians might argue that this is only true of exceptional circumstances[78] and here it may be equally problematic not to condone action such as the torture of one person in order to save potential victims of a planted bomb. However,

---

[72] Raphael 1994, p.54; Warnock 1971, pp.29–30; Beauchamp 1982, p.97.
[73] Harman 1977, p.137.   [74] cf Wolf 1982, esp pp.427–30.
[75] See eg Williams 1978, p.64.
[76] But cf Mill's arguments discussed eg by Frankena 1963, pp.33–4.
[77] But cf utilitarians' reliance on the 'law' of diminishing marginal returns to argue that egalitarian redistribution would be required: Simmonds 1986, pp.31–3; Goodin, pp.247–8.
[78] cf also Edel 1986, p.324 noting that one can never judge ethical theories in terms of their response to extreme situations.

utilitarianism also seems prepared to accept human rights violations on a more every-day basis. It may, for instance, condone punishing the innocent if this would deter crime or enslaving a minority if this would maximise welfare. For many, there are certain values—often expressed in terms of rights (to life, liberty, and physical integrity, etc.)—which must always trump[79] considerations of utility.

An equally tricky problem for utilitarianism is that it may sometimes be self-defeating. In certain circumstances, if everyone followed utilitarian principles, the overall level of utility may be reduced even though each single act might satisfy the utilitarian calculus. For instance, if one person were to disobey a rule prohibiting walking on the grass there might be very little harm as compared to the overriding benefit to that individual. But if everyone did so, the grass would eventually be ruined, thus reducing overall welfare.

It is usually responded that utilitarianism was always intended as a theory of jus-tification for institutional action rather than individual decision-making and it is here that it has always proved most useful. Indeed, it is sometimes argued that it would be better if individuals refrained from utilitarian calculations when faced with moral dilemmas. Not only does this rather undercut utilitarianism's value as moral theory, but it raises the problem of having to ensure that people promote utility while at the same time abjuring utilitarian calculations. The usual response is to rely on the traditional distinction between act- and rule-utilitarianism.

4.3.3 *Rule-Utilitarianism*

Due to utilitarianism's many problems, it has long been suggested that, instead of each utilitarian always deciding how each individual act will affect utility, rules should be laid down designed to maximise utility. Thus, whereas act-utilitarians will decide what best maximises utility in every single case, irrespective of its potential long-term effect on utility, perhaps referring to (but not considering themselves bound by) certain rules of thumb, rule-utilitarians follow rules thought likely to increase overall utility over the long run, even if they decrease utility in particular cases. In this way, individual rule-utilitarians are excused from making their own utilitarian calculations—an approach which can be adopted by all consequentialist theories.[80]

At first glance, this seems to answer many of the criticisms of utilitarianism. Indi-viduals are no longer required to be incessant calculators. Rule-utilitarianism can also be used to address act-utilitarianism's inadequate consideration of personal relation-ships, human rights and duties such as not lying. This is because prohibitions on acts such as torture, lying, and punishing the innocent may be said to be ultimately in the long-term interest of all because they promote stability and the necessary con-ditions for social co-operation. Moreover, all forms of rule-consequentialism avoid the problems of individual act-consequentialists being fallible, biased, or insuffi-

---

[79] cf Dworkin 1977.
[80] cf the discussion of what may be called rule-egoism at text following n.55.

ciently informed.[81] Rule-consequentialism saves time and allows for moral problems to be debated once and for all by the experts.[82]

On the other hand, these alleged advantages point to a serious danger with all forms of rule-consequentialism.[83] Even if, for example, rule-utilitarianism remedies all the flaws in act-utilitarianism, it is likely to lead to what Williams[84] has called 'Government House utilitarianism' whereby utilitarian calculations are made by an informed elite imposing their views on the unthinking masses. Moreover, it may be doubted whether rule-utilitarianism can be substituted for act-utilitarianism. What happens when two utilitarian rules conflict? Unless the rule designers can success-fully construct a hierarchy of rules weighted according to utility, utilitarians are forced back to act-utilitarianism in order to decide as to which rule it is best to follow. More importantly, Williams has argued that committed utilitarians are unlikely to follow rules when doing so will definitely decrease utility, especially as they are required to balance the imagined consequences of everyone breaking a rule against the actual consequences of upholding it.[85] If this is the case, we are back to act-utilitarianism.

5. VIRTUE ETHICS[86]

5.1 Introduction

Thus far, our discussion suggests that, while morality should not be simply a matter of following abstract rules irrespective of context or consequences, it is also prob-lematic to require moral agents to act as permanent casuistic calculators of the con-sequences of their actions. For some, this suggests that a moral theory along the lines of Gewirth's sophisticated system, which allows for a weighting of moral considera-tions, is most desirable. For others, however, the whole tradition of seeing morality primarily in terms of principles and obligations is misconceived. Instead, a call is made for a return to the earlier moral tradition of virtue ethics, which began with the Greeks, limped on through the Medieval period and was largely killed off by the Enlightenment. Given the failure of later traditions to provide an authoritative or even coherent basis for morality there has been a marked revival of this pre-modern approach. According to its most prominent proponent, MacIntyre, only virtue ethics can rescue society from the current malaise of moral fragmentation and interminable moral disagreements.[87]

'To be or to do' is the question raised by virtue ethics.[88] Whilst deontology and consequentialism focus on action, virtue ethics cuts across the deontological/

---

[81] Wasserman 1990, p.401.   [82] Luban 1988, p.120.
[83] In addition to the criticisms below, see Warnock 1971, p.34–70.
[84] Williams 1985, p.108ff.   [85] Williams 1972, pp.105–8.
[86] See Frankena 1963, ch.4; Beauchamp 1982, ch.5; Pence 1984 and 1991.
[87] MacIntyre 1985. See also eg Williams 1985.   [88] Frankena 1963, p.52.

consequentialist division by concentrating on character rather than action—on being rather than doing. Whereas deontology and consequentialism treat ethics as a matter of obligations, virtue ethicists see ethics as largely a matter of the presence or absence of fixed character traits, dispositions or habits of behaviour which are regarded as morally worthy. The focus is on what counts as moral goodness and the virtuous life, and on how people can make themselves morally 'better' and live the good life by developing virtues. Virtue ethicists concentrate on defining what character dispositions are virtues (for example, loyalty, honesty, and courage) and which are vices (for example, selfishness, bad temper, immodesty) and on analysing the type of social circumstances best suited to developing the virtues and counteracting the vices.

5.2 The Virtues of Character[89]

Deontologists and consequentialists do not entirely ignore the question of character. Character dispositions are important to their ethics in that they ensure that individuals obey the obligations laid down for them. Indeed, without the development of relevant character dispositions, obligation-based ethics could not get off the ground. However, virtue ethicists contend that the question of character should be central to morality or at the least far more prominent than it is in obligation-based ethics.

Concentration on obedience to obligations does not, it is argued, capture the whole ethical story. There are many aspects of good character such as displaying gratitude or personal integrity which are relevant to morality, but which cannot be squeezed into obligation-based ethics.[90] Moreover, the fact that people obey moral obligations tells us little about their morality. They might, for instance, do so out of self-interest. According to virtue ethicists, even obedience out of a sense of duty is less morally praiseworthy than moral actions stemming from dispositions, traits and sentiments which lie at a fairly deep level of psychological motivation. Those who do not murder or steal because their prior dispositions rule out even considering such actions are more morally praiseworthy than those who begrudgingly resist the temptation out of a feeling of obligation. Indeed, in direct contrast to Kant's argument that those who are charitable out of a sense of duty have more moral worth than those who obtain pleasure from giving, Aristotle argued that the truly virtuous person is one who derives pleasure from virtue.

Virtue ethicists also argue that those persons held up as moral exemplars—moral saints and heroes like Gandhi, Mother Theresa, Nelson Mandela, and Oskar Schindler—are people motivated by deep-seated and spontaneous feelings of compassion, empathy, etc., rather than just by pious adherence to duty. Similarly, whereas duty-based ethics only looks at isolated acts of individuals, virtue ethics recognises that we judge others as a whole and that even the highly virtuous may at times

---

[89] In addition to the above citations, see Blum 1988 and Kupperman 1988.
[90] cf Williams 1985, ch.10.

commit individual immoral acts or have ongoing minor vices. Whereas one either obeys or disobeys obligations, virtue ethics recognises that there are degrees of being virtuous and that one can be vicious even while punctiliously obeying a duty.[91] This emphasis on moral motivation similarly distinguishes virtue ethics from consequentialism's focus on the outcome of individual actions.[92] Moreover, unlike most deontologists and consequentialists, virtue ethicists recognise that even if one moral consideration can be regarded as trumped by another, virtuous people nevertheless feel remorse at having to violate or neglect the trumped moral consideration.[93]

A final argument by virtue ethicists is that duty-based moral theories are insufficient to equip individuals with the moral tools necessary to resolve all moral problems.[94] Moral decisions, they argue, derive from character habits rather than the analytical application of rules or principles. As we have seen, deontological and consequential principles are often indeterminate or internally inconsistent. They also fail to cover all situations raising ethical issues. But even where deontology or consequentialism provides relevant and non-conflicting principles, they are often too abstract to cope with complex and multi-faceted problems. Moral agents still need to recognise that situations are morally problematic in the first place. They need the ability to identify the salient features, to be sensitive to psychological aspects, such as the feelings, attitudes or life plans of others, as well as their own, and, perhaps most importantly, to care about all these features of moral situations. Additionally, they need to be able to recognise that many moral issues are not simply one-off events but involve ongoing relationships, values and projects requiring the virtues of commitment and loyalty. According to virtue ethicists, it is here that moral character is central.

5.3 The Virtue Tradition

While the issues of virtue and character were central to all Greek philosophers, it is in Aristotle that we find the fullest and most plausible account of virtue ethics.[95] A central feature of Greek ethical theory is that questions of ethics are treated as part of Socrates' question, 'How should one live?' For Aristotle, as for many other Greeks, the answer to this question is teleological in that every action and every project has a good at which it aims. According to Aristotle, the highest good of human lives is *eudaimonia*, which can best be translated as 'well-being' or 'flourishing'. The aim of ethics is thus the study of the conditions necessary for human well-being. According to Aristotle, humans achieve well-being by successfully performing the functions associated with their social position and occupation. Given that the good life is

---

[91] eg where one hurts another's feelings by piously avoiding white lies. See also Barry, above n.32.
[92] Slote 1998, pp.172–3.   [93] See eg O'Neill 1991, p.183, regarding Kant; Williams, above n.75.
[94] Much of this paragraph is taken from Kupperman 1988.
[95] For an overview see eg MacIntyre 1967, ch.7; and 1985 *passim* but esp ch.12; Beauchamp 1982, pp.154–63; Williams 1985, ch.3; and as regards Greek ethics generally, see eg MacIntyre 1967, chs.2–8; Rowe 1991.

both prosperous and virtuous, this requires possession of the relevant 'excellences' including—but not limited to—the moral virtues.

However, individuals also have a capacity common to their species. Reason enables humans to harmonise the exercise of the various non-moral virtues or excellences with the moral virtues. But since intellectual reason cannot always be relied upon to ensure the good life, individuals must not only develop dispositions to act morally— the virtues—but they must also develop *phronesis*—'practical wisdom'[96]—which enables them to see what should be done in practical situations. The virtues and *phronesis* are not inborn or formally taught, but are gradually acquired through ex- perience and practice which leads to fixed habits of behaviour. Consequently, the development of virtue is inextricably tied to each individual's community.

To a large extent, modern virtue ethics involves a working through and critical response to Aristotle's ideas. Thus MacIntyre and others argue that modernist ethics went wrong when it abandoned the idea that morality is aimed at some *telos*. However, he sought to replace Aristotle's 'dubious metaphysical biology', which locates this *telos* in human biological functions, with the idea that virtues are acquired qualities enabling people to achieve goods internal to various social practices and that these in turn help to provide a narrative order and coherence to their lives.[97] Flowing from Aristotle's lead, virtue ethicists have engaged in a number of useful debates, for instance, over whether all virtues exist to counter natural passions or inclinations and whether moral virtues can ever be exercised for immoral purposes. And in order to illustrate the nature of virtue, some virtue ethicists have analysed the lives of real life saints and heroes.[98] However, perhaps the most important and controversial outgrowth of virtue ethics has been the development of a communi- tarian critique of the liberalism that underlies most deontological and consequential theories.[99]

While this critique began with virtue ethicists like MacIntyre,[100] it was also taken over by political philosophers who have criticised Western political traditions for unduly emphasising individuals over communities. It is argued that the liberal tra- dition of Kant, Mill, and, more recently, Rawls and Gewirth all treat individuals as independent, autonomous, rational, and wholly competent choosers. In contrast, communitarians argue that individuals are implicated selves, whose identity is embedded in and shaped by the traditions of their communities and accordingly that their 'deepest and most important obligations flow from identity and relatedness, rather than from consent'.[101] By focusing on atomistic individuals with apparently pre-formed identities as the source or foundation of morality and in seeing moral- ity as a matter of individual rights, it is argued that liberalism de-emphasises com-

---

[96] For a useful overview, see Douzinas and Warrington 1994, pp.179–81.
[97] MacIntyre 1985, esp chs.14 and 15 and for a detailed critique, see Cornell 1985, pp.314ff.
[98] See eg Blum 1988; Flanagan 1991, preface. See also the postmodernist, Wyschogrod 1990.
[99] See eg MacIntyre 1985; Selznick 1987; Sandel 1998.
[100] Communitarianism is, however, a broad church, drawing *inter alia* on the philosophical pragmatism of John Dewey, the sociology of Emile Durkheim, and on Hegel and Heideggerian phenomenology.
[101] Selznick 1987, p.451.

mitment and obligation, especially those not deriving from consent,[102] while also undermining the benefits of being part of vibrant and supportive communities. The central communitarian value is thus belonging rather than freedom or independence. It is argued that only by treating people as concrete, situated selves, rather than abstract holders of rights, can the goal of treating people as ends not means be fulfilled. While milder forms of communitarianism recognise that rights might be important, they are treated either as secondary to communitarian interests or more critically as simply symptomatic of community breakdown. Consequently, there is a call for the revitalisation of communities and communitarian values.

Moreover, a communitarian ethics rejects the idea that morality can be based on universal principles. Instead, it must rest on agreed values within communities, established under conditions of 'co-operative enquiry' involving open, collective deliberation.[103] Accordingly, belonging to communities requires individuals to be committed to social participation and requires communities to provide individuals with the resources and opportunities[104] to develop the character and virtues necessary for social participation. Finally, like consequentialists, and unlike deontologists, communitarians expect individuals to advance the good over the right.

5.4 Evaluation

Undoubtedly, the revival of virtue ethics and the communitarian critique of liberalism have been extremely important developments. A duty-based ethics is simply not capable of capturing the rich complexity of morality nor providing the individual with all the necessary tools to resolve ethical dilemmas. Communitarianism has rightly emphasised that as moral agents we are not isolated actors, but part of communities who shape our identities and to whom we should give due respect. However, this has not led to an abandonment of deontology and consequentialism or their liberal character. A common criticism[105] of both virtue and communitarian ethics is that, at least at present, they are far too vague to replace their rivals. For instance, MacIntyre's view that we can rely on the moral traditions within existing communities ignores the fact that, because there are myriad moral communities even within specific social contexts, individuals have always to choose which community's set of values to develop and by definition this cannot be done according to a communitarian ethic.

More specifically, liberals point to the dangers of seeking morality in community values which often tend to be highly conservative if not bigoted and intolerant to those perceived as outsiders.[106] Moreover, while communities might be significant

---

[102] eg those deriving from being part of families or nations responsible for past evils like anti-semitism or slavery.

[103] See Tam 1998, pp.227–34.

[104] cf Bell 1993, pp.13, 174–5, 215–16 regarding the role of education.

[105] The following criticisms are taken from Pence 1984 and 1991; Gutman 1985; Buchanan 1989; Pepper 1990; Wells 1990; Flanagan 1991, chs.5 and 6. See also Cornell 1985 as regards MacIntyre and Roberto Unger.

[106] See also from a postmodernist perspective, Bauman 1993, 1994, and 1995.

sources of meaning and support for us, liberals argue that they are also the source of our greatest fears, oppression and pain and that hence it would be retrogressive to return to societies where the group subsumes the individual. Individuals need autonomy as well as belonging; to be separate as well as connected. Thus some liberals argue that, as long as certain political rights are retained, communitarian ideals can and should be incorporated into liberal political theory. While the libertarianism of writers like Nozick[107] is likely to undermine community commitments, it is argued that Rawls' welfare liberalism[108] is pluralistic rather than individualistic and is perfectly compatible with individuals choosing to reflect community values.

As regards virtue ethics, more generally, similar moves have been made by both duty-based ethicists and virtue ethicists to attempt to incorporate the best of both traditions.[109] The former argue that without moral principles the virtues remain too vague and may indeed end up being used to further immoral ideals. One still needs to determine the morality of certain types of action. Consequently, while attention to character is important, its role remains the secondary one of ensuring that individuals form the dispositions necessary to ensure obedience to obligation. Conversely, on the basis that not all moral issues can be resolved by duties, virtue ethicists insist that questions of character remain central, with ethical duties playing an important secondary role in helping to form moral character and enabling individuals to adopt a critically reflective attitude to existing community practices.[110] In other words, just as deontology has embraced consequential considerations and consequentialism has been unable to escape the pull of moral rules, we see that the difference between duty- and virtue-based ethics boils down to a matter of emphasis rather than exclusive validity.

6. PSYCHOLOGY, FEMINISM, AND THE ETHIC OF CARE

By contrast to the gender-blindness of existing ethical theories, from the 1980s some feminists began to argue that women speak morality 'in a different voice'. This phrase comes from the title of Gilligan's groundbreaking and highly inspirational book.[111] Here she takes to task the idea, almost as old as moral philosophy itself, that women have an inferior sense of morality to men; that, being ruled by the heart rather than the head, they are unable to sufficiently distance themselves from their emotions in order to be able to make proper moral judgements.

Gilligan's ideas emerged from her criticism of the work of her fellow developmental psychologist, Kohlberg, which is of interest to ethics in its own right.[112] Based on experiments, Kohlberg concluded that individual morality develops in three definitive stages, each with its own two sub-stages. At the pre-conventional level,

---

[107] Nozick 1974.   [108] Rawls 1971.   [109] See eg O'Neill 1996.
[110] See Kupperman 1988.   [111] Gilligan 1993.
[112] For an overview and critique, see eg Hartwell 1990; Fishkin 1984, pp.3–18, 150–3, 158–76; Thomas 1991; Flanagan 1991, chs.7 and 8; Tronto 1993a, pp.68–76; the essays in Larrabee (ed.) 1993 *passim*.

individuals are ruled by self-interest. First stage agents learn how to behave through threats of punishment and are only concerned with the interests and concerns of others if they impinge on their own. Second stage agents acknowledge others' interests but treat them as instrumental to self-interest through mutually beneficial exchanges. At the conventional level of morality, individuals become genuinely concerned with the needs of others. At first, they seek to fulfil the expectations of others due to a desire for their approval and the need to maintain loyal and trusting relationships like those of the family, but by the fourth stage loyalty switches to social institutions, and morality is commensurate with obeying its partial rules and obligations. The highest, post-conventional level of moral development is reached when individuals develop their own principled approach to morality. Stage five largely correlates with utilitarian morality, although rights to life and liberty are regarded as absolutely inviolable. Finally, the very few[113] individuals who reach stage six behave like Kantian or Rawlsian deontologists in regarding moral behaviour as that which accords with certain universal, impartial, and rationally derivable principles which outweigh all social obligations, institutional rules and consequentialist considerations.

Kohlberg clearly sees moral development as always moving towards greater altruism and greater theoretical complexity. For this and other reasons, his theory has attracted considerable criticism from moral psychologists and ethicists in general. For example, the claim that deontology is more complex and sophisticated than utilitarianism has been challenged, as has his argument that moral development parallels cognitive development.[114]

However, by far the most significant criticism of Kohlberg is that he ignores the gender dimension of moral thinking—hardly surprising as his experiments were originally confined to male subjects. Consequently, the postulated trajectory of moral development is aimed at what men appear to regard as the most superior form of moral thinking, namely the sort of abstract, unemotional and impersonal moral reasoning associated with deontology and utilitarianism. This masculinist approach to ethics, which stresses objective, impartial, and universalistic principles and rights, Gilligan terms the 'ethic of justice'.

On the basis of experiments with both sexes, Gilligan argues that women and girls tend to favour an 'ethic of care' which is based on connectedness, subjective emotion, and responsibility for maintaining relationships. Here she refers to psychoanalytical theory[115] which argues that men tend to see themselves as autonomous from others whereas women see themselves as continuous with and connected to others. This is because children develop their sense of self-identity in relation to their mothers. Since boys soon learn that they are different to their mothers, their conception of self is

---

[113] According to some estimates only 5 per cent of the population: Tronto 1993a, p.68. See also Thomas 1991, p.467; Hartwell 1990, p.1994; Flanagan 1991, p.227, questioning whether this stage is not simply a hypothetical end-point. If true, this rather undermines the plausibility of deontological ethics.

[114] ie the development of the ability to reason, to imagine and conceptually categorise.

[115] Chodorow 1978. See also Dinnerstein 1987.

more distinctly autonomous than that of girls, who come to see themselves as embedded in and defined by their relationships. These they see as web-like networks rather than ladder-like hierarchies; as involving co-operation rather than competition.

According to Gilligan, these differing perspectives translate into two different ethical voices. Whereas the ethic of justice is founded on the idea that everyone should be treated equally, the ethic of care requires that no one should be hurt. Whereas men tend to stand on principle and act according to people's rights irrespective of the consequences, women are more pragmatic, being more concerned to uphold relationships and protect their loved ones from harm. Whereas the ethic of justice assumes that one can resolve moral dilemmas by abstract and universalistic moral reasoning, the ethic of care requires due attention to context and the specific circumstances of each moral dilemma. And in resolving such dilemmas, men tend to rank ethical principles, whereas women attempt to address the concrete needs of all and to ensure that if anyone is going to be harmed it should be those who can best bear the harm. Along similar lines, Noddings has argued that a rule- or principle-based ethics fails to capture what is distinctive and valuable about female morality.[116] Attempting to resolve ethical dilemmas through abstract principles capable of universalisation conceals the sort of questions which need answering and which are an essential part of moral judgement.

Undoubtedly, the assertion of a feminist ethic has given many women an enhanced sense of moral worth. Thus, instead of relegating the female mode of morality to stage three of Kohlberg's model, Gilligan has argued that it should be valued equally alongside the ethic of justice as an equally mature form of moral reasoning, whereas Noddings has argued that it is in fact morally superior.[117] Given its concentration on consequences and context, connection and community—and hence its similarities with consequentialist, virtue, and communitarian ethics—feminist ethical theory adds considerable weight to the criticism, not just of deontological ethics, but of all theories which privilege abstract, rational thought and which treat moral agents as atomistic, unconnected and abstract thinkers. For instance, Benhabib has argued that unless morality takes seriously the specific needs of concrete others, it can never achieve the sort of universalisability rightly stressed by the Kantian tradition but which is undermined by its notion of the 'general other' as persons devoid of any history, context and characteristics.[118] Moreover, the ideas of Gilligan and Noddings have been drawn upon to call for wide-ranging changes to myriad social activities and institutions, including law's content, legal processes, the legal profession, and professional legal ethics.[119]

However, the idea of a specifically feminist ethic has come under attack from feminists as well as non-feminists.[120] One line of attack has questioned whether moral-

---

[116] Noddings 1984.   [117] See Flanagan 1991, ch.11 for the various positions taken on this issue.
[118] Benhabib 1982. See more generally Benhabib 1992.
[119] See eg Menkel-Meadow 1985 and 1995; Bender 1990; Cahn 1990 and 1992; Rhode 1994.
[120] For a discussion of the debate, see Bender 1990; Flanagan 1991, chs.9–11; Grimshaw 1991; Cahn 1992; Tronto 1993a, p.82ff; Larrabee (ed.) 1993; Rhode 1994; Menkel-Meadow 1995.

ity is in fact gendered.[121] Thus Kohlberg later altered his model to include a caring orientation and, like others, reported no gender differences in further experiments.[122] On the other hand, Gilligan and others have continued to report gender differences, albeit not on the scale originally suggested. Moreover, she has never claimed that the two ethics are exclusively male or female.[123] Instead, she argues that, while all people use both orientations at different times, each gender starts with a preferred orientation, and while women can equally use both orientations, men are far less inclined towards a caring ethic.[124]

But even if gender differences in moral thinking can be shown to exist, many feminists regard their celebration as problematic. For one thing, they ignore the many differences between women related to their different life experiences, stemming from factors like race, class and sexual orientation. More importantly, however, speaking of a female ethic ties in with the essentialist idea that women are naturally or at least immutably different from men. This is inherently dangerous in that gender differences are rarely asserted without, at least, an implicit assumption of the superiority of stereotypical male values, ways of behaving and forms of thinking.

Some feminists go further and argue that the caring female voice has been constructed by a male dominated society in order to maintain female oppression.[125] Indeed, pointing to the fact that post-colonial African men also display a caring ethic, it has even been argued that this ethic derives from oppressive social relations rather than gender differences in psychological development.[126] Moreover, it is no surprise that women display a greater caring orientation given their traditional relegation to the private sphere of society—the home and the family—and to caring occupations like nursing and teaching, which are less valued and less rewarded than the traditionally male dominated public sphere of politics and economics. In this context, to celebrate a female ethical voice can be said to reinforce existing assumptions that women should be responsible for nurturing and maintaining relationships while men dominate those spheres of society which provide access to power. To foster a caring orientation manifesting itself in an overriding concern to maintain relationships even to the extent of self-sacrifice may even undermine women's ability to assert themselves and to escape abusive relationships.[127]

Accordingly, many have called for the ethic of care to be disassociated from its gender connotations and valued in its own right. Thus Tronto sees caring broadly as including everything done to maintain, continue and repair the world so that we

---

[121] See also the criticisms of her methodology in the essays in Larrabee (ed.) 1993 *passim*.

[122] See Benhabib 1982, pp.270–2; Flanagan 1991, ch.10; Nicholson 1993, pp.78ff.

[123] See Gilligan 1982, p.2 and 1993.

[124] See Menkel-Meadow 1985, pp.28–30 regarding her further research and Flanagan 1991, pp.228–32, questioning it and arguing that if differences exist they probably stem from the fact that the sexes face different moral dilemmas.

[125] See eg MacKinnon 1984, pp.38–9.

[126] See Card 1988, p.128; Tronto 1993a, pp.83–4; and 1993b, pp.243–4. More plausibly, it might be argued that the ethics of justice owes more to the values of capitalist economies, which have generally excluded women and minority groups from their benefits.

[127] Card 1988, pp.129–30.

can live in it as well as possible.[128] In this way, she expands the ethic of care from its maternal connotations of being confined to those nearest and dearest to us. While acknowledging its inherent dangers of parochialism and paternalism, she claims that an ethic of care is also able to pay due regard to distant others. Indeed, it is arguably better able to address their needs than the austere equality and limited obligations of many other ethical approaches.[129] At the same time, like others,[130] Tronto recognises that an ethic of care is a necessary, but not a sufficient, basis for morality. Because of problems such as the difficulty of weighing competing needs and the dangers of concentrating our care on those closest to us, it needs to be supplemented by notions of justice, equality and rights. Thus, unlike the hegemonic claims of most other ethical theories, many supporters of an ethic of care recognise that different moral theories may be appropriate to different issues. Nevertheless, given the problems with an ethics of justice and the fact that most people spend most of their lives involved in caring rather than in the abstract weighing of principles of justice, it is argued that the ethic of care should take precedence over or, at the least, rank equally with other ethical orientations.

7. POSTMODERNISM AND THE ETHICS OF ALTERITY

7.1 Introduction

According to some contemporary thinkers, we have reached a radical historical juncture.[131] This new age is marked by globalisation of markets and the media, rampant consumerism juxtaposed with widespread starvation, large-scale environmental problems stemming from unrestrained technological developments and market forces, as well as widespread political apathy and uncertainty, partly caused by sound-bite politics and the fact that the end of the socialist dream has not revealed the triumph of its capitalist rival. Morality also appears to be in crisis.[132] The demise of the moral influence of religious and secular authorities, the disintegration of social homogeneity, the annihilation of moral communities, and the concomitant plurality of lifestyles and values confront the individual as never before with the apparent relativism of morality and the burden of personal moral choice.

No doubt many—especially *fin de siècle*—generations have seen themselves living through a new beginning. However, what is less important than whether we live in a period of postmodernity or simply one of late modernity is that there is a distinctly postmodernist approach to theorising and thinking about our world, in general, and to moral philosophy, in particular. At the very least, the 'post' in postmodern indicates a rejection of modernism and the Enlightenment project.[133] Thus postmod-

---

[128] Tronto 1993a and 1993b.   [129] Flanagan 1991, pp.203–4.   [130] See eg Benhabib 1982.
[131] The following discussion of postmodernity and postmodernism draws *inter alia* on Harvey 1989 and Best and Kellner 1991.
[132] See eg Wolfe 1989; Bauman 1995; Gardiner 1996a, p.121. See also Giddens 1994.
[133] Bauman 1993, p.10.

ernism can be characterised[134] as involving a thoroughgoing scepticism about the ability of knowing subjects to harness reason and science to the yoke of human progress. Not only has science failed to deliver the benefits it promised, but it seems to create as many problems as it solves. Reason has not simply been used in order to understand and improve the world, but as a means of control and oppression. The same can be said for the notion of objective truth, which is rejected in favour of the view that truth—like the knowing subject herself—is a matter of social construction, language, and discourse in general and hence is implicated in power relations. Accordingly, postmodernists prefer small-scale accounts of the world based on local knowledge and a plurality of different voices rather than modernist attempts to reduce complex, contradictory and arbitrary reality to univocal 'grand narratives'. All of these features are found in the postmodernist critique of modernist ethics and in its proffered alternative.

7.2 The Meta-Ethical Debate

Central to postmodernist ethical theory is a rejection of modernist ethics' meta-ethical foundations and their claim to objectivity. This criticism is unique to postmodernism. However, while some modernists embrace moral scepticism, postmodernists go further and concentrate on moral realism's political implications. We shall thus explore both the plausibility and politics of moral realism.

At its most rigorous, moral realism involves:

(1) the ontological[135] claim that there exists an objective moral reality 'out there', which is part of the 'furniture' or 'fabric' of the world, just as real as material phenomena, real numbers and the rules of logic;

(2) the epistemological claim that this moral reality is discoverable and representable as knowledge which corresponds to moral reality; and

(3) the semantic claim that moral judgements may involve objective descriptions of moral reality.

This allows moral realists to claim that moral judgements are based on foundations that are both unquestionable and universally applicable. In rejecting this position, moral sceptics rely on a number of arguments.

Most obvious, but perhaps least persuasive,[136] is 'empirical relativism'.[137] This relies on the fact, first noted by the Sophists, that moral values differ over time and from place to place, if not person to person. Accordingly, it is concluded that moral values

---

[134] This description of postmodernism is highly personal, given the difficulties of defining a theory which rejects large-scale theorising, is wary of definitions, stresses the radical indeterminacy of meaning and the opaqueness of language, and many of whose leading lights resist the tag 'postmodernist'.

[135] Ontology involves theories of what things are.

[136] cf the even less persuasive argument that the indeterminacy of moral principles, the fact that they often clash and are frequently subject to exceptions establishes that there are no moral truths: Fishkin 1984, pp.52–6, 111–19; Moore 1982, pp.1101–2, 1149–52.

[137] Described by Frankena 1963, p.92 as 'descriptive relativism'. For general discussions of relativism, see Frankena 1963, pp.92–4; Williams 1972, ch.3; and 1985, ch.9; Moore 1982, pp.1088–97.

cannot be said to be universally valid and also that no one is entitled to criticise the values of cultures other than their own.

This latter 'normative relativism'[138] is easily dismissed. As we shall see, it forms no necessary part of the postmodernist position. Indeed, in relying on the apparently objective value of tolerance, it seems to contradict ethical scepticism.[139] Moral realists also counter-argue that the contingency of moral values is greatly exaggerated and that in fact there is a surprising degree of moral consensus across cultures and historical epochs.[140] Apparent moral differences stem from different opinions as to the facts relevant to moral judgements rather than the applicable moral principles. For example, it has been argued that we all agree over the value of human life. Differences over issues like abortion and capital punishment may stem, for instance, from disagreements over whether humans are ensouled at conception or birth, and whether capital punishment deters or is applied in discriminatory fashion.[141] This refutation of empirical relativism seems unpersuasive. There do seem to be significant differences in moral views both between and within cultures. Not all abortion opponents are Catholic, while many oppose the death penalty irrespective of its deterrence value and pattern of imposition.

Nevertheless, even if moral views do differ radically, this is only circumstantial evidence, rather than conclusive proof, of ontological relativism. While different cultures and different people within cultures may have competing moral values, there may still exist an objective moral reality behind these differences.

An alternative sceptical argument is that moral reality cannot be said to exist given that moral statements or judgements do not refer to or describe moral facts.[142] One form of this 'semantic subjectivism'[143] argues that, when people say that actions, thoughts or character traits are morally good or bad, they merely mean that they approve or disapprove of them. This simple form of subjectivism is, however, alleged to ignore salient features of our common usage of ethical language.[144] Most people when they say that things are wrong arguably mean that they are wrong in an objective sense.[145] More importantly, it is argued that, if moral statements merely refer to one's attitude, feelings or emotions about some issue and hence, unless insincere, will always be true, then we cannot speak of such views as wrong or of two people disagreeing with each other.

---

[138] Frankena 1963, p.93. cf also Williams 1972, pp.37–8, referring to 'vulgar relativism'.

[139] See also Rachels 1991, p.433, regarding the semantic version of subjectivism discussed below.

[140] See eg Frankena 1963, p.93; Raphael 1994, pp.16–17. cf also Williams 1972, p.33 who nevertheless accepts empirical relativism; Warnock 1971, pp.120–1 and Moore 1982, pp.1095–6 who question whether one can infer a lack of moral consensus from the mere fact that moral views appear to differ.

[141] Luban 1990b, pp.129–30.

[142] The following discussion is based on Frankena 1963, pp.88–92; Warnock 1971, pp.125–31; Beauchamp 1982, pp.358–76; Hare 1991; Rachels 1991; Raphael 1994, ch.3. See more generally on the value of the debate about moral language, Williams 1985, ch.7.

[143] Note that we are using subjectivism in a rather broader fashion than linguistic theorists who confine it to its first two variants discussed below.

[144] For other less important criticisms, see Moore 1982, p.1076.

[145] cf Warnock 1971, p.118; Atkinson 1992, p.875.

Other semantic subjectivists argue that moral statements express rather than refer to moral attitudes, feelings or emotions. They take the form of 'hurrah or boo for X' rather than 'I approve/disapprove of X' and hence can be regarded as wrong or in conflict. 'Moral emotivism' has, however, also been largely rejected. For instance, it fails to analyse what sort of attitudes, feelings, or emotions moral statements express[146] and more importantly it fails to capture the fact that moral statements differ from other expressions of attitudes—such as 'hurrah/boo for Manchester United/City'—in implicitly holding out the promise of reasoned justification.

The final form of semantic subjectivism holds that moral statements are pre-scriptive in exhorting their addressees to act in particular ways. Moreover, they are a special kind of prescription in applying equally to all people in similar situations. This 'universal prescriptivism' has been criticised for ignoring the fact that other types of prescriptions, such as the pragmatic 'look before you leap', may also apply universally[147] and the fact that moral statements can only be prescriptive if they are also descriptive.[148]

In our view, many of the technical problems with the various forms of semantic subjectivism are potentially surmountable.[149] Moreover, the more fundamental criticisms only work on the assumption that there is a moral reality which moral statements can describe. Even if semantic subjectivism is flawed, this does not establish that moral reality does exist. In other words, moral realism's plausibility rests on its ontological and epistemological claims. Here, however, the debate[150] is so complex and seemingly interminable that we will only sketch the central strategies of both sides before concentrating on the specifically postmodernist critique.

While all realists claim that there are moral facts 'out there', they differ as to what sort of things they are and how we come to know them. 'Naturalists' hold that moral facts are part of the natural world and are thus knowable in the same way as any other fact.[151] However, they differ substantially as to what these natural foundations are. The most popular secular suggestions refer to human nature,[152] our biological function,[153] the 'human predicament',[154] and human practices or institutions.[155] In reply, sceptics argue that, not only does the lack of agreement between naturalists undermine their position, but that they come up against one or more problems. One is the fact-value gap raised by Hume's 'no ought from is' query, which suggests that

---

[146] See MacIntyre 1985, pp.11–14 for this and other criticisms of emotivism.

[147] cf Warnock 1971, pp.130–1.   [148] Moore 1982, p.1085.

[149] Thus one can distinguish expressions of moral attitudes, feelings or emotions from expressions of other attitudes, etc., and one can distinguish moral prescriptions from other universal prescriptions by their subject matter rather than by their form: cf Warnock 1971, p.131. Moreover, there is nothing problematic about describing some person's reference to their own views as wrong if wrong is understood not in the sense of being untrue but as a reference to the unpersuasiveness of their view.

[150] For an overview, see eg Fishkin 1984; Atkinson 1992, pp.872–87; Singer (ed.), chs.35–40 and 42; Raphael 1994, ch.2.

[151] For an overview of naturalism, see eg Beauchamp 1982, pp.339–52; Pigden 1991.

[152] See eg Hume, section 4.3.1, above.   [153] See eg Aristotle, section 5.3, above.

[154] Warnock 1971, esp ch.2.

[155] See eg the argument of MacIntyre in section 5.3, above and Pigden 1991, p.429.

the arguments of naturalists tend to be of a pragmatic rather than moral nature.[156] Another problem is that the factors relied on are too indeterminate to ground objective moral foundations and are decisively determined by the particular conditions of different societies.[157] In addition, there remains the common intuition that moral facts are open to question in ways that non-moral facts are not and that moral judgements are qualitatively different to scientific discovery and justification.[158]

One response to this accepts that moral facts differ from non-moral facts, but argues that they are still real in the same way that mathematical or logical rules are no less real because they cannot be empirically observed. Thus 'non-naturalists' like Kant hold that moral facts are matters of necessary and self-evident truth revealed by intuition to all rational people for use as first principles. But, even if we assume that mathematical and logical rules are objectively true as matters of intuition, it is far less plausible to regard intuitions about morality as being universally valid. It is revealing that the list of moral duties which deontologists derive from intuition tends to vary between intuitionists[159] and that intuition has been claimed as the meta-ethical foundation of utilitarianism as well as deontology.[160] More importantly, many are suspicious of basing morality on the exercise of intuition. According to Bentham, intuition can easily be used as a smokescreen for self-interest.[161] Even genuine attempts to base moral duties on intuition run into problems. One is that, if our intuitions are regarded as inborn aspects of human nature, then they are unlikely to cover many of the issues arising in complex social interaction. Alternatively, if they are regarded as based on socialisation, then intuitionists have to jettison any claim to the universality and objectivity of their moral theories. Moreover, intuitively derived duties are likely to be heavily influenced by past common moral traditions, which may well be outdated, prejudiced and parochial.[162]

The second and more contemporary response to the criticisms of moral realism argues that it only fails if one expects it to establish moral truth to a standard not even required of knowledge about material facts or axiomatic principles. Most contemporary epistemologists have jettisoned the idea that knowledge is only true if it corresponds to some objective reality for the view that truth is a matter of our knowledge cohering with all other propositions believed to be true. Thus, while realism might fail according to a 'correspondence' standard of truth, there can be said to be moral truths of a 'coherentist' nature. Accordingly, a modified objectivist position holds that moral truths can be said to exist when the beliefs of all reasonable people who have engaged in 'reflective equilibrium' behind a 'veil of ignorance'[163] or under conditions of an 'ideal speech situation'[164] would converge on some belief.[165] If this approach is applied to morality, moral knowledge can be said to be as secure

---

[156] See section 3.4, in relation to Gewirth.   [157] See section 4.2, above.
[158] Moore 1982, p.1113.   [159] cp eg Ross 1930, pp.21–2 with Nagel 1986, p.176.
[160] See Schneewind 1991, p.153.   [161] ibid, p.152.   [162] Davis 1991, p.212.
[163] See Rawls 1971.   [164] See Habermas 1973.
[165] See also Frankena 1963, pp.94–6; Warnock 1971, pp.122–5; Fishkin 1984; Williams 1985, ch.8; Smith 1991. This approach can also be seen in the 'perfectly sympathetic spectator' of utilitarianism and the 'ideal observer' stance of other moral theories.

as other forms of knowledge and moral facts to be no less 'queer'[166] than non-moral facts.

In response, sceptics can argue that the attempts by these 'minimal objectivists'[167] to derive objective moral principles from the hypothetical conversations of hypo-thetical rational people in hypothetical situations are unpersuasive.[168] Either such hypothetical situations are so devoid of reality as to be unable to produce principles useful for real life or the small amount of reality read into the hypothetical situation is such as to defeat the attempt at impartiality. Even slight changes in the appropri-ate decision-making procedure make substantial differences to the values derived, thus rendering the outcome subjectivist or relativist. As postmodernists and femi-nists, for example, have argued, what is regarded as rational is not an abstract quality, but a function of particular societies and their power relations.

But, even if these problems could be overcome and a coherentist account given of objective morality, this would not establish the existence of moral reality. The modified objective approach addresses issues of epistemology, not ontology. Radical sceptics, especially those of postmodernist hue, might argue that there are no such things as facts—moral or otherwise[169]—there are simply opinions, which bear the influence of social construction through language and other discourses.[170] In other words, the belief that moral facts are no less secure than other facts does not assist the objectivist because no knowledge is secure. Arguably, the reason why we speak of moral 'reality' is because of our desire to see our beliefs reflected onto the world in the same way that we continue to speak of the sun 'setting' and 'rising'.[171]

In any event, milder sceptics who retain the belief that moral facts are ontologi-cally different to at least some non-moral facts can argue that nothing moral realists have said has established the existence of moral truth even by the standards of a 'coherentist' epistemology. We are still left in the dark as to what moral reality looks like and how it can be said to exist independently of individuals and communities. Equally, however, realists argue with considerable justification that none of the arguments denying moral truth have coherently undermined the case for moral reality.[172]

7.3 Meta-Ethics and the Postmodernist Critique

In the light of this impasse, it could be argued that there is no harm if realists con-tinue to speak as if the moral values they espouse represent moral truth, whereas sceptics use the language of opinion rather than reality. This is where the specifically postmodernist critique of meta-ethics becomes relevant.

---

[166] cf Mackie 1977, pp.38–42; Moore 1985, *passim*.   [167] Fishkin 1984, ch.2.
[168] See generally Atkinson 1992, pp.887–8. In relation to Rawls, see eg Fishkin 1984, pp.95ff; Williams 1985, pp.77–80 and 99ff; Simmonds 1986, ch.2; Wyschogrod 1990, pp.66–9; Kymlicka 1991, pp.191–3; Douzinas and Warrington 1994, pp.173–4.
[169] cf, however, Moore 1982, p.1153, who doubts whether moral sceptics are also fact sceptics.
[170] See Nicolson 1994.   [171] Atkinson 1992, p.880.
[172] See esp Moore 1982. This is not surprising given the difficulty of proving a negative.

In general terms, postmodernists would argue that claims to truth—moral or otherwise—are not simply misguided. They are never neutral, but an important component of the exercise of power. Even if the proto-postmodernist, Nietzsche, exaggerated by stating that the will to truth always involves the will to power, it can be argued along with Foucault that 'truth is not outside power or lacking in power'.[173] Throughout history various forms of morally outrageous conduct have been legitimated by dominant groups through recourse to grand concepts such as 'Truth', 'Reality', 'Normality', 'Human Nature', etc.[174] Moreover, the hegemony of their views is then defended by portraying relativism and scepticism as leading to a moral abyss.

More specifically, Bauman[175] has noted the irony that, while the Enlightenment proclaimed the individual's power to make his[176] own morality, modernism in fact leads to the suffocation of individual moral conscience by heteronomously applied moral and legal codes. For example, philosophers like Hume regarded morality and law as a means of ensuring through rules, rewards and punishments that the animalistic masses acted, not in terms of their apparent human nature, but in terms of the 'real' human nature revealed by the experts. Similarly, for those who believed that reason revealed universal principles to rational individuals, the fact that the masses seemed incapable of rationality was once again seen as justifying their imposition on the 'hoi-polloi' by professional and political elites. In other words, modernism could not escape St Augustine's complaint that giving individuals the freedom to choose what is right only leads to immoral actions. Consequently, it was seen as necessary for individuals to surrender their freedom to externally set standards, to replace individual conscience with moral codes and to shape ethics after the pattern of law. That such codes were used as instruments of social domination can be seen in the way they supported racism, slavery, colonialism, and sexism, all the while purporting to be based on absolute moral foundations like nature or reason.

Instead of desperately and dangerously seeking objective and universal foundations to morality, postmodernists urge individuals to recognise their own moral responsibility for their actions and look inwards to their own moral conscience rather than outwards to external standards of morality. This has, however, led to the common criticism that postmodernist ethics is an oxymoron, in that without truth there can be no morality, and that it leads to amorality and moral nihilism.[177] From the right, it is argued that without moral foundations there can be no social standards and that without standards there is simply a moral free for all. From the left, it is argued that if there are no objective values then all views are equally valid and

---

[173] Foucault 1980, p.131.

[174] cf Best and Kellner 1991, p.231. A recent example is the papal encyclical *Veritatis Splendor*, in which the 'Splendour of Truth' dictates that Catholics must continue to eschew 'artificial' means of contraception, notwithstanding the tragic consequences of overpopulation for both humans and the environment.

[175] Bauman 1993; esp 'Introduction' and ch.1; 1995, ch.1. See also Douzinas and Warrington 1994, esp ch.4.

[176] The Enlightenment was unconcerned about, if not antagonistic towards, female emancipation.

[177] cf eg Best and Kellner 1991, esp pp.283–94; Crook 1991, pp.158–61.

it is impossible to criticise the sort of immorality and injustice associated with fascism, racism, etc.

The alleged problem of moral nihilism is a red herring. Individuals who believe that nothing matters morally are rare indeed.[178] They would seem to be suffering from an extreme form of melancholia in displaying an extraordinary lack of feeling about anything, if not something approaching madness in apparently not caring whether they are themselves subject to grossly immoral acts. For most moral sceptics, something does matter—the values they and their communities believe in.[179] Just because one does not claim to be objectively right does not mean that one lacks all morals. There is no such thing as a moral vacuum. We all have consciences or at least are socialised into some form of morality.

But even if the nihilism argument is confined to ethical subjectivists and relativists, it does not logically follow that they are 'condemned to silence'[180] on issues of morality.[181] Moral scepticism does not logically entail normative relativism. One can deny the existence of universally applicable and objectively valid moral values yet still claim that some values are better than others. This will involve reliance on and an attempt to justify the values in which one believes. To a large extent, we are likely to refer to the values prevalent in the communities in which we grew up but we may also rely on ideas adopted more reflectively over time. Thus, instead of being condemned to silence, the moral sceptic is condemned to questioning, persuasion and rational argumentation. What postmodernism denies is the power to claim to speak the truth. It does not deny the right to attempt to persuade and to challenge prevailing ideas.

Moral realists might, however, argue that, while moral scepticism does not logically entail normative relativism, in practice it inevitably leads to moral complacency and an 'anything goes' attitude. But this is unproven. Moreover, sceptics may persuasively counter that it is moral realism which is more likely to encourage ethical complacency. Thus it is a short step from believing in objective notions of morality to accepting that particular moral claims reflect that objective moral truth. Rather than inculcating complacency, the denial of objective morality may compel one to constant reflection, evaluation and critique. Constant awareness that claims to truth can never be more than just claims discourages complacency and constantly invites the questions: under what conditions has this truth-claim been made, by whom and whose interests is it likely to serve?

An alternative and opposite complaint is that moral sceptics end up arbitrarily 'imposing' their views on others.[182] This is somewhat ironic given that it is precisely the tendency towards such moral imperialism that motivates much of the postmodern argument against moral realism. It is also left unclear how moral sceptics

---

[178] Rachels 1991, p.434. cf also Williams 1972, p.17; Atkinson 1992, p.884–5 n.115.
[179] See eg Atkinson 1992, p.885.   [180] Twining 1988, p.1545.
[181] The following argument is taken from Nicolson 1994. See also Douzinas and Warrington 1994, p.204; Cornell 1985, p.378.
[182] See eg Fishkin 1984, pp.140ff.

can impose their views on others other than through the force of their arguments. Moreover, there is likely to be far more chance of moral compulsion if arguments are backed up by claims to moral truth than if they are admitted simply to be personally held opinions. Conversely, the latter position is far more likely to lead to greater openness to the views and values of other individuals and their communities. Indeed, one can argue that postmodernism's rejection of the sort of moral interventionism that has characterised modernism is by itself a superior moral position.

7.4 The Ethics of Alterity

The content of postmodernist ethics is also argued to have a number of superior moral qualities. While many early postmodernists saw ethical theorising as so prone to the dangers associated with foundationalism as to be best avoided altogether[183] or simply preferred to 'slide around in the joys of textual analysis',[184] later postmodernists have sought to 're-ethicise' ethics. In doing so, many[185] have turned to the late modernist tradition of dialogical ethics[186] represented by Buber, Bakhtin and, most influentially, Levinas,[187] in order to develop a postmodern 'ethics of alterity'.

These writers share with postmodernists (as well as communitarians and feminists) a rejection of ethical theories that dissolve the concrete particularities of specific individuals in systems of abstract concepts and relations imposed from above. By contrast, dialogical ethics emerge from the actual lived relationships of corporeal moral agents with concrete others. The starting point for this understanding is the typically postmodern critique of modernity's notion of the self as an abstract thinking ego which constructs others and the world as products of its own mind. This ignores the concrete particularity of flesh and blood individuals and involves treating the world and its occupants instrumentally. The dialogical tradition denies that one can separate the self from others because individuals only come to selfhood through alterity. We only acquire self-consciousness through our engagement with 'the Other'. According to Bakhtin, 'I realise myself initially through others: from them I receive words, forms, and tonalities for the formation of the initial idea of myself'.[188] But this does not result in the self's total fusion with the Other. Instead, there is a return to self; not to Kant's atomistic self or the threatened, agonistic self of Sartre's 'Hell is other people',[189] but one whose awareness of alterity is rendered ethically meaningful by respect, compassion and love for the Other.[190] As moral selves we take responsibility for the Other not because of her merit, qualities, or rights or because of our contractual or other obligations, but simply because of her existence.

---

[183] See Gardiner 1996a, p.123 in relation to Lyotard.

[184] Douzinas and Warrington 1994, p.9. See also Bauman 1993, pp.2–3.

[185] But see also the extreme, agonistic subjectivism of Foucault: Gardiner 1996b.

[186] For an overview, see Gardiner 1996a and 1996b. See also Cornell 1985, regarding the slightly different dialogical approach of Hegel.

[187] See eg Wyschogrod 1984; Cornell 1988 and 1990; Bauman 1993 and 1995; Cooke 1993; Douzinas and Warrington 1994. The following discussion of postmodern ethics is based on the above writers.

[188] Quoted in Gardiner 1996a, p.137.

[189] cf Bauman 1993, p.77 and more generally Warnock 1970, ch.4.

[190] cf Levinas' use of the allegory of caress, discussed by Bauman 1993, pp.92–4.

The mere presence of the Other—the gaze of her face in Levinas' terminology—acts as an epiphany summonsing an immediate and spontaneous response from us. Moreover, Levinas stresses that responsibility is one-sided and asymmetrical rather than reciprocal. Concern for the Other must be concern for the Other's sake, not for our own sake. I must be for the Other whether she is for me or not. Reciprocation is accidental, not necessary.

Given the source of ethical responsibility in the immediacy, materiality and uniqueness of the face to face relation, and given that the Other's needs are unpredictable and infinite, it is clear that the ethics of alterity cannot be reduced to moral rules, principles and codes, particularly those which seek to impose symmetry and universality. Nor can such codes limit our responsibility to the Other.[191] For Levinas, the moral state is one of anxiety and tension. As moral selves we are denied the comfort of already existing norms to guide and reassure us that we have reached the limit of our duties, so sparing us the anxiety of guilty conscience. The Other's demand is not expressed aloud nor is its content specified. Because I have to interpret what she requires, I can always misinterpret her needs. Accordingly, I can never know whether I have done the right thing—that I have not caused rather than cured the Other's pain—nor whether I have done enough. To think that one has done enough for the Other is to stop caring for her and thus to abnegate one's responsibility.

The ethics of alterity recognises that life's essential messiness renders ethical dilemmas incurably irresoluble and that attempts to reduce morality to universal, rational and non-ambiguous principles are doomed to failure. Instead of top-down attempts to impose universal norms based on reason, postmodern ethics seeks to listen to the voices of those usually silenced and to use their stories of 'pain, joy, hope and despair'[192] to challenge the established categories and content of modernist ethics. Postmodern ethics thus marks a shift from normativity to narrativity. It also seeks to 're-enchant'[193] morality by recognising that it is best left to human spontaneity, emotions, impulses and inclinations and that moral action is not necessarily morally inferior just because it cannot be explained and justified. Furthermore, postmodern ethics hopes to counter many of the deleterious effects of modernist ethics and modernism itself. It seeks to re-awaken the individual's moral conscience which has been anaesthetised by the replacement of individual responsibility with moral and legal codes, by cynicism in the face of seemingly unstoppable wars, genocide and environmental destruction, by bureaucratic organisations in which moral responsibility appears to 'float' within the organisation without attaching to anyone in particular or at all, by businesses whose worship of economic efficiency rules out questions of morality and by the fact that we increasingly see our lives as involving fragmentary episodes lacking in continuity, consequence and connection to those who live alongside us but whom we do not know.[194]

However, while the ethics of alterity challenges modernist ethics, it also raises

[191] cf Bakhtin's memorable phrase: 'There is no alibi in being', quoted by Gardiner 1996a, p.139.
[192] Cook 1993, p.2458.   [193] cf Bauman 1993, p.33.
[194] In addition to the references at n.187, see Bauman 1994.

problems for postmodernists. Some might be troubled by the realist overtones in references to the 'primordial'[195] relation with the Other as the 'essence'[196] and 'foundation'[197] of morality. On the other hand, given the uniqueness and immediacy of this relationship, this is hardly the sort of foundationalism which casts such a shadow over modernist ethics.[198] In any event, we can always read the ethics of alterity as a call to ethical responsibility rather than a privileged description of reality.

More problematic is the fact that postmodernist ethics appears to be too demanding. Not only is responsibility to the Other unlimited and hence always liable to be unsatisfied,[199] but once we move away from the primary 'I–Thou' moral relation into general social relations we are faced with many others. Are we expected to care for everyone equally when our resources for compassion are limited? One response is to say that there is nothing wrong with setting high moral standards as ideals and allowing people to work out for themselves how much they can manage to achieve without making their own lives miserable.

Another response comes from Levinas himself who recognises that with the entry of 'the Third' we are forced to make comparisons and to weigh the competing demands of different individuals. This requires a basis for comparison which requires the sort of principles of justice enacted in laws or other normative codes. In other words, according to Levinas, we are always fated to 'fall into' law; into codes and those relations of symmetry and reciprocity which conflict with the original ethical relation. This does not, however, simply return us to modernist ethics. While moral and legal codes might be inevitable, postmodernists regard them as inferior to the morality of the self–Other encounter and dangerous in always reducing difference to sameness, thus effacing the Other's specific needs. The ethics of alterity reminds us that our responsibility is unlimited and cannot be extinguished by codes. It acts as a 'star'[200] calling upon us to constantly recover the traces of otherness which have been obliterated by symmetry. Indeed, respect for otherness is inherently implicated in the postmodern methodology of deconstruction, which seeks to uncover the hidden and disprivileged meanings of texts, including those that reduce morality to codes.[201]

Related to this is another way of limiting the infinite nature of responsibility to otherness. Thus it might be argued that postmodernist ethics is not simply concerned with any Other, but with those regarded as the excluded Other: 'the stranger, the outsider, the alien or underprivileged';[202] 'the wretched of the earth', 'suffering through war or natural catastrophe, through poverty, illness or psychic injury'.[203] Under this view alterity is marked not so much by proximity—as in dialogical

---

[195] eg Wyschogrod 1990, p.150.			[196] eg Douzinas and Warrington 1994, p.165.

[197] Bauman 1993, esp ch.3.			[198] cf Bauman 1993, p.80; Douzinas and Warrington 1990, p.165.

[199] cf Derrida's criticism from within postmodernism that this renders the ethical relation devoid of any fun: Cornell 1988, p.1619.

[200] Cornell 1990, p.1697; Bauman 1993, ch.5.			[201] cf Cornell 1990.

[202] Douzinas, Goodrich and Hachamamovich 1994, p.22.

[203] Wyschogrod 1990, pp.xv, 233 and 254. See also Cook 1993, p.2458.

ethics—but by lack and destitution, while ethical standards are regarded as discoverable in the lives of self-renouncing moral saints rather than moral rules.[204]

Bauman suggests a further concretisation of postmodernist ethics.[205] Relying on Beck's analysis of contemporary 'risk society',[206] he points out that many of the celebrated aspects of modernity such as technological development and economic development have consequences which are frequently unintended, not immediately recognised and far removed both in time and space. The scale of possible consequences of human actions has long outgrown our current moral imagination. Focusing on persons in our sight and reach, and actions having visible and predictable effects, modernist ethics tends to limit our responsibility to those 'near and dear'. It prompts us to ensure our own children's well-being, but not to deal with the environmental problems facing all children and future generations, or with world poverty.

According to Bauman, ethics needs very long hands to reach those beyond our sight and beyond the present. Moreover, because it must cope with an endemically uncertain and potentially catastrophic future, a postmodern ethics must be one of self-limitation and one that does not seek excuses in ignorance. We need to visualise the long range effects of our actions and to give the prophecy of doom greater heed than the prophecy of bliss. We need an ethics of preservation and prevention rather than of progress and perfection.

No doubt these elaborations on the ethics of alterity are unlikely to satisfy those seeking certain solutions to moral problems; still less those who would prefer easily satisfied duties which do not impinge too greatly on their day to day lives. Communitarians, on the other hand, might regard postmodern ethics as placing too much autonomy in the hands of individuals at the expense of respect for community values.[207] Postmodernists are likely to respond that, while our moral values and inclinations will always bear the deep trace of our communities, ultimately moral responsibility is uniquely our own and cannot be evaded by reference to the will of community or its moral or legal codes.

8. CONCLUSION

For those seeking enlightenment from philosophical ethics in order either to rethink the current professional legal ethics or to obtain guidance in their professional and personal lives, a number of lessons can be drawn from our admittedly simplistic sketch of the main ethical approaches.

---

[204] ibid. [205] Bauman 1993, esp ch.7 and 1994, pp.34–8. [206] Beck 1992.

[207] cf Lash 1996, who makes the slightly different point that Levinas' and Bauman's ethics are insufficiently grounded in real world practices. See, however, the call of other alterity ethicists for the establishment of dialogical communities based upon pluralism and full participative democracy: Gardiner 1996b, p.140 and Cornell 1985 regarding Hegel; and Bauman's criticism of communitarianism: Bauman 1993, p.43ff; 1994, pp.30–4; and 1996.

Deontological ethics reminds us that it is the essence of immorality to have standards of behaviour which some but not others are expected to follow. It also suggests that there may be certain moral values that are so fundamental as to require precedence over any social good which can be achieved by violating these values. By contrast, consequentialism urges that such an ethics is likely to be too inflexible to meet the exigencies of real-life dilemmas and that an ethics which is distinct from notions of the 'good life' is likely to be empty and sterile.

By contrast to these two traditions, virtue ethics reminds us to pay attention not simply to what moral actors do, but also to their intentions, motivations, and the way they live their lives as a whole. Without a focus on character and moral development, ethics is likely to end up as a set of formal injunctions with little impact on moral behaviour. Communitarians, feminists, and postmodernists all emphasise that morality is and ought to be something that involves real people, situated in real social contexts, rather than the abstractions of competing theories. They also argue that love or the needs of others is as good a starting point for ethics as moral rights or respect for abstract individuals. Finally, postmodernists urge us to abandon as naive and dangerous the notion that it is possible to find and elaborate 'true' ethics and to recognise the unlimited and uncertain nature of moral obligations.

In later chapters we will argue that professional legal ethics ignores the large variety of competing ethical theories in favour of an approach influenced by liberalism and formalism, and which largely derives from deontological ethics, but also owes something to utilitarianism. Accordingly, we will draw on the competing ethical traditions to interrogate both the form and content of professional legal ethics and to explore new ways of envisioning the ethics of lawyers.

3

The Social Context: Professional Ideals and Institutional Settings

The importance of the professions, and the professional classes can hardly be over-rated, they form the head of the great English middle class, maintain its tone of independence, keep up to the mark its standard of morality and direct its intelligence.

H. Byerley Thomson[1]

We do not do anything but run a business. We sell a service which is the stuff between our ears. What is this thing about learned profession? It is the stuff of sherry talk . . .

Law Firm Complaints' Handler[2]

1. INTRODUCTION

'Lawyers aren't made, they are born—out of wedlock', runs a current anti-lawyer joke. Yet no one would seriously argue that lawyering is simply in the genes. Instead, a complex of dispositional factors, social background, education, training and work experience go to make up the 'legal persona'.[3]

Exploring the social setting of the legal profession is extremely important for a number of reasons. In the absence of much concrete information on how lawyers actually deal with ethical issues, it helps us predict how they will behave both in terms of whether they are likely to follow the norms found in written discourses on professional legal ethics, and how they are likely to act where there are no governing norms. Sociological insights into the realities of modern practice help us to understand not just the generic constraints upon ethical behaviour to which all practitioners are subject, but also that these constraints vary according to the practitioners' particular social setting. Ethical behaviour will be influenced by the type of legal work performed, by lawyers' position in organisational hierarchies, their client base, etc. In short, lawyers' social context is essential to understanding the micro-ethics of practice.

This context, however, also raises ethical questions of a macro nature. Like most professions, lawyers have always made a number of eloquent claims about their mode of operations which can either be seen as setting out important professional ideals or, more cynically, as an attempt at legitimating their high fees, status, and power.

---

[1] *The Choice of a Profession* (1857), p.5, cited in Corfield 1995, p.200.
[2] Quoted by Christensen *et al* 1999, p.36.   [3] Elkins 1978.

Many theorists[4] have sought to identify a middle path between these competing versions by characterising professionalism as underpinned by an implied 'social contract' between professions, on the one hand, and consumers and government, on the other, in which professions guarantee certain levels of competence, accessibility, a service ethic, high moral standards and public protection (in the shape of indemnity insurance, compensation funds, etc.) in return for high status, independence, financial rewards, and restricted competition. However, in the last twenty years or so, the growth of inter- and intra-professional competition, of consumerist concerns over poor client care and professional standards, and the apparent triumph of the notion of law as a business over law as a profession have placed the contractarian version of professionalism in jeopardy. This has led some writers to suggest that we are witnessing 'the end of professionalism' as we know it,[5] or at the very least a substantial renegotiation of the 'social contract'.[6] In this light, we are entitled to ask what has happened to the professional ideals of altruism and high ethical standards and, indeed, whether the legal professions have ever really upheld their side of the bargain. If not, they may themselves stand condemned as fundamentally unethical.

In order to explore these micro- and macro-ethical issues, we shall first consider in more detail the nature of the professions' core ideals and then examine the institutional settings and contexts which are relevant to understanding both the claims of professionalism and how lawyers are likely to resolve ethical issues.

2. THE IDEALS OF THE LEGAL PROFESSIONS

Much of the earliest sociological theorising about lawyers took the profession's claim to ethical status largely at face value. Durkheim, for example, located the professions as key intermediate institutions which, existing between citizen and state, acted as the guardians of moral authority in modern society.[7] The so-called trait theories,[8] which emerged in the mid-twentieth century, and focused on the professions' social functions,[9] followed this trend by emphasising the distinctively professional notions of community, altruism and the regulation of conduct. Theoretically speaking, this narrow functional approach has fallen into academic disfavour since the late 1960s, not least for its failure to articulate theoretically the relationship between traits.[10] Nevertheless, of all the major strands of sociological theorising, it remains the only one really to stress the importance of ethics to the professional project.[11] Moreover,

---

[4] See eg Halliday 1987; Glasser 1990; Paterson 1996.
[5] See eg Abel 1986; Hanlon and Shapland 1996.   [6] Paterson 1996.
[7] Durkheim 1992.   [8] See eg Millerson 1964; Moore with Rosenblum 1970.
[9] This 'functionalist' approach, which can be traced back to the work of Durkheim, dominated mid-twentieth century sociology. Its primary concern was to describe how social groups and institutions operate to maintain each other and the totality of the social system in which they are located. An integral part of this process was to describe those institutions—including the professions—in terms of their defining characteristics or 'traits'.
[10] See notably Johnson 1972, pp.23–32; Macdonald 1995, pp.2–4.
[11] Abel 1988a, p.7; though it said little of substance about those ethics.

when the legal professions have entered debates about their own professionalism,[12] they have tended to subscribe most readily to this 'trait model', perhaps because it has corresponded most closely to their ascribed self-image in its mixture of 'pious hopes and self-interest'.[13] For these reasons we have retained the trait approach as a primary means of organising the material in this chapter, and as a basis for critique, whilst also drawing on much recent, more theoretically informed, work on the legal professions.[14]

In essence the trait theories agree on a relatively small number of characteristics that are said to define professional work and organisation.[15] We intend to concentrate on six of these which are clearly reflected in professional discourse,[16] though a number of them are closely interlinked and for that reason will be considered together. First, it is said that professions are characterised by their deployment of technical knowledge and skills, developed from specialised and frequently lengthy education and training. This also underpins a second trait which is the tendency to require some certification of competence, usually based on examination. Thirdly, professionals are said to share a sense of collegiality[17] and homogeneity with members of the same profession. This is commonly reinforced by membership of a professional association or body. Fourthly, intra-professional collegiality is combined with a high level of autonomy in the organisation and delivery of professional work. Professions traditionally lack the strong emphasis on hierarchical bureaucracy displayed by more managerial occupations. Fifthly, professions are also characterised by a commitment to principles of altruistic service and high ethical standards, creating a mutual expectation of trust between professional and client.[18] Finally, these standards and expectations are usually supported by codes of professional ethics which are normally established as part of a self-regulatory system.

These traits are (or can easily be) represented as positive consequences of professionalisation. They uphold an image of the professions as highly educated, highly skilled, independent yet socially responsible 'communities within the community',[19] ethically grounded in the *noblesse oblige*[20] tradition of legal service—that is, an ideal-type that makes the patrician assumption that service is rendered as a matter of public duty, rather than calculated commercialism. It is thus important to ascertain the empirical foundation for these claims. We will do so by looking at the extent to

[12] Notably, in the UK, the Ormrod Committee 1971, para. 86; Benson Commission 1979, para. 3.2; Marre Committee 1988, paras. 4.13, 4.22, 6.9, 13.2; Bar Council 1989, ch.4; and, in the USA, the Stanley Commission 1986, p.10.

[13] Atkinson 1983, p.225.

[14] See Macdonald 1995, ch.1, for an overview of the various theoretical models. Note that some of these functionalist themes have re-emerged in the 'neo-contractualist' approach being advanced by writers like Halliday 1987; Glasser 1990; and Paterson 1996, 1997.

[15] Millerson 1964.   [16] See n.12 above.

[17] Note that 'collegial' is used in two distinct senses in the literature. One, as here, refers to the ideal-typical collective group identity of lawyers; the other, following Johnson 1972, describes the classical lawyer-client relationship in which the lawyer exercises substantial control over client decision-making. Both senses are used in this and subsequent chapters.

[18] cf Watkins *et al* 1993, p.10.   [19] Goode 1957.   [20] Luban 1988b.

which the classical professional traits are upheld or undermined by a range of important institutional settings, starting with the procedural context, moving on to the professional-institutional, demographic, educational and, finally, the business contexts.

3. THE PROCEDURAL CONTEXT

Clearly, a key characteristic of the Anglo-Welsh procedural model is its adversarial nature, characterised by the classical image of litigation as the modern equivalent to trial by battle, in which the lawyers act as their clients' champions. Indeed, adversarialism can be regarded as the defining feature of lawyering in our system, being reflected in both institutional structures and ideology. This can be shown by reference to three important and inter-connected characteristics.

3.1 Characteristics of the Adversary System

The first characteristic is its competitiveness. The adversary system, unsurprisingly, treats its protagonists as adversaries, characterised in its most extreme form by the notion of 'zealous advocacy'.[21] Procedures have evolved in the expectation that litigation is party-led both at pre-trial and trial stages. The emphasis on orality[22] and judicial detachment (the judge as umpire as opposed to inquisitor) at the trial stage has also served to emphasise the representative and combative nature of the advocate's role. Arguably, this competitiveness encourages manipulation and tactical abuses of the system, whereby lawyers use their power to subvert due process by strategic use of procedural devices.[23]

Secondly, as we shall see in much greater detail, the existence of the adversarial system plays an important and *prima facie* plausible role in justifying the current conception of the lawyer's proper function.[24] The division between barristers and solicitors itself reflects the centrality of specialist advocates who are capable of playing an independent but representative role in proceedings, while the ethical focus of the codes of conduct, as we shall see,[25] shows a clear bias in its concern with the activities of advocates. This idealises not just the adversary system but the place of advocacy within the system so that the advocate's role becomes fundamental to the liberal social order. As one professional insider claims:

. . . advocacy is central not only to our legal system but also to our way of life. Advocacy has, in its manifestation of freedom of expression, its protection of liberty, and its vital contribu-

---

[21] See Ch.6, section 2.
[22] Though this has been a key feature of the Anglo-American model, it is probably not a definitive characteristic of adversarialism *per se*—see Ch.7, n.21.
[23] See eg Woolf 1995, p.13; and Ch.6, section 3.2.   [24] See Ch.6, section 2.2; Ch.7, section 2.
[25] Ch.4, section 3.3.3.

tion to the rule of law, an essential morality which justifies its practice, excuses its excesses, and makes intolerable any society which lacks its presence.[26]

Thirdly, adversarialism casts a long shadow over the legal system.[27] Many conduct rules, not just on advocacy, but on more generic issues such as confidentiality and conflicts of interest, also reflect adversary assumptions by obliging lawyers to behave in an (in)appropriately adversarial fashion, even in non-contentious matters.[28] The importance of the adversarial system is reinforced not just by practice itself, but by prior socialisation processes which draw on powerful images of the legal process presented by the media, and by the system of legal education, which draws heavily on the adversary principle, albeit through the more rarefied medium of appellate rather than trial court advocacy, as the grounding for legal analysis and argumentation.[29] The power of this image is such that it can colour the whole of lawyers' approaches to legal practice. Lawyers often have difficulty converting to a non-adversarial paradigm.[30] The formal competitiveness underpinning litigation roles and rules becomes translated into a 'stylistic competitiveness'[31] that may be ethically dubious,[32] even in the litigious context, but which may also influence lawyers inappropriately to adopt low-level, often competitive, negotiation strategies, or skew their perspective on using mediation or other forms of alternative dispute resolution (ADR) for their clients.[33] However, this adversarial outlook is likely to become increasingly problematic as the Anglo-Welsh system undergoes some fundamental stylistic and substantive changes.

3.2 Challenges to Adversarialism

There is, even within litigation, a marked shift away from the classical adversarial paradigm, particularly in civil disputes. The emphasis on orality has been in decline for some years,[34] hastened by greater judicial demand for case papers and outline ('skeleton') arguments in an attempt to speed up litigation. Pre-trial judicial management of cases has also become increasingly important since the Civil Justice Review of 1988; a process that has largely been completed by the Woolf reforms. As a consequence, cases will become far more subject to judicial control early in the pre-trial stage, and are likely to exhibit less opportunity for tactical abuse and delay.[35] Similarly, the increased emphasis on pre-trial disclosure of evidence (in both civil and criminal proceedings) not only changes the character of trials, but also brings

---

[26] Pannick 1992, p.10.   [27] See Mnookin and Kornhauser 1979.
[28] See Ch.6, section 2.2.   [29] See further section 6, below.
[30] Menkel-Meadow 1996; cf data in Davies *et al* 1996; Genn 1998, pp.36–8. The fact that most disputes never reach the courts does not necessarily invalidate this argument. Cases that settle do so in the shadow of the court, and may be carried on in a combative and adversarial fashion to the point of settlement.
[31] Lowenthal 1982, p.74.   [32] See Ch.8, below.
[33] See variously Lowenthal 1982; Genn 1987, 1998, pp.35–41; Boon 1995; Tur 1995; Davies *et al* 1996.
[34] See eg Glasser 1993.   [35] cf Dingwall *et al* 1990; Glasser 1993.

into question some of the assumptions underlying the ethics of lawyer-client confidentiality.[36]

Moreover, there is mounting concern, particularly in 'private plight'[37] as opposed to corporate work, that adversarialism is simply becoming too expensive. The essence of this argument is threefold. First, the increase in corporate litigation has changed the character of the process for all: 'refinements of due process . . . require more submissions, hearings and findings . . . elaborations of the law . . . require more research, investigation, evidence and use of experts'.[38] Consequently transaction costs rise. Secondly, routinised litigation practice, particularly as computerised litigation support facilitates document production, etc., builds up costs because lawyers will take certain steps out of habit rather than strict necessity.[39] Thirdly, adversarialism may, in some (though not by any means all) contexts, increase rather than dissipate 'the heat' of disputes, thereby either reducing settlement rates, and/or increasing the amount of legal work that clients demand. This heat may be generated as much by clients as their lawyers, but the adversarial nature of the system may make it difficult for lawyers to advance non-adversarial alternatives for fear of seeming insufficiently zealous or supportive of clients.[40] Consequently the courts frequently find themselves 'unable to make appropriate provision for the parties . . . because of their liability for legal costs'.[41] Critics also point to the problem of supplier-induced demand for legal aid: because legal aid services are both purchased and delivered by lawyers, it is argued that lawyer self-interest has ensured incentives for escalation of costs have become inherent to the system.[42]

By contrast, however, in criminal litigation, there has been concern that lawyers are not being adversarial enough; that the intended checks and balances are being undermined by an ideology among lawyers, particularly defence lawyers, that clients are likely to be guilty, and that their role is therefore primarily concerned with the 'routine production of guilty pleas'.[43]

In addition, the growing emphasis on ADR, however reluctantly embraced by some lawyers, cannot be ignored. ADR is already a key part of many areas of civil practice. The arbitration of both large scale commercial disputes and of small claims are now so well established that they barely justify the epithet of alternatives to court proceedings. Successive governments have also declared their commitment to extending the use of mediation[44] in family proceedings.[45] The proportion of 'non-family'

---

[36] See further Ch.9.   [37] ie non-commercial work for private clients, particularly litigation.

[38] Galanter 1992, p.20.

[39] This concern is particularly voiced in matrimonial work—see eg Tur 1995, pp.148–9 for examples. This is not to suggest routine lawyer misconduct. The failing is essentially, as Tur argues, systemic rather than individual.

[40] See Davis 1988, pp.96, 104–6; Genn 1998, pp.39–40. Though lawyer self-interest may also impact on the likelihood of settlement because of its consequence for fees—Kritzer 1987; Genn 1998, pp.38–9.

[41] *Evans v Evans* [1990] 1 FLR 319, 321.

[42] See eg Abel 1982 p.6; Bevan *et al* 1994; but cf Wall 1997.

[43] McConville *et al* 1994, p.41. See further Ch.5, section 2.1.

[44] Whereby a neutral third party assists disputants to a negotiated settlement.

[45] Though the Government has recently delayed indefinitely the implementation of Part II of the Family Law Act 1996, which would require couples to attend information meetings to see if there is scope

civil disputes mediated is likewise almost certain to grow following the Woolf reforms, which have empowered the courts to consider any unreasonable refusal of, or unreasonable behaviour during, ADR when awarding costs.[46]

The resultant picture is a complex one. Adversarialism is traditionally seen as the driving force behind our legal system and lawyers' ethics. In practice, however, the adversarial context is not only becoming less adversarial—a practice which may or may not be deemed ethically problematic, depending perhaps on the form of action involved—it is also being displaced in a number of fields by practices such as negotiation, arbitration, and mediation. As a consequence, at the very least we must acknowledge that too much emphasis on an adversary ethic may give 'a false unity to the field of legal ethics'.[47]

4. PROFESSIONAL STRUCTURES AND INSTITUTIONAL CONTEXTS

4.1 Introduction

English lawyers, it has been said,[48] form part of a distinctive European tradition of professional organisation, in which the legal professions are characterised by their 'separateness'. What this means is that the legal professions are distinguished from other occupational groups and, in some cases, each other by a number of characteristics. These include formalised role incompatibilities whereby a professional group is legally protected from competition;[49] constancy of institutional structures;[50] and (claimed) adherence to general, but often tacit, professional standards.[51] As Glenn argues,[52] professional ethics cannot be understood separately from these professional structures and traditions. The creation of politically autonomous professional associations has in many respects been the key to this process.

The creation of such associations supports many of the professions' value claims, most notably to both collegiality and autonomy (self-governance[53]). These particular values underpin the professions' claims to authority over their members, and help construct a sense of ethical/disciplinary control as a form of 'community sanction'.[54] Historically, the perceived need to maintain a group identity and ethos were

for reconciliation or informal resolution of matters in dispute. These were expected to divert a significant proportion of cases to mediation, but this was not borne out by the pilot schemes. The Lord Chancellor's Department (LCD) has nevertheless affirmed its long-term commitment to mediation in family proceedings, the structures for which are already implemented in Part I of the 1996 Act. See LCD Press Releases of 17 June and 25 June 1999 at http://www.open.gov.uk.

[46] See Part 44, Civil Procedures Rules; also more generally Woolf 1996, pp.64–5.

[47] Haber and Baumrin 1988, p.117.   [48] Glenn 1990, pp.426–9.

[49] eg the reserved activities, such as probate practice.

[50] eg the Inns of Court, the Law Society.

[51] See Burrage 1988, p.228, for a similar typology.

[52] Glenn 1990, p.425.

[53] We use the word governance deliberately in this chapter to embrace both the representative and regulatory functions of professional institutions: the issue of self-regulation is addressed in detail in Ch.4.

[54] cf Greenwood 1957.

key motivations behind the emergence of both the professional associations and their conduct rules. This is manifestly evident, historically, in the Bar's ideology and practices, in particular in the way the Inns of Court[55] and the Circuit Mess, by controlling admissions, training, discipline and much of the social life of practitioners, sought to construct an *esprit de corps* within the independent Bar.[56] The formation, from the mid-eighteenth century,[57] of both local and national law societies in England and Wales was also motivated by a desire not just to increase solicitors' 'clubability' but to better control their admission, training, and discipline.[58] It was also, perhaps even more fundamentally, part of a concerted project to raise the profession's occupational status.[59]

4.2 The Modern Institutions

This collegial ideology is largely reflected in the current professional institutions, though, clearly, it also has its limits. The existence of a divided profession in England and Wales is the most obvious of these, leading to separate representation of the interests of solicitors and barristers.[60] Though the Law Society and the Bar display distinctive organisational characteristics,[61] they have both sought to maintain management systems in which policy is largely determined by practitioner representatives sitting on the professional governing bodies.[62] This system of governance involves extensive powers of self-regulation, as we shall see.[63] Whereas the professions' disciplinary bodies have, to some extent, been opened up by the introduction of lay participation, the Law Society and Bar Councils themselves consist solely of

[55] Which, until the expulsion of solicitors and attorneys in the mid-C16th and C17th, had, with the inns of chancery, provided a common form of association for both branches of the profession.

[56] As late as the 1980s a Treasurer of Gray's Inn described training as a barrister as including 'not merely the acquisition of a sound knowledge of the law, but the attainment through mutual association and companionship of an honourable status and code of professional conduct'—cited in Seldon 1987, p.89. History in fact suggests that the unifying effect of these institutions is overestimated, even in respect of the smaller and more socially cohesive Bar of the nineteenth century—cf Cocks 1983, pp.23ff.

[57] The Society of Gentleman Practisers was founded in London, *circa* 1739. The first provincial societies were founded in Bristol (1770), Yorkshire (1786), and Somerset (1796), followed by a handful more in the early 1800s. See Kirk 1976, pp.36–41.

[58] Corfield 1995, pp.83–5, 206; Sugarman 1996, pp.87–91.　　　　[59] Sugarman, ibid, pp.90–2.

[60] This is not to suggest there is no co-operation between the legal professions. As Corfield 1995, p.85, notes, even as the formal divisions between solicitors and barristers hardened in the nineteenth century, there emerged a growing rhetoric, underpinned by professional etiquette, which stressed the unity of lawyers in a profession 'with a shared knowledge and a common set of operating conventions', but it does mean that both branches begin from a formal assumption that they must speak with a separate voice. For an 'insider' perspective on this see Gaskell 1984, p.2600.

[61] The Law Society is a larger and administratively more complex body than the Bar Council. Both operate through a diverse committee structure, but the Law Society relies far more on an extensive professional secretariat and bureaucracy for support.

[62] The key governing bodies are the General Council of the Bar and the Council of the Law Society. However, the organisation of the Bar is somewhat less centralised, particularly given that the Inns of Court retain some autonomy. See Allaker and Shapland 1994, p.13; Thornton 1995, pp.53–4.

[63] Ch.4, esp section 2.

lawyers. However, these existing structures, and their underlying ideologies, now face a number of challenges to which we now turn.

4.3 Professionalism: In Whose Interests?

There has always been an inherent tension between the regulatory and representative functions of the professional bodies, in that their representative role requires them to act in the profession's best interests, whereas their regulatory role is grounded in their ability to act in the public interest. While it would be wrong to accede wholly to the marxian view of the professions as conspiracies against the laity, there is strong empirical evidence that the professional bodies are ready to trade-off public interest against self-interest, in such a way as to put their members' interests first. Examples of this can be seen in the jostling for position by the Law Society and Bar over rights of audience in 1986,[64] and in the deal struck with government in the early 1970s, whereby the Law Society gave way on the abolition of conveyancing scale fees, in exchange for the continuing right to act for vendor and purchaser in domestic property transactions.[65]

The rise of a new and vociferous consumer movement, backed since the early 1980s by government policies that were, first, hostile to professional monopolies and then more positively supportive of mechanisms for enabling 'assertive citizens',[66] has made it harder for lawyers to hide behind the mystique of professionalism. Bodies like the National Consumer Council and the Consumers Association have published highly critical, widely publicised accounts of the legal system's workings and lawyer (in)competence. Lawyers have sometimes been their own worst enemies, by adopting an arrogant approach to client care and complaints, while the professional bodies have in turn proved themselves somewhat inept at dealing with incipient crises of public confidence in lawyers.[67] Consequently, as Mears acknowledges, '[t]he public's perception of what amounts to a first class service has changed radically. Fifty years ago, none of the professions had to work to gain the respect of the public or their

---

[64] Following abolition of the solicitors' conveyancing monopoly. As a *New Law Journal* editorial at the time noted, discussion documents issued by both professional bodies were 'partisan statements in which self-interest is paramount . . .': see Zander 1988, p.28. The battle over advocacy rights has continued through the 1990s—see eg Zander 1988, pp.24–31, and 1997. For recent government proposals to further extend rights of audience to employed lawyers and a wider pool of solicitors in private practice, see Lord Chancellor's Department 1998 and the Access to Justice Bill 1999, clauses 31–39.

[65] See Kirk 1976, p.152. See also Sheinman 1997, Lunney 1997 for earlier examples. It would be wrong to suggest, however, that the professions always won these encounters. Consider eg the Law Society's unsuccessful attempts in the mid-70s to use its control over practising certificate waivers to force the government to fund Law Society-backed rather than independent law centres—Fennell 1976, pp.17–18.

[66] Thomas 1992, pp.2–6; Williams 1996, p.2.

[67] eg the Law Society's failure in the early 1980s to deal appropriately with the 'Glanville Davies affair' (involving a serious complaint of overcharging against a member of Council) can be seen as a defining moment, which paved the way for the political attacks which followed. See Burrage 1996, p.69, and cf the Marre Report 1988, para. 4.21.

clients. They operated in a climate of deference. The simple reality is that those days are gone and we must adapt to the fact.'[68] As we shall see in Chapter 4, the possibility that adaptation might necessitate the complete separation of representative and regulatory functions cannot be excluded.

4.4 Representation and Intra-Professional Segmentation

The continuance of existing structures of governance has been threatened *inter alia* by the increasing segmentation[69] or fragmentation[70] of professional interests. This too has undoubtedly created tensions in professional legal ethics. A small number of examples will suffice for now.

First, the notion of collegiality has always had a mythical edge to it. Professions, like other forms of social organisation, display conflicts over authority, status and control. At an institutional level, as we have seen, this has long been evident in relations between the Law Society and the Bar, reflecting the contradictory tensions between their mutual interests and antagonisms.[71] However, there are also quite frequent clashes between the grassroots and government within each profession (particularly when times are financially hard). Concerns thus tend to focus on the representativeness of the professional bodies, and their ability to lobby effectively for the interests of the whole profession, rather than just a privileged element. For example, in the mid-1980s the Bar Council was heavily criticised for being out of touch with the junior Bar, and a number of changes were forced through at Annual Conference aimed at making the Bar Council more representative and more democratic.[72]

Within the solicitors' profession these tensions reflect the increasing divide between the interests of large and small law firms—hence the long-standing grievance of 'rank and file' members that the Law Society Council is dominated by the representatives of the City and large firms more generally.[73] The other side of that coin is the question put by one City solicitor: 'Why do . . . firms like [this] subscribe to the same trade union as a man above a betting shop in Billericay High Street?'[74] Doubts about the representativeness of governance were also reinforced by the oligarchic system of 'election' of senior officers, whereby successive Presidents, Vice-Presidents, and Deputy Vice-Presidents were selected from the ranks of Council members and elected unopposed at the Law Society's Annual General Meeting.[75] This system was finally blown apart only by the vociferous and populist campaign

---

[68] Mears 1997, p.1.   [69] Bucher and Strauss 1961; Bucher 1962.

[70] The distinction is primarily one of degree. Segmentation, as we shall see, suggests the professions have split along a particular fault line, nowadays commonly identified as the corporate/private client 'hemispheres' (Heinz and Laumann 1982) whereas fragmentation suggests a more radical diffusion of groups and interests.

[71] See the previous section and Hughes 1994 p.37.   [72] See Abel 1988a, pp.130–1.

[73] Sugarman 1996, pp.105–6; Zander 1988, p.249.   [74] In Goriely and Williams 1996, p.122.

[75] See eg *Law Society's Gazette*, 26 April 1995, p.10.

of Martin Mears, who was one of two members to stand against the 'official' candidate in 1995.[76] The Law Society's growing bureaucratisation also became a source of frustration in the early 1990s, both because of the direct demands it made on practitioners,[77] and because of a growing sense that the profession's grassroots had lost control of the agenda.[78] Though the latter are only the latest examples of long-standing power struggles between elite and non-elite members, and between traditionalists and modernisers, affecting both professions, they indicate the fragility of professional collegiality in increasingly large, fragmenting, professions.

Secondly, the increase in specialisation, and the recognition of special constituencies within the professions, has also fostered the growth of special interest groups such as the Legal Aid Practitioners' Group, the Solicitors' Family Law Association, the Association of Personal Injury Lawyers and the Commercial Bar Association. Constituency groups include bodies like the Society of Black Lawyers (which cuts across the professional divide), the Association of Women Solicitors, or the Bar Association for Commerce, Finance and Industry (for employed barristers). The functions of such groupings may range from the purely social and educational to more deliberate lobbying (both within and outside the profession) and related 'political' activities. There is, however, some evidence of special interest groups not simply lobbying for (or against) changes to practice rules and practices, but creating their own sub-sets of 'rules' which seek to (re)define the notion of good lawyering within their domain. The role of the Solicitors' Family Law Association, which has had its own code of practice since the mid-1980s, is probably the paradigmatic example of this in Britain.[79]

Thirdly, the growth of in-house lawyers also adds additional strains and tensions, not least because the functions and needs of in-house lawyers are often vastly different, and, it is sometimes felt, poorly served by professional bodies which are dominated by private practitioners.[80] The ethical duties of employed lawyers continue to generate difficulties for the professions, not least because employed lawyers fit uncomfortably with traditional expectations of professionalism, apparently lacking the 'normal'[81] degree of independence from clients, and subject to potentially conflicting duties to employers and profession.[82]

---

[76] Every presidential election since then has been contested.

[77] See eg Sommerlad 1995, p.179; Goriely and Williams 1996, pp.106–8; Christensen *et al* 1999, p.36.

[78] See eg *Law Society's Gazette*, 19 March 1997, p.24. cf also *Gazettes* of 15 December 1995, p.14; 9 May 1996, p.10.

[79] See Webley 1998; Neale and Smart 1997, p.377.   [80] Mackie 1989, ch.12.

[81] In anthropological terms this suggests their 'outsider' status reflects the fact that they breach certain 'purity taboos' of the profession. cf Abbott 1981, p.824: 'the impure is that which violates the categories and classifications of a given cultural system'.

[82] See eg the partial rejection of the Law Society's application for extended rights of audience for employed solicitors. See ACLEC 1996b, Appendix C; 1997, pp.15–16. More problematic has been the restrictions placed by the European Court of Justice on lawyer-client confidentiality (for the purpose of its proceedings) which effectively exclude most corporate counsel because of their perceived lack of independence: see *AM&S Europe Ltd v EC Commission* (Case 155/79) [1982] 2 CMLR 264.

4.5 Globalisation and Cross-Border Practices[83]

The internationalisation of legal practice has become a major complicating factor in mapping the professional terrain. The mega-law firms, with offices in several jurisdictions, today act for multi-national and even supra-national clients in complex transactions which may themselves span multiple national and legal boundaries.[84] The growth of transnational, or even 'global', legal practice has been facilitated by the free market ideology dominating the major trading blocs, such as NAFTA and the European Union, which have tended to support cross-border trade in services, including legal services.[85] It is widely acknowledged that globalisation, in its pursuit of the 'possibility of a borderless world',[86] presages the demise of many institutions of the traditional nation state. It is not fanciful therefore to suggest that the globalisation of legal practice potentially challenges the regulatory pre-eminence of the national professional associations. Within the legal sphere this process can be seen through the increasing role of both supra-national political (such as the European Union) and professional institutions[87] in determining standards of professional regulation. This can be illustrated through the problem of 'double deontology', which underlies the ethics of cross-border practice.

The process of transnational practice obviously begs questions as to the professional standards to be adopted in such contexts. The principle that has been adopted internationally is that lawyers practising outside the jurisdiction as 'foreign legal consultants' are bound both by the local ethical code and (to some degree) their 'home' professional standards. This principle has its foundation in an international code— the International Bar Association's International Code of Ethics, first promulgated in the late 1950s. However, in Europe it is now also enshrined in both the CCBE[88] Code of Conduct, which governs cross-border practice within the EU, and Community law.[89] It remains a cumbersome principle, not least because professional responsibilities in many areas, and particularly those involving principles of confidentiality or conflicts of interest, may be widely divergent between states and difficult to determine. It is perhaps unsurprising then that greater harmonisation of conduct standards is increasingly presented as a solution to the difficulties created by double deontology.[90]

---

[83] The growth of global and cross-border practice also has implications for the business context, discussed in section 7, below, though there is so far insufficient research on UK practices to justify extensive consideration. cf also Arthurs and Kreklewich 1996 and Flood 1989 on the cultural and economic significance of the US big law firm ('Cravath') model.

[84] Flood 1996; Arthurs and Kreklewich 1996; Boon and Flood 1999.

[85] See eg Skarlatos 1991; Pardieck 1996.   [86] Waters 1995, p.118.

[87] cf Evetts 1995 (on the internationalisation of the engineering professions).

[88] Comité Consultatif des Barreaux Européens, *Code of Conduct for Lawyers in the European Community*. See Annex 10B LSG.

[89] See Art. 4 of the Lawyers' Services Directive 77/249/EEC, which also lays down rules for dealing with conflicts arising from the application of double deontology.

[90] Toulmin 1991–92; Bruyninckx 1997. For a more critical view, see Arthurs 1999; Boon and Flood 1999.

The other force for change on the international scene is the rise of the multi-national, mega-law firm, which is itself a significant feature of professional segmentation. This creates a number of interesting issues concerning the development of a global legal culture.

Mega-law firms, in many respects, represent a distinct layer of professional institutions, better resembling the big accountancy firms than other law firms.[91] Their size and power[92] may make them at least semi-autonomous from the local profession and mean that their interests will not always coincide with those of the professional association in any (particular) host country. The rise of such firms may thus weaken the capacity of local associations to mobilise the profession on local issues, or to compete collectively for new jurisdictions.[93] However, while the globalisation of legal practice often involves the transplanting of North American structures and ideologies, from activities such as 'lateral hiring'[94] down to techniques for internal organisation of the firm,[95] there is little evidence to date that this has extended to the widespread importation of US styles of lawyering.

Thirdly, at a micro-ethical level, one might ask how far national ethical standards may be eclipsed by the culture of the international law firm? It is conceivable that, say, a law firm based in the United States and operating in London may employ US, British and possibly even other European lawyers, thereby generating potentially multiple problems of double deontology. The solution, adopted by at least one multi-national (and as described to one of the present authors), is for the firm itself to establish its own practice standards, which meet at least the minima likely to be demanded by double deontology, but which may seek in some instances to set 'higher'[96] standards than those prevailing in the locale. To that extent the firm itself may be becoming the primary site of ethical regulation in multi-national practice.

5. THE DEMOGRAPHIC CONTEXT

Prior to the growth of the modern law schools, the majority of lawyers qualified for practice through lengthy apprenticeships either at the Inns of Court or in law firms. This enabled the profession to firmly police the professional fenceline and to ensure that lawyers were made of the 'right stuff'. Even when graduate entry had become

---

[91] Flood 1996, p.201.

[92] Both political and economic. cf Flood, ibid, p.170 on the extent to which mega-law firm lawyers have influence in national and international political arenas.

[93] Halliday and Karpik 1997, pp.368–9.

[94] ie headhunting lawyers from other firms, to develop or strengthen a specialism, or even to disable the competition. See Galanter and Palay 1992, pp.50–1; Flood 1989, pp.579–80. This was virtually unheard of in the UK pre-1980s.

[95] See Flood 1996, pp.175, 188–9.

[96] Obviously a loaded term which we have not sought to unpack here, but reflecting some sense that 'best practice' is good for business.

more or less normalised,[97] until the late 1960s, when the former polytechnics first began to establish vocational courses to rival those run by the Law Society and Bar, considerable control was retained by the professions' virtual monopoly over entry to vocational training. Their ability to select neophytes in their own image was further enhanced, particularly at the Bar, by the fact that, for many years, training—a minimum of a year's pupillage at the Bar, or a two-year period of articling to a solicitor—was unpaid, requiring the majority of trainees to be of independent means, or at least to have access to significant private financial assistance. Moreover, although women have been legally entitled to join the professions since 1919,[98] the proportion to do so remained very small up until the 1970s.[99] The number of ethnic minority entrants, until the mid-1980s, was proportionately even less.[100]

Thus the profession has traditionally been dominated by white (upper) middle class men. As well as having important implications for the range of experiences and values of lawyers, the demographic construction of the legal profession is, we argue, an important macro-ethical issue, raising questions about the social diversity of the profession and its capacity to deliver access to justice. We will illustrate this through three interrelated points.

First of all, existing education and recruitment practices act as a crude process of 'social closure',[101] controlling market supply through training and credentialisation, and thereby restricting access to the profession (and hence to justice) from the supply side. Despite the universities' gatekeeping role, access to the professions is ultimately controlled through recruitment by firms and chambers. The threefold expansion in the number of law students since the late 1980s[102] has ensured that, while the profession's control over entry may formally have declined, its actual selection powers have increased because it is now operating in a buyer's market. Whereas about 66 per cent of the 14,000 or so law students who graduate annually will find places on the vocational courses, only a third are likely to find training places,[103] notwithstanding that around 60 per cent aspire to become legal professionals.[104] The increase in competition for jobs[105] is likely to increase the advantages held by those from

[97] Via either the law degree or the postgraduate conversion courses—Common Professional Examination or Diploma in Law. Henceforth we shall refer to the holders of these as simply law graduates.

[98] Sex Disqualification (Removal) Act 1919.

[99] See Abel 1988b, pp.36–7. Women now constitute annually about 40% of those entering pupillage, and just over 50% of those becoming solicitors. In global terms, however, women constitute only some 20% of the practising Bar and 30% of solicitors in private practice.

[100] Ethnic minorities now comprise over 6% of the practising Bar—an unusually high proportion by comparison with most other British professional and managerial occupations, including solicitors. See Hamylton and Bhalla 1994, p.79.

[101] See eg Larson 1977; Witz 1992, pp.36, 197.

[102] See Webb 1999. The total number of undergraduate law students in 1994–95 was estimated to be 34,466: Harris and Jones 1997, p.67.

[103] See Bell and Johnstone 1998, p.12.

[104] McDonald 1982; Webb 1986; Sherr and Webb 1989; Bell and Johnstone 1998.

[105] See Halpern 1994, p.7. Shiner and Newburn 1995 identified the average number of applications successful applicants for training contracts must make as 30.2 and 46, respectively. In 1998 there were over 1,800 applicants chasing under 700 pupillages: information provided to the authors by the Bar Council.

certain backgrounds, thus further narrowing the social base of the profession. The process may also operate against particular classes of applicant—for example, mature students with families who may find it difficult to take up work experience opportunities (especially if they are unpaid) during vacations. Ethnic minority or working class students are likely to be disadvantaged on multiple counts, particularly if they are studying at lower status institutions. Their ethnicity,[106] class, and educational background[107] are all likely to tell against them in the recruitment process. Moreover, such students will often lack the kinds of cultural capital[108] which might help them overcome such disadvantages.

Secondly, whereas the tight social homogeneity, historically so characteristic of the legal professions, is being disrupted by the rising number of female and ethnic minority lawyers, inroads into the (upper) middle-class bias of lawyers have been not nearly as marked as the increased levels of participation in higher education might suggest.[109] In the early 1980s about 70 per cent of law students were drawn from professional and managerial backgrounds. By the mid-90s this figure was still in excess of 60 per cent,[110] while the 25 per cent rate of law students educated in private schools remains much higher than for non-law students in general.[111] Such statistics tend to confirm the general picture whereby professions have recruited predominantly from the professional classes, creating a kind of circulation of elites.[112] Indeed, even more specifically, the level of 'occupational inheritance'—the tendency for children to follow in the occupational footsteps of parents or close relatives—remains high among lawyers.[113] Such data seem to support the views of educational sociologists who argue that changes throughout the education system are in fact reinforcing the power of a middle class 'parentocracy' to purchase the credentials their offspring require to enter higher status occupations,[114] and thereby helping to sustain patterns of social exclusion from occupational groups like the legal profession.

Thirdly, this all begs the question, what are the values that this social group espouses? Although it is very difficult to determine the impact of the social background of lawyers[115] on their values, there is limited empirical data which suggests students enter law school with a conservative orientation towards the function of law and of lawyers, and with career objectives which tend to emphasise the prestige

[106] Shiner 1997, p.65. The same research found no clear statistical evidence of sex or race discrimination in the allocation of pupillage, though cf TMS Consultants 1992.

[107] On the interaction of class and education, see Shiner, ibid, pp.61, 66, and 75–9.

[108] Cultural capital can be broadly defined as the socialised cognitive and social skills that bring material success. See Bourdieu and Passeron 1977.

[109] Though cf the view conveyed by an established barrister to one of the authors, that the profession felt it could no longer assume that new entrants were 'chaps like us'.

[110] McDonald 1982; Webb 1986.

[111] Approximately 1 in 6 non-law students come from private schools and only 5% of the general population: Shiner 1997, p.158.

[112] See eg Egerton 1997.

[113] Estimates of close relatives in the legal profession vary from 14% (Webb 1986, p.85) to 20% (Shiner 1997, p.158, estimating that young people are between 10 and 20 times more likely to study law if they have a lawyer parent).

[114] Brown 1990, 1996.   [115] cf Nicolson 1992, in relation to judges.

and financial advantages of lawyering over its social functions.[116] As we will attempt to show in the rest of the chapter, the hegemony of such values is also likely to be enhanced by legal education and the business context to modern practice.

6. THE EDUCATIONAL CONTEXT

In earlier years, when lawyers received all their legal training 'in house' as articled clerks and pupils, control by practising lawyers of professional socialisation was substantial.[117] This control has slowly eroded as legal education has moved into the hands of the universities (and other independent educational institutions) which claim to provide a 'liberal arts' education. However, contrary to the anticipated liberalising effect of higher education, socialisation studies suggest that students' conservative orientations are maintained, if not actually reinforced, by the law school experience.[118]

Although the evidence is sketchy and often based on nothing more than individualised experience,[119] it would seem that legal education still primarily constitutes a 'training for the hierarchy',[120] in terms of which students learn to play the game of law and to participate in sustaining the status quo. This can be deduced from a number of common features of the law student's educational experience.

Perhaps most important is the essentially formalistic and 'technicist'[121] nature of legal education. In terms of the 'black-letter tradition' the focus is on describing the written content of laws and analysing fundamental legal concepts rather than their purpose, social context or substantive justice. Critical evaluation, if undertaken at all, is confined to examining the logic and rational coherence of particular legal decisions and areas of law.

This formalistic approach dominated the British legal academy until relatively recently and still characterises much of legal education. It emerged due to the triumph of legal positivism over natural law theory in the nineteenth century. Legal positivism insists on the strict separation of law and morality, but only for the purpose of determining the validity of legal norms,[122] rather than for the further question of their evaluation. However, under the influence of legal positivists like

---

[116] Webb 1986; Sherr and Webb 1989. See also McDonald 1982.

[117] This was particularly true of the Bar. Aspiring barristers were likely to be a highly homogenous group because the expense of training and the requirement that non-graduates prove their proficiency in Latin and Greek served as significant class barriers to entry: see Abel 1988a, pp.17–18. In addition, pupils were expected to reside in the Inns of Court. For the argument that pupillage and articles constituted a 'moral training' (in the widest sense of that term) see Burrage 1996, p.54.

[118] Notably Webb 1986. cf Erlanger and Klegon 1978; Hedegard 1979; Granfield 1992; Erlanger *et al* 1996, regarding the US position.

[119] See eg Stanley 1988; Goodrich 1996; and in the USA, Kennedy 1982; Turow 1988.

[120] Stanley 1988; Kennedy 1982.

[121] Thornton 1998. Similar arguments have been developed by English writers, notably Twining 1994.

[122] Hart 1958; Steir 1991, p.580ff.

Austin[123] who insisted that students should not be exposed to questions of the politics or morality of law 'lest it inflame their passions',[124] generations of law students have grown up seeing law in purely technical terms. Its social role and the justice of its rules were simply assumed. Indeed, the trend in modernist ethics to replace moral autonomy or community values with codified systems meant that morality came to be conflated with law.[125] While liberalism insisted on an inviolable sphere of autonomy regarding issues of 'private morality', issues of justice were reduced to a concern with the fair and equal administration of law. As regards the latter process, classical legal formalism inherited from the common law tradition the declaratory myth of adjudication, which insists that judges merely declare rather than make the law. Accordingly, the process of adjudication and legal argumentation is presented as an exercise in formal logic, whereby clear law is applied to clear facts in the form of the deductive syllogism.

These ideas have come under increasingly critical attack this century. In the 1920s and 1930s the American Realists persuasively argued that adjudication is a creative process involving policy and morality as well as logic, that the law and facts relevant to its application never exist in a neat pre-packaged form waiting to be applied, that law cannot be understood in isolation from its social context and that law is best regarded as a process involving not simply the courts but all legal actors who can influence the outcome of legal issues.[126] However, these jurisprudential developments had little impact on British legal education before the late 1960s. Only then, spurred on by a wider questioning of the liberal social order and its laws, did it begin to reflect the influence of Realism,[127] sociological theories of law[128] and, later still, the emerging feminist critique.[129]

However, even today, the influence of legal formalism remains strong. While the picture differs quite dramatically between law schools and between courses within law schools, the dominant focus remains on technical legal knowledge and skills, and the prevailing message is that legal rules and arguments can be understood and deployed in a value-neutral or context-free way. Relatively rarely are issues of law's morality and politics suffused throughout the curriculum. Instead, they tend to be relegated to 'soft' subjects like jurisprudence, sociology of law, gender and law, etc., freeing the rest of the curriculum for the detailed description and analysis of legal rules and for practice in the sort of technical and formalistic reasoning for which lawyers are famed. The implicit message in this is that there is a distinction between 'law' which is rigorous and useful, and 'non-law' which is 'soft' and of purely academic interest, if that.

[123] The first professor of jurisprudence at University College, London, the first 'modern' English law school.
[124] See Cotterrell 1989, p.81.   [125] eg Douzinas and Warrington 1994, ch.1.
[126] For an overview see Freeman 1994, ch.8.
[127] Initially through the development of 'law in context' and latterly socio-legal studies: see eg Thomas 1997; Bradney 1998.
[128] See eg Bankowski and Mungham 1976.
[129] On feminism and the inherent masculinism in law teaching, see Thornton 1996; Collier 1991.

This has a number of important consequences. One is that the concentration on law's detail and techniques leaves unquestioned its context, including its ethical values. Consequently, students are subtly inculcated into the worldview which underlies the content and institutions of the law they study. According to one commentator, knowledge and dispositions that emerge from legal education 'become part of a new common sense that is fundamentally consistent with the predominance of a market-based understanding of social-relations and a particular form of democratic life that is elitist, as opposed to participatory'.[130]

Individual freedom, particularly that of property owners and economic actors, and respect for the Rule of Law with its emphasis on certainty and procedural justice is portrayed as more important than substantive justice. Gender differences appear as an inevitable feature of social relations and heterosexuality the natural form of private relations. The analytical style of legal reasoning also plays a role in suppressing values and ways of thinking likely to challenge the legal and professional status quo. The focus on formal logic plays a particularly important role in confining legal argument to those considerations relevant to the application of established law to relevant facts.[131] For example, whereas, as we have seen,[132] many argue that women, or possibly all oppressed groups, favour a form of ethical reasoning that is intuitive and concerned to preserve relational connections, rather than driven by conventional rights discourse, such ideas have barely been acknowledged by mainstream legal discourse. Instead, law students are likely to learn that legal success depends not on compassion or moral concerns but on the ability to exercise the instrumental rationality of *homo oeconimicus*.

The overriding concentration on analytical technique has other important consequences. It may disguise the extent to which there is an underlying cultural and social curriculum that is assessed but never taught.[133] This is likely to disadvantage those working class, ethnic minority and female students who do not share the cultural capital of white (upper-) middle class men.[134] The focus on doctrinal complexity and analytical rigour also tends to lead to students devaluing courses that concentrate on socio-economic context or moral considerations. This is specifically problematic for courses that examine ethical issues—whether professional or otherwise.[135]

In fact, however, ethics currently plays a very small part in law curricula. The discussion of philosophical ethics is usually confined to the margins in jurisprudence courses or, in its applied form, to courses like medical or health care law. However, such courses are not always compulsory or available.[136] Exposure of undergraduates

---

[130] Granfield 1998, p.303.   [131] See Nicolson 1994, pp.734–40.   [132] Ch.2, section 6.

[133] Bourdieu and Passeron 1977; Atkinson and Delamont 1990, pp.106–7.

[134] What Thornton 1998, p.370, calls 'benchmark masculinity'.

[135] cf Pipkin 1979. One study conducted in the mid-1980s showed that students felt that little emphasis was placed on legal ethics in the undergraduate law curriculum. On the other hand, while they thought that it deserved greater emphasis, they still rated ethics the second *least* important of 12 curricular elements. See Sherr and Webb 1989, p.239.

[136] Barnett 1995. Even when jurisprudence is compulsory, ethics is not an inevitable curriculum component.

to issues of professional legal ethics is even less likely. So far as we can ascertain, only a handful of law schools teach such courses and then only as optional subjects. The topic of 'professional conduct'—which, as we shall see,[137] is in many respects different from legal ethics—is a compulsory part of vocational training. However, it is taught primarily as a substantive 'black-letter' topic, oriented fairly uncritically around the content of the professional codes of conduct, with little regard to the larger normative questions associated with the lawyer's role.[138] The vocational courses are heavily supported by instruction manuals, which largely reinforce the ethos and discourses of the vocational stage. And if this is true of the current position, then it is even more true of those earlier generations of lawyers whose legal education contained no reference to professional conduct norms and who were exposed, at most, to guides to professional conduct which were even more complacent towards professional legal ethics than the current teaching manuals.[139] The style and content of these texts[140] suggest standards of conduct are not important for fundamentally moral reasons, but because they enable lawyers to 'protect their backs' and so help support the status and reputation of the profession as a whole and the success of individual practitioners.[141] Moreover, when we turn to those manuals that cover the specific areas of legal practice, they either ignore ethical issues altogether or simply outline the relevant professional rules.[142] Once again the focus is on technical skills and legal knowledge rather than ethics. Consequently most teachers and practice supervisors currently have few meaningful points of reference from which to develop an ethical legal education.

This absence of an ethical dimension to legal education fails to redress a further consequence of the technicist nature of legal education—the encouragement of an 'instrumental morality'.[143] Most students will learn that law and legal outcomes are far from certain, especially because of the concentration on 'hard'[144] cases as teaching tools. Even if not directly exposed to the ideas of American Realism, students are likely to learn that law, legal reasoning and possibly also[145] facts are malleable. They may even come to recognise (perhaps unconsciously) the importance of

[137] Ch.4, section 3.3.1.   [138] See Webb 1998a. cp Granfield 1998, regarding the US situation.

[139] See Silverman 1989, which dilutes the importance of ethical issues by long discussions of practical issues; also Boulton 1975, which is particularly marked by a concern for the detailed niceties of etiquette rather than ethics.

[140] Though cf Inns of Court School of Law 1997, ch.4, which, based on Cranston 1995, emphasises some of the wider ethical issues.

[141] 'There is nothing more important to practice at the Bar than the way in which barristers conduct themselves and the regard in which they are held by their peers, lay and professional clients and those holding judicial office' (Inns of Court School of Law 1997, p.1); 'success at the Bar depends more than anything upon the way that you treat other persons' (ibid, p.3).

[142] See Webb 1998a, pp.275–6.

[143] Luban 1988a, p.16. See further Ch.6, section 3. cf Pepper 1986a, p.624ff; Luban ibid, ch.2; and 1987, pp.646–8 over whether this instrumentalism stems from the dominance of legal realism in American legal education.

[144] cf Dworkin 1977, p.119ff.

[145] But see Nicolson 1997 on the dearth of attention to facts in law and the consequent loss in terms of opportunities for ethical discussion.

retaining an indeterminate core of professional knowledge to preserving professional power and autonomy.[146] However, in the absence of a moral and political context to legal education, the message is that there are no limits to lawyer instrumentality other than those of a pragmatic nature—logic, the persuasiveness of any competing argument, the tribunal's sympathy, etc. Not even legal values can be said to deserve overriding respect given that they are likewise malleable.[147] The upshot is that students are likely to become cynical about the law and to value personal success rather than more altruistic or political goals.[148] Similarly, if the law routinely becomes a problem to be dealt with by 'creative compliance',[149] lawyers may also learn to defeat not simply the letter of the law, but also its *spirit* in an equally cynical manner.[150] And if this is the case, it would surely be surprising if lawyers did not treat their own rules of professional conduct as technical obstacles to be avoided when necessary.[151]

These tendencies towards cynical instrumentalism are themselves likely to be reinforced by general features of the law school experience which foster feelings of stress, competitiveness and ultimately an ethical pragmatism or even amoralism among students.[152] This process starts with the competition to get into law school and continues with the stress of successive assessment hurdles, further competition for vacation placements and mini-pupillages, and the pursuit of places on the vocational courses. Indeed, so fierce is the drive for grades and competition for jobs that law students seem increasingly prepared to cheat and plagiarise the work of others, hide, vandalise, or even steal scarce library materials and lie on their curricula vitae. This is then replaced by the chase for training contracts and pupillages, permanent contracts and tenancies. Moreover, this is all done in the knowledge that these relatively short-term struggles are to be replaced only by ongoing competition for clients, partnerships or the taking of silk, and even elevation to the bench. The 'massification'[153] of higher education may also itself have increased students' sense of competitiveness and alienation, so that students feel that they are being processed through the law[154] rather than educated in the idealised fashion we associate with a liberal education.

7. THE BUSINESS CONTEXT

7.1 Introduction

The process of professional socialisation does not, of course, end with training. As the classical model of lawyers as a moral community implicitly acknowledges, so-

---

[146] Atkinson 1983.   [147] Granfield 1998.

[148] On the decline of altruism during legal education, see Erlanger and Klegon 1978; Tomasic 1985; Granfield 1992. cf in the UK context Economides 1997; and Webb 1986.

[149] See McBarnet and Whelan 1991.   [150] McBarnet 1994, p.82.

[151] See eg Wilkins 1990, p.483; Pannick 1992, p.162; Blake and Ashworth 1998, pp.51–2.

[152] See eg Stanley 1988; Economides 1997; and, for an overview of the US literature, Iijima 1998. For empirical support see eg Foster 1981; Elkins 1985; Benjamin *et al* 1986.

[153] ie the process whereby higher education has moved from relatively small scale delivery to the social and educational elite, to a mass delivery to a broader cross-section of the population: Scott 1995; Webb 1999.   [154] See quotes in Webb 1995, p.193.

cialisation processes are, in theory, reinforced by the professions' collegial culture and by the particular culture of the locale in which lawyers work. The question is: what impact do these contexts have on the attitudes and behaviour of lawyers? We have already seen that education in its current form appears to have little positive effect. If this is combined with ambivalent or negative ethical messages sent out by the practice context, the result is a potentially powerful 'double whammy' which will restrict the capacity of new lawyers to develop an ethically informed perspective on legal practice.

The service ethic prescribed by traditional ideologies of professionalism and the classical view of professions as homogenous communities together perform a powerful legitimating role. Not only do they imply a shared commitment to common values, but they encourage abuses of professional standards and morality to be explained away as the work of 'rotten apples'. In this view there is room 'for some variation . . . some out-of-line members, even some conflict [because], by and large, there is a steadfast core which defines that profession, deviations from which are but temporary dislocations'.[155]

By contrast to the classical model of professions, sociologists working with an 'interactionist' perspective stress the mutability of professions, patterns of role differentiation and conflict, leading to the segmentation[156] of professions through specialisation, competition and intra-professional differences in work methods, interests, associations, and clients. In this light, evidence of substantial segmentation or, more critically, fragmentation in professional structures and practices might represent a threat not just to the viability or power base of existing professional associations, but a threat to the very legitimacy of the profession and its ethical norms. The fragmentation thesis has not been extensively developed in the context of the Anglo-Welsh professions and the structural differences—not least the existence of a divided legal profession—make comparison with the USA somewhat difficult. It is thus necessary to examine the empirical evidence for and against fragmentation in the legal professions, given that the nature of legal practice has changed so enormously in the last thirty years or so, before exploring any possible implications for legal ethics.

7.2 An Overview of Practice Trends

The solicitors' profession today involves a greater range of practices than probably at any time previously. Historically it has been dominated (numerically at least) by the generalist small firm and sole practitioner. On the face of it, little has changed. In 1996, 83 per cent of firms were either sole practitioners/sole principals, or small firms with four partners or less. However, there were also by 1996 111 mega-law firms with 26 or more partners, generating over twice the level of gross fees per solicitor than the average sole practitioner/principal. Moreover,

---

[155] Bucher and Straus 1961, p.326.   [156] See above, section 4.4.

nearly 48 per cent of fee earners are now employed in firms of eleven partners or more.[157]

The growth of the large firm has also been accompanied by an associated increase in specialisation. Throughout the 1960s and 70s many City firms, and some of their larger London and provincial colleagues, began to focus their efforts on corporate and commercial work and to downgrade or eliminate much of their (traditional) private client activity. This itself enabled a trend of specialisation and growth which was initially capped (to an extent) only by restrictions on firm size, which were not eliminated until 1967.[158] Growth thereafter remained relatively steady until the explosion of the legal services market in the mid-1980s.[159] The Thatcherite-inspired 'Big Bang' which saw the de-regulation and subsequent re-regulation of the finan-cial markets, the commercial property boom, and the growth in both volume and complexity of corporate work, especially in areas such as mergers and acquisitions, generated a significant volume of work for lawyers in an increasingly competitive environment. Specialisation has, moreover, extended beyond the large City firms. A number of medium-sized and even some small commercial firms have rationalised their functions to become niche market players, dealing in narrow technical spe-cialisations, often on referral from the big players.[160] Even on the private client side, the need for critical mass and the capacity to undertake relatively high volume work has become more important as the declining profitability of the residential con-veyancing market[161] and the rationalisation of legal aid[162] have made it harder for small generalist firms to survive.

Similar trends are also beginning to emerge at the Bar. Despite some sharing of resources, chambers traditionally operated more as loose aggregations of indepen-dent practitioners rather than single economic units. However, economic pressures seem now to encourage chambers to function increasingly as single units, particu-larly in terms of adopting a more managerial approach to practice.[163] Expansion and/or more specialisation has also become something of a priority. Chambers are increasingly dividing into either very large, relatively generalist, sets or smaller niche sets, with the smaller generalist chambers being squeezed in the middle. The largest chambers (which are in any event no larger than many medium-sized solicitors' firms) tend to be concentrated in London,[164] and may now contain between 50 and

---

[157] Law Society 1998, p.34. This is reflected, of course, in a growing disparity in profitability, and hence income. Figures published in 1997 indicated that profit per equity partners in the largest law firms averaged £84,000 while sole practitioners averaged £22,000: Law Society 1997. *Legal Business* in 1998 estimated the gross profit per partner at Slaughter & May, which topped its profit 'league', at £875,000: *Independent*, 11 September 1998, section 2, p.24.

[158] Until the passing of the Companies Act 1967, s.120(1)(a), solicitors were prohibited by statute from forming partnerships of more than 20 partners. [159] See further Flood 1989; Lee 1992.

[160] See eg Hanlon 1997. [161] See eg Blacksell *et al* 1991, pp.85–8; cf Domberger and Sherr 1989.

[162] See eg Smith 1996; Moorhead 1998.

[163] eg, in terms of complaints procedures, marketing, etc.

[164] Though the largest set in the country, with 78 tenants, has recently been created by the merger of two Birmingham chambers: *The Lawyer*, 12 May 1998, p.1. The limited evidence available suggests that the provincial Bar has also grown, and become more specialised, albeit at a slower rate than in London: see eg *Marre Report* 1988, para. 5.16.

80 tenants. However, these remain the exception rather than the rule. One outcome of expansion has been an increasing migration beyond the geographical confines of the Inns of Court, as chambers have been obliged to seek larger or otherwise more suitable accommodation, thereby diluting the territorial exclusivity enjoyed by much of the Bar. Consequently, as Hughes notes, 'chambers have superseded the communal life of the Inns as the source of Bar culture. . . .'[165]

There is thus clear evidence of some increasing fracture along the corporate/private client divide. At the same time, however, we should be wary of over-generalisation. Even within a single sphere of private client work, such as criminal defence, there is a significant range of professional cultures and values at play.[166] Whatever the exact extent of fragmentation, it is clear that the traditional image of the collegial, unitary legal profession is at the very least substantially under threat, if not already a thing of the past, given the growing ideological distance between firms driven by specialisation (both within and across the corporate/private client 'hemispheres') and differing organisational imperatives.[167]

7.3 Professional Organisations and Ethics

Although, as we have seen, an emphasis on collegiality is still reflected to some degree in the institutions of the modern legal professions,[168] their rapid growth in the late twentieth century has left the professional bodies with considerably less influence on legal culture than they had a century ago. This is particularly true for the solicitors' profession, which is significantly larger, more socially diverse and geographically dispersed than the Bar. Consequently, today, the key site of occupational socialisation in practice will be the firm or chambers. These environments will serve to define and reinforce certain values and expectations among their members through their organisational structures (management hierarchy, departmental structures, etc.) and work expectations.

The organisational structures of legal practice are important in shaping a significant part of the social networks that give order and stability to the working lives of professionals.[169] Here there are three key features.

The first is the management structure. Lawyers have tended to rely on 'collegial'[170] as opposed to bureaucratic systems. Management functions are commonly vested in central 'charismatic' (in the Weberian sense) figures—heads of chambers, or senior or managing partners.[171] In most law firms this tends to be supported by a shallow hierarchy in which substantial power is exercised by a few elite members—the equity

---

[165] Hughes 1994, p.37.   [166] McConville *et al* 1994, ch.3. cf also Sommerlad 1995.

[167] Note the argument in the US that there is no longer 'enough interchange among the specialities to produce a bar that functions as a community of shared fate and common purpose': Heinz *et al* 1998, p.774. We suggest the data discussed in this chapter discloses a similar trend in England and Wales.

[168] See above, section 4.2.   [169] Hanlon 1996; Arnold and Kay 1995.

[170] Weber 1978, pp.263, 271–82; Cook and Waters 1998, pp.333–4.

[171] McConville *et al* 1994, p.17; Abbey 1993.

partners, or some grouping within the partnership.[172] The Bar has tended to retain a more democratic structure, based around the chambers meeting, but day-to-day management also fits the collegial rather than bureaucratic model. Decision-making in such collegial settings is often informal and self-validating.[173] Decisions on recruitment and promotion in particular tend to be risk-averse, and may be based on peer evaluation and judgements grounded in the organisational culture, rather than on published procedures and criteria.[174] Employment conditions and remuneration are also frequently negotiated individually and informally. Such processes may, whether incidentally or deliberately, foster competitive and individualistic tendencies within organisations. Charismatic management styles can also increase the tendency of organisations to reproduce themselves in their own image and to reinforce social exclusion and closure on the basis of often discriminatory 'collectivist criteria'[175] such as class, race, and gender. Exclusion by gender may be particularly significant in ethical terms, given the argument, based on Gilligan's ethic of care, that women lawyers display distinctive styles of lawyering and ethical reasoning.[176]

The second important organisation feature is the management ethos. Here we have seen a shift (less evident in chambers) towards a more corporatist[177] or managerialist[178] approach. This trend is often identified as central to the transformation of legal practice from a professional to a business paradigm. The new corporatism/managerialism emphasises the development of internal management systems and marketing, more sophisticated methods of time costing for legal work, greater standardisation and routinisation of work outputs (particularly through information technology applications), and, in the larger solicitors' firms, departmentalising and otherwise streamlining working practices. These changes have also been accompanied by increased expectations as to productivity, reflected in long working hours, pressures to bill as much time as possible, and a career structure which both rests on (masculine) assumptions that fee earners will be almost endlessly available to meet often arbitrary and unpredictable calls on their time.[179] These developments have imposed new performance pressures on fee earners, already operating in a context

---

[172] cf Lee 1992, p.38. Firms may draw a variety of distinctions eg between 'finders' or 'rainmakers' who bring the clients in, and 'minders' who take on administrative tasks within the organisation. See Flood 1991; Kelly 1994, pp.50–1. In large firms even those at (salaried) partnership level may have only a restricted managerial role and little sense of control over the organisation: Drummond 1997, p.1856.

[173] See Waters 1989, pp.957–8; Cook and Waters 1998, p.334; Lazega 1992. Unless otherwise indicated the following points are all derived from these sources.

[174] Although promotion to partnership is increasingly predicated on rainmaking and managerial skills, the package of qualities still tends to be defined in charismatic terms. As the regional partner of one large law firm has expressed it: 'it's very difficult to define, it's just a feeling, will this person command respect, will they bring in work and have they got a business perspective . . .'. Cited in Hanlon 1996, p.9.

[175] Cook and Waters 1998, p.335.

[176] See Ch.1, section 6, above; also Jack and Jack 1989.

[177] Whereby 'the firm adopts the body of a partnership but with the mind of a corporation.': Lee 1992, p.38.

[178] ie bureaucratic: Sommerlad 1995.

[179] See Seron and Ferris 1995; Sommerlad 1994, pp.37–41; Drummond 1997.

of decreased job security and continuity than has historically been the norm. Consequently lawyers, especially in the larger firms, may develop a sense of powerlessness—an inability to control even their own working practices.[180]

This new ethos and its consequences sit uncomfortably with traditional notions of professional autonomy, and the expectation of bespoke service delivery. Moreover, increased financial pressures may create a greater risk that practitioners will cut corners or otherwise behave unethically in order to meet targets. More tangibly, there is evidence that they reduce not just a lawyer's quality of working life[181] but also the quality of legal services.[182]

The third important feature is the structuring of working relationships between lawyers in the organisation. The Bar's structure has not undergone many of the changes experienced by solicitors. Barristers in private practice remain self-employed, independent practitioners. Because of its smaller size, the Bar has, arguably, been able to retain a more collegial structure and working environment. Specialisation within chambers may actually have enhanced that capacity, even though, at the same time, competition between chambers has apparently increased.[183]

By contrast, the increase in law firm size has transformed the solicitors' profession into one in which a greater proportion of solicitors are now employees—as trainees, assistant solicitors and, relatively recently,[184] salaried partners—rather than the independent practitioners characteristic of classical legal professionalism. This has a number of implications for ethics.

First, the pressures of practice may have had an impact on interpersonal relations between members of the firm. For example, senior fee earners must themselves carry a heavy burden of cases, so that, particularly in smaller firms, the volume of supervision trainees receive may be very limited, thereby weakening and to some extent depersonalising the apprenticeship model.[185] This may have important implications for the ways in which ethics are transmitted, as it were, inter-generationally, and more generally for trust relations within the firm.[186]

Secondly, although the classical model has long acknowledged that employed lawyer status carries the potential for conflict between lawyers' ethical commitments to the profession, and their obligations as employees and executives of corporations,[187] the same logic has not been carried across into a private practice environment where the majority of lawyers are actually employees. Here it is assumed that

---

[180] Drummond 1997.

[181] Sommerlad 1995, p.182 and cf Moorhead and Boyle 1995.

[182] These are not unconnected. High levels of stress among lawyers may lead not only to absenteeism and health problems for those involved, but to increasingly dysfunctional working groups, operating at a higher risk of errors. See Berney 1995, p.255.

[183] See Morison and Leith 1992, p.40.

[184] See Flood 1989, p.580.

[185] See Shiner 1997, pp.87–8; Goriely and Williams, 1996, pp.10, 37–40.

[186] cf 'Survey shows assistants lack confidence in senior partners', *Law Society Gazette*, 29 January 1997, p.9.

[187] See eg Gunz and Gunz 1994, p.124. Hence the creation of specific conduct rules for the employed sector, notably the Employed Solicitors Code 1990 (see ch.4, LSG) and Part IV, CCB.

the professional obligations which bind each firm member are adequate to deal with the possibility of ethical conflicts arising between fee earners. This may occur, for example, between senior members of firms and their juniors who may feel more uncomfortable about bending the rules.[188] As a number of studies suggest, the current assumption side-steps many issues of power and status within the law firm, and perhaps overestimates the institutional support for,[189] and logic of, traditional, individualised, notions of professional responsibility.

But it is not just that the lawyer's status has changed. The whole way of working is different from the historical norm. Much legal work (particularly in the corporate sphere) has become both more specialised and more team-based as transactions become too complex for single fee earners to take sole responsibility. At the same time, in many respects, work has also become more routinised (as we shall see), not just in the context of high volume transactions, but in the sense that information technology and information systems have facilitated the repackaging and reusing of information, so that service delivery is designed less on a 'one-for-one' and increasingly on a 'one-for-many' basis.[190] These processes have, as with production lines, reduced the various workers' control over the final 'product'. For example, teams of lawyers will tend to report to and often work on cases brought in by senior fee earners (particularly the firm's rainmakers). This raises two ethical concerns. Firstly, these senior individuals are likely to participate in complex patronage relationships with both their clients and the team working on 'their' cases.[191] This of itself may generate conflicting ethical responsibilities for those involved.[192] Secondly, such processes of bureaucratisation and routinisation raise an important ethical consideration: who takes responsibility for the ethics of a transaction? The danger is that in bureaucratic settings ethical responsibility for a specific act becomes too dispersed, so that it is simultaneously everyone's, but ultimately no one's.[193]

7.4 Client Relations: Business Versus Ethics?

The changing nature of legal work and in particular the fragmentation process has directly influenced lawyer-client relations in ways which raise important ethical questions. We shall explore these via Sherr's division of lawyers into 'super heroes' and

---

[188] If this seems unduly idealistic, it is notable that Carlin's classic study found a lower level of ethical concern among large firm partners than associates: see Carlin 1966, p.140. See also the case studies cited by Lamb 1995, pp.232–3.

[189] For example, one might reinterpret current and widespread calls for the extension of limited liability to law firms from the corporate end of the profession as a negation of an important element of individual responsibility.

[190] Susskind 1996, p.287; also Flood 1991.   [191] Flood 1991, p.68.

[192] This in turn is likely to create a difficult and often ambiguous ethical position for the more junior fee earners who may not only have a limited responsibility for those cases, but also become caught in a variety of ethical traps. For example, they may be put under pressure to act unethically by the client and the lawyer managing the case acting in unison, or they may be caught in a dilemma between their duty to the clients and their dependence on superiors in the firm—for instance where the partner running the case wants a junior to inflate the hours she has billed.

[193] Bauman 1994, p.8, calls this the problem of 'floating responsibility'. See also Luban *et al* 1992.

'slaves',[194] which emphasises the complex and sometimes contradictory images of legal practice.

The super hero image is usually characterised by traditional 'private plight' work. Here the lawyer as expert swoops down to save clients in their moment of crisis—an image most commonly associated with criminal defence lawyers.[195] However, given that the bulk of cutting edge, creative, technical lawyering is now performed for commercial clients, the classical image of lawyer as skilled craftsman is one to which many corporate lawyers would adhere, albeit with the caveat that their solutions are as much 'commercial' as 'legal'. Moreover, in some respects, the corporate model may in fact come closer to the idealised service ethic. This can be seen in both the (relative) growth of *pro bono*[196] work in large law firms[197] and the style of client-handling required by corporate lawyers.

Despite its apparent novelty, *pro bono* work has a long tradition, largely uninterrupted by the rise and subsequent decline of legal aid.[198] Moreover, it has not just been the preserve of large law firms, contrary to the impression given by the media.[199] Smaller firms[200] and barristers also undertake free legal work in a variety of forms and contexts, ranging from high-profile Caribbean death penalty cases, through routine private plight work conducted 'in-house', to voluntary work in law centres, etc. Nevertheless, the *pro bono* activity of large law firms is ethically significant because of the potential contradiction it creates in our understanding of organisations that, according to some commentators, have abandoned the traditional service ethic and replaced it with an entrepreneurial view of practice that is at odds with the more humanistic values of benevolence, altruism and a concern for justice.[201] Unsurprisingly, there has been some attempt to link *pro bono* activity in large law firms to this new entrepreneurial turn. Large law firms have obtained considerable positive publicity for their *pro bono* activities and have exploited the training opportunities such work provides.[202] However, recent empirical data suggest that *pro bono* motivations (both for the firms and individuals involved) are more complex than just advancing self-interest and economic advantage, building also on a tradition of voluntarism, ideas of individual self-development,[203] worries about lawyers' image[204]

---

[194] Sherr 1995 and cf Flood 1994. We have taken some liberties with Sherr's basic premise, however.

[195] See further Ch.7, section 3.2.1.

[196] *Pro bono publico* is the American usage, increasingly adopted in the UK, to describe the provision of no fee/low fee legal services.

[197] See Boon and Abbey 1997.

[198] However, evidence to date suggests that the overall volume of *pro bono* activity remains relatively small. See Flintoff 1995; Boon and Abbey 1997.

[199] See eg *The Lawyer*, 15 October 1996, p.1; *Guardian*, Section 2, 15 July 1997, p.17, and the publicity garnered by the annual Legal Protection Group *Pro Bono* awards: see eg *New Law Journal*, 5 May 1995, p.623. cf *Guardian*, Section 2, 14 March 1995, p.10, for a more sceptical appraisal.

[200] Statistical data is scarce. However, Chambers and Stephenson-Harwood 1990 found that 41% of solicitors surveyed in a representative sample undertook some work for free. See also Webley 1999, p.16, who found a very strong *pro bono* commitment in legal aid practices.

[201] Edwards 1990; Stanley 1991 and cf Hanlon 1997, p.820.

[202] Galanter and Palay 1995; Boon and Abbey 1997.   [203] Webley 1999, p.19.

[204] Which may admittedly be linked to preservation of status and prestige rather than a direct defence of the service ethic. See Boon and Abbey 1997, p.651.

and, for many of those involved, a self-ascribed ethical commitment to serving the community.[205]

As regards the issue of client-handling, there is evidence of a marked difference in approach between much corporate and private client work. Contrary to the traditional image, it must be recognised that there are elements of private plight work which make it difficult for lawyers to deliver a personalised service. Much private client work is reactive, 'one-shot' case-handling.[206] Like the comic-book hero, the lawyer cannot stop and talk, but has to fly off to deal with the next crisis. There is little opportunity to develop a relationship with clients. This tendency has been increased by the financial and organisational pressures discussed in the next paragraph. Consequently, commercial work may, in some instances, offer a more individualised and continuing lawyer-client relationship. Corporatisation has demanded a significant rethinking of the relationship,[207] making it more responsive to clients and the commercial constraints within which they operate,[208] thus coming closer to the traditional ideal of bespoke service. On the other hand, while corporate clients will generally enjoy an individualised relationship with their lawyers, it is at the same time less personalised.[209] They are perceived increasingly to demand 'value for money', to expect that firms work to the same kinds of management standard seen in the corporate sphere, and generally to ensure that services are provided according to 'commercial as opposed to purely legal logic'.[210] Such demands may not be for just specialist, bespoke services, for there are equally areas of 'low diagnosis/high process'[211] work for commercial clients, such as volume debt collection or uninsured loss recovery where clients want a highly efficient output at low unit cost. In other words, it is an approach to legal work that demands a consistent and routinised mode of production, more dependent on effective use of support staff and information technologies, than the 'high diagnosis' skills of professional fee earners. This shift in processes and values is not unique to the large law firms, and contributes to the creation of the alternative image of lawyer as slave.

The slave image also cuts across the corporate/private divide. In the corporate sphere, fee earners may see themselves as slaves to the law firm and the clients whose power drives the logic of large modern practices. The pressures of corporate work are now legendary. Trainees, associates and partners are often under considerable

---

[205] eg Sweet 1998, p.11. For empirical evidence, see Boon and Abbey 1997, pp.652–3; Webley 1999, p.18.

[206] The distinction between 'one-shot' (one-off) and 'repeat player' clients is taken from Galanter 1974.

[207] Flood 1989, pp.570–1; Galanter and Palay 1992.

[208] Jim Edmunds, managing partner of one City firm, puts it thus: 'I've known many of my clients for 20 years. In some cases I began by advising their predecessors. Nonetheless, I can't afford to let up very much. My field is intensely competitive and if I neglect my people, my competitors will be in there in a second.': Leigh-Kile 1998, pp.91–2.

[209] See Hanlon 1997, p.802, which points out that the corporate client today is less likely to be the owner/entrepreneur, with whom partners may have enjoyed a more personal or social relationship, than non-owning managerial staff. cf the comment by 'Andrew', a corporate lawyer interviewed by Drummond 1997, p.1856: 'I couldn't cope with people and their problems'.

[210] Hanlon 1997, p.813. See also Flood 1991, p.41.   [211] Maister 1997.

pressure to make and complete deals. Long working hours and high billing targets are the norm.[212] This can encourage not just an unquestioning, treadmill response to the job—a tendency to take the money and run[213]—but also the risk that lawyers begin to adopt a slave perspective which treats the client/master as the enemy.[214]

In the private client sphere, the nature of the lawyer-client relationship may vary significantly by virtue of the kind of work, and the type of firm, involved. The bureaucratic and routinised 'managerialist' approach to legal work, while sharing some of the organisational characteristics of the corporatist model, demands a largely dichotomous approach to clients. While corporate clients have come to expect a tailored approach (even though that may involve a routinised solution), the clients of the managerialist firm will generally have little option but to accept a standardised service. Such clients are seen essentially as 'files' to be processed in as efficient and speedy a manner as possible.

This approach can clearly be seen in criminal defence work, which is fast becoming the paradigmatic example of managerialist, private client lawyering in Britain. McConville *et al* thus stress that much defence practice directly contradicts 'the professional rhetoric of providing an individualised service with continuous representation'[215] by operating systems of routinised, discontinuous and often deprofessionalised client service in which most client representation outside the court is undertaken by paralegal or unqualified staff.[216] At the same time, even in the context of lower status private client work, there is evidence of marked differences in lawyer behaviour towards fee paying and legally aided clients, even if this is only at the level of 'handholding'.[217] Lawyers here may seek to develop a more personalised service in order to justify higher fees in an attempt to avoid the descent into 'pure' low cost/high volume legal practice. Equally, there are clearly firms that are ideologically committed, or still expected by the market (particularly in rural settings where the traditional 'family firm' may still survive) to provide a relatively personalised and individual service.[218] This does not detract, however, from the fact that the overall trend is away from a relational[219] model of service delivery to one that is in many respects 'de-humanised'.

These developments are significant in terms of what is often called 'client patronage'—the need to accommodate and defer to client wishes. Patronage is likely to have significantly different meanings in different practice settings. For example, barristers will tend to cultivate a patronage relationship with solicitors. As the Bar's 'professional clients', solicitors are their key repeat player and so, in many ways, of more

---

[212] Flood 1994; Leigh-Kile 1998, pp.92–3.

[213] One trainee surveyed has put it rather differently: 'most firms are astute enough to realise that by increasing your salary by just enough each year, it will guarantee that it will become harder and harder to leave the profession as time goes on': 'Trainees who bluffed their way in, want out', *The Lawyer*, 19 May 1998, p.2.

[214] cf US lawyer Steve Kumble's saying: 'Praise the adversary. He is the catalyst by which you bill your client. Damn the client. He is your true enemy.': quoted in Flood 1994, p.400.

[215] McConville *et al* 1994, p.41.   [216] See ibid, pp.37–45.

[217] ibid, p.36; also Van Hoy 1997.   [218] cf Blacksell *et al* 1991; McConville *et al* 1994.

[219] Though possibly a paternalistic relationship: see Ch.5, below.

long-term (economic) importance than their lay clients. However, this pragmatic perspective is not reflected in the CCB which emphasises the primacy of duties to lay clients.[220] Similarly, the kinds of patronage relationships which develop in small firm/private client work are likely to be significantly different from those required in large firm/corporate work; though, as we have already seen, it is not always easy simply to generalise across the corporate/private divide.

Although a lawyer's reputation, as a marketable asset, may in part be built on traditional notions of professionalism and integrity,[221] the maintenance of reputation, status, and economic success also demands strategies of accommodation and patronage between lawyers and (especially) their landed or business clients.[222] The lawyer's ability to develop such strategies depends on a complex of personal, social and economic ties (through class and cultural allegiances, family connections, financial networks and business interests, etc.)[223] and socialisation into the expectations of particular client groups.[224] The changes to the practice environment already considered have important implications for client patronage and its 'ethical' basis.

Patronage has always raised difficult ethical problems, because it hints at the risk of over-identification with client interests,[225] and hence a loss of lawyer independence and objectivity. This risk may be increased in more competitive environments, where the chase for business may make it harder for lawyers to resist client demands. Underlying this is the further problem that some lawyers feel they can no longer rely on client loyalty. This problem is most commonly identified in the commercial sphere, where the greater volume of repeat players is to be found. The conventional notion of professionalism has largely assumed that patronage involves a reciprocal relationship in which client accommodation is rewarded by clients' loyalty to lawyers.[226] This seems more doubtful now, as commercial clients exercise choice in an increasingly competitive and specialised legal services market.[227] However, the opposite of patronage can also be ethically troubling since it may indicate under-identification with client interests.[228] As we have already seen, the increased pressures to routinise and depersonalise some categories of private client work, particularly criminal defence, appear to have substantially increased the risk of under-identification.

This discussion reflects in microcosm wider concerns about the ethical capacities of different kinds of law firms. There is considerable evidence that unethical behaviour is a response to particular situational pressures which have a disparate impact on small firms and sole practitioners.[229] Lawyers in small firms have more opportu-

---

[220] Para. 203, CCB.   [221] cf Carlin 1966, p.141; Arnold and Kay 1995.
[222] Rhode 1985, p.627.
[223] What Dezalay and Garth label the practice of 'relational capitalism'. See Dezalay and Garth 1997, pp.111–13. Specific examples litter the histories of the major law firms, such as Slinn 1984, 1987. See also Kelly 1994, pp.53–4 for a graphic account of the birth of 'Mahoney, Bourne, and Thiemes'. See more generally Sugarman 1993.
[224] Hanlon 1996; Moore and Moore 1991.   [225] We develop this further in Ch.6, section 2.2.
[226] See above, n.16 and accompanying text.   [227] Hanlon 1997, pp.813–14.
[228] See Chs.5 and 6, below.   [229] Arnold and Kay 1995; also Carlin 1966, p.120.

nities to violate conduct norms. They are also less subject to supervision or the possibility of peer pressure than their large firm counterparts, and are unlikely to have sufficient influence with the professional body to affect patterns of enforcement. On the other hand, large law firms are significantly better equipped to prevent ethical violations than many smaller firms. Lawyers with stable client bases of wealthy clients are less likely to take the opportunity to violate ethical norms than practices with a poor and unstable client base, while the 'embeddedness' of juniors in large law firm culture, with its greater emphasis on training, monitoring, and supervision, and concern for its reputation, should reduce opportunities for trust violations.[230] At the same time, this is not to suggest that problems of ethical violation will not arise in the corporate/mega-law sectors. It does suggest, however, that they are likely to be qualitatively different. Large-firm lawyers will tend to have less need or opportunity to defraud clients. Levels of competition for commercial work place pressure on firms to price their services competitively, particularly as more and more commercial clients seek a fixed fee 'for the job' rather than accept time-based billing. By virtue of their repeat player status, commercial clients will also tend to have a better sense of the cost of specific transactions. On the other hand, they may put their lawyers under greater pressure to behave unethically *for* them, by acting against the interests of innocent third parties, the environment, etc., or by acting according to hyper-adversarial[231] or even counter-adversarial[232] role assumptions.

Consequently, it is hardly surprising that professional disciplinary proceedings are most commonly commenced against small firms/sole practitioners.[233] Given the skewed demography of entry to the legal profession, this has a worrying corollary. If lawyers from disadvantaged groups are more likely to enter the less prestigious areas of small-firm practice, they are more likely to confront the issues we have discussed, and perhaps disproportionately likely to suffer disciplinary sanctions.

7.5 Summary

In sum, then, the business context adds considerably to the complexity of the background against which lawyers resolve ethical dilemmas. The business context largely determines lawyers' organisational culture, client interests and work relations. These structures in turn will do much to define the opportunities for and pressures against unethical behaviour, and to suggest the likely victims of any ethical violations which do occur. While there is evidence that distinctive practices have developed in the

---

[230] Arnold and Kay, ibid. Note that their analysis relates more to cases of serious professional misconduct involving mostly criminal behaviour or gross negligence by lawyers.

[231] See eg Mintz 1986. See also Ch.6, section 3.2.

[232] This can be a direct consequence of specialisation. For example, the 'small world' of much specialised commercial work makes it difficult for firms to avoid conflicts of interest in representing different clients, or for individual lawyers who may act as arbitrators or mediators in such disputes. See Menkel-Meadow 1996.

[233] Arnold and Hagan 1992; a similar pattern emerges from so far unpublished research by Mark Davies of Sussex University into trust account violations by English solicitors.

corporate and private client sectors, there is also evidence that patterns of organisational change are more complex than the segmentation thesis necessarily implies.
This in its complexity creates a major challenge for professional ethics and regulation: it is not just a question of whether the conventional individualistic and adversarial ethical assumptions can be sustained, but of how long the professions can
maintain the practice of aiming regulations at unitary professions which, perhaps,
no longer exist.

8. CONCLUSION

As Economides has usefully emphasised, citizens' access to justice is in part predicated on a supply of trained lawyers who are equipped to deliver 'justice'.[234] Yet our
analysis raises doubts on a number of fronts. Cultural and structural constraints
affecting both access to and the delivery of education and training bring into question the representativeness of lawyers in our society, and their preparedness to deal
with the problems of ethical uncertainty and value conflict raised by the practice of
law at the start of the twenty-first century.

While claims to professional collegiality and a strong service ethic have always
been contestable, the trend towards professional fragmentation constitutes a significant threat to, but also an opportunity to reconsider, the ethical basis of professionalism at a number of levels. First, it reinforces material resource and skills
inequalities in a kind of legal 'Matthew effect'.[235] This has been especially, though
not exclusively, apparent in certain kinds of public interest litigation. Mega-law firms
internationally have represented defendants in much of the multiple plaintiff
and disaster litigation of recent years, often against opponents considerably less
well resourced and, perhaps, represented.[236] It has also threatened to create or at
least enhance a skills/knowledge gap which is developing in respect of the non-
commercial areas of law. This is the result of two trends. First, there is already a substantial tranche of lawyers who, unless they are in firms (or even chambers, as the
Bar becomes more specialised) which have a significant commitment to *pro bono*
activities, have had little direct contact with work for the disadvantaged, or even with
more general private client work.[237] The other factor is the extent to which large
commercial firms have had a significant influence on the content of solicitors' train-

[234] Economides 1998; Economides and Webb 1998a.
[235] The 'Matthew effect' essentially describes any process whereby more is given to those who already
have.
[236] Resource inequalities may be exacerbated by the introduction of CFAs and legal aid contracting in
England and Wales, eg consider the financial effect of the war of attrition by Gallaher and Imperial
Tobacco in the recently collapsed tobacco litigation: see Ch.6, section 3.2; though cf also the collapse of
the Opren litigation in the 1980s: Berlins 1987.
[237] This is itself largely a consequence of the fact that most solicitors today undertake the final stages
of professional training in the larger, commercial, law firms. Shiner's study indicated that 42% of trainees
in 1996 were in 'high street' (including both general and legal aid practices) as opposed to city, large
provincial or niche firms. See Shiner 1997, p.69.

ing, skewing it increasingly towards their needs.[238] Secondly, our analysis affirms the extent to which the quality of lawyers' ethics and of access to justice may be influenced by factors beyond the immediate control of the professions collectively, let alone of individual firms and chambers. Changes to the underlying adversarial system, or to the ways in which lawyers are paid, have major implications for the quality of justice. Such changes are too often debated in an ethical vacuum, and professional responses likewise may take little cognisance of their impact on the ethical dimension of practice. Lastly, fragmentation, particularly in its globalised dimensions, should also lead us to examine the focus and 'neutrality' of conduct regulation, and the continuing capacity of the domestic professional bodies to regulate uniformly and police effectively the professions as a whole. Yet, at the same time, the large law firms' increasing autonomy could provide us with useful examples of how issues of ethics might be more effectively regulated at local levels.

This picture, which is deeply postmodern in its complexity and elusiveness, suggests to us that, at minimum, there is a need to develop a more contextually sensitive ethics through processes of legal education and training, more open ethical debate and consultation, and in revised structures and systems of professional regulation. We will develop this theme in the following chapters.

---

[238] Note the changes made to the Legal Practice Course in 1996, placing greater emphasis on Business Law at the expense particularly of Wills and Probate, which was downgraded despite its status as (in part) a reserved area of solicitors' practice.

4

The Regulatory Context: Ethics and Professional Self-Regulation

[A]ny association with the profession dispels the suggestion that the profession's ethical codes are self-interest writ large. There is a genuine concern with high ethical standards, not least so as to maintain the profession's public standing.

Ross Cranston[1]

In reality the worlds of ethics and professional ethics only partly intersect. Not a few aspects of professional regulation . . . owe their origins to questions of policy rather than reality.

Alan Paterson[2]

1. INTRODUCTION

In the last chapter we explored the extent to which the institutional and social background of lawyers affected their claim to being an ethical profession both as a collectivity and in responding to ethical dilemmas as individuals. In this chapter we extend these macro and micro concerns into a discussion of another major source of lawyers' moral standards—the regulatory frameworks laid down by the professions themselves which guide the way in which solicitors and barristers conduct their professional life. This will involve an overview of the regulatory institutions, the codes of conduct and the mechanisms for their enforcement. In providing such an overview, we have not forgotten that the profession's own regulatory framework does not constitute the full range of norms that may affect the way in which lawyers behave. In addition to those informal norms which stem from lawyer socialisation, there exist, as we have already noted, isolated legislative provisions, cases on tort, contract, fiduciary and adjectival law, as well as decisions of judges acting in their supervisory capacity over the professions.[3] Nevertheless, for a number of reasons, we consider it both acceptable and necessary to study the professions' own regulatory frameworks in isolation from these other written sources.

One is the practical point that the professional codes tend to be treated as a separate, enforceable set of rules and principles. While they lack direct legal force, they can be said to constitute, primarily for their own purposes, though sometimes also for the purposes of the general law, 'proper and accepted practice'.[4] Although, as we shall see in Part II, there may well be significant disjunctures between externally

---

[1] Cranston 1995, p.1.   [2] Paterson 1995, p.177.   [3] Cranston 1995, pp.2–3.
[4] *Kenyon-Brown v Desmond Banks & Co* (1998) unreported. Lawtel transcript, No. C8600213.

imposed law and internally promulgated regulation, the latter is largely based upon statutory and especially Common Law regulation of lawyer conduct. Indeed, as a guide to solicitors' professional conduct rather than a code in the traditional sense, the LSG includes references to many of these relevant legal provisions along with the rules promulgated by the Law Society itself. And while the conduct rules need not be coterminous with the law, it has been said that the codes commonly set higher conduct standards than the Common Law.[5]

Secondly, the codes of conduct and their enforcement mechanisms are likely to provide the most significant influence on lawyer behaviour. Not only do the codes provide a more readily accessible guide to professional norms than the numerous rules scattered throughout the legal *corpus*,[6] but, as we have seen, they form the basis for the first exposure most legal neophytes have to the issue of professional conduct.[7] The professional codes largely set the tone and determine the content of most other written discourses on professional legal ethics. Indeed, the fact that breaches of the codes can lead to disciplinary action means that lawyers ignore them at their peril, unless their disciplinary mechanisms are a dead letter. For both these reasons, it can be said that the profession's own regulatory framework plays a significant role in inculcating behavioural norms both initially and throughout a lawyer's career.

Finally, the profession's own regulatory framework, while possibly prioritising the interests of professional elites,[8] is the closest one comes to a collective statement about lawyers' values and ideals.[9] In addition to the internal function of informing lawyers what ethical values are regarded as important and how they should behave, it has the external function of signalling to the public what they can expect from lawyers. As such it is the most important source for evaluating the macro-ethical claims of the profession.

In looking at the profession's own regulatory framework, our aim is thus not simply the practical one of obtaining an overview of the various ethical duties of lawyers as a step to evaluating their adequacy for resolving ethical problems. It is also aimed, first, at examining whether the codes and, indeed, the regulatory framework in general merely represent 'self-interest writ large'[10] or whether lawyers do indeed display 'a genuine concern with high ethical standards' and, as professional elites are fond of asserting, owe duties to truth, justice, and the general public.[11] Secondly, by drawing upon general ethical theory, specific discussions of professional legal ethics and the growing corpus of regulatory theory, we will explore possibilities for reforming the regulatory framework in ways which both increase the chances of lawyers attaining those high ethical standards and for making the professions more responsive to the needs and concerns of the communities which they are meant to serve.

[5] See *Lee & Co Ltd v Coward Chance* [1991] Ch.259, 266.
[6] cp Holland 1995, regarding the law relating to solicitors.   [7] See Ch.3, section 6.
[8] See eg Shuchman 1968; Schneyer 1992; Sugarman 1996; de Groot and van Leuwen 1998, p.159.
[9] Woolley 1996, p.71.
[10] See Sampford with Parker 1995, pp.12–13; O'Dair 1997, p.2; Sheinman 1997, pp.146–7. cf also Paterson 1997, p.37.
[11] See Ch.6, section 2.2.

2. THE INSTITUTIONS OF SELF-REGULATION

2.1 Introduction

In the previous chapter we saw that one of the defining characteristics of the professional project has been the power of professions to regulate and control their own activities, including the setting of codes of conduct and their enforcement. This feature of professions has significant ethical implications.

The classical *noblesse oblige* professional tradition[12]—endorsed overwhelmingly by both the 1979 Royal Commission on Legal Services and the 1988 Marre Committee[13]—defends self-regulation as upholding the public interest in five ways. The first is that it preserves lawyers' independence, which in turn is said to be necessary to ensure that they play their role in ensuring the effective operation of the adversarial system and upholding the dignity and autonomy of citizens through vindicating their substantive and procedural rights. Secondly, it is claimed that the professions are best placed to regulate themselves, because only they have the necessary expertise to monitor practice.[14] Thirdly, it is asserted that self-regulating organisations (SROs) can more easily 'funnel-in' deviant behaviour for monitoring and, if necessary, sanction through rules of professional conduct than could external regulators through more formal kinds of regulation.[15] Fourthly, it is also sometimes suggested that self-regulation has positive 'dispositional' effects, in that it encourages lawyers to use their power and independence responsibly.[16] Lastly, it is also commonly argued that there are substantial cost advantages to self-regulation. Since SROs have in-house expertise and information, their information costs in formulating standards and providing guidance will be lower than those incurred by external agencies, as will monitoring and enforcement costs.[17]

While we shall later critically evaluate the role of lawyers in the adversarial system and in upholding human dignity and autonomy, there is much to be said for these arguments. At the very least, it would be extremely problematic to place lawyers under complete state control since they play an important role in protecting individuals against state power. On the other hand, self-regulation can be criticised as a cover for the pursuit of self-interest.[18] This, as we shall see, may affect the codes'

---

[12] See Ch.3, section 2.

[13] Though both also acknowledged that the professions had not been sufficiently responsive to public concerns about self-regulation: Arthurs 1982, pp.163–8; Marre 1988, pp.29–30. Marre is particularly striking in its dismissal of accountability problems as, essentially, a public relations failure.

[14] See eg Marre 1988, pp.29–30.

[15] See Brockman and McEwen 1990, pp.3, 9–15.

[16] Williams 1984, pp.266–7.

[17] Ogus 1994, p.107. Of course, since these costs in a self-regulating system will be borne by the profession and its clients rather than by the taxpayer, they may not be lower for professionals than they would be if regulation was externally imposed and monitored.

[18] For an overview of these arguments, see eg Paterson 1997, p.28; Parker 1997b, pp.388–90; Brockman and McEwen 1990, p.3. cf Mew 1989 for evidence that Canadian lawyers are aware of, if not uncomfortable with, the tensions created by self-regulation.

content and their enforcement. Professions possess, by definition, considerable monopoly power over markets that display substantial information asymmetries.[19] If consumers are poorly placed to judge quality, or identify abuses of that monopoly position, there is limited potential for pure market control over the service. Since those same information asymmetries may protect the professions' collective and individual interests, there is, perhaps, a strong inherent risk not just of conflicts of interests, but also of 'regulatory capture',[20] whereby regulatory agencies lose their independence by being subverted or dominated by the regulated to the extent that they begin to reflect the latter's worldview. This may limit the capacity of SROs to 'get tough' with their members. Indeed, professional bodies may use their autonomy to downplay or condone much minor deviance by filtering it out of the disciplinary system at an early stage, or by imposing relatively minor sanctions.[21] Secondly, it is also sometimes argued that SROs are not even uniformly partial to the interests of their own. Self-regulation may operate in the interests of a dominant professional group, or groups, thus helping to determine the outcomes of intra-professional power play.[22]

2.2 The Current Position

Given these criticisms, we need to ascertain the current position as regards self-regulation of the legal professions, noting that professional self-regulation does not always exist in its purest, 'voluntarist' form, neatly distinguished from external regulation by bodies such as the state.[23] Admittedly, *voluntary* self-regulation has tended to be seen as the dominant mode of professional regulation. It serves important ideological functions in suggesting a 'social contract' whereby professions undertake to regulate their own professional standards and ethics in exchange for the collective[24] and autonomous control of their market and members, and all the other advantages of professional status.[25] In reality, however, professional self-regulation is often *coerced*—in that professions have only acted in the face of government threats to impose statutory controls. Alternatively, self-regulation may be *mandated* by governments requiring professional bodies to operate within designated frameworks or

---

[19] ie consumers are not in a strong position to judge quality of services: see Bowles 1994; Dingwall and Fenn 1987.

[20] Ogus 1994, p.108. The risk of capture is now generally thought to be overstated in regulatory theory: see eg ibid, pp.57–8; Rees and Vickers 1995, pp.366–7, but a question mark still remains over professional SROs.

[21] Steele and Nimmer 1976; Brockman and McEwen 1990. This consequence may also flow in part from the indeterminate nature of many conduct rules. See Wolfram 1978, p.626.

[22] See sources above, n.8. See also Fennell 1982, pp.150–1, on the Law Society's development of anti-touting regulations in the 1930s as a weapon against the 'legal aid societies' who were widely suspected of ambulance-chasing and entering into champertous contingent fee arrangements with accident victims.

[23] See Black 1996, p.27, from whom the following terminology is taken.

[24] Note that self-regulation may also be individually tailored to individual economic units (firms, chambers, etc.), while collective and individualised regulation may co-exist in the same regulatory framework. See Black ibid, p.27.

[25] eg Menkel-Meadow 1985, pp.39–40 and see more generally Ch.3, section 1.

sanctioned by governments reserving the power to sanction systems and rules designed and proposed by professional bodies. Such state-sponsorship of professions has grown since the early 1980s and shifted the balance of the 'regulatory bargain',[26] hence blurring the distinction between self- and external regulation.

On exploring the legal professions' position along this continuum between voluntary self-regulation and purely external regulation, we discover an extraordinarily complex picture, involving a range of governmental[27] and non-governmental organisations[28] with some regulatory control over the market for legal services and, hence, over lawyers. Moreover, there is no common regulatory framework. Barristers are regulated by the Bar, solicitors by the Law Society and both by the Legal Services Ombudsman. Nevertheless, by tracing the evolution, roles and approach to conduct regulation and discipline of the latter three institutions, we can see that day-to-day control remains pre-eminently with lawyers themselves.

Historically, the organisation and control of barristers was primarily vested in the various Inns of Court, a set of medieval voluntary 'guilds' of lawyers lacking significant statutory footing.[29] Today, each Inn remains an essentially self-governing body to which all practising and non-practising barristers must belong. Since the 1960s, however, collective control has substantially moved away from the individual Inns, first to the Senate of the Inns of Court, and latterly to the Bar Council, a governing body of some 120 elected[30] barristers. The latter has exclusive power to promulgate and amend the CCB. It has a fairly small secretariat, which includes a Professional Standards and Legal Services Department. This administers the conduct aspects of the Bar Council's work, provides ad hoc advice in response to specific inquiries by practising barristers and prospective written guidance on professional standards, and administers the Bar's complaints procedures. The Inns themselves, however, have retained ultimate authority over discipline through their Disciplinary Tribunals. Significantly, none of these institutions owes their authority to legislation. To that extent, the Bar remains more truly self-regulating than its sister profession.

Solicitors only really attained national collective self-regulation through the forum of the Law Society during the last two decades of the nineteenth century.[31] While membership of the Law Society remains voluntary, its regulatory authority extends to cover all solicitors. The governing body is its Council, made up of 70 elected

---

[26] Macdonald 1995, p.115; Paterson, 1996.

[27] Notably the Lord Chancellor and the Lord Chancellor's Department, and the Attorney General. See Baldwin 1997.

[28] Notably the Legal Aid Board, the Securities and Investments Board (SIB), the Office of Fair Trading (OFT) and the Monopolies and Mergers Commission (now the Competition Commission). The soon to be disbanded Lord Chancellor's Advisory Committee on Legal Education and Conduct also best fits within this category. Set up under the Courts and Legal Services Act 1990 (CLSA), it has made a distinctive contribution to professional regulation as the first lay-dominated body to have a substantial say in the setting of conduct rules for the Anglo-Welsh legal professions.

[29] See further Cocks 1983; Abel 1988a, ch.9.

[30] Either in person or as representatives of the circuits, specialist bar associations or the Inns.

[31] Although the Law Society's origins can be traced back to the 1820s, it took years before its membership reached representative proportions: Abel 1988a, pp.242–3.

representatives of local constituencies. The Council's work is supported by an extensive secretariat. This includes the Professional Ethics Division, which has some responsibility for drafting conduct rules and standards, and also provides an advice and guidance service to practitioners, but is not involved in complaints or the disciplinary process. There is also a Monitoring Unit,[32] which has responsibility for advising and monitoring firms on compliance with the regulation of various aspects of practice, such as insolvency, investment business and the keeping of accounts, and various obligations to gather fraud intelligence.[33] In addition, there are 121 autonomous local law societies which exist in a somewhat ambiguous relationship to the Law Society. While the larger local societies may play a role in advising on and dealing with complaints, they have no formal regulatory or disciplinary powers over members.

The Law Society gained control of disciplining solicitors in the 1880s with the establishment of the Disciplinary Tribunal. This remained the basic framework until political pressure in the early 1970s resulted in the establishment of the more independent Solicitors' Disciplinary Tribunal.[34] This involved a one-third lay membership in all hearings and broke the link between membership of the Council and the disciplinary tribunals. In 1986, following the 'Glanville Davies affair'[35] and the growth of consumerism in the 1980s, new semi-autonomous investigation and adjudication procedures were created, managed by a separate arm of the Law Society, the Solicitors Complaints Bureau (SCB). In 1996, the SCB was itself reorganised and renamed the Office for Supervision of Solicitors (OSS). This operates under delegated authority from the Law Society's Council, through the Compliance and Supervision Committee, whose members are formally appointed by the Master of the Rolls. Like the SCB, it is not therefore a truly independent body; a point which has led to much criticism.[36]

The third key regulatory institution, the Legal Services Ombudsman (LSO), was created in 1991 partly to replace the relatively ineffectual Lay Observer scheme which, since 1976, had exercised a supervisory role over complaints to the Law Society.[37] The LSO's jurisdiction is statutory in origin,[38] and covers complaint-handling by both the Law Society and Bar. Unlike most ombudsman schemes, the LSO is distinctive in lacking power to adjudicate original complaints. Instead, her[39] role is to review the conduct and manner of complaint-handling. Moreover, since this may sometimes involve further investigation of the original claim,[40] and because she can, where the complaint has already been investigated, make compensation orders against individual practitioners rather than against the relevant professional body,[41] the distinction between investigating complaints and investigating their management can seem a fine one.

---

[32] Within the Professional Standards and Development Directorate.
[33] Baldwin 1997, pp.24–5.   [34] See Solicitors Act 1974, s.46.   [35] See Ch.3, n.67.
[36] See eg Hansen 1994.   [37] See Abel 1988a, pp.254 and 255.   [38] Under s.21, CLSA 1990.
[39] The current LSO is Ann Abraham.   [40] See James and Seneviratne 1995, p.203.
[41] See s.23, CLSA 1990.

Apart from ordering compensation, the LSO can require complaint-handlers either to reconsider complaints *ab initio*, or to reconsider exercising its disciplinary powers over complaints she has investigated. She can also require reimbursement of a complainant's legal costs in addition to compensation for distress or inconvenience. The LSO is also meant to exert a more general influence on good practice in complaint-handling in one of three ways. First, she can make general recommendations on complaints-handling to the professions, independent of any individual complaint;[42] a power which has to date been used sparingly.[43] Secondly, she may seek to influence the professional bodies informally through meetings with their representatives. Finally, she may use her Annual Report to 'name and shame' professional bodies guilty of poor practice or inadequate responses to earlier criticisms and may publicise, in anonymous terms, poor complaints-handling by individual lawyers, firms or chambers.[44]

The LSO has, however, been criticised for her limited powers of enforcement.[45] In particular, she lacks power to enforce compliance with compensation orders and recommendations.[46] There has also been the problem that, because she cannot deal with the primary cause of complainants' grievances, around a quarter of complaints received annually are rejected.[47] This creates a risk—borne out by research conducted in 1998[48]—of the failure to meet consumer expectations. The same study also revealed concerns with delay and a lack of effective complaint-handling within the LSO's office.

2.3 Reform of Self-Regulation

We thus see a relatively complex, multi-layered system of institutional control of the legal profession covering a wide range of matters concerning professional service delivery. Despite the existence of some external accountability for and control of lawyer behaviour, the system remains largely one of self-regulation. At the same time, this position is under constant threat. Self-regulation has long been exercised in the shadow of actual or threatened external control. Indeed, the incremental rise of external control appears likely to continue given the current strength of consumerist concerns, on the one hand, and the professions' waning influence over government and their apparent inability to mobilise public support, on the other.[49] Consequently, they are forced constantly to remake the same 'regulatory bargain': 'agree to this particular change, and we, the state, will allow you to retain the appearance of self-

---

[42] See s.24, CLSA 1990.   [43] James and Seneviratne 1995, p.199.   [44] See ibid, p.200.

[45] See James and Seneviratne 1995. Though these limits are not unusual in terms of the 'standard' ombudsman model.

[46] See at n.41 and 42, above.   [47] James and Seneviratne 1995, p.194.

[48] Customer Management Consultancy Ltd (no date).

[49] See Burrage 1996, pp.66–9. On the other hand, were a complete system of external regulation to be proposed, the profession is likely to be able to successfully rely on the cost argument referred to at n.62, below.

regulation'.[50] Moreover, self-regulation increasingly takes a sanctioned rather than voluntary form, in that rule changes must be made with an eye to the reaction of other regulatory bodies, such as ACLEC and the OFT.

As we have seen, while there are valid public interest arguments in favour of independent self-regulatory professions, there are equally persuasive public interest arguments that powerful institutions like the legal profession should be more accountable to the public they serve. In other words, while self-regulation should not be totally abandoned, we argue that there is a need to build more positively upon the current pressures for accountability by introducing greater responsiveness into the regulatory relationship.[51]

In essence, this would involve creating conditions which support dialogue and understanding between the regulator, the regulated and the consumers, as well as what Braithwaite and Makkai call a positive conception of trust. However, many regulatory systems may contain elements of responsiveness, without being fully-fledged responsive systems. According to Selznick the latter involves the acceptance of a 'reflexive' mode of rationality characterised by integrity, flexibility and participation in decision-making, by diffusion of authority and less top-down, authoritarian administration.[52] There are limited signs that the legal profession is moving slowly down that path,[53] and lay representation in the disciplinary process is now also well established. But such piecemeal initiatives are by themselves insufficient. It remains the case that there is often 'a profound gap between what angers clients . . . and what lawyers and their professional associations see as important enough to merit serious attention'.[54]

In making suggestions for reform throughout this chapter we shall be guided by the goal of responsive regulation. In specific regard to the institutional framework of professional regulation, there are at least three important ways of ensuring this goal: accountability, reflexivity, and transparency.

As regards the first way of ensuring this goal, professional regulators should be at least accountable[55] to some external institution, if not wholly independent.[56] As Arthurs points out, public accountability is important because it provides the basis whereby professions gain social trust.[57] Indeed, given that the professions have

---

[50] See Sheinman 1997, regarding solicitors. The latest instance of this trend was the announcement by the Lord Chancellor's Department in March 1999 that self-regulation would continue, subject to the LSO being granted increased supervisory powers: *The Law Society's Gazette*, 24 March 1999, pp.1, 18. See also the Law Society's latest attempts to shore up self-regulation at n.282 below.

[51] We recognise that what we propose in this chapter is an ideal, but offer it in the hope that it will generate further discussion as to what might be more immediately achievable.

[52] Selznick 1993, pp.286–7.

[53] eg OSS initiatives like its Lawyerline helpline, and the guidance functions carried out by both Law Society and Bar Council, may help break down some of the barriers and establish greater dialogue between professional regulators and 'grassroots' lawyers.

[54] Quotation from the summary to the New South Wales Law Reform Commission's 1993 Report, but equally applicable to the English experience.

[55] For a useful discussion of the meaning of accountability, see Holdsworth 1994, pp.45ff.

[56] See Arthurs 1982; Marks and Cathcart 1974, pp.229–30, 233–4.   [57] ibid, p.183.

increasingly acknowledged that individual practitioners should be accountable to their clients and that much professional conduct is already regulated (indirectly) outside professional disciplinary fora,[58] the creation of greater collective account-ability appears to be merely a logical extension of current trends.

Assuming that the case for collective accountability is accepted, we need to ask what it involves. In brief, it may be built into regulatory schemes either as an alter-native to direct external regulation—that is, as a process of making internal proce-dures more 'visible'—or as part of (normally) hierarchical external systems of checks and balances. In either case, accountability is likely to be predicated on some matrix of procedures requiring openness to (public) scrutiny, lay participation, and an element of external monitoring.[59] However, it is widely acknowledged that creating external regulatory control does not automatically resolve concerns about profes-sional accountability; it simply relocates them by creating—in the form of an infinite regress—*quis custodiet* ('who regulates the regulator') questions.[60] The con-ventional approach to this problem is to place any statutory bodies created under judicial and Parliamentary supervision, requiring them to submit a regulator's annual report to Parliament and subjecting them to the National Audit Office's supervisory authority. However, while this may provide enough hierarchical supervision, it will do little to ensure the regulator's own responsiveness.

Consequently, we propose a more nuanced approach involving a cyclical rela-tionship in which regulators and regulated act as each other's guardians, with suffi-cient transparency for the process to be observed from outside the circle.[61] With this in mind, we tentatively offer the following suggestions for reform:

(1) There needs to be a single independent regulatory body. This would help sim-plify the regulatory system by reducing the number of key players and hence the number of organisations that need to be accountable.[62] For the sake of argu-ment, we will call it the Legal Services Commission. It could take on all the existing functions (and funding) of the LSO, the OSS and the Lay Commis-sioner, the monitoring and at least some of the guidance functions of the Law Society Monitoring Unit and Professional Ethics Division, and the equivalent functions of the Bar Council's Professional Standards Department. The profes-sions would thus retain initial control over setting their internal rules and regulations, though this power might be made subject to some duty to consult with and, possibly in some contexts, even to obtain the Commission's approval. The professions would also retain ultimate control over their disciplinary procedures, though the Commission might act as an independent 'prosecution' service.

---

[58] Notably through professional negligence claims, or judicial controls such as wasted costs orders, etc.
[59] See eg Law Reform Commission 1993, paras. 3.58–3.91.
[60] ie the only way to ensure accountability of an nth-level regulator is to create another regulator at level n + 1. See generally Dingwall and Fenn 1987, pp.55, 61–2.
[61] Braithwaite and Makkai 1994, p.9. cf also Dingwall and Fenn ibid on the problem of regression.
[62] This would also have cost advantages, which would be desirable in preventing dramatic increases in regulation costs.

(2) We might look at ways of funnelling certain disputes away from the Commission's investigative activities, such as through formal (independent) mediation of complaints, rather than exclusive reliance on conciliation by the Commission. There might even be a case for following the example of some US jurisdictions and imposing mandatory arbitration of fee disputes on request by clients.[63] The cost of such services could be met at point of supply by the disputing parties, rather than, as at present, indirectly by the profession as a whole. Inevitably this raises, admittedly surmountable, issues of access and of fairness for aggrieved clients, who may be unable, or unwilling, to pay to pursue legitimate grievances against the profession.[64]

(3) There is the question of the Commission's own accountability. In the spirit of reflexivity, it ought to be required to consult with and to consider the views of both professional bodies and consumer groups in fulfilling its role. This will ensure accountability without giving either interest group hierarchical power over the Commission, while simultaneously obliging the Commission to listen and justify its actions to those groups.

The second, and at times overlapping, means of ensuring greater institutional responsiveness is through 'reflexivity'. A reflexive regulatory system is one that encourages participants to engage in reflection and dialogue.[65] It is thus particularly apt for the pursuit of a postmodern approach to ethics which calls for a plurality of voices and dialogue in relation to ethical issues. Pursuit of reflexivity as a regulatory objective has major implications not only for the operation of regulatory systems,[66] but also, as we shall see, for the form of ethical codes.[67] Most important as regards the former is the need for sites of dialogue between regulator, regulated and legal service consumers.[68] Dialogue may be located at various points in the regulatory relationship—at rule formation, implementation and/or at enforcement stages—and indeed should arguably be located at all stages.

In support of such dialogue sites, one can argue that the legitimacy of regulation is enhanced when the standards have been first agreed through public debate. Professions, on the other hand, are not used to discussing their standards publicly and fostering open debate, sometimes even within their own ranks. For example, grass-roots criticism of the LSG's requirement that firms run internal complaints

[63] See Stretch 1995, p.25.

[64] Cost disincentives could, of course, be mitigated by cost-shifting rules on a conventional 'loser pays' basis.

[65] cf Black's reference to 'conversations' about regulation: Black 1998, pp.77–9, 91ff.

[66] The analysis that follows possibly underplays the risks associated with regulatory regimes that rely heavily on responsive/dialogical input: see eg Black ibid, pp.92–6, but note also her conclusion at p.105: 'conversations are both an inevitable and, in certain circumstances, desirable part of the regulatory process. Ways therefore need to be found to structure, use and accommodate them whilst not shifting them to another, more private, forum or silencing them altogether.'

[67] Thus reflexivity is best ensured by 'aspirational' rather than 'disciplinary' codes: see section 3.1, below.

[68] cf Sampford with Parker 1995, pp.16–17, calling for 'ethical circles' to work through real and hypothetical ethical dilemmas, but narrowly confining them to practitioners.

procedures (Practice Rule 15)[69] largely saw it as an unwanted bureaucratic measure foisted on the profession by the Law Society.[70] Parker's research on issues of regulation and accountability in the Australian legal profession also stresses, not surprisingly, that where regulatory reforms were advanced in contexts involving dialogue and 'strategies of persuasion', voluntary reform in the public interest was far more successful than where reforms had been imposed without consultation with the profession.[71]

But our argument is not just about the range of professional opinion that ought to be involved. Public debate requires public participation and there is a strong case, we suggest, for introducing substantial lay representation on bodies setting and applying professional standards.[72] Because professional activities like law impact on the wider community, it can be said to be essential that they should accommodate community reflection on the ethical standards involved.[73] Otherwise, the profession's collective moral autonomy will be privileged over the values of the community it is intended to serve. Lay members of the disciplinary committees and tribunals would obviously have relevant expertise, but there might also be grounds for extending representation to a range of consumer and community interests.

Dialogue at the enforcement stage is also particularly useful if this process is transformed from being aimed mainly at imposing sanctions *ex post facto* for code breaches to being more about promoting a general willingness to maintain high conduct standards.[74] As we shall see later,[75] much of the research on regulatory strategies suggests that responsive conversations between the regulator and the regulated can play an important part in building trust and ensuring compliance.

The third way of ensuring more responsive professional regulation is through transparency. To be trustworthy, social institutions need to operate in ways that are visible and comprehensible to consumers. If their functions, rules and operating procedures are unknown, or hard to understand, this will help generate confusion and a culture of distrust. The evidence to date indicates that solicitors often fail the transparency test at both firm and regulatory levels.[76] For instance, Practice Rule 15, which is primarily intended to provide information on service standards, is too often ignored in spirit if not in the letter. This failure to provide adequate information at an early enough stage in the professional relationship also rebounds on the OSS, which has faced consumer criticism both for its expectation that all complaints must first be channelled through the firm complained of, and for the limits in its jurisdictional rules, which place various species of complaint outside its remit. At present, there is no equivalent data available on the practice in chambers, though it is likely that achieving transparency there will at least be complicated by the fact that the professional and lay client's information needs are likely to be signifi-

---

[69] Paras. 13.01–3, LSG.   [70] cf Christensen *et al* 1999, p.28.   [71] See Parker 1997a.
[72] cf Arthurs 1982, pp.168–74, 176–7; Law Reform Commission 1993, paras. 3.63–3.74.
[73] Coady 1996, p.281.
[74] Black 1998, p.88; see also p.89, quoting Schauer that 'rules doom decision-making to mediocrity by mandating the inaccessibility of excellence'.
[75] Section 4.3.
[76] See Christensen *et al* 1999; Harris 1994, pp.366–7.

cantly different. The obvious danger is that 'he who pays the piper, calls the tune' and that chambers will be far more ready to address the needs of the former rather than the latter, unless their dissatisfaction is channelled through professional clients. At the regulatory level, the quality of information given to complainants by the Lay Commissioner and the disciplinary procedures have already been heavily criticised.[77]

A number of practical developments could be explored to increase the system's transparency. For example, more uniform information requirements could be imposed on the professions. For all its practical failings, the Citizens' Charter model illustrates the range of information that ought routinely to be provided to clients, such as the specification (so far as possible) of normal performance targets, complaints procedures, and rights to compensation for inadequate services. Information on the regulator's role and power should also be made available at the outset, so that clients are not misled or confused as to the procedures and powers of such bodies should they wish to pursue their complaint beyond the firm or chamber concerned. The adoption by the professions of a more inclusive approach to complaints, involving less reliance on the jurisdictional boundaries between complaints which have disciplinary implications and those that might merit court action, would also be consistent with building a more comprehensible and transparent system. Moreover, the professions could engender greater openness on the disciplinary front. In particular we could follow the trend in the United States to make all disciplinary proceedings open.[78] This approach has been said to lead to greater accountability and greater comprehensibility of the system—to both lawyers and public.[79] Finally, disciplinary tribunal decisions could also be more widely publicised, as already occurs in some jurisdictions.[80]

3. THE CODES OF CONDUCT

In turning our attention to the second major dimension of the regulatory framework—the professions' codes of conduct—we will not abandon the responsiveness theme. However, our main concerns will be the macro-ethical issue of whether the codes are mostly concerned with the professions' own interests, as self-regulation might suggest, and the micro-ethical issue of their likely impact on the behaviour of individual lawyers. We will then consider reform of the codes in the light of the need for responsiveness and to ensure high ethical standards. First, however, it is necessary to look at the possible functions of codes in general in order to provide an idea of what aims the CCB and LSG might seek to achieve.

[77] Legal Services Ombudsman 1998.
[78] Usually, once a decision has been made to file formal charges, though some states have allowed files to be treated as open from the point of laying a complaint: Stretch 1995, p.24.
[79] ibid. See also Wilkins 1992, pp.884–5.
[80] eg the Law Society of Upper Canada publishes summaries of disciplinary sentences on its website.

3.1 The Functions of Ethical Codes[81]

As we have already suggested, codes play an obvious function in educating both legal neophytes and qualified lawyers as to how they should behave. They also act as written proof of the bargain entered into by profession, state and the community, which is often said to underlie the professional project and which will reflect the current state of play in the conflict between professions' desire for autonomy and the demand by the state and the public for accountability. More generally, codes can be regarded as public statements of the values and standards to which the profession has committed itself[82] and, hence, possibly as attempts to create 'a bridge with society'.[83] Whether or not, however, they can be taken at face value or are better seen as cynical attempts to head off external regulation or to legitimate the professional project and, in particular, the pursuit of professional self-interest[84] is an issue that will be pursued below.

In this way codes may act normatively both as a means of socialising professional insiders and as statements addressed externally to clients and the general public. However, these ideological functions do not exist in the abstract. They flow, either deliberately or inadvertently, from attempts to regulate professional behaviour for more prosaic reasons which, in the context of the legal professional, are largely about protecting both external and internal interests. Thus codes may attempt to protect those who might be harmed or manipulated by lawyers—clients, third parties and/or the general public. They may also attempt to protect the professions' interests by upholding their image as upright professionals, preventing the unscrupulous obtaining unfair market advantages over the scrupulous, and protecting individual professionals from excessive and immoral demands by clients.

There are, however, many different regulatory strategies[85] for achieving these goals which are usually combined rather than adopted exclusively.[86] First and most obviously is the *'command and control'* technique whereby certain behaviour is mandated, either negatively by actions being prohibited or more positively by action being required, with sanctions being provided for breaches. Such sanctions usually take the form of disbarment, suspension and fines, which can be coupled with 'naming and shaming' measures, though breaches of mandated behaviour may also lead to compensation awards.[87] To a large extent this strategy works through the deterrence effect of the fear of disciplinary action or compensation awards and the

---

[81] See generally, Rhode 1981; Frankel 1989; Moore 1989; Harris 1994; Coady 1996; Lichtenberg 1996; de Groot-van Leeuwen and de Groot 1998.

[82] Woolley 1996, p.76.   [83] De Groot-van Leeuwen and de Groot 1998, p.165.

[84] See the British commentators at n.10; and see eg Morgan 1977; Abel 1981, pp.653–7, 667ff; Rhode 1981, pp.692–706, regarding the US codes.

[85] See eg Baldwin 1997, pp.81–5.

[86] It is important to note that these must be understood in ideal type terms and as interrelated rather than as hermetically sealed.

[87] Note that this approach need not rely solely on provisions in the codes, but may also take into account the existence of legal sanctions and compensation usually for more extreme forms of professional misconduct, such as defrauding clients: Wilkins 1992, pp.806–7. On the other hand, professional regulatory regimes may funnel some of these cases away from the courts: see Brockman and McEwen 1990.

associated bad publicity. However, deterrence may also be achieved more informally through the 'internal sanction of professional conscience' and the 'external sanction of peer criticism'.[88] Secondly, codes can adopt a *licensing* strategy[89] which regulates standards of entry and practice management or involves prior contracting, such as the Legal Aid Franchising arrangement,[90] and which is likely to be supported by some element of *ex post* monitoring. Thirdly, regulation may operate through the *provision of incentives* for desired behaviour, such as kite-marking services to give providers a competitive edge.[91] Finally, and perhaps least determinative of required behaviour, is the provision of internal frameworks to *guide* decision-making and to help professionals make choices which are both more informed and more consistent than they might otherwise be. Thus whereas command and control works largely through deterrence, this guidance strategy works more through positive encouragement.

Before looking more specifically at the CCB and LSG it is important to note two points. The first is that in practical terms one cannot easily distinguish their ideological and practical functions. For instance, prohibiting, requiring or encouraging particular forms of behaviour will often have an educative function as regards lawyers, while they and the licensing and incentive techniques will convey important ideological messages to clients and the general public. Secondly, while it is possible to combine most of the four regulatory strategies, they cannot be given equal priority in any one code. This is because of factors relating to the form of codes.[92] Thus the command and control and licensing techniques are most effectively and most fairly pursued by provisions drafted in detailed language. Codes drafted in this style are often described as 'disciplinary codes'.[93] They tend to have a highly legalistic, regulatory form and prescribe only minimum, 'lowest common denominator', standards which can be strictly reinforced by disciplinary sanctions. By contrast, the guidance function is better achieved by broader principles couched in the language of 'moral suasion'. Such 'aspirational codes' are aimed at aiding, rather than minimising, decision-making. They aim to set higher standards, but, like the incentive technique, operate on a principle of voluntarism.

Given this link between the function and form of codes, examining the form of the CCB and LSG might provide some indication of their purposes. Before moving to such an analysis, it is important to appreciate the differences between the CCB and the LSG in this regard.

3.2 An Overview of the Codes

Along with most other professional codes, the CCB and LSG are of relatively recent origin. In line with the *noblesse oblige* tradition, for centuries the professions relied

---

[88] Moore 1989, p.14.   [89] Baldwin 1997, p.84.   [90] ibid, p.82.

[91] Ogus 1994, pp.137–8.

[92] The following discussion draws on Patterson 1981, pp.722–5; Frankel 1976; Hazard 1992; Glendon 1994; Sampford with Parker 1995, p.14ff. See also Jackson 1994.

[93] Also called 'criminal codes': Hodes 1981, p.751, comparing these with a 'vague platitudes' approach.

extensively on informal peer pressures and unwritten systems of etiquette to control professional conduct, albeit ultimately backed up by some formal judicial control.[94] As gentlemen, and therefore men of honour who knew instinctively how to behave, formal control of lawyers was regarded as otiose.[95] At most what was needed was control of entry into the profession in order to ensure those made of the 'right stuff' gained the privilege of practising.

Against this backdrop professional regulation has emerged and grown in two primary ways. The first has been the steady accretion of practice rules, primarily governing solicitors and largely on technical matters such as client solicitation, accounting rules and so on, which owe their origins more to political and economic, rather than ethical concerns.[96] The second has been a small trickle of texts, starting with Maughan's *Treatise*,[97] concerned in some ways with professional ethics and etiquette. For the solicitors' profession the shift from treatise to 'code' occurred in 1974 when Lund's lectures, first published in 1960, were converted into the first edition of the LSG. Since then these have grown from a relatively slim volume into its current 762 densely packed pages. By contrast, building on earlier texts on ethics and etiquette,[98] the Bar only published its first Code of Conduct in 1980. And even today it only comprises 196 pages including numerous blank pages, title pages, content pages and an index.[99]

Ascertaining why ethical regulation happened when it did is not easy. The reasons seem, perhaps inevitably, to be varied, rather than reflective of some single, seismic event, such as Watergate. One reason is the gradual deregulation of the market for legal services, which has created a continuing need to regulate the new, more competitive, environment.[100] Another reason is the expansion of the professions, and in particular the break-up of their homogenous communities by the entry of women, ethnic minorities and working class members through the increasing control of universities over the supply of lawyers.[101] Finally, there is the collective desire to support practitioners (and to protect standards), both symbolically and practically, in the face of an increasingly complex professional role.

While the exact impact of these factors requires further investigation, at this stage

---

[94] This is even less apparent today. The judges' disciplinary role has increasingly taken a back seat since the development of an internal regulatory dimension. The judges have thus proven themselves deeply reluctant to discuss the conduct dimension as such, even in cases concerning quite fundamental ethico-legal issues arising out of the retainer. See eg *Lee & Co Ltd v Coward Chance* [1991] Ch.259, 259H.

[95] See Thornton 1995, pp.55–6, regarding the Bar. See also Burrage 1996, p.49, regarding solicitors.

[96] See Sheinman 1997; Lunney 1998.

[97] *Treatise on the Laws of Attornies and Solicitors* (1825): see Sheinman, ibid, p.142n. See also Samuel Warren's *Popular and Practical Introduction to Law Studies* (1845) and *The Moral, Social and Professional Duties of Attornies and Solicitors* (1848). Warren, as a barrister, was, of course, well placed to advise attornies as to the standards expected of gentlemen practitioners!

[98] Notably, Boulton 1975.

[99] Much of the main body of the code is also repeated in Annexe H (Written Standards for the conduct of work). Where this occurs we will only refer to the former.

[100] Particularly activities like advertising, the creation of multi-disciplinary practices, and regulating direct access to barristers.

[101] See Ch.3, section 5.

it is possible to offer a number of reasons why the LSG is around four times longer than the CCB. Perhaps the most significant is the fact that, whereas the work of barristers is confined largely to advocacy, opinion writing, and the drafting of pleadings and other documents, solicitors are involved in a much wider range of activities. The variety of such activities has frequently prompted the Law Society to clarify how general rules of practice, such as those on conflict of interests, confidentiality and publicity, are to apply in specific contexts. In particular, the many areas of solicitor's practice which involve commercial activities, such as property selling and investment business, have attracted highly detailed external regulation designed to protect clients. Chapters on these topics, together with other specific types of solicitor activity, such as advocacy and litigation, ADR, insolvency, probate work and conveyancing, account for over a third of the LSG.[102]

Another crucial difference between barristers and solicitors affecting the amount of regulation in their respective codes flows from the divided nature of the profession. Most importantly, barristers' relationships with clients are mediated by instructing solicitors. It is solicitors who have to deal with clients on a regular basis, who negotiate fees, have to render accounts, and who hold their clients' money. Detailed regulation of such matters amounts to almost 12 per cent of the LSG.[103] Their direct financial relationship with clients also means that certain statutory provisions, such as those on money laundering, apply to solicitors only and are thus not found in the CCB.[104]

Differences in the source and history of the two codes are also important factors. Thus, given the apparent tendency for codes to become increasingly detailed over time,[105] the LSG's earlier origins might be important. In addition, solicitors have been subjected to external control by Parliament and the courts to a greater extent and for a far longer period than barristers. Consequently, there is a far greater body of regulation that can be incorporated into the LSG than into the CCB.

Nevertheless, even when the above 'material' differences between the two professions are taken into account, the Law Society exhibits a far greater preference for detailed regulation in contrast to the broad principles favoured by the Bar Council.[106] For example, the LSG devotes separate and fairly lengthy chapters to precise definitions of the solicitor's general duties regarding conflicts of interest and maintaining confidentiality, whereas the CCB contains only a handful of paragraphs merely exhorting barristers to avoid conflicts of interests and breaching confidentiality.[107] Perhaps the most striking example of the differing approaches is the fact that the LSG provides more detailed regulation of advocacy than the CCB.[108] Here one can speculate that the Bar's preference for an 'aspirational' type of code reflects the greater

---

[102] See Part V.   [103] See chs.13, 14, and 28.
[104] See Annex 3B, para. 16.07 and Annexes 16C and D, LSG.   [105] See eg Kagan 1989.
[106] One major exception involves rules regarding disciplinary proceedings: cp chs.30 and 31 of the LSG with Part VIII and Annexes M-P of the CCB.
[107] See below at nn.165 and 161, respectively. See also below at nn.164–74 on the differences in the two codes regarding the duties of integrity and independence.
[108] See ch.21, LSG.

tenacity of the *noblesse oblige* tradition in the Bar's culture, which in turn can be said to reflect the relatively exclusive nature of the Bar, both in terms of numbers and class, race and gender origins, and their geographic concentration in the London Inns and smallish chambers in other urban areas. By contrast, the large number of solicitors, their geographical dispersal, the existence of solo and small firm practices, and the wider social origins of solicitors might appear to require a greater need for written norms promulgated by the leaders of the profession.

3.3 The Form and Focus of the Codes[109]

3.3.1 *Introduction*

When we turn to a detailed analysis of the CCB and LSG, we also see differences of form within each code according to the type of issue regulated. As we have already seen, there are a number of reasons why codes subject particular issues to detailed rules rather than general principles or even vague admonitions. Nevertheless, one reason may well be that they are perceived as too important to be left to the discretion of individual lawyers. But whether true or not, the form of particular norms is likely to convey an implicit message about the relative importance of the matter regulated. And while the relative amount of regulation of particular issues conveys a subtle message, a far more explicit message is conveyed by the fact that some issues are subjected to little or no formal regulation at all. In other words, in order to gain a better understanding of the educative function of the codes, we need to analyse what can be called their focus, both in relative terms—the amount of regulation of particular issues as compared with others—and in absolute terms—what issues receive *any* regulation. This inquiry is also important for evaluating the question of the extent to which self-regulation has resulted in the dominance of lawyers' own interests over those of clients, third parties, and the general public.

In examining the codes' form and codes for these purposes, we can address two more specific questions. The first is whether the norms are in fact about ethical issues. Many are in fact concerned with etiquette[110] or matters of 'mere regulation'. The latter tend to be rather like traffic or VAT regulations in that they 'require knowledge and implementation', but no 'thought and understanding'.[111] They are largely laid down for bureaucratic reasons relating to the profession's internal management requirements, economic self-interest or self-image and are consequently sometimes called 'guild' or 'trade association' rules.[112] Here we shall describe rules of etiquette and 'mere regulation' as rules of 'conduct' to distinguish them from ethical

---

[109] The following discussion is based upon Nicolson 1998, esp pp.53–66, from which passages are reprinted with the generous permission of Hart Publishing.

[110] Note, however, that etiquette norms can easily shade over into ethical norms given that both involve the treatment of others. However, the distinction between the two can be justified on the basis that the former is concerned with behaving properly as a question of form and convention—the done thing—rather than concern for the interests of the others—the right thing. cf Phillips 1990, p.109ff.

[111] Crawley and Bramall 1995, p.105.　　　　[112] Freedman 1975, pp.110 and 115.

norms.[113] As we have seen,[114] ethics can be loosely defined as the question of what is 'right' or 'good' behaviour from a moral, as opposed to an aesthetic, practical, etc., point of view. The second relevant question focuses on whether particular norms involve what may be called the private or the public faces of ethics and conduct.[115] The former involve the interests of lawyers themselves and those close to them: their clients, fellow professionals, and the legal profession as a whole, whereas the latter involve duties to the general public, third persons, the environment, future generations, and to 'justice'.

Bringing together these two questions, we can subdivide the professional rules into the following categories: private face conduct norms; public face conduct norms; private face ethical norms; and public face ethical norms. However, it is important to keep in mind that these categories are intended merely as ideal types, designed to provide a convenient means of classifying and analysing the vast and confusing array of professional norms. As we shall see, many areas of regulation do not fall neatly on one or other side of the two classificatory axes. Nevertheless, the advantages of having a language for discussing the various regulatory norms will hopefully compensate for inevitable disputes over particular classifications.[116]

3.3.2 *Rules of Conduct*

While both codes commence with high sounding commitments to ensuring that professional legal ethics serve the interests of justice and the public interest,[117] in reality a large proportion of their norms has little or nothing to do with ethical issues. Thus, while the CCB's 'general purpose' does acknowledge the 'public obligation' of barristers to ensure public access to justice[118] its main aim purports to be to provide rules which 'preserve and enhance the strength and competitiveness of the independent Bar'.[119] Moreover, the twelve paragraphs containing the CCB's fundamental principles appear rather more concerned with protecting the Bar's reputation and image, barristers' independence and self-interest than with the needs of clients and the public at large.[120] However, far more indicative of the CCB's focus is the fact that roughly 70 per cent of it involves conduct norms.

Ascertaining the equivalent figure in the LSG is impossible given its length, complexity and the fact that many of its norms straddle the conduct/ethics distinction.[121] Nevertheless, it is illuminating that of the 22 Practice Rules promulgated by the Law Society summarising 'the basic principles of professional conduct',[122] the vast

---

[113] cf Crawley and Bramall 1995, p.105ff, referring to 'core ethics', thus begging the question as to the content of 'non-core' ethics.

[114] Ch.1, section 2.

[115] cf Disney 1986, p.82, who draws a distinction between intrinsic and extrinsic matters.

[116] cf de Groot-van Leuwen and de Groot 1998, p.162 where this scheme is relied upon.

[117] See para. 102, CCB; principle 6 of para. 102, LSG.

[118] Para. 102(a) (iii). However, this manifests itself in the so-called cab-rank rule: see at n.203, below and Ch.7, section 3.2.2.

[119] Para. 102(a).   [120] Paras. 201–12.   [121] See section 3.3.4, below.

[122] Para. 1.04 n.1, LSG.

majority deal with matters of internal bureaucracy or the protection of the interests and self-image of the profession. And, taken as a whole, a substantial portion of the LSG is devoted to matters of mere regulation[123] and a fair amount to etiquette.[124]

Both codes give pre-eminence and considerable attention to protecting the image of solicitors and barristers as independent, financially upright professionals, and as above trade, unseemly commercial competition, and crude self-interest. Thus, two of the six 'basic principles' in Practice Rule 1 of the LSG prohibit solicitors from doing anything to compromise or impair their own independence, integrity or good repute, or the profession's good repute.[125] Similarly, the first substantive provision of the CCB exhorts barristers not to engage in conduct which is 'dishonest or otherwise discreditable to a barrister', 'likely to diminish public confidence in the legal profession . . . or otherwise bring the legal profession into disrepute' or engage in any occupation which might 'adversely affect the reputation of the Bar'.[126]

Lacking any further clarification, some of these high sounding principles remain just that. However, a vast amount of regulation, particularly in the LSG, is devoted to ensuring an image of lawyers as upright professionals free from the taint of commerce. Thus there are myriad rules, for instance, controlling publicity about a lawyer's services,[127] contingency fees,[128] the giving and receiving of gifts and commissions[129] and ensuring that solicitors honour professional undertakings, which are as much about lawyer image as protecting the public.[130]

The apparent importance of these matters to the professions can be seen in the attention to detail in the rules. For instance, the LSG's publicity rules allow solicitors to claim to be specialists or experts in particular fields, send unsolicited mailshots, and name members of their staff on notepaper, but not to use the Law Society's Coat of Arms, or make unsolicited visits or telephone calls to potential clients.[131]

However, while the profession might like to portray itself as being above coarse business practices, the codes are by no means totally devoid of provisions serving the economic self-interest of lawyers, notwithstanding recent assaults on traditional restrictive practices. There are rules protecting lawyers' monopolies in the provision of legal services,[132] protecting their fee earning capacities[133] and allowing solicitors

---

[123] See esp chs.1–4, 8–10, 14, and 29–31, LSG.   [124] See esp chs.19 and 20, LSG.

[125] Para. 101(a) and (d).   [126] Para. 201(a)(i) and (iii) and (b).

[127] Para. 307, CCB; paras. 11.02, 11.03, 26.06, 26.14, 27.19 and Annexes 11a, 21B, and 27E, LSG.

[128] Para. 211, CCB; paras. 14.04–06 and Annex 14B, LSG.

[129] Paras. 205 and 207(d), CCB; paras. 11.01 n.3, 14.14–14.15, 15.05, 23.04, 23.07 and Annex 14G, LSG.

[130] Ch.18, LSG. Rules on fee-sharing, arrangements with claims assessors, and introductions and referrals (see at nn.166–8) could also be said to come into this category. See also the various similar provisions in the regulation of specific areas of practice like insolvency, conveyancing and investment business (chs.25–7, LSG).

[131] Para. 11.03 and paras. 2(e) and 3 of Annex 11A, LSG. See also paras. 307.1–2, CCB regarding the Bar's rules on advertising.

[132] eg para. 212, para. 2 of Annexe B and Annexe J, CCB; paras. 2.06, 3.06, 17.04, 21.05, and 25.07, and Annex 25A, LSG.

[133] Paras. 308, 502(b)–(d) and 503, para. 8.2 of Annexe H, CCB; paras. 5.05, 12.12, and 25.14, ch.14 *passim* and Annex 25A, LSG.

to limit their liability for negligence.[134] In many cases such provisions are highly detailed. An example is the Bar's rules on practice in Law Centres and Legal Advice Centres,[135] which go into minute detail as to what exactly a barrister may or may not do if employed by or attending these types of centres.

The importance of protecting professional self-interest can be seen in the significant amount of regulation—especially in the CCB—devoted to protecting and facilitating the split nature of the profession;[136] an important restrictive practice, protecting certain traditional activities of barristers and solicitors, and ensuring the increased fee earning capacity of lawyers through the duplication of legal representation.[137] It is significant that this restrictive practice is considered to be one of the main aims of the CCB, meriting two paragraphs dealing with its fundamental principles and a single annex on this issue constituting just over 10 per cent of the CCB.[138]

It is also noteworthy that, by comparison to this detail and its prohibitions on contingency fees and those fixed irrespective of the work done,[139] the CCB leaves fee-setting largely unregulated.[140] Thus, whereas barristers must provide proper financial remuneration for work done on their behalf by their colleagues,[141] the CCB contains no clearly defined notion of the overcharging of clients and expressly exempts barristers from their 'public obligation' to provide prospective clients with access to justice where the latter cannot afford their fees.[142] By contrast, the LSG contains a substantial amount of regulation relating to payment for solicitors' services. While much of it does protect clients, it is also true that these rules largely emanate from external legal sources[143] and that a fair number are designed to protect the financial interests of solicitors.[144]

Less controversial is the substantial amount of regulation on the internal running of the professions, although some of this—like rules on the entry into and certification within the professions[145]—can easily shade into protectionism and hence self-interest.[146] Thus there are rules relating to pupillages and other training schemes,[147] the efficient running of chambers and law firms,[148] indemnity insurance and

---

[134] Para. 12.09, LSG.   [135] Para. 703.

[136] Paras. 102(a)(ii), 207(b) and (c), 210, 402.1, Annexe D, Annexe E, rules 2.1 and 11.6 of Annexe H, Annexe I; Ch.20, LSG.

[137] See Zander 1968, chs.12–13. But cf recent limitations on this restrictive practice; see Zander 1997. See also the rules controlling entry into the profession: eg paras. 301–2, 401; CCB ch.2, LSG *passim*.

[138] Annexe D. See also paras. 102(a)(ii), 207(b) and (c), 210, 402.1, Annexes E, F and G, rules 2.1 and 11.6 of Annexe H, CCB; paras. 21.05–21.06 and ch.20, LSG.

[139] Paras. 211 and 303, CCB, respectively.

[140] Para. 308, CCB.   [141] Paras. 309.1 and 309.2, CCB.

[142] Para. 502. cf also para. 503 which protects the fee-earning capacities of QCs and junior barristers.

[143] Solicitors' fees have long been controlled by Parliament: see Abel-Smith and Stevens 1967, p.53ff.

[144] Paras. 5.05, 12.12, 14.01, and 25.14, and para. 2.5 of Annex 21A, LSG.

[145] eg Annexe A, CCB; ch.2 and 3 *passim*, LSG. See also the relevant provisions in Part V of the LSG, which deals with specific areas of practice by solicitors.

[146] Abel 1988.

[147] Paras. 701.1–7.02, Annexes A and C, CCB; para. 2.08 and Annex 2E, LSG.

[148] Paras. 303–4, Annexe B, Equality Code, CCB; chs.3 and 7 *passim*, LSG. See also para. 21.06, Annex 21H, LSG.

compensation,[149] membership of the professional bodies and their powers,[150] disciplinary proceedings and other control mechanisms by the professional bodies,[151] and provision for lawyers practising outside England and Wales and for 'foreign' lawyers practising here.[152] Here we find a substantial amount of highly specific regulation on issues relatively insignificant as far as professional conduct and ethics are concerned. Over 7 per cent of the CCB is devoted to regulating the pupillage system,[153] while the LSG contains four pages of highly detailed guidance on matters of the proper nomenclature for firms, their notepaper and publicity.[154]

The final category of conduct rules is those involving matters of etiquette. In the CCB's case, earlier detailed guidance[155] has been eschewed in favour of exhortations to barristers to display courtesy to the court and all with whom they have professional dealings,[156] and to dress decorously in court.[157] The LSG is far more detailed on the equivalent duties of solicitors, even to the extent of devoting two, albeit relatively short, chapters to 'relations with other solicitors' and 'relations with the Bar, other lawyers and professional agents'.[158]

3.3.3 *Ethical Rules*

Code provisions concerned with ethical issues can be classified according to three types of duties owed by lawyers: to clients; to the administration of justice; and to specific third parties and the general public.

There is no doubt that duties to clients are taken seriously by both professions, though the LSG provides far more regulation here than the CCB. Such duties are sometimes subdivided into loyalty, diligence and confidentiality,[159] although confidentiality can plausibly be regarded as part of the loyalty duty.[160] Here, the difference between the two codes is most stark, with only the LSG providing any detail as to the exact ambit of the confidentiality duty and its exceptions.[161]

Apart from confidentiality, loyalty to clients can be said to comprise three further duties: zeal, independence and integrity. The first requires lawyers to do their best for clients; an obligation which is painted in warmer colours[162] and in far more detail as regards barristers and solicitor-advocates than other solicitors.[163] The duty of inde-

---

[149] Paras. 301(b) and 302, CCB; ch.29, LSG.
[150] Para. 301(c), 302A, 401(b) and 401A(b), CCB; ch.2 *passim*, LSG.
[151] See at n.106 above.
[152] Paras. 602 and 704.1–2 and Annexes F, I and L, CCB; Part II, LSG.
[153] Annexes A and C, CCB.
[154] Paras. 2.03 n.12, 3.10–3.12, paras. 6 and 7 of Annex 11A.
[155] cp the CCB with Boulton 1975, its precursor.
[156] Para. 5.5 of Annexe H.   [157] Para. 5.12 of Annexe H.
[158] Chs.19 and 20, respectively. See also paras. 12.05 and 21.17 and paras. 6.1(a) and 6.3 of Annex 21A. Note, however, that these provisions contain a mixture of rules on etiquette, conduct and ethics.
[159] Cranston 1995, p.6.   [160] cf Paterson 1980.
[161] cp paras. 501(f), 504(b)(ii), 603, CCB with ch.16, LSG.
[162] cp para. 101(c), LSG with para. 203(a) and para. 5.1 of Annexe H, CCB, and para. 2.3 of Annex 21A, LSG.
[163] See especially para. 606 and Annexe H, CCB *passim*; ch.21 *passim*, LSG.

pendence requires lawyers to avoid situations where their zeal might be compromised. It comprises one of the LSG's 'basic principles' and one of the CCB's 'fundamental principles'.[164] It is fleshed out, albeit in far more detail in the LSG, in rules governing conflicts of interests between a lawyer's different clients and between clients and third parties or conflicting duties.[165] In addition, the LSG also contains rules on fee-sharing,[166] arrangements with claims assessors,[167] and introductions and referrals.[168] The duty of integrity is designed to prevent lawyers taking advantage of clients financially or otherwise. In the LSG it receives far more attention than the other two duties, but in the CCB it is confined to a paragraph simply prohibiting barristers from acting for clients whose interests conflict with their own.[169] While the LSG leaves the general notion of taking advantage of clients rather vague[170] and says no more on 'culpable overcharging' than that it is 'a question of fact in each case',[171] numerous rules regulate fees[172] and provide other forms of financial protection to clients,[173] including 60 pages of detailed rules on solicitor accounts.[174]

As regards the duty of diligence, although it receives far more attention in the LSG than in the CCB, both codes contain general principles as well as highly detailed requirements. Thus, barristers and solicitor-advocates are urged to 'act promptly, conscientiously, diligently and with reasonable competence',[175] while solicitors are required to uphold a 'proper standard of work'[176] and to 'carry out a client's instructions diligently and promptly'.[177] All lawyers are required to refrain from acting or continuing to act if they lack sufficient experience, time or opportunity for the work involved.[178] Examples of more specific obligations are those on barristers to give advice on chances of an appeal following conviction[179] and those on solicitors to deal promptly with letters, other communications, and requests for information.[180] In addition, following pressure from consumer groups, there are now detailed obligations on solicitors to provide clients with information relevant to their case[181] and for law firms to operate complaints-handling procedures.[182]

When we come to public face ethical norms, we find that they are dominated by lawyers' duties to the administration of justice and to the courts, more specifically.

---

[164] Para. 205(a) and (b), CCB; para. 101(a), LSG.
[165] Paras. 501(e), 504(b)(ii), 605 and paras. 3.3, 3.4 and 3.5 of Annexe H, CCB; paras. 15.01, 15.02, 15.03, 15.06, 25.01 and 25.02, and Annex 15A, LSG.
[166] Paras. 14.02 and 14.03.   [167] Paras. 11.08 and 11.09.
[168] Paras. 11.04–5, 26.07, 26.15, and 27.19, and Annex 11b.
[169] Para. 501(e), CCB. For the LSG equivalent, see paras. 15.04 and 25.03.
[170] See para. 12.07, LSG.   [171] Para. 14.13, LSG.   [172] Ch.14, LSG.
[173] See eg the rules on gifts and commissions, at n.129 above.   [174] Ch.28, LSG.
[175] Para. 601 and para. 5.4 of Annexe H, CCB; para. 6.1 of Annex 21A, LSG.
[176] Para. 101, LSG.   [177] Para. 12.06, LSG.
[178] Paras. 501(a) and (b), 504(a), 601 and paras. 5.4, 5.6, 5.7 and 11.3 of Annex H, CCB; para. 12.02 (which also speaks of competence) and para. 4.1(a) and (b) of Annex 21A, LSG.
[179] Para. 17 of Annexe H, CCB. See also paras. 5.9, 12.2, and 16 of Annexe H.
[180] Para. 12.08, LSG. See also paras. 12.10, 14.07, and 20.06, LSG.
[181] See, generally, paras. 5.01, 14.08 and 51.02 and ch.13, LSG *passim*.
[182] See paras. 13.01–13.03, LSG.

Thus, 'the solicitor's duty to the Court' is one of the six Basic Principles enacted by Practice Rule 1,[183] whereas barristers and solicitor-advocates are stated to have 'an overriding duty to the Court to ensure in the public interest that the proper and efficient administration of justice is achieved', to 'assist the Court in the administration of justice' and not to 'deceive or knowingly or recklessly mislead the court'.[184] Given the close association between the administration of justice and respect for courts, it is not surprising that the majority of duties relate to litigation and advocacy, although the LSG does impose certain requirements as regards the administering of oaths and alternative dispute resolution which protect the due administration of justice.[185]

As regards advocacy and litigation, there are specific duties of honesty in adducing evidence, drafting pleadings and the drafting and use of other documents.[186] What is striking about the CCB provisions—repeated in the LSG's Code for Advocacy[187]—is that, while they are not entirely free from vagueness or the delegation of important decisions to the discretion of individual advocates,[188] they contain the sort of detailed regulation only found in the CCB as regards areas of 'mere regulation'. Here there seems to be a careful attempt to spell out what advocates can do in representing their clients. This tendency is even more marked in the LSG, which closely details what lawyers must disclose to the court, when they should check the veracity of clients' stories, when they should decline to act for lying clients, and, in the case of criminal defendant clients, what they can do depending on whether the latter do or do not admit guilt. Again, however, the potential for avoiding these provisions is created by the occasional use of 'get-out' phrases such as 'where practicable'[189] and 'best endeavours'[190] and distinctions of which the most skilled sophist would be proud.[191] For instance, it is declared to be unbefitting conduct for a solicitor to call a witness 'whose evidence is untrue to the solicitor's knowledge as opposed to his or her belief'.[192]

There are also a substantial number of rules designed to avoid the possibility or the appearance of justice miscarrying. For example, lawyers involved in litigation are prohibited from making press statements calculated to interfere with the fair trial of a case,[193] interfering with witnesses,[194] privately communicating with the

---

[183] Para. 1.01, LSG.

[184] Para. 202, CCB; para. 2.2 of Annex 21A, LSG. See also para. 201(a)(ii), CCB; para. 2.1(a)(ii) of Annex 21A, LSG.

[185] See paras. 17.06–7 and ch.22, LSG.

[186] Paras. 504(e)–(g), 606, 610 and paras. 5.8, 5.10(d), 7.1, 7.2, 7.3, 7.4 and 17.3 of Annexe H, CCB; paras. 21.07, 21.20, 21.21, 21.13 and paras. 2.1, 2.2, 5.1(e)–(g), 6.6, 7.1(d) of Annex 21A, LSG.

[187] Annex 21A, LSG.

[188] eg para. 606, CCB and para. 6.6 of Annex 21A, LSG speak of 'not properly arguable' contentions, 'reasonably credible' supporting evidence and a 'reasonable belief' in certain types of contentions.

[189] Paras. 21.20 n.4 and 21.21 n.4, LSG.   [190] Paras. 21.20 n.7.

[191] cf Lord Diplock in *Saif Ali v Sydney Mitchell & Co (A Firm)* [1980] AC 198, 220A.

[192] Para. 21.07 n.5, LSG.

[193] Para. 21.18, LSG. See also para. 6.3 of Annex 21A, LSG; para. 604, CCB.

[194] See para. 607.1–607.3 and paras. 6.1, 6.2 and 11.5 of Annexe H, CCB; paras. 21.10, 21.11 and para. 6.5 of Annex 21A, LSG.

Court,[195] and from acting in cases where they are likely to be called as witnesses.[196] Once again, while the provisions in the CCB, although on fairly specific topics, are couched in general terms, the LSG frequently provides considerable detail in defining the exact ambit of its duties.[197]

Both codes also place a number of positive duties on advocates in relation to the Court and the administration of justice. Some are of a very general nature, such as barristers' duties to act courteously towards the Court[198] and solicitors' duties to obey Court orders.[199] Others, however, are more specific, such as the duties to assist the Court by disclosing relevant law and by bringing any procedural irregularities to its attention during the hearing, rather than subsequently using them as grounds for appeal.[200] Finally, these general duties are somewhat modified and customised by highly detailed rules regulating the different situation of lawyers acting for the prosecution, for an accused, in criminal proceedings generally or in civil proceedings.[201]

By contrast to the plethora of provisions protecting the interests of clients and the administration of justice, there are very few provisions concerned with protecting the general public or specific others who might be affected by lawyers' actions. Assuming that it is in the public interest that people have access to legal advice and a free choice as to their lawyer, a number of rules can be said to fall within this category. For instance, the so-called cab-rank rule attempts to guarantee everyone (or at least those sufficiently wealthy or fortunate enough to be legally aided)[202] access to a barrister or solicitor-advocate.[203]

There are also a number of protections extended to third parties and the general public. Thus lawyers are prohibited from causing unnecessary harm to the reputation or dignity of third parties.[204] However, this protection is strictly limited. First, it is almost entirely[205] confined to the context of litigation, suggesting perhaps that the codes are as much concerned with the dignity of the law and the courts as with

---

[195] Para. 21.09, LSG.

[196] Para. 501(d); para. 3.6 of Annexe H; para. 21.12, LSG.

[197] eg para. 21.10 nn.2–7 and cp the detail in the notes to 21.12, LSG with the broad statement of principle in para. 501(d) and para. 3.6 of Annexe H.

[198] Para. 5.5 of Annexe H, CCB.

[199] Para. 21.14, LSG. Note that these duties can be classified as public face rules of etiquette rather than ethics.

[200] Para. 610(c), CCB; para. 7.1(c) of Annex 21A, LSG; para. 21.07 n.3, LSG. See also para. 601(a) and paras. 5.11 and 14.1 of Annexe H, CCB; para. 21.01 n.6, and paras. 6.1(a) of Annex 21A, Annex 21F, LSG.

[201] Paras. 11.1–11.8, 12.1–13.6, 14.1–17.6 of Annexe H, CCB; paras. 21.13, 21.16, and 21.19–21, and Annex 21E, LSG.

[202] See para. 502(b)–(d), CCB; para. 2.5 of Annex 21A, LSG.

[203] Paras. 102(a)(iii) and 20 and para. 2.1 of Annexe H, CCB; para. 2.4.2 of Annex 21A, LSG. See also para. 503A and para. 3.1 of Annexe H, CCB; paras. 12.02, 21.03, Annex 21I and para. 4.1 and 4.3 of Annex 21A, LSG (requiring barristers and solicitor-advocates to assess their suitability for the work required of them) and paras. 11.01, 11.07, 12.03, and 21.03, and Annex 21I, LSG (protecting freedom of choice in instructing a solicitor).

[204] See para. 610(e)–(h), CCB; para. 7.1(e)–(h) of Annex 21A, LSG; para. 21.08, LSG. See also para. 606(c), CCB.

[205] But para. 12.02 n.6 and para. 17.01 n.5, LSG.

that of affected persons.[206] Secondly, the protection provided is somewhat undercut by allowing scope for evasion, both because important terms are left undefined and because the prohibitions are hedged with qualifications allowing, for instance, allegations which are not 'merely' scandalous or 'only' intended to vilify. Admittedly, such qualifications are necessary to balance the interests of third parties against those of clients, but at the same time lawyers will rarely be unable to argue that they had good grounds for believing that one of the qualifications applied.

Somewhat more ambitious in aim are recent rules[207] designed to eradicate discrimination by lawyers on the grounds of race, sex, sexual orientation or disability and in the case of barristers also on the grounds of ethnic origin, marital status, religion, or political persuasion. While these provisions are commendable, one wonders why it took so long and so much external pressure for lawyers to bring themselves into line with discrimination policies adopted legislatively from the late 1960s. More importantly, it remains to be seen how their ambit will be interpreted. At present, the codes are mostly concerned with equal opportunities within the profession[208] and with discrimination in the choice of clients.[209] They do not appear to prohibit, for instance, the reliance on sexist and racist stereotypes in arguing cases. What is clear is that neither code addresses perhaps the most important source of discrimination in society, namely that flowing from socio-economic class. The right to refuse to act for clients who cannot afford legal fees is expressly protected[210] and there are no provisions exhorting, let alone requiring, lawyers to ensure access to justice for the needy.

The above constitute the CCB's only public face norms. The LSG, however, goes a little further. Most are highly specific and very narrowly confined.[211] Of greatest *prima facie* import is para. 17.01 which prohibits solicitors acting 'towards anyone in a way which is fraudulent, deceitful, or otherwise contrary to their position as solicitors' and from using 'their position as solicitors to take advantage either for themselves or another person'. However, the protection afforded to third parties depends very much, firstly, on what is regarded as action contrary to a solicitor's position—in other words, on what harm to third parties caused by solicitors acting for clients is generally regarded as justifiable—and, secondly, on what is regarded as an unfair advantage. Currently, this provision is unlikely to have much impact since it is not generally seen as contrary to a solicitor's position to cause harm to the public interest or third parties when acting on behalf of clients.[212] Indeed, in elaboration

---

[206] cf the approach of the professional conduct manuals: ICSL 1996; Silverman 1997.

[207] See para. 204, CCB; Annex 1B, LSG, for the general principles.

[208] Paras. 6 and 1 of Annexes B and C, respectively, CCB and the new Equality Code (discussed in Inns of Court School of Law 1997); ch.7 *passim*, LSG.

[209] Para. 7.02 nn.3 and 4 and para. 2.4.4(a) of Annex 21A, Annex 21C, LSG.

[210] See also para. 502(b)–(d), CCB; para. 2.5 of Annex 21A, LSG.

[211] See eg paras. 3.16, 16.07, 25.13, and 27.19 n.10 and Annexes 3B, 16C and D regarding money laundering and para. 25.12 and Annexes 25F and G regarding mortgage fraud. See also paras. 17.02–3, 17.05 and 25.04 for even more narrowly confined duties to third parties.

[212] See eg Silverman 1997, p.128: 'a solicitor does not owe a duty to the world at large'. See further Ch.6, section 2.1. A similar response would apply to attempts to base limitations on lawyers harming the public interest or third parties on a number of general provisions prohibiting lawyers from acting in ways

of para. 17.01 the only examples given of prohibited action are very narrow and insignificant.[213] Ultimately, this provision appears to be designed as much to protect the image of solicitors as upright professionals as the interests of third parties.

The only provisions protecting the public interest or third parties which can be said to be anything other than very narrowly confined or overly vague are those allowing solicitors to breach their confidentiality duty to prevent, for instance, their being used to facilitate crimes or frauds, crimes likely to result in serious bodily harm, and child abuse. But even here, such disclosure is only permissive rather than mandatory.

3.3.4 *Evaluation*

In mapping the codes' focus and form, two factors prevent a completely clear picture emerging. The first is the frequent difficulties of categorising particular issues in terms of the ethics/conduct and public/private axes. Minor problems are caused by the fact that certain aspects of a particular duty may fit into one category, while other aspects fit into another.[214] Far more problematic are norms that straddle both sides of the two axes because they *simultaneously* protect more than one type of interest.[215]

Similar problems are encountered in ascertaining whether certain norms are solely about self-interest or whether they serve more elevated purposes.[216] This problem is most acute in relation to the plethora of rules, mostly in the LSG, which protect clients, especially those involving the duties of independence and integrity. Although they are commendable, it can be noted that such rules simultaneously, albeit indirectly, play an important role in serving the profession's self-interest in retaining the trust of the public—their potential clients—and the dignity and image of integrity and independence of lawyers.[217] And in many cases, one gets the distinct impression that it is their dignity and image rather than the protection of clients which is more important to the profession.

The second factor muddying the focus and form waters is the significant differences between the two codes. Thus, in very broad terms and taking into account the caveats about classification just noted, the CCB provides far less detailed regulation

which bring their profession into disrepute or discredit (para. 201(a)(i) and (iii), CCB; para. 1.01(d), LSG) or compromise their professional standards (para. 205(c), CCB).

[213] Thus apart from even more insignificant matters of etiquette, lawyers are required to ensure that no retainer arises between themselves and third parties, that third parties who submit draft documents have opportunities to correct them, that they do not write offensive letters, and that they provide truthful references: see notes to para. 17.01.

[214] Thus some rules on confidentiality protect clients and others the public interest, some rules on conflicts of interests deal with maintaining lawyer integrity and others with lawyer independence, whereas some rules relating to fees uphold lawyer self-interest while others protect clients.

[215] eg while the rules requiring solicitors to honour professional undertakings can be said to uphold their image as honourable professionals, they also help protect those to whom the undertakings have been made and consequently can be said to constitute private face conduct as well as public face ethical norms.

[216] eg the cab-rank rule is frequently portrayed as serving the public interest, yet it clearly also protects the economic interests of barristers who can represent clients without having to concern themselves with ethical issues raised by representation: see Ch.7, sections 3.1 and 3.2.2.

[217] cf Zander 1968, pp.156–7; Morgan 1995, p.221.

and is largely devoted to private face conduct norms, followed some way behind with a fairly even spread in focus between public and private ethical norms. The LSG provides roughly as much emphasis on private face ethical norms as private face conduct norms, but substantially less on public face ethical norms. Moreover, where it does provide regulation, it tends to be in a 'disciplinary' form. Although the norms are not free from vagueness and occasional get-out clauses, especially in relation to the few public face norms not concerned with the administration of justice, the attempt appears to be to provide specific directions to solicitors which can be reinforced by sanctions for breach rather than provisions designed simply to guide decision-making.

Nevertheless, despite these differences, it is clear that the conflicting pictures of the codes as, on the one hand, self-interest writ large and, on the other, involving a commitment to the interests of justice are both misleading caricatures. Unlike in past years,[218] the codes are no longer largely devoted to protecting lawyer self-interest, at least in a direct sense.[219] This is probably not all that surprising. It is well recognised that empty rhetoric has little or no sustainable ideological force.[220] In order to maintain their legitimacy the professions must, at least to some degree, be bound by their own public service discourse.

At the same time, the codes can only be said to be seriously concerned with the interests of justice and the general public if one defines these interests narrowly and formalistically as referring, respectively, to procedural rather than substantive justice and 'that section of the public that is in need of legal advice, assistance or representation'[221] by loyal, diligent and confidence-keeping lawyers. However, if one regards public domain ethical issues as also involving how far client representation should be able to harm the interests of affected third parties, the general public, future generations and the environment, then only a fraction of either code concerns public face ethical norms. Moreover, those norms that do exist suffer either from being too narrowly confined or conversely overly vague.

It seems that neither the Bar nor the Law Society is particularly concerned with public face ethical issues. Admittedly, the imbalance between the detailed regulation of the private face of lawyering, particularly as regards matters of professional self-image and self-interest, matters of internal regulation and client protection, on the one hand, and the largely unregulated or loosely regulated areas of public face ethics, on the other hand, cannot be said to be due solely to the profession's overriding concern with protecting itself either directly or indirectly through protecting their clients. This imbalance is partly because many aspects of the internal management of the profession and the protection of clients require detailed regulation, whereas many public issues are inherently more difficult to regulate than, for instance, pupillages, lawyer publicity, etc. Nevertheless, there are notable silences on many important public face ethical issues which could be regulated without undue difficulty.

---

[218] See eg Zander 1968, *passim*.   [219] But cf the argument at n.217, above.
[220] cf E.P. Thompson's famous account of the Rule of Law: Thompson 1975, ch.10, pt.iv.
[221] *Swain v The Law Society* [1983] AC 598, 608E–F.

Examples are the propriety of whistle-blowing to prevent harm to health, safety and the environment,[222] the appropriate stances to be adopted towards unrepresented opponents and the abandonment of clients who run out of funds during the course of representation.

At the very least, the codes' silence on issues of general justice and the public interest as compared to the detailed regulation of matters such as how solicitors' firms should be named, what matters can be referred to in lawyers' publicity, and the ownership and storage of documents, suggest that they are more important than questions of acting justly and morally in regard to specific others, the general public or the environment. This imbalance in form and focus is likely to convey the impression that it is the areas of mere regulation, and the relationship of lawyer with client and the court, which raise the 'real' conduct issues and that their primary duties are to the profession, clients and the courts, and not to justice, morality, their fellow human beings, or the environment. The implication to be drawn is that the lawyer can use her discretion in regard to most public face ethical issues and, if so desired, indulge more pragmatic motivations such as money-making, the acquisition of status and kudos through winning cases, and maintaining good relationships with fellow lawyers and other actors in the legal process.

3.4 Reforming the Codes[223]

When one considers the centrality of the codes to the teaching of legal ethics and the general inculcation of ethical values, the above imbalance can be regarded as requiring reform. If one owes one's general ethical stance to more sophisticated deontologists like Gewirth, communitarians, feminists, postmodernists, or even most utilitarians, one is likely to reject an ethical system which so strongly favours self-interest and the interests of those linked to one largely because of a cash nexus and which largely takes the form of absolute duties of a formalistic deontological nature. However, making concrete suggestions for reforming the codes is complicated by the need to ensure that their form is best suited to the encouragement of an ethically informed and sophisticated profession, yet at the same time capable of being fairly applied and knowable by those affected by lawyer behaviour.

Thus, as regards the first concern, some argue for replacing the sort of highly detailed regulation currently favoured in relation to most conduct issues with more general statements of principles which operate as professional aspirations and ideals rather than as strict rules backed up by disciplinary sanctions.[224] More radically, some commentators favour abolishing professional codes altogether and leaving the

---

[222] See Ch.9, below.

[223] This section draws on Nicolson 1998, pp.66–9 and Nicolson and Webb 1998, pp.115–19, from which passages have been reprinted with permission of Hart Publishing and Carfax Publishing, respectively. See also Hutchinson 1998.

[224] eg Sampford with Parker 1995, pp.14–18. Cf also Phillips 1990, who, however, might also be taken as opposing codes altogether.

resolution of ethical dilemmas completely to the discretion of individual lawyers.[225] These total and partial deregulatory strategies are supported by a wealth of cogent arguments.

In resembling the sort of ethical approach favoured by deontologists,[226] codified ethics draw the fire of competing ethical traditions. Thus the attempt to resolve ethical dilemmas simply by laying down behavioural duties ignores the important dimension of character development highlighted by virtue ethics,[227] the importance of moral autonomy for strict Kantians,[228] and the summit of moral development proposed by Kohlberg.[229] Equally, the absolute nature of the ethical norms—their failure to consider the context of moral dilemmas and the highly specific needs of those involved, and to provide effective means of resolving competing ethical duties—will be rejected by (especially act-) consequentialists, and those influenced by feminist and postmodern ethics, not to mention deontologists like Gewirth. Indeed, for most postmodernists and many others, following ethical codes is the very essence of immorality.

More specifically, echoing Bauman's criticism of modernist ethics,[230] one can argue that reducing ethics to formalised systems of rules, especially those of a detailed nature, increases the chances of lawyers being implicated in unjust and immoral conduct by undermining ethical evaluation. Such an approach is likely to replace individual ethical decision-making with mindless conformity to rules especially as detailed codes suggest that all possible ethical dilemmas have been considered by the experts.[231] Rule-based ethics are likely to cocoon lawyers from constantly looking to their conscience and sense of right, and from questioning the notions of justice and morality contained within law and the legal system. Ethical codes may also lead to lawyers becoming cynical and unconcerned about questions of politics and morality. They tend to force lawyers to reduce issues of ethical judgement down to a matter of risk analysis and risk management; to making 'good guesses as to the level of malpractice at which they should operate in any given situation'.[232] Codes, especially detailed ones, are said to prevent the development of deeply felt ethical commitments, which are necessary to enable lawyers to be able to resist institutional pressures to act other than in a morally upright fashion.[233] In other words, codes are inimical to the development of the sort of ethical character highlighted as so important by virtue ethics.[234] Thus ethical discretion may well be preferable to the consciences of lawyers being constantly anaesthetised by their formalistic reliance on professional rules, particularly if they are drafted largely as an exercise in professional self-protection.

---

[225] eg Simon 1978; 1988; and 1998; Atkinson 1992; Salbu 1992. cf also Dawson 1994, p.153; Jennings 1991, regarding professional ethics generally.
[226] cf Harris 1994.   [227] See Jennings 1991.   [228] Harris 1994, p.108ff.
[229] cf Hartwell 1990, p.155.   [230] Ch.2, section 7.3.
[231] Salbu 1982, p.106.
[232] Practitioner quoted in Hazard 1978, p.153. See also Phillips 1990, pp.12 and 129.
[233] See Burbank and Duboff 1974, esp p.107.
[234] Kleinberger 1989, pp.370–1; Jennings 1991; and see further Ch.2, section 5.

There are also a number of pragmatic objections to the current form of professional ethics. An obvious point is that, even if the professions can be said to be truly striving for high ethical standards, the codes are subject to evasion by lawyers whose training and experience is designed to equip them to avoid unwanted legal consequences.[235]

Here it is often said that codes which depend on high levels of rule-specificity, interpretative literalism and case by case analysis and application[236] are more likely to encourage what is called 'creative compliance'—namely, post hoc manipulation by the regulated.[237] Moreover, no code can ever foresee and adequately resolve all ethical problems likely to arise. There will always be dilemmas which escape regulation either because they were not foreseen by rule-makers or because of the inherent ambiguity of language.[238] Here, conventional wisdom suggests that lawyers should give primacy to the codes' 'spirit'.[239] This, however, overlooks the fact that such a spirit may be difficult to identify[240] if indeed such a thing exists. Given that neither code contains references to the underlying reasons for their rules, their 'spirit' has to be discerned from lengthy documents. And, even if it could be discovered, individual lawyers are unlikely to be equipped for this task, especially if detailed codes of ethics do indeed militate against them developing an ethical orientation.

Detailed codes also freeze professional ethics at the moment of drafting. Without constant revision, the codes then become outdated and rest upon increasingly irrelevant assumptions about the constantly changing nature of the professional role and the lawyer-client relationship.[241] Conversely, constant modifications to codes, as opted for by the Law Society, may make them seem less relevant to practitioners, especially if, because of partial revisions, they can be shrugged off as 'a ragbag of things that have been important at one time or another'.[242] Such constant revisions may undermine the ability of practitioners and those affected by lawyer behaviour to be aware of relevant norms. This in turn may encourage a crude intuitivism among practitioners in which ethical solutions become a matter of simple common sense.[243] In the case of the former, this will render the codes less effective in guiding behaviour.[244] In the case of the general public, complicated and constantly changing rules

---

[235] See Ch.3, section 6.   [236] McBarnet and Whelan 1991, pp.848–9.

[237] On the other hand, though, there is little evidence as to the possibility of aspirational codes avoiding this problem, not least because systems of regulation appear subject to a tendency to drift back to formalism: cf McBarnet and Whelan 1991, pp.870–1.

[238] cf Hampshire 1949, p.476.

[239] Inns of Court School of Law 1997, p.2; Silverman 1997, p.71. See also Hazard 1992, arguing that gaps in codes are probably filled by stories about professional ideals such as those found in Harper Lee's *To Kill a Mocking Bird*. See also Edgar 1994, for a similar approach.

[240] See Sheinman 1987, p.143.

[241] cf McBarnet and Whelan 1991, pp.848–9 regarding the comparative advantages of general principles and broad standards in this regard.

[242] Law Society respondent cited in Allaker and Shapland 1994, p.32.

[243] De Groot-van Leeuwen and de Groot 1998, p.165; Hutchinson 1998, p.172.

[244] For evidence of this in the US, see Burbank and Duboff 1974. This could even lead to arguments that it is unfair to punish lawyers for breaching a range of norms too large to know, though such arguments have never held water in criminal law.

undermine the requirement of transparency which, as we have argued, forms part of the notion of responsive professional regulation. Indeed, even without constant revisions, highly detailed, lengthy and legalistic codes like the LSG are likely to lead to these problems.

A final problem with codes is raised by the increasing fragmentation of the profession.[245] Either codes become increasingly detailed and unwieldy in attempting to cover the different problems and circumstances of mega-law firms, high street practices, solo practitioners, employed lawyers, etc., or they continue to work with a universalistic ethics, which not only is philosophically questionable, socially unsustainable, and politically suspect in a pluralistic (post)modern society, but also increases the likelihood that professional elites will impose their values on less powerful groups for their own economic or political ends.[246]

On the other hand, there are serious problems with both deregulatory strategies.[247] First, total deregulation of professional legal ethics goes much further than the existing regime of self-regulation in freeing lawyers from public accountability. Instead, it relies heavily on the outdated *noblesse oblige* tradition and a 'professional mystique'[248] which disregard calls for greater accountability and transparency as misguided. Secondly, as Paterson persuasively argues,[249] the idea that the solutions to ethical dilemmas in professional life are self-evident and derivable from first principles involves naive wishful thinking. As we saw in Chapter 2,[250] the claims of moral realists that there exist universalist and foundational moral principles are now under serious attack. Moreover, as Paterson also notes, under the intuitive, first-principle approach lawyers might become heavily embroiled in problems like conflict of interest without even realising it.[251] Thirdly, deregulation may well lead to a lowering rather than a raising of ethical standards. Deregulation assumes educational and institutional frameworks capable of developing and sustaining the moral character and reflexive moral capabilities of individual professionals.[252] As we argued in Chapter 3, the current position in this regard is unlikely to encourage anything like the developed ethical orientation amongst lawyers which would equip, never mind incline, them to resolve ethical problems in ways which give due attention to issues of morality and justice, while the dominance of the idea that lawyers ought to be amoral technicians prepared to represent any client who can afford their services is also likely, as we shall see in Part II, to undermine their ability to exercise the sort of independent moral judgement required by code deregulation.

[245] See Ch.3, section 4.4.

[246] See Shuchman 1968, p.249, noting that ethical codes are frequently aimed at small law firms but formulated by large law firms to whom they are irrelevant. Whether this also applies in Britain, especially after the reform of rules on advertising, touting, etc., is a topic in need of further research.

[247] cf Cranston 1995, pp.5–6; Paterson 1995, pp.176–7 and 1997, p.37, calling for more detailed regulation.

[248] Crawley and Bramall 1995, p.105.

[249] Paterson 1995, p.177. See also Paterson 1997, pp.36–7, describing arguments for deregulation as a sophisticated form of relativism.

[250] Sections 7.2 and 7.3.   [251] Paterson 1995, p.177.

[252] See Atkinson 1992.

There are thus convincing arguments both for and against deregulation. How is one to square the circle? As a starting point, it is essential to place the arguments in context. The possibility of lawyers abandoning their ethical codes seems remote. In particular it seems highly unlikely that they would want to deregulate activities such as the running of the pupillage system and the keeping of client accounts given the importance of such issues for the profession's smooth operation and its image of integrity.

What, however, is more susceptible to reform is the form of the current codes: their level of specificity. In other words, we need to distinguish the question of *whether* we codify from *how*. Even accepting that professional legal ethics should be subjected to formal rules, we can ask whether the current codes are drafted with sufficient or excessive detail. Here the question of their focus resurfaces. As we have seen, at present matters of internal self-regulation, professional self-interest and certain rules, such as those relating to client accounts, which undoubtedly relate to ethics but are of an uncontroversial nature, are subjected to detailed regulation. By contrast, most ethical issues are dealt with by broad principles and vague admonitions. Given the dangers of subjecting ethical issues to detailed rules, this is arguably as it should be. However, as we also argued, this imbalance in focus and form suggests that the 'real' professional conduct issues involve matters of conduct and duties to clients, whereas the need to act morally as regards third parties, the general public and the environment are simply optional extras. Accordingly, the solution might lie in separating the regulation of matters of ethics and 'mere regulation' so as to avoid this impression. The latter can then be subjected to the sort of detailed rules which characterise 'disciplinary codes' and matters of ethics could remain defined in the sort of broad principles found in 'aspirational codes'.

On the other hand, merely subjecting lawyers to the sort of vague admonitions which characterise the few current public face ethical norms not devoted to protecting the administration of justice may result in them pursuing the same minimal standards which characterise the more detailed regulation of 'disciplinary codes'. Consequently, we propose laying down broad ethical principles which would guide ethical decision-making by being fleshed out by the statement of factors relevant to their implementation in the context of particular ethical dilemmas. Following the administrative law approach, such factors would have to be taken into consideration before a decision is reached but they could not by themselves determine the decision. In this way, it is hoped that both the problems of unregulated gaps in the codes and the anaesthetisation of moral conscience would be avoided. Indeed, by requiring lawyers to consider a wide range of relevant considerations in resolving dilemmas and hence to become well acquainted with the ethical codes, it is likely that they would become more ethically aware.[253] Moreover, such ethical awareness could be increased if the codes were to include commentaries on their principles' rationale and purpose and perhaps also the rulings and reasoning of relevant professional

---

[253] See Frankel 1976, esp p.883.

bodies adjudicating disciplinary matters and responding to requests for guidance by lawyers faced with particular ethical dilemmas.[254]

Of course, what will be lost will be the same degree of certainty with which the public could predict lawyer behaviour and lawyers could predict the likelihood of such behaviour attracting disciplinary sanctions. As regards the former, we would argue that the benefits to the public will far outweigh these disadvantages in that lawyers are more likely to refrain from the sort of immoral behaviour discussed in Part II of this book. As regards the latter, it could be argued that the codes' deterrence function could be abandoned or that there should be a combination of both disciplinary and aspirational norms, as has been attempted in other jurisdictions.[255] In response to the latter suggestion, one can ask whether the function of aspirational norms would not be undermined by the existence of another set of norms with a lower standard and which, importantly, are backed up by disciplinary sanctions. How many lawyers would actually strive to meet the higher standards of the aspirational norms if they can get away with a lower standard, especially when institutional factors encourage lawyers to cut moral corners? A similar response can be made to total abandonment of disciplinary sanctions. We would therefore argue for their retention notwithstanding the more aspirational form of the norms. The consequent dilution of certainty for lawyers faced with particular dilemmas can be met by increasing the professional bodies' guidance role. More importantly, the possibility of lawyers being unfairly disciplined for behaviour which does not clearly breach the codes can be avoided in a number of ways. First, by analogy with criminal law statutes, the codes could be read '*pro libertatem*'. Secondly, evidence that action was in accordance with institutional guidance could provide an absolute defence. Thirdly, lawyers found to have acted unethically could be punished only on proof of bad faith or when no reasonable lawyer would have so acted.

4. THE ENFORCEMENT MECHANISMS

4.1 Introduction

The final dimension to lawyers' regulatory framework is that of enforcement. Here the design of enforcement mechanisms is important because of what it may tell us about the professions' commitment to being responsive to the needs of clients and the general public. Furthermore, the extent to which the codes are enforced will send an important message to lawyers, clients and the general public, either reinforcing or undermining the codes' functions and whatever values and ideals they purport to espouse. They will also provide an indication as to whether regulation is dominated by professional self-interest rather than a desire to ensure high ethical standards. Similarly, problems such

---

[254] cf Annex 21A, LSG.
[255] Most notably the US: see eg Brown and Brown 1976, p.453; Hazard 1978a, pp.5–6; and see also Parker with Sampford 1995, pp.14–17, making a similar recommendation.

as non-enforcement, permissiveness, bias, etc., may undermine both public confidence in lawyers as a whole, as well as in those bodies charged with enforcement.

However, lest one too readily infers ethical complacency on their part from a failure to apply strictly sanctions to breaches of regulatory norms, it is necessary to note that such an approach is not the only or even the most effective way of responding to regulatory breaches.[256] At the opposite end to an *ex post* coercive enforcement strategy modelled on criminal law's attempt to deter through punishing breaches is a compliance approach based upon co-operation between regulator and regulated in which the former aims to work with the latter at seeking to ensure compliance through encouragement, persuasion, cajolement, etc. Where particular enforcement strategies fall along this continuum will depend on a number of factors.

One is the regulatory techniques adopted by particular codes. While there is no necessary connection, 'disciplinary' codes will tend to be accompanied by a coercive strategy and 'aspirational' codes by compliance strategies. A second factor is the way that regulators determine whether codes have been breached. Do they adopt a legalistic approach or do they try to apply the rules flexibly, building in operative levels of discretion? Although the style of determination is likely to be affected by the form of the norms, once again there is no necessary connection. Regulators need not necessarily apply formalistic regulations in a strict, literal fashion. Instead, they may try to use their discretion to ameliorate the rules' impact and to find compliance where stricter interpretations might suggest otherwise.

Thirdly, there is the question of what officials actually do once they identify non-compliance. Do they seek to punish or try to negotiate change to enable the regulated to 'come into compliance'?[257] This will depend heavily on the regulator's assumptions as to the regulations' rationale, but, again, we should not just assume that a highly legalistic regulatory regime will necessarily result in a stringent enforcement policy, nor that stringent enforcement is necessarily a precondition to deterrence.[258] Enforcement decisions in any regime will reflect a complex range of factors, including the regulators' resources, their assessment of the social and economic costs of preventing non-compliance, the extent of regulatory capture and the risks attached to either an accommodationist or punitive policy, the impact of attempted enforcement on regulatory relationships and compliance,[259] and the symbolic importance of enforcement in particular cases. As Hawkins observes, enforcement may well have a strong symbolic dimension, reflecting moral notions of right and wrong, and thereby 'placing the behaviour complained of in a framework which [is] familiar and comprehensible to all'.[260] In such a context it may be that it is just the 'bad cases', about which there is no moral ambivalence, that will receive punitive treatment.

---

[256] For an overview of enforcement strategies see eg Hawkins 1983; Scholtz 1984; Kagan 1989.

[257] Kagan, ibid.

[258] Maiman *et al* 1999 make the point that the institution of grievance procedures can itself be a deterrent (because of the stress and extra work involved in responding to formal complaints), so that the likelihood of actual punishment is relatively insignificant.

[259] See section 3.1, above, regarding the impact of the codes' form on compliance strategies.

[260] Hawkins 1990, p.449.

4.2 The Professions' Disciplinary Procedures

In looking briefly at the professions' disciplinary procedures and considering, as far as we can, their enforcement policy, a broad distinction needs to be made between complaints of inadequate professional services (IPS)[261] and the charge of professional misconduct, which has more serious disciplinary, and hence career, consequences for the lawyer. IPS is an umbrella concept to describe conduct or professional services which falls below 'the proper standard of work'[262] or 'significantly short of that which is to be reasonably expected'.[263] Most public concern at present relates to forms of IPS, such as delay, poor communication, etc., rather than breach of ethical norms. This is not to say that such matters are devoid of ethical implications. IPS may well flow from breach of ethical duties such as loyalty, fidelity or candour to the client.

In 1997, after considerable debate, the Bar introduced a revised complaints and disciplinary procedure. This involves a three-tier process, plus appeals.[264] Complaints from lay clients are dealt with initially by a Lay Complaints Commissioner. The Commissioner may, if the complaint shows no evidence of misconduct or IPS, dismiss it summarily, with or without advising counsel to try to conciliate the claim. Otherwise the complaint will be investigated further. This involves the Commissioner obtaining documentary evidence, usually from the barrister concerned and any instructing solicitor, as well as from relevant witnesses. Only if the Commissioner finds a *prima facie* case of inadequate professional services must he[265] refer the complaint to the Professional Conduct Committee (PCC).[266] The PCC must then determine whether there is a *prima facie* case of IPS or professional misconduct. It may dismiss complaints, or refer them either to its adjudication panel[267] (in pure IPS cases) or to a disciplinary panel for either an informal hearing (in respect of minor cases of misconduct, and possibly IPS) or a summary hearing (in more serious cases). The latter are heard by the third tier: the full disciplinary tribunals of the Inns. They are chaired by a High Court or Circuit judge, sitting with three practitioners and one lay member, and, unlike the other fora, in public.

Findings of IPS result in limited sanctions: an apology to the lay client, repayment or reduction of fees, or compensation of up to £2,000. Proven misconduct, on the other hand, is subjected to an intriguing hierarchy of sanctions, which range from being advised (by the panel) as to future conduct, or being admonished (the strongest penalty that may be imposed at an informal hearing) through orders to

---

[261] The introduction by the Bar of penalties for IPS under the 1997 scheme (below) marks the completion of a significant volte face, since the Bar had historically taken the view that the market rather than the profession should regulate much of what we would now call inadequate professional service: see Zander 1978, pp.119–20. Significantly, however, findings of IPS cannot be made in respect of work for which barristers could claim immunity from negligence claims: para. 43(d)(ii) of Annexe M, CCB.

[262] Para. 30.02, LSG.   [263] Para. 48(d) of Annexe M, CCB.

[264] We do not discuss the appeal process here; for further information see eg Inns of Court School of Law 1997.

[265] The present Commissioner is Michael Scott.

[266] The PPC has a mixture of professional and lay members; the former in the majority.

[267] Which, unusually, has four members: the Lay Commissioner, one lay member and two barristers.

forego or repay fees, to suspension or disbarment. The outcomes of the less serious disciplinary processes remain private between the barrister and complainant, unless the former requests publicity, whereas the results of tribunal and summary hearings are normally published both within the profession and outside.[268]

Solicitor discipline is managed through a semi-autonomous structure.[269] At its heart is the relationship between firms' internal complaints procedures and the OSS. Since April 1998, the OSS has operated a strict referral policy, whereby all complainants are expected first to have addressed their complaint to the firm concerned, despite strong evidence that many lack the required complaints procedures, and that many clients are deeply dissatisfied at having to complain to the very firm that gave rise to their complaint.[270]

Generally if problems are not resolved at this level, either by the firm involved under Practice Rule 15 or by conciliation, cases are passed to specialist OSS investigation units, or, exceptionally, directly to the Compliance and Supervision Committee. The latter's functions are reflected in a split between a lay-dominated[271] Client Relations Sub-Committee, which deals with IPS, and a professionally dominated Professional Regulation Sub-Committee, which can impose sanctions for professional misconduct, but also deals with a number of associated, procedural, appeals.[272] Where there is evidence of serious professional misconduct,[273] the Committee usually refers cases to the Solicitors' Disciplinary Tribunal, which, unlike the Committee, is a statutory body. Referral will tend to follow a lengthy (and costly) process of investigation, comment, and, often, appeal. Consequently, in 1993, the Law Society Council approved a 'fast track' procedure, which enables the Committee to remit certain cases (usually the more clear-cut or blatant cases of misconduct) to the Tribunal more speedily.

The range of sanctions available for IPS and misconduct is roughly similar to those applied by the Bar, though the OSS has a wider range of sanctions at its disposal than does the PCC, particularly in respect of powers to order inspection of a firm's accounts and to intervene in a practice.[274] Similarly, the Disciplinary Tribunal may impose penalties ranging from a fine, through suspension to disbarment ('striking-off').[275]

While research on the professions' practice and policy as regards disciplinary enforcement is patchy, such evidence as is available suggests that relatively few complaints lead to disciplinary action and that, of those that do, sanctions do not always

---

[268] As to where, see CCB Annex N, para. 26(2).

[269] For discussion see Sherr and Webley 1997; Swift 1996; Christensen *et al* 1999.

[270] See further Lewis 1996; Harris 1994.

[271] Lay members have, since March 1997, been appointed by open competition following public advertising of vacancies.

[272] An explanation of the various procedures can be found in Swift 1996, pp.6–8.

[273] Proceedings are normally commenced on the ground that the solicitor has been guilty of 'conduct unbefitting a solicitor' (see *Re a solicitor* [1972] 2 All ER 811; *Ridehalgh v Horsefield* [1994] 3 All ER 648) or for breaches of specific rules made under statutory authority (most commonly breaches of the Solicitors Accounts Rules).

[274] See para. 30.04, LSG.   [275] Para. 31.05, LSG.

reflect the gravity of misbehaviour.[276] For example, in the first year of the new Bar complaints scheme, 60 per cent of complaints were rejected outright by the Lay Commissioner, and in only about 65 cases (20 per cent of those investigated) was disciplinary action taken by the PCC.[277] In a detailed critique, Abel has documented the professions' reluctance to discipline their own.[278] He found that, out of every 100 grievances experienced by solicitors' clients, only two were reported, 0.2 per cent were investigated, and less than 0.001 per cent received serious punishment. Similarly, complaints to the Bar between 1968 and 1985 led to serious disciplinary action (suspension or disbarment) in only 4 per cent of cases. While the structures have changed since Abel's analysis, and possibly some of the culture too, there remains a very real problem of defensiveness. Despite the greater use of lay representation, the system of professional governance (including discipline) has largely remained closed to the participation of those outside the profession, and has tended to sustain what is potentially a rather paternalistic relationship between regulator and regulated. This point has been made on a number of occasions by the Legal Services Ombudsman. For example, in 1993, the first Ombudsman criticised the Diagnostic Unit of the SCB (the complainant's first point of contact with the SCB) for acting 'too much as a defensive operation on behalf of the Law Society'.[279] In her 1998 report,[280] the current LSO also criticised the Bar Council for its reluctance to take complaints seriously, concluding that the changes made in 1997 remained more symbolic than real. At the same time, attempts by the professional bodies to open up the complaints process have infuriated, or at least discomforted, many in the profession, who have not bought in, or been brought in, to the complaints culture.[281]

4.3 Reforming the Enforcement Mechanisms

The discussion above suggests that complaints of lawyer misbehaviour seem often to be regarded as an issue of little more than risk management. In our view, however, they strike closer to the ethical heart of professionalism, both because they raise issues of institutional trust and accountability which are central to the professions' ethical mandate, and because they beg wider questions about the relationship between the professions and the communities they serve.

---

[276] Recent examples include solicitor Angus Diggle's suspension from practice for one further year following his two years imprisonment for attempted rape: see Lees 1996, pp.88–92. Similarly, the Disciplinary Tribunal recently suspended a solicitor for three years for making a false document in order to deceive a client. The Tribunal commented that, despite the serious nature of the misconduct, leniency was appropriate, *inter alia* on the grounds that his work was 'of a proper standard in all other matters and that he [was] liked and trusted within the firm': *The Law Society's Gazette*, 1 March 1995, p.34.

[277] *The Times* 19 May 1998, p.9.

[278] Abel 1988a, pp.134–5 and 252–5. See also Disney *et al* 1986, p.83; Schnapper 1978, pp.202–3, who notes reasons for this reluctance.

[279] Legal Services Ombudsman 1993, p.8.   [280] Legal Services Ombudsman 1998.

[281] Christensen *et al* 1999. Note also that in the CMC survey of 250 practitioners 41% agreed with the proposition that 'we give in too often to unfounded complaints': Customer Management Consultancy Ltd (no date).

The profession could obviously do better in this regard by taking disciplinary issues more seriously.[282] However, they could also explore a more sophisticated strategy designed not only to ensure greater compliance but also greater responsiveness. Evidence suggests that strictly deterrent regulatory strategies may generate less long-term compliance than more flexible co-operative models.[283] Key variables within this process seem to be the opportunities for dialogue and interaction between regulator and regulated. A number of studies indicate that regulators who ignore opportunities for dialogue with, and participation by, regulatees generate opposition to regulation and, conversely, that those who use co-operation and dialogue build trust, and that trust, in turn, builds compliance.[284] This is not to say that compliance can be achieved without resort to punitive measures, but it does support the argument that punishment needs to be used discriminately, and, perhaps, chiefly as a response to breaches of regulatory trust.[285] Similarly, from the perspective of the consumers of legal services, there is evidence to suggest that clients are not particularly concerned about which enforcement strategies are adopted; most simply want their problems resolved, rather than their lawyers being disciplined.[286] Provided of course that a compliance strategy is applied efficiently, most clients should be satisfied.

Consequently consideration could be given to implementation of more responsive enforcement which operates through a 'trust but verify' system.[287] One version, developed by Ayres and Braithwaite,[288] involves a pyramid of regulatory strategies. These seek first to establish co-operation on a voluntary basis. If that fails, increasingly interventionist approaches can be instigated until, finally, a coercive approach is taken once it is clear less stringent options are ineffective. Such a strategy requires both effective implementation and verification systems.

Responsibility for the implementation of compliance measures cannot be other than localised. A possible solution, which really underpinned thinking behind the original complaints procedures proposal for solicitors,[289] and which already exists in some larger firms and chambers, involves each firm and chamber appointing its own compliance officer. The latter would not only deal with complaints, but also ensure compliance with the full range of legal and professional regulation, and deal with the verification needs of the regulator.[290]

A verification system would not only provide a check on compliance, but offers opportunities for dialogue and interaction between regulator and regulated. This may increase the risk of regulatory capture, but, as some writers stress,[291] such activities

---

[282] Though note the Law Society's recent proposal to inject £5.7 m into the OSS in an attempt to improve efficiency, and stave off the threat of government intervention: *Guardian*, 19 June 1999, p.7.

[283] See Kelman 1988; Rees 1988.

[284] See Kagan and Scholz 1984; Braithwaite and Makkai 1994; Parker 1997.

[285] Braithwaite and Makkai, ibid. See also Hawkins 1990, p.462.

[286] Christensen *et al* 1999; James and Seneviratne 1995.

[287] Braithwaite and Makkai 1994, p.9.   [288] Ayres and Braithwaite 1992, ch.2.

[289] Personal communication with Tony Holland, President of the Law Society at the time.

[290] Though the cost implications could make this difficult, if not impractical, for the smaller firms and chambers.

[291] Ayres and Braithwaite 1992; Axelrod 1984.

are central to engendering co-operative solutions.[292] Consequently problems of capture are probably best addressed as a matter of regulator accountability.[293]

A two-tier system of preventive audit and investigation, and follow-up of formal complaints would have considerable advantages over the present system. Powers to follow up complaints with firms are important, and need to be used because compliance with single formal rulings does not necessarily lead to changes of culture or practices. Moreover, non-compliant firms should routinely be required to identify what steps they have taken to reduce the likelihood of such complaints recurring. Random preventive audits[294] could provide a basis for giving compliance guidance to firms, and a valuable forum for dialogue between regulator and regulated. Although such audits need not and ideally should not have direct disciplinary consequences, if at the time of formal complaints there is evidence that the solicitor, barrister, firm, or chamber had failed to respond to previous audit guidance, that could be regarded as increasing the offence's gravity. Alternatively, non-random preventive audit could be introduced as a kind of incentive control, resulting perhaps in a quality rating or 'kite-mark' for those firms and chambers that achieve good levels of compliance.

---

[292] See Ayers and Braithwaite, ibid, p.134.

[293] eg James and Seneviratne 1995, p.206 have argued that the LSO's powers could usefully be extended to include inspection of the professional regulatory bodies, supported by the creation of direct enforcement powers over those professional bodies.

[294] If preventive audit is deemed desirable then this begins to push us towards the possibility of an external inspectorate. Peer audit techniques have been developed in the services sector, notably in the Health Service, but it is clearly doubtful that peer review would be either appropriate or acceptable in a more overtly competitive and privatised market environment, like the market for legal services. Our thanks to Robert Dingwall for drawing this distinction more clearly to our attention.

5

Duties to the Client: Autonomy and Control in the Lawyer-Client Relationship

> ... I tell you, that in becoming attornies and solicitors, you are about to enter ... into a solemn CONTRACT with us—with society at large that we may employ you not only advantageously but safely, without compromising our best and dearest interests. . . . And there is one very material circumstance to be here adverted to, which will have infinite weight with an honourable mind; namely that we are, to a great extent, compelled to take you, as it were, on trust.
>
> Samuel Warren[1]

1. INTRODUCTION

The lawyer's *raison d'être* is to serve client interests. Thus professional ethics discourse speaks of the duty of loyalty[2] to put their clients before all others, subject only to their overriding duty to the courts.[3] This, as we shall see in later chapters, raises major problems because of the harm lawyers may inflict on other persons, the general public and the environment in representing their clients. But even within the lawyer-client relationship difficult ethical questions are raised concerning the balance of power and control between lawyer and client. The key problem is seen as determining the acceptable degree of (lawyer) paternalism that is permitted in a system that, in theory, privileges the individual's (essentially the client's) right to autonomy.

Ethicists have long been concerned with the lawyer's ability to control or manipulate clients in ways that limit their self-determination.[4] For instance, when Gary Gilmore, awaiting execution on Death Row, wrote to his lawyers: 'Quit fucking around with my life. You're fired . . . ',[5] were they right to judge it in his best interests to file a notice of appeal regardless? In other words, are lawyers entitled to override their clients' wishes to act in what *they* see as their clients' best interests? However, in addition to lawyer paternalism, lawyers may also limit client autonomy in order to pursue their own interests—what can be called egoism—or in order to protect the interests of third parties, the general public or the environment—what can be called moralism or moral activism. Equally, one can also ask how much, if any, loyalty lawyers can expect from their clients.

---

[1] Warren 1848, p.11.   [2] Sometimes also called the duty of fidelity.
[3] See Ch.4, section 3.3; Ch.6, section 2.2.
[4] See eg Wasserstrom 1975; Lehman 1979; Luban 1981b; Bayles 1981, p.68; Pepper 1986a and 1986b; Ellman 1990.
[5] From Norman Mailer's *The Executioner's Song* (1979), cited in Luban 1981b, p.454.

Underlying these questions is a set of fundamental tensions between lawyer and client autonomy. The aim of this chapter is to try to expose these tensions chiefly through an analysis of power and control in lawyer-client relations. In so doing we shall ask whether the root of the problem lies in defining the acceptable limits of lawyer control, or in certain conceptual weaknesses in the established notion of autonomy. This will lead us to ask whether a different conception of autonomy might help us re-envisage that relationship. Specifically we shall explore three broad scenarios: where lawyers use their control over clients in their own self-interest; where they use their control (as they see it) in the interests of clients; and conversely where clients seek to exercise control over lawyers. First, however, we need to define the notions of autonomy, paternalism, egoism, and moralism.

2. BOUNDARIES OF AUTONOMY

2.1 The Meaning of Autonomy[6]

The notion of autonomy indicates a strong sense of personal freedom and self-identity: the idea that 'one's life is one's own'. It is also widely regarded as a multi-dimensional construct, possessing more or less distinct political and institutional, social, and moral dimensions. Having touched on the first two dimensions in Chapters 3 and 4,[7] we will concentrate on the latter two here. Social autonomy, we suggest, demands that we are free from the illegitimate pressures by non-political institutions in making our life choices. Moral autonomy, as we saw in discussing Kant[8] and as its literal meaning suggests, involves individuals being able to choose or accept their own moral values. For most philosophers a key significance of moral autonomy is that it substantially affects or even determines our capacity as moral agents.[9] It is hard to argue that someone is acting as a 'true' moral agent if their reasons for acting are not fully their own. Autonomy in this way exists as a *practice*, not just some idealised construct. As such, it requires a set of institutional and personal circumstances and characteristics that enable 'the full exercise of the capacity for choice'.[10]

The problem, of course, is that in the social world nobody can be wholly autonomous, since for one person to achieve absolute autonomy would inevitably constrain the autonomy of others. Liberal theory has sought to deal with this problem by using civil institutions to rule citizens through rather than in spite of their autonomy.[11] Such institutions seek to preclude the arbitrary subordination of individuals by finding rational justifications for constraining autonomy.[12] For the

---

[6] See generally Luban 1990b for a detailed discussion of autonomy in the context of legal ethics; note particularly the debate between Luban 1986; Pepper 1986b; and Ellman 1990 as to how far autonomy is a good in itself.

[7] Ch.3, sections 2 and 4.1; Ch.4, section 2.1. [8] Ch.2, section 3.2.

[9] See our discussion of Kant, Gewirth, and postmodernist ethics in Ch.2, sections 3.2, 3.4, and 7.4, respectively. See further Doyal 1990, p.4.

[10] Ellman 1987, p.761. [11] See Rose 1996, pp.19–20. [12] cf Luban 1990b, p.1036.

professions it is thus 'part of their rationale that the expert is someone whose work consists in judging of an individual's situation *in accordance with reason*, and hence in a way that that person, *if acting autonomously*, would do him/herself if s/he had the time, skills, knowledge and inclination necessary to do so'.[13] This accords with the standard notion of lawyers as their clients' 'mouthpiece'. The expert is, in effect, acting purely as the client's agent or cipher.

2.2 The Problems with Paternalism

As we noted above, paternalistic lawyers are those who usurp client decision-making in the belief that this furthers the clients' interests. It is important to note that it is not paternalistic *per se* for lawyers to make decisions for clients. But it is paternalistic when such decisions are made in ways which deny clients an effective say in the process,[14] since that is to treat the client as less than a moral equal.[15] As Luban emphasises, paternalistic interventions are inherently manipulative.[16]

2.2.1 *Just a Matter of Degree?*

For some ethicists, paternalistic interventions in any voluntary self-regarding choices made by individuals are forbidden, even if those choices are by some standards 'irrational' or the product of faulty reasoning.[17] In other words, we are obliged to respect those values freely and authentically[18] held by individuals even if we fundamentally disagree with them. This does not create an absolute bar on paternalism, but limits intervention to decisions which are non-voluntary, coerced, or flow from some mental incapacity on the decision-maker's part.[19] Although this latter situation does not correspond neatly with 'lay' understandings of paternalism, most philosophers accept that the assumption of control over another in such cases is a species of (usually justifiable) paternalism. In a sense, this form of paternalism can be said to make up for the deficit in that other's autonomy.

A wider approach permits paternalistic interference if the individual's self-regarding choice is by some standard irrational, and the well-informed and rational chooser would consent to that interference.[20] The standard of rationality chosen is

[13] D'Agostino 1998, p.31 (emphasis in the original).

[14] eg Buchanan 1978, p.372 characterises paternalistic interventions as requiring 'interference with a person's freedom of action or freedom of information, or the deliberate dissemination of misinformation'.

[15] Dworkin 1988, pp.123–4.   [16] Luban 1981b, p.458. cf also Ellman 1987, pp.726–7.

[17] See Arneson 1980.

[18] The difference between rational and authentic behaviour and beliefs is important here. For example, we would generally regard it as non-rational to depend extensively on Tarot readings before making major personal decisions, but if the belief in their power is freely and strongly held, it is authentic behaviour, and hence ought not to be lightly overridden.

[19] eg, *contra* Strauss 1987, p.340, one could argue that the decision of Odysseus' crew to ignore his pleas to be released from the mast after he had fallen under the Sirens' spell was not even short-term paternalism justified as advancing his long-term autonomy. Rather, it distinguished rationally between his non-authentic pleas and original authentic instruction not to be released under any circumstances.

[20] Dworkin 1971 and 1988, pp.124–5; Rawls 1971, pp.248–50.

of course critical here. We might for instance say that all new age travellers should be obliged to adopt a settled lifestyle, because otherwise they expose themselves to numerous social and environmental disadvantages relating to education, health care and economic well-being. But this assumes that choices many of us would define as imprudent are in fact also irrational. In short, we are faced with the problem that there are few common standards of rationality or definitions of 'the good' that justify intervention.

Both the above approaches underpin what are commonly called 'soft' versions of paternalism.[21] Most codes of lawyers' ethics thus set 'soft' paternalistic limits on representation on the first ground of 'non-voluntariness', according to relatively uncontroversial criteria of minority and mental incapacity.[22] Even here, though, the distinction between paternalistic and non-paternalistic acts is a fine, but sometimes significant, one. For example, assume a solicitor has a rich elderly client who, fearing the onset of senility, executed a power of attorney in favour of the solicitor some time ago. On the basis of medical advice that her client is now unable to manage his affairs, the solicitor adopts the powers vested in the deed. Even if the client objects to that course of action, the lawyer's adoption of power of attorney is not itself paternalistic. She has a basis for saying that the client's authentic and autonomous wish was expressed at the time the power was executed, rather than now. On the other hand, any steps taken by the solicitor under that power will be paternalistic, but that paternalism is justified by the client's inability to exercise full autonomy.

However, some commentators go much further in allowing soft paternalism over means and ends. For example, Kronman's model of the lawyer-statesman—a moral activist imbued with Aristotle's 'practical wisdom'[23]—takes as its starting point a very strong form of soft paternalism, since Kronman assumes a high degree of client incompetence in positing that the lawyer's initial function is to educate clients in the legal system's values. Unless and until lawyers are satisfied that such understanding has been achieved, they apparently have full moral responsibility for decision-making.[24] Similarly, on the underlying assumption that rational clients would not really wish to violate their own fundamental values, Luban argues that lawyers should not assist clients to pursue goals that would have this effect.[25] Such approaches may go so far in redefining competence that they ultimately override any meaningful client autonomy.[26] From the client's point of view, soft paternalism is not necessarily a softer option than hard paternalism.

The latter goes further and allows for at least some paternalistic intervention even where subjects are fully competent (however that is defined). Hard paternalism tends to be defended by reference to notions of preventing harm to self. The philosophical case for hard paternalism, however, has not been well made out.[27] As Lyons notes, the problem with relying on the 'harm condition' is that 'we are too

---

[21] Dworkin 1988, pp.124–9.   [22] See eg para. 12.02, LSG.   [23] See Ch.2, section 5.3.
[24] Kronman 1993. cf also Simon 1978, pp.130–44.
[25] Luban 1981b, pp.468–73.   [26] See Ellman 1987, p.778.
[27] cf Dworkin 1988, pp.124–9; Lyons 1984, pp.176–7.

prone to judge what is good for others on the basis of what we take to be good for ourselves'.[28]

The distinction between hard and soft paternalism has not been clearly drawn in professional legal ethics discourse. Hard paternalism undoubtedly exists in legal practice, though it seems most commonly to extend to the means to client ends rather than to the ends themselves. A prominent example is the apparent absolute discretion of advocates to dictate trial tactics.[29]

2.2.2 *Lawyers, Clients, and the Pathology of Paternalism*

The temptation for lawyers to be paternalistic is deeply embedded in both the ideological and institutional basis of the professional relationship. First, because of liberalism's emphasis on individual autonomy and the important role law and legal rights are seen as playing in protecting such autonomy,[30] the fact that individuals are ignorant of or unable to exercise their rights appears, by itself, to be a denial of their autonomy. Accordingly, by enabling individuals to exercise their rights, lawyers can claim to advance client autonomy almost regardless of the means used. Obeying instructions that enable clients to exercise their rights thus becomes a good in itself.[31] In this context, the exercise of lawyer paternalism, particularly over the means used to pursue clients' ends, may not even be brought into question.

Secondly, as we have already argued,[32] lawyers are trained to take a strategic and functional view of law. The lawyer's defining skill is to translate client needs into legal solutions by, if necessary, as much legal manipulation as the system will permit.[33] This is also an important source of lawyers' power over clients, and a further explanation for lawyer paternalism. Because lawyers possess information that is unavailable to clients, it is psychologically easy to translate the knowledge that there are things lawyers know that clients do not into a belief that they therefore know what is best for the client in general.[34] This tendency may, ironically, be reinforced by client-centred approaches to ethics, which emphasise the lawyer's duty to act in their clients' best interests. This can be contrasted with the experience of medical ethics, where power inequalities inherent in the doctor-patient relationship, combined with a principle of beneficence, have together generated a 'pathology of paternalism'.[35] It is for this reason that medical ethics has, as we shall see,[36] increasingly laid stress on increasing patient participation in clinical decision-making.

Thirdly, there are various structural features of the lawyer-client relationship which may also encourage lawyer paternalism. Cost constraints, for example, may restrict opportunities for exploring relevant issues, because neither lawyer nor client will

---

[28] Lyons 1984, p.176.

[29] See *Hall v Stothard* (1816) 2 Chit 267; *R v Greenwich CC Registrar* (1885) 15 QBD 54; *Ellender v Wood* (1888) 4 TLR 680. See also Graham Swanwick QC's observation: 'The wise advocate resists the twitch of the gown and shuts his ears to the suggestion . . . that [the client] knows best': *Rondel v Worsley* [1967] 1 QB 443, 490.

[30] See further Ch.7, section 3.2.2.   [31] Pepper 1986a, p.617.   [32] See Ch.3, section 6.

[33] cf Cain 1983; Pepper 1986a, 1995.   [34] Wasserstrom 1975, p.22.

[35] Downie 1996, pp.5–6.   [36] See section 4.2.3, below.

necessarily be willing to carry the cost of the extra time involved.[37] Possible cultural gaps between lawyer and client can also impede dialogue. Lawyers and clients may inhabit different social and moral universes that are difficult to bridge.[38] Clients, moreover, may take the view that one important reason why they employ a lawyer is to have decisions made for them.[39]

Thus professionalism justifies expert intervention on behalf of clients in two ways. The first, as we saw in section 2.1, seeks to deny the existence of paternalism at all, by deeming that lawyers, once acting on client instructions, are thereby advancing client autonomy. The second, by contrast, seeks to legitimate certain forms of paternalism by finding rational justifications for lawyers constraining client autonomy. Taken together they create an ideology, which suggests that lawyer paternalism is neither a wholly normalised feature of lawyer-client relations, nor a significant deviation from the norm. This is a point to which we shall return. First, however, it is also important to distinguish paternalism from the other types of interference with client autonomy, which we have labelled egoism and moralism.

2.3 Egoism and Client Interests

Invasions of client autonomy are egoistic when they are undertaken for reasons of lawyer self-interest. However, even if one accepts egoism as a general ethical theory, there seems to be little justification for lawyers putting narrow self-interest before the interests of clients. The lawyer's duty is always to act in the latter's best interests. This is apparent in both the underlying duty of loyalty,[40] and the myriad rules designed to discourage lawyers from acting in situations where conflicts of interest arise.[41] Yet the problem of egoism remains, and may be disguised from view by the often incoherent way in which we identify (or fail to identify) lawyer and client interests.

The issue of fees is a key example. Lawyers almost inevitably expect to get paid for their services, and to that extent have a direct professional (and personal) financial interest in the cases they run. It is often assumed that there is thereby an alignment of lawyer-client financial interests: lawyers' best chance of justifying their fees and attracting new and repeat work is to be seen as successful and committed to clients. But this overlooks the extent to which the financial interests of lawyer and client will, in fact, often be opposed.

Conditional fee arrangements (CFAs) provide an important, recent, illustration

---

[37] cf Pepper 1986a, pp.631–2.   [38] Wexler 1970, p.1052; Pepper, ibid, p.632.
[39] Pepper 1995, p.1557.   [40] See Ch.4, section 3.3.3.
[41] See eg ch.15, LSG and para. 203, CCB. Conflicts have been defined as arrangements which are 'adverse' to the interests or 'to the disadvantage' of present or former clients: see eg ABA *Model Rules of Professional Conduct*, Rules 1.8 and 1.9; *Spector v Ageda* [1971] 3 WLR 498. There is no equivalent general definition in the LSG or CCB. All such formulations are, ultimately, limited because they do not and probably cannot address the fundamental question of what precisely is a conflict, or when exactly the interests of lawyers oppose those of clients. One of the chief problems with conflicts of interest thus lies in their identification: Cranston 1995, p.17; Paterson 1995, p.177.

of this problem. They and their nearest equivalent, the American contingent fee, have been widely criticised for generating a direct financial conflict between lawyer and client.[42] This argument is, in some senses, counter-intuitive, and requires some justification. The basic argument advanced for CFAs or contingent fees is that they create a greater commonality of interest between lawyer and client precisely because they align the lawyer's financial interests with the client's through the element of the 'uplift'[43] or 'success fee', which only becomes payable on settlement or an award of damages. However, there is another side to the coin. The image of litigation as a joint venture between lawyer and client may re-cast the lawyer in the role of 'general partner managing the investment'.[44] Precisely because they give the lawyer a personal stake in the outcome, CFAs may therefore be subject to built-in conflicts between lawyer and client. Most notable are the possibilities that lawyers will over-estimate the risk,[45] 'cherry pick' cases, under-prepare relatively low value cases, pressure (non-institutional) clients for early settlement, and, conversely, in strong, high value cases, use obfuscatory and delaying tactics to postpone settlement and maximise fee income.[46]

2.4 Moralism and Lawyer Autonomy

It is not paternalistic for a lawyer to tell the partner of a client who has approached the lawyer to make a will that the client has AIDS, even though disclosure is against the client's wishes.[47] Interventions are paternalistic if they involve interference in what clients decide is good *for themselves*[48] (what we will call their 'self-regarding choices'),[49] as opposed to interventions which are designed to prevent clients harming others.[50] The belief that it may be right to restrict another's autonomy in order to protect others or uphold fundamental moral values can be regarded as 'moralism',[51] or 'moral activism'[52] rather than paternalism. The essential difference between

---

[42] See eg Bar Council 1989, p.259; Clermont and Currivan 1978; Graffy 1998; Rosenthal 1974, pp.96ff; Thomason 1991, pp.221–2.

[43] The maximum uplift currently allowed is 100% of profit costs and fees. The Law Society and Bar Council have recommended voluntary caps of 25% and 10% respectively. Further amendments to CFAs are proposed under the Access to Justice Bill 1999.

[44] Goodpaster 1992, p.233.

[45] See Yarrow 1997, pp.xii–xiii: 'The uplift appears to be too low or (more often) too high, in almost half the cases . . . a cynical interpretation is that some solicitors might be deliberately overestimating risk to justify charging clients a higher uplift.' cf Luban 1995, p.121, arguing that the higher rate for conditional/contingent fees is only justified because they include a risk premium; where there is little or no risk, lawyers should advise clients to select the hourly rate rather than a contingent fee basis.

[46] See eg the data produced by Rosenthal 1974, pp.98–9. Although their findings were more ambivalent, Kritzer *et al* 1985 noted that contingent fee arrangements were likely to generate less lawyer effort than an hourly fee in the case of lower value claims.

[47] On whether disclosure might breach extant confidentiality rules, see Ch.9.

[48] Luban 1981b, p.458.

[49] This phrase is taken from Scoccia 1990, p.319.

[50] The example given could, however, involve an element of paternalism, since the lawyer may reason that what is bad for the children is also against the interests of the client.

[51] See eg Harris 1985, pp.194ff.   [52] See further Ch.8.

moralism and paternalism is that it is no longer the (material) interests of the client which come first. Activist lawyers are primarily concerned with balancing their obligations to the client against their wider moral obligations to others. Whether such moral activism is justified will be discussed in the next four chapters. For now we can note that from the point of view of clients the effect of moralism and paternalism on their autonomy is likely to be the same, but the justifications underlying and potential scope for action flowing from paternalism and moralism are significantly different. For example, morally activist lawyers may intervene in or make decisions about the *ends*[53] clients wish to pursue, whereas the paternalistic lawyer will usually interfere only with the *means* by which clients' ends are pursued.[54]

3. THE LEGAL BASIS OF LAWYER-CLIENT RELATIONS

3.1 Introduction

In looking at the problems of egoism and paternalism, we will start with an analysis of the extent to which they are grounded in the legal basis of the lawyer-client relationship. The primary foundation of this relationship[55] is the retainer,[56] which, so far as solicitors are concerned, 'puts into operation the normal terms of the contractual relationship, including in particular the duty of the solicitor to protect the client's interest and carry out his instructions in the matters to which the retainer relates, by all proper means'.[57] In more general terms, the lawyer-client relationship is based, not in 'pure' contract law, but in agency law principles largely as translated into the codes of professional conduct.[58] Nevertheless, the quasi-contractual basis of the lawyer-client relationship is in itself ethically significant. Contractualism, in the liberal tradition, seems to offer an alternative to paternalism because it suggests an

---

[53] See Ch.8, sections 2.2 and 4.

[54] This is not to suggest either that activist lawyers are never concerned with means (see Ch.8, sections 2.2 and 5) or that paternalistic lawyers cannot interfere with client decisions as to ends.

[55] In fact, the legal profession's divided nature makes it unusually difficult to generalise about the legal basis of lawyer-client relationships. Thus barristers usually have two clients—lay and professional (usually a solicitor)—and are connected to neither by contract (see *Kennedy v Broun* (1863) 13 CBNS 677). We will therefore deal with the lawyer-client relationship primarily from the perspective of solicitors given that they are the lay person's primary and, in many cases, sole point of contact with the legal profession. The barrister-client relationship will be considered so far as possible in tandem with solicitors' duties, though specific differences will be emphasised where necessary. Although in-house solicitors work for their 'clients' under a contract of employment, the notion of being retained applies equally to them. See para. 4.01 n.2, LSG. Their ambiguous status is more clearly recognised by the CCB, which considerably restricts the rights of appearance of employed barristers: see Part IV.

[56] For simplicity's sake we have used the term retainer to describe the terms on which both barristers and solicitors are 'employed'. This reflects historically accurate usage, though today barristers tend to be 'instructed' rather than 'retained'.

[57] *Groom v Crocker* [1939] 1 KB 194, 222.

[58] cf *Rondel v Worsley* [1967] 1 QB 443, 481. It is also important to remember that agency is not a purely contractual relationship, but is grounded in wider principles: see Fridman 1996, pp.15–16 and 182–3.

interactive relationship in which each party's rights and obligations are negotiated and voluntarily agreed between them.[59] The reality of contract can be very different from this image, and the lawyer-client relationship is no exception.

The evolution of the principles governing this relationship has, in classic common law fashion, tended to be deeply casuistical and rather fragmentary, often reflecting the wider problems the courts have encountered (or generated) in negotiating the troubled relationship between contractual, tortious and equitable (fiduciary) rights and duties.[60] This has not been helped by the lack of any clear symbiosis between the common law and the codes.[61]

Much of the fine technical detail created by this complex falls beyond the scope of our work. Instead, we shall try to identify the key principles and issues under two broad heads. First, we shall explore the retainer's general scope, since that identifies the professional relationship's express terms and, by virtue of its basis in agency, also does much to define both the legal and power relations between lawyer and client. Secondly, we shall consider the main duties that are implied into the lawyer-client relationship, and their ethical significance.

3.2 The General Scope of the Retainer

The retainer's duration is normally determined by the nature and extent of each transaction.[62] Consequently, in general, where solicitors are employed over indefinite periods of time, each specific transaction is treated as a separate retainer. The possibility of any kind of 'general'[63] or continuing retainer to advise, outside of specific transactions, has not been widely accepted by the courts, and those few cases which seem to offer limited support for such a concept have turned on particular facts which are equally consistent with findings that solicitors are under an ongoing obligation tied to a particular transaction or set of transactions.[64] As we shall see in section 5.3, the law's failure to acknowledge the long-term, relational, basis of much legal work is itself ethically problematic.

The retainer's scope can also be defined functionally in terms of the powers and duties that attach to the parties in respect of given transactions. The (quasi-)contractual basis of the relationship means that this is determined primarily by any express terms agreed between lawyer and client. These may either serve to extend the retainer beyond the normal bounds of lawyers' responsibilities in given transactions, or restrict them in some way, provided in either case that express terms are not inconsistent with wider duties imposed by professional

---

[59] Veatch 1972, pp.5–7.   [60] See eg Fletcher 1995; DeMott 1992.

[61] See also the discussion in Ch.4.

[62] See *Anon* (1661) 82 ER 952; *Underwood, Son & Piper v Lewis* [1894] 2 QB 306; *Milner (JH) & Son v Percy Bilton Ltd* [1966] 2 All ER 894; *Warmington v McMurray* [1936] 2 All ER 745.

[63] *Gordon v Gordon* [1904] P 163; *Midland Bank Trust Co v Hett, Stubbs and Kemp (a firm)* [1979] Ch 384.

[64] *Midland Bank v Hett, Stubbs & Kemp* at 438; *George v Rimmer* Unreported, 14 November 1997 (Lexis transcript). cf *Bell v Peter Brown & Co* [1990] 2 QB 495.

rules.[65] In reality, however, the retainer's scope will be determined largely by a range of terms implied by the parties' conduct[66] or through the action of the common law or equity. In order to understand the operation of these legal rules we need to begin, more generally, with the agency relationship itself.

3.3 The Agency Relationship

The agency relationship is ethically significant because it underpins certain key assumptions about how lawyers may behave in representing clients. This can be seen both in the authority which flows from that relationship and the specific duties which are also, largely, grounded in agency.

The common view of agency relationships is one in which clients have most of the authority and responsibility for decision-making[67]—a view represented by the popular conceptions of lawyers as the client's 'mouthpiece' or 'hired gun'.[68] According to Bayles, by contrast, this underplays the professional's own autonomy and independence.[69] Closer analysis, however, reveals that neither view acknowledges the complexity of the agency model.

First, entailed within the agency model is a recognition that lawyers act as special kinds of agent, more specifically, as fiduciaries. This implies both that professionals are required to act in ways consistent with clients' need to trust them and, at the same time, given the inequalities of knowledge and power between lawyer and client, that clients have a lesser degree of decision-making power. The fiduciary element of the relationship is commonly said to be emphasised by lawyers' duties of loyalty,[70] confidentiality,[71] and even diligence,[72] but also by the fact that they are generally required only to ensure that clients *consent to* rather than *decide on* certain courses of action.[73]

Secondly, and closely related to the latter point, the agency relationship does

---

[65] See para. 501(c), CCB. Following *Parry-Jones v The Law Society* [1969] 1 Ch 1, the Law Society is empowered to override any contractual term or duty that runs counter to the solicitor's greater duty to comply with rules of professional conduct. This latter duty used to be expressly identified by the LSG as an implied retainer term. Today it has been replaced by a possibly more legalistic obligation (albeit relegated to a guidance note) to refuse instructions in breach of professional conduct rules: cp Principle 7.14 of the 1986 ed. of the LSG, with para. 12.02 of the 1993 ed. ('When instructions must be refused') and now para. 12.01 ('Freedom to accept instructions'). This principle is probably best seen as an example of the lawyer's wider duties as an officer of the court and member of the legal profession, which the written discourse shows cannot be superseded by client interests. See Ch.6, section 2.1, below.

[66] *Allen v Bone* (1841) 4 Beav 493.   [67] Bayles 1981, pp.61–2.   [68] See further Ch.6.

[69] Bayles 1981, pp.62–3. Bayles also emphasises the extent to which the agency element underplays professional obligations to third parties. See further Ch.6, below.

[70] See Holland 1995, para. F/87. This is an overarching duty, which we suggested in Ch.4, section 3.3.3 incorporates the more specific obligations of zeal, independence, integrity and confidentiality.

[71] cp *Rakusen v Ellis, Munday and Clarke* [1912] 1 Ch 831 and Ch.9, below.

[72] See *Bristol & West Building Society v Mothew* [1998] Ch 1 at 17. Note, however, that there is no wholly distinct *fiduciary* duty of care and skill. Instead, fiduciaries may be held in equity to owe a duty of care and skill equivalent to that owed at common law. See also section 7, below.

[73] Bayles 1981, p.69. For situations where lawyers will be required to obtain clients' consent, see eg paras. 12.09, 16.02, 16.04, and 25.01, LSG.

provide lawyers with a legally accepted sphere of autonomy. Like any agent, they have a range of authority to act on behalf of clients. Lawyers obtain not only *express* but also *implied* and *usual*[74] authority from the retainer and the circumstances surrounding them. The scope of express authority is, of course, a matter for agreement, and should properly be confirmed by any written retainer.[75] Such express instructions will override the lawyer's usual or implied authority to act insofar as the latter is inconsistent with the former.[76]

Nevertheless, implied authority may be extensive. As Fridman states: 'Every agent has implied authority to do everything necessary for, and ordinarily incidental to carrying out his express authority according to the usual way in which such authority is executed'.[77] In the lawyer-client relationship, the power to take such major steps as reaching settlements, signing contracts, making representations regarding loans, giving undertakings and receiving payment under court orders are all potentially within lawyers' implied or usual authority.[78] Beyond this a lawyer will also have considerable *ostensible* authority as against third parties.[79]

These rules are significant for the legal power[80] and autonomy they grant to lawyers. Clients will normally be bound by any acts that are within lawyers' actual, implied and even ostensible authority.[81] This, theoretically, appears to offer lawyers considerable freedom even in determining the ends of legal work, though, should lawyers exceed their instructions, they will be answerable to clients for any breach of warranty of authority. Moreover, the courts, and to some extent the codes, have generally shown a marked reluctance to enquire into the *means* by which lawyers seek to pursue instructions.[82] As a consequence of these various rules, for most of their normal and routine functions, lawyers have the power to act without a correlative *legal* duty to consult the client.[83] This legal position may be affected by two factors.

---

[74] See Fridman 1996, pp.46, 68–70, and 122. The term 'usual authority' extends implied authority beyond the specific retainer to include acts which are within lawyers' normal or usual business: *Waugh v HB Clifford & Sons Ltd* [1982] Ch 374.

[75] Note, however, that there is no general duty to reduce retainers to writing, though in some cases solicitors must have written instructions before acting: see Holland 1995, paras. E/408; K/451ff, whereas failure to provide clients with written terms of business may constitute inadequate professional service in contravention of Rule 15 of the Solicitors Practice Rules: see LSG Ch.13.

[76] See eg *Fray v Voules* (1859) 1 E & E 839.

[77] Fridman 1996, p.69.

[78] See further *Halsbury's Laws*, Vol. 44(1) paras. 121ff.

[79] See eg *Re Debtors No 78 of 1980* (1985) *The Times*, 11 May (regarding the conduct of litigation); *Connolly-Martin v D* (1998) *The Times*, 17 August (regarding the giving of undertakings). Distinguishing between usual and ostensible authority can be difficult, but cf Fridman 1996, p.70 for a suggested solution.

[80] In relation to agency generally, see eg Dowrick 1954, p.37; Fridman 1996, pp.20–2.

[81] *Waugh v H B Clifford & Sons* [1982] Ch 374. Where solicitors exceed their actual authority, clients will not be liable for costs, and may have an action for breach of warranty of authority: *United Bank of Kuwait v Hammond; City Trust Ltd v Levy* [1988] 3 All ER 418.

[82] See Ch.6, section 2.1 and Ch.8, section 5.

[83] As stated (admittedly in the context of the courtroom) in *R v Greenwich CC Registrar* (1885) 15 QBD 54.

The first is the client's power *vis-à-vis* the lawyer. In Johnson's famous analysis, professions may be divided into those that are 'collegial', in that the professional has considerable power to define the needs of clients/consumers, and 'patronage' professions, where clients define their 'own needs and the manner in which they are to be met'.[84] It is empirically likely that the modern legal profession transverses these ideal types.[85] What the data indicate, unsurprisingly, is that lawyer autonomy tends to be negatively correlated to client power and status. In short, wealthy, high status, clients are more likely than their poor and/or low status counterparts to have patronage relationships with their lawyers.[86] How far clients are likely to seek to abuse that power is a point to which we will return later in this chapter.[87]

The second factor to consider is the conduct rules themselves. In sum, the barrister's authority is derived from her ordinary authority at common law and the instructions of professional clients (solicitors).[88] To that extent, solicitors are answerable to lay clients (henceforth, simply 'clients') for those instructions, though barristers may be liable to clients directly for breaches of their warranty of authority.[89] Solicitors, on the other hand, are expected to make clear the extent of their authority when taking instructions,[90] and are subject to a number of specific duties to consult and inform, which are discussed below.[91] While it is difficult to generalise, one can view this duty with some scepticism, particularly in collegial practice settings. This is not necessarily to suggest that it is routinely ignored by solicitors acting in bad faith.[92] But the duty is largely at odds with what Rosenthal has called the traditional model of lawyer-client relationships, which gives

the determination of how much information the client should be given about his problem and the possible ways of dealing with it to the discretion of each professional. The professional's judgment may be based on a case-by-case assessment of what each client wants to hear, how much trouble the client is likely to make for the professional in added demands, how much time and energy it is worth spending on the case, how easy it is to communicate with the client, and related factors.[93]

Moreover, compliance with this duty is likely to be difficult precisely because it relates to steps which form much of what is taken for granted *by lawyers* about being a lawyer, and about which there is likely to be little (perceived) need for discussion, let alone dispute. Indeed, the duty to advise clients as to the scope of the lawyer's authority is somewhat undermined by the conduct rules themselves. The LSG thus advises only that 'it would not be appropriate for a solicitor to rely upon implied authority *for non-routine matters*'.[94] The obvious correlative of this is that reliance on

---

[84] Johnson 1972, pp.45–6. Note that this collegial/patronage distinction is somewhat different to that discussed in Ch.3, esp section 7.3.

[85] cf the 'two hemisphere' model discussed in Ch.3 and Heinz and Laumann 1982, pp.360–5.

[86] See eg Carlin 1966; Heinz 1983; Hanlon 1997.

[87] See section 4.3, below.   [88] cf para. 2.1, Annexe H, CCB.

[89] See *Connolly-Martin v D, The Times*, 17 August 1998.

[90] Para. 12.06 n.1, LSG.   [91] Section 4.1.

[92] Indeed, to our knowledge, no research has looked directly at this issue.

[93] Rosenthal 1974, pp.19–20.   [94] See para. 12.06 n.2, LSG (our emphasis).

implied authority is unproblematic in routine situations, and that, virtually by defi-nition, the question as to what is or is not routine lies with the lawyer.[95] There seems to be no particular obligation on lawyers to assess likely knowledge of the retainer's scope from the perspective of particular clients. One consequence of this is that the 'standard' terms to be implied into retainers are likely to be critical in determining the scope of the lawyer's responsibilities. Just how critical can be seen if we turn our attention in more detail to the conduct rules and standard practices which operate in the lawyer-client relationship, and determine where power and control lies in that relationship.

4. CONTROL IN THE LAWYER-CLIENT RELATIONSHIP

4.1 Manipulating the Client in the Lawyer's Interest

In theory, as we have seen, the duty of loyalty should prevent clients being manip-ulated in the lawyer's own interests. But there is much that loyalty and the conflict rules do not guarantee clients—particularly if their interests run counter to the finan-cial or other business interests of the lawyer.

Thus, the rules do not guarantee representation *ab initio*, at least in the case of solicitors.[96] Loyalty obligations (with the exception of confidentiality) only bind solicitors once retainers are established. In theory, of course, the Bar is obliged to provide representation to all comers by virtue of the cab-rank rule. This obligation is not taken lightly by barristers, but neither is it an absolute guarantee of repre-sentation. The personal, referral, basis of the relationship between firms and cham-bers means that there are informal ways in which barristers can let their preferences be known, so that they do not, on the whole, get offered work they would be likely to reject 'on principle' (if they could).[97] It is also legitimate to reject a brief that is not within one's field of expertise or which generates a potential conflict of interest, or, if all else fails, because one is too busy.[98] Moreover, given the way in which lawyer-client relations are organised in the modern profession, loyalty cannot even be said to commit individual lawyers to continuity of representation. While retainers cannot be terminated by lawyers without good cause,[99] this does not prevent solicitors from passing clients down the line to more junior colleagues in the firm,[100] or even to outside consultants or agencies (especially if legal aid has run out).[101] While it is probably harder for barristers to withdraw,[102] nevertheless the rules do not necessarily prevent them from passing on briefs because other

---

[95] Since for many private clients nothing about the legal process is likely to be 'routine': Galanter 1974.
[96] Though note that the rules governing solicitor-advocates are more restrictive: see Annex 21A, LSG.
[97] Scheingold 1994.   [98] Para. 501, CCB.
[99] Para. 12.10, LSG; the phrase is not used in the CCB, but see paras. 504–5.
[100] See Davis 1994, pp.102–3.
[101] cf the criticisms of standards in immigration cases noted in ACLEC 1998, p.22.
[102] See paras. 504–6, CCB; also Pannick 1992, p.40.

engagements clash or overrun, or because they have suddenly discovered a conflict of interest.[103]

The conduct rules also offer clients only limited protection from lawyer mendacity. Work both here and in the United States identifies four particular problem areas. First there is the risk that lawyers may 'puff' or exaggerate their expertise to win or retain business.[104] English and Welsh lawyers are under a general duty to be candid about their competence to act, at least insofar as they are obliged to refuse instructions in matters outside their competence. Both codes explicitly prevent lawyers acting where they lack the requisite skills and experience,[105] and this is reinforced by cases on professional negligence.[106] Whether lawyers are *obliged* to withdraw from retainers because they subsequently realise that they are out of their depth is unclear. The issue is not directly addressed by the codes, though common sense suggests that similar considerations should apply. Solicitors may legitimately side-step some competence issues by using counsel, or possibly even by expressly limiting retainers to areas of work within their competence, though the burden of proving such restrictions will fall on them, and may be difficult to discharge.[107] Candour also extends to publicity in so far as solicitors may not advertise themselves as 'specialists' or 'experts' in particular fields, unless that claim can be supported by specialist qualifications or experience.[108] This will not, of course, catch any puffing of expertise made 'one to one' in the privacy of lawyers' offices.

Secondly, lawyers may lie to hide their mistakes.[109] Lying may be aimed at preventing serious professional consequences (disciplinary or legal) or damage to lawyer-client relationships. Examples of the former might include covering up missed litigation deadlines, the provision of erroneous legal advice, or blaming breaches of confidentiality on support staff.[110] The latter cases are more likely to incorporate more 'minor' instances of neglect, such as withholding information from clients which might show their work in a poor light, albeit not as actually negligent.

---

[103] See eg the decision of Lord Neill QC, Chair of the Committee on Standards in Public Life, first to accept the brief to represent Dame Shirley Porter's appeal against surcharging over the 'homes for votes' scandal at Westminster City Council, and subsequently to withdraw because of the public 'perception' of a conflict of interest. See *Guardian*, 24 June 1998.

[104] Lerman 1990, pp.721–3.

[105] Para. 12.02 and Annex 21A, para. 6.1, LSG; para. 501(b), CCB.

[106] Which set the standard of work at the level expected of the reasonably competent solicitor or barrister. See *Midland Bank Trust Co Ltd v Hett, Stubbs & Kemp* [1979] Ch 384, 434–5, also *Edward Wong Finance Co Ltd v Johnson Stokes & Master* [1984] 1 AC 296; *Mortgage Express Ltd v Bowerman & Partners* [1996] 2 All ER 801.

[107] cf *Hurlingham Estates v Wilde* [1997] 1 Lloyd's Rep 525, 528–9. The Privy Council decision in *Clarke Boyce v Mouat* [1994] 1 AC 428 also suggests that limited retainers may come about where clients explicitly place limits on the advice to be given, even when such limits are potentially contrary to their interests.

[108] Para. 11.03 n.5 and para. 2(b) of Annex 11A, LSG. The CCB is less explicit on specialisation, noting only that advertisements and publicity may include statements 'about the nature and extent of the barrister's services', but not about 'the quality of the barrister's work . . .': paras. 307.1(c) and 307.2(d).

[109] Lerman 1990, p.725ff.

[110] eg if privileged documents are sent to the wrong party: see generally ibid, pp.727–9. The last of these examples would not, of course, ultimately excuse lawyers from liability.

Thirdly, and closely related to this, lawyers may engage in strategic deception in casework. One example is when they mislead clients in personal injury matters by playing down expectations as to likely compensation so as to encourage earlier settlement.[111] However, it is the covering-up of delay that is one of the most common problems and causes of client complaint.[112] This is often justified on the basis that many clients start off with unrealistic expectations, and most lawyers with unrealistic workloads.[113] In other words, there is a certain inevitability in the need for some deception if lawyers are to maintain both the kind of turnover deemed necessary in today's business context and their sanity. Indeed, such strategic deception may even be justified on paternalistic grounds: 'the client feels better if deceived than if he or she knew that the piece of work was at the bottom of the in-box'.[114]

The codes do not greatly reduce opportunities for lawyers to hide their mistakes or engage in strategic deception. Obviously, the more extreme forms of negligence and strategic deception might constitute breaches of their diligence duty, while lesser breaches might still amount to inadequate professional services, *if they are discovered*. However, the codes do little to encourage discovery of such abuses, because they place little real onus on lawyers to keep clients informed of events. The CCB makes no explicit reference to general duties to consult or inform clients, reflecting the fact that communications are normally to be channelled through professional clients.[115] Nor are the boundaries of consultation clearly drawn by the LSG, which fragments the obligation to keep clients informed into various heads. In the context of the retainer, the code 'front-loads' the duties to consult and inform,[116] requiring solicitors to confirm instructions and, 'at the outset of the matter', to discuss the steps necessary to pursue the action under consideration.[117] They are also required to 'consider with clients' whether the outcome of the matter will justify the risks or expense involved.[118] Thereafter, solicitors are under a continuing duty to 'keep clients informed of the progress of matters', and to answer requests for information 'promptly'.[119]

---

[111] Rosenthal 1974, pp.110–11. See also Boon 1996.

[112] cf the ample data which shows delay to be one of the primary causes of client complaint: see eg Lewis 1996, p.11. Other client avoidance tactics, such as using secretaries as buffer zones, lying about one's whereabouts, etc., constitute similar and perhaps more common, albeit possibly less serious, erosions of candour.

[113] cf the discussion of working practices in Ch.3, section 7.3.

[114] See Lerman 1990, pp.726, 739.

[115] Barristers are under a duty to notify professional clients if they are unable to provide an advice or document draft within either the agreed or a 'reasonable time': para. 5.6 of Annexe H, CCB.

[116] Despite the risk of client expectations changing significantly in the course of the retainer: see Spiegel 1979, p.84.

[117] See para. 13.04 n.2, LSG.

[118] Para. 13.11, LSG. According to n.1, this issue should be revisited as appropriate during the retainer.

[119] Para. 13.04 n.3, LSG. Note that these principles are drawn only implicitly rather than explicitly in the client care provisions of Practice Rule 15. Barristers are also required to act promptly and diligently in undertaking all their professional tasks (para. 5.4 of Annexe H, CCB) which would implicitly incorporate a duty to respond promptly to communications from professional clients.

These duties are hedged about by exceptions,[120] or by terms such as 'as appropriate',[121] which both dilute their impact and beg the question: by whose standard are these things to be judged? The LSG seems to assume that it is the solicitors' standards which are relevant, albeit with some recognition that they must be prepared to justify decisions.[122] Although the obligation to respond promptly to clients can be seen as part of the duty of diligence, it is also significant here because it reinforces the generally *passive* character of solicitors' duties. If clients do not ask about progress, it is debatable as to when, or possibly even whether, solicitors must say anything, and indeed, the evidence from complaints clearly suggests that solicitors are poor at keeping clients informed, whatever the rules might say. This conspiracy of silence is reinforced by existing charging practices, particularly in respect of disbursements, whereby clients know (or are likely to become aware) that any enquiry they make as to progress may well cost them money.

Lastly, lawyers may engage in inflated billing practices, as we have already seen in relation to discussing CFAs. In its more blatant form this will involve direct overcharging, whether by hourly billing or fixed fee,[123] or it may be indirect, as where lawyers delay early settlements to maximise the fees charged, or otherwise benefit their financial interests.[124] The general rules on solicitors' costs have certainly tried to restrict the opportunities for direct overcharging. Responsibility for costs and billing lies with solicitors, who are responsible for counsel's fees as well as their own. Solicitors are required to give clients the 'best possible' information on costs at the time of taking instructions, including an actual estimate, wherever this is possible,[125] and should subsequently confirm any fee agreement or oral estimate in writing.[126]

In respect of privately-funded retainers, both solicitors and barristers are under a continuing duty to keep clients informed as to costs.[127] Legally-aided clients are also entitled to advice on the effects of any contribution required and of the statutory charge, and should be warned as to any potential liability for an opponent's costs.[128] Such advice should be reviewed 'at appropriate stages' in the case.[129]

Again, such rules are either hedged about by qualifications and/or framed in ways that give individual lawyers considerable discretion. Although the LSG makes over-

---

[120] eg the duty to disclose material information may be excluded on 'therapeutic' grounds because disclosure might harm the client's physical or mental state (para. 16.06 n.4, LSG and cf Wheat 1998, p.190) or where disclosure would be unlawful or an abuse of another lawyer's privilege over documents (see notes to para. 16.06).

[121] See Practice Rule 15(2) and paras. 13.03 n.3, 13.04 n.7 and 13.11 n.1, LSG.

[122] Para. 13.03, LSG.

[123] See eg reports of a secret memorandum circulated to members of the Bar Council's professional standards committee expressing concern at evidence of barristers overcharging and submitting excessive legal aid claims: *The Times*, 11 August 1998, p.9; *Independent*, 11 August 1998, p.1.

[124] Rosenthal 1974, p.107.   [125] Para. 13.06, LSG.   [126] Para. 13.07, LSG.

[127] See paras. 13.08 and 13.09, LSG. There is no equivalent provision in the CCB, but see *Singer v Sharegin* [1984] FLR 114, 119, which appears to extend the duty to barristers. In practice, the latter's obligation is met by delivering appropriate fee notes to professional clients, disclosable to lay clients: see para. 8.2, Annexe H, CCB.

[128] Para. 13.10, LSG.   [129] ibid.

charging a disciplinary offence, it must be established that 'the charge is so excessive as to amount to culpable overcharging'.[130] Clearly, this standard leaves open the question of what *is* so excessive as to be culpable? The LSG itself offers no descriptive guidance. The Law Society does publish advisory (non-statutory) fee scales for certain non-contentious and contentious work. These express the scale element in the form of recommended or average percentages of the value of transactions, which might provide some limited indication of when fees have been calculated on an unusual and excessive basis.[131] Under the LSG it is also improper for solicitors to front-load bills by demanding payments on account[132] that are disproportionate to the overall value of the work to be done.[133] Given the supposedly negotiated basis of barristers' fees, it is not wholly surprising that by comparison the CCB deals with overcharging far more obliquely.[134] Thus barristers may charge a 'proper' fee,[135] which appears to be whatever the market will bear,[136] and then places the onus on instructing solicitors to challenge any element of the bill when presented.[137]

Billing practices have proved particularly difficult to police, not least because of many lawyers' reluctance to offer itemised billing, with the result that the extent of non-essential work or the amount of 'padding' may be difficult, if not impossible, to identify.[138] Moreover, there is substantial evidence that many solicitors simply ignore the written standards on costs.[139]

In sum, then, the current rules allow lawyers considerable control over the flow of information to clients. They encourage sophistical and paternalistic analysis of what, when and whether to disclose, rather than obliging lawyers to ask: 'what right have I to keep this information from my client?' It is tempting to view this structuring of the codes as part and parcel of the ways in which lawyers have sought (consciously or otherwise) to retain their professional mystique and power. As Ellman points out,[140] the narrower the range of decisions clients can make, the greater the scope of lawyers' authority, and, we would add, autonomy to act in their own interests rather than those of clients.

---

[130] Para. 14.13, LSG.

[131] See further the discussion on scale fees in Shapland and Sorsby 1996, p.222.

[132] ie in advance.

[133] Para. 12.07.

[134] So oblique that it was reported in 1998 that, following both adverse publicity and more private concerns over excessive fees within the Bar itself, the Bar's professional standards committee was contemplating both making it a specific disciplinary offence to overcharge by 50% or more, and requiring barristers to inform on any colleague known to be submitting excessive claims to the Legal Aid Board: *The Times*, 11 August 1998, p.9.

[135] Para. 502(b), CCB. This is presumably equivalent to the requirement that fees charged are to be 'fair and reasonable' in para. 3.4.1 of the Code of Conduct for Lawyers in the European Community.

[136] cf Zander 1988, p.39: 'the fee fixing process, with the [barrister's] clerk having a direct financial interest in the level of the fee, has a directly inflationary effect on the overall level of fees . . . in what is in effect a cynical assertion of monopoly power.'

[137] See para. 14 of Annexe D, CCB.

[138] cf the comments by 'Winston Hall' and 'Michael Williams' in Lerman 1990, pp.707 and 709, respectively.

[139] See eg Lewis 1996, p.12; Christensen *et al* 1999.

[140] Ellman 1990, p.123 n.17.

4.2 Manipulating the Client in the Client's Interest

In terms of the agency and fiduciary principles already outlined, formal precedence is given to the client's instructions, although lawyers have considerable discretion in framing those instructions. The only significant qualification provided by the codes is the lawyer's duty to act in the best interests of clients. This works to an extent because it assumes that the client's instructions and best interests elide because of the lawyer's intervention as professional adviser. Lawyers will not necessarily see this role as manipulative. Indeed, they will, with some justification, view this kind of advice and intervention as exactly what clients pay for.[141] But this also overlooks the strong possibility that the duties to act on client instructions and in their best interests will conflict.[142] What if lawyers' definitions of clients' interests are inconsistent with their instructions?

In other words, how much autonomy can the duty to act in the client's interests override? In looking at this question, we can distinguish two different situations: manipulation of client interests that is justified on the basis that a lack of technical or strategic awareness makes clients poor judges of cases; and manipulation which is justified because their judgement is in some way impaired by the situation.

4.2.1 *The Client's Lack of Technical Knowledge and Strategic Awareness*

A central justification of the professional role is that lawyers possess skills and expertise which clients do not. The lawyer's task therefore is to use these skills for the benefit of clients. The issue of manipulation arises not so much at the level of whether or when lawyers should use their expertise, but *how*. Yet the codes fail to recognise the importance of the latter question, first, by simply assuming that clients are responsible for defining their own ends, and secondly, by saying very little about the means lawyers may use to achieve client ends.[143] These silences can be illustrated with examples.

Firstly, the problem of plea-bargaining shows how far lawyers may go to determine clients' ends. The ethical duty of defence lawyers when plea-bargaining is laid

---

[141] See eg Pepper 1995, p.1557.

[142] See eg Gostin and Rassaby *Representing the Mentally Ill and Handicapped* (1980), p.4, on the problems created by the obligation to represent clients' 'best interests' in mental health review cases: cited in Disney *et al* 1986, p.656. An analogous problem arises under the Children Act 1989, where the strong presumption that contact with both parents is in the child's best interests will often cause lawyers to apply considerable pressure to clients who are opposed to contact with absent parents. See eg Neale and Smart 1997.

[143] cf the ABA Model Rules, Rule 1.2(a), which states that 'A lawyer shall abide by a client's decisions concerning the objectives of representation . . . and shall consult with the client as to the means by which they are to be pursued. . . .' Indeed, para. 11.01 n.2, LSG seems to go further in the opposite direction by requiring solicitors *not* to let clients override their professional judgement. However, from the examples given, this rule may be restricted to cases where client instructions would result in breaches of the law or rules of professional conduct. cf also Sherr 1999a, p.114, essentially arguing that major decisions as to ends are for clients, while the means are for lawyers. To this he adds the caveat that, where clients clearly wish to participate in certain detailed decisions about the handling of cases, those wishes should be followed provided this does not affect 'the proper running of the matter'.

down in *R v Turner*,[144] which starts from an assumption of lawyer, not client, autonomy. The advocate, we are told, must be 'completely free to give the accused his best advice, *albeit in strong terms*. This will often include advice that a plea of guilty . . . is a mitigating factor. . . .' Nevertheless, it then proceeds to say that 'the accused . . . must have a complete freedom of choice whether to plead guilty or not guilty' without any recognition that this meeting of lawyer and client autonomy is an extraordinary counsel of perfection. Empirical evidence has consistently shown that defendants who receive such advice 'in strong terms' are likely to follow it.[145] They have neither the technical expertise, nor the opportunity, to challenge the lawyer's advice.[146] But lawyers will object that by offering such advice they are only acting in clients' interests by attracting the sentence discount that flows from a guilty plea and/or (indirectly) from a charge bargain. This may be true, so long as lawyers are upholding the values of due process along the way. As Baldwin points out, 'everything hinges upon the competence and the professional integrity of the representatives'.[147] This conclusion is not wholly reassuring in a system where pressures created by the routinisation of practice and the pursuit of (cost) efficiency have created a culture built increasingly on the processing of guilty pleas, in which matters of lawyer self-interest or the legal system's bureaucratic imperatives may take precedence over the client's proper representation.[148] In this context, the idea that the plea is the client's sole decision risks perpetuating a myth of defendants as legally empowered individuals. Moreover, the assumption of conventional discourse that lawyers only 'advise' as to plea, and then only in the best interests of clients, in turn further obscures the actual power relations that exist between criminal lawyer and client.

Secondly, Lerman offers a telling illustration of the kind of problem of means that is not addressed by code-based duties. In a personal injury action run by a respondent to her study, the client got very upset whenever she spoke about the accident and her injuries. Her lawyer took a unilateral decision, albeit with some anxiety, as the case progressed not to discuss those matters which upset her because he wanted to increase the likelihood that she would break down in court. This is exactly what happened, to considerable effect. While this may have helped the client win her case, it paternalistically judged the client's best interests solely in terms of the financial outcome, and ignored the possibility that she might have preferred to take a lower cash settlement rather than face what may have been the considerable embarrassment and stress of breaking down in public.[149]

Codified duties to consult cannot easily define *how much* consultation is required in given cases. For instance, let us assume that the lawyer in the above example told

---

[144] [1970] 2 QB 321. The principles laid down are reflected almost verbatim in para. 12.3 of Annexe H, CCB; there is no equivalent in the LSG.

[145] See Baldwin and McConville 1977; McConville *et al* 1994.

[146] Even if the analysis is in some regards wrong. See eg McConville 1998, pp.572–6.

[147] Baldwin 1985, p.102.

[148] See McConville 1998; a slightly moderated version of this argument is also advanced by Blake and Ashworth 1998.

[149] Lerman 1990, pp.736–7.

the client at an early point in the case: 'if you are to obtain the level of compensa-tion we think this claim is worth, you will have to testify. This is likely to be dis-tressing for you. Are you willing to proceed on that basis?' If the client assented, the lawyer has discussed the means to be used in general terms, but not the specific tactics to be adopted. He might argue that he could not discuss the specific tactics because that of itself would have undermined the efficacy of the approach (and hence in Sherr's terms 'the proper running of the case'). It might even be argued here that, in deontological terms, the express duty to do the best for clients must override any (implied) duty to discuss tactics. This, however, begs, in turn, a further question which codes are also unable to answer: how do lawyers balance clients' financial inter-est against their psychological welfare? These sorts of issues are presently recognised as matters for lawyer judgement. However, as both plea-bargaining and Lerman's examples show, they involve questions that may not be asked unless respect for client autonomy is acknowledged to be a strong value underlying the lawyer-client rela-tionship.

4.2.2 *Client Irrationality*

It is axiomatic that many clients approach lawyers with problems that are deeply troubling at an emotional level. In such situations, clients may be so emotionally involved that lawyers construe their instructions or behaviour to be 'irrational' and contrary to their own interests. Here, lawyers might respond in one of two ways.

On the one hand, they might simply exercise a high level of control over cases. Such a view could be wholly consistent, as we have seen, with a 'best interests' approach. If clients lack the capacity to judge their best interests, then so long as they are capable of giving the necessary instructions to establish the relationship, lawyers can take over from there. The decision by Gary Gilmore's lawyers to mount an appeal against his execution, contrary to his express wishes, offers a powerful example of the problems underlying this approach. One can argue that intervention was justified because it could not have been in his interests to die. However, on closer analysis, this argument is less than watertight, not least because (as the debates around euthanasia show) the relationship between an individual's wishes and their rationality and best interests may be far more complex than at first appears. Thus, arguably it is not so irrational to wish to die if the only other alternative is to remain incarcerated in a brutal and impersonal prison system for the remainder (or a sub-stantial part) of one's life. The point is that a commitment to client autonomy means that lawyers can only meaningfully begin to determine what is in clients' best inter-ests if they enter into a process of engagement with them. But this, of course, may be emotionally a lot harder on lawyers, even when not representing clients like Gary Gilmore, than simply making the judgement for themselves.[150]

On the other hand, in line with the modern trend towards 'empathic' or 'client-centred' practice, lawyers might try to adopt a more counselling-oriented

---

[150] cf Lehman 1979, pp.1082–3.

role.[151] The lawyer-as-counsellor acknowledges the emotional dimension to practice and recognises that psychological stress may to some extent 'disable' clients as decision-makers. Such lawyers aim not only to support clients accordingly, but to find ways to enable clients to engage more effectively in decision-making. In terms of client autonomy, however, this approach is somewhat double-edged. Client-centred practice is, in theory, essentially participative and places much of the burden for decision-making on clients, or at least on lawyers and clients equally. But, at the same time, client-centred approaches can involve counselling techniques that may be inherently manipulative, not least because they can result in clients becoming to some degree emotionally dependent on lawyers.[152] The strategic advantages of this may not be lost on lawyers and there is certainly evidence that they use the relationship in ways that exploit the vulnerability of clients, which would be regarded as fundamentally unethical within caring professions like counselling or nursing.[153]

Thus we see that codified ethics have so far achieved little by way of restricting lawyer manipulation of clients and enhancing the latter's opportunities for self-determination. This problem is well recognised in the context of medical ethics, where a substantial literature and case law has emerged around the issue of patient self-determination and consent to treatment. In our view, the codes need to consider imposing duties on lawyers to obtain client consent as a means of protecting their autonomy.

4.2.3 *The Case for Client Consent*

Informed consent is a relatively highly developed concept in the medico-legal domain. Doctors are obliged (at least as regards competent patients) to obtain consent to treatment based on explanations of the procedures involved and any likely side-effects or other associated risks. The standard of informed consent is a flexible one, with most medical ethicists now acknowledging that the duty is determined by the patient's critical autonomy—in other words, their capacity to act for reasons that have been subjected to critical appraisal.[154] Beyond this minimum threshold, the more patients ask, the greater is their right to know. To that extent, the role of informed consent is very much an educative one, whereby the patient/client's dependency on the professional as decision-maker is reduced as the relationship progresses.

This approach sits uneasily with the codes' current model of the lawyer-client relationship, which allocates most decision-making responsibilities at the transaction's commencement. Although in limited contexts[155] the codes and case law have required lawyers to obtain 'informed' client consent before acting, this is exceptional.

---

[151] See eg Binder and Price 1979; Maughan and Webb 1995. cf Ellman 1987 on the risk of manipulation inherent in this approach also.

[152] See eg Ellman 1987, pp.769–70.

[153] cf the comments of one family lawyer quoted by Neale and Smart 1997, pp.388–9: 'You've also got to be a psychiatrist . . . it's very important to be extremely approachable and if you can get your client's confidence you can often talk them into looking at things in this [ie my] way.'

[154] Doyal 1990, pp.5–6.   [155] Mostly associated with conflicts of interest.

Generally, lawyers are not expressly obliged to obtain consent in respect of the normal steps in representing clients. Opportunities for meaningful client consent are mini-mised by 'compressing the burden of information transmittal and evaluation into one short time span', and more particularly to that point at which the knowledge asymmetries between lawyer and client are likely to be too great to allow clients much effective participation.[156]

There is also a close connection between legal duties to consult and the right to give informed consent. The less extensive or clear the duty to consult, the less oppor-tunity clients will have to exercise critical autonomy and give informed consent. Moreover, even where there is an obligation to obtain informed consent, the stand-ard this implies is somewhat unclear. In *Clarke Boyce v Mouat*[157] it was said that lawyers must disclose material facts. Consequently informed consent means consent given in the knowledge of the material facts. In some instances, applying this stand-ard may be relatively straightforward, such as where the failure to obtain consent goes to a central, often taken for granted, feature of the relationship as, for example, lawyers' competence to act.[158] But other instances emphasise the test's potential sub-jectivity and circularity. The courts have been at pains to suggest that materiality is assessed in the light of what clients want. This rather overlooks the fact that what they want will depend on what they know, which in turn will depend on what their lawyers have told them. In other words, materiality is first determined by lawyers estimating what clients want or need to know.

The underlying problem relates to how far should lawyers be required to go to ensure, as Eekelaar puts it in the medico-legal context, 'a field of choice' is opened up to clients, so that 'what clients want' becomes a meaningful standard. As Strauss acknowledges,[159] a commitment to client autonomy does not of itself resolve the question as to who should make what decisions, but it does suggest a presumption in favour of client decision-making.[160] It is a presumption which, if it is to be com-patible with the principle of authenticity discussed above,[161] should operate in rela-tion to all aspects of the retainer *which matter to individual clients*. In particular, this means that clients should be given the choice of caring about means as well as ends. The obvious objection is, of course, that such a duty on lawyers is inevitably going to be difficult to define in specific terms. So should we try, or is it sufficient to raise the presumption, not as a specific duty, but as an overriding matter of principle? Our approach to codified ethics suggests the latter option. As we argued in Chapter 4, it is only by eschewing, so far as is sensible, the formulation of detailed positive duties that we can encourage practitioners to take a more reflective approach to problems of ethics.

---

[156] See Spiegel 1979, pp.82–3 and 105.
[157] [1994] 1 AC 428. See also the New Zealand case of *Haira v Burbery* [1995] 3 NZLR 396.
[158] See eg *Hurlingham Estates v Wilde and Partners* [1997] 1 Lloyd's Rep 525, discussed above at n.107.
[159] Strauss 1987, p.339.
[160] And hence rebuttable in cases where client autonomy is legitimately overridden by other more fundamental values. See ibid, pp.340–1; see also Luban 1990 on the limits of autonomy.
[161] Section 2.2.1.

4.2.4 Can Clients Sanction Lawyer Paternalism?

If models of client-centred practice are pushing us down the path of informed consent, we also need to ask whether clients can consent to paternalistic lawyering on their behalf. We have already noted that clients may take the view that the reason they hired a lawyer is because they want to be relieved of the bother of making particular decisions. There is thus a seemingly attractive argument that it is paternalistic for lawyers to say to clients 'you must act autonomously and decide for yourself'.

At one level this must be right. For clients freely and voluntarily to surrender responsibility to make certain decisions is an exercise of their autonomy. Client autonomy does not demand active participation in decision-making; it simply demands that clients retain the freedom to choose who should make decisions.[162] On the other hand, client-sanctioned paternalism tends, as with all consent-based arguments, to stand or fall around the preconditions we set for lawyers' authority to act. Such evidence as exists suggests that lawyers may too readily assume authorisation from the circumstances surrounding the retainer, or take insufficient steps to empower clients with the necessary knowledge to make decisions.[163] A principle of client-sanctioned paternalism is sustainable, but its ultimate validity, we suggest, depends on client consent being obtained on an informed basis. The main effect of this would be to minimise the element of paternalism[164] by requiring lawyers to obtain more explicit authorisation for their acts, thereby placing the onus on clients genuinely to determine what they need to know or to authorise. One way of achieving this might be to encourage lawyers to obtain a limited waiver from clients of their right to be consulted in respect of specific aspects of the transaction.

4.3 Client Control of Lawyers

The other side of the autonomy coin is the argument that power inequalities do not always favour lawyers. They may themselves be subject to the control and machinations of their clients. Client control is, of course, central to the agency model, which, in theory, treats lawyers as having little autonomy or individual responsibility for their actions.[165] This is most apparent, for example, in the 'hired gun' model of lawyering.[166] As we have seen, however, the extent of lawyer power and control is far greater than this model assumes.

The argument about powerful clients has been most commonly advanced in contexts where lawyers 'enjoy' a patronage relationship with their clients—in short, in mega-law practices where clients are most likely to be in charge.[167] However, here

---

[162] On the relationship between autonomy and choice, see Dworkin 1988, pp.18, 23, and 78–9.

[163] Ellman 1987, pp.764–5; cf Spiegel 1979, p.104ff on the necessary conditions for client decision-making under an informed consent model.

[164] Since paternalism by definition is exercised by the assumption of authority rather than by authorisation.

[165] See Luban 1988a, pp.324–6.   [166] See Ch.6, esp section 2.2.

[167] See eg Luban 1986.

we must distinguish two different aspects of the relationship. It is one thing to say that lawyers' autonomy may be more constrained in relationships with patronage clients because they know that clients have the power and knowledge to make them answerable for the strategies adopted.[168] It is another to say that such clients are more likely to seek to manipulate their lawyers. Clearly clients may manipulate lawyers, for example, where they lie to their lawyers or try to get their lawyers to lie for them,[169] where they use their economic muscle and position to influence (or initiate) action on their behalf, or seek to influence decision-making between members of the same firm.[170]

In fact, however, there is relatively little empirical support for the view that it is corporate lawyers who are most subject to client manipulation, or indeed that the risk of client manipulation is ever that great.[171] Rather, one of the distinctive features of (corporate) practice is the extent to which lawyers and clients share common objectives.[172] As a result, there does not seem at present to be much need for the codes to play what is sometimes seen as an important 'defensive role' in providing lawyers with protection from client pressure.[173] Whether the codes do in fact offer much scope for this role and whether lawyers can be encouraged to adopt greater moral autonomy from clients are, however, issues which we will turn to in later chapters.

5. AUTONOMY: A CRITIQUE AND RE-EVALUATION

5.1 'Autonomy-in-Relation'

Thus far our discussion suggests that we cannot achieve full lawyer *and* client autonomy in the same relationship. This is, in fact, wholly consistent with liberalism's emphasis on an individualistic notion of autonomy, which is an autonomy of opposition. In other words, each individual's sphere of autonomy is carved out in competition with others. This may be contrasted with what Schmitt, drawing heavily on works of feminist ethics and social theory, has characterised as 'autonomy-in-relation'.[174]

To understand this concept we need to begin with the importance of separateness for conventional definitions of autonomy. Put simply, what this means is that if I make a decision, it is mine; if you make a decision, it is yours. If I freely adopt your

---

[168] See eg Galanter 1983, p.152; Wheeler 1991, p.250.

[169] eg where clients have 'salted away' money or property and try to pressurise lawyers into ignoring those assets in relation to debt, insolvency or matrimonial proceedings: see de Groot-van Leeuwen 1998, p.239.

[170] See eg Lamb 1995, pp.225, 227; Lerman 1990, p.739.

[171] See Carlin 1966; Heinz and Laumann 1983; Nelson 1985, pp.531–9. Indeed, one might argue intuitively that one of the few areas where clients may routinely attempt to manipulate lawyers is criminal defence work. Whether the ethical limits on representation encourage lawyers to enter complicitly into that process remains a more open question, though see McConville *et al* 1994, p.69.

[172] Nelson 1985, pp.525, 527.   [173] See Ch.4, section 3.1.   [174] Schmitt 1995, pp.90–7.

decision there remain two distinct decisions. Unless I have wholly surrendered my substantive independence to you, we are each still autonomous and responsible beings—you directly for the decision, and me indirectly by virtue of my decision to defer to you. It seems that if we are to maintain this version of autonomy it is at least arguable that there can be no truly *joint* decisions.[175]

In our view, separateness thus defined offers an impoverished basis for lawyer-client relations for three reasons. First, separate autonomy, as Schmitt suggests, privileges self-centredness over other values. This does not mean that autonomous individuals cannot be altruistic, but it does suggest that altruism is always conditional on subjects' overriding need to preserve their independence. Autonomous lawyers may choose to be instruments of their clients' purposes, but not to the extent of once and for all surrendering their own autonomy. Secondly, it follows that separate autonomy in fact conceals, even denies, the reality of dependence. The obvious, but still crucial, point here is that, whenever we commit to persons or causes—and this, after all, is what the duty of loyalty demands—we are no longer self-sufficient and free to follow our self-interest. Instead, as Dworkin argues, we become governed by what needs to be done for that person or cause.[176] Separate autonomy in such situations becomes a cipher. This Dworkin and Schmitt identify as 'procedural autonomy' because it exists only in the mind at the point at which one must choose whether to engage in certain tasks or relationships. The essence of such procedural autonomy is simply the consequentialist capacity to weigh choices. Thirdly, separateness may be morally unattractive. It may be self-absorbed, lacking in empathy, and generally incapable of obtaining the moral insight which flows from being in relation to another,[177] and which is the essence of caring and dialogical ethics.[178]

Autonomy-in-relation, on the other hand, seeks to recover for autonomy those values which are lost in the procedural version. Autonomy remains a good in so far as it describes a certain moral independence and ego-strength. These provide a basis for the critical reflexivity demanded by such as Dworkin. But autonomy-in-relation acknowledges that truly autonomous agents also draw strength from the ideas and support of others. They do not fear dependence. Moreover, autonomy-in-relation recognises that our distinctness itself forms the basis for the interdependence of, and reciprocity between, individuals. We are in reciprocal or interdependent relations when, in taking responsibility for the other, we recognise self and other as 'different but connected rather than separate and opposed'.[179] As Noddings defines reciprocity,[180] it is not the formally equal exchange of contractual relations, but the negotiation of joint projects through non-coercive and shared understandings; an idea which is echoed in Levinas' ethics.[181] This of itself undermines the validity of claims to exercise hard paternalism. We cannot know the other, her wants, needs, fears and weaknesses, without some meaningful contact and connection.

---

[175] Which Schmitt 1995, p.19 defines as decisions which neither party could complete individually.
[176] Dworkin 1988, pp.23–5.   [177] Schmitt 1995, pp.50 and 58–71.
[178] See Ch.2, sections 6 and 7.4.   [179] Gilligan 1982, p.147.
[180] Noddings 1984, p.4.   [181] See Ch.2, section 7.4.

Consequently, as Schmitt argues, 'I am in no position to define for others what is good for them without paying a great deal of attention to their perceptions of the world and their feelings and experiences of it.'[182] This obligation may extend beyond the most immediate other with whom we are engaged; moral decision-making requires us (as self plus other) to take account in our projects of the concrete needs of those to whom we are connected through the network of social relations.[183] The implications of this are radical, if, as Gilligan argues,[184] to adopt an 'inclusive' approach to social relations inevitably changes the character of (in our context) 'the game' of lawyering.

Using these concepts, we can critique the legal basis of lawyer-client relations, focusing on its contractual and transactional form, before suggesting some substantive reformulation of the duties involved.

5.2 The Problems with the Contractual Basis of the Retainer

The emphasis on the lawyer-client relationship's basis in agency, and more particularly its 'pure' contractual form as regards solicitors' retainers, is significant. By grounding lawyers' duties to clients in (contractual) agency, the law places legal services within a particular kind of power-liability relationship[185] which in turn operates within the domain of an individualistic, market ethic.[186]

The traditional approach to general contractual relations has been criticised for its content-neutrality; the fact that it tends to focus on the circumstances around the making of contracts rather than their content—particularly in determining vitiating factors. There are of course well-known exceptions, but they are viewed as just that. This approach inevitably assumes a high level of formal equality between contracting parties. The retainer is less content-neutral than many contractual arrangements, but even so, lawyers have in principle the capacity to negotiate around many of the retainer's terms, and to rely extensively on their implied authority. While it is not possible for lawyers to contract out of their duties under the codes, the absence of extensive principles on candour and client consent provides them with opportunities to exploit their power and knowledge to the detriment of clients. Equally, though, the assumption of formal equality offers lawyers little protection from clients who may seek to use their financial muscle to persuade lawyers to act in ways that may be regarded as unacceptable. The limitations of the existing ethical basis of professionalism are pretty obvious. Loyalty and fidelity remain, in theory at least, a one-way street. The agency basis of the relationship means that, formally, it calls for little

---

[182] Schmitt 1995, p.92.   [183] cf Gilligan 1982, pp.147–8.

[184] In du Bois *et al* 1985, p.45; just how radical will be considered in sections 5.1 and 6, below.

[185] See Fridman 1996, pp.21–2, asserting that, of all legal relationships, only agents have the necessary degree of power to represent and affect the contractual and property rights of principals.

[186] ibid, p.9. This particularly reflects the influence of classical contract law on the framing of the agency relationship: cf Gabel and Feinman (1982), esp pp.176–7; Maxton 1997, p.225, cf also Mazor 1968, p.1121, who makes the point that, historically, the lawyer-client relation is closely equated with the general agency relation.

or no reciprocity between client and lawyer.[187] There may be some moral, but certainly no legal, duties on clients to be loyal to lawyers, even where the patronage basis of the relationship vests most of the power in the client.

The contractual model also tends to assume that the front-loading of rights and duties is largely inevitable, perhaps even desirable, whereas this is in fact inimical to an informed approach to client decision-making, which requires client participation throughout the retainer.[188]

At the same time, however, the contractual basis of lawyer-client relations does provide some degree of mutuality of obligation. Obligations are not all on the lawyer's side. Thus the fact that solicitors can terminate existing retainers for cause, for example where clients have sought to involve them in wrongdoing or have positively misled them, creates some duty on clients to treat lawyers with integrity. But these obligations are generally of an imperfect nature[189] and do not relate to matters usually regarded as 'ethical'. Thus, the client's primary contractual duty is to remunerate their solicitor for work done. The best that can be said of this is that the Common Law duty generally applies regardless of whether clients obtain the benefit sought.[190] This at least avoids encouraging the sort of excessive zeal that might flow from a more explicit 'payment by results' culture.[191] On the other hand, the fiduciary nature of some obligations of lawyers not only does not encourage clients to act in good faith, but also places responsibility for client ends firmly with the lawyer.[192] To that extent the fiduciary principle can be seen as a major justification for lawyer instrumentalism and paternalism.

In this light, there may be a strong argument based on what Wilhelmsson[193] calls the new 'material contract paradigm' for restructuring the relationship more around external legal and social policy standards, such as the principle of good faith,[194] or expectations of more formalised standards of 'product information', etc., and less around the presumed intent of the parties.

5.3 The Problems with the Transactional Form of the Retainer

As we have seen, the retainer is formally constructed around a transactional, not relational (in the Noddings' sense), conception of the lawyer-client relationship. This has a number of implications. First, the transaction model focuses chiefly on the ends rather than means of legal representation and does little to arrest the

---

[187] At the same time, the formal case can be overstated. As Lee 1992, p.32 points out, because of the practical costs and difficulties associated with changing lawyers, particularly in 'mid-stream', client loyalty may extend beyond the point predicted by the agency model.

[188] See Spiegal 1979, pp.83–4.   [189] See Ch.2, section 3.2.

[190] See eg *Fisher v Drewett* (1878) 48 LJ QB 32.

[191] Though cf now the debates around conditional fees. See above, section 2.3, and the references cited there.

[192] See Developments in the Law 1981, p.1265.   [193] Wilhelmsson 1993, p.19.

[194] cf the Unfair Terms in Consumer Contracts Regulations, SI 3159/1994, which introduces a principle of good faith dealing into certain consumer contracts.

consequent objectification of clients—as the 'problem' and perhaps also lawyers—as the 'solution'. Secondly, as part of this transactional model, the relationship is treated as both 'bipartite' and 'binary'. It is bipartite in that lawyer and client interaction is treated as essentially distinct from their other legal and social arrangements. To create a lawyer-client relationship which disregards the context of those other relations is implicitly to deny that they have consequences for that relationship. This is at best unrealistic and at worst damaging. It leaves lawyers exposed to potential contradictions which have no acknowledged existence. For example, most lawyers today are caught between two duties of loyalty: to the firm and to clients. In legal aid cases, the clash of obligations may be even greater given additional duties to the Legal Aid Board, such as to avoid unjustifiable expenditure and to waive client confidentiality in prescribed circumstances,[195] and to their firm which will have to bear the cost of any work not chargeable to the Legal Aid Fund. The model is also binary in that lawyers and clients are treated as mutually autonomous. This can be seen in the current debates around consent generally, and client-sanctioned paternalism specifically, which suggest there may be a conceptual weakness with the current contractual view of lawyer-client relations. Legally speaking, the binary model tends to assume decisions must be either the lawyer's or the client's, but ultimately cannot be both. This underplays the relational character of service agreements, such as those between lawyer and client.

Moreover, by formally denying the often continuing nature of lawyer-client relationships, the transactional basis forces retainers back into the traditional 'adversary' contractual model, as opposed to what Collins[196] calls a co-operative model. While the adversary approach treats contracts as the clash of two individual wills driven by autonomous self-interest, the co-operative model emphasises the relationship's long-term nature, the interests of both those within and outside the contract, and concrete obligations such as loyalty and candour.[197] Indeed, this approach might provide a more accurate view of what the fiduciary basis of the lawyer-client relationship really means. It is perhaps notable that in Canada, where the courts have been most pro-active in extending the scope of fiduciary obligations, it has been acknowledged 'that not all fiduciary relationships are characterised by a dynamic of mutual autonomy'.[198]

6. RECONCEPTUALISING DUTIES TO THE CLIENT

The current emphasis on loyalty is, we have suggested, problematic, but not merely because of its undue emphasis on zeal,[199] and its other very real limitations as a foundation for the lawyer-client relationship. At the very least, we suggest loyalty fails because it is normatively incoherent. Loyalty is certainly too much of an umbrella

---

[195] See the Civil Legal Aid (General) Regulations 1989, noted eg in para. 16.02 n.9, LSG.
[196] Collins 1997, p.160ff. [197] Wilhelmsson 1993, pp.20–1.
[198] *Hodgkinson v Simms* (1994) 117 DLR (4th) 161, 186c. [199] This is developed in Ch.6.

term to be a useful description of any kind of discrete 'duty'. Virtually all the major obligations owed by lawyers to clients can be described as involving loyalty. The positive obligations of zeal, confidentiality, competence and diligence, and the negative obligations to eschew secret profits and conflicts of interest all reflect elements of loyalty. At the very least, one must question what advance 'loyalty' offers as a descriptive tool over these more specific characterisations of the lawyer's duties. At the same time, loyalty is too restrictive and too one-sided to constitute a satisfactory overarching principle for the professional relationship.

We argue, therefore, that loyalty, as an overriding principle, needs to be replaced by two more fundamental considerations—which we shall call 'good faith' and 'trust'—and which might better serve as the twin pillars supporting a more ethically sensitive lawyer-client relationship.

6.1 The Principle of Good Faith

Good faith is notoriously hard to define in the abstract, certainly once one tries to move beyond the blanket definitions of dealing reasonably, honestly, and in clear conscience.[200] There is little assistance at present from case law, where, although there are many passing references to the lawyer's duty of good faith, there has been little analysis of what it involves. Exceptionally, the duty of good faith was explained by Lord Esher MR as follows:

A professional man (*sic*) . . . [is] bound to act with the utmost honour and fairness with regard to his client. He [is] bound to use his utmost skill for his client but neither a solicitor or barrister [is] bound to degrade himself for the purpose of winning his client's case. Neither of them ought to fight unfairly though both [are] bound to use every effort to bring their client's case to a successful issue. Neither [has] any right to set himself up as a judge of his client's case. They [have] no right to forsake their client on any mere suspicion of their own or on any view they might take as to the client's chances of ultimate success.[201]

Despite the rather amorphous and, perhaps, wistful language, this quotation is instructive in a number of respects. It seems to suggest that good faith should be very much the overarching duty, so that obligations of zeal and diligence function within the limits set by expectations of fair dealing (whatever they may be).[202] It supports our doubts as to the logic of suggesting that loyalty either subsumes or is synonymous with good faith.[203] Rather, we suggest that it is good faith which in turn calls for loyalty to clients,[204] but a good faith duty also can and must (in theory) transcend loyalty to clients because in some situations we cannot act with honesty

---

[200] See eg Summers 1982; Adams and Brownsword 1995, p.212ff.

[201] *In re G. Mayor Cooke* (1889) 5 TLR 407, 408.

[202] cf the assertion that to call for a general (contractual) standard of good faith is to require 'a minimal standard rather than a high ideal': Summers 1982, p.834.

[203] cf Cranston 1995, p.13.

[204] See *Bristol and West Building Society v Mothew* [1998] Ch 1, 19.

and integrity and in accordance with a client's wishes.[205] The good faith/loyalty distinction appears to draw on the recognition that, while a professional should not divide her loyalty between her different clients, she cannot give them absolute loyalty. Rather, as Lord Esher seems to acknowledge, lawyers owe wider duties to have regard to a number of specific others in their professional relations.[206] The duty to act in good faith must be a standard that extends beyond the duties *to* clients, so that it serves also to imply some limits on how far lawyers may go in acting *for* clients. This idea has some, albeit limited, historical support from dicta which suggest that good faith underpins the notion of professional independence and hence, one might argue, the conflicts principles which flow from that.[207]

The modern contractual approach may also be helpful to a degree. It provides many examples in which the obligation of fair dealing will penalise poor quality of service and dishonesty—especially the misrepresentation or 'puffing' of products or expertise, the exercise of undue influence, and even moral impropriety, such as sex between lawyer and client. This approach also has some value in stressing the procedural dimension of good faith, particularly as to the formulation of duties of disclosure and commitment to published standards of fairness. Nevertheless, it remains a concept that is significantly underdeveloped in English jurisprudence,[208] and grounded too much on exclusionary rules rather than general principles.

Enunciation of a general good faith principle might then provide us with some basis for delineating in an ethically sensitive fashion the legitimate expectations of both lawyers and clients, consistent with an expectation of autonomy-in-relation. As a minimum, these would seem to involve mutual expectations of honesty, loyalty (within the limits of fair dealing) and respect. Equally, good faith notions may take us further, and closer to acknowledging formally the three-way nature of trust in professional relationships: in other words, as mutual trust between lawyer, client and public, and the need, therefore, for client as well as lawyer accountability for what is done in the course of representation. This may help us to acknowledge, for example, that to negotiate coercively breaches good faith and similarly that to lie breaches good faith and subverts autonomy, even when done at the behest of clients.

At the same time, while a good faith principle shares many characteristics with, and may help instil or enhance, trust, it is not of the same order as a general principle of trust, particularly if our focus remains primarily at the contractual level. It has been suggested that 'contractual trust' (of which our conventional notions of good faith are arguably a form) is a very limited form of trust, grounded primarily in our expectation that performance can be specified and monitored.[209] Indeed, a

---

[205] cf Finn's argument (1989, p.10ff) that duties of loyalty are not in fact fiduciary obligations, though often represented as such, but good faith obligations. cf also Austin 1996, pp.159–60.

[206] See similarly Koehn 1994, p.145.

[207] See *Re Holmes' Estate* 3 Giff 337; *Savery v King and King* (1856) 25 LJ Ch 482, 487; *Bristol & West Building Society v Mothew* above n.204.

[208] cf Adams and Brownsword 1995, pp.225–43, who are a significant exception given their argument at pp.247–53 for a general principle of contractual good faith based on Gewirthian principles.

[209] Little and Fearnside 1997.

number of ethicists go further and suggest that contract is actually inimical to trust, since it removes much of the discretionary element which forms the basis of 'true' trust relationships.[210] This suggests that good faith of itself may not be enough, and that some wider notion of trust needs to underpin lawyer-client relations.

6.2 Trust as a Professional Duty

The lawyer-client relationship has long been portrayed as a highly personalised one, built on trust and (mutual) respect for professional integrity. Without wishing to over-romanticise the image, the ideal lawyer has been portrayed, like Atticus Finch in *To Kill a Mocking Bird*,[211] as a respected and long-established member of the community. Indeed, in the classic scenario the interests of several generations of clients might well have been looked after by the same 'family firm' (with all its cultural connotations of altruism and long-term connection); a pattern that still pertains particularly to elements of rural practice.[212] In this kind of relatively stable community, trust, once established, is likely to be fairly easy to maintain, and hard to destroy.

However, modern society is generally more complex. As social theorists like Giddens and Beck[213] have shown, there is a paradox at the heart of modernity. The scale, complexity and sheer anonymity of modern institutions (firms, corporations, governments, etc.) make it difficult for us to make sensible decisions about who we can trust. Yet, by the same token, such abstract institutions are so central to our existence we are obliged to trust them. As Giddens puts it, trust is fundamental to the social management of risk in modern society. The difference between the historical ideal and the modern reality of lawyer-client relations is that, in most instances, the assumption of trust today cannot readily be made on an individualised or local[214] basis. Instead, one has to assess whether or not to trust the institution. In other words, our decisions are necessarily driven by generalised cultural assumptions as to who or what can be trusted.[215] We cannot easily judge the trustworthiness of individual lawyers, but we do make decisions based on the perceived trustworthiness of the profession. If, however, as Bok asserts,[216] their power means that professions are likely to be perceived as, to some degree, inherently untrustworthy, then there appears to be a problem.

Professions have long argued that part of their collective role is to sustain public trust through the operation of devices such as ethics codes and disciplinary procedures.[217] Clearly this approach has been of limited effectiveness.[218] Consequently, we

---

[210] See Koehn 1994; Baier 1995, p.117. If one accepts the logic of this argument, one might go one stage further and argue that contract itself may discourage, or at least not advance, the creation of trust: cf Bok 1990, p.920.

[211] Harper Lee (1960).   [212] Blacksell *et al* 1991, pp.89–90.

[213] See eg Giddens 1990; Beck 1992.   [214] cf Little and Fearnside 1997.

[215] See Sztompka 1998.   [216] Bok 1990, p.919.

[217] See eg *Bolton v Law Society* [1994] 1 WLR 512, 518.

[218] See Watkins *et al* 1992, and the studies of complaints against lawyers discussed in Ch.4, section 4.2.

must not only question whether lawyers' existing collective approach is sufficient to curtail the apparent erosion of public trust and confidence,[219] but at the same time consider more fully the place of trust in the individual lawyer-client relationship. If enhancing trust in the profession as a collectivity can help ensure trust in individual lawyers, then the reverse ought also to be true. We should not overlook the fact that individual lawyer-client relationships are also fundamentally built on trust. As the Louisiana Supreme Court once put it: 'In no other agency relationship is a greater duty of trust imposed than in that involving an attorney's duty to his client'.[220] It is this dimension that is our present concern.

The individual duty of trust is presently reflected in the fiduciary nature of the lawyer-client relationship and specifically in the expectations of honesty and secrecy. It may be objected that trust so conceived is practically indistinguishable from the loyalty duty already described. But this is precisely our point. Loyalty and trust *should* be distinguishable, and at present they are not.

For two main reasons, the notion of trust reflected in current professional rules and standards is somewhat impoverished. First, it reflects the fact that society is not entirely comfortable with the lawyer-client relationship. The *Concise Oxford Dictionary* defines trust as 'confidence in, reliance on, some quality of person'. Yet the lawyer-client relationship does not seem to satisfy the demand for trust in this sense. Trust is of particular importance where there are asymmetrical power/knowledge relationships.[221] As we have already suggested, clients are constrained to 'trust' lawyers as a condition of access to their special skills. This need to trust itself places clients (even patronage clients) in lawyers' power. However, this necessity does not guarantee that clients are confident that lawyers will exercise power in their best interests. The conduct rules, in theory, act as a corrective by imposing an obligation of trust on lawyers and hence creating a source of confidence in the profession. But this is in fact a special 'institutionalised' trust, of the kind that Thomas Jefferson had in mind when he described 'free government' as founded on 'limited constitutions, to bind down those whom we are obliged to trust with power'.[222] Such a one-sided obligation, in which virtually the whole duty is carried by the lawyer, not only reflects *in extremis* the imbalance of positive duties between agent and principal in lawyer-client relations, it also fails to constitute 'real' trust, freely given, because its very existence involves a *denial* of the confidence that underpins trusting relationships. Moreover, as Shapiro argues, the formalisation of such norms has a contradictory effect in simultaneously enabling fiduciary relationships and increasing the risks associated with them by institutionalising the possibility of conflict between fidelity to principal and agent self-interest.[223]

---

[219] See further Ch.3.
[220] *Plaquemines Parish Commission Council v Delta Development Co* (1987) 502 So 2d 1034, 1040.
[221] Baier 1995, p.102ff. Some theorists, eg Shapiro 1990 and Brien 1998, suggest that it can only exist where there are power asymmetries, but as Braithwaite and Makkai 1994, p.3, note, this is not necessarily reflected in lay descriptions of trust relationships.
[222] Cited in Selznick 1993, p.18.
[223] Shapiro 1990, pp.348–50.

Secondly, the tendency to conflate loyalty and trust also weakens our understanding of the lawyer-client relationship. Loyalty and trust are not the same thing. One may act in a manner that is 'loyal' for many reasons—such as a fear of disciplinary consequences or hope of financial gain—that have nothing whatsoever to do with trust. Trust, properly understood, will engender loyalty, not least because trust demands reciprocity.[224] But loyalty—at least as understood in lawyer-client relations—does not generally demand reciprocity and will not imply, or necessarily engender, trust. We therefore need to rethink fundamentally what we mean by trust in the lawyer-client relationship.

6.3 Towards a Principle of Trust

To understand why a reinvigorated notion of trust is important to lawyer-client relationships we need first to consider the necessary conditions of trust in social relations. First, we can note that trust flourishes in contexts of empowerment. As Ayres and Braithwaite argue, trust and power are 'mutually constituting' whenever trust is viewed as 'a relationship where the other player can be taken at his or her word, where there is a commitment to honest communication, to understand the needs of the other, to agreed rules of fair play and a preference for co-operation'.[225] This view of trust shares characteristics with both Schmitt's autonomy-in-relation, and Adams and Brownsword's model of good faith contracting. Despite obvious differences, both are strongly grounded in the need to achieve mutually acceptable ends through an 'ethic of co-operation'.[226]

The empirical validity of the co-operative model is reinforced by game theorists' work on the 'prisoners' dilemma' (PD).[227] PD is a simple game which models the so-called 'social trap' in which both parties to interactions have essentially two choices: to co-operate to their mutual advantage or to 'defect'[228] by engaging in the naked pursuit of self-interest. The latter choice may bring higher one-off rewards for defectors but at the risk of retaliation, leading to both parties' mutual harm—a so-called 'lose-lose' outcome. Axelrod's work on the development of co-operation stresses the importance of understanding and responding to the needs of the other in engendering 'win-win' solutions to PD problems.[229] Braithwaite and Makkai also emphasise how the process of empowerment will often vest clients with 'dangerous knowledge' that could be used against professionals should they discontinue acting in a trustworthy way.[230]

Secondly, the co-operative model also serves to emphasise another characteristic of trust relationships, namely that trust demands transparency. Trust relations are

---

[224] This is a major theme of much organisational sociology: see eg Fox 1974; Sennett 1998.
[225] Ayres and Braithwaite 1992, pp.84 and 86.
[226] The phrase is from Adams and Brownsword 1995, p.251.
[227] For descriptions of the prisoners' dilemma, see eg Axelrod 1984, ch.1.
[228] Axelrod's term for non-co-operation or cheating, ibid.
[229] See ibid, p.134.   [230] Braithwaite and Makkai 1994, p.10.

more likely to be built with individuals and organisations who make their operations, functions and *raison d'être* visible, easy to understand and open to question.[231]

Thirdly, opportunities for trust are increased by continuity of representation. Again, this seemingly self-evident point can be supported by work on the PD. In many social traps, the risks of defection may be kept in check by formal or informal controls, most notably the 'shadow of the future'[232] represented, for example, by the risk of retaliation or loss of business reputation. In the absence of effective formal controls, individuals and organisations are more likely to co-operate where the players are already known to each other. In business contexts, for example, it is known that companies may shun better deals available on the open market for the security of contracting with established suppliers.[233] Translated into the legal context, this suggests that the advantage is firmly with (corporate) 'repeat players' who are in a better position to build up a relationship with their lawyers over time. By contrast, the 'one-shot' nature of much private client work leaves both lawyer and client more exposed to the risk of the other's defection (particularly in the absence of effective institutional protection) and to the risk that one of the parties will neither co-operate nor defect, but simply walk away from the transaction.[234] As many law firms are only belatedly coming to understand, it pays to hold onto clients, not just financially, but perhaps for more fundamentally ethical reasons than they had imagined.

Finally, as noted above, trust effectively demands reciprocity. It is not a one-sided obligation. This can be supported by a number of analogies. In employment, for example, high trust relations between management and workers have been shown to be characterised by the parties' sense of reciprocal long-term obligation to each other.[235] Similarly, in a study of compliance with nursing home regulations, it was found that regulators who developed a culture of trust with nursing home directors saw rates of legal compliance improve.[236] In other words, those who are trusted are inclined to reciprocate by being trustworthy. As Putnam concludes: 'stocks of social capital, such as trust, norms and networks, tend to be self-reinforcing and cumulative'.[237]

7. CONCLUSION: IMPLICATIONS FOR THE FORM AND FOCUS OF THE CODES

Our project of reconceptualising the core ethical duties to the client cannot be completed without taking cognisance of the issues of the codes' form and focus raised in Chapter 4. To continue with the existing duty-based system of codification is, as we

---

[231] Sztompka 1998, p.23.   [232] Axelrod 1984.   [233] Yamagishi and Yamagishi 1996.
[234] cf Orbell and Dawes 1993.   [235] Fox 1974, p.98.   [236] Braithwaite and Makkai 1993.
[237] Putnam 1993, p.177. cf also Axelrod's emphasis on reciprocity in building co-operation: 1984, p.118ff, though it should be noted that Axelrod's model extends to reciprocity of defection as well as co-operation.

have argued, problematic because it both underplays the need for aspirational standards, and the separation of 'ethics' from matters of 'mere regulation', and, given our primary objective of using the codes to increase lawyers' ethical awareness and in this way hopefully increase the professions' stock of trust, does not do enough to empower clients and to make lawyers responsible for their actions.

Our analysis suggests that principles of trust and good faith are central to that project. However, these are both umbrella terms which would need to be further spelt out in terms of more specific principles. In so doing, we are not suggesting that the core duties identified in Chapter 4[238] are now irrelevant but that both their interrelationship and form may need to be reconsidered.

Loyalty obviously remains a key principle, since failures of loyalty would be contrary to expectations of trust and good faith. Nevertheless, the boundaries of loyalty, and particularly of lawyer zeal, are now more contestable given our suggestion that good faith dealing may extend to those beyond the retainer. As we have already said, this is a difficult issue to which we need to return at some length in the chapters which follow.

The obligation of *diligence* obviously is also integral to the lawyer's role, though ethically speaking it is probably the least contentious or problematic of the existing 'core' duties. However, the duty of diligence, in theory at least, does reinforce the zealous character of lawyering. Diligence in particular demands that the lawyer is answerable to the client for the means used to advance her cause. Undue delay, cutting corners, or a failure to exercise (or advise) caution on the client's behalf may all constitute a lack of lawyerly diligence. Consequently, the scope of diligence also needs to be considered in tandem with the obligation of loyalty. The principles of lawyer *independence* and *integrity* are similarly significant. The former primarily requires lawyers to avoid situations in which their loyalty might be compromised, whereas integrity requires them to be honest in dealings with clients and others, and offers lawyers an area of moral autonomy from clients—though at present (as we shall see in the next chapter) largely only in theory.

Nevertheless, we have argued that, even within the confines of the lawyer-client relationship, the lawyer's duties do not go far enough to ensure that all clients are given sufficient information to make informed choices about the work being undertaken in their name.[239] This, together with our concerns about the ways in which lawyers represent themselves and their competence, indicates a need for a general principle of *candour*. Clients are entitled to expect lawyers who are frank and open both as regards their own capacities to take on cases, and in the advice and information they give. As a variant on the Kantian Principle of Universality,[240] Menkel-Meadow[241] has argued that 'lawyers should reveal to their clients that which they

---

[238] ie loyalty, itself comprising zeal, independence, integrity, and confidentiality, and diligence: section 3.3.3.

[239] In particular, the existing rules do not seem to deal with the fact that most information is withheld from clients unthinkingly rather than dishonestly.

[240] See Ch.2, section 3.2.   [241] Menkel-Meadow 1990.

would want revealed to them if they were clients'.[242] The standard has much to commend it. It is simple, understandable and can be easily applied. It is context-sensitive and wide enough to encompass acts of both strategic (client-interested) and self-interested deception by lawyers. It is even, at least in Menkel-Meadow's vision, capable of some kind of relational turn.[243] On the other hand, given the evidence we have about the assumptions lawyers make about client needs or desire for information, it may still leave the door too open to lawyer paternalism. For example, empathic lawyers may feel so in tune with their clients' wants and needs that they regard it as redundant to ask for consent. In the light of Axelrod's work,[244] one might also doubt the efficacy of a duty of candour framed as a 'golden rule', since this demands a purely altruistic approach that may be hard to achieve within the pragmatic context of professional relations. At the very least, we suggest that there is a need for a more explicitly reciprocal expectation of candour. This has the obvious merit of giving lawyers the option of withdrawal in cases where clients have sought to mislead them in some material respect.

As a final principle governing the lawyer-client relationship, we have suggested that lawyers need to be subject to a principle of *informed consent*. Its applicability should be assessed in each retainer according to whether the information given reaches the standard required to enable that client to achieve critical autonomy, and should extend to a duty to consult over means as well as ends. This is not inconsistent with existing binary obligations under contract or tort. For example, evidence of informed consent would also protect lawyers by providing them with a *volenti*[245] or contributory negligence defence. Moreover, as Spiegel points out, informed consent may enable clients to better police the progress of cases and, hence, the lawyer's performance.[246] Although client-sanctioned paternalism, as we have defined it, is not inconsistent with these principles, good faith should preclude lawyers from seeking to establish, at the time of entering the retainer, a blanket waiver on client decision-making authority.[247] In many transactions, clients are unlikely to be able confidently to determine all their potential objectives at that stage. Such a waiver would thus act as a serious barrier to client autonomy.

The emphasis on broad principles of trust and good faith, backed up by more specific (but still generalised) expectations of loyalty, etc., potentially provides both an aspirational and contextually sensitive framework for lawyer-client relations. At the same time, while our main aim is not to offer an exact blueprint for reform, we recognise that it is essential to provide a codified structure that offers standards which are sufficiently meaningful to offer some guidance, rather than just pious hopes. General principles of the type we have described are unlikely to be enough to increase

---

[242] ibid, p.771.
[243] See Menkel-Meadow's emphasis on the empathic dimension of lawyers' judgement: ibid, p.770.
[244] See at n.227 and text following.
[245] ie a defence based on the voluntary assumption of risk.
[246] Spiegel 1979, p.105.
[247] ibid, p.82; Strauss 1987, p.347.

the potential for the normalisation of a relational ethics. Consequently, we suggest two possible ways of achieving this goal.

One involves rethinking the retainer so as to create a framework for relationships that are in certain key respects less flexible and more transparent as to the obligations involved (particularly those which may be implied), while perhaps also more flexible as to their duration and scope. There are a number of specific principles within the scope of retainers that our analysis has brought to the fore, and which ought to be considered. For example, it might be desirable to tighten up the rules on continuity[248] and withdrawal of representation. Much also remains to be achieved under the maligned title of 'client care': improved systems for information exchange; greater transparency in billing practices; visible and effective complaints mechanisms and so on. Here, as our analysis suggests, there may be a case for both greater rather than less prescriptive regulation, and more efficient use of professional sanctions, as well as some sensitive positive reinforcement to overcome the substantial cultural resistance to regulation apparent in local professional arenas.[249]

A second means involves building upon the approach to codes we proposed in the last chapter and our general argument about the importance of context to professional legal ethics. More specifically, we suggest that application of the general principles governing the lawyer-client relationship should be dependent on consideration of a number of contextual factors, which will guide but not determine the way in which lawyers treat clients. Consideration of such factors will be particularly relevant to questions such as identifying the information needs and objectives of clients, the degree of control lawyers exercise over clients and the extent to which they should consult clients as to means and ends, and whether lawyers undertake, continue or withdraw from representation. Based upon the discussion in this chapter, we can list these factors as: the client's status (individual or corporate), knowledge and abilities, vulnerability and decision-making competence; whether the lawyer has an ongoing professional relationship with the client, or is a 'one-shotter' or simply meets the lawyer on a referral basis;[250] the extent to which mutual expectations of honesty and candour have been met in the relationship, and particularly the aspects of the case which should be considered 'material' under the candour principle; and what steps in the process of representation are likely to be sufficiently 'major' to require the client's informed consent. This list should not, however, be regarded as exhaustive. No doubt other relevant factors would emerge were our relational and contextual approach to the retainer to be adopted.

---

[248] Even though this may have its downside. After all, unwilling representatives may be less prepared to develop the kind of relational understanding that we have sought to describe.

[249] See Christensen *et al* 1999, pp.58–61.

[250] As with specialist advocates or 'paper barristers' ie those who only write opinions.

6

The Lawyer's Amoral Role and Lawyer Immorality

[Is it] right that a man should, with a wig on his head and a band around his neck, do for a guinea what, without those appendages, he would think it wicked and infamous to do for an empire?

Lord Macauley[1]

1. INTRODUCTION

Implicit in Lord Macauley's rhetorical question is the age old criticism of lawyers that they are subject to a morality different to that of ordinary citizens; a morality which allows, if not encourages, them to perform actions on behalf of clients which would be regarded as immoral if performed by non-lawyers. Given the importance of serving client interests to the lawyer's role, it thus seems impossible for 'a good lawyer [to] be a good person'.[2] The conflict between what can be called 'ordinary morality'[3] and the expectation that lawyers favour client interests over those of particular or general others is said to arise in three ways.

First, lawyers might be asked to pursue client goals which are legal, but which the lawyer or others regard as immoral. For example, lawyers might be asked to help confessed rapists seek acquittals or oil companies desecrate the environment and the human rights of the inhabitants of oil rich countries. From a different political or moral perspective, defending IRA suspects or challenging the refusals of abortions might be regarded as equally suspect. Secondly, client goals might be best achieved through immoral, unjust, or unfair means. For example, lawyers might be expected to humiliate rape complainants by reference to irrelevant details of their sex life or attempt to defeat meritorious claims through abuse of procedural rules. Thirdly, lawyers might be given information relating to their clients whose disclosure could prevent serious harm to others or the public interest but is prevented by the duty of confidentiality.

Notwithstanding the apparent immorality involved in upholding client interests in these three types of situations, there are powerful arguments that lawyers should always put client interests over those of affected others and the general public. The following four chapters will explore the extent to which lawyers are in fact expected to do so and whether these arguments actually stand up to scrutiny. Given that client confidentiality raises specific issues and has its own specific justifications, we will

---

[1] Thomas Macauley, *The Works of Lord Macauley* (1900), quoted, *inter alia*, by Frankel 1980, p.30.
[2] Fried 1976, p.1060 (arguing, however, that the apparent conflict is resolvable: see Ch.7, section 3).
[3] See section 3.1 below.

discuss it in Chapter 9 after first looking at the interrelated issues of the pursuit of immoral means and ends by lawyers. Thus we will concentrate in this chapter on the relevant professional norms and criticisms of these norms. Then in Chapter 7, we will look at the justifications offered for these norms and in Chapter 8 at the possibilities for the current positions as regards immoral means and ends issues.

2. THE LAWYER'S AMORAL ROLE

2.1 Introduction

When lawyers are criticised for engaging in immoral behaviour on behalf of their clients, it is not usually suggested that the legal profession is peculiar in attracting individuals who lack moral fibre.[4] Admittedly, some lawyers might, for instance, regard pursuing company profit at the expense of human rights or humiliating rape complainants as unexceptionable. But if the problem was simply one of personal immorality, it would be one of general socialisation. Because, however, most examples of immoral or harmful behaviour on behalf of clients are not simply allowed but in many cases required by professional norms and in particular what is called the lawyer's 'role morality', we can clearly see that the problem is one of professional ethics.

The idea of role morality reflects the importance of social roles in human society.[5] In all but the earliest, smallest and most homogenous societies different social statuses or positions develop—hunter, gatherer, mother, father, etc.—representing 'patterns of reciprocal behaviour between individuals or groups of individuals'.[6] These patterns are necessary in order that individuals may entertain 'more or less dependable expectations about each other's behaviour'.[7] Roles represent the dynamic aspect of social statuses: the enactment of the rights and duties attached to them. Moreover, they have built into them some notion of appropriate and inappropriate conduct. Following the term's original dramaturgic origin, social roles can be said to provide their incumbents with a 'social script' as to what acts they are entitled and expected to perform, and how they should perform them, while also informing others what behaviour they might expect from role incumbents. As such, social roles are extremely important to morality, providing a bridge[8] between particular social statuses (parent, lawyer, etc.) and the behaviour expected of its holder (e.g. caring for one's children, representing clients zealously, etc.). In other words, occupation of a particular social status necessarily connotes a particular 'role morality'. In the case of professionals, this is called a 'professional role morality'.[9]

---

[4] But cf Frankel 1980, pp.21ff.
[5] The discussion of social roles draws upon Linton 1936, pp.113–14; Goffman 1959 and 1961, ch.2; Emmet 1966; Downie 1971. See also Cohen 1966 and, in relation to lawyers, Elkins 1978, esp p.746ff.
[6] Linton 1936, p.113.   [7] Emmet 1966, p.13. See also Linton 1936, p.114.
[8] See Emmet 1966, p.15.
[9] cp Luban 1983a and 1988a; with Luban 1994 and Williams 1983, respectively.

2.2 Written Discourses on Professional Legal Ethics

The professional role morality of lawyers which is found in written discourse on professional legal ethics can be described as 'neutral partisanship'.[10] This conception contains two interlinking principles. The *principle of partisanship* requires lawyers to act as their clients' 'partisan'.[11] Arguably, it includes all duties owed to clients. What partisan would not, for instance, display diligence or protect confidential information? However, in the context of the immoral means and ends debate this principle is most closely associated with the idea of lawyer zeal,[12] famously expressed by Lord Brougham:

An advocate, by the sacred duty that he owes his client, knows in the discharge of that office but one person in the client and none other. To save that client by all expedient means, to protect that client at all hazards and costs to all others, and among others to himself, is the highest and most unquestioned of his duties; and he must not regard the alarm, the suffering, the torment, the destruction which he may bring upon any other. Nay, separating even the duties of a patriot from those of an advocate, and casting them, if need be, to the wind, he must go on reckless of the consequences, if his fate it should unhappily be to involve his country in confusion of his client's protection.[13]

Although this melodramatic piece of rhetoric was probably intended as a 'menace' to George IV who was seeking the House of Lords' permission for divorce,[14] judicial dicta sing the same tune with a libretto hardly less florid. Thus barristers and solicitor-advocates are urged to defend their clients 'to the end', exercise zeal as 'warm as [their] heart's blood', to 'exert every faculty and privilege and power in order that [they] may maintain [their] client's right' and 'fearlessly to raise every issue, advance every argument, and ask every question, however distasteful, which [they think] will help [their] client's case'.[15] More sedate are the codes, which require barristers and solicitor-advocates to 'promote and protect fearlessly and by all proper and lawful means the client's best interests . . . without regard to their own interests or to any

---

[10] This term is taken from the US literature: see eg Luban 1994, p.xiv.

[11] Rogers 1899, p.259. Also described as a gladiator: Du Cann 1993, p.46.

[12] cf the dictionary definition of a partisan as one 'excessively devoted to a particular cause': *Collins Paperback English Dictionary* (Glasgow: HarperCollins Publishers 1990). The term 'zeal' is used more formally in the American discourse on legal ethics, leading some English lawyers to suggest that the duty to act in the best interests of clients involves a less zealous approach. 'Best interests', it is said, includes 'a special duty . . . [on the lawyer] to advise his [*sic*] client as to the legal and ethical standards which should be observed' rather than to 'take every step he can, whether legal or extra-legal, to gain advantage over the other party': Marre Committee 1988, para. 6.2. While the emphasis on best interests may invite a rather more paternalistic approach to clients' instructions, it imposes no greater formal side constraints than the US *Model Rules*, emphasising, as we shall see, only the limits of law and the professional conduct rules.

[13] Quoted *inter alia* in Rogers 1899, p.269.

[14] See eg Rhode 1991, pp.30–1. However, the view that the advocate should 'reckon everything subordinate to the interests of his client' was later advanced by Lord Brougham in a more neutral setting: Rogers 1899, p.270.

[15] Quotations from, respectively, *Rondel v Worsley* [1967] 1 QB 443, 502; *Queen v O'Connell* (1844) 7 Ir LR 261, 312; *Kennedy v Broun* (1863) 13 CB(NS) 677, 737–8; *Rondel v Worsley* [1969] 1 AC 191, 227.

consequences to themselves or to any other person . . .'.[16] Moreover, solicitor-advocates are required to say on behalf of civil and criminally accused clients what the client 'should properly say for himself or herself if the client possessed the requisite skill and knowledge'.[17] As regards non-advocates, written discourse on professional legal ethics is less expressive. The LSG requires all solicitors to act in their clients' best interests,[18] and early judicial authority urges them to 'use utmost skill . . . [and] every effort to bring their client's case to a successful issue.'[19]

While the partisanship principle requires lawyer zeal in pursuing client ends, the *principle of neutrality*[20] insulates lawyers from considerations of morality, justice or politics in relation to these ends or the best means to them. Lawyers are not required to be morally neutral in the sense of having or expressing no opinion about the morality of client goals or the most effective means to them.[21] Indeed, they can attempt to dissuade their clients from what they regard as morally repugnant action. Rather, the neutrality principle can be said to involve two related ideas. The first is that 'no moral obliquity' [*sic*][22] attaches to lawyers who represent clients to the best of their abilities. As Pannick puts it: 'it is the client, not the advocate, who decides whether—and how—to enforce his legal rights in a democratic society. If such conduct causes unfairness to others, it is the client, not the advocate, who should be criticised.'[23] Thus when faced with criticism, lawyers are entitled to file what may be called an 'ethical demurrer'.[24] But perhaps more important than deflecting external criticism—only partially successful in any event—the neutrality principle holds secondly that lawyers are at the very least entitled, without moral disquiet, to pursue clients' ends zealously no matter how immoral or unjust they or the means necessary to their achievement may be.[25] And, in the case of barristers and solicitor-advocates, the cab-rank rule *obliges* them to act irrespective of moral considerations for anyone who can afford their services.[26]

Admittedly, written discourse on professional legal ethics contains a competing conception of professional role morality. This denies that lawyers are mere mouthpieces of clients[27] or should seek to achieve client ends 'at all

---

[16] Para. 203(a), CCB repeated in para. 2.3 of Annex 21A, LSG.

[17] Paras. 21.20 and 21.21, LSG.   [18] Para. 1.01(c).

[19] *In re G. Mayor Cooke* (1889) 5 TLR 407, 408.

[20] Also called the principle of professional detachment: Lawry 1990; the principle of non-accountability: eg Schwartz 1978 and 1983, begging the question of who lawyers would be accountable to in the absence of this principle.

[21] See Pannick 1992, pp.92 and 153; du Cann 1993, pp.46–7.   [22] Rogers 1899, p.267.

[23] 1992, p.168. See also Stephen 1861, p.453: '[T]here is no moral difference at all between the advocate who conducts to a successful termination a prosecution instituted from the vilest motives, and the judge who passes sentence on the verdict. No one blames the latter, nor ought one to blame the former'; *Johnson v Emerson* (1871) LR 6 Ex 329, 367.

[24] cf Schwartz 1978, p.674.

[25] See eg du Cann 1993, p.46: 'like the mercenaries through the ages [the lawyer] has no right to ask if the cause which he fights is just.'

[26] See Ch.4 at n.203.

[27] *O'Connell*, n.15 above, p.313; *Strauss v Francis* [1866] LR 1 QB 379, 381; *Rondel v Worsley* [1967] 1 QB 443, 502.

costs'.[28] Instead, in rather outdated and chauvinist language, the lawyer has been exhorted to act as 'a gentleman and man of honour', or 'as a man and as a Christian', to temper zeal 'with self-respect', and not to degrade himself 'for the purpose of winning'.[29] On the other hand, such exhortations are vacuous to the point of insignificance.[30] One may wonder how many city lawyers are likely to refrain from zealously helping companies to avoid environmental laws or to shed costly employees on the grounds that such actions are degrading, unchristian, or ungentlemanly. And if lawyers were to be given pause for thought by such considerations, written discourse on professional legal ethics contains a far more specific countervailing message which states unambiguously that lawyers have no duty towards their adversaries[31] or 'the world at large'.[32]

More recently and somewhat less vaguely, lawyers are said to owe allegiance to the 'higher cause'[33] of truth, justice, and the public interest.[34] Yet closer examination reveals that what is meant by truth, justice and the public interest are the formalistic concepts of factual truth, the administration of justice and the public interest in the administration of justice,[35] rather than moral or political truth,[36] substantive justice or the general public interest, respectively. Accordingly, the content of 'higher cause' duties is almost entirely encapsulated by the idea that, as officers of the court[37] or ministers of justice,[38] lawyers owe 'overriding'[39] duties to the courts and the administration of justice, primarily to be truthful and candid, but also to represent their clients by fair and proper means.[40] Moreover, these duties simply entail com-

---

[28] Napley 1991, p.59.

[29] Quotations taken from Lund 1960, p.54; *O'Connell*, n.15 above, p.312; *In re G. Mayor Cooke, loc cit* n.19. See also *Smith v Smith* (1882) 7 PD 84, 89: 'There is an honourable way of defending the worst of cases'; *Kennedy v Broun*, above n.15, referring to the lawyer's duty to 'himself'; *Rondel v Worsley* [1967] 1 QB 443, 502D–G; Hilbery 1959, p.1; Ward 1995, p.135; Bird and Weir 1989, p.189.

[30] See the discussion of this issue in Ch.4, section 3.3.3.

[31] *In re G Mayor Cooke, loc cit* n.19; *Orchard v South Eastern Electricity Board* [1987] 1 QB 565, 571, questioning the contrary *obiter dicta* in *Kelly v London Transport Executive* [1982] 1 WLR 1055, 1064–5.

[32] Silverman 1997, p.128.   [33] *Rondel v Worsley, loc cit* n.27.

[34] See eg *Hutchinson v Stephens* (1837) 1 Keen 664, 668; *O'Connell*, above n.15, pp.312–13; *Strauss v Francis*, above n.27, p.381; *Batchelor v Pattison and Macakersy* (1876) 3 R 914, 918; *Kennedy v Broun*, above n.15, p.737; *Rondel v Worsley*, above n.27, pp.502 and 517; *Rondel v Worsley* [1969] 1 AC 191, pp.227, 243, 247, 259–60, 271, 282 and 283. See also *Tombling v Universal Bulb Company, Limited* [1951] 2 TLR 289, 296, quoting Macmillan 1937, p.17, who refers also to a duty to the State. With the extension of advocacy rights proposed by the Access to Justice Bill 1999, this duty is likely, by virtue of clause 41, to become a statutory obligation on all advocates and others 'conducting litigation' to observe 'a duty to the court to act with independence in the interests of justice'.

[35] See esp *Rondel v Worsley* [1969] 1 AC 191, pp.247 and 283.   [36] cf Nicolson 1994, p.739.

[37] eg *Rondel v Worsley*, above n.27, p.470, and above n.35, p.227. cf, however, Napley 1991, pp.60–1, who notes that, strictly speaking, only solicitors are officers of the court and only in relation to the Supreme Court.

[38] *Hutchinson v Stephens, loc cit* n.34; *O'Connell*, above n.15, p.312; *Rondel v Worsley, loc cit* n.27. cf also *Rondel v Worsley*, above n.35, p.247 ('*amicus curiae*'); *Beevis v Dawson* [1957] 1 QB 195, 201 ('helper in the administration of justice').

[39] Para. 2.02, CCB. See also para. 1.02 n.6, LSG.

[40] eg *R v Berens* (1865) 4 F & F 849, 854–5; *In re G Mayor Cooke, loc cit* n.19; *Rondel v Worsley*, above n.27, p.469, and above n.35, pp.282–3; *Saif Ali v. Sydney Mitchell & Co (A Firm)* [1980] AC 198, pp.219–20, 233, and 235.

plying with the codes' rules, which limit the tactics lawyers may use in representing their clients,[41] and which, as we have seen,[42] focus predominantly on ensuring honesty and fairness in litigation, while imposing few limitations on lawyer behaviour which are likely to protect third parties, the general public or the environment from the consequences of lawyer zeal.

It thus appears that lawyers are indeed conceived of as 'hired guns'[43] or 'amoral technicians'[44] prepared to do anything for anyone capable of paying their fees. Admittedly, the rules limiting lawyer zeal mean that they are not the hired guns of the lawless Wild West, but the modern mercenary operating according to the Hague Convention's 'civilised' code of killing.[45] However, these limitations are either narrowly concerned with the due administration of justice or alternatively too vague to ensure that lawyers will refrain from pursuing immoral ends or means.

At the same time, we have also seen that neutral partisanship does not apply monolithically to all lawyers. The duty of zeal is painted in vibrant colours as regards advocates and the cab-rank rule expressly endorses a strong principle of neutrality for barristers and solicitor-advocates. They are not simply entitled, but are required, to represent clients irrespective of moral considerations. By contrast, non-advocate solicitors are subject to a weaker principle of neutrality in that they are entitled but not obliged to ignore morality in deciding whether and how to represent clients.[46] Nevertheless, it can be argued that even without a strong principle of neutrality most lawyers will tend to regard their role as the zealous representatives of clients irrespective of moral, political, or justice considerations. This flows from a number of ideological, institutional and psychological factors.

2.3 The Ideological and Institutional Background to Neutral Partisanship

We have already come across one such ideological factor. Thus the very notion of professionalism is said to require professionals to devote themselves to serving client interests even at the expense of others.[47] This is not just a matter of professional ideology but a reflection of a deeper legal ideology emerging from the relationship's basis in agency law. Agency principles, as we have seen,[48] emphasise the duty of loyalty, and in fact (subject to legal limits) place it above all other duties lawyers may owe.[49]

---

[41] cf *Saif Ali*, ibid, 219H: 'To say of a barrister that he owes a duty to the court, or to justice . . . may seem to be no more than a pretentious way of saying that . . . a barrister . . . must observe the rules . . .' See also *Abse v Smith* [1986] 1 QB 536, 546B.

[42] Ch.4, section 3.3.3.

[43] eg Phillips 1990, p.38; Wheat 1998, p.193ff. This image is not always seen in negative terms: see Pye 1978, p.951; du Cann at n.25.   [44] Wasserstrom 1975, p.6.

[45] cf Quintilian's distinction between the assassin and the warrior: Rogers 1899, pp.270–1. See also Sherr 1993, p.59.

[46] See *Ridehalgh v Horsfield* [1994] Ch 205, 234.

[47] Pepper 1986a, pp.615–16. See further Ch.7, section 3.2.2.   [48] Ch.5, section 3.3.

[49] This can be seen in the rules which privilege client confidentiality—and hence the sanctity of the lawyer-client relation—over all other relationships. See Ch.9.

Another important factor is the existence of *prima facie* persuasive justifications for a strong principle of neutrality, although they are only partly articulated and probably only partially digested by English and Welsh practitioners. Thus it is argued that without neutral partisanship the adversary system of justice would not be able to operate effectively, that the liberal values of dignity, autonomy and equality would be thwarted, and the institutions of liberal government would be usurped, thus undermining democracy and the rule of law.[50] And in addition to these general arguments for neutral partisanship, the cab-rank rule is often justified on the basis that it ensures that the 'unpopular people', 'minority interests', the 'underprivileged' and those whose conduct is generally regarded as reprehensible do not go unrepresented.[51] Accordingly, it is frequently asserted that neutral partisanship represents a moral position itself and hence that those who follow its dictates are thereby both good lawyers *and* good persons.[52] Indeed, in the absence of such arguments, it would be virtually impossible to describe neutral partisanship as a role *morality*.

In the next chapter, we shall attempt to show that these justifications are far from watertight. Nevertheless, they are likely to be persuasive[53] given the current absence of critical evaluation of professional legal ethics, the fact that the justifications for neutral partisanship draw upon revered values and that they conveniently provide a principled argument for responding to institutional and psychological pressures.[54]

Undoubtedly, a crucial—if not the most crucial—institutional factor is the adversarial system. In general, much of professional legal ethics takes its cue from the adversarial system and from the advocate's role.[55] Written discourse is disproportionately concerned with ethical issues raised by advocacy and, in addition to providing the most commonly articulated justification for neutral partisanship, the adversarial system is an important source of lawyer socialisation, helping to foster an adversarial ethos, which largely coincides with neutral partisanship, and which is likely to spread to all legal work even when far removed from the natural home of this ethos—the courtroom and litigation. Indeed, it is arguable that neutral partisanship emerged, at least partly,[56] because of the adversarial system's need for the opposing parties to do their utmost to win their cases so that the passive adjudicator hears all relevant facts and arguments. From here it is a short step to advocates seeing legal proceedings as civilised battles[57] or sporting contests[58] in which the

---

[50] See Ch.7.   [51] ibid, section 3.1ff.
[52] See Pannick 1992, esp p.167 and ch.7.   [53] Pye 1978, p.937.
[54] Indeed, it is possible that the neutral partisanship conception and the justifications for it only clearly emerged relatively recently as part of the legal professions' increasing commercialisation and the demise of earlier more altruistic professional ideals (for examples of which see Rogers 1899; Orkin 1958, p.172; Pannick 1992, p.131; Crispin 1995, p.173; the judicial dicta cited at nn.28, 32, and 33, above). See further Luban 1988b; Gordon 1988; Shaffer 1988.
[55] See Ch.4, section 3.   [56] cf at n.47, above.
[57] Lord Diplock, quoted in Phillips 1990, p.115 (referring to 'bloodless fisticuffs'); Evans 1983, p.74; Napley 1991, p.85. See also Frank 1970, ch.VI; Frankel 1980, p.32.
[58] eg John Stuart Mill, quoted in McKenzie 1996, p.34; Pound 1906, p.404; Frankel 1980, p.11; Gerber 1987, p.5. For examples of this discourse, see eg Curtis 1951, p.21; Caplan 1978, p.133; Elkins 1992, pp.764ff, esp p.765.

display of skill and winning through tough, albeit fair, means is the sole measure of their worth. Such an attitude is given support by high-profile role models. For example, Lord Denning confessed that as a young barrister, he 'wasn't concerned so much with the rightness of the cause, I was concerned only . . . to win it if I could',[59] whereas Lord Donaldson commented that the highest praise reserved for lawyers is that they can 'dress up the wholly unarguable as if it had a scintilla of a basis of reason'.[60]

Equally, if not more, important in lawyer socialisation is their training, at least if advocacy manuals are anything to go by. Here, the few restraints on lawyer zeal are buried under a consistent message that winning is all and that in the fight for victory 'truth' and 'justice' may be taken as hostages. As one critic put it: 'Lawyer's texts on cross-examination teach the classic wisdom of successful veterans concerning the disaster of asking one question too many on cross; that blundering next question may give the entrapped witness a chance to *explain*, heaven forfend, to tell how it really was . . .'.[61] Such pearls of wisdom are often illustrated by apocryphal tales of legal skills triumphing over factual truth. Although designed to amuse, they simultaneously play 'a latent socialisation function into manipulation and persuasion rather than "truth"'.[62]

While these discourses valorising winning and skill at the expense of morality, politics and justice are aimed largely at advocates, a number of factors suggest that they are likely to influence all lawyers. One is the well recognised fact that the adversarial nature of formal legal proceedings casts a long shadow over all legal work.[63] The differences between litigation and other legal work are not so clear-cut that lawyers are likely to drop an adversarial stance once they move out of litigation. While ADR may be intended to be less adversarial, like negotiation, it may still involve opposing lawyers seeking to maximise client interests. Even where there are no formal opponents, lawyers may perceive themselves as facing opponents in the form of, for instance, taxing authorities in tax planning cases, consumers in the case of *pro forma* insurance contracts, or environmental and human rights groups in the case of companies wanting to exploit overseas oil deposits.

Another important factor is that it is the image of the combative advocate—the Kavanaghs, Perry Masons, and even the Rumpoles[64]—which dominate popular

---

[59] Quoted in Pannick, p.130. See also his comment in *Tombling*, above n.34, p.297: 'Cicero makes the observation that it is the duty of the judge to pursue the truth, but it is permitted to an advocate to urge what has only the semblance of it.' But note an earlier, more ethically informed, approach, described by Pannick, ibid, pp.130–1.

[60] *Attorney-General v Barker* [1990] 3 All ER 257, 261e–f. cf also Lord Cross, quoted in McBarnet 1981, p.18: 'I have seldom felt more pleased with myself than when I persuaded three out of five law lords to come to a conclusion I was convinced was wrong'.

[61] Frankel 1980, p.16. Although written about US instruction manuals, this description applies equally to their Anglo-Welsh equivalents.

[62] McBarnet 1981, p.19. As she notes, the very use of such tales nicely demonstrates the advocate's concern with good rather than accurate stories.

[63] Luban 1986, pp.645–6 and 1988a, pp.11–12; Menkel-Meadow 1996, pp.802–3.

[64] cf Pannick 1992, *seriatim*.

culture and hence the minds of legal neophytes. Subsequently, undergraduate legal education focuses largely on litigation, with students mostly being taught how to mount appellate legal arguments in an adversarial setting rather than how to draft wills, contracts and other documents. Nor are law students likely to have much contact with ideas critical of neutral partisanship and its supporting adversarial ethos, given the current state of ethical education and the fact that not all students are exposed to criticisms of the adversary system. Indeed, the way in which neutral partisanship treats as irrelevant considerations of justice, morality and politics for practitioners neatly echoes the general formalism of legal education.

More generally, as we saw in Chapter 3,[65] the emphasis on craft and competitiveness is a pervasive feature of legal careers, starting with the competition to get into law school and ending with possible elevation to the bench. Conversely, at no stage is an interest in or concern for issues of morality or justice likely to earn much kudos, respect, or status.

This factor is crucially reinforced by the commercial nature of modern legal practice. As we have already seen,[66] particularly with recent moves towards professional deregulation, there has been a growing move away from the *noblesse oblige* conceptions of legal practice towards one dominated by commercial considerations. Moreover, in so far as they ever existed, the common ethical standards of legal professionals, based on ideas of honour and fair play, have been threatened by increases in the numbers, social heterogeneity and geographical dispersion of lawyers.[67] Consequently, legal practice is increasingly seen like any other business, the main aim of which is profit-making through the provision of efficient services to those who can afford them. As in the general business world, doubts as to the morality of how profit is made are likely to be regarded as indicating weakness and a lack of business acumen. For lawyers who can attract wealthy clients, zeal is a highly profitable product.[68] To paraphrase Rhode, the temptation to leave no stone unturned on behalf of clients is great when the lawyer is being paid by the stone.[69] And for those whose profit margins are small, budgets are tight and the aim is simply a fairly comfortable lifestyle, turning down work on moral grounds is likely to be seen as an unaffordable luxury. Nonetheless, whether lawyers work for mega-law firms or high-street practices, even attempting to persuade clients to consider the moral implications of representation is likely to be avoided for fear of their loss to competitors.[70] Similarly, an amoral stance is likely to be a condition of continued employment for the many lawyers who are employed by large law firms or other businesses.

The business context to lawyering also reinforces the neutrality principle where

---

[65] Section 6.   [66] Ch.3, section 7.
[67] Ipp 1998, p.84. See Ch.3, section 5.   [68] Galanter 1983, pp.158–9.
[69] 1985, p.635; 1994, p.679. See also D'Amato and Eberle 1983, p.770: 'the more an attorney is a "gun", the more likely she will be hired'.
[70] cf Lawry 1990, p.330: 'Whatever the pro-client stance means in psychological or moral terms, the economic factor is hidden not too far from the surface.'

large firms and other organisations have highly developed divisions of labour.[71] Here individual lawyers are likely to see moral responsibility for their activities as somehow 'floating' throughout the organisation[72] or 'falling between the players'[73] rather than attaching to them personally. Finally, the increasing specialisation of legal work is likely to reinforce the tendency of lawyers to see their work solely in terms of technical skill with a concomitant reduction in their concern with morality.[74]

3. CRITICISMS OF LAWYER BEHAVIOUR

3.1 The Role-Differentiation Thesis

We thus see that there is a strong case for arguing that all lawyers—whether acting as advocates or not—are likely to adopt a stance of neutral partisanship in their professional life. In the next chapter we will examine the alleged justifications for this role morality. First, however, it is necessary to understand what exactly is wrong with this role morality.

The starting point for most criticisms is the 'quite fundamental' universalistic dimension of morality[75] most strongly associated with Kant's categorical imperative which, as we have seen,[76] requires that ethical norms apply to all equally. Morality 'is not, after all, like a jacket which you may put on or take off perhaps exchanging it for a white coat'[77] (or, more pertinently, a wig and bands). From this perspective, professional role moralities are necessarily suspect in appearing to provide professionals with a special pleading[78] in resisting what is variously called 'universalistic', 'common', 'ordinary', or 'personal' morality.[79] However, notwithstanding the impression created by some of these terms and some critics,[80] this 'role-differentiation' criticism[81] does not necessarily entail a belief in objective moral standards which apply universally or which everyone shares in common. Nor, as the terms 'ordinary' and 'everyday' suggest, are lawyers necessarily being criticised for conduct that would be immoral if done in non-professional contexts by non-lawyers. Frequently, there are no 'everyday' analogues to specifically legal acts such as cross-examining witnesses,[82] whereas 'ordinary' people may be incapable, for example, of providing ingenious interpretations of laws to defeat their purpose. What is really being said is that their role morality requires or at least allows lawyers to do for clients what the lawyer or, if they were capable, most others would *not* do for

---

[71] See Ch.3, section 7.   [72] Bauman 1993, pp.19–20.   [73] Luban 1988, pp.123–5.
[74] Teschner 1970, pp.817–22.   [75] Wasserstrom 1983, p.28. See also Goldman 1980, pp.20–1.
[76] Ch.2, section 3.2.   [77] Freedman 1978a, p.1.
[78] Luban 1988a, p.109 and 1994, p.xiii. Cf also Luban 1981a, p.462.
[79] See eg Wasserstrom 1975 and 1983; Postema 1980, pp.64–5; Goldman 1980, ch.3; Luban 1980, p.462ff, 1983, pp.1–3, 1988a, esp ch.6, 1994, pp.xii–xiv; Bok 1990, pp.922–3; Elkins 1992, p.735.
[80] See Ch.8, section 3 regarding Goldman and Luban.
[81] See generally Emmet 1966; Veatch 1972a; Goldman 1980; Freedman 1978–79 and 1981; Martin 1981a and b; Gewirth 1986; and cf the more ambivalent approach of Bradley 1927, ch.V.
[82] Williams 1983, p.260; Haber and Baumrin 1988, pp.115–16.

themselves.[83] In other words, the complaint is that lawyers are claiming to be able to bring about with impunity the sort of consequences which they or others would clearly regard as immoral or unjust were the context not that of legal representation.

Before examining this complaint in more detail, it needs to be noted that it is only the strictest of Kantians or existentialists like Sartre,[84] who require individual authenticity of the purest kind, that are likely to reject role morality *per se*. Many social scientists would argue that we always act in terms of one role or other[85] and hence that all morality is role morality.[86] Indeed, it is clear that the complexity of social existence makes it difficult to speak of morality without reference to the contexts in which individuals act and the roles they occupy.[87] While there may be an 'ordinary' morality, certain principles may only pertain to certain persons in certain roles.[88] For example, only debtors are expected to pay debts, doctors and nurses to care for patients, etc. The idea of an undifferentiated 'universalistic' morality has also been rejected as undesirable.[89] Most obviously, a moral division of labour facilitates the achievement of certain valuable social functions.[90] Thus, to enable surgeons to cure patients we excuse them from the general moral prohibition on wounding—indeed, we rename their acts as 'surgery'.[91] Moreover, according to Held, if everyone was 'equally concerned about the whole of morality all the time' they might dismiss all morality as 'hopelessly complicated, irrelevant or vague' and hence be less likely to be moved by moral considerations and more likely to seek to evade responsibility for their actions. It is thus better for moral agents to concentrate on manageable segments of morality reflected in roles, rather than trying to do 'the entire job of morality all at once and single-handedly'.[92] Consequently, when 'ordinary' morality recognises the complexity of social existence and the diversity of role-differentiated behaviour, it can be said to be 'just doing what it does everywhere ordinarily'.[93]

For two reasons, however, this does not mean that all morality is role morality.[94] First, individuals sometimes have to make choices about their role moralities: whether to occupy or abandon a role and its associated morality; how to resolve conflicts between the moral requirements of different roles or between competing interests within a particular role. Here, they cannot rely on the role morality in question; they must rely on moral values not specific to particular role moralities. Secondly, the idea that all morality is constituted by role morality simply does not accord

---

[83] cf Luban 1983a, p.1; Heffernan 1985, p.44.   [84] See Sartre 1957.
[85] See eg Park 1950, p.249; Goffman 1959, p.19. cf also Held 1983, pp.66–7. Indeed, some go further and argue that an individual's sense of self (or more accurately, selves) is indistinguishable from their roles.
[86] cf Luban 1988, p.107ff.
[87] As a result many commentators regard the role-differentiation criticism of lawyers as misplaced: see eg Held 1983, pp.66–7; Williams 1983, pp.259–63; Schneyer 1984, pp.1534–7; Haber and Baumrin 1988, pp.115–17; Hazard 1989; Stier 1991, pp.560–4; Tur 1994, esp p.64.
[88] See esp Luban 1980, p.462.
[89] As long ago as Plato 1975, p.129 (iv. 433). See also Durkheim 1933, Preface, and 1992.
[90] Postema 1980, p.72.   [91] Luban 1988a, p.113.
[92] Held 1983, pp.64–5. See also Goldman 1980, pp.23–4.
[93] Held ibid, p.67, cited with approval by Haber and Baumrin 1988, p.116.
[94] See Downie 1971, p.129ff; Wasserstrom 1983, p.34; Luban 1988a, pp.109–10.

with our moral understandings. Thus when we say that it is wrong to murder we do not mean that it is wrong for parents to murder, for lawyers to murder, etc. What we mean is that murder is wrong for persons, as persons, not as occupants of particular roles that just all happen to include the injunction against murder. In other words, there is a morality that exists over and above particular role moralities.

However, as we have seen, instead of being directly in conflict with ordinary morality, particular role moralities might be simply an extension of it to specific situations. We thus need to see whether the role morality of neutral partisanship is so out of line with 'ordinary morality' that it requires the sort of specific justification discussed in the next chapter. That it does is suggested by the vitriol directed at lawyers over the centuries[95] and the fact that lawyers themselves seem incapable of completely assuaging their doubts about their role.[96] More specifically, it is argued that, in encouraging either excessive or insufficient zeal by lawyers, neutral partisanship leads to considerable harm to third parties and the general public, to lawyers themselves and even to the clients who are meant to benefit from this amoral role.

3.2 Excessive Zeal and Harm to Others[97]

The main criticism of neutral partisanship is that it leads to what is frequently called 'excessive zeal',[98] which in turn causes harm to a wide variety of interests.[99] One of the most oft-heard complaints relates to the 'instrumentalist'[100] approach of lawyers—and especially advocates—to truth, law and justice. As long ago as 1726, Jonathan Swift described lawyers as a 'society of men . . . bred up from youth in the art of proving by words multiplied for the purpose, that white is black and black is white, according as they are paid'.[101] Similarly, John Stuart Mill complained that '[The lawyer] hires himself out to do injustice or frustrate justice with his tongue'.[102] More recently, it has been said that, in being prepared to 'bend, fold and spindle, if not mutilate the facts and the law', the lawyer 'either cheats her way to justice or cheats justice'.[103]

[95] See Ch.1, section 1.

[96] See Pannick 1992, pp.6–7, 127, 156, and 165–7; Elkins 1992, p.764ff.

[97] This section draws on Frank 1973, ch.IV; Frankel 1980, Part I; Luban 1988a, chs.1 and 2; Pannick 1992; Rhode 1985, pp.597–604 and 1994, pp.667–73; Gerber 1987; Lawry 1990; McKenzie 1996, pp.34–40. More specific criticisms are referred to in the footnotes. Although the above works are largely North American, we take the view that the underlying situation is not so very different in the Anglo-Welsh system, though the manifestations of zeal may be sometimes less extreme or flamboyant given the rather more understated traditions of advocacy on this side of the Atlantic. We have sought to illustrate the points relied on so far as possible by reference to British cases and materials.

[98] In the UK see eg Ipp 1998, p.83. Other phrases include 'hyperzeal', 'overzealous representation', 'over representation' or the 'overvaluing' of client interests, 'hardball' lawyering and 'Rambo' mentality. In addition to the references in n.97 above, see Elkins 1992, p.738; Stier 1991, p.570ff.

[99] Sometimes conceded by neutral partisanship supporters: see Pannick 1992, pp.165–6.

[100] Luban 1998a, ch.2.

[101] *Gulliver's Travels* (1726) ch.5, quoted in Pannick 1992, p.128.

[102] In Bentham 1843, Vol.7, p.479.   [103] Luban 1988, pp.13–15.

It is the legal professions' cavalier attitude to 'truth'[104] which has perhaps generated most criticism: the fact that in order to achieve client goals, lawyers may go to
great lengths to make 'the true look false and the false look true'.[105] Lawyers have
even argued for one interpretation of the facts of a case one day and then, because
it suited their clients, for exactly the opposite the next day. While lawyers are prohibited from the most direct forms of dishonesty,[106] there are many ways of being
'economical with the *actualité*' as it has famously been put.[107] More specifically, 'not
merely believing but knowing a statement to be true', lawyers may 'do all that can
be done by sophistry, by rhetoric, by solemn asseveration, by indignant exclamation,
by gesture, by play of features, by terrifying one honest witness, by perplexing
another, to cause a jury to think that statement false'.[108] In addition to notorious
devices of cross-examination, advocates sometimes employ 'dirty tricks'[109] such as
distracting the court's attention from unfavourable testimony or argument,[110] pretending to possess a determinative document in order to intimidate a witness into
providing favourable evidence,[111] or using their client's children to help garner court
sympathy.[112]

Attempts to suppress the truth may also begin before trial. In this vein we should
not overlook the extent to which lawyers are actively engaged by clients to use the
law as a blunt instrument to suppress unpalatable truths. A recent example of this,
and many of the other problems of lawyer zeal, is the 'McLibel' case where lawyers
went to great lengths in attempting to prevent the unrepresented and indigent defendants from presenting, both publicly and before the court, their allegations of aggressive marketing of non-nutritious food, low wages and involvement in animal cruelty
and environmental destruction by the plaintiff corporation.[113] Once proceedings are
under way, in terms of what is sometimes called the 'Anatomy of a Murder' tactic,[114]

---

[104] cf the criticism of objective, absolute and foundationalist notions of truth in Ch.2. Nevertheless,
the criticisms remain valid even with a subjective notion of truth. See Frankel 1980, p.73; Nicolson 1994,
p.739.

[105] Schwartz 1988.   [106] See Ch.4, section 3.3.3; Ch.8, section 5.2.

[107] By Alan Clark, a lawyer turned politician, who was one of the Government ministers implicated
in the Matrix Churchill affair. For a brief account, see Economides and Webb 1998b, pp.103–5.

[108] Lord Macauley, quoted by Frankel 1980, p.30. Though cf *R v Foran* (1995) *The Times*, 31 March,
where the Court of Appeal expressed its disapproval of the practice of 'muck-raking' by defence lawyers
in attempts to discredit police officers, often with only the flimsiest of bases for their allegations.

[109] Luban 1993, p.1761.

[110] Described as 'dumb shows' by Gerber 1987, pp.15–17. See also Pannick 1992, p.28; du Cann
1993, p.53.

[111] See Napley 1993, pp.134–5. For other egs see Disney *et al* 1986, pp.899–901. This may come peri-
lously close to misleading the court.

[112] Pannick 1992, pp.27–8.

[113] Following the longest ever UK trial, McDonald's libel action was upheld by the High Court
in respect of 6 out of the company's 12 allegations made against London Greenpeace. On appeal
the company's damages of £60,000 were reduced by a further £20,000 when the Court of Appeal agreed
that two further allegations in the leaflet constituted fair comment. The trial is estimated to have cost
McDonald's £10m. See http://www.mcspotlight.org/case/index.html.

[114] After the 1958 book by Robert Travers. cf eg Bress 1966, pp.1496–7; Heffernan 1985, p.57
and the more ambivalent approach of Freedman 1966, pp.1478–80; 1975, pp.69–74; and 1990, pp.
156–9.

lawyers may outline the law to their clients before hearing their story in order to avoid being hampered by ethical rules[115] which limit court tactics when clients admit liability or make otherwise adverse admissions. They may shop around for favourable expert evidence, and perhaps even put pressure on experts to adapt or amend their opinions if they are not sufficiently favourable.[116]

In relation to discovery, lawyers may provide incomplete or evasive responses to discovery applications, or overlook or even connive in the non-disclosure of material evidence. Thus in the prosecution of Judith Ward, despite a duty on prosecutors to act as officers of the court, rather than as zealous partisans,[117] the prosecuting solicitor and a barrister (who has since taken silk) failed to disclose important information which helped contribute to her unjustified conviction.[118] Even more effective in obstructing the truth are the various tactics associated with 'rule exploitation',[119] and designed to prevent cases from getting to court at all by sapping the energy and resources of opponents. Examples include the creation of inordinate delays, frivolous counter-claims, spurious procedural manoeuvres,[120] misleading negotiation strategies, excessive requests for discovery, or 'Hiroshima'[121] responses to discovery which bury the opponent under a mound of irrelevant documents.[122]

Criticisms of lawyer tactics are not confined to positive attempts at being economical with the truth. Also included is the exploitation of an opponent's legal misunderstandings,[123] or the failure to reveal information likely to affect a client's negotiating position[124] or the court's decision.[125] Lawyers are also condemned for

[115] This is distinct from witness coaching *per se*, which the Anglo-Welsh codes prohibit, at least in the case of advocates: para. 607(b), CCB; para. 6.5(b) of Annex 21A, LSG (cf para. 21.10, LSG regarding non-advocate solicitors). See further Wydick 1995, pp.5–8, for a comparative analysis of US and English practice.

[116] 'Lawyers lean on expert witnesses to alter opinions' *The Times*, 13 October 1997, p.8.

[117] See Ch.8 at nn.68 and 168–9.

[118] Tur 1992a, p.231. See also Ashworth 1998, pp.11–16, regarding similar prosecutorial abuses in other miscarriages of justice.

[119] 'Such exploitation is endemic in the system: the complexity of civil procedure itself enables the financially stronger or more experienced party to spin out proceedings and escalate costs by litigating on technical procedural points or peripheral issues instead of focusing on the real substance of the case': Woolf 1995, p.27.

[120] cf the recently collapsed English tobacco litigation. Here the companies took the claimants through the courts twice on procedural issues, first (quite legitimately) on their potential liability for costs (see *Hodgson v Imperial Tobacco Ltd* (1998) *The Times*, 12 February), and then again, successfully alleging that the majority of claims were statute-barred under the Limitation Act. The combined effect was to close down the claimants' capacity to continue with the main action, both procedurally and financially. The companies' costs have been estimated at around £9 million. See *Financial Times*, 7 December, 10 February 1998; *The Times*, 27 June 1998 and 27 February 1999.

[121] Rhode 1985, p.597. But cf du Cann 1993, p.95, who argues that delaying tactics are rare in Britain. If so, then the McLibel case (above n.113) provides one such 'rare' example. Cf also the assumptions underpinning the Woolf reforms, n.119 above; though whether the primary cause of delay is tactics or inefficiency is unclear.

[122] In part these problems have also reflected failure by the judiciary to use their powers to curb discovery excesses. See Woolf 1995, pp.27, 106.

[123] But cf Ch.8, n.111, regarding the lawyer's duty to disclose adverse legal provisions.

[124] See eg Luban 1988a, pp.149–50.   [125] See further Ch.8, section 6.2.1.

manipulating law and the legal process to suit client ends.[126] Examples include the pleading of procedural technicalities—like the parole evidence rule—to defeat meritorious claims, sophistical interpretations offered to defeat the spirit and purpose of laws, and 'forum shopping' for the most favourable court.[127]

In deontological terms, lawyer instrumentalism can be regarded as intrinsically wrong irrespective of its consequences. If not actually dishonest, it fails to uphold the standards of probity and honourable behaviour one might expect of professionals. The willingness of lawyers to dance to their clients' tune also suggests (to the public at least) hypocrisy, and a failure of the sort of moral integrity emphasised by virtue ethics.[128] For instance, advocates may appear to put not just their technical skills, but their reputation and even soul into arguing their cases.[129] They can express indignation at suggestions of client wrongdoing, pull the heartstrings of juries and make self-righteous appeals to the very notions of truth and justice that they seem intent on bending to their purpose. Yet if retained by the other side, they can just as easily and with equal warmth argue the opposite.[130] They may push the boundaries of legitimate zeal to the detriment of others even where they have sympathy for the causes of those others.[131]

Lawyer behaviour is criticised not just for its alleged intrinsic immorality, but also for its harmful consequences. Some critics are worried about the impact on law's authority, which is said to be based on the premise of equal applications to all, and which is undermined by lawyers manipulating law, procedure and facts in order to ensure that their clients 'need not play by the same rules as the rest of us'.[132] Similarly, Gordon has argued that evasion of the law provides 'a recipe for total sabotage of the legal framework', given that law requires a large degree of voluntary compliance.[133]

Other critics are more concerned that excessive zeal leads 'to atrocities against other combatants and mounting casualties among the civilian population'.[134] The harm to litigants with meritorious cases who suffer defeat at the hands of excessively zealous lawyers is obvious. Less obvious is the more widespread harm caused when such cases establish unjust precedents. Moreover, whatever the outcome of cases, litigants and witnesses may have to undergo abusive cross-examination or similar indignities, or face additional costs, vexation and strain when cases are unduly extended by litigation tactics. A particular target of criticism (and not just for feminists) is the use of past sexual history and innuendo to cast aspersions on the *mores* of complainants in

---

[126] cf Louis XII, quoted in Luban 1988a, p.15: 'Lawyers use the law as shoemakers use leather; rubbing it, pressing it, and stretching it with their teeth, all to the end of making it fit their purposes'.

[127] ibid, p.14.

[128] See esp Wasserstrom 1975, p.14 and the writers referred to in section 3.3, below.

[129] See eg Pannick 1992, pp.153–4.   [130] See at n.172, below.

[131] See Nadel 1993, chs.7–8 *passim* and p.152, regarding the prosecutor in Sara Thornton's trial and see generally Pannick 1992, esp pp.1–2.

[132] Luban 1988a, esp ch.2. See also Simon 1978 and 1988; Lowry 1990.

[133] Gordon 1988, pp.20–1.   [134] Atkinson 1992, pp.857–8.

rape and other sexual offence cases.[135] Nor has this reliance on sexism by lawyers been confined to defence lawyers. As Sara Thornton's trial for the murder of her violent spouse illustrates,[136] prosecutors may similarly play the sexual morality card, notwithstanding its doubtful relevance and the codes' prohibition on prosecutorial zeal.[137]

The potential for lawyers causing widespread harm is perhaps even greater outside litigation. For instance, the interests of company employees and consumers may be prejudicially affected by lawyer involvement in negotiations and the drafting of *pro forma* contracts. There are well-documented cases of lawyers advising and assisting profit-driven companies with activities leading to death, serious injury, huge financial loss to investors and widespread environmental damage.[138] And lest it be thought that such incidents are confined to America, we might well ask how the sale of weapons to repressive regimes, the lobbying of government by cigarette companies or the current desecration by British-based oil companies of the environment and human rights of those who live in underdeveloped countries could occur entirely without lawyer knowledge or assistance. Finally, there are also instances of more indirect harm, such as where ingenious tax evasion schemes reduce the amount of money available for public spending, or where the social or regulatory objectives of state agencies are obstructed by lawyers on spurious technical grounds.[139]

3.3 Harm to Lawyers[140]

For the critics of lawyers, at least, the above examples of lawyer behaviour encouraged or at least condoned by neutral partisanship are immoral. On the other hand, such conduct might not breach lawyers' own personal morality or, if it does, they might—for the reasons discussed in the next chapter—regard it as justified by the overall value of client representation. For example, criminal defence lawyers may argue that zealously defending clients who have confessed guilt, even if this requires abusively cross-examining rape complainants, is ultimately justified by the need to ensure that no one is convicted without clear proof.[141] Nevertheless, as this example might suggest,[142] most lawyers will probably be troubled at some time or another by having to commit unsavoury acts in the fulfilment of their allegedly valuable amoral role.

[135] See eg Adler 1987, ch.6; Luban, 1988a, pp.150–2 and 1990b, pp.1026–35; Kennedy 1992, pp.114–15; Wright 1994–95; Lees 1996; and, more ambivalently, Blake and Ashworth 1998, pp.26, 33. The legislative attempt in English law to make this strategy exceptional has been substantially undercut by judicial practice: Temkin 1993; Lees 1996, ch.5.

[136] Nadel 1993, ch.7.   [137] See Ch.8 at nn.68 and 168–9.

[138] See Heyman and Liebman 1988, pp.184–97.   [139] Gordon 1988, p.72.

[140] This section draws heavily on Postema 1980 and 1983. For similar analyses, see Flynn 1976; Williams 1983; Eshete 1983; Kleinberger 1989. cf also Simon 1988, ch.5 for a rather different but equally apt analysis.

[141] But cf Ch.8, section 5.3.   [142] cf Hall 1990; Raymond 1990; Elkins 1992, p.764ff.

Now it is possible that some will respond to this problem of 'dirty hands'[143] by facing up to and dealing with the tension and strain arising from any conflict between personal and professional morality. According to Postema, 'responsible' lawyers do not abandon the moral precepts they bring to their professional work but attempt to reconcile them with the demands of professional morality by '*taking* responsibility (or at least sharing responsibility) for the harm done, the rights violated, the values sacrificed, and acting in ways appropriate under the circumstances to assuming such responsibility'.[144]

The alternative approach[145] to perceived conflicts between professional and personal morality is exemplified by Montaigne's assertion that he was able to

concern myself with public affairs without moving the length of my nail from myself, and give myself to others without taking anything from myself. . . . The mayor and Montaigne have always been two people clearly separated. There's no reason why a lawyer or a banker should not recognise the knavery that is part of his vocation. An honest man is not responsible for the vices or stupidity of his calling, and need not refuse to practise them. They are customs in his country and there is profit in them. A man must live in the world and avail himself of what he finds there.[146]

Under this 'strategy of detachment', lawyers ignore the apparent conflict between their 'ordinary' morality and professional obligations and shift their attachment to more material goals such as the attainment of wealth, power and status, and/or to gaining pleasure through winning cases and exercising their technical skills.[147] Psychologically this involves lawyers viewing their 'self' as hermetically sealed from the morally problematic aspects of their professional role. Accordingly, they can refuse to accept any responsibility for harm caused or values violated by their professional acts. Such acts are simply not their own. Instead, responsibility is that of the client, their profession, the law or other institutions which allow such acts.[148]

At least two psychological factors suggest that lawyers are more likely to adopt the Montaigne response to moral dilemmas. First, it is seductive in making life comfortable.[149] What would otherwise be intractable moral dilemmas giving rise to anxiety and uncertainty[150] can be deftly avoided by adopting the reassuring position

---

[143] cf Walzer 1973. cf also Postema's reference to 'professional knavery': 1983, p.288, echoing Montaigne, quoted at n.146, below.

[144] 1983, pp.290–1 and see also at p.309.

[145] In fact Postema distinguishes two sub-strategies in this approach—the 'schizophrenic' and 'restricted identification'. However, as the subtle differences between them are irrelevant to our discussion, we shall treat them as one.

[146] *IV Essays de Montaigne* (1876), quoted (with approval) in Curtis 1951, p.20.

[147] For an example of such an attitude, see Curtis 1951, p.19ff. See also Pannick 1992, p.1.

[148] cf Fried's distinction between institutional and personal harms: 1976, pp.1084–7.

[149] See Wasserstrom 1975, p.9 and 1983, pp.29–30; Simon 1978, p.103. But cf Freedman 1978, p.195, who argues that it is at least as seductive for lawyers to impose their morality on clients.

[150] Psychological theory emphasises that we cannot long sustain positions of 'disequilibrium' or 'cognitive dissonance' caused by threats to our attitudes or values, but need to find a resolution. See Flanagan 1991, pp.191, 288. This of course does not determine that we choose the easy over the hard path, or the better over the worse one.

that it is the lawyer's job to pursue client interests, not to stand in moral judgement over them, and that moral responsibility for the consequences rests elsewhere. In this way, moral dilemmas can be turned into purely technical legal problems and the exercise of specialist knowledge and skills can be seen as a source of public status, power over clients and personal satisfaction. Secondly, the very nature of legal representation may require lawyers to act as extensions of their clients' moral personality, by using their skills to put the client's point of view in the best possible light, even when fundamentally rejected by the lawyer.[151] This creates a huge temptation to see the moral implications of legal representation as the client's responsibility.

Moral detachment has, however, important implications for the lawyer's moral integrity. In terms of virtue ethics, 'integrity' implies not just a sense of honesty and honour, but a moral 'wholeness' that sits uncomfortably with modern notions of role-differentiated morality. Just as truck drivers might be expected to display regret and feel responsibility for accidentally causing serious injury,[152] so might one expect lawyers to regret any harm they cause, even if it can be justified. Moral detachment may also involve self-deception and bad faith. Lawyers cannot so easily wish away the apparent conflict between one's ordinary morality and professional obligations by attempting to place responsibility for all harmful action on clients, the profession and the institutions of law, not least because they have freely entered their profession.[153] Seeking pleasure in the exercise of technical skills may similarly evidence bad faith. To experience such pleasure requires an identification with one's work. But how many lawyers are likely to disown the morally creditable, as well as the morally discreditable, consequences of the exercise of their skills? Finally, along with Aristotle and other virtue ethicists, one may take issue with Montaigne's claim that individuals can entirely separate their professional from their non-professional life. It seems inevitable that an individual's character will bear the traces of their work.[154] With lawyers, this is likely to result in their organs of moral conscience atrophying.[155] At best, they will become morally cynical or amoral in their non-professional dealings.[156] At worst, they may begin to prize attributes like cunning, manipulation and humiliation, which may be necessary for success in professional life but offensive in private life.[157]

---

[151] See Wasserstrom 1975, p.14.

[152] See Postema 1980, pp.68–9, echoing certain virtue ethicists, and Ch.2, section 5.2.

[153] cf Mellinkoff 1973, p.250. Pepper 1986a has argued, *contra*, that the obligation to adopt the amoral role is stronger because one has freely chosen that role. Given the lack of discussion of lawyers' ethics in the UK, it is doubtful whether this element of 'informed' choice applies here. In any event, we have argued that it is at least equally arguable that to adopt the role without taking responsibility for its consequences is an implausible abnegation of lawyer autonomy and dangerous denial of social responsibility.

[154] In addition to the references in n.140, see eg Hazard 1974, p.28; Wasserstrom 1975, p.15; Elkins 1978, pp.749 and 760; Kronman 1987.

[155] See also Rhode 1985, p.626; Atkinson 1992, pp.57–8.

[156] As even apologists for neutral partisanship are willing to admit: Pannick 1992, p.235. See also Wolf 1983, pp.51–3; Rhode, ibid.

[157] cf Eshete 1983, pp.274–5, who notes that over time lawyer amorality may develop into general immorality.

This invites the cynical response that lawyers are amply compensated for this particular 'occupational disease'.[158] But this response comes too quickly if one is concerned about the harmful acts flowing from neutral partisanship. Lawyers who have become amoral or even immoral in their private lives are less likely to be perturbed by having to dirty their hands at work. Moreover, a lawyer who is untroubled by causing harm necessary for some greater good is far less likely to be vigilant about causing harm when it is unnecessary.[159] In other words, the moral detachment to which many lawyers are driven by neutral partisanship is likely to increase the chances of lawyers being inclined to exercise all necessary zeal on behalf of clients irrespective of moral considerations. Moral detachment and its causes form a vicious circle. Lawyers may come to the profession with a personal morality which values integrity, respect for the law and the avoidance of harm to others. However, either persuaded to exercise excessive zeal because of the perceived values of neutral partisanship or forced to do so because of the institutional factors, lawyers may over time retreat into moral detachment. This, in turn, is likely to lead to a shutting down of moral conscience, thereby making it easier for lawyers to exercise zeal irrespective of the harm caused or other moral values violated.

3.4 Insufficient Zeal and Harm to Clients

Paradoxically, the moral detachment strategy associated with neutral partisanship may also lead to the opposite problem of excessive zeal, namely the provision of inferior legal services and the exercise of insufficient zeal. Numerous studies[160] have established that lawyers frequently provide inadequate services and that zeal is often diluted because of various institutional constraints on lawyers, such as the demands of profitability or the unwillingness to jeopardise harmonious relationships with their colleagues, judges, court officials and others who they have to deal with on a day to day basis. Indeed, it is arguable that this 'under-representation'[161] of clients is as great an ethical problem as their over-representation through excessive zeal and that what is really needed is a strengthening of the neutral partisanship conception to ensure an uncompromising attachment to client interests. This, however, ignores that a lawyer's ability and willingness to provide adequate and sufficiently zealous client representation might well be undermined by the principle of neutrality and its related strategy of moral detachment.[162]

Moral detachment can be said to lead to alienation from others. According to Postema, being unable to reconcile or integrate conflicting images of themselves as professionals and non-professionals, lawyers are less likely to be able to understand

---

[158] Pannick 1992, p.235.   [159] cf Williams 1978, p.64.

[160] See eg Baldwin and McConville 1977; McConville 1998; Davis 1994. See also Pannick 1992, p.3 and ch.7 regarding the incompetence of many advocates.

[161] See Rhode 1994, pp.676–82 *passim*.

[162] In addition to the arguments canvassed below, see Eshete 1983, pp.280–2. See also Ch.7, section 3.2.2, regarding the problem of the 'non-representation of clients' (Rhode 1994, pp.680–2).

others and their roles.[163] Similarly, having shut down or compartmentalised their own moral consciences, it is likely that lawyers are less able to recognise the moral personality of their clients and will thus tend to treat them not as whole persons, but simply in terms of their perceived material interests.[164]

As Simon argues,[165] many clients will approach lawyers without clearly defined goals, especially when they are unaware of the legal options open to them. Clarification of these goals necessarily involves exploring the moral implications of the various legal options. However, the principle of neutrality discourages lawyers from such an examination. Consequently, relying on their own values or on paternalistic assumptions about those of the clients, lawyers might lead clients to agree to legal solutions which they would have rejected had the various possible alternatives been explored. For example, women charged with killing their batterers might not want to attempt to escape imprisonment because they feel the need for moral expiation through a brief jail sentence which could follow pleading guilty to manslaughter.[166] But seeking an acquittal might be the obvious road to a lawyer unwilling to engage with his client in the sort of way required by feminist and dialogical ethics.

Neutral partisanship and moral detachment is also likely to prevent the development of *phronesis* which, as we have seen,[167] is rooted in 'ordinary moral beliefs, attitudes, feelings and relationships'[168] and which is extremely useful in professional contexts where novel situations arise.[169] Moral detachment may also hamper effective lawyering in the sense that moral arguments may play important roles in legal argumentation.[170] Lawyers who have shut off their moral faculties are less able to manufacture such arguments than are those with deep moral sentiments. To this extent, it can be said that the neutrality principle undermines rather than complements that of partisanship even where lawyers strive to do their best for clients.

However, as we have seen, by no means do all lawyers strive to do their best for their clients. While written discourses on professional legal ethics certainly encourage lawyers to exercise the utmost zeal, the rules allow them a broad discretion to exercise greater or lesser zeal. Such zeal can be so warm as to run the risk of breaching professional norms on proper behaviour, or it can be so minimal as to come close to incompetence. However, according to the neutral partisanship conception and its allied strategy of detachment, the question as to how much zeal lawyers should exercise in particular cases ought not to be answered by considerations of morality.

Moreover, with the shutting down of moral feeling may also come a shutting down of related feelings of empathy, sympathy and concern. Having detached themselves from moral sentiments, lawyers can no longer see clients in their full humanity. The lawyer becomes interested only 'in that part of the client that lies within his or her

---

[163] Postema 1983, p.298.   [164] Postema 1980, pp.80–1.   [165] 1978, pp.52–9.
[166] cf ibid, pp.56–8.   [167] Ch.2, section 5.
[168] Postema 1980, p.78. See further Postema 1980, p.68ff and 1983, p.306ff.
[169] See also Kronman 1987 and 1993.
[170] cf Postema 1980, p.79. Cf Hunt 1999 on the implications for lawyers of the Human Rights Act 1998.

special competency'.[171] The plight of clients and the possibility of them possessing the moral high ground are unlikely to lawyers who come to see clients as 'the divorce', 'the taking without owner's consent' or 'no. 20, Queens Road'. This situation is given bathetic force by the comment of Paul Hill, one of the Guildford Four who spent years in jail following his wrongful conviction for murder, that he 'got the impression that any of our barristers could easily have . . . taken over the running of the prosecution.'[172]

Having detached themselves from feelings of morality and humanity, it is likely lawyers will ration zeal according to more material considerations: by the client's status, whether they are one-off or regular clients, by the need to maintain salubrious relationships with those with whom they regularly deal, etc., but above all by their ability to pay. A lawyer's time and energy are not infinite and given the pressures to provide legal services as a profitable business, money is likely to be the quid pro quo for zeal, and to paraphrase Luban: the more quid, the more pro. Consequently, there is no paradox in saying that the lawyer's amoral role both encourages excessive and insufficient zeal. Everything depends on who the client is, how wealthy and powerful she is and on other material constraints on the lawyer. Conversely, little or nothing depends on the morality, politics or justice of the particular case.

4. CONCLUSION

It should be obvious from our discussion why, as an occupation, lawyers are particularly singled out for criticism and public opprobrium. On their own, the principles of partisanship and neutrality appear relatively innocuous.[173] Many professional and non-professional occupations are prepared to assist or provide services to the public without vetting them on moral grounds. No one criticises doctors for helping to cure those with morally reprehensible beliefs even if they go on to cause harm on recovery. Equally, there are professions and occupations which act as partisans, such as politicians who zealously pursue their constituents' interests. Indeed, lawyer zeal is often highly desirable and it is its absence that may equally be the subject of criticism. History and popular culture[174] are replete with examples of zealous lawyers fighting against all the odds to ensure that truth will out, justice is done and the civil liberties of the downtrodden are protected. Who would not want a lawyer to do their utmost for one's own case?

It is thus not lawyer zeal *per se* which is problematic, nor indeed moral neutrality, but the fact that such zeal is exercised irrespective of considerations of morality; the fact that lawyers will act zealously whether or not this ensures truth or justice,

---

[171] Wasserstrom 1975, p.21.

[172] *Stolen Years* (with Ronan Bennet) 1990, p.126, quoted in Pannick 1992, p.132.

[173] Simon 1978, p.37; Luban 1994, pp.xiv–xv.

[174] See eg Lawry 1990, pp.336 and 362; Elkins 1992, pp.740–3; Pannick's discussion of Rumpole 1992 *seriatim*.

whether their clients are oppressed or oppressing, and whether this protects or violates civil liberties. The only other occupations with a similar role morality are civil servants and mercenaries. However, the loyalty of civil servants is not available to the highest bidder; it is—or ought to be—owed to democratically elected governments, whereas mercenaries—the original hired guns—hardly represent a plausible model for professional ethics. We can thus see that, unlike in the case of doctors and nurses whose social functions seems to be intrinsically good, it cannot be said of lawyers that 'it is intrinsically good to try to win every lawsuit or help every client realise his or her objectives'.[175]

And when we turn to the ethical theories canvassed in Chapter 2, whether of an orthodox or critical nature, they appear to give neutral partisanship little support. Thus many deontologists would condemn as intrinsically wrong the sort of lawyer behaviour which approximates lying and the causing of harm to others. Virtue ethicists, as we have seen, would regard the impact of neutral partisanship on the lawyer's character as invidious, while feminists and postmodernists would reject neutral partisanship for preventing lawyers from weighing up client needs against those of others as well as discouraging lawyers from paying proper attention to client needs. It is only on rule-consequentialist grounds and on the basis of respect for the values of some contemporary deontologists that neutral partisanship can be justified. It is to these justifications we now turn.

[175] Wasserstrom 1975, p.13.

7

Justifying Neutral Partisanship

Devoted and unequivocal representation of a particular client will *ex proprio vigoro* satisfy a lawyer's duty to society. . . .

Paul A. Teschner[1]

[T]he individual lawyer does a morally worthy thing whomever he serves. . . .

Charles Fried[2]

1. INTRODUCTION

In classic role-differentiation terms, supporters of neutral partisanship regard the lawyer's role as justifying or at least excusing their actions on behalf of clients. The fact that lawyers act not in terms of their personal morality—what we shall call moral activism—but in terms of the accepted morality of their role is said to make the moral difference. Indeed, the lawyer's role is itself said to be a moral good and moral activism a moral evil.

The argument is not that every individual act by morally neutral lawyers is justi-fied. Instead, along rule-consequentialist lines,[3] it is—or at least has to be[4]—argued that, while neutral partisanship might lead to isolated cases of harm and immoral-ity, on balance it results in more good than harm.[5] When it comes to justifying this conclusion, British professional legal ethics discourse has largely focused on crimi-nal defence work, apparently assuming that the image of lawyers as fearless knights in shining armour protecting defenceless individuals against an oppressive state applies equally to all legal work.[6] In fact, as we shall see,[7] special considerations apply to criminal defence work. When it comes to justifying neutral partisanship outside criminal defence work, we have to draw on a well-developed American literature[8] which is only faintly echoed in Britain and even then only in relation to advocacy.[9] From this literature we can identify three main[10] arguments supporting neutral partisanship: it is essential to the adversary system; it promotes human dignity,

---

[1] Teschner 1970, p.838.   [2] Fried 1978, p.1078.
[3] See Williams 1983, p.261ff; Luban 1981a, pp.464–5 and 1988a, pp.116–17.
[4] Although the arguments in section 3 are not framed in this way, we will argue that in fact they can only work in consequentialist form.
[5] But cf Held 1983, p.67, who relies simply on lawyers' specialist skills and knowledge—an argument which would be enough to justify public executions if performed by skilful executioners (cf Martin 1981b, p.633).
[6] This is especially true of the cab-rank rule's supporters: see section 3.1, below and more generally, Pannick 1992, ch.5. But cf contra Cranston 1995, pp.22–3, 33; Brindle and Dehn 1995, p.130.
[7] Section 3.2, below.   [8] For an excellent overview, see Goldman, 1980, ch.3.
[9] See at nn.16–18, 77.   [10] See section 5 for supporting arguments.

autonomy, and equality; and it upholds the institutions of the liberal state. These claims are supported by a number of narrower arguments.

However, it does not take much reflection to realise that the argument that neutral partisans are necessary for certain institutions or values cannot justify the lawyer's amoral role unless they are themselves justified. Otherwise, for instance, South African security policemen could justify committing human rights atrocities simply because their actions were essential to apartheid. In other words, justifying neutral partisanship must involve a two-tier form of argumentation.[11] First, it is argued that neutral partisanship is necessary for some institutions—the adversary system or the system of liberal government—and certain social values—dignity, autonomy, and equality. Second, it is argued that these institutions or values are themselves valuable. In order to be persuasive, both tiers of the argument need to be satisfied.

2. NEUTRAL PARTISANSHIP AND THE ADVERSARIAL SYSTEM

2.1 The Arguments

Given the close links between neutral partisanship and adversariality which we noted earlier,[12] it is not surprising that the most pervasive—indeed, almost the only—justification for neutral partisanship in Britain[13] is its alleged necessity for the effective operation of the adversarial system. This overlooks the obvious point that if the system's fair and effective operation assumes both a neutral arbiter and opponents seeking to ensure a favourable result by the fullest investigation and presentation of the facts and law, then the 'adversary system excuse'[14] cannot be relied upon where either neutral arbiters or the clash of equal adversaries is missing. In other words, this argument can only justify neutral partisanship in litigation (and at a push perhaps also negotiations in the shadow of the courts). Moreover, given the many constraints on the prosecution in criminal cases, the argument can only apply to civil litigation.

The first tier of the 'adversary system excuse' argues that without zealous advocates unconcerned by the immorality of client ends or the means to those ends, one cannot be sure that everything that could be said for each competing party will be brought before the courts, thus harming the quality of decisions and litigants' interests. For the purposes of this discussion, we can assume that neutral partisanship is at least extremely useful for the adversarial system's functioning, although—as we shall see—some of its excesses may be counter-productive. What is important is to establish that the adversarial system itself is justified. And here British

[11] A fact not generally appreciated in Britain: but cf section 2.1.
[12] Ch.6, section 2.2.
[13] Macmillan 1937, pp.175–6; Napley 1991, p.61; Pannick 1992, pp.149 and 152–3; Ipp 1998, p.64.
[14] Luban 1983b.

discourse has largely[15] relied on unsubstantiated references to 'belief',[16] the lessons of 'experience'[17] and a rhetorical comparison with 'totalitarian' legal systems in which civil liberties were deliberately repressed in favour of state interests.[18]

In North America,[19] however, the adversarial system is more explicitly linked to the promotion of three goals: truth, the citizen's legal rights, and perceptions of procedural fairness. Some argue that these goals are *best* promoted by adversariality, whereas others simply assert that the adversarial system does promote them, without any comparative claim being made. In our view only the comparative argument is appropriate. It is pointless establishing that the adversarial system promotes certain admittedly valued goals, when another procedural system does as good a job yet eschews neutral partisanship. All things being equal, the non-comparative arguments may effectively work to justify the system's retention, but not the practice of neutral partisanship. Consequently, we will assume that to justify neutral partisanship the adversarial system must be shown to promote truth, the citizen's legal rights, or perceptions of fairness more effectively than procedural systems where neutral partisanship does not apply.[20]

In addressing this question, we will compare those aspects of Anglo-Welsh procedure which seem to be intrinsic to adversariality with an ideal type of inquisitorial procedure used in continental Europe,[21] given the socio-economic and political similarities between Western European countries and the United Kingdom, and the fact that lawyers in inquisitorial systems do not act as neutral partisans.[22] By contrast to party control over the investigation and presentation of cases, and the adjudicator's limited and passive role in adversarial trials, inquisitorial proceedings are structured more like scientific investigations. Here, neutral investigators investigate the facts of cases, presenting their written findings to the court which seeks to determine the correct decision by examining witnesses under the parties' guidance but not control.

---

[15] But cf at nn.24 and 25.   [16] Pannick 1992, p.149.

[17] *D v NSPCC* [1978] AC 171, 231F–G. See also Sydney Smith *Sydney Smith's Works* vol ii, p.19, cited in Rogers 1899, pp.262–3 ('found, experimentally'); and MacMillan 1937, p.175 ('proved')—neither of which are substantiated.

[18] *D v NSPCC*, ibid; Pannick 1992, p.168.

[19] For an overview, see Landsman 1984, ch.5; Freedman 1990, ch.2 and from a more critical stance, Luban 1983a; and 1988a, ch.5; Belliotti 1988, pp.23ff; Mackenzie 1996. The subsequent discussion draws heavily on these writers with more specific references being provided where relevant.

[20] Consequently, we will ignore arguments that could apply equally to inquisitorial systems: cf Simon 1978, pp.92ff; Hazard 1978a, p.120.

[21] We have opted for this approach because all Western legal systems contain adversarial or inquisitorial elements mixed in different proportions and because there are a number of aspects of common law and civilian legal procedure which do not seem intrinsic to adversarial or inquisitorial methods, respectively, but which for various historical reasons have become closely associated with one or other of the two procedural families: see Damaska 1986, pp.3–6. For example, juries, orality, the 'day-in-court' idea and most importantly, the 'overprotection' of criminal defendants against state power are commonly but mistakenly associated with adversarial justice. By contrast, Continental systems are usually thought to involve career judges, rigid rules, and reliance on official documentation.

[22] While they are subject to the principle of neutrality, they are not expected to act solely as their clients' partisan: Simon 1978, p.47.

2.2 Evaluating the Arguments

2.2.1 *The Adversarial System and Truth*

Whatever other values dispute resolution systems might seek to promote, few would deny that truth should rank very highly. In the absence of strong reasons,[23] there seems to be little justification for judicial fact finders not seeking maximum factual accuracy. Consequently, one argument for the adversary system's superiority is that it is best suited to ascertaining true facts.[24] As one English judge asserted: 'truth is best discovered by powerful statements on both sides of the question.'[25]

Unfortunately, however, this claim is impossible to verify empirically.[26] Not only is it impossible to establish the comparative factual accuracy of particular systems since none exists in pure adversarial or inquisitorial form, but it is impossible to verify the accuracy of any adjudicative decision. No one can ever really know what the 'true' facts of particular disputes are. Litigants and witnesses know when they are consciously lying, but human errors in memory, perception and recall[27] mean that even honest witnesses can seriously distort the 'truth'. As Luban puts it: 'A trial is not a quiz show with the right answer waiting in a sealed envelope.'[28] Consequently, the arguments for the adversarial system's superiority rest upon a mixture of analogies with other disciplines, conjecture, and intuitive 'armchair psychology',[29] backed up by some laboratory experiments. Nevertheless, the influence of this cocktail makes it necessary to examine its ingredients more closely.

The argument by analogy relies on the allegation that other disciplines develop knowledge through claim and counterclaim.[30] But even if true, it can hardly be argued that courtroom proceedings imitate the generally sincere and honest investigation and presentation of evidence by scientists and social scientists.[31] Their research is not hampered by evidentiary rules preventing the disclosure of decisive information on the grounds of some greater value. It might occasionally happen, but it hardly fits with the scientific ethos, that researchers act like lawyers and conceal and ignore all evidence that does not support their hypotheses.

Initially more persuasive are two 'armchair psychology' arguments. The first—sometimes called 'the Fuller thesis'[32]—argues that there is a 'natural tendency' for fact investigators and evaluators to convert into fixed conclusions theories of cases developed as preliminary diagnoses in order to bring cases into some order and to

[23] See at section 3.2 below, regarding criminal trials.
[24] See Pannick 1992, pp.149, 152, and 247. The advantages of the adversary system as regards truth-finding are even accepted by some of its fiercest critics: see Frank 1973; Frankel 1980.
[25] Lord Chancellor Eldon in *Ex parte Lloyd* (1822) Montagu's Reports 70n, 72, cited with approval in *Jones v National Coal Board* [1957] 2 QB 55, 63.
[26] cf the endless stream of contradictory claims and findings cited by Freedman 1990, pp.26–39 *passim* and Schlesinger *et al* 1989, pp.337ff.
[27] See eg Jackson 1995, ch.10.
[28] 1988a, p.68.   [29] ibid, p.69.   [30] eg Held 1983, p.69.
[31] Luban 1988a, pp.69–70; Belliotti 1988, p.24. See also Gross 1987, p.742.
[32] Fuller and Randall 1958 and Fuller 1971. Quotations below are taken from Fuller and Randall 1958, p.1160.

provide a basis for evaluating testimony. Consequently 'all that confirms the diagnosis makes a strong imprint on the mind while all that runs counter to it is received with diverted attention'. This, however, is remedied by an adversary's presentation of evidence holding the case 'in suspension between two opposing interpretations', leaving 'time to explore all of its peculiarities and nuances'. The second argument alleges that those seeking to win cases have greater incentives than neutral investigators to investigate the facts thoroughly, especially where the facts initially found are unfavourable. Consequently, courts are likely to be presented with more facts under the adversarial system.

Both hypotheses have been confirmed by experiments simulating evidence gathering and presentation in adversarial and inquisitorial settings.[33] However, not only has their methodology been criticised,[34] but one can question whether laboratory experiments effectively replicate the special atmosphere, undercurrents and dynamics of trials and in particular the dramatic personal confrontations of adversarial trials.[35] Reading statements of facts to students hardly resembles the presentation of facts by advocates relying on rhetoric and various tactical devices to persuade fact adjudicators.[36] Nor does 'buying' facts from experimenters resemble frequently harassed lawyers deciding whether to fully investigate a case or to fall back on their courtroom skills.

But even at the level of conjecture and intuition, there are a number of counter arguments to both arguments. Regarding the first,[37] Simon has noted that even if the adversarial system ' "holds the case . . . in suspension between two opposing interpretations" while all the "peculiarities and nuances" are explored', it has yet to be established that allowing lawyers to attempt to distort or obfuscate the facts 'increases the likelihood that the balance will ultimately be struck in favour of the correct interpretation. . . . Prejudices, after all, are often very accurate, and in a world of shared values and common experiences, one expects "familiar patterns" to have a certain reliability.'[38]

In answer to the second argument, one may offer the equally intuitive counterargument that, while partisans may investigate more facts, neutral investigators may present facts that neither adversarial party may wish to be heard.[39] Furthermore, if having two investigators is so effective, one may ask why the lawyers of sufficiently wealthy clients do not use competitive fact investigation.[40] And, even if one ignores many of the more deliberate attempts at ensuring witness bias, it seems likely that

---

[33] Thibaut and Walker 1975. And see Freedman 1990, pp.30–1; Schlesinger *et al* 1989, p.435, citing anecdotal evidence from lawyers who have practised in both systems.

[34] Brett 1973; Damaska 1975, pp.1095–1100.

[35] Admitted by Freedman 1990, p.33.

[36] Gross 1987, p.740 n.22.

[37] See also Gross 1987, p.743, who notes that properly trained and sufficiently intelligent fact finders should be able to remain sceptical about first impressions, irrespective of procedural context.

[38] Simon 1978, p.76, quoting Fuller and Randall 1958, p.1161.

[39] Brett 1973; Frankel 1975, pp.1037–8; Damaska 1975, p.1093.

[40] cf Rhode 1985, p.597.

some witnesses will subconsciously alter their evidence in subtle ways to accord with the perceived interests of those calling them.[41]

However, the main problem with the claims for the adversarial system's superiority at truth-finding stems from the very practice requiring justification: zealous advocacy. As we have seen,[42] professional socialisation and pedagogical discourses encourage an attitude whereby winning, albeit according to minimal rules of fair play, is regarded as paramount and 'truth' is something to be relied on in rhetorical discourse rather than a professional ideal. It may be that cross-examination is the 'greatest legal engine ever invented for the discovery of truth'[43] and that 'litigators' devices . . . are useful for testing dishonest witnesses, ferreting out falsehoods, and thus exposing the truth. But to a considerable degree these devices are like other potent weapons, equally lethal for heroes and villains.'[44] Moreover, when we recall the numerous litigatory tactics expressly designed to prevent truth emerging or cases even getting to trial,[45] the adversarial trial could be regarded as equivalent to throwing 'pepper in the eyes of a surgeon'.[46]

Furthermore, the temptation on all advocates to concentrate on persuasion and the production of belief rather than truth[47] is likely to be exacerbated under adversarial conditions. According to Luban:

Adversarial tactics, in law as in elsewhere, tend to escalate more or less independently of anyone's intentions. Game theorists call the structure that compels escalation a Prisoner's Dilemma: a lawyer engages in the practice because not to do so would put him at a disadvantage relative to other lawyers who do. All the lawyers might recognise that it would be better for all concerned if no one engaged in the practice, but this recognition, even buttressed with the knowledge that other lawyers share in it, does not help anyone unilaterally refrain from it.[48]

In response, it may be argued that while partisan lawyers do engage in truth-obstructing tactics, the adversary system's very design involves a delicate web of checks and balances whereby each party's tactics are countered by those of the other, an impartial arbiter ensures fair play and an appeals procedure rectifies mistakes.[49] These latter procedural considerations can be easily dismissed. The ability of trial judges to ensure that truth is not obstructed by dishonest and unfair tactics is limited by current rules which condone a wide variety of tactics inimical to truth-finding.[50] Similarly, appeal courts have very limited scope to reverse findings of fact and even if they do so, the process may be time-consuming, costly, and stressful.

However, the biggest problem with the checks and balances argument is that it suffers from the same delusion that underlies the classical laissez-faire economic theory with which it is ideologically linked.[51] Just as it seems a pious hope to expect

---

[41] Damaska 1975, p.1094.   [42] Ch.6, section 2.   [43] Wigmore 1974, para. 1367.
[44] Frankel 1975, p.1039.   [45] See Ch.6, section 3.2.   [46] Frank 1973, p.85.
[47] See Ch.6 at n.59.   [48] Luban 1981a, pp.460–1.
[49] See Luban 1981a, p.470; 1988, pp.78–81; Schwartz 1978, esp p.677.
[50] See Ch.6, section 3.2 and Ch.8, section 5.
[51] cf Frank 1973, p.72; Wasserstrom 1975, p.13; Frankel 1980, pp.10–11.

some 'invisible hand' to ensure that the general public benefits from the aggressive pursuit of individual self-interest,[52] so it seems naive to expect that truth will emerge if two adversaries do their utmost to obstruct it.[53] There is no more reason to suggest that true versions of events will emerge from the clash of two false versions than that overall confusion will reign, or some third false version will emerge.

Indeed, it is the possibility of such inequalities which justifies most scepticism about the truth-finding qualities of the adversarial system. Sociological studies have shown the adversary system's assumption of equality to be a hollow myth. When a legal system which allocates access to lawyers on a market basis (only partially ameliorated by state legal aid schemes) combines with a socio-economic system riven by huge wealth differences, some will inevitably receive more competent and more zealous legal representatives than others. Money also buys advantageous access to expert witnesses and a greater ability to engage in truth-obstructing tactics, like delay and discovery abuses. Reinforcing wealth differences in many cases are the advantages enjoyed by 'repeat players' in the legal process, such as superior knowledge of the workings of the legal process, ready access to legal specialists, economies of scale, low start-up costs, the opportunity to develop informal relations with institutional incumbents, and an ability to play for higher stakes than 'one-shotters'.[54]

There may, of course, be even greater flaws with the inquisitorial system. However, as yet, these have not been established.

2.2.2 *The Adversarial System and Legal Rights*

The claim that the adversarial system is the best procedural context for the protection of legal rights is usually articulated in the criminal context and then simply assumed to apply equally to civil cases, despite their different goals and essential features. Thus, the argument that the goal of truth-finding in criminal trials is specifically watered down in order to protect procedural rights[55] has considerably less purchase in civil cases. Most rules of procedure and exclusionary rules of evidence which are not designed to ensure reliable truth-finding are aimed at protecting general public interests rather than the individual's rights. Moreover, the procedural rights of criminal defendants in adversarial systems are designed to protect them against a state perceived to be overly powerful—a consideration that does not normally apply in civil proceedings.

In this light, the argument about adversariality and the rights of civil litigants appears to be confined to substantive legal rights and the argument that 'by good disputing shall the law be known'.[56] This, however, could refer to the adversarial system's advantages in protecting extant legal rights or in creating valuable new legal rights.

The former alternative invites a battle of intuitive hypotheses similar to that discussed in the previous section. Thus the argument regarding incentives for thorough

---

[52] See Ch.2, n.53.   [53] Rhode 1985, p.595ff.   [54] Galanter 1974.
[55] See section 3.2.1 below.   [56] *Cordell v Second Clanfield Properties* [1969] 2 Ch 9, 16–17.

fact investigation could be modified to apply to legal investigation, whereas critics could point to the incentives for lawyers to attempt aggressively to ensure legal findings that support their clients' interests. Admittedly, lawyers have less opportunity to conceal legal materials than facts; both because they are in the public domain, and because advocates are obliged to reveal adverse legal materials.[57] At the same time, all but the most naive of formalists now recognise that there is no such thing as the 'true' law locked away awaiting judicial discovery. Judges frequently—some would say, invariably—make law. Consequently, as with findings of fact, we can never know whether cases are based on 'true' law and thus can never make comparative evaluations of accuracy. In addition, if judges do make law, zealous counsel are likely to use their rhetorical skills to ensure that the final product favours their clients. This means that once again we have to assume that some 'invisible hand' will ensure that the correct path is steered between competing versions of legal truth, while turning a blind eye to the possible impact of inequalities in access to legal zeal, competence and litigatory resources.[58]

Alternatively, Freedman has argued that the adversarial system provides the best means for 'advances in individual rights and liberties'.[59] Without lawyer zeal many disputes would be settled instead of being pushed to full trial, thus undermining the important role litigation plays in creating new legal rights and placing constraints on state and other forms of power. Admittedly, civil litigation can play this and other important roles.[60] However, to be persuasive Freedman's argument requires empirical support in the form of comparative research indicating that lawyers in inquisitorial systems more readily encourage their clients to settle cases that ideally should go to court. And even if this evidence were to emerge, one would have to weigh these advantages against the possibility that in areas such as those involving civil liberties the courts might make matters worse[61] and that in other areas, such as those involving intimate and business relations, the parties might be better avoiding adversarial legal proceedings altogether.[62]

2.2.3 *The Adversarial System and Fairness*

The final comparative argument in favour of the adversarial system contends that it best accords with our sense of fairness, hence providing a more effective means of ending disputes and ensuring acceptable decisions.[63] Three reasons for this are proffered. One is that the adversarial system provides individuals with maximum involvement in and control over proceedings leading to decisions that affect their lives, whereas inquisitorial systems are largely controlled by public officials.[64] Secondly, without adversarial advocacy it is said that people will fear 'that perhaps more might have been said for the losing side and suspicion is cast on the decision reached'.[65]

---

[57] See Ch.8, n.111.   [58] See Gordon 1988, pp.21–2.   [59] Freedman 1990, pp.18–20.
[60] See the discussion in section 4.1.   [61] Griffith 1997; Ewing and Gearty 1990.
[62] See eg Tur 1995 and more generally Goldman 1980, pp.153–4; Menkel-Meadow 1996.
[63] cf Macmillan 1937, p.174.
[64] Freedman 1990, pp.39–41. See also Damaska 1986, pp.120–1.
[65] Fuller and Randall 1958, p.1216.

Thirdly, it is argued that neutral investigators who develop a working hypothesis of cases are likely to be seen as biased by whichever party is disfavoured by this hypothesis irrespective of whether actual bias plays a part.[66]

However, even if these arguments were to be empirically tested,[67] one still has to ask whether the fact that litigants' perceptions of adversarial proceedings as fairer should be sufficient to justify neutral partisanship. It is conceivable that the impact of any inequalities between the parties in terms of abilities, commitment and resources may make adversarial litigation less fair in fact than inquisitorial litigation. If this were the case, the idea that *perceptions* of fairness should take precedence over *actual* fairness would be an outrageous example of the triumph of form over substance. Admittedly, the argument that the inquisitorial system is fairer than the adversarial has not been tested, let alone established. But, by the same token, neither has the contrary argument. Consequently, it does not seem as if the argument from fairness—perceived or actual—can take us any further.

2.3 Conclusion

It would seem that the arguments based on the adversarial system collapse on close analysis into, at best, intuitive hypothesis, and, at worst, mere rhetorical assertion. At the same time, while it is impossible to say that this system is any better than the inquisitorial system at finding truth, upholding legal rights or engendering perceptions of fairness, nor has it been established that it is any worse. We can thus conclude, along with Luban, that no case has been made for its replacement with the inquisitorial system.[68] Indeed, replacing the adversarial system would involve enormous costs in terms of effort, expense, confusion, anxiety, disorientation, and inadvertent miscarriages of justice due to unfamiliarity with a new system. In addition, the philosophy underlying the adversarial system is said to resonate with the social belief that things are best done by individual effort and in competition with others[69] and Anglo-American distrust of officialdom.[70]

This 'pragmatic justification'[71] for the adversarial system cannot, however, justify the immoral and harmful action flowing from neutral partisanship.[72] Indeed, by frequently subverting truth-finding and the protection of legal rights, and by detracting from the perceived fairness of litigation, it is neutral partisanship itself that provides one very important reason why many of the arguments for the alleged supe-

---

[66] Damaska 1986, p.120.

[67] This has only occurred in relation to the first argument and even then only by laboratory experiments (see Thibaut and Walker 1975), which do not tell us much about how real litigants rate actual adversarial proceedings. Indeed, such empirical evidence as does exist suggests that lay respect for the system of justice is reduced in those who have come into contact with the courts, especially as litigants—victorious or otherwise: see Genn 1982; Davis 1994.

[68] See Luban 1988a, pp.92–103.

[69] Kutak 1983, p.173.

[70] Freedman 1990, pp.38–9. cf also Luban 1998, pp.99ff.

[71] Luban 1988a, pp.93, 98–102, and 153–4. See also Croft 1992, pp.1302–3.

[72] cf contra Ellman 1990, pp.143–5 and Luban's persuasive response in 1990b, pp.1020–1.

riority of the adversary system fail. And while there remains the possibility of gross inequalities in resources and legal assistance between parties, the idea that zealous lawyers will cancel out each other's adversarial abuses and ensure an increase in the sum total of truth finding, legal rights protection, and perceived fairness, the very existence of neutral partisanship will scupper attempts to rely on the adversarial system's alleged superiority.[73]

In response, it might be argued that neither of these factors is intrinsic to the adversarial system. Thus, it could be argued that without those tactics that detract from truth-finding, the upholding of legal rights and perceptions of fairness, the adversarial system would still remain superior to the inquisitorial system.[74] Indeed, its qualities would be greatly enhanced. Similarly, one could dismiss any substantial inequalities between legal adversaries as stemming from capitalism or some other social evil rather than the adversary system itself.[75]

No doubt, the adversary system could and should operate in conditions of parity between opponents. However, neutral partisanship needs to be justified in actual rather than utopian conditions. Currently there is nothing like the parity which would ensure that it functions in the way assumed by its supporters. Until differences in access to justice and to the resources useful for winning cases are radically reduced, it is arguable that the adversary system will not provide the best means for advancing its alleged functions, but merely the best means for the powerful to further their interests. Somewhat more persuasive is the argument that neutral partisanship could be reformed to prohibit excessive adversarial zeal. However, we would then not be justifying neutral partisanship as we currently know it. Moreover, by emasculating the partisan lawyer without reforming the principle of neutrality it is possible that we would lose the benefit of lawyer zeal where it is in fact justified.[76]

3. NEUTRAL PARTISANSHIP AND LIBERAL VALUES

3.1 The Arguments

The second major set of arguments justifying neutral partisanship rely on the central liberal values of 'individual dignity, autonomy, and equality'.[77] By contrast to the argument based upon adversarial justice, the arguments here bear far more resemblance to deontological theory in that the above values are all closely associated with the Kantian tradition and the supporters include some of the contemporary deontologists discussed in Chapter 2.[78] Moreover, the arguments seem to regard neutral

---

[73] cf Donegan 1983, pp.123–4, who, however, fails to draw the logical conclusion from his recognition of this point.

[74] cf Frank 1973; Frankel 1980; Held 1983, p.69ff regarding the adversary's alleged truth-finding qualities.

[75] cf Landsman 1984, p.40.   [76] See Ch.8.

[77] Pannick 1992, p.247, a point, however, which he fails to develop.

[78] See esp sections 3.2 and 3.3.

partisanship as intrinsically rather than consequentially required by the liberal values, although we shall show that this latter claim is misplaced and that in fact the argument can only succeed if it is claimed that on balance neutral partisanship does more good than harm by promoting human dignity, autonomy and equality.[79]

The argument from dignity has been most eloquently put by Donegan.[80] Since humans cannot be blamed for acting on opinions defensibly reached and honestly held or for their failings regarding observation, memory and impartiality, Donegan asserts that '[r]espect for the dignity of every human individual requires that even if prospective clients are mistaken in their beliefs about either the facts of a case or its moral rights and wrongs, they have a right to have their view considered in negotiations and legal proceedings'. Equally, they require 'a fair opportunity to raise questions about what is due to them under the law before properly constituted courts and to defend themselves against claims upon themselves or charges against them'. However, because law 'will at best be imperfectly understood by nonprofessionals', citizens must be able to hire lawyers.

While Donegan's argument is limited to litigation and negotiation, Pepper has extended it to all legal work by relying on the values of autonomy and equality.[81] His starting point is the belief that law is 'a public good', which has created various mechanisms to enable the private attainment of individual or group goals. Companies, contracts, trusts, wills, and the availability of courts to settle private grievances are, he argues, vehicles for individual or group empowerment. His second premise is that society is committed to upholding individual autonomy and allowing diversity rather than imposing its view of 'right' or 'good' conduct. His third premise is that in highly legalised societies autonomy frequently depends upon access to the law and that '[f]or most people, most of the time, meaningful access to the law requires the assistance of a lawyer'. Consequently, lawyers are necessary for meaningful individual autonomy and those who refuse assistance on moral grounds wrongly 'substitute their beliefs for individual autonomy and diversity'. This is particularly problematic given the unequal nature of the lawyer-client relationship, which flows, on the one hand, from the lawyer's technical expertise, experience and monopoly of services and, on the other hand, from the client's dependency on the lawyer and possibly their lower educational and socio-economic status.[82]

---

[79] See section 5.   [80] 1983, esp pp.128–35. cf also Freedman 1975, pp.2 and 4.

[81] 1986a, esp pp.616–19. See also Pepper 1986b, pp.662–7 and 1995, esp p.1598; Fried 1976; Freedman 1978, esp p.204. Fried bolsters the argument by analogising the lawyer-client relationship to that of what he calls a 'special purpose' friendship. This led to almost universal derision (see esp Simon 1978, p.109: 'Fried's lawyer is like a friend in the same sense that . . . Canada Dry Ginger Ale "tastes like love" ', cf Wolf, p.59n.4; Luban 1988a, p.83 and 1994, p.xxi), given the commercial nature of the lawyer-client relationship, its difference to the reciprocity, affection, admiration, intimacy, and vulnerability involved in the sort of friendship valorised by Aristotle, and the absurdity of having a friendship with corporate entities: Freedman 1978, p.198; Donegan 1983, p.128; Wasserstrom 1983, p.37; Dauer and Leff 1977; Simon 1978, pp.108–9; and 1998, pp.19–21; Haber and Baumrim 1988, p.108. Most importantly, this argument ignores the fact that we are not expected to do immoral things for our friends, a fact later admitted by Fried 1977, who also concedes that the justification for neutral partisanship does not need the friendship analogy.

[82] cf also Gordon 1988, pp.68–71.

Moreover, given that access to the public good of law should be available to all, Pepper argues that the refusal of legal assistance offends the idea of equality. It results in 'unfiltered access to the law [being] available only to those who are legally sophisticated or to those able to educate themselves sufficiently for access to the law, while those less sophisticated—usually those less educated—are left with no access or with access limited by the lawyer's moral judgement and veto'.[83] In a similar vein, it has frequently been argued that without neutral partisanship and, in particular, the cab-rank rule, 'the unpopular and the unmeritorious', 'minority interests', the under-privileged in society and those, like alleged rapists or child molesters, whose conduct is regarded as reprehensible will go undefended.[84] The cab-rank rule is said to encourage representation by insulating lawyers from criticism.[85] Because lawyers cannot pick and choose their clients, it is argued that the public will not perceive them as endorsing their clients' views or actions. And in support of the need for such a shield, attention is drawn to the difficulties those such as Irish nationalists and members of the Red Brigade have had in obtaining legal representation.[86] Finally, neutral partisanship is justified on the grounds that equal access to lawyers is important because law 'significantly equalizes' power between government and citizenry and between powerful and weak citizens.[87]

3.2 Evaluating the Arguments

There is much that is persuasive in the above arguments. At least in the abstract, dignity, autonomy[88] and equality are values worth protecting. The idea that no one should be subject to legal consequences without being heard is undoubtedly an extremely important value, upholding not just human dignity but also protecting citizens against potentially unjustified interference with their life, liberty, and other legal rights. Similarly, we recognise that lawyers can and ought to play an important role in equalising imbalances in power in society and in protecting the underprivileged and unpopular. Finally, as we have already seen,[89] the problem of lawyer manipulation of clients is a serious one.[90]

However, while these arguments would need to be addressed if neutral partisanship were to be abandoned, we shall argue that they do not provide a blanket justification for neutral partisanship. Instead, the justification for lawyers acting as neutral partisans depends on the type of work they perform.

---

[83] Pepper 1986a, p.619.

[84] *Ridehalgh v Horsfield* [1994] Ch 205, 234C; Pannick 1992, pp.141 and 146; Kennedy 1992, pp.47–8; Thornton 1995, p.69.

[85] *ex parte Lloyd* n.25, above; *Rondel v Worsley* [1969] 1 AC 191, 227; Zander 1968, p.282; Pannick 1992, pp.140–2.

[86] Caplan 1978, p.134. See also Pannick 1992, pp.142–4. Similar arguments have been made regarding, for instance, Afro-Americans in the Deep South and the victims of McCarthyism: eg Pollitt 1964; Rhode 1991, p.33.

[87] Pepper 1986b, p.667. See also Freedman 1975, p.4.

[88] But cf Luban 1990b, p.1037ff and see further Ch.5.

[89] Ch.5, section 4.   [90] But see at section 3.2.2.

3.2.1 *Criminal Defence Work*

The need for lawyers to represent all prospective clients facing criminal charges zealously is accepted by even neutral partisanship's strongest critics.[91] For most, the justification for the hired gun role in criminal defence work lies in the reasons behind the special civil libertarian protections that the law accords to criminal defendants.

These reasons usually[92] start with the fundamental imbalance in power and resources between state and defendants.[93] While prosecution counsel may or may not have advantages in terms of competence, experience and preparation time, they have substantial investigative advantages because of the police, other investigative agencies and state forensic laboratories, the ability to appeal to the public for information, usually greater financial resources than defendants and the ability to obtain damaging admissions through arresting and interrogating suspects. By contrast, defence counsel frequently cannot rely on client assistance because they are either incapable or incarcerated. In court, the state has the advantage of greater credibility. Judges and juries tend to believe police witnesses and disbelieve defendants, commonly assuming that defendants would not be in the dock without good reason. Whereas the prosecution of crime seems legitimate and in accordance with democratic government, attempts by defendants to evade criminal liability are likely to be viewed with much greater suspicion. Sociologists observe that the whole nature of legal proceedings and court atmosphere operate to make criminal convictions more likely than not,[94] frequently persuading defendants to opt for plea bargains even when convinced of their own innocence.[95]

The second stage in the argument refers to the grave consequences of being criminally charged. The possibility of being convicted, as well as the tension of criminal proceedings, imposes tremendous anxiety on suspects and possibly also financial expense, lost employment, disrupted family life, and a damaged reputation, even if acquitted.[96] And if convicted, defendants may lose their property or liberty. In addition, there is the humiliation of public condemnation, the loss of reputation and social discrimination against those with criminal records.

For some, the 'cruel and degrading' nature of punishment justifies zealous representation irrespective of guilt or innocence.[97] For others, it is needed to protect the dignity of criminal defendants. According to Freedman,[98] the rights to trial by jury,

---

[91] See eg Wasserstrom 1975, pp.6–10 *passim*; Goldman 1980, pp.117–20; Schwartz 1983, pp.155–6; Rhodes 1985, pp.605–6 and 1991, pp.32 and 37; Luban 1988a, pp.58ff and 1993. See also Cranston 1995, pp.22–3 and 33. Note, however, that not all accept all the tactics currently employed by criminal defence lawyers. See Ch.8, section 6.

[92] See also Simon 1993, pp.1714–21, who refutes some minor and more dubious arguments.

[93] In addition to the references in n.91, the following discussion draws upon Freedman 1975 and 1990; Kaplan 1986; Mitchell 1980; Babcock 1983. See also Humphreys 1955, pp.739–40.

[94] See eg Carlen 1976; McBarnet 1981; Rock 1993.

[95] See eg Baldwin and McConville 1977; McConville 1998.

[96] See Freedman 1975, p.84: 'merely to be charged with a crime is a punishing experience'.

[97] Eshete 1983, pp.272–4. See also Griffiths 1970, p.408; Mitchell 1980, p.329; and, more tentatively, Wasserstrom 1975, p.12.

[98] *Loc cit* n.14. Similar concerns inform Mitchell 1980.

due process, and the privilege against self-incrimination all mark society's respect for individual dignity, as do criminal defendants' 'rights'[99] to lawyers who will act as their 'champion' by protecting their interests 'zealously'.[100] For most commentators, however, zealous criminal defence is justified not just by the need to protect individual dignity—as important as that might be—or against punishment *per se*, but the need to protect against *unjustified* punishment.

Many are motivated by traditional liberal[101] mistrust of the state based on the belief that '[p]ower-holders are inevitably tempted to abuse the criminal justice system to persecute political opponents, and overzealous police will trample civil liberties in the name of crime prevention and order'.[102] Although support can be found for this concern in the well-publicised miscarriages of justice of recent years,[103] even in routine cases involving 'harassed over-worked bureaucrats' motivated by the desire to dispose of cases quickly rather than by excessive zeal, imbalances in power between state and defendant may result in punishment being imposed on the innocent or excessively on the guilty with consequent serious invasions of their rights to liberty, property, and reputation.[104]

In this light, the plethora of legal protections for criminal defendants already mentioned, as well as the high standard of proof in criminal trials, the so-called right to silence, rules against illegally obtained evidence and limits on the prosecution's adversarial stance,[105] are aimed not so much at ensuring that criminal courts accurately ascertain factual truth or protect human dignity, but at 'overprotecting'[106] defendants by placing significant obstacles in the way of convictions in order to equalise power imbalances between state and defendant. On the assumption that no rules could effectively protect the innocent from conviction while simultaneously allowing conviction of the guilty,[107] it is famously declaimed that 'rather a hundred guilty go free than one innocent is convicted'. This is sometimes supported by the argument that whereas the material consequences of conviction for the innocent are dire, and while the general public may be legitimately outraged or be exposed to further harm by freed criminals, no one is materially affected when criminals go free.[108] Moreover, protecting the freedom of criminal defendants can also be seen as indirectly protecting the freedom of all. As Babcock colourfully puts it, 'the civil libertarian tells

---

[99] Note that British criminal defendants do not have constitutional rights to counsel, as they do in the US.

[100] Freedman 1970, p.4.

[101] But cp Simon 1993b, pp.1767–8 with Luban 1993, p.1730.

[102] Luban 1988a, p.60. See also Gillers 1986, p.1024.

[103] See eg Ashworth 1994, pp.10–14.

[104] See Luban 1993, pp.1731–55 in response to Simon's argument (1993, p.1707) that most defendants do not face Leviathan.

[105] See Ch.8 at nn.68 and 168–9.   [106] See Luban 1988a, pp.60–3.

[107] cf, however, Simon 1993, p.1708.

[108] 1988a, p.59; Schwartz 1983, pp.162–3. However, this can be said to ignore the feelings of victims and the fact that acquittals may undermine criminal law's role in deterring crime and generally setting moral standards for society: see eg Williams 1955, p.258; Simon 1993, p.1708. On the other hand, when weighed against the prevention of unjustified convictions, such harms may well be regarded as a price worth paying.

us that the criminal accused are the representatives of us all. When their rights are eroded, the camel's nose is under and the tent may collapse on anyone'.[109]

From this perspective, the right to zealous advocacy is simply one of the plethora of protections afforded to criminal defendants in their unequal fight with the prosecution.[110] Without such representation, it is argued that unjust convictions will multiply.[111] This point is emphasised by the allegedly lacklustre approach of defence counsel in some miscarriages of justice cases[112] and reinforced by recent inroads on a defendant's procedural protections,[113] their evasion by the police[114] and prosecuting lawyers,[115] their erosion by the courts[116] and disregard by juries.[117] It is also suggested that zealous advocacy may force the state to investigate cases more thoroughly with a consequent uncovering of more exculpatory evidence and ambiguities in superficially strong cases.[118] Similarly, the threat of zealous advocacy may strengthen the hand of defence lawyers in plea bargaining negotiations.[119]

Recently, arguments for neutral partisanship in criminal defence work have gone beyond liberal justifications.[120] These focus on the particularly harsh and discriminatory nature of the modern criminal justice system: the fact that it operates disproportionately against the poor and other oppressed minorities; the fact that many are 'battered and mistreated in the process of arrest and investigation';[121] the fact that the cases of 'the vast majority of criminal defendants receive no individualized scrutiny, but instead are processed like carcasses at the meat-packing plant'.[122] In these circumstances preventing the punishment of even the guilty is justified. According to Babcock, criminal defence can also be said to be beneficial irrespective of its success. Providing defendants with a 'full panoply' of rights and concerns is not only a humanitarian act, but may 'promote rehabilitation' and decrease the 'anger and alienation' of friends, relatives, and members of their community.[123] Arguably, these arguments are no more than modern day correctives to the liberal arguments.[124] However, one can go even further and see criminal defence as always justified as a

---

[109] Babcock 1983, p.177.

[110] Implicitly recognised by the limits placed on the zeal of prosecutors: *loc cit* n.105.

[111] Rhode 1991, p.32.   [112] See Ch.6 at n.172.

[113] See the Criminal Justice and Public Order Act 1994, ss.34–37; the Criminal Procedure Investigation Act 1996, discussed by Walker and Starmer 1999, chs.5 and 7.

[114] See eg Walker and Starmer 1999, chs.3 and 4; Sanders and Young 1998, ch.4.

[115] See eg Ch.6, section 3.2.

[116] See eg Sanders and Young 1998, ch.9, regarding ss.76–78 of the Police and Criminal Evidence Act 1984.

[117] cf LSE Jury Project 1973; Simon 1993, pp.1717–19 regarding the inability of juries to understand the criminal standard of proof.

[118] Mitchell 1980, pp.303–10; Kaplan 1986, pp.231–2. But cf Simon 1993, pp.1711–12, who points out that the police and prosecutors may equally respond by adopting misleading and coercive tactics of their own, or by pressurising the legislature to reduce defence rights.

[119] Luban 1993, pp.1744–8.

[120] Described by Babcock 1983, pp.178–9, as the political activist's and the social worker's reasons. See also Simon 1993, pp.1722–8 and Luban 1993, pp.1749–55, confusing the two reasons and for a similar approach, see Mitchell 1980 *passim*.

[121] Babcock 1983, p.178.   [122] Luban 1993, p.1754.   [123] Babcock 1983, p.178.

[124] See Luban 1993, p.1750.

political act against the state when the crimes being prosecuted are those which reflect class divisions, racism, sexism and institutionalised homophobia.

Clearly, not everyone is likely to accept all the arguments in favour of neutral partisanship on the part of the criminal defenders. Indeed, the last argument has yet to receive any support, while the arguments that punishment is always an evil or that criminal defence may promote rehabilitation and community harmony have either been condemned[125] or ignored. Similarly, not everyone accepts all facets of the liberal argument.[126] In our view, however, the very few commentators who have attempted to shake its core have failed to do so. Consequently, we conclude that the liberal arguments along with some of the more radical arguments provide a persuasive case for neutral partisanship in criminal cases.[127]

3.2.2 *Other Legal Work*

By contrast to criminal defence work, justifications for neutral partisanship outside criminal defence work have to rely on the full range of arguments from dignity, autonomy, and equality. Some of these can be set aside relatively easily. Thus the argument that refusing to represent or act zealously for individuals subordinates the latter's autonomy to that of the lawyer is overly rhetorical. In such cases, lawyers simply decline to assist in pursuit of the individual's autonomy. It is still open to the latter to obtain the assistance of another lawyer. Only if the lawyer is the prospective client's last resort does the refusal of zealous representation nullify the individual's 'rights' to dignity, autonomy and equality. If indeed they are rights, they are like the human right to be free from starvation, in the nature of positive freedoms.[128] They cannot be said to impose obligations of zealous assistance on the first lawyer that the individual happens to approach. Moreover, citizens do not have rights to legal assistance[129]—let alone zealous assistance—and even if they did, it can be argued that any correlative obligation rests on the profession as a whole.[130] As long as this obligation is in fact met, individual lawyers should be free to decline to assist clients in immoral activities.

In support, one can point to the stubborn fact that legal need can never be fully met by a privatised system of legal services. Lawyers must inevitably make decisions as to whom to allocate this scarce resource. At present, such decisions are made largely on financial grounds—on the basis of ability to pay or qualify for legal aid. It seems counter-intuitive to hold that it is worse to make such decisions on moral grounds. Equally, no one in society has full autonomy. Apart from democratically justified state interferences, there are numerous informal filters on moral autonomy. Private citizens with influence or leverage over others can block what they regard as

---

[125] See Pye 1978, p.927 arguing that, even if evil, punishment has been democratically sanctioned.
[126] See Simon at nn.104 and 118 above; Heffernan 1985, pp.79–85, whose arguments are even less persuasive.
[127] However, see Ch.8, sections 5.2 and 6.3 for some minor qualifications.
[128] cf Goldman 1980, ch.1.
[129] See further at section 4.2.
[130] Raymond 1990; Schwartz 1978, p.692 and 1983, p.557ff; Hutchinson 1998, pp.177 and 178.

immoral activities.[131] Why should this 'Lysistratian prerogative'[132] be denied to lawyers? Indeed, why should client autonomy take precedence over that of lawyers?[133]

According to Pepper, one answer lies in the inherent advantages professionals have over their clients.[134] Admittedly, the dangers of lawyers taking advantage of clients' inferior economic position, vulnerability and inability to evaluate legal services are, as we have seen,[135] real and need to be addressed if neutral partisanship were to be abandoned. On the other hand, this problem only applies to established lawyer-client relationships and thus does not prevent lawyers refusing assistance. In addition, as we have also seen, because of lawyers' financial need for clients, power relationships are not one-way[136] and many clients may have the financial clout and expertise to negotiate on equal terms with lawyers. Problems of lawyer control are unlikely to be serious in the case of in-house lawyers, and those who act for repeat players and other wealthy private and corporate clients. Ironically, it is those clients who are able to cause most harm to the interests of others who are least subject to moral control by their lawyers.

Also ironic is the possibility of moral paternalism flowing from neutral partisanship itself. As we have already seen,[137] moral detachment may prevent lawyers from ascertaining their clients' true wishes and hence unwittingly imposing their morality on clients who unquestioningly accept what appear to be proffered solutions to technical problems by disembodied experts. Moreover, because lawyers are either required or strongly encouraged to act zealously for clients irrespective of their moral or political objections, they may be tempted to use all their powers to dissuade clients from objectionable legal actions and this in fact may involve greater invasions of client autonomy than the simple refusal to accept instructions.[138]

Another argument made by Pepper and others is that the benefit lawyers derive from a monopoly over legal services makes it particularly offensive for them to deny access to law's benefits.[139] Others, however, have argued that it is the very existence of this monopoly that obliges lawyers to ration their services according to morality and the public interest.[140] But, even assuming that socially sanctioned monopolies entail obligations to act for those needing legal services, lawyers' monopolies are limited. Apart from isolated monopolies such as the swearing of affidavits and

---

[131] cf Schwartz 1978, pp.693–4; 1983, p.559; Wolfram 1983, pp.232–3.

[132] cf Luban 1986, esp p.642, 1988, p.167. Lysistrata organised a sex boycott of the wives in order to dissuade their husbands from going to war.

[133] A point acknowledged by some supporters of neutral partisanship: eg Fried 1976, p.1083; Freedman 1978, pp.199 and 204 in relation to the lawyer's right to refuse representation, although not in relation to the right to limit zeal.

[134] Pepper 1986a, pp.615–16 and 634. Here Pepper also seems to think that moral activism is simply a question of lawyers putting their interests above those of clients, whereas it will usually—and indeed should always—involve concern for third parties, the general public or the environment: cf Luban 1988a, pp.126, 144–7 and 1990a, p.452.

[135] See Ch.5.

[136] Ch.5, section 4.3. See Luban 1990b, pp.1036–7 in the present context.

[137] Ch.6, section 3.4.   [138] See also Goldman 1980, p.126.

[139] cf Freedman 1978, p.204; Schwartz 1978, p.694; Wolfram 1983, p.223.

[140] eg Burger 1966, pp.11–12; Edwards 1990, pp.1156–7; Rubin 1975, pp.588–9.

possibly also the prohibition on litigants being represented in court by anyone other than qualified lawyers, lawyers enjoy *de facto* rather than *de lege* monopolies. It is their absence of legal knowledge and legal skills that may make lay persons dependent on legal assistance. Some legal acts are effectively impossible without legal assistance. But numerous other acts like making wills, suing for divorce, and conveyancing may be performed by lay persons. Here, lawyers do not control access to law and its autonomy, they merely enable more effective access. And in some cases, such as where they negotiate business deals or lobby politicians, lawyers do not even provide access to law or specialised legal skills. In other words, legal representation is not invariably necessary for the protection of individual dignity and autonomy under the law.[141] Instead, it merely ensures that citizens have an equal opportunity to obtain the more effective protection (hopefully) ensured by legal representation.

However, other professionals have similar *de facto* monopolies. Engineers who refuse companies assistance in developing weaponry for sale to oppressive regimes place such companies at a disadvantage *vis à vis* those who can hire less morally sensitive engineers. No one would consider criticising the former for substituting their own beliefs for 'individual autonomy and diversity',[142] so why should lawyers be criticised if they refuse their services to arms corporations?

According to liberals like Pepper, this is because lawyers deny access not just to some private means of furthering an individual's interest—such as the making of profit through selling weapons—but to a 'formal public good' which is 'fundamentally enabling and empowering' in promoting individual autonomy, equalising imbalances in social power and providing a civilised forum for the resolution of disputes. In the next section, we shall examine whether the fact that law is a 'formal creation of society' makes a difference, but for now we need to examine whether law is in fact a 'public good available to all'.[143] This in turn requires an examination of the social context in which law operates. Now it seems obvious and indeed is recognised by Donegan[144] that, while zealous legal representation may be extremely valuable to particular individuals, a blanket obligation of neutral partisanship is likely to cause far more harm than good in unjust societies with unjust legal systems. Yet the liberals simply assume or assert the 'generally just and decent'[145] nature of Western liberal democracies by a rhetorical comparison of such 'free societies' with Nazi Germany, apartheid South Africa, Cuba and other 'totalitarian' regimes.[146] Admittedly, Britain and the United States, for instance, do not suffer from the same human rights abuses found in the latter regimes, but this does not of itself establish their generally just and decent nature. The liberals beg the very question they need to address.

Instead, they rely, usually implicitly, on a familiar story about what constitutes a

---

[141] Impliedly admitted by Freedman 1978, p.204; Pepper 1986a, p.617 (but cf at p.646).
[142] Pepper 1986a, p.617.   [143] Quotations from Pepper 1986b, p.666.
[144] Donegan 1983, pp.124–6. cf also Fried 1976, p.1081ff.
[145] Fried 1976, p.1085. See also Pannick 1992, p.168; Donegan 1983, p.125.
[146] Fried, ibid. See also n.18, above.

just society; one which clearly bears the traces of classical liberal and neo-liberal socio-economic theories.[147] As we have seen, the moral of this story is that an important, if not *the* most important, social value is the freedom of individuals to pursue their own goals.[148] However, because unconstrained individual freedom may lead to anarchy and the domination of some by others through physical and other forms of illegitimate coercion, law lays down neutral rules designed to ensure a level playing field and maximum freedom for all. These rules provide individuals with rights against both the state and other individuals, while a principle of legality ensures that these rights are only infringed after due process of law and on legal grounds. Secure in the knowledge that their freedom will be protected and that they know what they can and cannot do, humans are thus left to flourish by pursuing their own ideas of the good life. In these circumstances, it is believed that the overall sum of human welfare will increase as if an invisible hand existed to ensure that general welfare flows from the pursuit of individual self-interest.

Allied to and often operating in tandem with this liberal story is a view of law and the legal process associated with legal formalism.[149] As we have already seen,[150] formalists not only see law and morality as separate entities but also conflate law with morality and justice with formal justice. Consequently, lawyers are discouraged from asking whether law is in fact moral or whether the judicial application of law accords with notions of substantive justice.

The formalist story, although still influential over practising lawyers, has been fundamentally refuted by numerous legal theorists, liberal[151] as well as critical.[152] It is argued that, even in democratic and 'generally just and decent' societies with 'reasonably just' legal systems,[153] the conflation of law with morality ignores the possibility that individual laws can be unjust. Not infrequently, significant harm may result to individuals, the public interest and the environment precisely because of the existence of legal rights. Consequently, there has been a rejection of the idea that morally lawyers can obtain for clients everything the law can be made to yield.[154]

However, we can go further and question assumptions about the just nature of Western societies and their legal systems. In competition to liberalism is a critical story (or, more accurately, stories), associated with marxism, communitarianism, feminism, race theory, queer theory, postmodernism, and Critical Legal Studies. According to these theories, law's neutrality and the universality of liberal freedom are but mirages. The rules are laid down and administered by those with power in

---

[147] cf Parker 1995, pp.76–7; Koniak 1996.   [148] See eg Hayek 1982; Raz 1986.
[149] See the Critical Legal Studies' criticism of liberal legalism: eg Hunt 1986.
[150] Ch.3, section 6.
[151] See eg the discussion of natural law theorists by Lloyd 1994, ch.3.
[152] eg Douzinas and Warrington 1994, ch.1.
[153] Quotations from Fried 1976, pp.1085 and 1081, respectively.
[154] Schwartz 1978, p.685; Luban 1988a, esp pp.74–8; Schneyer 1984, p.40; Kennedy 1984, p.1160; Simon 1988, pp.1123–4. cf also the similar point that the liberals have conflated legal with moral rights: eg Goldman 1980, ch.3 *passim*; Postema 1980, p.86; Schwartz 1983, p.555; Rhode 1985, pp.609 and 611.

society or, at least, in terms of ideologies which support the powerful (capitalists, men, heterosexuals, etc.). Consequently, these rules tend to promote their interests at the expense of others. Moreover, the type of freedoms protected are those which favour the powerful. For example, the freedom to exploit property is protected whereas freedom from starvation or unhealthy living and working conditions is downplayed if not completely ignored. Likewise, freedom of sexual expression is protected (at least for heterosexuals), but not women's freedom from sexual violence. Admittedly, the law does sometimes incorporate the interests of the powerless, otherwise it would not act as a legitimatory ideology. Nevertheless, whether one benefits from the liberal order ultimately depends to a large extent on one's place in the social hierarchy.

Although the liberal and critical stories of law and its social context outlined above present highly simplified versions of a complex debate, we tend to side with the latter. This leads us to a number of specific criticisms of the liberal argument which echo the criticisms of orthodox ethical theories we saw in Chapter 2 and in particular those of contemporary deontologists like Fried and Donegan who are leading proponents of the liberal justification for neutral partisanship.[155]

The first is that it rests on an impoverished view of dignity, autonomy, and equality. Humans are seen as atomistic, selfish entities concerned only with their own well-being and that of their nearest and dearest. In other words, individuality is reduced to individualism. Individuals are treated as abstract holders of rights and duties, rather than concrete individuals with differing needs, concerns and capabilities. Recognition of the differences between individuals based on class, race, gender, sexuality, etc., is jettisoned in favour of a concept of formal legal equality. Humans are also seen as isolated islands in a stormy social sea, rather than as having their individuality constructed in the context of complex social ties to others and being marked by vulnerability, need, and dependence.[156] This is perhaps no more apparent than in the notion that the protection of individual dignity and autonomy extends to artificial legal persons such as companies.[157]

The liberal conceptions of dignity, autonomy and equality are not simply impoverished. They are potentially oppressive. By promoting clients' dignity and autonomy, zealous lawyers will often impair that of others. As we have seen,[158] lawyers may intimidate or humiliate opponents or their witnesses, whereas concentration on that aspect of human dignity related to the right to be heard ignores the equally if not more troubling invasions of human dignity which can occur when clients are able, for instance, to evict tenants or sack workers.

As regards autonomy, in some cases, such as when one feuding neighbour obtains the right to disputed land, there may be no overall reduction in autonomy. However, in other cases there may be, such as when zealous advocacy enables landowners to block well-used public rights of way. And when one thinks of oil companies

---

[155] See section 3.2.   [156] cf Luban 1990b, p.1041.
[157] Goldman 1980, p.128; Rhode 1985, p.608.   [158] Ch.6, section 3.2.

destroying the environment and way of life of local inhabitants or hamburger chains preventing free speech in order to increase profits, it becomes apparent that the liberal defenders of neutral partisanship are not talking about autonomy in the pure sense of the greater ability by persons to pursue their own self-interest without constraint, but in the sense of their right to obtain as much freedom and material benefits for themselves as the law allows.[159] They are talking of 'legal' or 'formal' autonomy and dignity, rather than the real-life ability of individuals to flourish in meaningful and dignified ways. Under this formalist conception it is perfectly acceptable for the autonomy of artificial legal persons to take precedence over that of flesh and blood human beings.[160] And it is perfectly legitimate for companies to reduce the autonomy and dignity of unprofitable workers by dismissing them, but not for lawyers to refuse to assist them in doing so. What, however, is most problematic about the conflation of 'real' with 'legal' autonomy and dignity is that the law is not neutral. It does not protect the dignity, interests and freedoms of all equally. To take an obvious example, freedom of property might protect the freedom of those who own valuable property, but it results in invisible (at least to liberals) restraints on the behaviour of others. Legal freedom and rights offer far more to those whose interests are legally protected and who have greater and better access to legal procedures.

Consequently, the liberal claim that equal access to law ensures equality can be criticised for ignoring the possibility that the law itself is premised upon, and indeed is a significant means of ensuring, substantive inequality. It is not only marxists or other critical legal theorists who have noted that equal access to unequal law ensures only substantive inequality.[161] In other words, just as liberals have formalistically conflated 'real' or substantive dignity and autonomy with formal or legal dignity and autonomy so have they conflated substantive equality with 'equality under the law'.

This conflation also ignores that access to law and lawyer zeal is not distributed equally. As already noted,[162] a stubborn feature of societies where wealth and legal services are subject to the vagaries of the free market is the fact that, when it comes to access to lawyers, some in society are more equal than others. The liberal argument that full zeal by one lawyer is necessary to counter full zeal by her opponent is significantly limited by the possible absence of such countervailing zeal or even an opposing lawyer.[163]

Such absences may also result from the way that the liberal legal order treats certain issues as non-legal, certain disputes as non-justiciable or certain interests as lacking legal standing. Where large companies seek planning permission or monopolistic mergers, there is rarely the possibility for the effective legal representation of those interests directly affected: local inhabitants, consumers, employees, and the

---

[159] cf Goldman *loc cit* n.137, noting that in the corporate context autonomy can only mean freedom to maximise profit.

[160] See Goldman and Rhode, *loc cit* n.137.

[161] See Weber 1954, pp.188–91; Ehrlich 1936, p.238.

[162] Section 2.2.2, above.

[163] Admitted by Donegan 1983, p.136. cf also Schwartz 1983, p.547.

environment itself. It is perverse to argue that lawyers should zealously represent clients on the basis that weaker opponents would do so if they could.[164] Here un-mitigated legal zeal will simply result in inequality of outcome and the potential harming of poorly represented or unrepresented interests.

The arguments that neutral partisanship in general and the cab-rank rule in par-ticular are necessary to ensure that everyone, especially the unpopular, the under-privileged and the reprehensible, have equal access to lawyers and hence to justice are likewise undermined by social realities. Indeed, such arguments and the criti-cisms[165] of those lawyers who decline cases on moral grounds come across as rank hypocrisy. Most individuals lack access to the law, not because lawyers substitute their moral autonomy for that of their clients, but because most will only represent those who can afford their fees or qualify for legal aid.[166] The legal profession's professed concern about access to justice would also carry more weight if more lawyers engaged in *pro bono* work or other ways of assisting minority groups, the underprivileged, etc.[167] In this light, one can ask whether instead of being of 'great constitutional importance',[168] and 'a major contribution to the rule of law and to a fair society',[169] the cab-rank rule (and indeed neutral partisanship in general) can be more aptly described as 'just a way of making money from the most terrible people'.[170]

Some liberals blithely ignore the failures of the liberal order.[171] Others attempt to side-step the issue by calling for improved access to lawyers.[172] Given that legal aid and sporadic appeals by professional elites for more *pro bono* representation have failed to seriously reverse existing inequalities, such calls have a somewhat hollow ring.[173] And given the enormous expense and changes required to ensure true equali-ty of access to lawyers, this situation is unlikely to change.

Nor can the problem be wished away by asserting that the issue of neutral parti-sanship is separate to that of unequal access to lawyers.[174] It is true that abandoning neutral partisanship will not solve current problems of unequal access to lawyers. It is also true that, as individuals, lawyers cannot remedy the problem of access to

---

[164] cf Goldman 1980, p.132. And see also pp.124–6.

[165] Pannick 1992, pp.144–5; Thornton 1995, p.70.

[166] cf Mears 1990, 157: 'The so-called [cab-rank] "rule" [has] always smacked of barristerial humbug since of course the petty criminal would find it hardly less difficult to purchase a whole fleet of London cabs than to hire, say, Mr George Carman QC for a two week trial in the Crown Court.'; Phillips 1990, p.39: 'The taxi will take a rich man to the house of ill-fame, but not the poor man to his home.'

[167] See Hall 1990; Raymond 1990, but cf Pannick's unsupported rejection of this: 1992, p.146.

[168] Lord Ackner, 516 HL 207 (20 Feb. 1990) (debate on the Courts and Legal Services Bill), quoted in Pannick 1992, p.137.

[169] Pannick 1992, p.142.

[170] Mortimer 1988, p.18. See also Rhode 1985, p.630.

[171] See Fried 1976, p.1075: 'There is no wrong if a venture fails for lack of talent or lack of money—no one's rights have been violated. But rights *are* violated if, through ignorance or misinformation about the law, an individual refrains from pursuing a wholly lawful purpose.'

[172] See eg Pannick 1992, pp.169 and 186–90.

[173] See Goldman 1980, pp.123–4; Rhode 1985, pp.608–11, noting also lawyer support of restrictive practices. A similar point can be made about English and Welsh lawyers: see Zander 1968.

[174] Pepper 1986a, pp.619–21. See also 1986b, pp.667–8.

justice. On the other hand, zealous representation does not just provide neutral benefits to those who can afford lawyers.[175] It provides them with advantages over those who cannot. This may translate into material and other benefits, and even legal changes reinforcing these advantages.[176] It is not just a question, as Pepper argues,[177] of adding one evil (inequality of access to lawyers because of lawyers' moral discretion) to another (inequality of access because of cost). It is a question of whether we want the evil of unequal access to justice to continue to combine with the evil of social power differentials. One cannot justify neutral partisanship on the grounds of equality, when it exacerbates existing social inequalities.

Admittedly, given the likely coincidence between the morality of those with easy access to partisan lawyers and these lawyers themselves, abandoning neutral partisanship will not totally eradicate this exacerbation,[178] but retaining this role will certainly just ensure that the inequalities remain. In our opinion, the best argument for retaining neutral partisanship is that it benefits the weak in society. But even if this could be established, it does not follow that the only way to provide such protection is to continue to uphold a role morality which encourages lawyers to act for the powerful in harming the interests of the powerless.

Indeed, the cab-rank rule and neutral partisanship appear not to have prevented the very problem used to frighten critics into dropping calls for their abandonment, namely the difficulties minority groups, the unpopular, the reprehensible, etc., have in obtaining lawyers. It is an open secret that the various legitimate grounds for refusal of clients allowed to barristers[179] have always been used as smokescreens to conceal the refusal of unwanted clients.[180] According to the cab-rank rule's supporters, the answer lies in reaffirming its existence and extending it to solicitors in order to force or at least encourage them to uphold professional ideals.[181]

By contrast, it can be argued that neutral partisanship and the cab-rank rule actually militate against lawyers protecting civil liberties by preventing them from developing a personally felt commitment to these values. As we have seen, neutral partisanship tends to anaesthetise moral conscience.[182] So do rules.[183] They tend to cut off contemplation about their underlying reasons and their adequacy, especially if supported by high-sounding rhetoric. Indeed, developmental psychology suggests that those who obey rules because of a fear of sanctions are more likely to succumb to temptations to evade them than those with personally felt commitments.[184] This is particularly apposite to a profession whose training and working life is largely devoted to rule manipulation.

---

[175] Luban 1986, pp.643–5.   [176] See also Galanter 1974.   [177] Pepper 1986a, pp.618, 620.
[178] ibid, p.620 and 1986b, p.668.   [179] See Ch.5, at n.98.
[180] Zander 1968, p.283; Caplan 1978, p.134; Disney *et al* 1986, p.605; 'Editorial' 1990; Pannick 1992, p.144; Thornton 1995, p.69.
[181] An apparent recognition of the moral spinelessness of lawyers: see Lord Brougham, 55 *Parliamentary Debates, House of Lords* (5th series), 10 Aug. 1840, cols 1401–2, cited in Melinkoff 1973, pp.143–4; Caplan 1978, p.134. See also Pollitt 1964, pp.17–18.
[182] Ch.6.   [183] See Ch.4, section 3.4.
[184] See Richards 1981, p.368, relying on Kohlberg (see Ch.2, section 6).

Instead of a role which anaesthetises moral conscience, an easily avoided rule requiring representation and occasional rhetoric, we would argue that lawyers are far more likely to be socialised into developing personally felt commitments to service ideals if they are exposed from an early stage in their legal careers to a thorough and ongoing debate about questions of access to justice, civil liberties, morality and substantive justice, and if their role requires them to distinguish between those who really need assistance and those who simply want to pursue self-interest at the expense of others.

4. NEUTRAL PARTISANSHIP AND THE INSTITUTIONS OF LIBERAL GOVERNMENT

4.1 The Arguments

Even if we accept that law is not so self-evidently a social good such that lawyers are required to provide access to it in all cases, it nevertheless remains a 'formal creation of society'[185] and hence lawyers who decline to pursue citizens' legal rights can be said to undermine the institutions of liberal government, and particularly the principles of democracy and the rule of law.[186]

More particularly, lawyers who decline to assist individuals to gain access to beneficial legal provisions arguably usurp the legislature's right to set behavioural standards for society.[187] Moreover, they do so without popular mandate or special legislative expertise.[188] For some, this raises the prospect of lawyers becoming 'an oligarchy whose duty it is to nullify decisions made by the people's duly elected representatives'.[189] If lawyers object to laws relevant to cases, it is said that they should still vindicate their clients' rights, but seek reform through the democratic process, rather than surreptitiously substituting their views for those of the institutions of liberal government.[190] From this it flows that lawyers are obliged to obtain any benefit for clients which the law allows. Moral activism may also undermine the courts' authority. By refusing to argue cases the lawyer usurps the judiciary's role as the adjudicator of disputes[191] and, as we have seen,[192] by refusing to argue cases zealously lawyers can be said to undermine the adversarial system's effectiveness. Where it is not just the facts of cases that are disputed but also the law, the lawyer also usurps the courts' important role of legal clarification and development.[193] Lawyers who argue cases with which they have no sympathy can be said to benefit society whether

---

[185] Pepper 1996b.

[186] Only explicitly argued in Britain by Pannick 1992, pp.167–8. For an overview of the arguments raised elsewhere, see Goldman 1980, pp.96–7 and 111–12.

[187] Mellinkoff 1973, p.158.   [188] Ellman 1990, p.156.

[189] Freedman 1978, p.195. See also Pepper 1986a, p.617; Wasserstrom 1975, pp.10–11 (raising but not endorsing this argument).

[190] Freedman 1975, p.49; Mellinkoff 1973, p.158; Fried 1976, pp.1080–2; Pepper 1986, p.617.

[191] cf Sir Thomas Erskine at n.230, below.

[192] Section 2.   [193] See Gillers 1986, pp.1025–6.

they win or lose. Either way, they will make manifest any apparent need for legislative intervention. Moreover, litigation may provoke public debate, new insights into problems and moral pressure on the parties to modify their behaviour. Finally, by providing citizens with a court system, their grievances can be channelled 'into socially controlled non-violent means of dispute resolution',[194] thus averting violence and instability.

4.2 Evaluating the Arguments

The wider reaches of these arguments are easily countered. The idea that many lawyers will act as law enforcers during office hours and law reformers in their spare time seems rather naive,[195] as the profession's record on *pro bono* work suggests. Even if neutral partisanship does not anaesthetise lawyers' moral and political sensibilities as we have argued,[196] busy lawyers are unlikely to have the necessary time or energy for such 'schizoid lawyering',[197] whereas many lawyers are unlikely to want to be seen campaigning against laws which benefit their regular client base. It also seems absurd to have lawyers expending energy solving problems that they helped create in the first place. Equally, the idea that lawyers who exercise moral activism represent an 'undemocratic oligarchy' is little more than emotive rhetoric. As Luban caustically notes, 'The worry about a hidden Central Committee of lawyers evaporates when we realize that the committee will never hold a meeting, and that its members don't even know they are on it.'[198]

However, there still remains the argument that *individual* lawyers can subvert democracy, the rule of law, and the liberal organs of government by declining to enforce the citizens' legal rights. One response could track the earlier arguments made about law's limited value in societies riven with class, race and gender differences in order to make the point that democracy and the rule of law are not the unalloyed virtues they would be in more egalitarian societies.[199] Less radically, one can challenge the arguments for neutral partisanship based upon the values and institutions of liberal government from within the liberal tradition. Central to these arguments is the idea that if conduct is going to be prohibited this should be done by democratically elected institutions and, in interstitial cases,[200] by the courts.

Other criticisms go to the heart of the reliance on liberal government. Building on our earlier criticisms of legal formalism for conflating law with morality and justice, it can be argued that, despite disapproving intensely of certain behaviour, bodies with legislative power might decline to act where it would be 'too difficult to specify the conduct, or if the laws would of necessity be vague or over- or under-inclusive, or if enforcement would destroy our liberties'.[201] For example, English

---

[194] Freedman 1990, p.18.   [195] See Gordon 1988, pp.22–3.   [196] See Ch.6.
[197] Term taken from Gordon, *loc cit* n.195.
[198] Luban 1986, p.641. See also Goldman 1980, pp.129–30.
[199] See eg Fine 1984.   [200] See Bell 1983.
[201] Luban 1986, p.640. See also Postema 1980, p.86.

judges might regard as immoral the failure to rescue those in physical danger, but they have declined to impose general duties to rescue. Similarly, the law declines to prohibit activities like gambling and prostitution, yet at the same time withholds legal backing for related contracts.[202] Legislative bodies may also be 'too "anaesthetized or simply overworked" to remedy obvious deficiencies in legal standards',[203] while financial considerations are likely to have a similar inhibitory effect. In addition, certain behaviour might remain unprohibited simply because legislatures have never considered its morality. The lawyer who refuses to help exploit a new cybernetic form of transmitting child pornography into the country is hardly usurping the authority of a legislature as yet unaware of this activity. Consequently, it cannot be argued that all conduct that remains legal is necessarily legislatively and judicially condoned, and hence may justifiably be furthered by lawyers without moral criticism.

This argument is not implicitly based, as Pepper rhetorically suggests, on the assumption that the legislature has delegated 'to the individual lawyer the authority for case-by-case legislation and policing'. Even if lawyers have not been delegated power to refuse to pursue what they see as immoral ends or immoral means, this does not mean that they are obliged to assist clients irrespective of their moral beliefs. For Pepper's argument to work, it needs to be established that, by specifically sanctioning, defining and giving effect to certain acts, the law intends persons wanting to engage in such activities to have any necessary legal assistance.[204] Yet, particularly in the light of the recent inroads to legal aid, it is clear that English law provides no legally guaranteed right to legal representation. It merely facilitates legal assistance if it can be obtained. Even where the law places obstacles in the way of individuals maximising their autonomy, it cannot be said that it thereby impliedly requires lawyers to provide legal assistance in negotiating these obstacles. To say, for instance, that lawyers must assist munitions companies in obtaining administrative permission to export landmines would mean that such companies could also compel the assistance of accountants or engineers if their involvement was also required by law. Moreover, lawyers who refuse on moral grounds to act in these situations do not usurp the legislature's authority to impose the obstacle since their objection is not to the obstacle, but to the way in which the company wants to exercise its autonomy.[205] If they are second-guessing the legislature, they do so in relation to its decision to allow companies to make landmines and accordingly are in exactly the same position as the engineer and accountant.[206]

The final counter-argument against the claim that moral activism would usurp the institutions of liberal government is based upon the critique of some of the formalist assumptions underlying the liberal justification for neutral partisanship.[207] One assumption is that law and legal rights exist in a determinate form, waiting to

---

[202] Schwartz 1978, p.685.   [203] Rhode 1985, p.603, quoting Kennedy 1973, p.394.
[204] cf Fried 1976, p.1075.   [205] cf Gillers 1986, p.1028.
[206] The situation can, however, be regarded as different in the case of advocates: see Ch.8, section 5.4.
[207] Simon 1988, pp.1124–5; Wilkins 1990.

be used by their beneficiaries. As legal realism has convincingly established, law's content is fluid and subject to complex processes of construction both inside and outside courtrooms.[208] Zealous legal representation can often extend beyond vindicating rights to actually creating them, either because no rights existed beforehand or because the case involved competing rights. Accordingly, it is difficult to see how lawyers can escape involvement in law-making.[209]

However, zealous representation can also effectively negate rights, such as where lawyers rely on tactical devices to avoid what otherwise would be unwanted legal consequences.[210] Here, lawyers can be said to undermine the authority of those creating and enforcing such rights. Of course, extreme Realists would say that legal rights are simply what the law can be made to yield. As a description of the practical consequences for those asserting legal rights, this view is persuasive. But in ethical terms there comes a point when it can be said that the zealous lawyer is not simply putting into effect, but undermining, legislative and judicial decisions as to how people should behave.[211]

In fact, the lawyer's creative role extends beyond this. While the duties on litigators to reveal all legal sources (whether advantageous or not)[212] law's public nature and the fact that the plausibility of legal arguments can be fairly closely monitored make the scope for usurpation of the court's role of clarifying law somewhat limited, the same cannot be said as regards fact adjudication. Fact sceptics like Frank have persuasively argued that the facts of cases are even more determinate and subject to construction than the law.[213] One can accept that there are never 'true' sets of facts behind cases, or even if there are, that they can never be found, yet still recognise that lawyers have considerable scope through truth-obstructing tactics to distort what might otherwise be the impact of the facts. And when one considers that most cases turn on factual issues, it is clear that the willingness of lawyers to zealously pursue client interest can significantly undermine the courts' truth-finding capability.[214] Moreover, given the important link between factual and legal construction, fact construction by zealous lawyers can further influence what rights are created in cases.[215]

Also relevant is the fact that most legal disputes are settled out of court. Admittedly, they are settled in the courts' shadow, but that does not mean that settlements always represent likely judicial decisions, especially if there are differences in bargaining position between the parties and no court to see 'fair play'. Indeed, lawyers may well decide to keep matters out of court where they perceive weaknesses in their

---

[208] See eg Wilkinson 1990, pp.478–84.   [209] Simon 1988, p.1125; Gordon 1988, p.26ff.
[210] See Ch.6, section 3.2.
[211] cf Luban 1986, pp.646–8 and 1988a, p.18ff in response to Pepper 1986a, p.624ff and 1986b, p.668 *in fine*; Gordon 1990, p.261ff.
[212] See Ch.8, at n.111.
[213] Frank 1949, Preface and 1973. See further, Nicolson 1997, pp.132–5.
[214] cf section 2 where the idea that partisan tactics support rather than undermine the adjudicative process was refuted.
[215] Nicolson 1994 and 1997.

client's case. In these circumstances, zealous representation subverts rather than upholds the courts' function.[216]

5. CONCLUSION

If our criticisms of the various arguments supporting neutral partisanship are convincing, then it follows that there is no blanket justification for all lawyers acting as neutral partisans on behalf of anyone who can afford to pay their fees. We have argued that the essential nature of neutral partisanship and the socio-economic context in which it operates frequently undermine the very institutions (the adversary system, the legislature and the courts) and values (human dignity, autonomy and equality, democracy and the rule of law) relied on to support it. In addition to this, we still have to take into account the harm to others that prompted the criticisms of lawyer behaviour we saw at the beginning of our discussion.

To be sure, it can still be argued that, although neutral partisanship does cause harm and undermines the values and institutions said to justify it, nevertheless, over the long run, neutral partisanship supports these institutions and values on more occasions than it undermines them. Such an argument would be perfectly valid given the rule-consequentialist nature of the main arguments for neutral partisanship.[217] However, apart from the argument from adversariality, the arguments for neutral partisanship have at most only been implicitly couched in rule-consequentialist terms. Instead, it is generally assumed, along more deontological lines, that neutral partisanship is intrinsically justified because it upholds the liberal values of dignity, autonomy, equality, democracy and the rule of law. Yet, not only does neutral partisanship lead to the invasion of other values, most importantly the idea of non-maleficence and the concern for others required by the ethics of care and alterity, but it frequently undermines the very values and institutions which it is meant to uphold.[218] It can be regarded as still open to supporters of neutral partisanship to show that in the long run the benefits of lawyer amorality outweigh the harm it causes generally and to their favoured values, but as yet, no such attempt has been made.[219] And one wonders whether one could ever persuasively make the sort of calculation required by rule-consequentialism in regard to the wide variety of contexts, values and harms raised by neutral partisanship. It would seem far better to weigh up the advantages of zealous representation in particular contexts if not in

---

[216] cf Luban 1988a, p.77. Of course, lawyers who ensure out of court settlements assist the smooth running of the justice system by preventing the courts being clogged up with cases which could easily be settled. However, this can be said whether they display all necessary zeal or not. Indeed, it is possible that zealous advocates are more likely to ensure that cases are settled which should have gone to court and more likely to ensure that cases go to court which should be settled.

[217] See section 1, above.   [218] See Gordon 1990, pp.258–61.

[219] cf, however, the argument that the time of ethics is one of immediacy rather than the future (or diachronic rather than synchronic in Levinas' terminology): see Douzinas and Warrington 1994, pp.238–40.

individual cases against the harm it may cause, taking into account also any dangers involved in allowing lawyers to abandon their amoral role.

As has been intermittently stressed throughout our discussion, many of the justifications proffered for neutral partisanship, while not justifying a blanket ban on moral activism by lawyers, may have considerable force in requiring lawyers to represent particular types of clients in particular situations despite moral objections to their ends and perhaps also to exercise all necessary zeal despite moral objections to the means necessary to those ends. As even the fiercest of critics of neutral partisanship has acknowledged, when we seek the services of lawyers we may entrust 'a large chunk of our life' to them and the fact that they take 'on so intimate a burden and [handle] it in a trustworthy and skilful manner when the stakes are high seems commendable in itself'.[220] Lawyers can thus be seen as intrinsically valuable when they give succour to those in need,[221] such as criminal defendants, tenants facing eviction and victims of negligence by multinational corporations. However, as Luban points out, there is a difference between the 'person-in-trouble' and the 'person-in-no-trouble, but-who-troubles-others'.[222] Indeed, when the lawyer represents those who want to exacerbate the former's problems, it becomes difficult to see how zealous representation is intrinsically valuable.

Thus zealous representation may, but equally may not, be morally worthy in itself. Similarly, abandonment of neutral partisanship may in some circumstances be regarded as problematic over and above its alleged positive values. One such argument is found in Johnson's famous reply to the perennial lay question posed by Boswell as to how lawyers can in conscience pursue causes which they 'know to be bad':

Sir you do not know it to be good or bad till the judge determines it. . . . An argument that does not convince yourself may convince the judge to whom you urge it; and if it does not convince him, why, then, Sir, you are wrong, and he is right. It is his business to judge; and you are not to be confident in your own opinion that a cause is bad, but to say all you can for your client, and then hear the Judge's opinion.

Implicit in this reply is what has been called the epistemological demurrer[223] and what may similarly be called the ethical demurrer.[224] The former refers to the idea that 'often we cannot know who is right and who is wrong until the case has been argued' and relies on 'the inherent difficulty of knowing, on the basis of material available to one side, in advance of court proceedings, what will be revealed at trial'.[225] As an English judge noted, 'the path of the law is strewn with examples of open and shut cases, which somehow were not; of unanswerable charges which, in the event were completely answered; of inexplicable conduct which was fully explained . . .'.[226] In terms of the ethical demurrer, lawyers humbly admit that they

[220] Luban 1988a, p.82.   [221] Mellinkoff 1973, p.270; Freedman 1986, esp p.331.
[222] Luban 1988a, p.83.   [223] Rhode 1985, pp.618–20.
[224] cf Rhode 1985, pp.620–3, referring to 'the appeal to agnosticism'.
[225] Pannick 1992, pp.149–50.
[226] *John v Rees* [1970] Ch 345, 402. cf also *Rondel v Worsley* [1969] 1 AC 191, 275C–D.

are not qualified to make the moral and other normative evaluations of the kind necessary if they were to abandon moral neutrality.[227] Similarly, it is argued that moral activism would require lawyers to assess matters such as the public interest, which are 'too nebulous . . . to serve as a basis for any practical action or judgment regarding a lawyer's professional conduct'.[228]

To a large extent the two demurrers do no more than reinforce the arguments made in sections 3 and 4, above.[229] Thus, the harm to dignity and autonomy caused by lawyers who refuse to give individuals a voice in court or access to the autonomy provided by law can be said to be particularly offensive because of the lawyer's inability to ever know the facts of legal disputes or make moral or public policy judgements about the exercise of autonomy. Similarly, lawyers who refuse to represent clients because of what they think of their cases can be said to assume 'the character of the judge . . . before the hour of judgment'[230] as well as that of legislative bodies charged with formulating society's moral standards. Consequently, given that these arguments fail to provide a blanket justification for neutral partisanship, so must the epistemological and ethical demurrers.

Indeed, reliance on the ethical demurrer appears hypocritical or at best, self-deceiving.[231] Few complain about lawyers' inability to make judgements about morality or the public interest once elevated to the bench.[232] Similarly, the profession as a whole does not deny its ability to make normative evaluations when convenient.[233] In defending their restrictive practices, lawyers have always claimed to be able to understand the public interest better than the public itself.[234] At first glance, the epistemological demurrer appears more persuasive given that, speaking metaphysically, no one can ever be said to 'know' the 'truth'.[235] But, despite the adversarial system's alleged qualities, this applies equally to courts. Indeed, as the codes implicitly recognise,[236] lawyers may often be better placed to 'know' the facts.[237] Apart from the obvious point that most cases do not reach court and hence there may be no adjudicator likely to have better knowledge than lawyers, we have also seen that lawyers frequently do their utmost to ensure that the truth is kept from the courts.

At the same time, while not justifying a blanket ban on moral activism, both

---

[227] See eg Mellinkoff 1973, p.157; Donegan 1983, p.132; Ellman 1990, p.156.

[228] Krash 1974, p.33. See also Donegan 1983, p.132.

[229] Freedman 1975, ch.5.

[230] Sir Thomas Erskine: *R v Thomas Paine* (1792) 22 State Trials 357, 412.

[231] cf Rhode 1985, p.621.

[232] cf Simon 1988, pp.1120–3.

[233] Rhode 1985, p.622. See also Luban 1988a, p.170.

[234] cf Zander 1968. Cf also Pannick's patronising dismissal of the critics of the cab-rank rule as simply not understanding its supporting arguments: 1992, pp.144, 145, and 149.

[235] cf Nicolson 1994.

[236] Thus lawyers are prohibited from 'knowingly' deceiving, limits are placed on the defence of those who admit their guilt to their lawyers, while para. 21.07 n.5, LSG even explicitly distinguishes between proffering evidence which is untrue to the 'solicitor's knowledge as opposed to his or her belief'.

[237] Curtis 1951, p.14; Freedman 1975, pp.52–3; Rhode 1985, p.619.

demurrers, the latter particularly, legitimately raise the possibility of lawyers being too ready to refuse possibly justified cases or tactics on 'mistaken' views of the facts or morality of cases. Consequently, the epistemological and ethical demurrers correctly counsel moral activist lawyers to allow the individual's legal rights and the legal process to take their course whenever they are not convinced about the facts or ethical merits of what they are being required to do on behalf of clients.[238]

A similar caution about exercising moral activism relates to the fact that it might breach clients' 'legitimate expectations' that, having paid for their services, lawyers will pursue their interests fully within legal limits.[239] Such an argument cannot, however, provide a blanket justification for neutral partisanship. By definition it only applies once the retainer is established and hence cannot prevent lawyers refusing representation on moral grounds. Similarly, this argument cannot, without lifting itself up by its own bootstraps, preclude modification of the expectation of zeal by individual arrangements between lawyers and clients, or by wholesale rule changes. Nevertheless, in line with the duty of good faith argued for in Chapter 5, it does urge lawyers to be cautious and candid before they decline to exercise all necessary zeal on moral grounds lest they lull clients into a false sense of security. However, even if lawyers do betray client trust, one can ask whether this is always an overriding evil. Breaking promises is a wrong, but not an absolute wrong. Circumstances will always exist when the evil caused by zealous representation will outweigh the evil involved in not fulfilling the promise or expectation of lawyer zeal, such as when lawyers acting for oil companies learn of plans to flout environmental rules and cause enormous harm. In addition, as Goldman argues,[240] the failure to fulfil agreements or expectations carries less weight in the case of promises or expectation of immoral acts. Here the client's complaint is not so much that the agreement or expectation to do something immoral was not fulfilled but that it was created in the first place. The mere promise or creation of expectation that something will be done cannot make moral what would otherwise be immoral.

We thus see that there is much that is valuable about zealous legal representation of clients and that there are dangers in abandoning neutral partisanship, but that these values and dangers are not so universally applicable as to swing the balance in favour of a total prohibition on lawyer activism. It is therefore necessary to turn to an exploration of how far one can go in moving away from neutral partisanship without abandoning what is valuable about lawyer zeal and without running into problems associated with moral activism.

[238] See Heffernan 1985.
[239] For statements and criticisms of this argument, see Goldman 1980, pp.108, 134–5; Wasserstrom 1983, pp.31–2; Gillers 1986, esp p.1019; Stier 1991, p.464.
[240] ibid, pp.134–5.

8

Reforming the Lawyer's Amoral Role

Yes, we can doubtless gain your case for you; we can set a whole neighborhood at loggerheads; we can distress a widowed mother and her six fatherless children and thereby get you six hundred dollars to which you seem to have a legal claim, but which rightly belongs, it appears to me, as much to the woman and her children as it does to you. You must remember that some things legally right are not morally right. We shall not take your case, but will give you a little advice for which we will charge you nothing. You seem to be a sprightly, energetic man; we would advise you to try your hand at making six hundred dollars in some other way.

Abraham Lincoln[1]

1. INTRODUCTION

In rejecting the blanket justification for neutral partisanship in the previous chapter, we did not conclude that lawyers should *never* act zealously on behalf of clients. As the discussion of criminal defence work shows, lawyers may still be required to so act even when they have ethical or political objections to the ends or means of representation. Instead, our conclusion only entails rejection of the principle of neutrality. Although individual lawyers may be able to justify acting zealously for some clients, they are always morally responsible for their decision to do so. Lawyers cannot simply divert moral censure of their behaviour by an appeal to their role. More importantly, lawyers are not entitled to quieten their own moral conscience by taking refuge in the argument that pursuit of this role is a moral act in itself.

In this chapter we intend to sketch our view of how morally activist lawyers should approach the dilemmas of practice arising from the problems of immoral ends and means. The main body of the chapter will be devoted to developing an approach which tailors the various options open to lawyers in departing from neutral partisanship to the particular contexts of legal representation. Before that, however, we need to have an idea of what these options are.

2. ALTERNATIVES TO NEUTRAL PARTISANSHIP

In developing a contextual approach to the ends and means issue, we need to consider more closely what alternatives there are to the strong version of neutral

---

[1] Quoted in Luban 1988a, p.174.

partisanship—in other words, to requiring rather than simply entitling lawyers to exercise all necessary zeal on behalf of anyone able to pay their fees without consideration of the moral dimensions of such representation. Here three main options present themselves: 'moral dialogue'; the refusal of representation altogether; and the refusal to pursue every client end or use every effective means to client ends. In evaluating these options, we need to consider their moral implications not just in isolation from, but also in combination with, each other. An option may appear innocuous on its own, but be harmful when combined with another.

2.1 'It's Good to Talk'—Moral Dialogue

One option favoured by both critics and supporters of neutral partisanship,[2] and possible under current ethical rules,[3] involves lawyers discussing with clients the morality and possible harmful impact of the ends and/or the means of representation. 'Moral dialogue' may be conducted in the 'same matter-of-fact and . . . unmoralistic manner that one discusses the financial aspects of a representation'.[4] It may merely involve lawyers attempting to show that less immoral or harmful options are in fact in the clients' interests,[5] or it may involve lawyers actively trying to persuade clients to adopt less immoral or harmful ends or means.[6] The benefits of moral dialogue are not all one way. It may not just allow lawyers to resolve moral dilemmas by getting clients to come round to their way of thinking or at least reaching compromises over their moral differences. By abandoning an approach whereby moral issues are deemed off-limits, lawyers may—for the reasons discussed earlier[7]— actually provide a better service to their clients and avoid lawyer paternalism. Discussion and debate between client and lawyer can engender better self-awareness on the part of each as well as a deeper mutual understanding. Indeed, lawyers may learn that particular clients do not simply want what is best in material terms but may also want to 'do the right thing'.

At the same time, it has to be recognised that the efficacy of moral dialogue is limited.[8] For example, clients faced with serious consequences such as the loss of their liberty or considerable amounts of money are unlikely to be prepared to adopt less harmful means to their ends. Moral dialogue is also more likely to be effective in relation to immoral means rather than ends. Whereas some clients might be dissuaded from achieving their goals by any means, it is less likely that they will change their minds about what they initially wanted to achieve. Moral dialogue is also time-consuming and, especially in the legal world, time costs money. Ideally, the costs of moral dialogue should fall on both parties, given that lawyers benefit from the opportunity

---

[2] Simon 1978, pp.132ff; Heffernan 1985, pp.74–5; Pepper 1986a, pp.630–2; and 1995, p.1600ff; Luban 1988a, p.160ff; Edwards 1990, p.1160; Schneyer 1991, p.27.
[3] See Ch.6, section 2.1.   [4] Luban 1988a, p.173.
[5] For an actual example, see Simon 1998, p.129.
[6] cf Simon 1978, pp.132–3. But cf also Luban 1988a, pp.173–4.
[7] Ch.7, section 3.2.2.   [8] Pepper 1986a, p.332.

to integrate their personal morality with their professional obligations while clients obtain a better service. However, the difficulties of ascertaining how much extra time was devoted to discussing moral as opposed to legal and practical issues render such a solution unlikely. However, we would argue that, instead of billing clients for the extra time taken, thus further inflating legal costs and exacerbating access to justice problems, lawyers should be required to foot the bill for moral dialogue out of their current profit margins. It would be hypocritical for lawyers to claim to be an ethical profession and then immediately pass the bill to clients who already pay enough for the privilege of having a professional to represent their interests.

However, the most serious problem with moral dialogue relates to the possible invasions of client autonomy. As Pepper argues,[9] the fact that lawyers will generally have more knowledge and expertise than their clients, and the possibility of differences in their articulacy, social status, financial security, etc., creates the potential for lawyers either intentionally or unintentionally to ensure that their moral beliefs take precedence over those of their clients.

Although this problem is very real,[10] it does not arise equally in all contexts.[11] It does not therefore rule out moral dialogue in all cases. Instead, it counsels lawyers to be wary about the warmth with which they put forward their moral and political views. The level of persuasion employed where large companies want to engage in environmental degradation would be inappropriate where ill-educated, indigent clients are in dire need. The zeal with which lawyers advocate their own views should also depend crucially on whether or not they have the power ultimately to refuse to assist the client in pursuing behaviour perceived to be immoral. Indeed, without such a power, there is only so far that moral dialogue can both raise problems for client autonomy and resolve immoral ends and means dilemmas. We therefore need to examine the justifiability of a lawyer's right to 'conscientious objection'.[12]

2.2 Conscientious Objection—Refusal to Assist

Most critics of neutral partisanship and even a considerable number of its supporters[13] accept that lawyers should be able to refuse representation because of perceived immoral ends or means.[14] As we have seen, there is no justification for requiring

[9] See Ch.7, section 3.1.

[10] Although it pales into insignificance alongside other motivations for lawyers exercising undue control over their clients: see Ch.5. For an illuminating discussion of how moral activism may be made compatible with client autonomy, see Sisak 1997 (albeit in relation to client confidentiality).

[11] See Ch.7, section 3.2.2. cf also Postema 1980, p.84, who argues that moral paternalism is only a problem if lawyers already hold strongly paternalistic views.

[12] This phrase is used *inter alia* by Heffernan 1985, *passim*; Pepper 1986a, pp.332–3. cf also Luban 1988a, p.156, speaking of civil disobedience.

[13] See Fried 1976, pp.1082–6; Freedman 1978, esp pp.199 and 204–5, and 1990, pp.50–7 and 66–70; Donegan 1983, p.137; and, more tentatively, Pepper 1986a, p.634 and 1986b, p.660. cf comment to Rule 6.2 of ABA Model Rules: 'a lawyer ordinarily is not obliged to accept a client whose character or cause the lawyer regards as repugnant.'

[14] Indeed, it is sometimes even argued that lawyers should be able to refuse to represent clients on the basis of objections to their character or beliefs irrespective of what they want done on their behalf.

lawyers to obtain for or do on behalf of their clients everything the law and current rules of professional legal ethics allow. Rather than ensuring that those in need always obtain assistance, a strong principle of neutrality as exemplified by the cab-rank rule may actually ensure less personally felt commitments to protecting the needy.[15] There is a much stronger likelihood that a real commitment to these values will develop if lawyers as a group are obliged to debate when they should act for clients irrespective of personal morality, academics evaluate the solutions reached and students are exposed from an early stage to important questions of access to justice, civil liberties, morality and substantive justice. Indeed, lawyers might even develop a greater commitment to helping those currently unable to afford their fees.

With the abandonment of neutral partisanship and the cab-rank rule, the emergence of what Luban has called lawyers 'for a principle' or 'for the damned'[16] also becomes more likely. Like criminal lawyers who defend those they believe to be guilty in the belief that everyone is entitled to a fair trial, the former type of lawyers recognise that while they may personally object to clients, their ends or the means to those ends, some higher principle is at stake. For example, ardent supporters of civil liberties might represent racists in order to protect freedom of expression.[17] Lawyers 'for the damned', on the other hand, recognise a moral duty to defend those who no one else is prepared to represent. They respond to the plight of the Other.[18]

Abandonment of neutral partisanship and the cab-rank rule may also ensure more effective upholding of professional ideals in another way. Those in need of legal representation will generally receive greater zeal, more empathy and understanding, and generally better service from lawyers who either share their values or who regard it as their moral duty to provide representation than those who provide representation solely because of the force of professional rules.[19] Indeed, it can be argued that this need to ensure effective representation means that no lawyer should ever be required to act for clients whose ends, means to those ends or characters are so repugnant as to jeopardise committed representation. It would seem better for such clients to have to seek other lawyers than to be sabotaged by less than zealous representation.[20]

Consequently, there are strong arguments for allowing lawyers to withhold their services where they have strong moral, political or personal objections to the client, her ends or the means necessary to achieve those ends. While we shall later argue that there are certain types of clients who always deserve representation, for the reasons already noted, we do not think that forcing lawyers to represent such clients is likely to ensure that their needs are best met. Moreover, to do so can be said to be unfair in placing an obligation on the lawyer who happens to be first in line which ought to rest on the profession as a whole. It is true that money, status and other

---

[15] Ch.7, section 3.2.2.   [16] Luban 1988a, pp.160–6.

[17] cf Aryeh Neier (a Jewish lawyer who defended the right of free speech of Nazis) quoted in Elkins 1992, p.785 n.97.

[18] But cf Ellman's criticism (1990, p.150) of Luban's argument (1988a, p.163) that lawyers for the damned are obliged to transform and redeem their clients. Such an approach, as Luban (1990b, pp.1025–6) later admits, is excessively overbearing and invasive of the client's dignity and autonomy.

[19] cf Simon 1978, p.132; Wolfram 1983, p.224.   [20] See Wolfram 1983, p.224.

benefits create incentives for lawyers to represent clients irrespective of moral considerations. However, we cannot simply hope that no client will be refused by all lawyers.[21] For one thing, it is the poor and the unpopular, rather than the rich and powerful, who are most likely to find themselves unrepresented. For this reason alone, there needs to be a safety net to catch the 'victims' of conscientious objection.

One suggestion for ensuring representation without undermining the moral autonomy of individual lawyers is to limit the right of refusal to all but the 'last lawyer in town'.[22] In other words, lawyers may only refuse clients where there are other (competent) lawyers available. Such a solution is, however, impractical. When does one know that one is the last lawyer in town? How big is the 'town' for the purposes of the rule? If lawyers are expected to approach every available lawyer in a 'town' as big as London, by the time they find the 'last lawyer' it may be too late to vindicate their interests. A better solution would be to provide those whose interests are deemed to entitle them to legal representation with a legal right to approach the Bar or Law Society after being refused a certain number of times (say three) by lawyers.[23] These bodies would then appoint a lawyer from a list made up either of all lawyers in the relevant area or preferably by suitably remunerated[24] volunteers who are less likely to show weakened commitment because of having clients foisted onto them.

Such a solution is, however, not totally watertight. As Pepper has pointed out, 'finding one lawyer is hard enough, and if that lawyer says "no", the effort to find another may well be too great. Changing lawyers is costly psychologically as well as financially.'[25] Consequently, clients may abandon the search for a lawyer after only one refusal or, because of power differentials between them and the first lawyer approached, may be influenced to limit their ends or means to those ends in ways which may be regarded as limiting their autonomy. These problems are by no means likely to arise with all prospective clients, though once again they are far more likely to be prevalent with clients from lower socio-economic groups. Consequently, another way of ensuring access to legal services would be to prohibit lawyers from refusing to assist clients unless they are able to find a substitute of equivalent competence and experience.[26]

---

[21] cf Donegan 1983, p.137; Ball 1983, p.566; Disney *et al* 1986, p.607.

[22] The phrase appears to be that of Schwartz 1983, p.562. See also Freedman 1978, p.198; Wolfram 1983, p.222; Hall 1990; Rhodes 1991, p.40. This is the approach in New South Wales: Disney *et al* 1986, p.602.

[23] A similar scheme applies to Scottish solicitors: Phillips 1990, p.39. See also Pollitt 1964, pp.27–8; Schwartz 1978, p.695, 1983, pp.562–3, 1993, pp.562–3.

[24] Such remuneration is highly appropriate given that the volunteers take on the responsibilities of those who would prefer not to compromise their moral integrity or who are motivated solely by material considerations.

[25] Pepper 1986b, p.660.

[26] cf Hall 1990. The only drawback would be a residual sense of responsibility on the part of the first lawyer approached for any harmful or otherwise immoral actions pursued by a subsequent lawyer. However, such a feeling can be partly assuaged by the lawyer first attempting to dissuade the client from immoral ends or means before deciding to 'pass the buck'.

If lawyers are to have the right to 'conscientious objection' they need to exercise even greater caution when engaging in moral dialogue. Where clients are likely to be unduly deferential to lawyer opinion, the right may act as a Damoclean sword, compelling clients to jettison their own interests. Here it might be better that lawyers who have very strong objections to client ends or means which are unlikely to be met by minor modifications of the client's wishes should refrain from any attempt at dissuasion and simply decline representation. Where, however, clients are unlikely to be deterred from their chosen ends and means without a true 'conversion', moral dialogue might be appropriate even if its failure might end in the refusal of representation.

Thus far we have dealt with the withholding of assistance prior to a retainer being established. Clients might, however, initially conceal their true goals or other relevant information[27] or form an intention to pursue immoral ends or means in response to information given to them following research by lawyers or new developments in the case. Should lawyers have the same right to withdraw as to refuse assistance in the first place? For a number of reasons the answer must be no.

One practical problem involves having to ascertain who should bear the costs of lawyer withdrawal. For instance, should clients only pay when they have deliberately concealed their intentions regarding their ends or should they also pay for any benefits they receive prior to the lawyer's decision to withdraw? More importantly, the emotional energy required to find alternative lawyers is likely to be greater where the relationship has already begun. Most importantly, withdrawal from representation may sabotage the client's interests, for instance, by rendering litigation time barred or leaving the client without representation in court. Equally, it may signal to opponents or to adjudicators that there is some flaw in clients' cases.[28]

Consequently, having commenced representation, lawyers should only be allowed to withdraw where this would not substantially harm clients.[29] In addition, they should always be required to take into account any inconvenience and distress caused by withdrawal and should ensure that withdrawal does not place clients in a worse financial position.

2.3 Pulling Punches—Qualified Representation[30]

A final option for morally activist lawyers is to represent clients, but to refrain from actions that they regard as morally or politically objectionable. For example, advocates may seek to win cases, but decline to deliberately obstruct the truth, humiliate witnesses, rely on technicalities to defeat meritorious claims, etc. Similarly, lawyers may assist clients with their tax liabilities, but refrain from exploiting loop-

---

[27] cf *R v Courvoisier* (1840) 173 ER 869, discussed in detail by Mellinkoff 1973, where the defending barrister was surprised with an admission of guilt late in the proceedings.

[28] See the discussion of the perjury rules in section 6.2.2, below.

[29] cf para. 504(a) and (g), CCB; para. 5.1(a) of Annex 21A, LSG.

[30] cf Heffernan 1985, who speaks of 'qualified access'.

holes in relevant legislation. At first glance, this option appears the most innocuous of the three canvassed. However, depending on how it operates, it may prove to be the most problematic.

There can be little objection to lawyers failing to pursue all possible client ends or means to those ends where they have discussed their moral objections with the client and obtained consent to the reduction of zeal. Of course, there must be informed consent.[31] Clients must be informed that they are entitled to obtain another lawyer and the lawyer's right to refuse assistance must not be used as a weapon to compel client consent. Similarly, lawyers should be aware and take steps to counter any other imbalances in bargaining position between themselves and their clients. What is, however, objectionable is for lawyers simply to conceal from their clients the existence of legal options, such as loopholes in tax legislation, or, without any warning, refrain from all necessary zeal. By not giving clients the opportunity of finding less scrupulous lawyers, lawyers not only betray client trust, but also engage in sabotage through deception.

Consequently, we can conclude that lawyers should always inform clients of their objections to pursuing certain means on their behalf in the hope that they can dissuade them. If clients are unpersuaded, it can be argued that lawyers should either refuse assistance if they can or, if not, swallow their moral objections and do the best for clients. To fail to do so in the knowledge that clients expressly want the lawyer to pursue immoral ends and means can be regarded as equally, if not even more, unethical than surreptitious betrayal. It is thus arguable that morally upright lawyers should never contemplate either the surreptitious or blatant betrayal of clients.

In response, two points may be noted. The first is that the betrayal response is made more likely and more understandable if lawyers are prohibited from declining representation. This provides an additional reason for abandoning the cab-rank rule. Secondly, while morally responsible lawyers are rarely likely to 'betray' clients, it can be argued that this option should not be totally ruled out.[32] For instance, one could argue that the harm caused to the environment and to the health and human rights of the citizens of oil rich countries outweighs the immorality of betraying multinational corporations by declining to exploit all possible means to obtain mining rights and evade norms protecting the environment and human rights.

3. MORAL ACTIVISM AND ETHICAL FOUNDATIONS

Before looking at how the application of these options can be tailored to the various contexts of legal representation, we need to look briefly at the question of whether lawyers are simply expected to rely on their own personal moral values in applying our contextual approach, or whether professional norms can go further and lay down

---

[31] See Ch.5, section 4.2–3.
[32] Pepper 1986a, pp.332–3; Luban 1988a, esp at p.174 and 1990b, pp.1022 and 1026.

some more objective ethical foundations for moral activism. Of course, if there are persuasive suggestions for objective ethical standards guiding lawyer discretion, there are good grounds for writing them into our contextual approach. They would minimise the dangers of lawyers going off on 'frolics of their own', declining to extend all necessary zeal to clients on mere personal whim, and would help prospective clients predict what they can expect when they seek legal assistance.

On the other hand, from the perspective of moral scepticism, the claim to objective standards is necessarily suspect. As postmodernists persuasively argue, moral realism's search for objective foundations has proved fruitless and, more importantly, politically dangerous.[33] However, as not everyone is likely to be convinced by these criticisms, we shall briefly consider the three major suggestions for objective foundations for moral activism.

The first relies on the values within law. The most developed proposal comes from Simon[34] who argues that lawyers should have a Dworkinian-style[35] discretion to depart from neutral partisanship in order to promote law's ideals and values.[36] This, however, assumes that legal ideals and values are sufficiently clear and consistent to provide answers to the infinite variety of moral dilemmas raised by legal representation. Critical Legal Studies scholars, for example, have persuasively argued that law is inherently indeterminate and subject to a series of contradictions and conflicting values which render impossible clear and predictable answers to problems of legal interpretation.[37] Far more importantly, Simon fails to argue, let alone establish, that the law's spirit, values, ideals, or purposes are worth pursuing.[38] His approach will only be an improvement on neutral partisanship if the law itself is moral and just. In many cases, substantive and procedural injustice flows from the purpose and spirit of law itself. Simon's approach would, for instance, provide scant assistance to lawyers asked to prosecute battered women charged with murdering their assailants. For those critical of the Western legal order and many of its laws, Simon's approach does little more than deal with the worst excesses of neutral partisanship, namely where it leads to subversion of just laws and procedural values. And, as we have seen, even those who are generally supportive of this legal order recognise that the law, morality and justice do not always coincide.[39]

Somewhat wider is Goldman's argument that lawyers should refrain from pursu-

---

[33] See Ch.2, section 7.3.

[34] Simon 1988 and 1998. See also Simon 1978, p.130ff. For less developed approaches, see Gordon 1988 and 1990; Wilkins 1990; and cf Schwartz 1978, p.671; and 1983, pp.554–5, relying on the notion of 'unconscionability' in the US law of rescission, reformation, and torts, without developing his argument.

[35] See eg Dworkin 1977.

[36] Which he conflates with 'justice': Simon 1988, pp.1083 and 1090. Applied to conscientious objection, Simon argues that lawyers should ask whether acting would be an appropriate distribution of their limited ability to help those needing legal assistance. Applied to the question of the internal merits of client goals Simon argues that lawyers should strive to ensure that decisions should turn on their 'underlying merits', that legal procedures work as effectively as possible and that, where they cannot neutralise or repair defects in the relevant legal procedures, 'the most legally appropriate resolution' of their cases are reached. In addition, lawyers should seek to uphold the purposes of laws except where they are unclear or pose 'an especially grave threat to fundamental legal values'.

[37] See eg Hunt 1986.   [38] Atkinson 1992, p.894ff.   [39] Ch.7, at n.151.

ing clients' legal rights when this would violate the moral rights of others.[40] There are practical problems with the details of his suggestion, flowing from his failure to specify in much detail the content of his rights[41] or how lawyers should weigh their clients' moral rights against those of others. However, the main problem with Goldman's arguments, as with most rights theorists, is that the only difference between Goldman's approach and that of moral subjectivism is that he has chosen to translate those moral considerations which he values into the emotively charged language of moral rights in order to give them privileged protection. Nor, for the reasons also canvassed in Chapter 2,[42] can this impression be avoided by Goldman's reliance on a Rawlsian 'veil of ignorance'.

Our main problems, however, relate to the meta-ethical foundations and political implications of a moral rights approach. In our opinion, Bentham's dismissal of natural moral rights as 'nonsense upon stilts' has yet to be refuted.[43] The turn to veils of ignorance and ideal speech situations might make the ensuing moral rights less personal to the person asserting them, but it only replaces possible personal prejudices with those prevalent within particular social milieus. This is, in fact, clear from the way that Goldman ends up with a morality that favours individuals over the collective and self-interest over altruism by carefully limiting his rights to those of a negative nature. Indeed, as we saw in Chapter 2,[44] the very reliance on rights as the lawyer's yardstick involves a preference for individualism and other features of the social status quo. While recognising the political cachet accompanying rights discourse and hence its short-term utility to excluded groups, we remain highly sceptical both of the content of the rights privileged by liberals like Goldman as well as the very notion of rights. In summary, the content of these rights is closely linked to the liberal socio-legal order, which we have already criticised for privileging some over others and for focusing on the freedom of the powerful to pursue their interests while ignoring the fact that many lack the freedom necessary to enjoy a meaningful social existence. Moreover, as we also saw, rights may themselves play an important part in helping to support an oppressive status quo.

Consequently, it can be concluded that Goldman's approach might discourage lawyers from simply acting in ways supportive of the legal status quo, but it would not do much to challenge iniquities flowing from the socio-economic status quo. More specifically, it is unlikely to preclude lawyers from acting in ways that harm interests, such as those of the environment and future generations, which according to some postmodernists require urgent protection but which are not, at least currently, accorded moral rights.[45]

---

[40] Goldman 1980, ch.3, esp p.137ff.

[41] He merely says that rights are necessary to enable individuals 'to formulate and pursue their own plans of life' and to 'stake out a moral space in which individuals can develop and pursue their own values within a social context', and that they express 'the fundamental liberal values of individual autonomy and equality': ibid. pp.28–9.

[42] Section 7.2.   [43] Ch.2 at n.40.   [44] Section 3.4.

[45] It is doubtful whether 'third generation' rights, even if they were to become well established, would extend as far as Bauman and others would require. cf Ajei 1995.

The third suggestion of objective standards for the morally activist lawyers is Luban's reliance on 'common morality'.[46] However, he does not simply suggest that lawyers should always follow common morality when it clashes with neutral partisanship. Instead, they should weigh the moral reasons arguing for and against this role morality. More specifically, Luban recommends that lawyers engage in his inelegantly dubbed 'four-fold root of sufficient reasoning'. This requires them to justify (1) the institution(s) supported by neutral partisanship by showing its/their moral good; (2) neutral partisanship by appealing to the institution's structure; (3) lawyers' obligations by showing that they are essential to the neutral partisan role; and (4) the particular act required by neutral partisanship by showing that the above obligations require it.

Using this approach, Luban comes to similar conclusions[47] to us in relation to the representation of criminal defendants and those in similar positions of powerlessness in civil cases. However, out of concern at the damage to lawyers' moral and psychological integrity were they obliged to constantly decide that the morality of following their role is outweighed by common morality,[48] he concludes that in all other cases neutral partisanship should be a default position, acting as a defeasible presumption to be applied unless there are strong contrary considerations of common morality.

In our view, his conclusions as regards the latter type of cases should be rejected.[49] We do not think that the interests of lawyers are sufficient to justify a role morality that may require harmful and otherwise highly immoral conduct. If lawyers are going to act as neutral partisans it must be because the interests of clients and the general public are too important to be left to consequentialist calculations in each specific situation. Whether this can be said to be the case, however, requires the sort of argumentation provided in the next section.

More pertinently to the issue of objective standards, Luban's use of 'common morality' as the touchstone for overriding neutral partisanship runs into a number of problems. One is that he fails to specify how strong the demands of common morality need to be in order to bar zealous representation. More fundamentally, Luban fails to establish the existence of any 'common morality'. In elaboration of its practical operation, he states that lawyers should not inflict morally unjustifiable damage on others, be deceitful, use morally defensible laws in ways which violate their generality or spirit, or pursue substantively unjust results.[50] However, while defining what he means by deceit[51] and 'morally defensible law'[52] Luban declines to

---

[46] Luban 1988a, esp ch.6. See also the more limited use of common morality by Wolf 1983.

[47] Luban 1990a, pp.425–52 (retreating from his earlier conclusion in Luban 1988a, esp p.154ff, in response to criticisms by Wasserman 1990, that lawyers should only act as neutral partisans when its dictates are in accord with common morality).

[48] Acknowledged in 1998a, p.125, but not acted upon.

[49] cf also the criticisms of Wasserman 1990; Ellman 1990; Atkinson 1992.

[50] 1988a, p.157.

[51] ibid: 'actions that obscure truths or that lure people into doing business under misapprehensions'.

[52] See Luban 1988a, ch.3.

do likewise in relation to the crucial phrases 'morally unjustifiable damage' and 'substantively unjust results', presumably because of his belief in the existence of a social consensus on issues like abortion and capital punishment, gratuitous cruelty towards children, etc. These, however, are not the moral issues that routinely trouble practising lawyers. Even if we can say there is a consensus on such 'big' issues—which, as the issues of abortion and capital punishment illustrate, is naive[53]—this is far less likely to be true in respect of whether lawyers should, for instance, seek the acquittal of defendants who have confessed their guilt or use procedural technicalities to defeat meritorious claims. Indeed, there is likely to be serious disagreement on some of the bigger moral issues raised by client ends, such as the justifiability of tax evasion schemes or the sale of weapons to repressive regimes.

More importantly, even if there is a social consensus on particular moral issues, this does not entail that we ought to follow it. No doubt Luban would not have condoned earlier American lawyers using racist legislation to achieve client goals, notwithstanding that it was supported by most Americans. The problem with the reliance on 'common morality' is that it may go no further than cultural anthropology in merely identifying a society's moral consensus, without providing normative arguments why such consensus should be followed. As Atkinson persuasively argues, to answer Hume's 'is-ought' question,[54] Luban either has to argue that the common morality upon which he relies is grounded in objective values going beyond the mere fact of its acceptance or acknowledge that his decision to follow 'common morality' is based on no more than *his* personal values. Given that such objective grounds have yet to be persuasively established, and given our support for the postmodernist criticisms of previous attempts to do so, we thus conclude that lawyers can do no better than rely on their own moral values in resolving ends and means dilemmas.

4. A CONTEXTUAL APPROACH TO IMMORAL ENDS AND MEANS

This, however, does not mean that ethical discourse must begin and end with the recognition that there can be no moral standards other than those of each individual practitioner. In addition to the problems already noted in Chapter 4 with regard to deregulating professional legal ethics,[55] we accept that simply leaving lawyers to apply their own, hopefully well thought out, moral and political values to ethical dilemmas is unfair to both lawyers and their clients. Without any guidance on exercising their discretion, lawyers are likely to end up suffering from moral paralysis, given the enormous and difficult task of weighing up every single moral consideration relevant to every moral dilemma. On the other hand, for all the reasons also

[53] See Ch.2, section 7.2, where Luban's arguments are dealt with; Ellman 1990, pp.129–30 for similar criticisms.
[54] See Ch.2 at n.51.   [55] Section 3.4.

canvassed in Chapter 4, we do not think that the solution lies in attempting to reduce all the possible moral dilemmas over means and ends to rules. In particular, such a formalistic approach would not do much to rectify the anaesthetisation of moral conscience that flows from the lawyer's amoral role. Consequently, in line with the approach of 'aspirational' codes, we suggest that the professional codes should regulate means and ends issues by laying down a number of considerations relevant to particular dilemmas which lawyers would have to take into account before deciding how to respond. These considerations would guide rather than determine their decisions. Moreover, particularly if they were to include an elaboration of the rationale behind the various considerations, the codes thus formulated would play an important role in educating lawyers as to moral values, including that of providing legal representation to the needy.

For a number of reasons, we accept that the starting point for such a decision-making schema is the idea that there is a defeasible presumption in favour of neutral partisanship.[56] Not only is the zealous pursuit by lawyers of the interests of their clients the *raison d'être* of the lawyer-client relationship, but as we have seen there are valuable benefits to be gained from the principle of partisanship. Consequently, in some areas of practice and in relation to some types of cases, it may be appropriate for lawyers to adopt the neutral partisans' stance. The aim of the following discussion is to explore when this should be the case.

Here our discussion will be organised around two important contextual factors. The first relates to the type of dilemma involved: should lawyers represent the particular client given their moral objections to their ends (or even to clients themselves) and, if so, should they use all necessary zeal and available tactics in representing clients? The second involves the type of legal work involved: criminal defence, criminal prosecution, civil litigation, negotiation, the legal facilitation of personal or financial affairs through legal mechanisms or advice, or lobbying. Within these two contexts a wide variety of other factors will be relevant which either affect the applicability of the justifications for neutral partisanship or provide reasons for lawyers to pursue ends or means to which they have moral objections. These will be referred to as and when they arise.

5. IMMORAL ENDS AND DECISIONS TO REPRESENT[57]

5.1 Introduction

As we have seen,[58] the Anglo-Welsh approach to decisions to represent is one of wide contrast. Either—as in the case of barristers and solicitor-advocates—refusal is

---

[56] See Ch.7, section 5.

[57] We will only discuss the initial decision to represent. As we noted in section 2.2, above, additional considerations apply to decisions to withdraw.

[58] Ch.6, section 2.1.

limited to financial and practical considerations or—in the case of all other lawyers—refusal can be on any grounds whatsoever (excluding those of a discriminatory nature). Moreover, discussion of the issue is confined to calls for extending the cab-rank rule to all solicitors.

In seeking to provide a more nuanced approach for both branches of the profession, we will concentrate largely on the situations where lawyers are inclined to refuse representation because of immoral ends. Sometimes this relates solely to what the client wants done. For instance, some lawyers might be uncomfortable helping the wealthy to avoid paying tax or oil companies to exploit oil reserves in pristine environments. In other cases, lawyers' concerns relate to the nature of allegations made against their clients. For instance, lawyers might balk at defending those charged with paedophilia or with particularly brutal murders or rapes. However, lawyers' objections might have nothing to do with the prospective client's ends, but simply to who they are and what they have done in situations unrelated to the case in question. For instance, lawyers concerned about human rights or the environment might be unwilling to provide any form of legal service to Shell. Finally, lawyers might object to representation because they know that certain immoral means will have to be used, such as when rape defendants insist on raising complainants' past sexual history in cross-examination. While all these types of refusals might stem from the same moral objections and will have the same effect on the client, we shall see that they raise different ethical considerations. We will, however, consider the last type of objection in the next section given that it raises the question of immoral means, which is a separate issue.

5.2 Criminal Defence

The overwhelming arguments in favour of neutral partisanship in the context of criminal defence work logically entails the conclusion that lawyers should always represent criminal defendants irrespective of the nature of the charges or their past actions and even if they believe the client to be guilty. Given the serious consequences of wrongful convictions, it is here that the arguments in favour of the 'epistemological demurrer'[59] come into their own. While we do not accept that lawyers are never better placed than courts to 'know' whether clients are lying, the consequences of lawyer mistakes are too serious to allow them to supplant the courts' judgment.[60] Even confessions of guilt cannot be trusted. They may constitute a tired response to police pressure and the prosecution process, or be motivated by a desire for notoriety or to protect others, or the result of confusion, ignorance of the 'true facts' or a misunderstanding of the differences between moral and legal guilt.[61] Not all these

---

[59] See Ch.7, section 5.

[60] Also, as Kaplan 1986, pp.239ff points out, lawyers may base their belief as to guilt on inadmissible evidence, thus undermining the admissibility rules and truly rendering them 'judge and jury' of the client's guilt.

[61] See Lund 1960, p.106; Mellinkoff 1973, pp.150–1 and 163; Pannick 1992, pp.157–8; Blake and Ashworth 1998, pp.19–20.

considerations are equally persuasive. Client autonomy arguably dictates that defendants who sincerely want to protect others should be allowed to do so. And lawyers who do not ensure that confessions accord with the facts or the correct legal position can be said to be incompetent. Nevertheless, once again, the consequences of unjust convictions dictate an ethic of caution.

In any event, it is a central tenet of criminal justice values that, whatever the actual position on guilt, no one should be convicted unless proved guilty beyond reasonable doubt and in accordance with certain procedural safeguards. Consequently, as the codes correctly recognise,[62] even when clients confess or lawyers are convinced of guilt, they are morally obliged to ensure that the prosecution is put to proof[63] and that their client's procedural rights are not infringed. More radically, given that there is a difference between legal and moral guilt, it can be argued that defence of those thought to be guilty is particularly important where the crimes charged can be regarded as unjust and even more so where they have not received legislative approval.

Thus, we can conclude with many others that, in playing their morally justified role of protecting defendants against unjust convictions both by protecting their procedural rights and by zealous representation, the criminal defence lawyer may justifiably effect the acquittal of the guilty—even where the offence is heinous and the client potentially dangerous.[64] It is accepted that such lawyers do not defend their clients' criminal activities. Instead, they defend their clients against the *charge* of criminal activity.[65] In the words of the fictional anti-hero Horace Rumpole: 'I defend murderers. Doesn't mean I approve of murder.'[66]

Moreover, so strong is the lawyer's moral obligation to protect the rights of criminal defendants and thereby the civil liberties of all, that we believe that lawyers should provide representation even where there are other lawyers willing and able to take any rejected case. This is because a refusal of representation may exacerbate the stress associated with being a criminal suspect and reduce the chances of thorough preparation which is particularly necessary in criminal cases.

There are three possible exceptions to our conclusion that lawyers are always morally obliged to represent criminal defendants. One is where lawyers genuinely believe that their moral objections will prevent them from being able to perform their job properly[67] and they are able to find equally competent and zealous representation in sufficient time for proper preparation. But even so, it is arguable that this should be limited to defendants who are not particularly prone to anxiety about the process, such as those who have regular dealings with the police and courts.

A second possible exception flows from the fact that most of the persuasive justi-

---

[62] Para. 13 of Annexe H, CCB; para. 21.20 n.5, LSG.

[63] Although the difference between this and actively ensuring acquittals through controversial tactics is rather narrow: Luban 1993, pp.1761–2.

[64] cf Pannick 1992, p.165; Kennedy 1992, p.47; Luban 1993, p.1755.

[65] Gillers 1986, p.1024.   [66] Mortimer 1983, p.280.

[67] It might, however, be hoped that greater discussion of the ethics of criminal defence work will increase awareness of the value of defending 'the indefensible' (Kennedy *loc cit* n.64) over that likely to flow from the current amoral role, and hence that such situations will be rare.

fications for the representation of criminal defendants relate to the need to protect individual liberty and dignity. The loss of liberty represented by companies having to pay fines is likely to be less invasive than imprisonment or even the fining of individuals, whereas one cannot speak of harming a company's dignity by the loss of representation. Admittedly, the prosecution and punishment of companies may have deleterious human effects, ranging from company executives' anxiety over the prosecution process to company bankruptcy with consequent job losses. Nevertheless, the varied nature of these circumstances leads us to suggest that lawyers would be entitled to weigh up such circumstances in deciding whether to represent corporate defendants.

5.3 Criminal Prosecution

When it comes to decisions about representation, the codes treat prosecuting lawyers no differently to other lawyers. Although they are sometimes said to be 'Ministers of Justice' seeking convictions only where justice requires,[68] the requirements of justice are confined to the limits placed on prosecutorial zeal in seeking convictions.[69] Thus, barristers and solicitor-advocates are prohibited from refusing prosecution cases, whereas professional norms contain nothing to suggest that solicitors asked to act in private prosecutions or those employed by the Crown Prosecution Service (CPS) or various regulatory bodies[70] should depart from the neutral partisanship role. Instead, it would seem as if prosecuting lawyers are expected to pursue all alleged criminal law violations, albeit limited in the case of state prosecutions by guiding legislative principles and the CPS's *Code for Crown Prosecutors*.[71]

Whether the amoral role of prosecutors is justified is largely[72] ignored by professional ethics commentators. Whereas the actions of prosecutors generally protect collective community interests, most justifications for neutral partisanship rely, as we have seen, on the needs of individuals. Although the adversary system excuse could be said to justify prosecutors acting as neutral partisans, we have also seen that it is most suspect where—as in criminal prosecutions—there are gross imbalances in power; hence the limitations on prosecutorial zeal. Instead, justifications for extending the neutrality principle to prosecuting lawyers could be based on the community's interests in being protected from crime and the fact that both the identification of behaviour as criminal and the prosecutorial guidelines represent the community's will as expressed through its democratic representatives.[73] On the other hand, while the existence of democratic support for prosecutorial ends can be said to create a strong presumption in favour of prosecutorial moral neutrality, a case can be made

---

[68] See eg *Puddick* (1865) 1 F & F 497; Humphreys 1955, esp p.741.

[69] See below at nn.168–9.

[70] Such as the Inland Revenue, Customs and Excise, and the Serious Fraud Squad. See Ashworth 1998, ch.5.

[71] Crown Prosecution Service 1998.   [72] But cf at n.79, below.

[73] The Code is issued by the Director of Public Prosecutions in terms of s.10 of the Prosecution of Offences Act 1985.

for lawyers being entitled to consider their moral or political objections to particular prosecutions.

As we have seen,[74] the argument from democracy is not conclusive and is particularly suspect as regards common law crimes, whereas state prosecutorial policies are far from uncontroversial.[75] Far more important, however, is the potential for great harm caused by unjustified convictions, made very real in the case of state prosecutions by imbalances in power and resources between state and defendant. We already accept that this justifies many limitations on the state's ability to obtain convictions—including limitations on prosecutorial zeal—and that this in turn may lead to the guilty going free. Accordingly, it can be argued that criminal defendants should be further protected from unjust convictions by allowing—if not obliging—prosecuting lawyers to judge the morality of pursuing particular prosecutions, especially where the consequences for defendants are grave and the potential for unjustified convictions is great.

There are many areas where current state policy can be argued to potentially cause miscarriages of justice.[76] Discussion of all of these would, however, take us away from our aim of illustrating and exploring a contextual approach to ethical decisions about ends and means, and deep into complicated issues of criminal justice and the prosecutorial policies of the various regulatory agencies. Consequently, we will concentrate on two issues that are similar to those arising in other legal work.

Depending on the correct interpretation to be given to the test of evidential sufficiency for prosecution in the CPS code,[77] CPS employed or instructed lawyers may be required to seek convictions notwithstanding their strong or at least reasonable doubts as to the defendant's guilt.[78] For instance, courts may regularly disbelieve certain types of defendants even when some are innocent or prosecuting counsel may learn of evidence strongly suggesting innocence which would be inadmissible at trial.

In our view,[79] prosecutors should decline to prosecute (and to accept plea bargains) where they believe defendants are innocent or even where they think that there is insufficient evidence to persuade a reasonable court.[80] For one thing, it is dangerous to trust the courts always to get it right when the consequences of unjustified

---

[74] Ch.7, section 4.2.

[75] See eg Ashworth and Fionda 1994; Sanders 1994; Ashworth 1998; and, more generally, Crispin 1995, pp.178–83.

[76] See ibid and the lack of guidance in the codes or elsewhere on the proper approach to plea-bargaining. Should prosecutors, for instance, accept plea bargains where they believe that defendants have defences that might be accepted in court? See eg Blake and Ashworth 1998, pp.28–9.

[77] *Viz* that 'there is enough evidence to provide a "realistic prospect of conviction" ': para. 5.1.

[78] This would be compatible with the approach that requires prosecutors to predict how actual courts would react to the evidence. See Ashworth 1998, ch.6 for this and the alternative interpretation discussed in n.80, below. Given that CPS lawyers usually exercise their role of reviewing police prosecutorial decisions solely on the basis of the police file, such situations could be said to be rare. On the other hand, new evidence may arise at a later date particularly when lawyers interview prosecution witnesses.

[79] See also Humphreys 1955, p.741; Kaplan 1965; Freedman 1975, pp.84–8 and 1990, pp.218–21; Williams 1985, but cf *contra* Uviller 1973; Worboys 1985; Ashworth 1998, pp.204–5.

[80] As is required by the intrinsic merit test, which is implicitly supported by paras. 4.10 and 4.13 of the CPS's *Explanatory Memorandum: Crown Prosecution Service* 1996.

convictions are serious. Considerations of proper institutional role should not take precedence over harm to individual defendants. Secondly, even though prosecutors are prohibited from being 'economical with the truth' in order to obtain convictions, no morally responsible lawyer should take the risk of securing the conviction of those who they consider to be innocent. Merely acting on what courts are likely to do, as one interpretation of the evidential sufficiency test requires, is not an approach appropriate to individual ethics. It suggests that prosecutors can go ahead even when they think that courts will unjustly convict because of a consistent prejudice against types of offender or in particular types of cases. Thirdly, most accused do not get the opportunity of court trials but accept plea bargains based *inter alia* on their likely chances of conviction. If they are told that they are more likely than not to be convicted, they might accept offers of lesser charges even when innocent. Finally, even where individual defendants are acquitted, they are unlikely to emerge unscathed by the process of prosecution. For all these reasons, lawyers should decline to prosecute unless convinced beyond reasonable doubt of the defendant's guilt.

The second circumstance in which lawyers might be expected to refuse to prosecute is where they clearly believe particular offences to be unjust either in substantive content or in the procedures laid down for enforcement or proof. The obvious objection to this is that it would involve a usurpation of the power of the proper authorities to set behavioural standards.[81] However, even in the unlikely event that all other lawyers refuse to prosecute a particular offence, one has to weigh this private act of nullification[82] against opposing considerations. One involves the converse of the argument made earlier that not everything that is legal is moral. In other words, simply because state institutions have criminalised certain action does not mean that the offence is justified morally or otherwise. Criminalisation by the appropriate authorities does indeed create a strong presumption of lawyer obedience, but that presumption should always be capable of being negated by strongly felt moral or political objections. As already argued,[83] in a society riven with substantial class, gender, race and other power differentials, the democratic process does not confer an absolute legitimacy on its legislative products.

More importantly, some criminal offences emerge not from a democratically elected legislature but an unelected, unaccountable and unrepresentative judiciary. Although most long-standing judicially created offences can be said to have gained the implied consent of the community, the absence of legislative repeal may in some cases owe more to legislative indifference or preoccupation with more pressing concerns than, for instance, concerns about the (un)justifiability of the blasphemy offence in a modern multi-cultural community. Certainly in the case of more recently created offences like that of conspiracy to corrupt public morals[84] lawyers should

---

[81] Although the list of public interest factors militating against prosecution in para. 6 of the CPS code is not exhaustive, there is unsurprisingly no indication that the public interest might include the offence's perceived injustice.

[82] cf Simon 1998, esp pp.83–108 on nullification.   [83] Ch.7, section 4.2.

[84] See *Shaw v DPP* [1962] AC 220.

consider whether they are justified in prosecuting people for vaguely defined and unduly invasive offences created by a reactionary judiciary.

5.4 Civil Litigation, Negotiation, and Facilitative Work

As we noted earlier, British arguments for neutral partisanship largely take their force from criminal defence work where the lawyers are portrayed as superheroes rescuing citizens in distress or alternatively from the lawyer's role in the adversary system.[85] However, in reality most lawyers are not engaged in criminal defence work, nor indeed in formal litigation or even contentious civil work. Instead, they spend most of their time in negotiation, mediating and facilitating client affairs through legal advice, the setting up of legal instruments such as trusts, companies or wills, or even in lobbying activities.

These types of work may give rise to a wide variety of moral dilemmas related to the decision as to whether to accept instructions. Should lawyers help landlords evict poor tenants, hamburger chains use libel laws to gag welfare activists, or road builders obtain injunctions against environmental protestors? Should they defend cigarette companies against the claims of cancer sufferers? Should lawyers negotiate exploitative contracts with workers or favourable leases for massage parlour owners? Should they draft wills leaving money to racist organisations? Should lawyers provide clients with information about the law and the possibility of its enforcement to those who they know or suspect might use it for illegal and/or immoral purposes? We thus need to ask whether in all or any of these contexts lawyers can be said to be morally obliged to provide representation despite ethical objections.

5.4.1 *A Duty to Represent?*

Earlier we argued that lawyers do have a moral obligation to represent almost all criminal defendants because of the imbalances in power between state and individual and because of the latter's grave need for protection. Do similar considerations justify a duty to represent in civil legal work?

Clearly they might. Prospective clients may be faced with opponents more powerful than the state. Some large companies now exercise more power and control more resources than many of the world's governments. In addition to being able to afford the very best lawyers and long drawn out legal proceedings designed to sap the resources and will of opponents, large organisations may also benefit from various advantages flowing from being 'repeat players' in the legal process, such as economies of scale and beneficial relationships with legal actors. In some civil cases the prospective clients may in fact be the state. This alone might not require lawyers to provide representation despite moral objections. One would not compare companies wanting to avoid tax with criminal defendants facing unjustified convictions. What is also required is the possibility of the prospective client facing an outcome which, in terms

---

[85] See Ch.7, section 1.

of stigma, financial impact and general well-being, is similar to the harmful consequences of a criminal conviction.[86] This may also occur in civil cases. As well as
having to pay huge amounts of damages, defeated litigants may lose their livelihoods
or homes, while the health and quality of life of communities may be impaired by
environmental degradation. And in the case of immigration applicants, losing cases
may even lead to torture or death following deportation.[87]

Consequently, instead of making a strict distinction between criminal and non-
criminal cases, following Luban we can distinguish between the 'criminal defence
paradigm', where there are 'political reasons to aim at prophylactic, or pre-emptive,
protection of the individual from powerful institutions (including the state, but also
private institutions)' and the 'civil suit paradigm', involving disputes between 'relatively evenly matched private parties'[88] or where there is no discernible opponent. In
'criminal defence paradigm' cases, lawyers can be argued to be morally obliged to
represent irrespective of concerns about the morality of client ends or what they are
alleged to have done. Of course, there is no bright line between the two paradigms
and lawyers will inevitably make moral judgements in attempting to distinguish
them. This counsels lawyers to resolve any doubt in favour of representation.
Nevertheless, the possibility that prospective clients might have needs similar to
those of criminal defendants could provide a starting point for decisions to
representation.

As regards civil suit paradigm cases, our earlier discussion of the justifications for
neutral partisanship outside criminal defence work[89] suggests that possible arguments
for an absolute obligation of representation are limited to contentious civil work. In
the case of non-contentious negotiations[90] and facilitative legal work, the only supporting arguments are that lawyers ensure access to specialist skills and knowledge,
yet the same can be said of other professionals who are not under professional obligations to assist despite moral objections. We have also argued that law is not necessarily a public good, and that the argument from equality is undercut by the fact
that access to legal services is unequally apportioned in society.[91] The argument that
lawyers should be obliged to inform clients of the law and the legal consequences of
proposed or past action is also tendentious. *Prima facie* one could say that by unlock-
ing the mysteries of complex law, lawyers are fulfilling a public function by ensuring that law is known to the public and hence that the rule of law is met in both
substance and form. On the other hand, it seems counter-intuitive to hold that
lawyers must give clients information which they know will lead to illegal or harmful
behaviour, such as where clients ask whether their four-year-old children are

---

[86] Rhode 1985, p.608.
[87] See Douzinas and Warrington 1994, p.228. See also ACLEC 1998 regarding the standard of legal
representation in such cases.
[88] Luban 1988a, p.65. See generally pp.63–6.   [89] See Ch.7, section 3.2.2.
[90] ie those aimed not at disputes resolution but obtaining some future benefit for clients through entering into contracts or obtaining permissions relating to land use: see Menkel-Meadow 1984 (referring to
'transactional negotiations').
[91] Ch.7, section 3.2.2.

competent witnesses in sexual abuse cases.[92] And if a Realist approach to what counts as law is adopted, lawyers would be obliged to inform clients, for example, that certain types of offences are currently not being prosecuted or that procedural and other pragmatic factors will ensure that they will not be sanctioned for civil wrongs.[93] As even Pepper accepts, the issue of whether lawyers should always provide clients with information as to the law is far too complex to hold that lawyers simply act as neutral conduits of information.[94] At the most, the need for citizens to know the law may justify a rebuttable presumption in favour of lawyer assistance.

When we turn to contentious work, the arguments in favour of a duty to represent are, *prima facie*, stronger, especially in relation to advocacy.[95] Thus the privilege given to advocates by protecting them against competition from unqualified, non-litigant, advocates arguably suggests they should not be able to refuse representation because of personal moral feelings. It could also be argued that the right to legal assistance is implied in the legally sanctioned right to a court hearing. In addition, all litigators play a necessary and community sanctioned role by ensuring that litigants' interests are properly represented and that courts are able to adjudicate cases effectively on the basis of all relevant law and facts, both providing a non-violent forum for dispute resolution and perhaps also clarifying and developing the law.

These are weighty considerations. Nevertheless, we do not think that they establish a conclusive case for lawyers being obliged to represent parties to disputes, irrespective of ethical objections. We readily concede that the monopolies lawyers enjoy create reciprocal moral obligations to the community. Yet this establishes precisely the opposite of the liberal argument.[96] Lawyers can be said to exercise their monopoly in the community's interest when they refrain from assisting individuals to cause harm to the general public or to specific individuals rather than when they simply act for whoever can afford their fees. As we have already noted, the legal profession, at least as currently organised and funded, cannot fulfil all legal needs. Lawyers must choose how to allocate the scarce resource of their skills. The liberal argument might hold if it could be established that simply acting for those best able to afford their legal services most effectively contributed to the community interest. But, in our view, this has not been established. In this light, we can conclude that allocating legal skills on the basis of perceived moral worthiness furthers community interest at least as much as allocation according to ability to pay. It would be a rather strange community that explicitly[97] accepts that impecuniosity is a good reason for citizens to go unrepresented, whereas their perceived immorality is not.

Finally, one can question the assumption that lawyers are necessary for the adversarial system's proper working. In absolute terms, this is simply not true. Citizens

---

[92] Example taken from Pepper 1995, p.1551. Indeed, answering such questions may constitute aiding and abetting any consequent abuse.

[93] cf ibid, esp pp.1554–8 and 1654–71.   [94] ibid. See also Hazard 1981.

[95] See Ch.7, sections 3.2.2 and 4.2 *passim*.   [96] See Ch.7 at n.140.

[97] cf Fried, quoted in Ch.7, n.171.

can, albeit with differing degrees of difficulty and success, litigate and argue many types of legal cases. Legal assistance is usually an advantage rather than a necessity.[98] Lawyers may effectively be necessary when clients face powerful opponents and unduly complex law. But this does not establish that they should always represent litigants, merely that the strength of the case for providing representation varies from context to context. This suggests an approach whereby lawyers asked to represent those whose ends or character is regarded as immoral should weigh up those factors favouring representation against factors suggesting that the lawyer's personal morality should take precedence.

5.4.2 *Factors Relevant to Representation Decisions*

One set of relevant factors relates to certain institutional features of cases. Lawyers can be said to be required to play their allotted adversarial role whenever they face opponents capable of putting forward their case in front of impartial arbiters willing and able to see that fair play prevails. Conversely, where these factors are absent, lawyers are arguably either more or less justified in taking account of their own moral views depending, respectively, on whether the prospective client is likely to be benefited or prejudiced by the absence of these factors. Lawyers should take into account that opponents might be unrepresented, ill-educated, and indigent, or that prospective clients are large corporations with access to unlimited resources. Also relevant would be whether their own status and abilities might unfairly magnify their clients' advantages.

A second set of factors relates to the nature of the lawyer's moral objections. Arguably, lawyers are most justified in refusing representation where they object to client ends because otherwise they would be directly involved in immorality or injustice. Conversely, lawyers who simply object to the client's character or any past behaviour unconnected with their present goals can be said to be least justified in refusing representation. For example, making an otherwise unexceptionable will for a racist only assists racism in the indirect and marginal sense of lending legitimacy to the racists by treating them as normal members of the community. Defending allegations of conduct that the lawyer regards as immoral falls between these two extremes. On the one hand, lawyers who enable clients to escape the legal consequences of immoral action are at least accessories after the fact to such immorality[99] and may indeed encourage their clients to perform further immoral acts. On the other hand, by analogy with criminal defence cases, lawyers who defend clients in these situations can be said to play a morally valuable role in ensuring that no one suffers legal sanctions without due process. However, defending allegations in civil cases is not quite analogous to criminal defence work. Civil cases are more like a zero sum game in which the failure to prove liability may have serious consequences for opponents. Unlike the harmful consequences of acquittals which are usually only indirectly felt,[100] losing civil claims may affect litigants directly and may be disastrous for them

---

[98] But cf Pannick 1992, p.3 and ch.7, regarding the competency of advocates.
[99] cf Bentham's argument in relation to lawyers who act for confessed criminals: Orkin 1958, p.170.
[100] cf Ch.7, at n.108.

or the community as a whole. Lawyers representing those charged with immoral acts in civil cases do not therefore just defend clients against unjustified liability; they may also help harm others.

A more convincing argument for lawyers to provide representation where their moral objections are to the prospective client's alleged actions derives from the epistemological demurrer argument. Although, as we have seen,[101] this argument does not establish that lawyers can never 'know' or that courts are always better placed to 'know', it does counsel lawyers to be convinced that allegations against clients are well-founded before refusing representation. Similarly, while the ethical demurrer is even less convincing as justifying a blanket ban on conscientious objection, it also counsels lawyers to be sure of their moral objections.

The final factor relevant to the question of conscientious objection is whether the prospective client is likely to obtain legal assistance elsewhere. Objections to the refusal of legal assistance are substantially weakened, if not totally negated, where alternative, equally competent lawyers are available, especially since lawyers lacking moral objections to clients or their goals, or who provide representation as a matter of moral principle, are likely to provide more committed representation than those who act as amoral technicians. Similarly, where there exists a scheme ensuring legal representation for those refused representation, conscientious objection can always be said to be justified as long as refusal would not result in time bars being triggered or considerable distress to the individual seeking legal assistance. But even if the latter circumstances do pertain, or even if individuals would be left unrepresented by refusals of assistance, we still feel that lawyers should be free to weigh up all relevant factors in deciding whether the immorality and harm involved in representation outweigh the harm caused by conscientious objection.

5.4.3 *Conclusion*

Taken as a whole, our discussion suggests that the argument for a cab-rank rule applying to all lawyers involved in non-criminal work weakens as one moves from litigation through contentious negotiation and mediation to non-contentious negotiation and facilitative legal work. The social values of litigation, the litigating lawyer's adversarial role, the possibility of systemic checks and balances in litigation and the dangers of mistakenly assuming prospective clients guilty of alleged immoral acts provide a relatively strong, albeit rebuttable, presumption in favour of representing litigants and undertaking mediation work. In the case of advocates this presumption is reinforced by the partial monopoly over court representation. When it comes to contentious negotiation, the only arguments supporting a similar presumption flow from the existence of an opponent and the fact that certain forms of negotiated settlement, such as divorce settlements, custody disputes, etc., may have to receive the imprimatur of the court which can retrospectively ensure that fair play prevailed.[102]

---

[101] Ch.7, section 5.

[102] In addition, all settlements can be said to occur in the courts' shadow and this may inhibit parties from abusing the absence of an impartial arbiter.

This presumption becomes even weaker in the case of non-contentious negotiations, where only the existence of the other negotiating party provides some justification for the pursuit of immoral ends. Similarly, only the idea that all citizens are entitled to know the law provides any specific justification for lawyers performing counselling activities to clients with or suspected of immoral objectives. Finally, where lawyers are asked to facilitate a client's interests there does not seem to be any specific argument in favour of them being required to ignore their moral objections to the client or her ends, except possibly as regards notaries whose assistance is usually made compulsory by law.

6. IMMORAL MEANS AND LAWYER TACTICS

6.1 Introduction

Unlike the issue of immoral ends, the ethical problems raised by the means lawyers may employ in representing clients is subject to a fair amount of regulation and discussion in England and Wales. This is largely due to the lawyer's duties to the proper and fair administration of justice generally and to the courts in particular, which, as we have seen, are said to take precedence over those to clients.[103] Accordingly, the courts have laid down many rules—summarised in the professional codes,[104] most of which seek to prevent them being deceived or misled. In addition, there are also some rules designed to ensure that lawyers act fairly towards specific individuals. Sometimes overlapping with duties to the administration of justice, these latter obligations are also mainly confined to litigation.

As will become clear, the above rules leave unregulated a vast array of tactics which lawyers can use in furthering client ends. We will not attempt to discuss the morality of all such tactics—an enormous and complex task. Instead, we will concentrate on highlighting gaps in the rules and problems with the general approach to lawyer tactics, before illustrating how a contextual approach could be used to resolve dilemmas raised by a lawyer's perception of the immorality of various means to client ends.

6.2 The Current Approach

6.2.1 *Gaps and Uncertainties*

Unsurprisingly, professional norms prohibit the most blatant forms of lawyer dishonesty, such as lying to courts,[105] fabricating defences or devising facts.[106] Furthermore,

---

[103] Ch.6, section 2.1.
[104] Where this is the case, we will refer to the codes rather than the cases.
[105] See eg the code provisions in Ch.4 n.186, above.
[106] Paras. 606 and 610(d); n.3 to paras. 21.20 and 21.21; paras. 6.6 and 7.1(d) of Annex 21A, LSG. The standards are even higher as regards litigation documents: see para. 606, CCB; para. 6.6 of Annex 21A, LSG; *Myers v Elman* [1940] AC 282, 294; *Rockwell Machine Tool Co. Ltd v E P Barrus (Concessionaries) Ltd* [1968] 2 All ER 98, 99.

both codes devote considerable attention to ensuring that lawyers are not implicated in witness perjury, either by allowing witnesses to give perjured evidence or continuing to act where clients admit perjury.[107] There are also detailed rules designed to ensure that lawyers do not influence witness testimony or attempt to obtain false testimony,[108] while solicitors are prohibited from making payment to witnesses conditional on the evidence given or the outcome of cases[109] (but not from shopping around for favourable expert witnesses).[110] Lawyers are even positively required to disclose adverse precedents and statutes,[111] affidavits filed in the proceedings[112] and, in the case of prosecuting lawyers[113] and in certain civil proceedings,[114] adverse facts.[115]

However, the general approach[116] is that while lawyers must not actively mislead courts, they may stand back and watch courts act in ignorance of or in error as to facts adverse to their clients even where their silence is not required by the duty of confidentiality.[117] Not surprisingly, distinguishing between illegitimate active deception and legitimate passive concealment has not proved easy in practice.[118] For instance, no action was taken in one case when a lawyer asked a witness currently serving a three year jail sentence to confirm whether he lived at what was normally his home address.[119] However, in another case, a new trial was ordered because a lawyer failed to disabuse the court and opposing counsel of their mistaken impression that his client was still a chief inspector of police; an impression strengthened by the fact that the client had attended court out of uniform and he had addressed him as 'Mr' rather than 'Sergeant'.[120]

---

[107] See para. 13 of Annexe H, CCB; paras. 21.07 n.5, 21.20 nn.1, 5 and 6, para. 21.21 n.5 and para. 21.13, LSG.

[108] Para. 607, CCB; para. 21.10 and para. 6.5 of Annex 21A, LSG. See also Ipp 1998, p.92 regarding expert witnesses.

[109] Para. 21.11, LSG.

[110] But see now Woolf 1996, pp.140–2 regarding court appointed experts and cf rule 35.3 of the Civil Procedure Rules, which states that an expert's overriding duty is to the Court.

[111] Para. 610(c), CCB; n.3 to paras. 21.07 and 21.19, n.1 to 21.20 and 21.21, LSG.

[112] Para. 21.07 n.4, LSG.   [113] Para. 11.2, Annexe H, CCB; para. 21.19, LSG.

[114] *Viz ex parte* applications, Search Orders and family proceedings: Hilbery 1959, pp.15–16; Ipp 1998, pp.69–71.

[115] cf also the debate as to whether previous convictions need be disclosed during mitigation: Pannick 1992, p.163; du Cann 1993, p.42; Blake and Ashworth 1998, pp.32–3.

[116] See *Tombling v Universal Bulb Co Ltd* [1951] 2 TLR 289, esp p.297; *Saif Ali and Another v Sydney Mitchell & Co (A Firm) and Others* [1980] AC 198, 220A–B; *Vernon v Bosley (No. 2)* [1997] 3 WLR 683 *passim*; and, more implicitly, paras. 606 and 610(d), 5.8 of Annexe H, CCB; paras. 21.07, 21.20 and 21.21 and Annex 21G, LSG. But cf *Rondel v Worsley* [1967] 1 QB 443, pp.502B, 512E–F and 517E; Ipp 1998, pp.68–9, who, relying on *Vernon v Bosley*, argues that there is a trend towards more stringent duties of disclosure. However, of the three judges, only Thorpe LJ supports disclosure by lawyers and then only as regards information not subject to lawyer-client privilege which renders earlier honest representations untrue. Stuart-Smith LJ only required lawyers to resign if clients refused to make disclosure and Evans LJ rejected any duty of disclosure.

[117] cf para. 21.20, n.1, LSG.

[118] cf the notorious *Bridgwood* case (*The Law Society's Gazette*, 9 November 1988, p.53) considered in Annex 21G, LSG.

[119] *Tombling v Universal Bulb Co Ltd* above n.116.

[120] *Meek v Fleming* [1961] 2 QB 366. Note, however, that in both cases the issue was whether there should be a new trial, not whether the lawyers had breached ethical norms.

Notwithstanding the relatively large number of rules on the litigating lawyer's duty of honesty, there are many areas of uncertainty. Given that court cases are conducted adversarially and are subject to a burden of proof, few object to lawyers who believe their clients to be liable yet try to ensure they avoid liability by using rhetorical language and gestures, play acting, feigning emotions such as anger or surprise,[121] pretending to believe in facts or interpretations of the law,[122] or vigorously putting the other side to proof. By contrast, as we have seen,[123] many commentators criticise tactics apparently accepted by the profession, which can be described as being 'economical with the truth', such as only asking certain questions of witnesses, knowing that further questioning might allow the truth to emerge,[124] or by attempting to discredit witnesses known to be telling the truth by attacking their character, focusing on minor but irrelevant inconsistencies in their evidence or harassing them into contradicting themselves.[125] Also controversial are the tactics of arguing for factual inferences known to be false or saying things literally true but highly misleading in the circumstances.[126]

The current rules can also be criticised for encouraging a 'hear no evil' approach to truth.[127] While, on the one hand, the codes prohibit reckless as well as intentional deception of courts,[128] on the other hand, solicitors may even put forward evidence they believe (as opposed to know) to be false, as long as they check the truth 'where practicable' when put on inquiry.[129] While the idea that lawyers might prejudice clients because of their mistaken view of the facts might justify this approach—especially in criminal cases—far less justifiable is the apparent condonation of the 'Anatomy of a Murder' tactic, whereby lawyers outline the law to their clients before hearing their story.[130] However, because it is the client who chooses to take the hint

---

[121] See eg du Cann 1993, pp.63, 68–9, 133.

[122] See Pannick 1992, pp.153–4. Note, however, that advocates are prohibited from directly giving their opinion about a case: para. 610(b), CCB; para. 7.1(b) of Annex 21A.

[123] See Ch.6, section 3.2. In addition to the general references contained there, see Noonan 1966 and 1977; Blake and Ashworth 1998, pp.29–31. See also Wright 1994–95.

[124] See eg Evans 1993, pp.100–1 *passim*; du Cann 1993, pp.136–7; Sherr 1993, pp.103–4.

[125] See para. 13.5 of Annexe H, CCB, Pannick 1992, pp.159–60 and more generally the chapters on cross-examination in the references ibid. See also Freedman 1975, ch.4; and 1990, ch.8.

[126] See eg Simon 1993, p.1704; Blake and Ashworth 1998, p.31. In criminal cases where the defendant has confessed guilt, this may amount to setting up a false affirmative defence contrary to the codes (para. 13.3 of Annexe H, CCB; para. 21.20, LSG). In civil cases, solicitors are prohibited from acting 'in such a way that, in the context of the language used, a failure to disclose amounts to a positive deception of the court': para. 21.21 n.1, LSG. But cf Lord Denning in *Tombling v Universal Bulb Company Limited*, quoted in n.59, Ch.6.

[127] Luban 1993, p.1761. For other criticisms, see Cranston 1995, p.27 and for examples, see Heymann and Liebman 1988, pp.184–215; Napley 1991, pp.47, 65–6, and 69 (but cf at p.16); Disney *et al* 1986, pp.904–5.

[128] Para. 202, CCB; para. 2.2 of Annex 21A, LSG, but cf para. 21.07 where no mention is made of reckless deception.

[129] See para. 21.07 n.5, para. 21.20 nn.4 and 6 and para. 21.21 nn.4 and 5, LSG. A more ambivalent approach is adopted in para. 13.6 of Annexe H, CCB which states that the proper approach can only be ascertained after careful consideration of all the circumstances of the case (criticised by Blake and Ashworth 1998, pp.20–1).

[130] See Ch.6 at n.114.

and adjust their story, while the lawyer need never know that this has occurred, no professional rule is broken.

If, however, the current norms of honesty and candour in litigation are thought undemanding, they are almost totally silent as regards dishonesty outside litigation. Admittedly, as we saw in Chapter 4,[131] there are general requirements of honesty and honour as well as prohibitions on actions which are discreditable or likely to bring the legal profession into disrepute, while solicitors are prohibited from acting in ways contrary to their position as solicitors and enjoined to act with frankness and good faith towards other solicitors (but by implication not with unrepresented opponents or third parties). While high sounding in theory, these norms offer little guidance on the propriety of myriad ways of being economical with the truth outside formal litigation.[132]

Take, for instance, negotiations over the sale of a business, for which the lawyer has been told not to accept less than £1 million.[133] Is it acceptable to (a) avoid mentioning that a recent legal provision or a local authority decision will seriously hamper the business's future activities; (b) exaggerate the business's qualities; (c) conceal the latest financial figures which have been produced since negotiations started and which drastically alter the picture of financial health initially conveyed; (d) state that the company is poised for expansion despite having made losses over the last three years; (e) state that the client does not want to accept less than £1.5 million; or (f) state 'I have been told not to accept less than £1.5 million'?

The same disparity between fairly detailed regulation in relation to litigation and vague standards in relation to other legal work characterises the lawyer's duty of fairness. As regards litigation, in addition to some obvious and minor[134] duties,[135] advocates are prohibited from making allegations or asking questions solely in order to be scandalous or to insult, degrade, or annoy, from naming people in court where this would impugn their character unless unavoidable, and from impugning the character of witnesses in cross-examination without giving them a chance to reply and from accusing others of crimes, fraud or misconduct unless such accusations are relevant and supported by reasonable grounds.[136] This does not, however, prevent the notoriously controversial tactic of attempting to discredit the testimony of complainants in rape and other sexual offence cases on the basis of their past sexual history[137] since this can be said to be intended not simply to be abusive but to ensure

[131] See section 3.3.3.
[132] Feigning emotions, concealing information and pretending to believe in interpretations of the facts and law would, however, seem to be acceptable: see eg Halpern 1993; Tribe 1993.
[133] cf Rubin 1975; White 1980; O'Dair 1997.
[134] But cf *Ernst & Young v Butte Mining Plc* [1996] 1 WLR 1605 where it was stated without any support that advocates should refrain from taking advantage of mistakes by opponents.
[135] See Ch.4, at nn.193–6. See also eg para. 5.10(c) of Annexe H, CCB; para. 7.1 of Annex 21A, LSG.
[136] Para. 610(e)–(h), CCB; para. 7.1(e)–(h) of Annex 21A, LSG. See also Hilbery 1959, p.19; Napley 1991, p.77, who requires advocates to be satisfied of the factual foundation of damaging allegations as to character or credibility.
[137] But cf MacMillan 1937, p.191.

acquittals. For the same reason, lawyers may be able to rely on other forms of prejudice such as racism in advocacy[138] or more general forms of intimidation and harassment that undermine the dignity of witnesses.[139]

More generally none of the above rules deals, at least directly, with the 'dirty
tricks'[140] sometimes employed by advocates. In addition to the general prohibition
on impairing the administration of justice and making allegations and statements in
documents without factual foundation,[141] advocates are prohibited from making
contentions that they do not consider properly arguable[142] and enjoined to avoid
unnecessary expense or wasting court time.[143] However, most lawyers are likely to
find evasion of these rules rather easy.[144] Nor do they cover delays not involving court
time or expense, such as where negotiations are delayed until opponents' financial
circumstances are at their weakest because of the need to pay tax.

If pedagogical manuals are anything to go by, professional norms also accept
various underhand strategies designed to boost the client's bargaining position in
negotiations. Prospective lawyers are told that they could ensure the opponent's dis-
comfort by seating arrangements, threaten to walk out and even intimidate opposing lawyers by asking whether they are experienced enough for the case.[145] There also
does not seem to be anything preventing lawyers drafting unenforceable contractual
terms to be used as bargaining tools[146] or filing for joint custody on behalf of divorc-
ing husbands in order to drive down financial settlements. Apart from the criminal
law prohibition on blackmail and extortion, the only relevant ethical guidance is the
prohibition on solicitors demanding in a letter before action 'anything other than
that recoverable under the due process of law'.[147]

Similarly, there is no guidance on lawyers who deliberately advise their clients to
break the law in the belief that they are unlikely to be caught or that the legal penalties do not outweigh the practical benefits. Of course, if the law in question is penal,
such advice may amount to aiding and abetting an offence. But what if lawyers advise
clients to breach contracts with those whose livelihoods depend on their fulfilment?
The LSG prohibits solicitors from acting contrary to the law[148] but is silent regarding solicitors who advise others to do so.

It is thus clear that a wide variety of arguably unfair lawyer tactics are not specifically prohibited by professional norms. It is of course possible that at least some
unfair tactics may be held to contravene the more general norms of professional legal
ethics. Certainly lawyers who pursue unfair tactics could be said to be acting dis-
honourably or degrading themselves on behalf of their clients.[149] In the sphere of litigation or negotiation settlements which require a judicial imprimatur, their conduct

---

[138] See Ch.4, section 3.3.3.   [139] Accepted by Evans 1993, p.97.
[140] See Ch.6 at n.109.   [141] See Ch.4, nn.185–6.
[142] Para. 606 and para. 5.8 of Annexe H, CCB; para. 6.6 of Annex 21A, LSG. See further Ipp 1998,
pp.98–102.
[143] Para. 601a and para 5.11 of Annexe H, CCB; para. 6.1, LSG.
[144] As is also the case with breach of the discovery rules.
[145] See Halpern and Tribe, n.132, above.   [146] O'Dair 1997, p.317.   [147] Para. 18.05, LSG.
[148] Para. 12.01.   [149] See Ch.6, n.29.

might be said to prejudice the administration of justice. Furthermore, solicitors may be said to breach the LSG's general requirement of fairness which prohibits them, *inter alia*, from acting contrary to their position as solicitors or as using their position as solicitors to take unfair advantage of others. However, as we have seen,[150] this provision lacks teeth in that it begs the question of what is regarded as proper behaviour by solicitors and is subject to the solicitor's overriding duty to clients.

Whereas the propriety of at least some of the above tactics may be doubtful, it is clear that professional norms condone lawyers who rely on procedural technicalities to defeat otherwise meritorious claims or who mount sophistical legal arguments designed to defeat law's clear purposes.[151]

6.2.2 *General Criticisms*

From the perspective of those unpersuaded that maximum lawyer zeal benefits the adversarial system of justice, the institutions of government and the general public, current professional norms allow far too many dishonest and unfair lawyer tactics, with detrimental consequences to opponents, third parties caught up in legal disputes and other legal work, and to the general public. Current norms can, however, also be criticised on other grounds.

One is that their effectiveness is often undercut by their vagueness, or alternatively by subtle distinctions,[152] qualifications and get-out clauses.[153] Arguably, this is made inevitable by the impossibility of providing clear-cut answers to many irresoluble conflicts between duties to clients and those of honesty and fairness. However, for lawyers trained in exploiting legal language the rules are unlikely to pose too many obstacles in the way of furthering client interests.

Less justifiable, however, is the patchy nature of many rules. Thus, without any apparent justification, some distinguish between client and non-client witnesses[154] and between civil and criminal cases,[155] whereas others sometimes apply to barristers and not solicitors[156] and, even more frequently, vice versa.[157] This and the many silences in the rules strongly suggest that they have developed in an ad hoc manner as and when problems arise without thought being given to general standards of honesty and fairness.[158]

---

[150] Ch.4, section 3.3.3.
[151] Pannick 1992, p.114; Napley 1991, pp.72–3, but cf *Graham v Sutton, Carden & Co* [1897] 1 Ch 761, 766. See also Cranston 1995, p.19, who argues that lawyers should screen out unjustified claims and damp down abuses of the legal profession.
[152] Admitted in *Saif Ali, loc cit* n.116.
[153] See eg at n.129; the intimidation, harassment, etc., of witnesses and others is only prohibited where 'merely' designed to be abusive: para. 610(e), CCB; para. 7.1(e) of Annex 21A, LSG; the examples given in Ch.4, nn.189 and 190.
[154] See eg the CCB's silence on perjury by non-client witnesses; the LSG rule on past perjury: para. 21.13.
[155] eg there are no rules relating to civil clients who admit liability.
[156] cp para. 6 of Annexe H with para. 21.10, LSG; and see Napley 1991, pp.52–3.
[157] See eg the rules in paras. 17.05, 17.06, 21.09, 21.10 nn.2–3 and 21.13.
[158] cf Ipp 1998, p.65.

Moreover, many rules appear to be based on insufficient consideration of the issues involved. For instance, perjury rules arguably fail adequately to balance the competing interests of clients, the administration of justice and lawyers themselves.[159] Thus, requiring lawyers to cease acting for clients who intend to assert their innocence in court despite having confessed guilt may ensure the withdrawing lawyer's clean hands, but it will not necessarily prevent perjury since clients are unlikely to confess guilt to any subsequent lawyer approached. Furthermore, the codes ignore the timing of the client's confession. While it might be appropriate for lawyers to withdraw following confessions prior to court proceedings, withdrawal during proceedings may signal the possibility of past or future perjury to the court, thus breaching the lawyer's duty of confidentiality.[160] Undoubtedly, the issue of past and proposed perjury is one of the most complex ethical issues for lawyers and every solution proposed appears to carry with it its own problems. Nevertheless, more thorough consideration of the issue is needed.

Similarly, not only is the prohibition on 'rehearsing, practising and coaching' witnesses confined to advocates, but it fails to distinguish between attempts at taking witnesses 'down memory lane with predetermined destinations in mind'[161] and the vital task of checking the proposed testimony of witnesses. Relying on studies of witness psychology, Freedman has argued that, while also potentially creating the possibility of witnesses subconsciously inventing facts, thorough questioning by lawyers can be essential in aiding witness recall.[162] Given the split nature of the legal profession, it may be argued that this task should be performed by instructing solicitors. But this might prevent barristers and solicitor-advocates who are worried about breaching the rule from remedying poor initial interviews.

Our final and most important criticism of the current norms on lawyer tactics relates to their categorical nature: the fact that they are drafted in absolute terms with little or no consideration of consequences or context. In formalistic deontological fashion, it is assumed that the propriety of conduct is unaffected by the specific circumstances of particular cases. For instance, duties of honesty apply irrespective of the type of case, client, opponent and the justice of the applicable law, while 'truth' is understood as only encompassing factual events and situations. This ignores the fact that there are truths other than those of a factual nature—'truths' of a moral or political nature:[163] for example, that sexism and racism are wrong. Accordingly, lawyers are expected to display the same commitment to truth whether clients are faced with legitimate or manifestly oppressive laws. Similarly, no consideration is given to the relationship between the justifiability of client ends and the validity of the means used. Instead, along Kantian lines it is assumed that it is either absolutely right or absolutely wrong to use a particular means irrespective of the ends

---

[159] See eg Pannick 1992, pp.156–61; Blake and Ashworth 1998, pp.21–2; Ipp 1998, pp.87–9. For more thorough US analyses, see eg Freedman 1966; 1975, ch.3 and 1990, ch.6; Wolfram 1977; Pye 1978, pp.947–59; Harvey 1983.

[160] See Ch.9, section 5.2.2(b).   [161] Rhode 1985, p.600 and 1994, p.671.

[162] Freedman 1975, ch.6 and 1990, ch.7.   [163] Nicolson 1994, p.739. cf Curtis 1951, p.12.

sought.[164] For instance, under the codes it is always wrong to use the evidence of confessed perjurers, but almost[165] always right not to reveal adverse facts to courts, opponents or other relevant parties.

As we saw in Chapter 2, such an approach is rejected by consequentialists, most contemporary moral philosophies and probably intuitively by most people, who are likely to regard the propriety of legal tactics as crucially dependent on the merits of the client's case.[166] For example, it seems far more acceptable for lawyers to abusively cross-examine where they believe or even suspect that witnesses are lying or mistaken than where they 'know'—for instance, because of the client's admission—that the witness is telling the truth. Similarly, the use of dubious tactics to defend one's client seems to be far more acceptable where the law involved is perceived to be an unjust one, such as the Poll Tax, than where the client is charged, for instance, with drink-driving.

6.3 The Contextual Approach

By contrast to the current approach to the propriety of lawyer tactics, our contextual approach requires lawyers to weigh up the perceived immorality of the tactic in question considered in the abstract against all other relevant contextual factors. It is our belief that the limits to lawyer zeal cannot be laid down with mathematical precision, but must depend not only on the type of legal work involved but also on subtle variations in the lawyer's perception of the factual, legal, moral, and political merits of the particular case in question. In other words, the propriety of tactics which involve or come close to the codes' standards of dishonesty or unfairness depend on an assessment of the overall 'factual' truth of the client's case as well as an assessment of whether justice or morality requires an acquittal notwithstanding the question of factual truth.

Thus the state's enormous powers and the considerable harm caused to defendants by unjustified convictions mean that controversial tactics are, on the one hand, least justified in the case of prosecutors and, on the other hand, most justified in the case of criminal defence lawyers.[167] Indeed, this is currently accepted in official[168] and

---

[164] See *Queen v O'Connell* (1844) 7 Ir LR 261, 312: 'Let us never forget the Christian maxim, "that we should not do evil that good may come of it" ' Lawry 1990, p.324.

[165] But see paras. 21.07 n.4 (regarding affidavits); para. 11.01 of Annexe H, CCB, 21.19, LSG (regarding prosecutors).

[166] Recognised by Teschner 1970, pp.825–6; Simon 1978, p.136; Goldman 1980, p.118ff. See also Wright 1994–95.

[167] See eg Goldman 1980, p.118ff; Schwartz 1988; Luban 1993; Cranston 1995, p.22. But cf Simon 1993 who rejects tactics not aimed at helping courts to make informed decisions or vindicating procedural rights and Luban ibid, at pp.1759–62, noting the difficulty of applying such a test.

[168] Prosecutors are expected to argue their cases 'dispassionately and with scrupulous fairness' without attempting to obtain convictions 'by all means at their command', prohibited from using advocacy to obtain harsher sentences and obliged to disclose to the defence certain useful information: para. 11 of Annexe H, CCB and para. 21.19, LSG. As regards criminal defence lawyers, special rules seem to suggest that they can act more robustly for clients who admit liability than civil litigators: para. 13 of Annexe H, CCB, para. 21.20, LSG.

other professional discourse[169] on professional legal ethics—albeit not always explicitly. Moreover, one can go further and argue that if any of the most controversial means to client ends are to be allowed, they should be open to criminal defence lawyers.

One exception to this might be tactics that involve long-term harm to the community going beyond that caused by the acquittal of particular defendants. Here one thinks of the reliance on sexist and racist stereotypes in obtaining acquittals, and in particular on the attempt to portray female participants in trials as of loose character because of past sexual experiences.[170] Nevertheless, even here a nuanced approach seems preferable to an absolute ban on such tactics.[171] Certainly where defendants have made plausible and well-informed confessions to their lawyers, no justification can be offered for this tactic. However, where lawyers are fairly certain of innocence, the need to prevent convictions would seem to justify this evil where absolutely necessary. And where the lawyer is agnostic as to the defendant's guilt, the value of preventing potential miscarriages of justice impels us to the reluctant conclusion that here lawyers are entitled to rely on sexist and racist stereotypes, but again only if perceived as absolutely necessary.

Other possible exceptions mirror those made in discussing whether lawyers should ever be entitled to refuse to defend criminal suspects.[172] Thus it may be argued, albeit tentatively, that lawyers should be less inclined to use controversial tactics and certainly should never contemplate breaching current ethical standards on behalf of companies or private citizens who confess to particularly harmful offences and make it clear that they intend to re-offend in the future.[173]

Far more complex than criminal cases is the position in civil litigation. In 'criminal defence paradigm' cases, it can be argued that lawyers acting for the side seeking to cause harm and who have power and resource advantages ought to act more like prosecutors, particularly where (as in the McLibel case) the opponent is undefended and is faced with an unjust law.[174] Conversely, where clients are disadvantaged and potentially likely to suffer harm, lawyers can be said to be far more justified in using controversial tactics, especially where they are convinced that clients' cases are justified and/or they are prejudiced by unjust law.

In 'civil suit paradigm' cases where the parties are more or less evenly balanced and perhaps also where their clients, while disadvantaged by the imbalance in resources, are nevertheless seeking to impose harm on opponents, lawyers are perhaps justified in allowing the adversarial system to take its course. Here the existence of neutral arbiters and procedural rules designed to ensure fairness can be said to render appropriate all necessary and officially authorised zeal. This is not to say that current rules could not be made to uphold more effectively the truth-finding aims of

---

[169] Hilbery 1959, p.10; du Cann 1993, p.46. See also at n.68, above.
[170] But cf Freedman 1975, ch.4 and 1990, ch.8; Ellman 1990, pp.155–7 rejecting such an exception.
[171] cp Luban 1990b, pp.1026–35 with 1988a, pp.150–2.
[172] See section 5.2, above.   [173] Goldman 1980, pp.118ff.
[174] But cf Ellman 1990, pp.157–8, rejecting Luban's approach in 1988a.

adversarial trials.[175] For instance, attention could be given to the 'Anatomy of a Murder' tactic and to those 'dirty tricks' aimed solely at preventing the truth from emerging. More controversially, what is regarded as deception could be extended beyond knowledge of falsity based on client confession to situations where lawyers are for other reasons absolutely convinced that the client is lying. And, equally controversially, lawyers might also be required to refrain from those tactics involving being 'economical with the truth'. One suggestion which is unlikely to be accepted collectively by the professions, but which we think should be seriously considered by lawyers of conscience, is to avoid the use of procedural technicalities to defeat undeniably meritorious civil claims,[176] such as those of Thalidomide victims, where the consequent harm to the claimants is great, or the attempt to defeat the purpose of undeniably just laws, such as those tackling environmental degradation or upholding important civil liberties.

To complicate matters further, the above suggestions for reduced zeal in civil paradigm cases may nevertheless be regarded as inappropriate in special circumstances. For example, lawyers might be particularly convinced that clients are in the right or that the law is unduly favourable to opponents. Here, they could be regarded as justified in using tactics that would otherwise be regarded as involving excessive zeal.

Once one moves outside the sphere of litigation into negotiation it can be argued that the absence of neutral arbiters available to ensure fair play dictates that fundamentally different considerations apply, just as players are expected to display greater honesty and fairness in sports where there is no referee.[177] Contrary to the current approach in written discourse on professional legal ethics, which leaves unregulated tactics outside the sphere of litigation, it can be argued that the absence of a court requires higher standards of propriety rather than lower.[178] On the other hand, it is arguable that it is zealous opponents, not the courts, who offer the best means of preventing litigants benefiting from various tactics which come close to dishonesty, while the courts can only prevent unfair tactics if they are clearly prohibited by procedural or ethical rules. Moreover, in negotiations involving two roughly equal opponents there is probably an expectation and acceptance of a more robust approach to truth and fairness. Consequently, a case can be made for treating tactics in negotiation in the same way as tactics in civil litigation, with the important factors being whether or not opponents are capable of looking after their own interests and whatever behavioural norms are accepted in particular localities and areas of practice.[179] In the absence of effective opponents, lawyers could be expected to display even higher standards of candour and fairness than in civil litigation given that there is

---

[175] See eg Frank 1973; Frankel 1980; Davies and Sheldon 1995.

[176] But cf Simon 1988; Lawry 1990, pp.359–60.

[177] Schwartz 1978, p.678.

[178] ibid; Lawry 1990, p.346; O'Dair 1997, p.321. One could also argue that negotiations aimed at settling legal disputes should be treated somewhere between litigation and transactional negotiations given that they take place in the shadow of the court and hence any improprieties are potentially discoverable by the court if negotiations break down.

[179] White 1980, esp p.926.

no possibility of the court playing even the marginal role of assisting disadvantaged parties such as those without legal representation.

Finally, as regards legal work designed to facilitate client affairs, the potential tactics that can be employed are so varied that little guidance can be provided to lawyers other than the overriding consideration that they ought to ensure a correlation between the means used and the ends sought. The question of whether tax lawyers should be prepared to facilitate their clients' affairs through constructing tax avoidance schemes[180] or whether company lawyers should advise their clients to breach contracts in order to sack workers because of the financial advantages[181] is a matter of personal morality which could never be subjected to detailed rules. All that one can expect here is that lawyers take into account the harm that they might cause or the breach of any other moral principles when deciding whether to adopt particular means to client ends.

7. A DECISION-MAKING SCHEMA FOR MORALLY ACTIVIST LAWYERS

Having outlined how a contextual approach to immoral ends and means dilemmas differs from and, hopefully also, has numerous advantages over the current combination of an amoral role and formalistic rules, we can summarise our approach in the form of a decision-making schema for the morally activist lawyer. This schema is organised into three components.

The first involves examining the justifications for neutral partisanship in the particular context of cases in order to ascertain whether they should prevail. The most important of these factors involve power imbalances. As we argued in Chapter 7, virtually all justifications for neutral partisanship can be negated by power imbalances between prospective or existing clients and opposing interests whether they be litigation or negotiation opponents, campaign groups, governmental agencies relevant to facilitative schemes, etc. Also important are various factors relating to relevant state institutions, such as the absence of democratic support for legal provisions or the checks and balances necessary for legal procedures to operate effectively.

The second component of our decision-making schema involves evaluating a number of 'generic' ethical considerations. Even if lawyers decide that the arguments for neutral partisanship do not justify zealous representation in particular cases, they must still ascertain whether a number of other factors which apply irrespective of the case's context counsel against moral activism generally or the particular form contemplated. One factor relates to the problem of lawyer control and its impact on the moral autonomy of clients. Here, lawyers ought to consider whether the various

---

[180] See Disney *et al* 1986, pp.922–7 and cf Lawry 1990, p.349 who accepts tax avoidance but otherwise argues that the zealous lawyer role is an abomination in facilitative work.

[181] As regards lawyer involvement in action contrary to the law, see Freedman 1975, ch.6 and 1990, ch.7; Disney *et al* 1986, pp.918–22; Pepper 1995.

factors affecting the balance of power between lawyer and client raise the potential for invasions of client autonomy. As we saw earlier,[182] the extent of these problems varies according to the particular form of moral activism contemplated. For instance, it is better for lawyers to refuse representation than to limit zeal surreptitiously or attempt to dissuade clients from pursuing certain tactics by threatening withdrawal. Another relevant factor is that the timing of decisions to decline zealous representation may harm the client's interests.[183] Thus lawyers need to consider whether, for example, the refusal to act altogether or the limitation of zeal will reveal confidential information or leave the client insufficient time to obtain alternative assistance.

The third component of the decision-making schema involves 'specific' ethical considerations. Here lawyers can be expected to evaluate the strength of their moral objections to client ends or the best means to those ends, taking into account that not all moral objections equally justify refusing representation, whereas not all tactics are equally problematic. Also relevant here is the harm likely to be caused by zealous representation. This involves an assessment of its type—to dignity only or also to liberty, property, and even to life, as well as the number of likely victims and its likely magnitude. Where moral principles other than that of non-maleficence are involved, such as those prohibiting dishonesty or promise-breaking, or those encouraging charity or altruism, these need to be weighed in terms of perceived importance. For instance, where lawyers regard as unjust the laws favouring client interests, they need to consider both the degree of injustice and also whether there are other reasons, such as the law's democratic legitimacy, which suggest that they should vindicate clients' particular legal rights despite substantive legal injustice. Lawyers' assessments of the strength of their ethical or political objections to particular clients' ends or means should also include an assessment of the likelihood of any harm occurring and the confidence with which lawyers hold their beliefs. Given the presumption in favour of neutral partisanship, lawyers should be sure that harm will occur and that their moral objections are well founded and applicable. Similarly, given the arguments supporting the epistemological demurrer, lawyers should always hesitate before basing their decisions on their beliefs as to the facts of cases.

Application of the above schema for decision-making by morally activist lawyers is not meant to involve simply examining the various factors in each component in a mechanical fashion by placing ticks in boxes. For one thing, no lawyer is likely to work through each stage separately and consecutively. Instead, their moral objections to ends or means will probably alert them to the need for ensuring both that there are no strong objections to moral activism and that, if there are, that they are outweighed by the strength of their moral objections. This is likely to occur in the form of a gestalt reaction, perhaps followed by more careful rationalisation and even by the initial decision being reversed or modified as new information emerges or they are persuaded by moral dialogue with clients.[184] Nevertheless, setting out the three

---

[182] Section 2.   [183] Section 2.2, above.
[184] cf Frank's description of judicial decision-making: Frank 1973, ch.XII.

separate stages of the decision-making schema is important for alerting lawyers to the various considerations relevant to moral activism so that their more intuitive decisions are at least implicitly informed by the various relevant contexts and factors. More importantly, the questions raised in each component generally escape all-or-nothing answers, such that satisfaction of one component renders consideration of others irrelevant. Instead, almost all factors involve a dimension of weight[185] and their strength needs to be weighed against that of competing factors. Decisions can only be made once all applicable factors in all three components have been evaluated and weighed against each other.

Having set out the problems with the current approach to immoral ends and means, and our proposed contextual alternative, we now turn to the third area where the lawyer's amoral role can be regarded as problematic—the lawyer's duty of confidentiality.

---

[185] cf Dworkin's distinction between rules and principles: 1977, pp.23–8.

9

Confidentiality

The public interest in the efficient working of the legal system requires that people should be able to obtain professional legal advice on their rights, liabilities and obligations. This is desirable for the orderly conduct of everyday affairs. Similarly, people should be able to seek legal advice and assistance in connection with the proper conduct of court proceedings. To this end communications between clients and lawyers must be uninhibited. But, in practice, candour cannot be expected if disclosure of the contents of communications between clients and lawyers may be compelled, to a client's prejudice and contrary to his wishes.

Lord Nicholls of Birkenhead[1]

The legal profession, not clients or society as a whole, is the primary beneficiary of confidentiality rules.

Daniel R. Fischel[2]

1. INTRODUCTION

The requirement that lawyers keep secret their clients' confidences is one of their most fundamental ethical duties,[3] flowing from the fiduciary nature of the lawyer-client relationship.[4] As many real life dilemmas attest, it is also a duty which may conflict with other moral values and the public interest. For example, lawyers are prevented from revealing their client's intention to commit perjury or to rely on past perjury in court proceedings.[5] They cannot leak information uncovered by their own experts which shows, for instance, that their clients have caused opponents life-threatening conditions[6] even if instant treatment could prevent death. They cannot even disclose that clients have confessed to crimes for which others are presently serving life sentences,[7] even if their clients are immune from prosecution. And, depending on the nuances of criminal liability for corporate manslaughter,[8] they might not even be able to blow the whistle on companies who decide that it is

---

[1] *R v Derby Magistrates' Court, ex p B* [1995] 4 All ER 526, 543g–h.   [2] Fischel 1998, p.3.

[3] See Crawley and Brammall 1985, p.107. In the US, lawyers' confidentiality is described as a 'sacred trust' (Freedman 1975, p.5) and the 'glory of the profession' (Freedman 1990, p.87). See also eg Luban 1988a, p.186; Koniak 1992, p.1427ff, regarding the centrality of the duty.

[4] See Ch.5, section 3.3.

[5] See *Courvoisier* (1840) 173 ER 869, discussed by Mellinkoff 1973.

[6] *Spaulding v Zimmermann* (1962) 116 N.W. 2d 704, discussed *inter alia* by Luban 1988a, pp.149–50.

[7] See eg the case described by Tur 1994, p.73.

[8] cf text at n.50, below, regarding the exception allowing disclosure in relation to criminal acts likely to cause serious bodily harm.

more profitable to pay out a few claims for negligence than recall defective products.[9]

At the same time, apart from isolated voices like Bentham and, more recently, Fischel,[10] not even the fiercest critics of the current confidentiality duty call for its total abolition. As Lord Nicholls asserts, it is supported by powerful arguments. Consequently, as with neutral partisanship, we need to examine whether these arguments can justify the way in which the confidentiality duty requires lawyers to adopt a role morality which may require them to override ordinary morality. Admittedly, lawyers' confidentiality obligation does not require them to cause harm on behalf of their clients, but simply to refrain from preventing any harm their clients may cause. More importantly, as Lord Nicholls implicitly suggests, confidentiality can be regarded as essential to the very existence of the lawyer-client relationship rather than a mere optional extra, as arguably could be said of zeal. Nevertheless, these differences from the duty of zeal do not assuage the feeling that their secrecy obligation requires lawyers to refrain from disclosure in situations where many non-professionals would feel morally obliged to reveal confidential information. It is thus necessary to examine whether the current confidentiality duty adequately balances the needs of clients and the legal system more generally, on the one hand, against those of third parties, the general public interest and the environment, on the other hand. First, however, it is necessary to gain a more detailed idea of the current position.

2. THE CURRENT POSITION

Doing so is complicated by the fact that there are three distinct sources of the lawyer's duty to keep secret client confidences[11]—the codes, the common law, and legal professional privilege. The widest statement of this duty is to be found in the codes. Its essence is apparent from the CCB which states that '. . . a practising barrister must preserve the confidentiality of his . . . client's affairs and must not without the prior consent of his . . . client or as permitted by law . . . communicate to any third person . . . information which has been entrusted to him in confidence or use such information to his . . . client's detriment or to his own or another client's advantage'.[12] However, whereas this is the only paragraph on confidentiality in the CCB, the LSG

---

[9] cf the Ford Pinto *cause celebre* discussed eg by Luban 1988a, p.206ff; Dalkon Shield litigation discussed in Mintz 1986. Note that while the Public Interest Disclosure Act 1998 protects, in some circumstances, employees who blow the whistle from dismissal, it does not override lawyers' duty of confidentiality or legal professional privilege.

[10] Bentham 1843 vol. 7; Fischel 1998.

[11] Although there is currently no distinct law of privacy, this might change with the incorporation of the European Convention on Human Rights into English law by s. 1 of the Human Rights Act 1998, raising the possibility of a further source of the lawyer's duty; a rather remote possibility, especially given the Convention's rather different focus: cf Feldman 1993, Pt. III.

[12] Para. 603, CCB.

devotes a whole chapter[13] to the topic which provides detailed guidance on specific situations.[14]

Closely related and applying in tandem[15] to the professional obligations of confidentiality is the common law obligation not to breach confidences. Since at least 1849, English law has proscribed the unauthorised use of information received in confidence.[16] This is said to rest on the public interest justification that 'confidences, like contracts, "be held sacrosanct" '[17] and, in relation to personal confidences (as opposed to other types of protected information),[18] on the value of privacy. In the case of solicitors, the law implies a term into the retainer obliging them to keep their client's affairs 'secret and not to disclose them to anyone without just cause'.[19] Because of their fiduciary role and the fact that the confidentiality obligation is now regarded as a 'broad principle of equity',[20] barristers are under a similar obligation,[21] despite not being contractually bound to clients. While the codes simply prohibit lawyers breaching confidentiality on pain of disciplinary proceedings, the law of confidentiality enables clients to restrain by injunction threatened or continued breaches of confidentiality and to obtain damages for actual breaches.

Far narrower is the impact of legal professional privilege.[22] This is also based on public interest grounds, but on the specific need to encourage citizens to obtain legal assistance without fear of adverse information being revealed in court.[23] The older[24] 'litigation privilege' prevents evidence being given of confidential information communicated by clients or other sources to their lawyers in relation to proposed or contemplated litigation unless the client consents. The broader and more recently acknowledged 'legal advice privilege' provides the same protection to all communications between lawyers and clients, though not third parties, regarding advice sought going beyond litigation. While legal professional privilege may overlap with the common law and professional obligations of confidentiality, it has a distinct sphere of operation, merely acting as an evidential rule enabling clients to prevent lawyers revealing certain confidential information in pre-trial discovery and in judicial or quasi-judicial proceedings. Beyond such proceedings, it is the professional and legal obligations of confidentiality which are applicable. Moreover, only rarely will privilege prevent secondary evidence of confidential communications (usually in the

---

[13] Ch.16, LSG.

[14] eg regarding conflict situations, the sharing of office services or equipment with other firms, the selling of book debts to factoring companies, the use of postcards to acknowledge receipt of communications, insolvent clients and requests for clients' addresses.

[15] See para. 16.01 n.2 (referring to breaches of the duty leading to both disciplinary proceedings and civil actions) and cf n.1 which distinguishes these duties from privilege.

[16] See Gurry 1984, esp ch.I.

[17] ibid, p.325, quoting *Norwich Pharmacal Co v Commissioners of Customs and Excise* [1974] AC 133.

[18] *viz* business secrets, government information, and artistic and literary confidences.

[19] *Parry-Jones v Law Society* [1969] 1 Ch 1, 7.

[20] *Seager v Copydex* [1967] 1 WLR 923. See further Gurry 1984, Pt. Two.

[21] *Carter v Palmer* (1839) 1 Dr & W 722 and (1842) 8 Cl & F 657.

[22] See eg Tapper 1995, pp.470–94; Keane 1996, pp.519–38.

[23] See further section 4.2.   [24] For the history, see eg Hazard 1978b.

form of copies of privileged documents) from being led.[25] Here also the law of confidentiality and the codes fill the gap.

Because of the privilege's narrower scope and because our primary focus will be on the professional norms of lawyer conduct rather than the law, we shall concentrate on the lawyer's confidentiality duty as found in the codes and as influenced by the law of confidentiality (henceforth, 'the confidentiality duty'), making specific reference where relevant to legal professional privilege. This duty applies to all qualified lawyers including those employed 'in-house'.[26] It also extends to the agents and employees of lawyers;[27] the latter being required to ensure that the former uphold confidentiality.[28] To be protected, information must be entrusted to the lawyer in confidence[29] and cannot already be a matter of public knowledge.[30] Unlike the legal advice privilege, the confidentiality duty (like the litigation privilege) applies 'irrespective of the source of information'.[31] Thus the duty extends to oral communications made by clients or third parties and any letters, papers and documents entrusted to lawyers.[32] It applies even if no lawyer-client relationship is established subsequent to confidential information being communicated.[33] However, it appears that it must be imparted to the lawyer *qua* lawyer—in other words, for the purposes of seeking advice or assistance.[34] Finally, the duty does not cease with the retainer's termination or the client's death, but only by their waiver or, if deceased, by waiver of their personal representatives.[35]

This is of particular importance in lawyer-client relationships, since it prevents a lawyer once and for all from acting in any way that is inconsistent with the confidentiality duty owed to an existing or former client. In this way, the confidentiality duty merges into the duty to avoid conflicts of interest. The LSG allows firms to continue to act for two clients where potentially there are such conflicts, provided they can erect a 'Chinese wall'[36] to prevent confidential information leaking from one person or group to another in the firm. This is only explicitly authorised by the LSG in respect of non-contentious work following the merger of two firms.[37] In all

---

[25] See Tapper 1995, pp.481–3.

[26] *Alfred Compton Amusement Machines Ltd v Commissioner of Customs and Excise (No. 2)* [1973] 2 All ER 1169.

[27] Para. 16.01, LSG; Gurry 1984, ch.VIII.   [28] Para. 16.01, LSG.

[29] See para. 603, CCB and Gurry 1984, p.4 and ch.VI.

[30] Para. 16.02 n.8, LSG; Gurry 1984, chs.IV and V.   [31] Para. 16.01 n.3, LSG.

[32] See Gurry 1984, p.150 and regarding privilege, see Tapper 1995, pp.473–4 and 483–4; Keane 1996, pp.526–7.

[33] Para. 16.01 n.4.

[34] Gurry 1984, p.150, and cf Tapper 1995, pp.477–8, regarding privilege. According to Black 1982, p.300, if this condition does not apply the information may still be protected by the law of confidentiality, but this may be more difficult to establish (cf Gurry 1984, pp.150–1). See also Black ibid, regarding the position where information is imparted without lawyers' consent.

[35] Para. 16.01 n.3, LSG; para. 603, CCB ('whether or not the relation of counsel continues . . .'); Gurry 1984, ch.XII; Black 1982.

[36] That is, in effect, some kind of formal information barrier separating different parts of or groups in the firm. See Midgley 1992.

[37] Annex 15A, LSG.

other situations, it advises that it is 'doubtful' whether a Chinese wall will suffice to permit joint representation.[38] This advice reflects the extent to which the English courts have always been sceptical of Chinese walls,[39] but still leaves firms in some doubt as to the relative legal and disciplinary positions.

Whereas the law of confidentiality and the codes are relatively similar as regards the ambit and duration of the confidentiality duty, they differ as regards its exceptions. Indeed, the LSG appears to be more influenced by evidential rules which permit only a few exceptions to privilege.[40] By contrast, the legal duty of confidentiality is more easily overridden in that the courts are required to balance the public interest supporting confidentiality against any countervailing public interest which requires disclosure.[41] While the defences available are not fixed, lawyers are most likely to rely on that allowing disclosure of committed and contemplated 'crimes, frauds and misdeeds', including civil wrongs.[42] The confidentiality obligation may also be overridden by competing legal duties, duties to the court[43] and professional rules of conduct.[44] Finally, the duty's equitable roots mean that actions for breach are subject to the general defences to equitable remedies, such as 'unclean' hands and delay.[45]

The extent to which breaches of confidentiality can be excused in disciplinary proceedings is far less clear. The CCB only allows disclosure of confidential information with client consent or 'as permitted by law'. However, it is unclear on the face of the code whether the law referred to is that of confidentiality or, as is more likely,[46] privilege. The only other guidance is the requirement that barristers must withdraw from representation where clients refuse to sanction compliance with discovery rules and their duties to the court.[47]

The LSG is far more specific and far more clearly based on the law of privilege.

---

[38] Para. 15.03 n.4, LSG.

[39] See eg *Re a firm of solicitors* [1992] 1 All ER 353; *Re David Lee & Co* [1992] Ch 259, 268. The House of Lords has recently emphasised that the fiduciary basis of the relationship makes it unacceptable that solicitors should accept instructions without the consent of former clients, where there is *any* genuine risk of disclosure of information confidential to the former client—*Prince Jefri Bolkiah v KPMG (a firm)* [1999] 2 WLR 215, overruling *Rakusen v Ellis, Munday and Clarke* [1912] 1 Ch 831. This both reasserts the absolute nature of the confidentiality duty and the centrality of client consent, rather than some assessment of the quality of the arrangement itself, as legitimating Chinese walls.

[40] See Tapper 1995, pp.490–4; Keane 1996, pp.527–32.

[41] See Gurry 1984, ch.XV; Brindle and Dehn 1985, pp.115–19.

[42] Although perhaps not already committed civil wrongs: Gurry 1984, pp.331–4. See also Brindle and Dehn 1985, pp.117–18, distinguishing disclosure of 'mere mismanagement' from disclosure of serious illegality, fraud, risk to health and safety or the environment.

[43] *Rondel v Worsley* [1969] 1 AC 191, 277.   [44] *Parry-Jones*, above n.19.

[45] Gurry 1984, ch.XVI.

[46] This appears to be the effect of the Bar Council's practice of giving advice on para. 603, CCB which treats its scope as generally consistent with the guidelines in the LSG. See Stobbs 1999 and cf by implication, Cranston 1995, p.7; Brindle and Dehn 1995, p.123.

[47] Para. 504(e) and (f). Note here *Vernon v Bosley (No 2)* [1997] 1 All ER 614, and the disagreement therein between Stuart-Smith and Thorpe LJJ as to whether counsel should be required to make disclosure to the court after withdrawing. The Bar Council's interim advice pending clearer judicial guidance is that counsel should withdraw and say nothing. See *Bar News*, June 1998, p.8.

First, it *requires* disclosure of confidential information where ordered by court or police warrant, or required by the Legal Aid Board.[48] Disclosure of experts' reports may also be required in cases concerning children.[49] Secondly, it *permits* solicitors to reveal confidential information in four circumstances:[50] (i) where they are being used to facilitate the commission of crime or fraud; (ii) in order to prevent clients or third parties committing criminal acts likely to cause serious bodily harm; (iii) where they suspect 'continuing sexual or other abuse' which poses a 'sufficiently serious' threat to the 'life or health, both mental and physical' of children;[51] and (iv) where necessary to defend themselves against criminal, civil, disciplinary proceedings, or client complaints. Thirdly, the LSG refers to the existence of a number of statutory exceptions to the duty of confidentiality and privilege and in some cases provides solicitors with specific guidance on meeting their obligations under these statutes.[52] However, like the law on privilege and unlike the law on confidentiality, there is no broad exception allowing, let alone requiring, lawyers to reveal confidential information when required by the public interest more generally.

3. CRITICISMS OF THE CURRENT POSITION[53]

Given that our primary aim is to evaluate whether the confidentiality duty adequately balances the interests of clients and lawyers, on the one hand, against those of affected third parties and the general public, on the other, we shall concentrate on the exceptions to the duty rather than its ambit and duration.

A preliminary criticism relates to the codes' many uncertainties,[54] particularly as to the crucial expression 'as permitted by law' in the CCB.[55] Adding to this uncertainty is the patchwork nature of the various exceptions found in the law and the codes. Thus, depending on how the phrase 'permitted by law' is interpreted, the exceptions to the barrister's professional duty could be either narrower or wider than those provided by the LSG.[56] Moreover, the position for both barristers and solicitors differs according to whether the context is the admissibility of evidence, a civil

---

[48] Para. 16.01 n.9. See also paras. 5.03–5.04.   [49] Para. 16.02 n.5.
[50] Nn. 1, 3, 4, and 9 to para. 16.02, respectively.   [51] See further Annex 16A.
[52] Para. 16.02, nn.11 (regarding prevention of terrorism legislation) and 12 (regarding the solicitor's general response to government and statutory bodies authorised to obtain information); para. 16.07 and Annexes 16C and D (regarding money laundering).
[53] See eg Cranston 1985, p.7ff; Tur 1992b and 1994; Brindle and Dehn 1995, pp.121–5; Ipp 1998, p.72ff and for more specific criticisms, section 4, below. This section also draws on the following US commentators: D'Amato and Eberle 1983; Rhode 1985, pp.612–17; Subin 1985; Luban 1988a, chs.9 and 10 *passim*; Zacharias 1989, esp pp.353–61; Fischel 1998.
[54] eg does serious bodily harm in para. 16.02, n.3, LSG include psychological harm and, if so, does this include rape and other serious sexual offences which do not require proof of actual physical violence? Does the expression 'criminal act' in the same provision apply only to crimes committed in the UK or to those that would have been criminal if committed here?
[55] See at n.46, above.
[56] The fact that it is interpreted as broadly the same is a consequence of unpublished guidance, not the drafting of the code. See ibid.

action for breach of confidentiality or disciplinary actions for breach of the codes. Not only is this potentially anomalous in practice, but it raises questions as to whether these differences are deliberate or simply down to oversight.

The more serious and more frequent criticism of the current position on confidentiality is that it unjustifiably undervalues the administration of justice, the interests of legal opponents, other affected third parties, the general public interest and the environment.[57] Thus in general, lawyers cannot reveal confidential information in order to prevent physical or mental harm to adults, the imprisonment of the innocent, financial ruin of third parties or opponents, the total destruction of property, including residential property, as well as widespread environmental destruction and harm to animal life. This applies even if disclosure would not seriously damage client interests and even though the harm caused when disclosure is not permitted might in the long run outweigh that when it is. Compare, for instance, the risk of serious bodily harm (where disclosure is permitted), and the risks associated with deportation of refugees to repressive regimes or the lengthy imprisonment of innocent suspects (where it is not).

Admittedly, the exceptions which allow lawyers to disclose where they are being used to facilitate crime or fraud, or suspect that a crime likely to result in serious bodily harm might be committed, are potentially available for situations where lawyers might be expected to prevent harms, for example, where the failure to recall a defective product or the emission of toxic waste will seriously harm members of the general public. However, many regard this as not going far enough. The former exception will only prevent harm in fairly rare circumstances, while the latter stops short of many harms that arguably require prevention. It may not even extend to acts causing serious psychological harm or rape and other sexual offences which do not necessarily involve actual physical violence. Moreover, the fact that disclosure is permissive rather than mandatory, even where the likely harm is serious, might be argued to favour clients unduly, especially as the financial and other disincentives for lawyer disclosure fail to give those, such as in-house lawyers, the necessary support for doing 'the right thing'.

For some, the firmness with which lawyers' lips are sealed is particularly problematic given that, by contrast to other professionals who have less stringent confidentiality duties, they are especially well placed to discover and prevent serious immorality, harm, and injustice.[58] Obviously clients benefit where lawyers bow to professional and legal obligations rather than follow their personal morality. Indeed, clients can use confidentiality as 'a device for cover-ups',[59] for instance by handing over incriminating documents to lawyers. Even where there is no deliberate attempt to abuse confidentiality, the duty has been criticised for allowing clients intent, for

---

[57] In addition to the references cited in n.53, above, see section 5.1 regarding more specific calls for reform.

[58] See Tur 1992b, p.73: '[the] widespread loss and distress associated with massive banking, insurance and pension frauds . . . simply could not occur without . . . lawyers who, as professionals, must have at least an inkling of the true nature of their principals' activities. . . .'

[59] Hazard 1978b, p.1062.

instance, on escaping liability for heinous acts or engaging in highly immoral acts of dubious legality to obtain the legal assistance they need without fear of exposure.

In this way, the confidentiality duty increases the value of legal services to clients and gives lawyers an edge over other professionals who offer similar services,[60] but without the same level of confidentiality.[61] It is also said to protect not only lawyers' pockets but also their egos and social status[62] and to shield them from public scrutiny of the sort of dubious activities which flow from their neutral partisan role. Arguably, the confidentiality duty exacerbates the dominance of this role. It relieves lawyers of the psychological pressure of having to weigh up the ethical problems of whether to betray client confidences because of overriding moral or public interest considerations[63] and, as we have seen,[64] justifies excessive zeal whenever pulling punches would reveal client confidences. Consequently, many regard the confidentiality duty as being ultimately as much—if not more—about lawyer self-interest[65] than justice, loyalty, autonomy, and the other high-sounding supporting justifications for the duty offered by the profession.[66] The relative silence[67] with which the legal professions met the introduction of the European Union's money laundering regulations[68] provides a case in point. These regulations not only drive the proverbial coach and horses through the confidentiality duty, they may oblige lawyers actively to betray clients suspected[69] of money laundering by continuing to act for them while an investigation continues. Indeed, it is often argued that the superficiality, if not hypocrisy, of the profession's commitment to justice, loyalty, and autonomy is revealed by their insistence on at least one exception to their confidentiality obligation—namely where it is necessary to defend themselves.[70] Once such an exception is conceded, and

[60] eg tax advice by accountants, government lobbying by professional lobbyists.

[61] See Wolfram 1986, p.247: 'confidentiality is a product no-one else can sell'.

[62] cf Patterson 1980, esp p.966 with regard to the duty of loyalty which he regards as including the confidentiality duty.

[63] See Wigmore 1961, p.553 justifying a duty of non-disclosure 'if only for the sake of the peace of mind' of lawyers and cf Fischel's reply: 1998, pp.25–6.

[64] See Ch.8, section 2.3.

[65] On the other hand, it has also been argued that the duty harms lawyers by curtailing their freedom of speech (Zacharias 1989, p.354) and affecting their moral integrity in ways similar to neutral partisan-ship (Landesman 1983, p.208). However, most lawyers probably regard these consequences as outweighed by the benefits conferred by the duty.

[66] See section 4.2, below.

[67] cf the concerns, and indeed resistance, raised by other European legal professions. See Sherr 1999b.

[68] Introduced by the Criminal Justice Act 1993 and Money Laundering Regulations SI 1933/1993, which implemented the Money Laundering Directive of 1991. See para. 16.07 and Annexes 3B and 16C, LSG.

[69] Given lawyers' professed reluctance to sit in judgment over their clients, the decision to report is itself ethically problematic, though the evidence to date suggests that English lawyers are not exactly rushing to 'shop' their clients. Figures from the National Criminal Intelligence Service (NCIS) (see *The Lawyer*, 8 September 1998) show reports of suspicious transactions from solicitors fell from 300 to 236 cases between 1996 and 1997. The NCIS has, rather questionably perhaps, taken the view that this reflects a failure by lawyers to meet their obligations, rather than a tendency among the criminal fraternity to launder their funds in less sensitive jurisdictions. This nevertheless raises the interesting question as to how many solicitors may, by virtue of the regulations, now be implicated in clients' criminality.

[70] See text following n.49, above.

applied even to minor accusations, it becomes difficult to accept that the duty of confidentiality should allow lawyers to move so far from the possible demands of 'ordinary morality' without strong justification.

4. JUSTIFYING CONFIDENTIALITY

While no commentator advocates an absolute duty of confidentiality, many support the current general presumption of confidentiality subject to its few narrowly confined exceptions[71] or even regard the exceptions as going too far.[72] In doing so, they rely both on justifications for confidentiality in general and those that are specific to the lawyer-client relationship.

4.1 General Justifications for Confidentiality

Here one can rely on the arguments of deontologists and virtue ethicists who justify confidentiality on the allegedly intrinsic values of privacy, loyalty, promise-keeping, and non-maleficence.[73] Thus, as a starting point, confidentiality can be regarded as based on a complex human need to impart personal information[74] in order, for instance, to obtain advice or assuage feelings of guilt, while at the same time retaining control over such information.[75] Under the influence of liberalism's respect for personal autonomy, the idea that everyone should have a protected sphere of privacy, including the ability to keep information about themselves private, is now generally accepted in Western society and protected by some legal systems, including the European Convention on Human Rights. Accordingly, the unauthorised disclosure of another's personal information wrongly invades their privacy irrespective of any notion of confidentiality. Where, however, information is imparted in confidence, two additional values require the confidant's silence. The first is loyalty, which requires that we remain steadfast to those close to us—'friends, lovers, families, organisations, political movements and nations'[76]—and justifies providing them with special protection. The second is the value of promise-keeping, which is applicable because most communications of confidential information, especially to professionals, flow from an explicit or at least implicit secrecy pledge. Finally, rein-

---

[71] See, in the UK (albeit largely in the context of privilege), Stewart and Vaughan 1975; Napley 1991, pp.62–3; Ward 1995, pp.138–40; and, as regards the US, see eg Callan and David 1976; Callahan and Pitkow 1980; Alschuler 1981 and 1982; Fried 1986; Allen *et al* 1990.

[72] Freedman 1966, 1975, and 1990.

[73] See Bok 1980, pp.149–52 and 1984, pp.119–21; Bayles 1981, pp.83–5; Landesman 1983; Moore 1985, pp.188–91 and 197; Finn 1992, pp.320–1.

[74] ie information which most people would choose not to reveal about themselves or which specific individuals regard as particularly sensitive.

[75] Landesman 1983, esp p.196. But cf Phillips 1990, p.62, noting that communication of secrets is a familiar way to fortify trusting relationships.

[76] Fletcher 1996, p.174.

forcing each of these values is the duty of non-maleficence, which is particularly applicable because of the potential harm caused by the disclosure of confidential information.

However, none of these duties is sufficient to justify the width and rigidity of the lawyer's confidentiality duty, even when one considers that clients are particularly vulnerable to harm caused by breaches of confidentiality.[77] Thus, as the current legal position suggests, privacy rights are easily outweighed by competing legal rights, moral values and the public interest. Common examples include the need to stop the spread of contagious diseases or prevent crime. Indeed, to the extent that the duty of confidentiality is justified by the confider's rights to personal autonomy, such rights can be said to be forfeited when they threaten unjustifiably to invade the autonomy of others.[78] Irrespective of whether or not the contractual or even fiduciary nature of the lawyer-client relationship is sufficient to ground the sort of loyalty used to justify confidentiality[79] there are limits to what we can expect loyal and trusted others to do on our behalf.[80] To require great immorality of them may itself be an act of reciprocal disloyalty. Similarly, a promise to keep information secret cannot by itself support a duty of confidentiality.[81] The fact that a promise has been made would not be regarded by anyone but the strictest Kantian to outweigh any sufficiently strong duty to prevent harm or fulfil some other moral duty. Indeed, in most cases promises of confidentiality will implicitly exclude those disclosures one is morally required to make.[82] Moreover, reliance on promises as supporting a peremptory duty of confidentiality can easily be undermined by lawyers promising merely a *prima facie* obligation. Finally, whereas the non-maleficence principle provides the strongest single justification for a general duty of confidentiality, disclosure might not in fact cause any harm to confiders or the harm might be clearly outweighed by the harm caused to others by upholding confidentiality.[83]

Admittedly, privacy, promise-keeping, and non-maleficence can be regarded as 'perfect duties' under Kant's schema. Yet most ethical theorists, even fellow deontologists,[84] refuse to allow his formalistic distinction between acts and omissions to take precedence over the fact that values, such as life and liberty, might outweigh those of privacy, promise-keeping, and the prevention of lesser harms flowing from disclosures of confidences. It is also true that the values of privacy, loyalty, promise-keeping, and non-maleficence are far more powerful when combined than when treated separately. Yet no one who supports a general duty of confidentiality argues that it provides anything other than a *prima facie* obligation.

---

[77] But cf Moore 1985, p.208, noting that the clients of lawyers are more likely to cause harm than clients of other professionals.

[78] See Moore 1985, pp.194–5.   [79] cf Fletcher 1993, esp pp.22–3.

[80] cf Ch.7, n.81 regarding Fried's friendship analogy.

[81] But cf Alschuler 1981, pp.351–2.

[82] Donegan 1983, pp.141–2.   [83] cf Landesman 1983, p.197ff.

[84] See Ch.2, section 3 generally and 3.3 in particular.

4.2 Specific Justifications for Lawyer Confidentiality

Consequently, those who support the general and peremptory, rather than limited and *prima facie*, duty are usually[85] forced to rely on the particular benefits of confidentiality to lawyer-client relationships. Although articulated by commentators and courts largely in the context of legal professional privilege, it is reasonable to assume that this argument applies equally to the general confidentiality duty.[86]

Following the demise of the original justification for privilege, in the idea that, as 'gentlemen', lawyers do not betray confidences,[87] its supporters have come—as the opening quotation in this chapter illustrates—to rely on the privilege's importance to the public interest. This argument is essentially rule-consequentialist in that it acknowledges that legal professional privilege excludes relevant evidence and causes isolated harm to the public interest, yet asserts that in the long run it does more good than harm.

Crucial to the argument is the assumption that 'unless the client can be sure that his confidences would be respected', he might 'not venture to consult any skilful person or would only dare to tell his counsellor half his case'.[88] Having gained this additional information, lawyers can serve the public interest in two ways. First, they can provide clients with the effective representation necessary to help them know 'their rights and liabilities and obligations', to 'arrange their affairs in and out of court' and to argue their cases. This is said to promote the public interest in ensuring the efficient working of the adversary system, so that 'potential disputes, civil especially, [are] obviated or settled' and that human dignity, autonomy and equality are upheld. In response to Bentham's argument[89] that the privilege actually undermines the public interest by enabling the guilty to avoid justice without being needed by the innocent, it is persuasively argued that clients might fail correctly to distinguish incriminating from exculpatory or neutral information and, fearing lawyer disclosure, conceal what it is in their interests to reveal or even shy away from legal assistance altogether.[90] The second way in which lawyers can serve the public interest, once they learn of information which would not otherwise be disclosed, is by

---

[85] But see Alschuler 1982, p.73.

[86] cf Luban 1988a, p.187. It might be argued that, given its less absolute nature, the general duty requires less justification. Conversely, the fact that disclosure will usually be less harmful to clients outside litigation suggests a need for a stronger justification.

[87] See eg Radin 1928; Hazard 1978b.

[88] Quotations taken from *Greenough v Gaskell* (1833) 1 My & K. 98, p.103; *D. v NSPCC* [1978] AC 171, 231A–C; *R v Derby Magistrates' Court, ex p B* [1995] 4 All ER 526, 543g–h. See also the *Derby Magistrates' Court* case at pp.538–41; *Pearse v Pearse* (1846) 1 De G & SM 12, 29; *O'Rourke v Darbishire* [1920] AC 581, 615; *Harris v Harris* (1931) P 10; *Seabrook v British Transport Commission* [1959] 1 WLR 509, 513; *Waugh v British Railways Board* [1980] AC 521, 531.

[89] Bentham 1843 vol.7, supported by *Flight v Robinson* (1844) 8 Beav. 22, 36; Radin 1928, p.494; Fischel 1998, pp.22–6.

[90] See eg Wigmore 1961, pp.552–4; Freedman 1975, pp.4–5; a point accepted by even critics of a strong confidentiality duty: Bayles 1981, pp.84–5; Luban 1988a, pp.189–92. But cf at n.96 below regarding the possibility of lawyers educating clients about what information would be incriminatory and what sort exculpatory.

dissuading clients from litigating unjustified cases, breaking the law and even acting in an otherwise immoral fashion.

Critics, however, argue that the empirical claim and consequentialist calculus behind these arguments is based on pure conjecture. Thus the claim that abrogating or weakening confidentiality would dissuade prospective clients from approaching lawyers and have a chilling effect on disclosure is said to involve no more than a 'mixture of *a priori* theory and armchair psychology'[91] dressed up as empirical reality. It has never been proved and is perhaps unprovable.[92] Indeed, it runs up against equally intuitive counter-arguments.[93]

Thus it is questionable whether watering down or even abandoning the confidentiality duty would really scare away many potential clients. The growing complexity of law and its importance to people's lives arguably mean that many, if not most, prospective legal clients would approach lawyers even if not guaranteed the same level of confidentiality currently offered—a prediction confirmed by one survey.[94] More intuitively persuasive is the claim that the absence of protection would impede effective representation by discouraging full and frank disclosure. However, this too is based on some doubtful assumptions.

The argument that the innocent must be protected from unwittingly withholding useful information assumes that they cannot understand the relevant substantive rules which determine what evidence is exculpatory and what incriminating, yet can grasp what information will be protected by the confidentiality rules. According to Simon, 'in most cases the lawyer can educate the client about the substantive rules, but in cases where she fails to do so, she will also fail to make the client understand the confidentiality rules'.[95] Moreover, the alleged need for full disclosure in order to provide effective representation is somewhat undermined by the apparent practice of some lawyers of encouraging clients to fabricate facts by first outlining the law before asking clients to commit themselves to a version of the facts.[96] This might be ethically suspect; nevertheless, it suggests that lawyers do not regard as fatal the loss of possible exculpatory information. Moreover, one can query how many truly needy clients would withhold information if the importance of full disclosure were properly explained to them by empathetic lawyers genuinely concerned to help.[97] Unless lawyers regularly breach confidentiality, most clients are likely to opt for certain assistance as opposed to the mere possibility of disclosure. Finally, it is possible that out of emotional needs, such as the desire to confess, many clients may well reveal incriminating information irrespective of any secrecy pledge.

---

[91] Haber and Baumrin 1988, p.114, echoing Luban quoted in ch.7, at n.29.

[92] Moore 1985, p.179; Simon 1993, p.1720. cp also Kaplow and Shavell 1989 with Bundy and Elhauge 1991 over whether confidentiality increases the amount of information available to courts.

[93] See 'Note' 1977, pp.470ff; Subin 1985, pp.1163–6; Zacharias 1989, pp.364–7; Simon 1998, pp.56–62.

[94] Zacharias 1989, p.395.   [95] Simon 1993, p.1720. See also 1998, pp.61–2; Fischel 1998, p.24.

[96] See Ch.6, section 3.2.

[97] cf Fischel 1998, p.24. Indeed, the failure to obtain relevant information may owe as much to inadequate interviewing as to client worries about disclosure.

Although not free from methodological problems,[98] American empirical research confirms suspicions about the value of confidentiality to client disclosure. A substantial proportion of those interviewed (ex-clients and others) did suggest that the expectation that their secrets would be protected does encourage candour. However, when one takes into account the finding that clients are not usually informed of the duty and, if told, rarely understand it, that it already contains a number of exceptions[99] and that many clients apparently withhold information despite awareness of the confidentiality obligation,[100] the promise of strict confidentiality appears far less important than is commonly assumed. Zacharias concludes from this and the fact that lawyers were regarded as no more trustworthy than priests and other professionals with less stringent confidentiality obligations that client candour stems more from a general trust in lawyers as honourable professionals than from their strict professional and legal obligations.[101] Reform of the confidentiality duty is thus unlikely to have a serious impact on client disclosure.

However, even if we assume confidentiality does ensure even a small amount of additional important information—at the very least it cannot reduce the amount of information imparted to lawyers—we need to examine whether the benefits of confidentiality outweigh its disadvantages. The argument[102] that confidentiality leads to more clients eschewing illegal or immoral acts and vexatious litigation assumes that, while lawyers' inability to blow the whistle on clients detracts from the leverage they can exert, confidentiality ensures that more opportunities for lawyers to influence clients will arise in the first place because of the additional information gained. Not only is this unprovable, but even if lawyers are prepared to transcend their current amoral role and act as their clients' moral conscience, one may wonder how effective their attempts at persuasion can be when backed up by no more than, at best,[103] threats of withdrawal. More importantly, if lawyers are in fact so effective in dissuading client illegality and immorality, why is an exception to confidentiality made for perhaps the most serious type of immoral conduct: child abuse and serious bodily harm? Nor does advice from lawyers about the legality of future conduct necessarily lead to less client illegality. Clients who might not have otherwise risked action of uncertain legality may learn that the possibility of and likely degree of sanction justify the risks and may even learn of ways to avoid being caught, including the

---

[98] See Zacharias 1989, pp.377 and 396 regarding his own study and at p.379 regarding the study in 'Note' 1962; Thornburg 1993, pp.165–6 regarding the two studies she describes at pp.164–5.

[99] If clients are not being told of these exceptions, as Zacharias' study (ibid) also suggests, then clients' rights to effective representation through full disclosure have arguably been bought at the expense of their rights to autonomy. See Subin 1985, pp.1165–6.

[100] See Mann 1985, pp.40–2; also the studies cited by Zacharias 1989, p.367.

[101] ibid, esp p.386.

[102] See eg Burnham 1969, p.913; Hodes 1981, p.794; Freedman 1990, p.88, criticised by Radin 1928, pp.491–2; Shavell 1988 *passim*; Zacharias 1989, pp.369–70 and 389; Fischel 1998, pp.28–32; Simon 1998, pp.56–61. See further Kaplow and Shavell 1989; Bundy and Elhauge 1991.

[103] See at n.47 regarding barristers.

handing over of incriminating evidence to their lawyer.[104] Finally, the argument that lawyers can only dissuade clients from unnecessary litigation if they can coax adverse information from them assumes that honest clients would not otherwise disclose such information and that clients, who would have concealed adverse information in the absence of confidentiality, would follow advice to settle or drop cases rather than approach another lawyer and be less candid second time around. The only plausible argument in this regard is to the effect that full disclosure by clients may lead to them learning that *prima facie* incriminating facts are in fact exculpatory and thus remove any motive to commit perjury.[105] However, such cases are far from common. Nor can we assume every defendant is prepared to commit perjury to avoid liability.

Similarly suspect is the argument that the disadvantages flowing from confidentiality are outweighed by its promotion of effective legal representation. As we have already argued,[106] effective legal representation does not always ensure the efficient operation of the adversary system or the promotion of human dignity, autonomy, and equality.[107] It is only valuable to the extent that it is used for valuable ends. More specifically as regards litigation, even if confidentiality persuades some innocent clients to reveal *prima facie* incriminatory facts, this will not necessarily result in more accurate decisions than if the guilty lose the protection of confidentiality. Indeed, ineffective representation of the guilty may lead to an overall increase in accurate results especially as there is less likelihood of the innocent withholding exculpatory information than the guilty withholding incriminating information. Furthermore, it has also been argued that confidentiality might reduce accuracy by creating a general suspicion about the candour of all party testimony, thus making it difficult for the innocent to signal that, unlike the guilty, they have nothing to hide.[108] Although clients can waive privilege, their lawyers can still not testify that client testimony corresponds with their instructions.[109]

Nevertheless, while the consequentialist argument based on the need for effective representation is unproven, it may still succeed in non-consequentialist form.[110] Only strict utilitarians are prepared to accept the conviction of a few innocent defendants if it leads to overall accuracy. For those concerned about civil liberties, even the smallest possibility of the innocent withholding exculpatory information may be said to justify confidentiality. In particular it would be invidious in denying criminal defendants the opportunity of raising both substantive and procedural defences or obtaining lesser sentences through guilty pleas. Indeed, the civil libertarian argument goes

---

[104] This is subject, of course, to the crime/fraud exception already considered.

[105] Allen *et al* 1990. But see Thornburg 1993, pp.205–18 as regards the inapplicability of this argument to the corporate context.

[106] In Ch.7.   [107] cf Moore 1985, pp.203–4.   [108] Fischel 1998, p.18ff.

[109] See the conflict rule prohibiting lawyers from acting in cases where they might have to give evidence (para. 501(d), CCB; para. 4.1(d) of Annex 21A, LSG) and the evidential ban on previous consistent statements (Tapper 1995, pp.294–309).

[110] The following argument is taken from Luban 1988a, pp.191–2.

further and relies on the important idea, given legal recognition in the privilege against self-incrimination,[111] that it is abhorrent to force or trap persons into admitting to criminal liability even if in fact guilty.[112] The objection here is not to clients voluntarily imparting incriminating information to lawyers knowing that they may well reveal it, but to facing them with the invidious choice of having to forego effective representation through withholding possibly relevant information or revealing such information at the risk of it being made public by the lawyer.[113]

4.3 Conclusion

We thus see that the consequentialist arguments supporting a strict duty of confidentiality deserve, at best, the Scottish 'not proven' verdict. Given that a strict duty of lawyer confidentiality departs from 'ordinary morality' and thus requires strong justification, as with neutral partisanship, we can therefore conclude that the attempt to provide a blanket justification for this strict duty fails. Nevertheless, it does not follow that the duty should be totally abandoned. In addition to the civil libertarian arguments, there still remain the non-consequentialist arguments in favour of maintaining secrets discussed earlier. Combined, they suggest that lawyers should always start from a presumption of confidentiality. And, while the payment of money can never justify a promise to act immorally, in the absence of clear proof of such immorality, the fact that clients pay lawyers to act in their interests and at least implicitly expect that their secrets will not be betrayed establishes a strong argument for confidentiality. As we accepted in evaluating neutral partisanship,[114] the entire *raison d'être* of the lawyer-client relationship would be destroyed if lawyers were routinely to be concerned with interests other than those of their clients.[115]

However, it is also our opinion that these arguments do not justify the current strict duty of confidentiality. As we saw earlier, the values of privacy, loyalty, promise-keeping and non-maleficence can always be trumped by more weighty intrinsic values, if not by the public interest and other more consequentialist arguments. As regards the civil libertarian arguments, our discussion of the possible impact of reforming confidentiality suggests that few clients are likely to be adversely affected. Of course, the seriousness of the impact on their civil liberties might still justify a strict confidentiality duty. On the other hand, not all cases raise civil liberties issues. In other words, while a combination of the general and civil libertarian arguments might support a strict confidentiality duty as regards some clients, they do not suggest that it should apply to all clients and in all types of cases.

---

[111] See Tapper 1995, pp.453–9; Keane 1996, pp.510–19. The privilege also extends to other types of quasi-criminal penalties and, in criminal cases only, to forfeitures.

[112] See eg Radin 1928, p.493; Luban 1988a, pp.192ff (both, however, confining its relevance to criminal cases) and Callahan and Pitkow 1980, pp.162–4.

[113] Note that these arguments are usually made by US commentators relying on constitutional rights against self-incrimination and, in the case of criminal defendants, to legal representation.

[114] Chs.7 and 8.   [115] cf Moore 1985, pp.209–11.

This, in turn, suggests a need for the sort of contextual approach developed in the previous chapter.

5. A CONTEXTUAL APPROACH TO CONFIDENTIALITY[116]

5.1 Alternatives to the Current Position

The starting point of a contextual approach to confidentiality is an awareness of the possible alternatives to the current confidentiality position. Broadly speaking, there are two contrasting approaches to reform. The first and less controversial simply involves expanding the number and/or width of the current disclosure exceptions, which can continue to be of a mandatory or permissive nature depending on the issues at stake. Alternatively, confidentiality could be watered down into a *prima facie* duty capable of being defeated whenever the values protected by confidentiality are regarded as outweighed by the public interest, the interests of specific others, or the environment.[117] The balancing task could be put in the hands of professional bodies or even the courts.[118] However, in our view this would be unduly burdensome,[119] especially for the courts. It would also be inappropriate where disclosure must be immediate to be effective, and would undermine the advantages of placing discretion in the hands of individual lawyers, to which we have frequently referred.

On the other hand, providing lawyers with a disclosure discretion is particularly problematic in the context of confidentiality.[120] From the perspective of those wanting to ensure greater moral activism, permissive disclosure does not seem to go far enough. As we shall see, in some cases the balance lies so firmly in favour of disclosure that a discretion would invidiously allow lawyers to succumb to pressures to place client interests above those of others. It is even possible that lawyers might waive their right to disclose in return for additional payment by the very clients who can cause the most widespread harm—powerful repeat players and wealthy one-shotters. Finally, lawyers might eschew whistle-blowing out of a fear that professionally sanctioned disclosures might nevertheless attract civil liability. The latter fear is, however, not very realistic given the wider exceptions to the common law oblig-

---

[116] The suggestions made in this section are intended to apply irrespective of the position regarding legal professional privilege. Even if the latter remains wider than the professional duty, where appropriate—such as to protect innocent persons from criminal convictions—lawyer disclosure may still be effective in allowing opponents to discover independent admissible evidence or to produce copies of privileged documents.

[117] See 'Note' 1977; Hobin and Jensen 1980; Simon 1988, esp pp.1140–3 and 1998, esp p.56; Brindle and Dehn 1995, pp.122–4; and, more ambivalently, Wheat 1998, pp.197–8.

[118] See Hobin and Jensen 1980, pp.152–3; Tur 1992b, p.83.

[119] Reference is already frequently made to the Law Society (22% of all 1993 queries): Crawley and Bramall 1995, p.109.

[120] For general discussions of the merits and demerits of discretionary disclosure, see Subin 1985, pp.1174–5; Zacharias 1989, pp.404–6.

ation. And the concerns about lawyers selling their souls can be met by prohibiting them from prospectively agreeing to waive the right to disclose.

Far more problematic is the impact on clients of discretionary disclosure. As the comparatively more dramatic increase in the required disclosure of adverse facts under discovery rules shows, the expansion of specified exceptions to confidentiality is unlikely to drastically affect clients' faith in lawyers, particularly if they are clearly defined and explainable. By contrast, allowing disclosure in vaguely or completely undefined circumstances is, as Zacharias' study suggests,[121] likely to have a far greater adverse impact on client communications. Consequently, in making suggestions for reforming the current professional rules in areas where we regard strict confidentiality to be inappropriate, we will eschew a totally discretionary approach in favour of one which enables lawyers to give as much guidance as possible to their clients as to the safety of their secrets.

Nevertheless, we consider it unwise to rule out totally discretionary disclosure either in defined circumstances or in terms of a balancing test. Aside from the 'ethicising' effect of discretion, it is obviously impossible to cater for all possible situations where disclosure is appropriate through the provision of narrowly defined exceptions. Moreover, the permissive exceptions to the current duty *already* provide lawyers with a discretion as to disclosure, albeit only within clearly defined situations, apparently without adversely affecting the use of legal services or client communications. Finally, a general discretion to disclose need not entail an unguided discretion. As we have argued throughout this book, professional rules can and should set out relevant factors which lawyers have to consider before making their decision and which may even be conveyed to clients in outlining the confidentiality position. We therefore need to assess whether, in situations where disclosure might be appropriate, the advantages of allowing a general discretion to disclose outweigh the possible impact on clients and the public interest and, if not, whether disclosure under specified exceptions should be mandatory or permissive.

We thus end up with four possible alternatives for the various contexts in which problems of confidentiality might arise. In ascending order of liberality, they are: an absolute prohibition on disclosure; permissive disclosure in defined circumstances; mandatory disclosure in defined circumstances;[122] and a general discretion to disclose. However, before analysing where each of these alternatives might be appropriate, we need to look at a number of suggested ways of avoiding the need for disclosure or at least ameliorating its potentially harmful impact on clients.

---

[121] Zacharias 1989, p.403. Note, however, that the results do not take into account that the urgency of real situations (as opposed to the hypothetical used) might make clients more likely to disclose (and indeed also to approach a lawyer).

[122] Somewhere between the latter two categories is the possibility of a rule which does not simply allow disclosure but requires the lawyer to disclose unless convinced that it would do more harm than good. This would meet the objection that permissive exceptions are insufficient to encourage disclosure: see at n.130, below.

One[123] is termination of the lawyer-client relationship. While the cab-rank rule suggests that barristers can only do so in the limited circumstances defined in the CCB,[124] the absence of an obligation to accept instructions in the first place suggests that solicitors can end retainers rather than disclose client confidences. As we have already argued, lawyers contemplating withdrawal ought to consider the impact on the client, particularly if they are especially vulnerable[125] and also in the admittedly rare situations where this would be tantamount to disclosure.[126] In any event, however, withdrawal does not end the lawyer's dilemma over disclosure.[127] This dilemma remains as long as the disclosure could prevent harm to others or the public interest. Withdrawal does not even successfully pass the buck to subsequent lawyers instructed, given that the client might be less forthcoming second time around.[128]

Another suggestion is Subin's proposal that lawyer disclosure be made conditional on the existence of a 'vicarious immunity' which would protect clients against any disclosed information being used in criminal or even civil proceedings. In this way, harm to third parties and the general public could be avoided through disclosure without creating a chilling effect on client trust. At first glance such a provision appears to make acceptable even an unlimited disclosure discretion. Closer analysis, however, reveals that a vicarious immunity would not completely protect clients against self-incrimination and therefore should not assuage their doubts about full disclosure. Even if the immunity went beyond the current privilege to include protection against secondary evidence or client guilt or civil liability, there is always the possibility of lawyer disclosure leading to the state or civil opponents independently obtaining the incriminating evidence.[129]

A rather different way of attempting to allow wider lawyer disclosure without unduly undermining the value of confidentiality is to narrow the obligation's ambit down from all confidential information communicated to lawyers to only that related to the case for which assistance is sought or alternatively to that which is harmful to clients.[130] *Prima facie*, these 'particular case' and 'negative information' approaches obviate the need for exceptions to confidentiality given that its justifications relate to ensuring effective representation in particular cases and preventing clients

---

[123] cf also the optimistic suggestion that disclosure can be made without identifying the client, making public the confidential information and/or exposing the client to detrimental consequences, yet still achieve its purpose: Callahan and Pitkow 1980, p.172; Finn 1992, p.325. In reality, however, lawyers must typically either disclose any harm to clients (actual and potential) or refrain from whistle-blowing.

[124] See at n.47, above.   [125] See Ch.8, section 2.2.

[126] eg where it reveals intended or committed client perjury: see further section 5.2.2, below.

[127] cf Ferren 1978, pp.1257–8; Bok 1990, p.127; Freedman 1990, pp.115–16 (solely in relation to perjury); Tur 1994, p.61.

[128] cf Ferren ibid, p.1257 referring to a 1969 ruling by the Law Society's Professional Purposes Committee requiring disclosure to a new solicitor of an ex-client's intent to defraud an opponent.

[129] By analogy with the American 'fruits of the poisonous tree' doctrine (cf Tapper 1995, p.533), the vicarious immunity could be expanded to include all information obtained as a result of disclosure of client confidences, but this is unlikely to be workable and hence sufficiently protective of clients.

[130] See Landesman 1983, pp.204–7.

withholding what they think is harmful evidence. On the other hand,[131] because people naturally and, in many cases, unavoidably mix up the relevant and irrelevant in communicating information, it seems unreasonable to expect them to separate out information relating to the case from extraneous information or negative from positive or neutral information in deciding what to disclose to their lawyer—especially if the ultimate test is to be objective rather than subjective. Consequently, while the fact that information goes beyond the particular case or is unlikely to harm clients will be a relevant consideration in the exercise of any disclosure discretion, limiting the disclosure obligation cannot obviate the need for exceptions to it.

There remains, however, one effective way of making disclosure less invidious for both clients and lawyers. This is to require lawyers to remain silent until they have attempted to persuade clients to act in ways that would obviate the need for disclosure.[132] Such dialogue would have to be more than a formality. Nor should it be used by lawyers to undermine client autonomy through the various forms of manipulation discussed in Chapter 5.[133] It will usually be preferable to respect client autonomy at the expense of openly breaching confidentiality, than ensuring that clients act according to the lawyer's moral lights through underhand or oppressive invasions of their autonomy. On the other hand, the requirement that disclosure must be preceded by moral dialogue might have to be jettisoned in the rare circumstance that it would defeat disclosure, where, for example, clients could tip off accomplices or precipitate intended unlawful or immoral action.

5.2 Confidentiality and Context

In evaluating whether and when lawyer whistle-blowing ought to be absolutely prohibited, exceptionally mandated, exceptionally permitted or generally permitted in terms of a balancing discretion, we shall organise our discussion around two relevant dimensions. The first involves the various types of cases in which disclosure dilemmas arise. Given the importance of ascertaining the extent to which disclosure is likely to harm actual and prospective clients, this axis will focus on the type of client involved—individual or corporate entity—and their reasons for approaching lawyers—criminal defence, civil litigation, or general advice and assistance.[134] These categories will also provide a very general idea of the type of interests and values which might argue for disclosure, but a more detailed idea of these factors will emerge from our discussion of the second relevant dimension—the various types of information which are usually said to require disclosure. Using these two dimensions, a matrix of different disclosure contexts can be developed.

5.2.1 *The Case Typology*

If there is an argument for a category of absolutely protected client secrets, it applies most plausibly to criminal defendants. Indeed, as with neutral partisanship, the jus-

---

[131] ibid, pp.205–6.   [132] Subin 1985, p.1168; Zacharias 1989, p.404.
[133] And in relation to confidentiality, see the excellent discussion by Sisak 1997.
[134] For a sketch of a similar approach, see Popkin 1981.

tifications for a strict duty of confidentiality usually have in mind and take most of their force from criminal defence work. Even if, on closer analysis, these justifications reduce to the general arguments for confidentiality and those based on protecting civil liberties, the civil liberties of criminal defendants can be regarded as arguing for an absolute or, at least,[135] near absolute confidentiality duty. As we saw in discussing neutral partisanship,[136] the imbalances in power between state and individual and our acceptance of the consequent need to be prepared to countenance the acquittal of many guilty defendants rather than risk a few convictions of the innocent suggest a need to avoid even a faint possibility of a weakened duty of confidentiality discouraging defendants from obtaining effective legal representation. Moreover, it is in the context of criminal charges that the concern about forcing clients to choose between effective representation and self-incrimination has most resonance. And in order to fully put to rest the minds of criminal defendants it can be argued that, apart perhaps from exceptional circumstances,[137] the prohibition on disclosure should extend to all confidential information, not just to that relevant to the criminal charges or that which is likely to harm the defendant. Equally, it should apply irrespective of whether or not the context is the criminal proceedings for which representation is sought.

At the opposite extreme[138] to criminal defendants as regards the need for a strict confidentiality duty are large corporate entities.[139] Compared with private individuals and small businesses, they have a much greater ability to inflict serious and widespread harm, such as through environmental destruction and dangerous consumer goods, and are more likely to abuse lawyer confidentiality by deliberately handing over incriminating information.[140] As empirical research confirms,[141] they are also far less likely to refrain from legal representation or full disclosure if confidentiality is not absolutely guaranteed. Most large organisations have an ongoing and unavoidable need for legal assistance, which is likely to take precedence over the possibility of lawyer whistle-blowing. Such whistle-blowing is, in any event, likely to be rare given the control such organisations have over their lawyers. Furthermore, given their greater sophistication as compared with most individuals, organisational representatives are far less likely to eschew full disclosure because of mistakes about the incriminating nature of information. And, if they do regard such information as incriminating them personally, they should know that confidentiality protects the organisation, not its employees, who might in fact end up as scapegoats for any wrongdoing. Finally, there is already a great deal of uncertainty as to the safety of

---

[135] See the next section.   [136] Ch.7, section 3.2.1.

[137] See at text following nn.154 and 163, below.

[138] We have not discussed the position of prosecution lawyers because they are already under extensive disclosure requirements. In any event, as their client is theoretically the state, the same considerations that underlie the justifications for lawyer confidentiality do not apply. An extremely interesting issue, which is beyond the scope of this book, is the extent to which confidentiality duties ought to be extended to vulnerable complainants and witnesses—in other words, to what extent should the public interest in obtaining convictions yield to the needs of affected individuals.

[139] See 'Note' 1977, pp.473–7; Luban 1988, ch.10; Thornburg 1993; Wheat 1998, p.198.

[140] See the Dalkon Shield litigation, above n.9.   [141] See Thornburg 1993, pp.164–6.

company secrets given the difficulties which arise when there are clashes in the secrecy needs of particular elements of organisations, such as its shareholders and directors.

Moreover, the explicit reliance upon civil liberties, loyalty, privacy, and promise-keeping and the implicit reliance on human dignity, liberty, and equality do not apply so effectively here. Both come up against the obvious point that we are dealing with the interests of an abstract entity, not flesh and blood humans. It seems absurd to speak of corporate dignity and, even if we analogise organisations to humans, we are unlikely to be nearly as concerned about the 'civil liberties' of organisations facing criminal fines, civil damages or the loss of compensation. Moreover, in most cases whistle-blowing in the corporate and bureaucratic context will not involve litigation about past events but an attempt to prevent organisations causing future harm to others or the environment. Only the most extreme civil libertarian would argue that whistle-blowing interferes with a right to cause others harm, even where such harm is not expressly outlawed. It is not that we are unconcerned to protect organisational interests, it is just that we are far more likely to regard the harm they may cause to humans as being of overriding importance. Accordingly, we would suggest that in this context the arguments for client confidentiality are sufficiently weak to justify giving lawyers discretion to weigh up the values of confidentiality against the gains to be had from whistle-blowing, especially where the confidences relate to proposed or even ongoing activities rather than litigation about past wrongdoing.

Somewhere between corporate and criminal defence work are the various types of cases involving individual clients not facing criminal charges. Relatively easy to dispose of are those where powerful clients face vulnerable and powerless opponents. On the same reasoning used when discussing neutral partisanship, one can conclude that 'criminal defence paradigm' cases should be treated as if they were actual criminal defence cases. More difficult to resolve is the position regarding individuals not involved in the above type of cases.

On the one hand, they are far more likely to refrain from disclosure to lawyers if confidentiality is not protected, nor are they likely to be as capable of causing as much harm to others as companies.[142] Equally, the general arguments for confidentiality apply with full force here. On the other hand,[143] where there are two roughly equal litigants or clients seeking to pursue their financial or other personal interests, we are less likely to be concerned if they opt to withhold information from their lawyers. If their cases are in fact unfounded or their purposes immoral, then the confidentiality obligation will in fact prevent justice being done with possibly dire consequences to opponents. It is obviously different when they mistakenly withhold useful information, but given the uncertain effect of confidentiality on disclosure, such situations are likely to be less common than those where the existence of the confidentiality obligation leads to unjust results. And, unlike in criminal and criminal defence paradigm cases, there is no need to protect the client against the significantly superior resources of the opponent. The only relevant argument here is that

---

[142] 'Note' 1977, pp.477–8.   [143] The following argument draws upon Luban 1988a, pp.203–4.

which refers to the client's need for effective representation and protection against forced self-incrimination. However, neither have the same sway as in criminal cases. As already noted, there is no 'right' to representation let alone effective representation and even the privilege against self-incrimination is being slowly whittled down outside criminal cases.[144] Consequently, we can conclude that, while confidentiality should not be breached lightly, especially where it exposes the client to the possibility of criminal charges and other serious consequences, lawyers should have a discretion in appropriate cases to weigh the harm involved in breaching confidentiality against that involved in keeping silent. The only remaining question is whether this discretion is appropriate to all civil-paradigm cases or whether it should be limited to certain types of information where the client is an individual rather than an organisation. This requires a closer look at the second dimension to our contextual approach.

5.2.2 *The Information Typology*

This dimension can be divided into three categories based on the sort of harm disclosure is designed to prevent: to lawyers; to the administration of justice; to others (third parties, the general population, or the environment). While the last two categories overlap in that the suppression of relevant information in litigation harms litigants, the issues surrounding truth and justice in litigation can be regarded as sufficiently *sui generis* to justify a distinction between whistle-blowing designed to ensure just and fair resolution of legal disputes and that designed to prevent specific future harms to others.

(a) *Harm to Lawyers*

In calling into question the profession's sincerity in insisting on the need for a strict confidentiality duty, disclosure by lawyers to protect their own interests is *prima facie* the least justifiable exception to confidentiality. On the other hand, where clients initiate proceedings against lawyers it does seem unfair to prevent lawyers from relying on relevant information in defending such proceedings and accordingly the courts have held that privilege is implicitly waived in such circumstances.[145] However, the so-called 'self-defence'[146] exception in the LSG,[147] unlike the exception to privilege[148] upon which barristers must rely, is not dependent on clients commencing the criminal, civil or disciplinary proceedings in question.

Where they do not and solicitors breach confidentiality, they clearly abrogate to themselves a protection that is not extended to others who might avoid much greater penalties than mere professional discipline if confidentiality could be breached. In any case, it could be argued that lawyers are paid handsomely for the possibility of losing defences dependent on client confidences and that over the long run it

---

[144] See Keane 1996, p.105ff.   [145] eg *Lillicrap v Nalder & Son* [1993] 1 All ER 724.
[146] See eg Levine 1977 regarding the US equivalent.   [147] See at n.50, above.
[148] See *Nederlandse Reassurantie Groep Holding NV v Bacon & Woodrow* [1995] 1 All ER 976, esp pp.986–7.

benefits them far more than it prejudices them. While the profession might raise the spectre of clients deliberately using confidentiality to mount abusive claims against lawyers, it is instructive that they have been less concerned about abusive claims against others or the possibility that lawyers might threaten disclosure of highly harmful information to dissuade clients from commencing proceedings against them.

These arguments do not, however, necessarily justify removal of the self-defence exception. Instead, they can be said to support, on the one hand, the extension of a similar concern to clients' opponents and, on the other hand, treating this exception according to the same balancing approach applicable to other cases. The only difference should be that when clients institute proceedings against their lawyers we are entitled to infer that clients *knowingly* waive their right to confidentiality particularly if the self-defence exception has been pointed out to them. Indeed, one can go further and require that lawyers put clients on notice of the possibility of confidentiality breaches before disclosure in self-defence can be raised.

(b) Harm to the Interests of the Administration of Justice

Except where their own interests are at stake or following a court order, lawyers are obliged to remain silent in relation to criminal and civil proceedings even if aware of information necessary for truth to be found and justice to be done. This position is not only supported by all the justifications for client confidentiality canvassed above, but is also said to follow logically from the adversarial nature of legal proceedings. On the other hand, the natural link between adversariality and a litigant's right to conceal their hand and ambush opponents with unexpected information has been substantially undermined by expanding civil discovery and prosecutorial disclosure obligations. In addition, the (at present) largely rhetorical description of lawyers as court officers with supposedly overriding duties to the court could be relied on to argue for greater disclosure obligations in litigation. Thus, those like Frankel, who are concerned about the administration of justice and fairness between litigants, have called for professional rules to go even further and require disclosure of all material information which would probably substantially affect the determination of material issues in civil cases.[149] Indeed, confidentiality can be argued to be unnecessary to adversarial justice[150] if not detrimental in increasing the costs of case preparation.[151]

In response, it has been argued that, while the present position might undervalue truth and justice, fundamental changes to the adversarial system should come from Parliament or at least the courts rather than the professions.[152] Indeed, recent

---

[149] Frankel 1980, ch.6 and 1982 (reversing his earlier exemption of privilege from the proposal); tentatively supported by Moore 1985, pp.211–17. See also Popkin 1981, pp.769–70.

[150] Moore 1985, p.215.

[151] Fischel 1998, esp. pp.6–7 arguing that, being denied access to information in the hands of opponents, both sides have to increase fact investigation.

[152] Alschuler 1981 and 1982.

Parliamentary and judicial reforms suggest that proposals as wide as Frankel's have not been considered necessary.[153] On the other hand, our contextual approach to lawyers' ethics would only treat respect for these bodies as creating a presumption, albeit a very strong one, against lawyer disclosure going beyond these reforms. Lawyers may be faced with situations where justice overwhelmingly requires disclosure, such as where they represent powerful clients against weak opponents likely to suffer great harm if unsuccessful.[154] Nevertheless, if such disclosure is allowed by professional rules, they should be drafted to apply only to criminal defence paradigm cases. Otherwise the disadvantages of the possible chilling effect of such a potentially wide-ranging exception on client disclosure to lawyers may well outweigh any benefits in the few cases in which lawyer disclosure would be appropriate and indeed forthcoming.

Whether or not this suggestion is accepted, there remains the question of whether lawyers should disclose information where clients fail to authorise compliance with existing legal rules on disclosure. Currently, lawyers are simply required to withdraw[155] or at least refrain from aiding and abetting clients who refuse to comply.[156] Similar issues are raised by the fierce debate over whether lawyers should breach confidentiality by reporting their client's intention to commit perjury or rely on past perjury.[157]

In both cases, withdrawal might not be regarded as going far enough given that it still allows clients to shop around for less scrupulous lawyers or to conceal from subsequent lawyers their intention to breach litigation rules. On the other hand, withdrawal during trials might breach confidentiality by signalling to adjudicators and opponents that the client has failed to reveal disclosable information, has committed perjury or intends to rely on past perjury. The same dangers inhere in another compromise solution whereby, instead of lawyers being directly implicated in perjury by examining them in the normal way in court, clients give their testimony in the form of a 'free narrative'. Moreover, if free narrative does not in fact signal to adjudicators that it contains lies, then it must implicate the lawyer in the client's perjury.

While the complicated nature of this issue counsels against firm conclusions without the sort of analysis extending beyond our preliminary sketch of confidentiality reforms,[158] we tentatively suggest that lawyers should be able to breach confidentiality in order to ensure compliance with required disclosure and the prohibition

---

[153] See eg the Woolf reforms to civil justice, which emphasised the need for limiting and streamlining disclosure in order to increase access, despite some concerns that this might also increase the risk of evasion: Woolf 1996, p.126.

[154] An example would be the *Spaulding* case referred to above n.6.

[155] Para. 504(e) and (f), CCB.   [156] Para. 21.12 n.2, LSG.

[157] In addition to more general discussions cited in Ch.8, n.159, see eg Noonan 1966 and 1977; D'Amato and Eberle 1983, pp.785–9; Donegan 1983, pp.145–7; Landesman 1983, pp.209–10; Moore 1985, pp.217–21; Luban 1988a, pp.197–201.

[158] eg further thought needs to be given as to whether perjury is different to non-compliance with disclosure rules, whether there is a difference between past and prospective perjury and whether there is a difference between client perjury and that of the client's witnesses.

on perjury as long as clients are first warned of this possibility. Given the inadequacy of the current compromise between silence or whistle-blowing, it would be preferable to opt for one or other extreme and we are not convinced by the arguments put most forcefully by Freedman[159] that lawyer acquiescence in client wrongdoing is preferable. Admittedly, the possibility of whistle-blowing may have a chilling effect on client communications, but not necessarily any more than knowledge that withdrawal is mandatory. Moreover, there is a subtle but important difference between lawyers telling clients that they might not stand back while well-known litigation rules are flouted and telling them that their confidences might be betrayed on grounds whose applicability cannot be predicted in advance. Moreover, those clients prepared to commit perjury are not simply being faced with the stark choice of self-incrimination or ineffective representation; they can always ensure effective representation by candid disclosure but decline to give perjured evidence.[160] Indeed, if this is explained to clients, the dissuasion of perjury could be said to outweigh any possibility that the innocent might still be tempted to withhold what they regard as incriminating evidence. In any event, disclosure of future and perhaps even past perjury can be regarded as justified on the grounds that the lawyer is 'being used by the client to facilitate the commission of a crime'.[161]

At the same time, because of any residual possible negative impact on civil liberties, it is imperative that disclosure be permissive rather than mandatory and that it is regarded as exceptional, if not prohibited, in criminal defence and possibly also criminal defence paradigm cases. Lawyer discretion is also strongly indicated because of the possibility of a disjuncture between moral and legal truth,[162] as when the governing substantive law or adjectival law is unjust. In other words, lawyer disclosure may be inappropriate where it clearly works more injustice than justice. Moreover, if disclosure is to be allowed the rules should lay down a precondition that lawyers are convinced that perjury has been or will be committed.

(c) Harm to Others

Disclosure to prevent harm to others raises far more complicated considerations than the previous two categories discussed. First, there are myriad ways—criminal and non-criminal—in which clients can harm others. Second, such harm can be to identifiable individuals or to large groups like consumers, pension holders or the inhabitants of vast localities. Third, the harm might stem from past, continuing, or future events. Fourth, the probability of the harm occurring might range from a slight possibility to an overwhelming certainty. Fifth, the harm can be to physical or emotional health, to bodily and sexual integrity (such as through rape), to liberty (such

---

[159] Freedman 1966, 1975, ch.3 and 1990, ch.6.   [160] Luban 1988a, pp.200–1.
[161] Para 16.02 n.1, LSG. On the other hand, the privilege might still apply given that the common law only prohibits communications made with the specific purpose of obtaining advice as to how to effect a crime or fraud: see Newbold 1990, p.475. And cf Freedman 1990, pp.125–7, arguing that the US equivalent of this exception does not apply to crimes committed within the very case in which the lawyer is acting.
[162] See Nicolson 1994, pp.734–40.

as through false imprisonment), to privacy, to residential security or to proprietary and financial interests, as well as to the environment. Finally, within most[163] of these categories, the harm may range from very minor to very severe.

Apart from some narrowly defined exceptions, solicitors are only permitted to breach confidentiality in order to prevent *future* acts of a *criminal* nature *reasonably believed* to be *likely* to result in *serious bodily* harm, whereas barristers may not even be able to go this far.[164] Yet the way in which the above five variables might interrelate suggest that, for instance where widespread harm is certain, the fact that it is not serious or physical, or flows from a future or criminal act, should not necessarily rule out lawyer disclosure. Here one thinks of noxious emissions causing low level but constant and long-lasting interferences with health and comfort of many victims, large-scale pension fraud affecting many poorly paid workers and innocent persons condemned for crimes committed by the lawyer's client. In all such cases, it is arguable that lawyers need to be able to weigh the particular harms envisaged, their mode, certainty and seriousness against the actual harm likely to be caused to clients by disclosure and the consequent impact on future clients. On the other hand, the fact that there are so many variables influencing whether lawyers should disclose to prevent harm equally tells against a wide discretion here because of the difficulties clients will have in predicting whether their secrets will be safe. It is thus in the very situation where a balancing discretion seems so necessary that it is most likely to have a chilling effect on client disclosure.

However, we have argued that the chilling effect on corporate clients is likely to be minimal and that concern about its possibility should not be as decisive as in other cases. Moreover, given that it is usually corporations that cause the sort of harm which might justify whistle-blowing without necessarily involving serious physical harm, criminal acts or perhaps even future acts, it is arguable that lawyers should have a discretion to balance the likely harm to be avoided against the values flowing from maintaining confidentiality. Disclosure for non-criminal acts, past acts, and for non-serious and non-physical harm should be, and—given the financial dependence of corporate lawyers—is likely to be, rare. However, it is not inconceivable. For example, while the situation where lawyers are expressly retained to defend particular actions might be different, it might be justifiable for in-house lawyers or those on long-term retainers to leak information in a class action by numerous indigent claimants who have suffered enormous pain and suffering caused by the company's confessed negligence. Far more acceptable is disclosure of the company's intention to engage in future acts which are likely to cause widespread, but not necessarily serious, bodily harm or which would destroy natural habitats but not harm humans. Here, the threat of disclosure would certainly enhance the lawyer's ability to engage in moral dialogue effectively. Finally, the greater moral activism by corporate lawyers which such rules might encourage may lead them to be more inclined to report

---

[163] eg one can never regard the harm rape causes as minor, irrespective of the physical or even emotional damage to the victim.

[164] See section 2, above.

suspected harmful action to senior management, hence transforming some purely tortious acts or omissions into criminal conduct.[165] Indeed, such reporting could be regarded as a necessary precondition to whistle-blowing, apart from very exceptional circumstances where the potential harm is immediate and the likelihood of dissuasion highly unlikely.[166]

As regards non-corporate clients, the civil liberties and other non-consequentialist arguments are far stronger, while the potential for preventing widespread but non-physical harm is far smaller. Even here, however, the current exceptions arguably do not go far enough. Although lawyers can disclose information acquired while being used to facilitate crimes and frauds, such situations are likely to be rare. In fact, this exception arguably falls under the 'prevention of harm to self' category in being designed to protect lawyers from the consequences of deliberately being used to further crimes or fraud rather than to protect those harmed by such acts. Moreover, one wonders why all intentional harmful acts are not covered by this exception as provided by the law on confidentiality.[167] At the same time, given the possibilities for client abuse of confidentiality, this exception should continue to exist even in the case of criminal defendants and criminal defence paradigm clients. Not only are we mainly concerned that they obtain assistance regarding possible liability for past acts, but we are far less likely to regard them as having a right to commit future crimes or frauds. Equally, it should remain a permissive exception given that the crimes and frauds referred to are not confined to those that are serious and given that it does not always follow that law-breaking is immoral.

By contrast, consideration needs to be given to changing the current LSG exception *permitting* disclosure to prevent clients or others committing criminal acts reasonably believed to result in serious bodily harm into one which *requires* disclosure, at least in civil paradigm cases.[168] Moreover, by analogy with the crime of grievous bodily harm, the exception should extend to serious psychological harm and, as with the LSG exception relating to children,[169] to rape and serious sexual offences, whether or not physical violence is involved.

As regards the LSG's distinction between past and future acts,[170] this can be regarded as, on the whole, justifiable.[171] A client's civil liberties require that they obtain effective representation in respect of possibly false allegations, especially given the considerations underlying the 'epistemological demurrer', but clients have no moral, let alone legal, right to commit future wrongful acts. On the other hand, it is not easy to maintain the bright line between past and future acts. More importantly, there is at least one circumstance where the disclosure of past actions

---

[165] eg in cases like the Zeebrugge sinking, lawyer disclosure of inadequate safety to senior management might have ensured the existence of corporate liability for decisions in manslaughter.

[166] cf Brindle and Dehn 1995, p.118.

[167] See section 2, above.   [168] Para. 16.02 n.3, LSG.   [169] Para. 16.02 n.4, LSG.

[170] Note, however, that this distinction is ignored where lawyers are inadvertently used in the commission of crimes or frauds.

[171] On the distinction, see Hazard 1978a, pp.27–32; Moore 1985, pp.242–5; Fried 1986, pp.444–5.

should[172] and indeed used to be permitted.[173] This is where disclosure would prevent the criminal conviction of innocent persons and where it would not simultaneously expose the client to criminal charges.[174] Indeed, a similar argument can be made, albeit less persuasively, for the protection of innocent civil defendants. At the same time, given that disclosure might well expose clients to consequences other than legal liability, and given that innocent persons can face anything from life imprisonment to unconditional discharges, this exception should either be confined to serious consequences or be permissive.

The remaining situations which might call for disclosure are where the foreseen harm is not of a physical or psychological nature or, where it is, where such physical or psychological harm is not serious. In our opinion, disclosure of potential financial or property loss can only be justified where it will cause harm which is equivalent to serious bodily or mental harm. Similarly, disclosure of acts likely to cause less than serious bodily or mental harm will only rarely outweigh any potential harm to the client and hence justify the possible chilling effect on future clients. Consequently, in this context it can be argued that outside the corporate and possibly also criminal defence paradigm there should be no further extensions of the current exceptions to confidentiality.

6. CONCLUSION

Having made a number of quite specific recommendations for reform of the lawyer's duty to keep clients' secrets, it is necessary to make two further points by way of conclusion. The first is that our suggestions are aimed more at illustrating the advantages of a contextual approach to professional legal ethics than at providing definitive answers to specific problems of confidentiality. No doubt our suggestions will be controversial to some and may well contain flaws. However, if they succeed in placing on the agenda the possibility of a more nuanced approach to confidentiality allowing for some increase in the possibilities for whistle-blowing by lawyers, then this chapter will have achieved its goal. At the very least, we hope that it might lead to the justifications for the current position being subjected to closer evaluation.

The second point is that, in arguing for increased lawyer disclosure to protect third parties, the general public and the environment, we are mindful of the need to ensure that the balance does not tip too far away from protecting clients.

---

[172] This is accepted by even those British commentators who otherwise support a strict confidentiality duty: eg Pannick 1992, pp.163–4; Ipp 1998, pp.72–3, but cf contra Napley 1991, pp.62–3. See also Black 1982; 'Correspondence' 1982; Fry 1997.

[173] See *R v Barton* [1972] 2 All ER 1192 and *R v Ataou* [1988] 2 All ER 321 (overruled by *R v Derby Magistrates' Court, ex p B* [1995] 4 All ER 526); para. 16.04, n.8 of the 6th edn. (1993) of the LSG.

[174] eg because they have since died, been offered immunity, or are protected by the double jeopardy principle.

[175] Note that this requirement goes further than the need for moral dialogue after communication but

Consequently, we end this chapter by making more explicit two means of enhancing the presumption of confidentiality which have as yet only been touched on in passing. The first is a requirement that lawyers must be convinced beyond reasonable doubt that disclosure will do more good than harm. The second is that, apart from very rare circumstances, such as when it would precipitate serious harm to others, lawyer disclosure should not conflict with a client's legitimate expectation, gained through express promise or conduct, that the particular information disclosed would in fact be kept secret. In other words, lawyers should not breach confidentiality if they have not warned clients of the possibility of disclosure *before* communication of the relevant information.[175] Indeed, this may in fact improve the current position, whereby many lawyers fail to mention the few disclosure exceptions which do exist, and thus might enhance client autonomy and prevent possibilities of betrayal of trust by lawyers.[176]

No doubt, determining the timing and wording of disclosure warnings is fraught with difficulty. Providing a lengthy description of disclosure possibilities, not remotely relevant at the beginning of interviews, might unnecessarily affect client candour or even encourage dissimulation.[177] On the other hand, not mentioning possible exceptions at an early stage might lead to lawyers being caught out by the communication of information they would want to disclose. Nevertheless, it is surely within the abilities of most lawyers to balance the need for client candour with the need to put clients on notice about possible disclosure. Not all cases raise all disclosure exceptions, nor do full details of the relevant position have to be given until the first inkling of a possibility of disclosure. Where lawyers miscalculate and are surprised by the clients' communication of potentially disclosable information, blowing the whistle should be highly exceptional. In this way, lawyers can play a more morally activist role without undermining their whole *raison d'être*—responding to the needs of clients.

---

before disclosure (see text at n.132, above) in that it gives the client the option of not revealing incriminating information to the lawyer if they would prefer to lose effective representation rather than risk public disclosure of such information.

[176] Simon 1978, pp.133–4; Hodes 1981, pp.775, 786–7, 810.

[177] Alschuler 1981, pp.170–1; Freedman 1990, pp.111–13 (regarding perjury only).

10

Conclusion: Towards a More Ethical Profession

> The foolproof—universal and unshakably founded—ethical code will never be found; having singed our fingers once too often, we know now what we did not know then, when we embarked on this journey of exploration: that a non-aporetic, non-ambivalent morality, an ethics that is universal and 'objectively founded' is a practical impossibility; perhaps also an *oxymoron*, a contradiction in terms.
>
> Zygmunt Bauman[1]

Throughout this book we have made a number of criticisms and some specific proposals for the reform of various 'macro' and 'micro' issues relating to professional legal ethics. In this concluding chapter we intend to build upon these proposals in order to further our main aim of encouraging a more ethically aware and concerned legal profession. Accordingly, our suggestions for reform have not been designed to provide definitive answers to particular ethical dilemmas but to bring about an *approach* to ethics which requires lawyers to engage with the multitude of ethical issues raised by legal practice in a far more active and conscious fashion than is generally the case at present.

In this chapter we start by drawing together our discussions of what we regard as the main problem with professional legal ethics—the dominance of formalism and liberalism. This will lead us to a comparison with the advantages of our proposed contextual approach, both as a means of guiding ethical decision-making and enhancing the development of lawyers' moral character. By paying close attention to the way in which this approach may be embedded in the professional codes and taught as part of legal education, we hope to meet some of the possible objections. Finally, we shall briefly explore ways of reinforcing the contextual approach through other institutional changes in order to further reinforce our goal of encouraging a more ethical profession.

1. THE DOMINANCE OF FORMALISM AND LIBERALISM

In Chapter 2, we saw that both formalism and liberalism had their roots in the Enlightenment philosophy of Kant and his followers.[2] Given the middle class origins of lawyers and the affinity between legal values, market liberalism, and constitutional democracy, English and Welsh lawyers are likely to find persuasive the liberal justifications for the rules and roles of professional legal ethics. Given also the many

---

[1] Bauman 1983, p.10.   [2] Ch.2, section 3.

similarities between Kantian deontology, 'ten commandment' forms of Christianity, the structure and aims of law itself, and the dominance of legal formalism in law schools, unsurprisingly the professions turned to the deontological approach to ethics once it was realised that lawyers' social background could not sufficiently guarantee their moral character and ethical standards. Consequently, the new ethical codes were modelled on the most formalistically inclined of all ethical traditions, laying down narrow duties of a minimalist nature, which are meant to be applied in a legalistic and categorical fashion generally without reference to context or consequences.[3] As such, they invite concentration on the letter rather than the spirit of ethical norms; on form rather than substance. As in the case of legal formalism, ethical formalism tends to consider obedience to formally laid down norms as the beginning and end of ethical obligation.

Lawyers' ethics are also influenced by formalism in its more specific guise of legal formalism. Thus, as we have seen,[4] the latter's historical dominance has discouraged legal academics from focusing on issues of morality and justice, and, even more so, on lawyers' ethics. Instead, legal education tends to teach students to value technical skill and professional success. This ethical gap is left unfilled by the vocational courses, where the emphasis is more on rules of 'mere regulation'[5] than ethics and the pedagogical style focuses narrowly on compliance—teaching students to keep their noses clean by avoiding possible disciplinary proceedings.

The role of formalism is also central to the justifications for the current norms governing the lawyers' duties of zeal and confidentiality, and the underlying conception of neutral partisanship. Thus, as we saw in Chapter 7, neutral partisanship is justified on the basis that, by playing their allotted role in the adversarial system and in helping clients vindicate their legal rights, lawyers *ipso facto* act ethically and ensure justice. However, as we argued, this makes a number of dubious assumptions about the meaning and attainability of truth and justice in the legal system. The adversarial system is assumed to ensure that correct facts are found, thus ignoring the possibility that power imbalances between adversaries will simply mean that 'truth' follows power. Moreover, in line with 'fact positivism' with which legal formalism is closely associated,[6] truth is conflated with factual truth, thus ignoring that truths of a moral and political nature may also be at stake in the legal process. Similarly, justice is assumed to flow from the correct application of law to the facts, thus ignoring not only that lawyer creativity in relation to facts, but also that law itself, may be unjust. And in the same way that faith in the adversary system ignores the possible impact of power imbalances between adversaries, including as one important component their lawyers' zeal, so the legitimatory goal of vindicating clients' legal rights ignores the fact that the recognition and application of these rights might reflect wider power imbalances in society. Similarly, lawyers do not simply put into effect legal rights in a mechanical fashion; in many cases they may manipulate or even create such rights in the first place.

---

[3] Occasionally, consequences are referred to, but in the form of categorical rules rather than those requiring consequential calculations.

[4] Ch.3, section 6.   [5] cf Ch.4, section 3.3.1.   [6] See Nicolson 1994.

Challenges to the formalistic picture of the legal process also undermine the core liberal arguments that the lawyer's amoral role is justified as the necessary means to individual dignity, autonomy and equality, as well as the political values of democracy and the rule of law. However, the main problem with these liberal arguments is that, in formalistically conflating dignity, autonomy and equality with legal dignity, autonomy and equality, they conveniently ignore the actual invasions of these values wrought by upholding clients' legal rights. Law, we have argued, does not impartially protect everyone's dignity and autonomy, but in both its content and application is riven with discriminatory distinctions based on class, race, ethnicity, gender, etc.

Moreover, as we first argued in Chapter 5,[7] because of its assumptions of rational, self-seeking, and atomistic individualism, even within the context of the lawyer-client relationship itself, liberalism may ironically undermine its whole purpose—the enhancement of individual autonomy. Treating all clients as the *homo oeconimicus* of classic liberal theory may lead to paternalistic invasions of client autonomy where lawyers make unfounded assumptions about their clients' needs, desires and interests, and treat cases as purely technical problems of how most effectively to vindicate their legal rights. Moreover, unable to see beyond the client's formal autonomy, lawyers may ignore the extent to which power differentials based on knowledge, wealth, background and status may render clients dependent on them with a consequent usurpation of their effective decision-making.

The influence of liberalism can be seen, finally, in the professions' argument[8] that their collective autonomy in the form of self-regulation is necessary to ensure that lawyers play their role in protecting individual autonomy against state power and in helping to maintain the liberal scheme of government with its emphasis on the rule of law and the separation of powers. However, as we also saw in Chapter 4 and subsequently, much of the content and enforcement of self-regulation has reflected the needs and interests of the professions themselves rather than those they are supposed to serve. Indeed, the present system fails adequately to create that same separation of powers that lawyers are so ready to enforce elsewhere.

Thus, to summarise, we have argued that through the influence of formalism and liberalism, current professional ethical norms act to undermine lawyers' ability to play a truly positive social role. This does little to assuage public doubts about the amoral role and general function of lawyers, and the process by which even those who do enter law school with the aim of furthering justice are likely to end up as amoral ciphers for large corporations, unthinking technocrats in large or medium-size law firms or as high-street lawyers simply trying to ensure a comfortable living. Consequently, we have argued that a move away from an ethics based on formalism and liberalism to one which requires lawyers to consider the contextual factors relevant to their representation of clients and the impact on specific and general others would go at least some way towards encouraging a more ethical profession.

[7] See also Ch.6, section 3.4, Ch.7, section 3.2.2. [8] See Ch.4, section 2.1.

2. THE CONTEXTUAL ALTERNATIVE

As we argued in the Introduction, professional legal ethics needs to be contextualised both as a topic of study and as a set of norms governing lawyers' ethics. Throughout the book we have thus sought first to understand lawyers' ethics in terms of the various philosophical, sociological and regulatory contexts and, secondly, to develop an approach to ethics which requires lawyers to take cognisance of context in dealing with clients and in resolving the various dilemmas which may arise out of client representation. However, given that the basis of our contextual approach to ethical decision-making was first introduced in Chapter 4 and then developed incrementally in later chapters, it is necessary to provide an overview of how all aspects of the contextual approach may be incorporated into the codes.

As we have repeatedly argued, in contrast to the current narrow and categorical approach to ethics, lawyers should be required to take into account the real life situation of their clients, including all their needs, desires and interests, and the possible impact of their actions on third parties, the general public and the environment. This has led us, first, to a broader understanding of the content of the duties imposed on lawyers *vis-à-vis* clients and in particular to a deeper conception of what is meant by loyalty and autonomy.[9] Thus, instead of the current uni-dimensional and uni-directional understandings of these notions, we argued for a wider duty of good faith on the part of both lawyer and client, and a more contextualised understanding of 'autonomy-in-relation'. Secondly, we called for greater limits on the lawyer's general duty of loyalty as found in its specific manifestations of zeal and confidentiality.[10] This, we argued, should come in the form of decision-making schemas which require lawyers to consider a wide range of contextual factors in deciding how to resolve the conflict between duties to clients with their wider moral duties to act with integrity and concern for the interests of others. Thus, building on our discussion of the problems associated with, on the one hand, highly detailed codes containing categorical duties and, on the other, leaving lawyers absolute discretion as to how to act, in the hope that they will possess the appropriate character for the intuitive resolution of ethical problems, we suggest that in dealing with ethical issues[11] the codes should contain three normative levels.

The first would consist of a general statement of the underlying values which should underpin the lawyer-client relationship, set out at the beginning of the ethical codes, perhaps along the lines of the Preamble to the CCBE Code.[12] Based upon our conclusions in dealing with the issues of lawyer and client autonomy, immoral ends and means, and confidentiality, we suggest that the following values are primary: good faith and trust, which applies to both lawyers in their proximate 'face-to-face' dealings with clients and others, and to clients themselves; non-maleficence, which

---

[9] See Ch.5.   [10] See Chs.6–9.

[11] As opposed to conduct: see Ch.4, section 3.4, where we argue for a separation of the ethical and conduct issues in either different documents or in clearly differentiated parts of the same document.

[12] Referred to in Ch.3, section 4.5.

requires lawyers to refrain from harming others; and beneficence, which requires lawyers to do good and prevent harm to others.

The second layer would consist of more specific general principles which govern the lawyer-client relationship. These could be set out in much the same way as the general principles contained in Practice Rule 1 of the Solicitors' Practice Rules are found in paragraph 1.01 of the LSG. Based upon our discussion in Chapters 6–9 and combined with the requirements of lawyer diligence and independence which we have not discussed at length,[13] we propose the following four principles:

(a) *Loyalty.* The lawyer's primary duty is to uphold their clients' interests, needs and desires. This involves a presumption that lawyers will exercise all necessary zeal on behalf of their clients (the principle of partisanship) and will keep secret all their confidential information (the principle of confidentiality).

(b) *Integrity.* Notwithstanding the principle of loyalty, lawyers must recognise that they are implicated in and hence morally responsible for all actions taken on behalf of clients. They cannot pass on moral responsibility either to clients, who they have freely chosen to represent, or to the profession, which they have freely chosen to enter. Thus in deciding whether to undertake or to continue representation, or to engage in particular forms of representation, lawyers are obliged to consider the impact on their personal moral integrity, the integrity of the profession as a whole, and the interests of affected third parties, the general public, and the environment.

(c) *Candour.* Good faith representation requires a mutual expectation of honest and open communication between lawyer and client with regard to all material aspects of the transaction, and, as far as is compatible with the duty of loyalty, between lawyer and third parties. A failure of candour on the part of lawyer or client may be sufficient to justify termination of the retainer.

(d) *Informed consent.* It is an ethical presumption that clients are entitled to sufficient information to enable them to participate effectively in decision-making throughout the retainer's duration. This presumption extends to all major steps in the transaction, whether regarding means or ends, and their likely cost. Where lawyers are in any doubt as to whether clients would wish to be consulted before steps are taken, the presumption requires that consultation takes place. Lawyers may not override the presumption by obtaining a blanket waiver of consent from clients.[14]

In order that these principles do not remain at the level of pure aspiration without much meaningful content, they need to be fleshed out by commentaries setting out their rationale and underlying values. Moreover, in order to assist lawyers to put these principles into effect and, in particular, to resolve conflicts between them, we propose that the third layer sets out the contextual factors which are relevant to the way in

---

[13] Though see Ch.5, section 7.

[14] Admittedly, this is the sort of categorical rule we have largely sought to avoid, but it is critical if the whole principle of informed consent is not to be side-stepped. See ibid.

which lawyers should apply the general principles set out above when faced with the type of ethical dilemmas discussed in Chapters 6–9.[15] Given the importance of deciding micro-ethical issues in context, we suggest that separate sections or even chapters be devoted to the contextual factors relevant to the four separate issues we discussed. We have already sketched what we regard as the most important of these factors in Chapters 5, 8, and 9 in the form of broad decision-making schemas.[16] These, we have stressed, are aimed at alerting lawyers to and guiding their decision-making through specifying contextual factors which they must consider, but which will not determine their decisions in mechanical fashion. While some of these contextual considerations are specific to particular issues, others apply across the board, and may thus be usefully summarised here.

Perhaps the most general of these factors is the question of the relevant interests, desires and needs of those involved in and affected by legal representation—understood not only in material (financial or otherwise) but also emotional and psychological terms. This is crucial in determining, first, the informational needs and expectations of clients and, more particularly, what aspects of the case are 'material' for the purposes of the candour principle; secondly, when failures of candour will justify the retainer's termination; and, thirdly, what steps in the representation are 'major' for the purposes of informed consent. This factor is, however, equally important in relation to third parties and the general public whenever they are likely to be affected by actions of lawyers in representing clients. Moreover, lawyers are also justified in considering their own interests, not only in terms of the integrity principle, but also, to some extent, in earning the fees necessary to justify their continuation in private practice and in avoiding dismissal from employment.

The type of needs, interests and desires of those affected by client representation is obviously closely related to a second important contextual factor we have repeatedly stressed. This is the harm likely to ensue to third parties, the general public, the environment and even lawyers themselves both individually and collectively from the loyal representation of clients and conversely the type of harm likely to ensue to clients, those associated with them, and again also to lawyers if limits are placed on client loyalty. However, as we have seen, it is not just the type of harm that is relevant but also its degree and likely occurrence.

While the above questions will depend on many other more specific contextual factors, one factor which will frequently be relevant is the question of the balance of power both between lawyer and client, and between lawyers, as clients' representatives, and affected others. The former will be relevant to the informational needs and expectations of clients, the likely problems of manipulation by client or lawyer, and the extent to which moral activism may lead to problems of client control. Both types of power imbalances will affect the likely harm to clients and others where their interests are in opposition.

[15] Indeed, we would argue that similar approaches could be developed for other ethical principles such as lawyer diligence and in particular lawyer independence.

[16] See sections 7, 6, and 5, respectively.

Finally, because of the way that various contextual factors tend to recur in particular types of cases, we can note that, in evaluating the above, much depends on whether the case involves criminal defence, civil litigation, mediation, negotiation, facilitation or advice giving. Moreover, where the lawyer is not representing a criminal defendant, it will be important to ascertain where the case fits along the continuum between criminal defence paradigm and civil suit paradigm cases.

If ethical codes are to incorporate the sort of decision-making schemas we have outlined, in order to assist lawyers in developing a true understanding and appreciation of the importance of contextual decision-making, as with the general principles, it is essential that commentaries are provided explaining the rationale behind each contextual factor and possibly also giving examples of actual or even hypothetical cases. In this way, it is hoped that the codes will not simply guide ethical decision-making but also help educate lawyers as to the importance of ethics and the wide variety of ethical considerations relevant to the dilemmas they are likely to face. This in turn will ensure that the codes can play two further important functions.

The first is to assist development of lawyers' moral character, which virtue ethics emphasises is necessary to, at least, supplement obligation-based ethical approaches. Secondly, by exposing law students to the various dilemmas and moral considerations that apply in different areas of practice, the codes can help them make ethically informed choices as to what type of legal practice they pursue. It is perhaps a trite point that this is perhaps the most significant ethical decision in a lawyer's career.[17] From this flows the type of moral dilemmas they are likely to face as well as the likely constraints on their ability to exercise moral activism. It is therefore essential that aspiring lawyers are aware of these dilemmas and constraints *before* they make career choices and that they are encouraged to consider such choices in terms of their moral implications rather than simply in terms of financial rewards, career prospects and job satisfaction. Having to understand and evaluate a professional code containing general principles supported by a schema for moral decision-making should alert lawyers to the moral implications and the importance of career choices, as well as providing them with guidance as to how to integrate their personal moral values with their professional obligations throughout their legal careers.

3. POSSIBLE OBJECTIONS TO A CONTEXTUAL APPROACH

If the codes manage to perform these two functions, this will go some way to meeting possible objections to our contextual approach.[18] The first is the argument most likely to be voiced by professional insiders that it would be too demanding in terms of

---

[17] See eg Nicolson 1994, p.741; Hutchinson 1998, p.176.

[18] cf also the discussion by Simon 1988, pp.70–4 regarding the following and other, less weighty objections to a contextual approach.

time and effort to expect lawyers to use the decision-making schemas.[19] An immediate counter-response is that the considerable financial rewards and status which
can flow from the privilege of a practising certificate warrant the expectation that
lawyers spend some time working out for themselves whether any harm they cause
in using this licence can be justified. In any event, the amount of time involved is
likely to decrease as lawyers gain experience in using it. More importantly, given the
trend towards specialisation, few lawyers will have to get to grips with the various
factors raised by all the contexts of legal practice and with all specific and general
ethical considerations. For example, the arguments for neutral partisanship in criminal defence work limit the factors to be considered, whereas city lawyers will not
have to worry about abandoning 'criminal defence paradigm' cases and rarely about
the problems of paternalism.

A far more plausible variant on the possible objection that our approach is too
demanding might rely on the financial and other practical constraints facing lawyers.
These may make it unrealistic to expect lawyers to meet the requirements of good
faith and various forms of moral activism we have proposed. This argument is unpersuasive when applied to successful barristers in independent practice or partners in
thriving solicitor practices. But what about barristers needing to make their reputation in a competitive market? And what about the much greater number of solicitors who are employed by private law practices, the CPS, other public bodies or by
private companies? Clearly they risk being dismissed or, at the very least, spoiling
their promotion chances by taking the time to meet the requirements of candour
and informed consent, or by declining to take on clients, providing qualified representation, breaching confidentiality or even by attempting to engage their clients or
employers in moral dialogue. These problems cannot be evaded by stating, albeit
accurately, that they stem largely from the fact that legal services have become a
product like any other to be sold according to free market principles. We have to
deal with the lawyer's social context as it exists.

In response, one can point out that, especially in corporate practice, current fee
structures are already sufficiently beneficial to lawyers[20] to justify their having to bear
any additional costs imposed by the requirement of good faith or moral activism. In
our view, clients should not generally pay more for a quality of service they are entitled to expect nor should they be able to pay less in order to avoid the ethical consideration of representation issues which should be part and parcel of a professional
service. Consequently, if there is a cost, it should be borne out of existing profit
margins.

As regards moral activism more specifically, state prosecutors may be able to

---

[19] See Sheinman 1997, p.151 and cf also Ellman 1990, pp.139–41 and 152, regarding Luban's proposals discussed in Ch.8, section 3 and Luban's response in 1990b, pp.1022–3. cf, more generally, the
criticisms of consequentialism in Ch.2, section 4.3.

[20] The view that competitive pressures are keeping fees down can be found expressed almost weekly
somewhere in the legal trade press. Like many intuitive views it may not always be correct. Economic
research suggests that some areas of the legal services market are not, relatively speaking, as price-
sensitive as is commonly thought. See Domberger and Sherr 1989.

conceal their moral decisions beneath conclusions that the various tests for prosecution are not satisfied. Similarly, in-house lawyers and other employed lawyers could argue that certain ends or means to ends they regard as immoral are not financially viable or legally supported. But even if one is persuaded that the breach of good faith and candour principles involved is preferable to personal involvement in harm, immorality and injustice, it has to be conceded that the practical opportunities for such strategies are limited. There is only so far one can go in plausibly arguing that prosecutorial policy, financial considerations or the law itself do not support immoral ends or means. And there are only so many times employees can use this strategy before arousing employer or client suspicions.

However, to allow these considerations to trump the arguments for a contextual approach, good faith lawyering and moral activism would be to ignore the point made earlier that if legal neophytes are made aware of the type of ethical dilemmas and external constraints likely to arise in particular areas of practice they cannot later seek to deny moral responsibility for any actions they feel constrained to perform. Put simply, if one is not happy with being required, for instance, to assist in the laying off of workers to maintain profit levels or the destruction of the environment by oil companies and one is not prepared to engage in moral dialogue and other forms of moral activism in order to dampen down client immorality, one should seek alternative career options.

The second possible objection to our contextual approach is the direct converse of the above 'too hard' argument. Here, it may be argued that providing lawyers with discretion to resolve ethical dilemmas will make it *too easy* for those bent on immoral behaviour to get away with it, thus increasing the overall level of lawyer immorality.[21] The position, it might be argued, is already too lax given that many areas of potentially unethical behaviour are currently unregulated and the professions' casual attitude towards breach of those rules that do exist. Both these points are readily conceded, though the latter also rather undermines the call for a prohibition-based regulatory approach.

Nevertheless, as we argued in Chapter 4, the disadvantages in terms of the anaesthetisation of moral conscience, the likely encouragement of legalistic attempts at creative compliance and the likelihood that the profession will continue to baulk at the strict punishment of its own, not to mention all the practical problems with detailed ethical codes, strongly argue against a command and control approach. Without the development of appropriate moral character, strict duties are never going to be able to do all the ethical work necessary to ensure a more moral profession, whereas our contextual approach can, as we have argued, play an important part in the development of moral character.

In any event, it may be recalled that we have rejected a regulatory approach which totally eschews disciplinary sanctions for code breaches.[22] Admittedly, the

---

[21] cf the views of Cranston 1995, pp.5–6; Paterson 1995, pp.176–7 and 1997, p.37.
[22] See Ch.4, sections 3.4 and 4.3.

imposition of such sanctions may be less frequent than is possible under the current disciplinary approach to regulation.[23] However, by analogy with administrative law, action can be taken when lawyers fail to consider relevant factors in making ethical decisions or balance the various factors in ways which no reasonable lawyer would. Moreover, the process of taking disciplinary proceedings and the publicisation of decisions and the reasoning on which they are based is as important in its educative effect on other lawyers as the realisation that unethical behaviour might be sanctioned. Even if lawyers are ultimately acquitted on 'rule of law' grounds, decisions may establish precedents for the future with important educative effects on others. While our contextual approach may allow those bent on immoral behaviour to evade sanctions if they go through the motions of purporting to consider all relevant contextual factors before acting, although impossible to prove (or, indeed, to disprove), we believe that in the long run it may lead to an overall reduction in lawyer immorality. This is because fewer lawyers should engage in immoral behaviour due to ignorance, indifference or a failure of ethical imagination.

4. INSTITUTIONALISING AN ETHICAL PROFESSIONALISM

We are not, however, so naive as to think that this sea change in lawyer attitudes will occur solely through changes to the content and form of current regulatory norms. What is also needed is a plethora of changes to the legal professions' social and institutional contexts. Here the range of relevant factors is so wide and the possibilities for change so mixed that we intend to do no more than sketch the most important factors, concentrating on those possibilities for change which seem most promising and where we, as legal academics, might have most effect.

On that basis, we start with legal education itself. Incorporating a contextual approach into the codes is undoubtedly important if we are to ethicise the professions, not least because they would then be less susceptible to being taught in a narrow 'black letter' fashion. However, wider educational reform at both the initial and vocational stages of legal education needs to accompany if not precede code changes in order to enable students to develop moral character or help them deal with real-life ethical dilemmas. Admittedly, given the centrality to the Common Law tradition of reasoning by analogy and case distinguishing, law students are capable of understanding the importance of the factual context to legal cases. However, the tradition's separation of law from ethics means that it tends to bury issues of value under layers of technical and pragmatic justification thus rendering it insufficient as a grounding in ethical reasoning. Ethical lawyering within a contextual approach requires that students consciously develop the capacity for a more sophisticated form

---

[23] Though data from other Common Law systems suggest that sanctions for breaches of ethical rather than regulatory norms are relatively rare under disciplinary models. See the sources discussed in Ch.3, section 7.4.

of reasoning which recognises the centrality of ethical sensitivity and 'judgement' in the Aristotelian tradition of *phronesis*.[24]

Judgement in this sense is itself a virtue.[25] It describes both the capacity for ethical understanding, and the intellectual and practical skills necessary to convert ethical thought into ethical action.[26] It requires a sufficient knowledge and understanding of the ethical principles involved and the empathic capacities necessary to identify, first, that a situation has ethical dimensions, and then to recognise the range of considerations which define its moral terrain. It involves the capacity to select and justify morally appropriate courses of action as they arise in specific situations.

Given the length of time needed to develop these skills and given that lawyers and their ethics form an important constitutive part of the administration of justice, there is a strong case for locating professional legal ethics at the initial stage of legal education. Crucially, as we have sought to show, micro-ethical issues need to be discussed within their sociological and philosophical contexts, since this alone can give students the conceptual tools and language to step back and take a reflective view of the subject. This, however, creates practical challenges for law schools, not least regarding curriculum design. As we have seen, a small number of courses already exist in England and Wales, either teaching professional legal ethics as a subject in its own right or integrating it into some part of the curriculum, such as in introductory 'legal system' courses, jurisprudence, clinical or skills-based courses. These are welcome developments, but from a long-term perspective it is doubtful whether they are sufficient. An emerging body of educational literature suggests that, if professional legal ethics is not to be marginalised, it needs to pervade the curriculum.[27] Ideally, this requires not just its integration into the substantive subjects, but a separate course devoted to both macro- and micro-issues of legal ethics. At the very least, macro-issues, such as the impact and appropriateness of the adversary system and the role of the legal profession, could be discussed in 'English Legal System' or 'Law in Society' courses and remaining issues in courses dealing with legal theory or legal practice.

Teaching legal ethics needs to be considered not only as a matter of what and where but also how. Studies[28] suggest that the development of ethical judgement requires not just substantive knowledge, which could be delivered by relatively traditional means, but also processes of internalisation and reflection developed through

---

[24] See Ch.2, section 5.3. [25] See Webb 1998a, pp.144–5.

[26] This also requires sufficient strength of moral character, though it is probably beyond the capacity of any system of education to single-handedly ensure that individuals will act on their beliefs: see Rest and Narvaez 1994, esp ch.1. Hence the importance of creating other institutional structures which will encourage individuals to 'do the right thing'.

[27] Webb 1996, 1998a and 1998b. See also Rhode 1992; O'Dair 1997; Brayne *et al* 1998, p.273. The idea of pervasiveness would also seem to underpin ACLEC's call for education in legal ethics and values: ACLEC 1996, para. 2.4. This has been barely emphasised in the drafts of the revised Joint Announcement on Qualifying Law Degrees which will set the 'core curriculum' for the initial stage of professional training at least for the next five years.

[28] See eg Rhode 1992; Rest and Narvaez 1994.

ethical problem-solving, Socratic dialogue, role-play, group-work, and possibly even live client and/or simulated clinical experience.[29] These methodologies should be equally relevant to vocational training, even though the focus at that stage might more justifiably be as much on matters of 'mere regulation' as on ethics. Opportunities created for dialogue and reflection may serve not just to enhance individual moral development, but, at a minimum, may also support a socialising function by acculturating students to an environment in which ethical dialogue and reflection come to be seen as a normal part of legal work. Moreover, drawing on common themes in communitarian, feminist and postmodern theory,[30] we suggest it might also offer the potential to develop in students a sense of 'identity' and of moral self that is embedded more in social networks and interactions than the atomistic, self-centred, 'I' of liberal individualism.

Given the importance of moral communities to the creation of ethical character, it is important that the academy considers ethics not just as an educational topic, but in relation to its own practices. Factors such as staff acquiescence in widespread student cynicism and instrumentalism, the misuse of teacher power in the classroom, oppressive and discriminatory social practices both within the student body and the institution more generally, and the general lack of consensus or even discussion of the moral values of legal education all serve to undermine the capacity of law schools to act as appropriate moral communities.[31] Law schools could also assist the professions in their task of addressing the demographic biases of the system not just by maintaining, if not increasing, the social mix of their intake,[32] but by confronting more explicitly the extent to which their traditional mode of discourse silences the alternative voices of many women, ethnic minorities, and other disadvantaged groups.[33] This is not about 'political correctness'; it is, in authentic liberal fashion, a matter of making space for pluralism to flourish.

In a similarly educative vein, we have suggested that the processes of ethical standard-setting and enforcement within the professions move away from a simple command and control model to play a greater role in normative inculcation. Drawing on the dialogical approach to ethics discussed in Chapter 2,[34] in Chapter 4 we proposed that systems of responsive regulation are developed which enable regulators and regulated to build up through 'regulatory conversations' a deeper contextual understanding of legal practice.[35] Along postmodernist lines, this can be used to make the regulatory process sensitive to a multiplicity of voices. This may be achieved by wider representation of consumer interests on regulatory bodies, a greater willingness to use the expertise of philosophers and academic lawyers (assuming a sufficient body of expertise eventually evolves) on ethics committees, and a willing-

---

[29] See Webb 1998b, pp.295–7 for a tentative model.

[30] The nature of these links is developed more explicitly in Kupfer 1996.

[31] Indeed, it is probably the overriding sense of disinterest that creates the greatest barrier to change at present.

[32] See also ACLEC 1996, para. 3.12 for support.

[33] See eg Worden 1985, pp.1144–5; Thornton 1998; McGlynn 1998, p.22.

[34] Section 7.4.   [35] Section 2.3.

ness to consult on rule changes beyond the professions. Perhaps this kind of approach may, as Sampford suggests, even lead to the creation of localised 'ethical circles' in which practitioners meet to 'develop their own critical morality'.[36]

A third area requiring reform is the business and organisational context to legal practice. The commonly expressed view that law is no longer a profession but a business reflects the increasingly difficult economic and policy climate within which lawyers—and particularly the small to medium-sized solicitors' firms, and some smaller chambers—are operating. As our analysis in Chapter 3 suggested, balancing cost, quality, and ethics remains one of the key challenges for lawyers as we enter the twenty-first century.

No one denies that lawyers are entitled to make a living, or that the need for economic survival can create real difficulties in balancing professional self-interest and public responsibilities. This is, however, no reason for jettisoning the latter. Some lawyers who use the 'business defence' seem to assume that businesses have responsibilities to no one but themselves. This disregards the extent to which successful businesses are expected to adopt extensive responsibilities for their customers and employees,[37] and, perhaps (but not invariably), wider social responsibilities[38] as well. To be involved in business rather than a profession does not excuse one from the human race. What the current situation does demand, however, is both a wider debate about the kind of business strategies that are compatible with an ethical professionalism, and some incremental policy of change. Although we do not pretend to have a blueprint for reform, there are a number of areas where change may be sought.

First, at the level of micro-regulation the professions need to develop clearer practices and higher expectations as regards client care and professional responsibility. Firms and chambers could, for example, be required to appoint in-house compliance officers who are responsible not just to the organisation but to the regulator for creating and overseeing both complaints systems and perhaps wider mechanisms for enhancing 'ethical compliance'. Moreover, as trends like fragmentation and globalisation potentially reduce the power of national regulatory bodies, we would argue that there is a strong case for developing a more organisationally-based ethic within the broader kind of responsive framework offered in Chapter 4. Indeed, given the increasing mismatch between group-based working practices and a system of regulation that is predicated on largely individualistic rules and mechanisms of enforcement, there is an argument generally for creating principles imposing greater collective responsibility on firms and chambers for their members' failings.

Second, there is the question of fees. Fees are critical both to the public's access to justice and the profession's ethical image. And here, rightly or wrongly, lawyers

---

[36] Sampford with Parker 1995, p.17.

[37] See Company Law Steering Group 1999, ch.5. It is notable, for example, that standards of complaint-handling that have become normalised in business settings are still resisted in some quarters of the legal profession: Ch.4, section 4.2, above.

[38] See eg Company Law Steering Group 1999; Post *et al* 1995.

are not trusted by the general public. At a fairly basic level, the professions need to work far harder in ensuring that cost regimes—and particularly the new conditional fee arrangements—are transparent, and that mechanisms for complaining about or taxing costs are kept simple and inexpensive. The move, apparent in corporate work, towards more 'up-front' fixed fee agreements may also be one way of ensuring greater cost visibility and comparability,[39] provided that, if there is any consequent increase in the competitive tendency to reduce fees, this is not such as to depress quality of service to unacceptable levels.[40]

But there is also an institutional dimension to the fees issue. 'Better' ethics will almost certainly cost more. For some sectors of the profession that might take some of the sheen off partnership, but we suspect it is hardly likely to cause financial hardship. For a significant number of small firms and chambers or sole practitioners it almost certainly will, and here the professions face some conflict between their regulatory and representative roles. Many of the current assumptions about the professions' future seem to be predicated on a presumption that we must safeguard the smallest (and often least economically viable) units, despite the fact that they are also the part of the professions under the most pressure to undertake low quality, high volume work (to keep competitive), to 'borrow' from client accounts and engage in other unethical or unlawful pursuits,[41] and often the least able (or willing?) to pay for the infrastructure necessary for good regulatory compliance. Assuming many such firms are unable to afford the costs of a more localised compliance-based system of regulation, if the professions were to move towards a more compliance-based model, it may be necessary to maintain a two-tier system, involving a greater degree of command and control regulation than at present for those firms unable to achieve the 'professional responsibility standards' necessary to be entrusted with compliance. In that way, the threat of greater regulatory control may itself act as an incentive to firms and chambers to adopt the standards necessary to attain the greater autonomy of a compliance-based system.

Thirdly, there is the question of how firms and chambers, as legal businesses, should engage with their communities. As we have seen, the narrowly individualistic and partisan approach that characterises much legal work within a liberal market economy privileges the autonomy of individual actors over the interests of their communities. A more contextual approach, which enables the lawyer to advise from the perspective of an independent and morally active member of the local (or even national or international) community, could 'empower' clients to achieve autonomy in an ethical manner within the context of a 'just community'.[42] Such an approach might encourage lawyers to offer more creative forms of advice and assistance which

---

[39] See also Woolf 1995, p.200 for support.

[40] Price competition is of course itself a product of deregulation, so one partial answer to quality might be re-regulation through scale fees, etc., which prevent undercutting (this was a feature in recent Law Society debates on the future of the conveyancing market). However, this overlooks the problem that scale fees may not accurately reflect the value of the work done and can generate significant rents for practitioners.

[41] And hence increasing indemnity insurance costs for the profession as a whole.

[42] Eberle 1993, p.125.

benefit clients and community rather than clients over community.[43] Activities such as *pro bono* work or involvement in initiatives like 'Business in the Community' could play an important part in developing a 'just community' perspective by encouraging lawyers to work for and with a variety of agencies and peoples. Indeed, there are already some signs that clients' expectations may force lawyers in these directions anyway.[44] Such initiatives should be encouraged by the professions collectively, not necessarily using the stick of mandation, or a practice levy, but possibly by offering assistance, through registration and networking activities, to support firms committed to community action, and/or carrots such as continuing education points, practising certificate fee waivers, or waivers of the excess on any indemnity claims in respect of *pro bono* activities.[45]

Despite its costs, this process of ethicising the business side of legal practice may itself have commercial benefits, not just in terms of market advantages, but in the potential for creating new markets for lawyers as ethical advisers and risk managers for commerce, industry and the professions.[46]

A fourth important context involves the demography of the profession. While there are, as we have seen,[47] some important empirical and political problems with associating an ethics of care with gender, there is evidence that a greater influx of women, and perhaps also men from disadvantaged backgrounds, may create opportunities for developing a more caring ethos among lawyers affecting the way clients are treated, a greater concern for the context of ethical issues as well as a desire to avoid harm rather than simply vindicate rights.[48] It is thus important that the universities continue to encourage the opening up of legal education to previously excluded groups. More importantly, pressure needs to be exerted on the professions both to move away from their current tendency to privilege those who are white, middle class, public school educated and, still to some extent, male, and to question much of the inherent masculinism apparent in the traditional structures of and approaches to legal practice.

A fifth institutional factor that appears to reveal some hope for the advent of a more ethical profession is the apparent steady demise of the split profession. Given the tendency of barristers to become involved late in legal proceedings, preventing the establishment of empathetic understandings of the needs and desires of clients, and to treat cases as purely technical problems, it is possible that the increased ability of solicitors to undertake advocacy may result in greater attention to 'autonomy-in-relation' and a greater concern about the impact of client representation on others.

---

[43] For example, by finding structural solutions to company-induced environmental problems, or, when advising on layoffs, finding cost-effective ways of investing a proportion of the money that might have gone in redundancy payments into a community employment scheme, or facilitating a buyout.

[44] British Aerospace recently announced that it would expect all solicitors' firms on its 'panel' to undertake *pro bono* activity, since this was consistent with the company's own corporate ethos of developing a partnership with the community. British Aerospace's legal department was itself reputedly the first group of in-house lawyers to make a formal commitment to undertake *pro bono* work: see *The Lawyer*, 3 November 1998, p.13. Our thanks to Andy Boon for bringing this item to our attention.

[45] Some, but not all, of these options are considered by Abbey and Boon 1995, pp.273–5.

[46] See further Sampford and Blencowe 1998, pp.337–9, and more generally Kaptein 1998.

[47] Ch.2, section 6.   [48] Jack and Jack 1989; Menkel-Meadow 1985.

At the same time, as we noted in discussing the contextual factors relevant to the lawyer-client relationship in Chapter 5,[49] care needs to be taken to ensure that lawyers do not lose their critical perspective by over-identification with clients or that clients are not provided with specialist expertise when relevant.

A final institutional factor which, as we have repeatedly argued, has a crucial impact on the state of current ethical discourse is the adversarial system. Here, we need to consider the ethical case supporting moves towards more inquisitorial procedures. Despite our many reservations about the adversarial system, we have stopped short of calling for its wholesale abandonment—even outside of criminal cases, where there remain strong grounds for its retention, and indeed reinvigoration. In civil cases, we recognise that adversarialism has many failings, not least of which are its tendency to force disputes into win/lose outcomes, its capacity to swallow a disproportionate amount of the parties' resources, its ability to undermine continuing relationships between disputants, and to allow them to trample over other innocent and often unwilling participants in the competitive struggle. We have therefore suggested that the degree of adversarialism needs to be curbed, but that we should not lose sight of the many contextual factors that will affect the application of any procedural model, particularly the power and resource inequalities that frequently characterise disputes. Indeed, the move to more inquisitorial or informal fora may not only not reduce but actually *exacerbate* existing power inequalities unless adequate checks are put in place.

Moreover, if reform to something as fundamental as the adversarial system is to take place, it is important that this happens in the context of appropriate ethical debate. The recent Woolf reforms to the civil justice system illustrate this need. These have sought, quite paternalistically, to impose a new, more co-operative, processual model on litigants largely regardless of their wishes, and possibly even their best interests. As part of this system, Rule 1.3 of the Civil Procedure Rules now obliges lawyers, as the 'overriding objective' of civil litigation, to assist courts in dealing with cases 'justly'— a principle which, through its close association in the Rules with the aims of active judicial case management, may too easily translate into dealing with cases as cheaply and expeditiously as possible. This is likely to create challenging sets of conflicts for lawyers who, if they zealously pursue clients' (adversarial) instructions, may find themselves on collision courses with the courts, and if they do not, with their clients. There are already anecdotal indications[50] that these new rules of the game are causing lawyers, as our earlier analysis suggested, to adopt creative compliance to minimise the fall-out from such potential conflicts, strategies which might actually make it harder for the courts to identify those who are genuinely abusing the system. If adversarial legal procedures are to play a less significant part in the future (and we are convinced that they should) the process of reform must be accompanied by a far more thoroughgoing *ethical* debate than has taken place to date. Hopefully this book will have gone some way to informing the contours of this debate.

---

[49] Section 7.   [50] See Marshall 1999.

Bibliography

ABBEY, R. (1993) 'The Senior Partner: The Law Firm's Nucleus' unpublished paper to the *Third International Conference on Lawyers & Lawyering*, Lake Windermere, July 1993

ABBEY, R. and BOON, A. (1995) 'The provision of free legal services by solicitors: a review of the report of the Law Society's *Pro Bono* Working Party' 2 *International Journal of the Legal Profession* 261

ABBOTT, A. (1981) 'Status and Status Strain in the Professions' 86 *American Journal of Sociology* 819

ABEL, R.L. (1981) 'Why Does the ABA Promulgate Ethical Rules?' 59 *Texas Law Review* 639

—— (1982) 'The Politics of the Market for Legal Services' in P.A. Thomas (ed.) *Law in the Balance* (Oxford, Martin Robertson)

—— (1986) 'The Decline of Professionalism?' 49 *Modern Law Review* 1

—— (1988a) *The Legal Profession in England & Wales* (London, Basil Blackwell)

—— (1988b) 'England and Wales: A Comparison of the Professional Projects of Barristers and Solicitors' in R. Abel and P. Lewis (eds.) *Lawyers in Society, Volume One: The Common Law World* (Berkeley, University of California Press)

—— (1989) 'Between Market and State: the Legal Profession in Turmoil' 52 *Modern Law Review* 285

ABEL-SMITH, B. and STEVENS, R. (1967) *Lawyers and the Courts: A Sociological Study of the English Legal Profession, 1750–1965* (London, Heinemann)

ACLEC (1996a) *First Report on Legal Education and Training* (London, ACLEC)

—— (1996b) *Annual Report for 1995–96* (London, The Stationery Office)

—— (1997) *Annual Report 1996–97* (London, The Stationery Office)

—— (1998) *Improving the Quality of Immigration Advice and Representation: A Report* (London, ACLEC)

ADAMS, J. and BROWNSWORD, R. (1995) *Key Issues in Contract* (London, Butterworths)

ADJEI, C. (1995) 'Human Rights Theory and the Bill of Rights Debate' 58 *Modern Law Review* 17

ADLER, Z. (1987) *Rape on Trial* (London, Routledge & Kegan Paul)

ALLAKER, J. and SHAPLAND, J. (1994) *Organising UK Professions: Continuity and Change* (London, The Law Society)

ALLEN, R.J., GRADY, M.F., POLSBY, D.D., and YASHKO, M.S. (1990) 'A Positive Theory of the Attorney-Client Privilege and the Work Product Doctrine' XIX *Journal of Legal Studies* 359

ALMOND, B. (1995) *Introducing Applied Ethics* (Oxford, Blackwell)

ALSCHULER, A.W. (1981) 'The Preservation of a Client's Confidences: One Value Among Many or a Categorical Imperative?' 52 *University of Colorado Law Review* 349

—— (1982) 'The Search for Truth Continued: The Privilege Retained: A Response to Judge Frankel' 54 *University of Colorado Law Review* 67

ANSCOMBE, G.E.M. (1958) 'Modern Moral Philosophy' 33 *Philosophy* 1

ARNESON, R.J. (1980) 'Mill vs Paternalism' 90 *Ethics* 470

ARNOLD, B.L. and HAGAN, J. (1992) 'Careers of Misconduct: The Structure of Prosecuted Professional Deviance Among Lawyers' 57 *American Sociological Review* 771

ARNOLD, B.L. and KAY, F.M. (1995) 'Social Capital, Violations of Trust and the

Vulnerability of Isolates: The Social Organization of Law Practice and Professional Self-regulation' 23 *International Journal of the Sociology of Law* 321

ARTHURS, H.W. (1982) 'Public Accountability of the Legal Profession' in Thomas (ed.)

—— (1999) 'A Global Code of Legal Ethics for the Transnational Legal Field' 2 *Legal Ethics* (forthcoming)

ARTHURS, H.W. and KREKLEWICH, R. (1996) 'Law, Legal Institutions and the Legal Profession in the New Economy' 34 *Osgoode Hall Law Journal* 1

ASHWORTH, A. (1998) *The Criminal Process: An Evaluative Study* (2nd edn., Oxford, Clarendon Press)

ASHWORTH, A. and FIONDA, J. (1994) 'The New Code for Crown Prosecutors: (1) Prosecution, Accountability and the Public Interest' *Criminal Law Review* 894

ATKINSON, P. (1983) 'The Reproduction of Professional Community' in R. Dingwall and P. Lewis (eds.)

ATKINSON, P. and DELAMONT, S. (1990) 'Professions and Powerlessness: Female Marginality in the Learned Occupations' 38 *Sociological Review* 91

ATKINSON, R. (1992) 'Beyond the New Role Morality for Lawyers' 51 *Maryland Law Review* 853

—— (1995) 'How the Butler Was Made to Do It: The Perverted Professionalism of *The Remains of the Day*' 105 *Yale Law Journal* 177

AUSTEN, L., GILBERT, B., HEATH, J., and MITCHELL, R. (1998) 'Ethics in Practice' 1 *Legal Ethics* 15

AUSTIN, R.P. (1996) 'Moulding the Content of Fiduciary Duties' in A.J. Oakley (ed.) *Trends in Contemporary Trust Law* (Oxford, Clarendon Press)

AXELROD, R. (1984) *The Evolution of Co-operation* (London, Penguin)

AYRES, I. and BRAITHWAITE, J. (1992) *Responsive Regulation: Transcending the Deregulation Debate* (New York, Oxford University Press)

BABCOCK, B.A. (1983) 'Defending the Guilty' 32 *Cleveland State Law Review* 175

BAIER, A. (1995) *Moral Prejudices: Essays on Ethics* (Cambridge, MA, Harvard University Press)

BAIER, K. (1991) 'Egoism' in Singer (ed.)

BALDWIN, J. (1985) *Pre-Trial Justice: A Study of Case Settlement in Magistrates' Courts* (Oxford, Blackwell)

BALDWIN, J. and MCCONVILLE, M. (1977) *Negotiated Justice: Pressures to Plead Guilty* (London, Martin Robertson)

BALDWIN, R. (1997) *Regulating Legal Services*, LCD Research Series No 5/97 (London, Lord Chancellor's Department)

BALDWIN, R. and MCCRUDDEN, C. (1987) *Regulation and Public Law* (London, Weidenfeld & Nicolson)

BALDWIN, R., SCOTT, C., and HOOD, C. (eds.) (1998) *A Reader on Regulation* (Oxford, Oxford University Press)

BALL, M.S. (1983) 'Wrong Experiment. Wrong Result: An Appreciatively Critical Response to Schwartz' *American Bar Foundation Research Journal* 565

BANKOWSKI, Z. and MUNGHAM, G. (eds.) (1976) *Images of Law* (London, Routledge & Kegan Paul)

BAR COUNCIL (1989) *The Quality of Justice: The Bar's Response* (London, Butterworths)

BARNETT, H. (1995) 'The province of jurisprudence determined—again!' 15 *Legal Studies* 88

BARRY, B. (1979) 'And Who is My Neighbour?' 88 *Yale Law Journal* 629

BAUMAN, Z. (1993) *Postmodern Ethics* (Oxford, Blackwell)

—— (1994) *Alone Again: Ethics After Certainty* (London, Demos)

—— (1995) *Life in Fragments: Essays in Postmodern Morality* (Oxford, Blackwell)

BAYLES, M.D. (1981) *Professional Ethics* (Belmont, CA, Wadsworth Publishing Company)

BEAUCHAMP, T.L. (1982) *Philosophical Ethics: An Introduction to Moral Philosophy* (New York, McGraw-Hill)

BECK, U. (1992) *Risk Society: Towards a New Modernity*, trans. M. Ritter (London, Sage)

BECKER, H. (1962) 'The nature of a profession' in National Society for the Study of Education, *Education for the Professions* (Chicago, Chicago University Press)

BELL, D. (1993) *Communitarianism and its Critics* (Oxford, Oxford University Press)

BELL, J. (1983) *Policy Arguments in Judicial Decisions* (Oxford, Clarendon Press)

BELL, J. and JOHNSTONE, J. (1998) *General Transferable Skills in the Law Curriculum* (Department of Education & Employment)

BELLIOTTI, R.A. (1988) 'Our Adversary System: In Search of a Foundation' I *Canadian Journal of Law & Jurisprudence* 19

BENDER, L. (1990) 'From Gender Difference to Feminist Solidarity: Using Carol Gilligan and an Ethic of Care in Law' 15 *Vermont Law Review* 1

BENHABIB, S. (1982) 'The Generalized Other and the Concrete Other' from S. Benhabib and D. Cornell (eds.) *Feminism as Critique: Essays on the Politics of Gender in late-Capitalist Societies* (Cambridge, Polity Press)

—— (1992) *Situating the Self: Gender, Community and Postmodernism in Contemporary Ethics* (Cambridge, Polity Press)

BENJAMIN, G., ANDREW, H., KASZNIAK, A., SALES, B., and SHANFIELD, S. (1986) 'The Role of Legal Education in Producing Psychological Stress among Law Students and Lawyers' *American Bar Foundation Research Journal* 225

BENSON COMMISSION (1979) *Report of the Royal Commission on Legal Services*, Cmnd 7648 (London, HMSO)

BENTHAM, J. (1843) *The Works of Jeremy Bentham* (ed. J. Bowring) (Edinburgh, William Tait)

BERG, J. (1991) 'How ethics could depend on religion' in Singer (ed.)

BERLINS, M. (1987) 'Victims of medicine, victims of law' *Law Magazine*, 12 June 1987, 16

BERMINGHAM, V., HALL, C., and WEBB, J. (1996) *Access to and Participation in Undergraduate Legal Education: An Exploratory Study* (Bristol, University of the West of England)

BERNEY, C. (1994) 'Quality of Life and the Legal Profession' 2 *International Journal of the Legal Profession* 253

BEST, S. and KELLNER, D. (1991) *Postmodern Theory: Critical Interrogations* (London, Macmillan)

BEVAN, G., HOLLAND, T., and PARTINGTON, M. (1994) *Organising Cost-Effective Access to Justice* (London, Social Market Foundation)

BEYLEVELD, D. (1991) *The Dialectical Necessity of Morality* (Chicago, Chicago University Press)

BINDER, D., BERGMAN, P., and PRICE, S. (1991) *Legal Interviewing and Counseling* (St Paul, MN, West Publishing)

BIRD, P.M.K. and WEIR, J.B. (1989) *The Law, Practice and Conduct of Solicitors* (London, Waterlow Publishers)

BLACK, J. (1996) 'Constitutionalising Self-regulation' 59 *Modern Law Review* 24

—— (1998) 'Talking about Regulation' *Public Law* 76

BLACK, R. (1982) 'A Question of Confidence: Communications between solicitor and client' *Journal of the Law Society of Scotland* 299

BLACKWELL, M., ECONOMIDES, K., and WATKINS, C. (1991) *Justice Outside the City: Access to Legal Services in Rural Britain* (Harlow, Longman)

BLAKE, M. and ASHWORTH, A. (1998) 'Some Ethical Issues in Prosecuting and Defending Criminal Cases' *Criminal Law Review* 16

BOK, S. (1980) *Lying: Moral Choice in Public and Private Life* (London, Quartet Books)

—— (1984) *Secrets: On the Ethics of Concealment and Revelation* (Oxford, Oxford University Press)

—— (1990) 'Can Lawyers Be Trusted?' 138 *University of Pennsylvania Law Review* 913

BOON, A. (1995) 'Ethics and Strategy in Personal Injury Litigation' 22 *Journal of Law & Society* 353

—— (1996) 'Skills in the initial stage of legal education: theory and practice for transformation' in J. Webb and C. Maughan (eds.) *Teaching Lawyers' Skills* (London, Butterworths)

BOON, A. and ABBEY, R. (1997) 'Moral Agendas? *Pro Bono Publico* in Large Law Firms in the United Kingdom' 60 *Modern Law Review* 360

BOON, A. and FLOOD, J. (1999) 'Globalization of Professional Ethics? The Significance of Lawyers' International Codes of Conduct' 2 *Legal Ethics* (forthcoming)

BOON, A. and LEVIN, J. (1999) *The Ethics and Conduct of Lawyers in England and Wales* (Oxford, Hart Publishing)

BOULTON, W. (1975) *Conduct and Etiquette at the Bar* (6th edn., London, Butterworths)

BOURDIEU, P. and PASSERON, J.-C. (1977) *Reproduction in Education, Society and Culture* (London, Sage)

BOWLES, R. (1994) 'The Structure of the Legal Profession in England and Wales' 10 *Oxford Review of Economic Policy* 18

BRADLEY, F.H. (1927) *Ethical Studies* (2nd edn., Oxford, Oxford University Press)

BRADNEY, A. (1998) 'Law as a Parasitic Discipline' 25 *Journal of Law & Society* 71

BRAITHWAITE, J. and MAKKAI, T. (1994) 'Trust and Compliance' 4 *Policing & Society* 1

BRAYNE, H., DUNCAN, N., and GRIMES, R. (1998) *Clinical Legal Education: Active Learning in Your Law School* (London, Blackstone Press)

BRAUN, R.L. (1967) 'Ethics in Criminal Cases: A Response' 55 *Georgetown Law Journal* 1048

BRESS, D.G. (1966) 'Professional Ethics in Criminal Trials: A View of Defence Counsel's Responsibility' 64 *Michigan Law Review* 1493

BRETT, P. (1973) 'Legal Decisionmaking and Bias: A Critique of an "Experiment"' 45 *University of Colorado Law Review* 1

BRIEN, A. (1998) 'Professional Ethics and the Culture of Trust' 17 *Journal of Business Ethics* 391

BRINDLE, M. and DEHN, G. (1995) 'Confidence, Public Interest and the Lawyer' in Cranston (ed.)

BROCKMAN, J. and McEWEN, C. (1990) 'Self-Regulation in the Legal Profession: Funnel In, Funnel Out, or Funnel Away?' 5 *Canadian Journal of Law Society* 1

BROWN, L.M. and BROWN, H.A. (1976) 'What Counsels the Counsellor? The Code of Professional Responsibility's Ethical Considerations—A Preventive Law Analysis' 10 *Valparaiso University Law Review* 453

BROWN, P. (1990) 'The Third Wave: Education and the Ideology of Parentocracy' 11 *British Journal of Sociology of Education* 65

—— (1995) 'Cultural Capital and Social Exclusion: Some Observations on Recent Trends in Education, Employment and the Labour Market' 9 *Work, Employment & Society* 29

BRUYNINCKX, G. (1997) 'The European Lawyer in 2020: Deontology' unpublished plenary paper to *Stage 97: The European Lawyer in 2020,* London, October 1997

BUCHANAN, A. (1978) 'Medical Paternalism' 7 *Philosophy & Public Affairs* 372

BUCHER, R. (1962) 'Pathology: A Study of Social Movements within a Profession' 10 *Social Problems* 40

BUCHER, R. and STRAUSS, A. (1961) 'Professions in Process' 66 *American Journal of Sociology* 325

BUCKLE, S. (1991) 'Natural Law' in Singer (ed.)

BUNDY, S.M. and ELHAUGE, E.R. (1991) 'Do Lawyers Improve the Adversary System? A General Theory of Litigation Advice and Its Regulation' 79 *California Law Review* 313

BURBANK, D.O. and DUBOFF, R.S. (1974) 'Ethics and the Legal Profession: A Survey of Boston Lawyers' IX *Suffolk University Law Review* 66

BURGER, W.E. (1966) 'Standards of Conduct for Prosecution and Defense Personnel: A Judge's Viewpoint' 5 *American Criminal Law Quarterly* 11

BURRAGE, M. (1988) 'Revolution and the Collective Action of the French, American and English Legal Professions' 13 *Law & Social Inquiry* 225

—— (1996) 'From a gentlemen's to a public profession: status and politics in the history of English solicitors' 3 *International Journal of the Legal Profession* 45

BURNHAM, B.P. (1969) 'The Attorney-Client Privilege in the Corporate Arena' 24 *Business Law* 901

CAHN, N.R. (1990) 'A Preliminary Feminist Critique of Legal Ethics' 4 *Georgetown Journal of Legal Ethics* 2475

—— (1992) 'Styles of Lawyering' 34 *Hastings Law Journal* 1039

—— (1993) 'Inconsistent Stories' 81 *Georgetown Law Journal* 2475

CAIN, M. (1983) 'The General Practice Lawyer and the Client: Towards a Radical Conception' in Dingwall and Lewis (eds.)

CALLAHAN, J.C. (1988) *Ethical Issues in Professional Life* (New York, Oxford University Press)

CALLAHAN, M.S. and PITKOW, H.C. (1980) 'The Propriety of the Attorneys' Actions in the Lake Pleasant Case' from A. Gerson (ed.) *Lawyers' Ethics: Contemporary Dilemmas* (New Brunswick, NJ, Transaction Books)

CALLAN, J.M. and DAVID, H. (1976) 'Professional Responsibility and the Duty of Confidentiality: Disclosure of Client Misconduct in an Adversary System' 29 *Rutgers Law Review* 333

CAMPBELL, T. (1998) *The Left and Rights: A Conceptual Analysis of the Idea of Socialist Rights* (London, Routledge & Kegan Paul)

CAPLAN, J. (1978) 'The Criminal Bar' in R. Hazell (ed.) *The Bar on Trial* (London, Quartet Books)

CARD, C. (1988) 'Women's Voices and Ethical Ideals: Must We Mean What We Say?' 99 *Ethics* 125

CARLEN, P. (1976) *Magistrates' Justice* (London, Martin Robertson)

CARLIN, J. (1966) *Lawyers' Ethics: A Survey of the New York City Bar* (New York, Russell Sage Foundation)

CHADWICK, R. (ed.) (1994) *Ethics and the Professions* (Aldershot, Avebury)

CHAMBERS, G. and HARWOOD-RICHARDSON, S. (1990) *Solicitors in England and Wales: Practice, Organisation and Perceptions* (London, The Law Society)

CHODOROW, N. (1978) *The Reproduction of Mothering: Psychoanalysis and the Sociology of Gender* (Berkeley, University of California Press)

CHRISTENSEN, C., DAY, S., and WORTHINGTON, J. (1999) ' "Learned Profession?—the stuff of sherry talk." The response to Practice Rule 15' 6 *International Journal of the Legal Profession* 27

CLERMONT, K.M. and CURRIVAN, J.D. (1978) 'Improving on the Contingent Fee' 63 *Cornell Law Review* 539

COADY, C.A.J. (1996) 'On Regulating Ethics' in Coady and Bloch (eds.)

COADY, M. and BLOCH, C. (eds.) (1996) *Codes of Ethics and the Professions* (Carlton South, Melbourne University Press)

COCKS, R. (1983) *Foundations of the Modern Bar* (London, Sweet & Maxwell)

COHEN, G.A. (1966) 'Beliefs and Roles' 66 *Proceedings of the Aristotelian Society* 17

COLLIER, R. (1991) 'Masculinism, Law and Law Teaching' 19 *International Journal of the Sociology of Law* 427

COLLINS, H. (1997) *The Law of Contract* (3rd edn., London, Butterworths)

COMPANY LAW STEERING GROUP (1999) *Modern Company Law for a Competitive Economy— The Strategic Framework* (London, Department of Trade & Industry)

COOK, A.E. (1993) 'Foreword: Towards a Postmodern Ethics of Service' 81 *Georgetown Law Journal* 2457

COOK, C. and WATERS, M. (1998) 'The Impact of Organizational Form on Gendered Labour Markets in Engineering and Law' 46 *Sociological Review* 314

CORFIELD, P. (1995) *Power and the Professions in Britain 1700–1850* (London, Routledge)

CORNELL, D. (1985) 'Toward a Modern/Postmodern Reconstruction of Ethics' 133 *University of Pennsylvania Law Review* 291

——(1988) 'Post-Structuralism, The Ethical, and the Law' 9 *Cardozo Law Review* 1587

——(1990) 'From the Lighthouse: The Promise of Redemption and the Possibility of Legal Interpretation' 11 *Cardozo Law Review* 1687

'Correspondence' (1982) 'A Question of Confidence: Taking Issue' *Journal of the Law Society of Scotland* 389

COTTERELL, R. (1984) *The Sociology of Law: An Introduction* (2nd edn., London, Butterworths)

——(1989) *The Politics of Jurisprudence: A Critical Introduction to Legal Philosophy* (London, Butterworths)

CRANSTON, R. (1995) 'Legal Ethics and Professional Responsibility' in Cranston (ed.)

CRANSTON, R. (ed.) (1995) *Legal Ethics and Professional Responsibility* (Oxford, Clarendon Press)

CRAWLEY, A. and BRAMMALL, C. (1995) 'Professional Rules, Codes and Principles Affecting Solicitors (or What Has Professional Regulation to do with Ethics?)' in Cranston (ed.) 1995

CRISPIN, K. (1995) 'Prosecutorial Ethics' in Parker and Sampford (eds.)

CROFT, C. (1992) 'Reconceptualizing American Legal Professionalism: A Proposal for Deliberative Moral Community' 67 *New York University Law Review* 1256

CROOK, S. (1991) *Modernist Radicalism and its Aftermath: Foundationalism and Anti-Foundationalism in Radical Social Theory* (London, Routledge)

CROWN PROSECUTION SERVICE (1996) *Explanatory Memorandum* (London, Crown Prosecution Service)

—— (1998) 'The Code for Crown Prosecutors' in *Annual Report 1997–8* (London, The Stationery Office)

CURTIS, C.P. (1951) 'The Ethics of Advocacy' 4 *Stanford Law Review* 3

CUSTOMER MANAGEMENT CONSULTANCY LTD (nd) 'Satisfaction in a super-escalated complaint environment: Summary of findings and recommendations' (Office of the Legal Services Ombudsman/Lord Chancellor's Department)

D'AGOSTINO, F. (1998) 'Two Conceptions of Autonomy' 27 *Economy & Society* 28

D'AMATO, A. and EBERLE, E.J. (1983) 'Three Models of Legal Ethics' 27 *St Louis University Law Journal* 761

DAMASKA, M. (1973) 'Evidentiary Barriers to Conviction and Two Models of Criminal Procedure: A Comparative Study' 121 *University of Pennsylvania Law Review* 506

—— (1975) 'Presentation of Evidence and Factfinding Precision' 123 *University of Pennsylvania Law Review* 1083

—— (1986) *The Faces of Justice and State Authority: A Comparative Approach to the Legal Process* (New Haven, Yale University Press)

DANCY, J. (1991a) 'An ethic of prima facie duties' in Singer (ed.)

—— (1991b) 'Intuitionism' in Singer (ed.)

DAUER, E.A. and LEFF, A.A. (1977) 'Correspondence: The Lawyer as Friend' 86 *Yale Law Journal* 573

DAVIES, G.L. and SHELDON, S.A. (1995) 'Some Proposed Changes in Civil Procedure: Their Practical Benefits and Ethical Rationale' in Parker & Sampford (eds.)

DAVIS, M., DAVIS, G., and WEBB, J. (1996) *Promoting Mediation: A Study of the Bristol Law Society Mediation Scheme in its Initial Phase* (London, The Law Society)

DAVIS, G. (1994) *Partisans and Mediators* (Oxford, Clarendon Press)

DAVIS, N.A. (1991) 'Contemporary deontology' in Singer (ed.)

DAWSON, A.J. (1994) 'Professional Codes of Practice and Ethical Conduct' 11 *Journal of Applied Philosophy* 146

DE GROOT-VAN LEEUWEN, L.E. and DE GROOT, W.T. (1998) 'Studying Codes of Conduct: A Descriptive Framework for Comparative Research' 1 *Legal Ethics* 155

DEMARCO, J.P. and FOX, R.M. (eds.) (1986) *New Directions in Ethics: The Challenge of Applied Ethics* (London, Routledge & Kegan Paul)

DEMOTT, D. (1992) 'Fiduciary Obligations under Intellectual Siege: Contemporary Challenges to the Duty to be Loyal' 30 *Osgoode Hall Law Journal* 471

DENNING, A. (1981) *The Family Story* (London, Butterworths)

'DEVELOPMENTS IN THE LAW' (1981) 'Conflicts of Interest' 94 *Harvard Law Review* 1244

DEZALAY, Y. and GARTH, B. (1997) 'Law, Lawyers and Social Capital: "Rule of Law" versus Relational Capitalism' 6 *Social and Legal Studies* 109

DINGWALL, R., DURKIN, T., and FELSTINER, W. (1990) 'Delay in Tort Cases: Critical Reflections on the Civil Justice Review' *Civil Justice Quarterly* 353

DINGWALL, R. and FENN, P. (1987) ' "A Respectable Profession?" Sociological and Economic Perspectives on the Regulation of Professional Services' 7 *International Review of Law & Economics* 51

DINGWALL, R. and LEWIS, P. (eds.) (1983) *The Sociology of the Professions: Lawyers, Doctors and Others* (London, Macmillan)

DINNERSTEIN, D. (1987) *The Rocking of the Cradle and the Ruling of the World* (London, The Warren Press)

300 *Bibliography*

DISNEY, J., REDMOND, P., BASTEN, J., and ROSS, S. (1986) *Lawyers* (2nd edn., Sydney, The Law Book Company)

DOMBERGER, S. and SHERR, A. (1989) 'The Impact of Competition on Pricing and Quality of Legal Services' 9 *International Review of Law & Economics* 41

DONEGAN, A. (1977) *The Theory of Morality* (Chicago, University of Chicago Press)

—— (1983) 'Justifying Legal Practice in the Adversary System' in Luban (ed.) 1983

DOUZINAS, C. and WARRINGTON, R. (1994) *Justice Miscarried: Ethics, Aesthetics and the Law* (London, Harvester Wheatsheaf)

DOUZINAS, C., GOODRICH, P., and HACHAMOVITCH, G. (1994) 'Introduction: politics, ethics and the legality of the contingent' in C. Douzinas, P. Goodrich, and G. Hachamovitch (eds.) *Politics, Postmodernity and Critical Legal Studies: The legality of the contingent* (London, Routledge)

DOWNIE, R.S. (1971) *Roles and Values: An Introduction to Social Ethics* (London, Methuen)

—— (1996) 'Professional Ethics and Business Ethics' in S.A.M. McLean (ed.) *Contemporary Issues in Law, Medicine and Ethics* (Aldershot, Dartmouth)

DOYAL, L. (1990) 'Medical Ethics and Moral Indeterminacy' 17 *Journal of Law & Society* 1

DOYLE, C. (1993) 'Regulating Firms with Monopoly Power' in R. Sugden (ed.) *Industrial Economic Regulation: A framework and exploration* (London, Routledge)

DRUMMOND, H. (1997) 'Living to Work' *New Law Journal*, 19 December 1997, p.1855

DU BOIS, E., DUNLAP, M., GILLIGAN, C., MACKINNON, C., and MENKEL-MEADOW, C. (1985) 'Feminist Discourse, Moral Values and the Law: A Conversation' 34 *Buffalo Law Review* 11

DU CANN, R. (1993) *The Duty of the Advocate* (2nd edn., Harmondsworth, Penguin)

DURKHEIM, E. (1933) *The Division of Labour in Society*, trans., G. Simpson (New York, The Free Press)

—— (1992) *Professional Ethics and Civil Morals*, trans., C. Brookfield (2nd edn., London, Routledge)

DWORKIN, G. (1971) 'Paternalism' in R. Wasserstrom (ed.) *Morality and the Law* (Belmont, CA, Wadsworth)

—— (1988) *The Theory and Practice of Autonomy* (Cambridge, Cambridge University Press)

DWORKIN, R. (1977) *Taking Rights Seriously* (London, Duckworth)

DZIENKOWSKI, J.S. (1993) 'Positional Conflicts of Interest' 71 *Texas Law Review* 457

EBERLE, E.J. (1993) 'Three Foundations of Legal Ethics: Autonomy, Community and Morality' 7 *Georgetown Journal of Legal Ethics* 89

ECONOMIDES, K. (1997) 'Cynical Legal Studies' in J. Cooper and L. Trubek (eds.) *Educating for Justice: Social Values and Legal Education* (Aldershot, Dartmouth)

—— (1998) 'Introduction: Legal Ethics—Three Challenges for the Next Millennium' in Economides (ed.)

—— (ed.) (1998) *Ethical Challenges to Legal Education and Conduct* (Oxford, Hart Publishing)

ECONOMIDES, K. and WEBB, J. (1998a) 'Editorial: The Ethical Imagination' 1 *Legal Ethics* 1

———— (1998b) 'Editorial: Claiming Sanctuary from Truth and Justice' 1 *Legal Ethics* 101

EDEL, A. (1986) 'Ethical theory and moral practice: on the terms of their relation' in DeMarco and Fox (eds.)

EDGAR, A. (1994) 'Narrating Social Work' in Chadwick, R. (ed.)

'EDITORIAL' (1990) 'Taking Sides' *New Law Journal*, 9 February

EDWARDS, H.T. (1990) 'A Lawyer's Duty to Serve the Public Good' *New York University Law Review* 1148

EGERTON, M. (1997) 'Occupational Inheritance: The Role of Cultural Capital and Gender' 11 *Work, Employment & Society* 263

EHRLICH, E. (1936) *Fundamental Principles of the Sociology of Law* (Cambridge, MA, Harvard University Press)

ELKINS, J.R. (1978) 'The Legal Persona: An Essay on the Professional Mark' 64 *Virginia Law Review* 735

——(1985) ' "*Rites du Passage:*" Law Students Telling Their Lives' 35 *Journal of Legal Education* 27

——(1992) 'The Moral Labyrinth of Zealous Advocacy' 20 *Capital University Law Review* 735

ELLMAN, S. (1987) 'Lawyers and Clients' 34 *UCLA Law Review* 717

——(1990) 'Lawyering for Justice in a Flawed Democracy' 90 *Columbia Law Review* 116

EMMET, D. (1996) *Rules, Roles and Relations* (London, Macmillan)

ERLANGER, H. and KLEGON, D. (1978) 'The Socialization Effects of Professional School: The Law School Experience and Student Orientations to Public Interest Concerns' 13 *Law & Society Review* 11

ERLANGER, H., EPP, C., CAHIL, M., and HAINES, K. (1995) 'Law Student Idealism and Job Choice: Some New Data on an Old Question' 29 *Law & Society Review* 851

ESHETE, A. (1983) 'Does a Lawyer's Character Matter?' in Luban (ed.)

EVANS, K. (1983) *Advocacy at the Bar: A Beginner's Guide* (London, Financial Training Publications)

——(1993) *The Golden Rules of Advocacy* (London, Blackstone Press)

EVETTS, J. (1995) 'International Professional Associations: the New Context for Professional Projects' 9 *Work, Employment & Society* 763

EWING, K. and GEARTY, C. (1990) *Freedom under Thatcher: Civil Liberties in Modern Britain* (Oxford, Clarendon Press)

FERREN, J.M. (1978) 'The Corporate Lawyer's Obligation to the Public Interest' 33 *The Business Lawyer* 1253

FELDMAN, D. (1993) *Civil Liberties and Human Rights in England and Wales* (Oxford, Clarendon Press)

FENNELL, P. (1976) 'Solicitors, Their Markets and Their "Ignorant Public": The Crisis of the Professional Ideal' in Z. Bankowski and G. Mungham (eds.) *Essays in Law and Society* (London, Routledge & Kegan Paul)

——(1982) 'Advertising: Professional Ethics and the Public Interest' in Thomas (ed.)

FINE, B. (1984) *Democracy and the Rule of Law: Liberal Ideals and Marxist Critiques* (London, Pluto Press)

FINN, P. (1989) 'The Fiduciary Principle' in T.G. Youdan (ed.) *Equity, Fiduciaries and Trusts* (Toronto, Carswell)

——(1992) 'Professionals and Confidentiality' 14 *Sydney Law Review* 317

FINNIS, J. (1980) *Natural Law and Natural Rights* (Oxford, Oxford University Press)

FISCHEL, D.R. (1998) 'Lawyers and Confidentiality' 65 *University of Chicago Law Review* 1

FISHKIN, J.S. (1984) *Beyond Subjective Morality: Ethical Reasoning and Political Philosophy* (London, Yale University Press)

FISS, O. (1984) 'Against Settlement' 93 *Yale Law Journal* 1073

FLANAGAN, O. (1991) *Varieties of Moral Personality: Ethics and Psychological Realism* (Cambridge, MA, Harvard University Press)

FLETCHER, G.P. (1993) *Loyalty: An Essay on the Morality of Relationships* (New York, Oxford University Press)

—— (1996) *Basic Concepts of Legal Thought* (New York, Oxford University Press)

FLETCHER, R. (1995) 'Mortgages, Markets and the Fiduciary Principle' 11(4) *Professional Negligence* 137

FLINTOFF, J.-B. (1995) '*Pro Bono* or Promotion?' *Legal Business*, Jan/Feb, 44

FLOOD, J. (1989) 'Megalaw in the UK: professionalism or corporatism? A preliminary report' 64 *Indiana Law Journal* 569

—— (1991) 'Doing Business: the Management of Uncertainty in Lawyers' Work' 25 *Law & Society Review* 41

—— (1994) 'Shark Tanks, Sweatshops and the Lawyer as Hero? Fact as Fiction' 21 *Journal of Law & Society* 396

—— (1996) 'Megalawyering in the global order; the cultural, social and economic transformation of global legal practice' 3 *International Journal of the Legal Profession* 169

FLYNN, J.J. (1976) 'Professional Ethics and the Lawyer's Duty to Self' 3 *Washington University Law Quarterly* 429

FOOT, P. (1978) *Virtues and Vices* (Oxford, Basil Blackwell)

FOSTER, J. (1981) 'The "Cooling Out" of Law Students' 3 *Law & Policy Quarterly* 243

FOX, A. (1974) *Beyond Contract: Work, Power and Trust Relations* (London, Faber & Faber)

FOX, R.M. and DeMARCO, J.P. (1986) 'The challenge of applied ethics' in DeMarco and Fox (eds.)

FRANK, J. (1949) *Law and the Modern Mind* (London, Stevens & Sons)

—— (1973) *Courts on Trial: Myth and Reality in American Trials*, E. Cahn (ed.) (Princeton, NJ, Princeton University Press)

FRANKEL, C. (1976) 'Review of the ABA *Code of Professional Responsibility*' 43 *University of Chicago Law Review* 874

FRANKEL, M.E. (1975) 'The Search for Truth: An Umpireal View' 123 *University of Pennsylvania Law Review* 1031

—— (1980) *Partisan Justice* (New York, Hill & Wang)

—— (1982) 'The Search for Truth Continued: More Disclosure, Less Privilege' 54 *University of Colorado Law Review* 51

FRANKEL, M.S. (1989) 'Professional Codes: Why, How and with What Impact' 8 *Journal of Business Ethics* 109

FRANKENA, W.K. (1963) *Ethics* (Englewood Cliffs, NJ, Prentice-Hall)

FREEDMAN, B. (1978a) 'A Meta-Ethics for Professional Morality' 89 *Ethics* 1

—— (1981) 'What Really Makes Professional Morality Different: Response to Martin' 91 *Ethics* 626

FREEDMAN, M.H. (1966) 'Professional Responsibility of the Criminal Defense Lawyer: The Three Hardest Questions' 64 *Michigan Law Review* 1469

—— (1975) *Lawyers' Ethics in an Adversary System* (Indianapolis, Bobbs-Merrill)

—— (1978) 'Personal Responsibility in a Professional System' 27 *Catholic University Law Review* 191

—— (1986) 'Legal Ethics and the Suffering Client' 36 *Catholic University Law Review* 331

—— (1990) *Understanding Lawyers' Ethics* (New York, M. Bender)

FREEMAN, M.D.A. (1994) *Lloyd's Introduction to Jurisprudence* (6th edn., London, Sweet & Maxwell)

FRIDMAN, G.H.L. (1996) *The Law of Agency* (7th edn., London, Butterworths)

FRIED, C. (1976) 'The Lawyer as Friend: The Moral Foundations of the Lawyer-Client Relationship' 85 *Yale Law Journal* 1069–89

——(1977) 'Author's Reply' 86 *Yale Law Journal* 584

——(1978) *Right and Wrong* (Cambridge, MA, Harvard University Press)

FRIED, D.J. (1986) 'Too High a Price for Truth: The Exception to the Attorney-Client Privilege for Contemplated Crimes and Frauds' 64 *North Carolina Law Review* 443

FRY, E. (1997) 'Justice or Confidentiality' *New Law Journal*, 10 January 30

FULLER, L.L. (1971) 'The Adversary System' in H.J. Berman (ed.) *Talks on American Law* (revised edn., New York, Random House)

FULLER, L.L. and RANDALL, J.D. (1958) 'Professional Responsibility: Report of the Joint Conference' 44 *ABA Journal* 1159

GABEL, P. and FEINMAN, J.M. (1982) 'Contract Law as Ideology' in D. Kairys (ed.) *The Politics of Law: A Progressive Critique* (New York, Pantheon)

GALANTER, M. (1974) 'Why the "Haves" Come Out Ahead: Speculations on the Limits of Legal Change' 9 *Law & Society Review* 95

——(1992) 'Law Abounding: Legalisation Around the North Atlantic' 55 *Modern Law Review* 1

——and PALAY, T. (1992) 'The Transformation of the Big Law Firm' in Nelson, Trubek and Solomon (eds.)

——(1995) 'Large Law Firms and Professional Responsibility' in Cranston (ed.)

GALBRAITH, J.K. (1992) *The Culture of Contentment* (London, Penguin)

GARDINER, M. (1996a) 'Alterity and Ethics: A Dialogical Perspective' 13 *Theory, Culture & Society* 121

——(1996b) 'Foucault, ethics and dialogue' 9 *History of the Human Sciences* 27

GARFINKEL, H. (1956) 'Conditions of Successful Degradation Ceremonies', 61 *American Journal of Sociology* 420

GASKELL, R. (1984) 'The Wind of Change in Legal Practice' *The Law Society's Gazette*, 26 September, 2599

GEAR, C.A. (1998) 'The Ideology of Domination: Barriers to Client Autonomy in Legal Ethics Scholarship' 107 *Yale Law Journal* 2473

GENN, H. (1987) *Hard Bargaining* (Oxford, Clarendon Press)

——(1998) *The Central London County Court Pilot Mediation Scheme: Evaluation Report*, Research Series No 5/98 (London, Lord Chancellor's Department)

GERBER, R.J. (1987) 'Victory vs. Truth: The Adversary System and its Ethics' 19 *Arizona State Law Journal* 3

GEWIRTH, A. (1978) *Reason and Morality* (Chicago, Chicago University Press)

——(1986) 'Professional Ethics: The Separatist Thesis' 96 *Ethics* 282

——(1996) *Community of Rights* (Chicago, Chicago University Press)

GIDDENS, A. (1990) *The Consequences of Modernity* (Cambridge, Polity Press)

——(1994) *Beyond Left and Right: The Future of Radical Politics* (Cambridge, Polity Press)

GILLIGAN, C. (1982) *In a Different Voice: Psychological Theory and Women's Development* (revised edn., 1993, Cambridge, MA, Harvard University Press)

GILLERS, S. (1986) 'Can a Good Lawyer be a Bad Person?' 84 *Michigan Law Review* 1011

GLASSER, C. (1990) 'The legal profession in the 1990's: images of change' 10 *Legal Studies* 1
——(1993) 'Civil Procedure and the Lawyers—The Adversary System and the Decline of the Orality Principle' 56 *Modern Law Review* 307
GLENN, P. (1990) 'Professional Structures and Professional Ethics' 35 *McGill Law Journal* 425
GLENDON, M.A. (1994) 'Legal Ethics—Worlds in Collision' 41 *First Things* (March) 21
GOFFMAN, E. (1959) *The Presentation of Self in Everyday Life* (New York, Doubleday Anchor Books)
——(1961) *Encounters: Two Studies in the Sociology of Interaction* (Indianapolis, Bobbs-Merrill)
GOLDMAN, A.H. (1980) *The Moral Foundations of Professional Ethics* (Totowa, NJ, Rowman & Littlefield)
GOODE, W.J. (1957) 'Community within a community: the professions' 22 *American Sociological Review* 194
GOODIN, R.E. (1991) 'Utility and the good' in Singer (ed.)
GOODPASTER, G. (1992) 'Lawsuits as Negotiations' 8 *Negotiation Journal* 221
GOODRICH, P. (1986) 'Blackstone's Tower: Metaphors of Distance and Histories of the English Law School' in P. Birks (ed.) *What are Law Schools For?* (Oxford, Oxford University Press)
GORDON, R.W. (1988) 'The Independence of Lawyers' 68 *Boston University Law Review* 1
——(1990) 'Corporate Law Practice as a Public Calling' 49 *Maryland Law Review* 225
GORIELY, T. and WILLIAMS, T. (1996) *The Impact of the New Training Scheme: Report on a Qualitative Study* (London, The Law Society)
GRABOSKY, P. and BRAITHWAITE, J. (1986) *Of Manners Gentle: Enforcement Strategies of Australian Business Regulatory Agencies* (Melbourne, Oxford University Press)
GRAFFY, C. (1998) 'Conditional Fees: Key to the Courthouse or the Casino?' 1 *Legal Ethics* 70
GRANFIELD, R. (1992) *Making Elite Lawyers* (Cambridge, MA, Harvard University Press)
——(1998) 'The Politics of Decontextualized Knowledge: Legal Education, Ethics and Progressive Law Students' in Economides (ed.) *Ethical Challenges to Legal Education and Conduct* (Oxford, Hart Publishing)
GREENWOOD, E. (1957) 'The Attributes of a Profession' *Social Work* July 1957
GRIFFITH, J.A.G. (1997) *The Politics of the Judiciary* (5th edn., London, Fontana)
GRIFFITHS, J. (1970) 'Ideology in Criminal Procedure or a Third "Model" of the Criminal Process' 79 *Yale Law Journal* 359
GRIMSHAW, J. (1991) 'The ideal of a female ethic' in Singer (ed.)
GROSS, S.R. (1987) 'The American Advantage: The Value of Inefficient Litigation' 85 *Michigan Law Review* 734
GUNZ, H.P. and GUNZ, S.P. (1994) 'Ethical Implications of the Employment Relationship for Professional Lawyers' 28 *University of British Columbia Law Review* 123
GURRY, F. (1984) *Breach of Confidence* (Oxford, Clarendon Press)
GUTMAN, A. (1985) 'Communitarian Critics of Liberalism' 14 *Philosophy & Public Affairs* 308

HABER, R.G. and BAUMRIN, B.H. (1988) 'The Moral Obligations of Lawyers' I *Canadian Journal of Law & Jurisprudence* 105
HABERMAS, J. (1973) *Legitimation Crisis* (Boston, Beacon Press)

HAINES, P.L. (1990) 'Restraining the Overly Zealous Advocate: Time for Judicial Intervention' 65 *Indiana Law Journal* 445

HALL, A. (1990) 'We say no and we mean no!' *New Law Journal* 2 March 284

HALLIDAY, T. (1987) *Beyond Monopoly: Lawyers, State Crises and Professional Empowerment* (Chicago, University of Chicago Press)

HALLIDAY, T. and KARPIK, L. (1997) 'Postscript: Lawyers, Political Liberalism and Globalization' in T. Halliday and L. Karpik (eds.) *Lawyers and the Rise of Western Political Liberalism* (Oxford, Clarendon Press)

HALPERN, A. (1993) *Legal Practice Handbook: Negotiation Skills* (London, Blackstone Press)

HALPERN, D. (1994) *Entry into the Legal Professions: The Law Student Cohort Study—Years 1 & 2* (London, The Law Society)

HAMPSHIRE, S. (1949) 'Fallacies in Moral Philosophy' LVIII *Mind* 476

HAMYLTON, K. and BHALLA, P. (1994) 'Shifting Constituencies of Race, Gender and Class' in Law Society, *Proceedings from the Annual Research Conference 1994* (London, The Law Society)

HANLON, G. (1996) 'Embeddedness, Re-Organisation and the Market—Relationships as the Professions' Core' unpublished paper to the *Socio-Legal Studies Association Annual Conference*, Southampton, April 1996

—— (1997) 'A Profession in Transition?—Lawyers, The Market and Significant Others' 60 *Modern Law Review* 798

HANLON, G. and SHAPLAND, J. (1996) 'Professional Disintegration? The Case of Law' in J. Broadbent, M. Dietrich, and J. Roberts (eds.) *The Ends of the Professions? The Restructuring of Professional Work* (London, Routledge)

HANSEN, O. (1994) *The Solicitors Complaints Bureau: A Consumer View* (London, National Consumer Council)

HARE, R.M. (1991) 'Universal prescriptivism' in Singer (ed.)

HARMAN, G. (1977) *The Nature of Morality: An Introduction to Ethics* (New York, Oxford University Press)

HARRIS, J. (1985) *The Value of Life* (London, Routledge)

HARRIS, N. (1994) 'Do Solicitors Care for their Clients?' 13 *Civil Justice Quarterly* 359

HARRIS, N.G.E. (1994) 'Professional Codes and Kantian Duties' in Chadwick (ed.)

HARRIS, P. and JONES, M. (1997) 'A Survey of Law Schools in the United Kingdom, 1996' 31 *Law Teacher* 38

HART, H.L.A. (1958) 'Positivism and the Separation of Morals' 71 *Harvard Law Review* 593

HARTWELL, S. (1990) 'Moral Development, Ethical Conduct and Clinical Education' 35 *New York Law School Law Review* 131

HARVEY, D. (1989) *The Condition of Postmodernity* (Oxford, Blackwell)

HARVEY, D.A. (1983) 'Responding to the Criminal Defense Client Who Insists on the Presentation of Perjuring Non-Party Witnesses: The *Schultheis* Solution' 68 *Iowa Law Review* 333

HAWKINS, K. (1983) 'Bargain and Bluff: Compliance Strategy and Deterrence in the Enforcement of Regulation' 5 *Law & Policy Quarterly* 35

—— (1990) 'Compliance Strategy, Prosecution Policy and Aunt Sally: A Comment on Pearce & Tombs' 30 *British Journal of Criminology* 444

HAYEK, F. (1982) *Law, Liberty and Legislation* (London, Routledge & Kegan Paul)

HAYLES, N.K. (1986) 'Anger in Different Voices: Carol Gilligan and *The Mill on the Floss*' 12 *Signs* 23

HAYNSWORTH, C.F. (1976) 'Professionalism in Lawyering' 27 *South Carolina Law Review* 627

HÄYRY, H. and HÄYRY, M. (1994) 'The nature and role of professional codes in modern society' in Chadwick (ed.)

HAZARD, G.C. (1974) 'Rethinking Legal Ethics' 26 *Stanford Law Review* 1227

—— (1978a) *Ethics in the Practice of Law* (New Haven, Yale University Press)

—— (1978b) 'An Historical Perspective on the Attorney-Client Privilege' 66 *California Law Review* 1061

—— (1981) 'How Far May a Lawyer Go in Assisting a Client in Legally Wrongful Conduct?' 35 *University of Miami Law Review* 669

—— (1982) 'Legal Ethics: Legal Rules and Professional Aspiration' 30 *Cleveland State Law Review* 571

—— (1989) 'My Station as a Lawyer' 6 *Georgia State University Law Review* 1

—— (1991) 'The Future of Legal Ethics' 100 *Yale Law Journal* 1239

—— (1992) 'Personal Values and Professional Ethics' 40 *Cleveland State Law Review* 133

HAZARD, G.C. and RHODE, D.L. (1988) *The Legal Profession: Responsibility and Regulation* (2nd edn., Westbury, NY, Foundation Press Inc)

HEDEGARD, J. (1979) 'The Impact of Legal Education: an In-depth Examination of Career-Relevant Interests Attitudes and Personality Traits Among First Year Law Students' *American Bar Foundation Research Journal* 267

HEFFERNAN, W.C. (1985) 'The Moral Accountability of Advocates' 61 *Notre Dame Law Review* 36

HEINZ, J.P. (1983) 'The Power of Lawyers' 17 *Georgia Law Review* 891

—— and LAUMANN, E.O. (1982) *Chicago Lawyers* (Chicago, University of Chicago Press)

HEINZ, J.P., NELSON, R.L., LAUMANN, E.O., and MICHELSON, E. (1998) 'The Changing Character of Lawyers' Work: Chicago in 1975 and 1995' 32 *Law & Society Review* 751

HELD, V. (1983) 'The Division of Moral Labor and the Role of the Lawyer' in Luban (ed.)

HEYMANN, P.B. and LIEBMAN, L. (1988) *The Social Responsibilities of Lawyers: Case Studies* (New York, The Foundation Press)

HILBERY, M. (1959) *Duty and Art in Advocacy* (London, Stevens & Sons)

HOBIN, T. and JENSEN, D.J. (1980) 'The Impropriety of the Attorneys' Actions in the Lake Pleasant Case' in A. Gerson (ed.) (1980) *Lawyers' Ethics: Contemporary Dilemmas* (New Brunswick, NJ, Transaction Books)

HODES, W.W. (1981) 'The Code of Professional Responsibility, The Kutak Rules, and the Trial Lawyer's Code: Surprisingly, Three Peas in a Pod' 35 *University of Miami Law Review* 739

HOLDSWORTH, D. (1994) 'Accountability: The obligation to lay oneself open to criticism' in Chadwick (ed.)

HOLLAND, J.A. (ed.) (1995) *Cordery on Solicitors* (9th edn., London, Butterworths)

HUGHES, S. 'Barristers and Solicitors: Rivals or Cohorts' in Law Society, *Proceedings from the Annual Research Conference 1994* (London, The Law Society)

HUMPHREYS, C. (1955) 'The Duties and Responsibilities of Prosecuting Counsel' *Criminal Law Review* 739

HUNT, A. (1986) 'The Critical Legal Studies Movement' 6 *Oxford Journal of Legal Studies* 1

HUNT, M. (1999) 'The Human Rights Act and Legal Culture: The Judiciary and the Legal Profession' 26 *Journal of Law & Society* 86

HUTCHINSON, A.C. (1998) 'Taking It Personally: Legal Ethics and Client Selection' 1 *Legal Ethics* 168

HUTTER, B. (1989) 'Variations in Regulatory Enforcement Styles' 11 *Law & Policy* 153
HUTTON, W. (1995) *The State We're In* (London, Jonathan Cape)

IIJIMA, A.L. (1998) 'Lessons Learned: Legal Education and Law Student Dysfunction' 48 *Journal of Legal Education* 524
INNS OF COURT SCHOOL OF LAW (1997) *Professional Conduct* (London, Blackstone)
IPP, D.A. (1998) 'Lawyers' Duties to the Court' 114 *Law Quarterly Review* 63

JACK, R. and JACK, D.C. (1989) *Moral Vision and Professional Decisions: The Changing Values of Women and Men Lawyers* (New York, Cambridge University Press)
JACKSON, B.S. (1995) *Making Sense in the Law: Linguistic, Psychological and Semiotic Perspectives* (Liverpool, Deborah Charles Publications)
JACKSON, J. (1994) 'Common Codes: Divergent Practices' in Chadwick (ed.)
JAMES, R. and SENEVIRANTNE, M. (1995) 'The Legal Services Ombudsman: Form versus Function?' 58 *Modern Law Review* 187
JAMIESON, D. (1991) 'Method and moral theory' in Singer (ed.)
JENNINGS, B. (1991) 'The Regulation of Virtue: Cross-Currents in Professional Ethics' 10 *Journal of Business Ethics* 561–8
JOHNSON, T. (1972) *Professions and Power* (London, Macmillan)

KAGAN, R.A. (1989) 'Understanding Regulatory Enforcement' 11 *Law & Policy* 89
—— and SCHOLTZ, J.T. (1984) 'The "criminology of the corporation" and regulatory enforcement strategies' in K. Hawkins and J. Thomas (eds.) *Enforcing Regulation* (Boston, Kluwer Nijhoff)
KAPLAN, J. (1965) 'The Prosecutorial Discretion—A Comment' 60 *Northwestern University Law Review* 174
—— (1986) 'Defending Guilty People' 7 *University of Bridgeport Law Review* 223
KAPLOW, L. and SHAVELL, S. (1989) 'Legal Advice about Information to Present in Litigation. Its Effects and Social Desirability' 102 *Harvard Law Review* 565
KAPTEIN, M. (1998) *Ethics Management: Auditing and Developing the Ethical Content of Organizations* (Dordrecht, Kluwer Publishing)
KAUFMAN, A. (1981) 'Book Review' 94 *Harvard Law Review* 1504
KEANE, A. (1996) *The Modern Law of Evidence* (4th edn., London, Butterworths)
KELLY, M.J. (1994) *Lives of Lawyers: Journeys in the Organization of Practice* (Ann Arbor, University of Michigan Press)
KELMAN, S. (1998) *Regulating America, Regulating Sweden: A Comparative Study of Occupational Safety and Health Policy* (Cambridge, MA, MIT Press)
KENNEDY, H. (1992) *Eve Was Framed: Women and British Justice* (London, Vintage)
KENNEDY, D. (1973) 'Legal Formality' 2 *Journal of Legal Studies* 351
—— (1982) 'Legal Education as Training for Hierarchy' in D. Kairys (ed.) *The Politics of Law: A Progressive Critique* (New York, Pantheon)
—— (1987) 'The Responsibility of Lawyers for the Justice of their Causes' 18 *Texas Tech Law Review* 1157
KINGDOM, E. (1991) *What's Wrong with Rights: Problems for a Feminist Politics of Law* (Edinburgh, Edinburgh University Press)
KIRK, H. (1976) *Portrait of a Profession* (London, Oyez)
KLEINBERGER, D.S. 'Wanted: An Ethos of Personal Responsibility—Why Codes of

Ethics and Schools of Law Don't Make for Ethical Lawyers' 21 *Connecticut Law Review* 365

KOEHN, D. (1994) *The Ground of Professional Ethics* (London and New York, Routledge)

KONIAK, S.P. (1992) 'The Law Between the Bar and the State' 70 *North Carolina Law Review* 1389

——(1996) 'Law and Ethics in a World of Rights and Unsuitable Wrongs' IX *Canadian Journal of Law & Jurisprudence* 11

KRASH, A. (1974) 'Professional Responsibility To Clients and the Public Interest: Is There a Conflict?' *Chicago Bar Record* 31

KRITZER, H. (1987) 'Fee Arrangements and Negotiation: A Research Note' 21 *Law & Society Review* 341

KRITZER, H., FELSTINER, W., SARAT, A., and TRUBEK, D. (1985) 'The Impact of Fee Arrangement on Lawyer Effort' 19 *Law & Society Review* 251

KRONMAN, A.T. (1987) 'Living in the Law' 54 *The University of Chicago Law Review* 835

——(1993) *The Lost Lawyer* (Cambridge, MA, Bellknap Press)

KUPFER, S.G. (1996) 'Authentic Legal Practices' 10 *Georgetown Journal of Legal Ethics* 33

KUTAK, R.J. (1983) 'The Adversary System and the Practice of Law' in Luban (ed.)

KYMLICKA, W. (1991) 'The social contract tradition' in Singer (ed.)

LACEY, N. (1996) 'Normative Reconstruction in Socio-Legal Theory' 5 *Social & Legal Studies* 13

LADD, J. (1980) 'The Quest for a Code of Professional Ethics: An Intellectual and Moral Confusion' extracted in D.L. Rhode and D. Luban, *Legal Ethics* (2nd edn., Westbury, NY, The Foundation Press 1992)

LAMB, D. (1995) 'Ethical Dilemmas: What Australian Lawyers Say About Them' in Parker and Sampford (eds.)

LANDSMAN, S. (1984) *The Adversary System: A Description and Defense* (Washington, DC, American Institute)

LANDESMAN, B.M. (1983) 'Confidentiality and the Lawyer-Client Relationship' in Luban (ed.)

LANGEVOORT, D.C. (1993) 'Where Were the Lawyers? A Behavioral Inquiry into Lawyers' Responsibility for Clients' Frauds' 46 *Vanderbilt Law Review* 75

LARRABEE, M.J. (ed.) (1993) *An Ethic of Care: Feminist and Interdisciplinary Perspectives* (New York, Routledge)

LARSON, M.S. (1977) *The Rise of Professionalism: A Sociological Analysis* (Berkeley, University of California Press)

LASH, S. (1996) 'Postmodern Ethics: The Missing Ground' 13 *Theory, Culture & Society* 91

LAW REFORM COMMISSION (1993) *Scrutiny of the Legal Profession: Complaints Against Lawyers* (Sydney, Law Reform Commission)

LAW SOCIETY (1997) *Annual Statistical Report 1997* (London, The Law Society)

——(1998) *Annual Statistical Report 1998* (London, The Law Society)

LAWRY, R.P. (1990) 'The Central Moral Tradition of Lawyering' 19 *Hofstra Law Review* 311

LAZEGA, E. (1992) 'Analyse de réseaux d'une organisation collégiale: les avocats d'affaires' 33 *Revue Française de Sociologie* 559

LEE, R.G. (1992) 'From Profession to Business: The Rise and Rise of the City Law Firm' in P. Thomas (ed.) *Tomorrow's Lawyers* (Oxford, Blackwell)

LEES, S. (1996) *Carnal Knowledge: Rape on Trial* (London, Penguin Books)

LEFF, A.A. (1979) 'Unspeakable Ethics, Unnatural Law' *Duke Law Journal* 1229

LEGAL SERVICES OMBUDSMAN (1993) *Annual Report* 1993 (Manchester, Office of the Legal Services Ombudsman)

——(1998) *Seventh Annual Report* (Manchester, Office of the Legal Services Ombudsman)

LEHMAN, W. (1979) 'The Pursuit of a Client's Interest' 77 *Michigan Law Review* 1078

LEIGH-KILE, D. (1998) *Lawyers on the Spot* (London, Vision)

LERMAN, L. (1990) 'Lying to Clients' 138 *University of Pennsylvania Law Review* 659

LEVIN, J. (1994) 'An Ethical Profession?' (Inaugural Lecture, Swansea, University of Wales Swansea)

LEVINE, H.D. (1997) 'Self-Interest or Self-Defense: Lawyer Disregard of the Attorney-Client Privilege for Profit and Protection' 5 *Hofstra Law Review* 783

LEWIS, V. (1996) *Complaints Against Solicitors: The Complainants' View* (London, The Law Society)

LICHTENBERG, J. (1996) 'What are Codes of Ethics for?' in Coady and Bloch (eds.)

LINTON, R. (1936) *The Study of Man: An Introduction* (New York: Appleton-Century-Crofts Inc)

LITTLE, M. and FEARNSIDE, M. (1997) 'On Trust' 2(1) *Online Journal of Ethics* at http://www.depaul.edu/ethics/ethg16.html/

LORD CHANCELLOR'S DEPARTMENT (1998) *Rights of Audience and Rights to Conduct Litigation in England and Wales: The Way Ahead* (London, Lord Chancellor's Department, June 1998)

LOWENTHAL, G.T. (1982) 'A General Theory of Negotiation Strategy, Process and Behavior' 31 *Kansas Law Review* 69

L.S.E. JURY PROJECT (1973) 'Juries and the Rules of Evidence' *Criminal Law Review* 208

LUBAN, D. (1981a) 'Calming the Hearse Horse: A Philosophical Research Program for Legal Ethics' 40 *Maryland Law Review* 451

——(1981b) 'Paternalism and the Legal Profession' *Wisconsin Law Review* 454

——(ed.) (1983) *The Good Lawyer: Lawyer's Roles and Lawyer's Ethics* (Totowa, NJ, Rowman & Allanheld)

——(1983a) 'Introduction' in Luban (ed.)

——(1983b) 'The Adversary System Excuse' in Luban (ed.)

——(1986) 'The Lysistratian Prerogative: A Response to Stephen Pepper' *American Bar Foundation Research Journal* 637

——(1988a) *Lawyers and Justice: An Ethical Study* (Princeton, NJ, Princeton University Press)

——(1988b) 'The *Noblesse Oblige* Tradition in the Practice of Law' 41 *Vanderbilt Law Review* 717

——(1990a) 'Freedom and Constraint in Legal Ethics: Some Mid-Course Corrections to *Lawyers and Justice*' 49 *Maryland Law Review* 424

——(1990b) 'Partisanship, Betrayal and Autonomy in the Lawyer-Client Relationship: A Reply to Stephen Ellman' 90 *Columbia Law Review* 1004

——(1993) 'Are Criminal Defenders Different?' 91 *Michigan Law Review* 1729

——(1994) 'Introduction', in D. Luban (ed.) *The Ethics of Lawyers* (Aldershot, Dartmouth)

——(1996) 'Introduction: A New Canadian Legal Ethics' IX *Canadian Journal of Law & Jurisprudence* 3

LUBAN, D., STRUDLER, A., and WASSERMAN, D. (1992) 'Moral Responsibility in the Age of Bureaucracy' 90 *Michigan Law Review* 2348

LUND, T. (1960) *A Guide to the Professional Conduct and Etiquette of Solicitors* (London, The Law Society)

LUNNEY, M. (1997) ' "And the Lord Knows Where That Might Lead"—the Law Society, the Fraudulent Solicitor and the Solicitors Act 1941' 4 *International Journal of the Legal Profession* 235

LYONS, D. (1984) *Ethics and the Rule of Law* (Cambridge, Cambridge University Press)

McBARNET, D. (1981) *Conviction: Law, the State and the Construction of Justice* (London, Macmillan)

—— (1994) 'Legal Creativity: Law, Capital and Legal Avoidance' in M. Cain and C. Harrington (eds.) *Lawyers in a Postmodern World* (Buckingham, Open University Press)

—— and WHELAN, C. (1991) 'The Elusive Spirit of the Law: Formalism and the Struggle for Legal Control' 54 *Modern Law Review* 848

McCONVILLE, M. (1998) 'Plea Bargaining: Ethics and Politics' 25 *Journal of Law & Society* 562

—— HODGSON, J., BRIDGES, L., and PAVLOVIC, A. (1994) *Standing Accused: The organisation and practices of criminal defence lawyers in Britain* (Oxford, Clarendon Press)

MACDONALD, K.M. (1995) *The Sociology of the Professions* (London, Sage)

McDONALD, P. (1982) ' "The Class of '81": A Glance at the Social Class Composition of Recruits of the Legal Profession' 9 *Journal of Law & Society* 267

McDOWELL, B. (1991) *Ethical Conduct and Professional Dilemmas* (New York, Quorum Books)

McELDOWNEY, J.F. (1995) 'Law and Regulation: Current Issues and Future Directions' in M. Bishop, J. Kay, and C. Mayer (eds.) *The Regulatory Challenge* (Oxford, Oxford University Press)

McGLYNN, C. (1998) *The Woman Lawyer: Making the Difference* (London, Butterworths)

MacINTYRE, A. (1967) *A Short History of Ethics* (London, Routledge)

—— (1985) *After Virtue: A study in Moral Theory* (2nd edn., London, Duckworth)

McKAY COMMISSION (1991) *Report of the Commission on Evaluation of Disciplinary Enforcement* (Chicago, American Bar Association)

MACKENZIE, G. (1996) 'Breaking the Dichotomy Habit: The Adversary System and the Ethics of Professionalism' IX *Canadian Journal of Law and Jurisprudence* 33

MACKIE, J.L. (1977) *Ethics: Inventing Right and Wrong* (Harmondsworth, Penguin)

MACKIE, K. (1989) *Lawyers in Business* (Basingstoke, Macmillan)

MacKINNON, C. (1984) *Feminism Unmodified: Discourses on Life and Law* (Cambridge, MA, Harvard University Press)

MACMILLAN, LORD (1937) *Law and Other Things* (Cambridge, Cambridge University Press)

MAIMAN, R., McEWEN, C., and MATHER, L. (1999) 'The Future of Legal Professionalism in Practice' 2 *Legal Ethics* (forthcoming)

MAISTER, D.H. (1997) *Managing the Professional Service Firm* (London, Pocket Books)

MANN, K. (1985) *Defending White-Collar Crime: A Portrait of Attorneys at Work* (New Haven, CN, Yale University Press)

MARKS, F.R. and CATHCART, D. (1974) 'Discipline Within the Legal Profession: Is It Self-Regulation?' 2 *University of Illinois Law Forum* 219

MARRE COMMITTEE (1988) *A Time for Change: Report of the Committee on the Future of the Legal Profession* (London: General Council of the Bar/The Law Society)

MARSHALL, D. (1999) 'Putting Your Clients First?' 2 *Legal Ethics* (forthcoming)

MARSHALL, T.H. (1963) *Sociology at the Crossroads* (London, Heinemann)

MARTIN, M.W. (1981a) 'Rights and the Meta-Ethics of Professional Morality' 91 *Ethics* 619

—— (1981b) 'Professional and Ordinary Morality: A Reply to Freedman' 91 *Ethics* 631

MAUGHAN, C. and WEBB, J. (1995) *Lawyering Skills and the Legal Process* (London, Butterworths)

MAXTON, J.K. (1997) 'Contract and Fiduciary Obligation' 11 *Journal of Contract Law* 222

MAZOR, L.J. (1968) 'Power and Responsibility in the Attorney-Client Relation' 20 *Stanford Law Review* 1120

MEARS, M. (1997) 'Foreword' in M. Mears (ed.) *Keeping Clients: A Client Care Guide for Solicitors* (Leamington Spa, Office for the Supervision of Solicitors)

—— (1990) 'Rape and the Radical Lawyer' *The Law Society's Gazette*, 28 March 16

MELLINKOFF, D. (1973) *The Conscience of a Lawyer* (St Paul, MN, West Publishing)

MENKEL-MEADOW, C. (1984) 'Toward Another View of Legal Negotiation: The Structure of Problem Solving' 31 *UCLA Law Review* 754

—— (1985) 'Portia in a Different Voice: Speculations on a Women's Lawyering Process' 1 *Berkeley Women's Law Journal* 39

—— (1990) 'Lying to Clients for Economic Gain or Paternalistic Judgment: A Proposal for a Golden Rule of Candor' 138 *University of Pennsylvania Law Review* 761

—— (1995) 'Portia *Redux*: Another Look at Gender, Feminism and Legal Ethics', in Parker and Sampford (eds.)

—— (1996) 'The Trouble with the Adversary System in a Post-Modern, Multi-Cultural World' 1 *Journal of the Institute for the Study of Legal Ethics* 801

MEW, G. (1989) 'Lawyers: The Agony and Ecstasy of Self-Government' 9 *Windsor Yearbook of Access to Justice* 210

MIDGLEY, J.R. (1992) 'Confidentiality, Conflicts of Interest and Chinese Walls' 55 *Modern Law Review* 822

MILLERSON, G. (1964) *The Qualifying Associations* (London, Routledge & Kegan Paul)

MINTZ, M. (1986) *At Any Cost: Corporate Greed, Women, and the Dalkon Shield* (New York, Pantheon)

MITCHELL, J.B. (1980) 'The Ethics of the Criminal Defense Attorney—New Answers to Old Questions' 32 *Stanford Law Review* 293

MOORE, M. (1982) 'Moral Reality' *Wisconsin Law Review* 1061

—— (1989) 'The Interpretive Turn in Modern Theory: A Turn for the Worse' 41 *Stanford Law Review* 871

MOORE, M. and MOORE, M. (1991) *Managing Lawyers: Recruiting and Retaining Staff in Private Practice* (London, Chancery Lane Publishing)

MOORE, N. (1989) 'The Usefulness of Ethical Codes' *Annual Survey of American Law* 7

MOORE, N.J. (1985) 'Limits to Attorney-Client Confidentiality: A "Philosophically Informed" and Comparative Approach to Legal and Medical Ethics' 36 *Case Western Reserve Law Review* 177

MOORE, W.G. (1970) *The Professions: Roles and Rules* (New York, Russell Sage Foundation)

MOORHEAD, R. (1998) 'Legal Aid in the Eye of the Storm: Rationing, Contracting, and a New Institutionalism' 25 *Journal of Law & Society* 365

MOORHEAD, R. and BOYLE, F. (1995) 'Quality of life and trainee solicitors: a survey' 2 *International Journal of the Legal Profession* 217

MORGAN, D. (1995) 'Doctoring Legal Ethics: Studies in Irony' in Cranston (ed.)

MORGAN, T.D. (1977) 'The Evolving Concept of Professional Responsibility' 90 *Harvard Law Review* 702

MORISON, J. and LEITH, P. (1992) *The Barrister's World* (Milton Keynes, Open University Press)

MORTIMER, J. (1983) *The First Rumpole Omnibus* (London, Penguin)

——(1988) *Rumpole and the Age of Miracles* (London, Penguin)

MNOOKIN, R.H. and KORNHAUSER, T. (1979) 'Bargaining in the Shadow of the Law: The Case of Divorce' 88 *Yale Law Journal* 950

NADEL, J. (1993) *Sara Thornton: The Story of a Woman Who Killed* (London, Victor Gollancz)

NAGEL, T. (1986) *The View from Nowhere* (Oxford, Oxford University Press)

NAPLEY, D. (1991) *The Technique of Persuasion* (4th edn., London, Sweet & Maxwell)

NEALE, B. and SMART, C. (1997) ' "Good" and "Bad" Lawyers? Struggling in the Shadow of the New Law' 19 *Journal of Social Welfare & Family Law* 377

NELSON, R. (1985) 'Ideology, Practice and Professional Autonomy: Social Values and Client Relationships in the Large Law Firm' 37 *Stanford Law Review* 503

NELSON, R., TRUBEK, D., and SOLOMON, R. (eds.) (1992) *Lawyers' Ideals/Lawyers' Practice* (Ithaca, Cornell University Press)

NEWBOLD, A.L.E. (1990) 'The Crime/Fraud Exception to Legal Professional Privilege' 53 *Modern Law Review* 472

NICHOLSON, L.J. (1993) 'Women, Morality and History' in Larrabee (ed.)

NICOLSON, D. (1992) 'Ideology in the South African Judicial Process: Lessons from the Past' 8 *South African Journal on Human Rights* 50

——(1994) 'Truth, Reason and Justice: Epistemology and Politics in Evidence Discourse' 57 *Modern Law Review* 726

——(1994) 'Facing Facts: The Teaching of Fact Construction in University Law Schools' 1 *The International Journal of Evidence & Proof* 132

——(1998) 'Mapping Professional Legal Ethics: the Form and Focus of the Codes' 1 *Legal Ethics* 51

NICOLSON, D. and WEBB, J. (1999) 'Taking Lawyers' Ethics Seriously' 6 *International Journal of the Legal Profession* 109

NODDINGS, N. (1984) *Caring: A Feminine Approach to Ethics and Moral Education* (Chicago, Chicago University Press)

NOONAN JR, J.T. (1966) 'The Purposes of Advocacy and the Limits of Confidentiality' 64 *Michigan Law Review* 1485

——(1977) 'Professional Ethics or Personal Responsibility?' 29 *Stanford Law Review* 363

'NOTE' (1962) 'Functional Overlap Between the Lawyer and other Professionals: Its Implications for Privileged Communication Doctrine' 71 *Yale Law Journal* 1226

'NOTE' (1977) 'The Attorney-Client Privilege: Fixed Rules, Balancing and Constitutional Entitlement' 91 *Harvard Law Review* 464

O'DAIR, D.R.F. (1997) 'Ethics by the pervasive method—the case of contract' 17 *Legal Studies* 305

OGUS, A.I. (1994) *Regulation: Legal Form and Economic Theory* (Oxford, Clarendon Press)

——and VELJANOVSKI, C. (eds.) (1984) *Readings in the Economics of Law and Regulation* (Oxford, Oxford University Press)

O'NEILL, O. (1991) 'Kantian ethics' in Singer (ed.)

ORBELL, J. and DAWES, R. (1993) 'Social Welfare, Co-operators' Advantage and the Option of Not Playing the Game' 58 *American Sociological Review* 787

ORKIN, M.M. (1958) 'Defence of One Known to be Guilty' 1 *Criminal Law Quarterly* 170

ORMROD COMMITTEE (1971) *Report of the Committee on Legal Education* Cmnd 4595 (London, HMSO)

PAGONE, G.T. (1984) 'Legal Professional Privilege in the European Communities: The *AM & S* Case and Australian Law' 33 *International & Comparative Law Quarterly* 663

PANNICK, D. (1992) *Advocates* (Oxford, Oxford University Press)

PARDIECK, A. (1996) 'Foreign Legal Consultants: The Changing Role of the Lawyer in a Global Economy' *Indiana Journal of Global Legal Studies*, vol. 3(2), at http://www.law.indiana.edu/glsj/glsj.html

PARK, R.E. (1950) *Race and Culture* (Glencoe, IL, The Free Press)

PARKER, C. (1997a) 'Converting the Lawyers: The Dynamics of Competition and Accountability Reform' 33 *Australian & New Zealand Journal of Sociology* 39

——(1997b) 'Competing Images of the Legal Profession: Competing Regulatory Strategies' 25 *International Journal of the Sociology of Law* 385

PARKER, S. (1995) 'Change, Responsibility and the Legal Profession' in Parker and Sampford (eds.)

——and SAMPFORD, C. (eds.) (1995) *Legal Ethics and Legal Practice* (Oxford, Clarendon Press)

PATERSON, A. (1995) 'Legal Ethics: Its Nature and Place in the Curriculum' in Cranston (ed.)

——(1996) 'Professionalism and the legal services market' 3 *International Journal of the Legal Profession* 137

——(1997) 'Legal Ethics in Scotland' 4 *International Journal of the Legal Profession* 25

PATTERSON, L.R. (1980) 'Legal Ethics and the Lawyer's Duty of Loyalty' 29 *Emory Law Journal* 909

——(1981) 'The Function of a Code of Legal Ethics' 35 *University of Miami Law Review* 695

PELLEGRINO, E.D. (1993) 'The Metamorphosis of Medical Ethics' 269 *Journal of the American Medical Association* 1158

PENCE, G. (1984) 'Recent Work on Virtues' 21 *American Philosophical Quarterly* 281

——(1991) 'Virtue theory' in Singer (ed.)

PEPPER, S.L. (1986a) 'The Lawyer's Amoral Ethical Role: A Defense, A Problem, and Some Possibilities' *American Bar Foundation Research Journal* 613

——(1986b) 'A Rejoinder to Professors Kaufman and Luban' *American Bar Foundation Research Journal* 657

——(1995) 'Counseling at the Limits of the Law: An Exercise in the Jurisprudence and Ethics of Lawyering' 104 *Yale Law Journal* 1545

PEREIS, G.L. (1982) 'Legal Professional Privilege in Commonwealth Law' 31 *International & Comparative Law Quarterly* 609

PETTIT, P. (1991) 'Consequentialism' in Singer (ed.)

PHILLIPS, A. (1990) *Professional Ethics for Scottish Solicitors* (Edinburgh, Butterworths)

PIGDEN, C.R. (1991) 'Naturalism' in Singer (ed.)

PIPKIN, R. (1979) 'Law School Instruction in Professional Responsibility: A Curricular Paradox?' (1979) *American Bar Foundation Research Journal* 247

PLATO (1975) *The Republic of Plato*, trans. F.M. Cornford (Oxford, Oxford University Press)

PLEASANCE, P., MACLEAN, S., and MORLEY, R. (1996) *Profiling Civil Litigation: The Case for Research* (London, Legal Aid Board)

POLLITT, D.H. (1964) 'Counsel for the Unpopular Cause: The "Hazard of Being Undone"' 43 *North Carolina Law Review* 9

POPKIN, W.D. (1981) 'Client-Lawyer Confidentiality' 59 *Texas Law Review* 755

POSNER, R. (1974) 'Theories of Economic Regulation' 5 *Bell Journal of Economics* 335

POST, J.E., FREDERICK, W.C., and LAWRENCE, A.T. (1995) *Business and Society: Corporate Strategy, Public Policy, Ethics* (New York, McGraw-Hill)

POSTEMA, G.J. (1980) 'Moral Responsibility in Professional Ethics' 55 *New York University Law Review* 63

——(1983) 'Self-Image, Integrity and Professional Responsibility' in Luban (ed.)

POUND, R. (1906) 'The Causes of Popular Dissatisfaction with the Administration of Justice' 29 *ABA Reports* 395

PRESTON, R. (1991) 'Christian ethics' in Singer (ed.)

PRICE, D. (1989) 'Taking Rights Cynically: A Review of Critical Legal Studies' 48 *Cambridge Law Journal* 271

PUTNAM, R. (1993) *Making Democracy Work: Civic Traditions in Modern Italy* (Princeton, NJ, Princeton University Press)

PYE, K. (1978) 'The Role of Counsel in the Suppression of Truth' 4 *Duke Law Journal* 921

RACHELS, J. (1991) 'Subjectivism' in Singer (ed.)

RADIN, M. (1928) 'The Privilege of Confidential Communication Between Lawyer and Client' 16 *California Law Review* 487

RAPHAEL, D.D. (1994) *Moral Philosophy* (2nd edn., Oxford, Oxford University Press)

RAWLS, J. (1971) *A Theory of Justice* (Oxford, Oxford University Press)

RAYMOND, B. (1990) 'The profession's duty to provide; a solicitor's right to choose' *New Law Journal* 2 March 285

RAZ, J. (1986) *The Morality of Freedom* (Oxford, Clarendon Press)

REES, J. (1988) *Reforming the Workplace: A Study of Self-Regulation in Occupational Safety* (Philadelphia, University of Pennsylvania Press)

REES, R. and VICKERS, J. (1995) 'RPI-X Price-cap Regulation' in M. Bishop, J. Kay, and C. Mayer (eds.) *The Regulatory Challenge* (Oxford, Oxford University Press)

REGIS, E. (ed.) (1984) *Gewirth's Ethical Rationalism: Critical Essays with a Reply by Alan Gewirth* (Chicago, University of Chicago Press)

REST, J. and NARVAEZ, D. (eds.) (1994) *Moral Development in the Professions: Psychology and Applied Ethics* (Hillsdale, NJ, Lawrence Erlbaum Associates)

RHODE, D.L. (1980–1) 'Why the ABA Bothers: A Functional Perspective on Professional Codes' 59 *Texas Law Review* 689

——(1985) 'Ethical Perspectives on Legal Practice' 37 *Stanford Law Review* 589

——(1991) 'An Adversarial Exchange on Adversarial Ethics' 41 *Journal of Legal Education* 29

——(1992) 'Ethics by the Pervasive Method' 42 *Journal of Legal Education* 31

——(1994) 'Gender and Professional Roles' 63 *Fordham Law Review* 39

RICHARDS, D.A.J. (1981) 'Moral Authority, the Developmental Psychology of Ethical Autonomy and Professionalism' 31 *Journal of Legal Education* 359

ROCK, P. (1993) *The Social World of the English Crown Court* (Oxford, Clarendon Press)

ROGERS, S. (1899) 'The Ethics of Advocacy' 15 *Law Quarterly Review* 25

ROSE, N. (1996) *Inventing Our Selves* (Cambridge, Cambridge University Press)

ROSEN, R.E. (1998) 'Devils, Lawyers and Salvation Lie in the Details: Deontological Legal Ethics, Issue Conflicts of Interest and Civic Education in Law Schools' in Economides (ed.)

ROSENTHAL, D.E. (1974) *Lawyer and Client: Who's in Charge?* (New York, Russell Sage Foundation)

ROSS, W.D. (1930) *The Right and the Good* (Oxford, Clarendon Press)

ROTUNDA, R.D. (1976) 'Book Review' 89 *Harvard Law Review* 622

RUBIN, A.B. (1975) 'A Causerie on Lawyers' Ethics in Negotiation' 35 *Louisiana Law Review* 577

RUSE, M. (1991) 'The significance of evolution' in Singer (ed.)

RUSSELL, I.S. (1997) 'Cries and Whispers: Environmental Hazards, Model Rule 1.6, and the Attorney's Conflicting Duties to Clients and Others' 72 *Washington Law Review* 409

SALBU, S. (1992) 'Law and Conformity, Ethics and Conflict: The Trouble with Law-Based Conceptions of Ethics' 68 *Indiana Law Journal* 101

SAMPFORD, C. and BLENCOWE, S. (1998) 'Educating Lawyers to be Ethical Advisers' in Economides (ed.)

SAMPFORD, C. with PARKER, C. (1995) 'Legal Regulation, Ethical Standard-Setting, and Institutional Design' in Parker and Sampford (eds.)

SANDEL, M.J. (1998) *Liberalism and the Limits of Justice* (2nd edn., Cambridge, Cambridge University Press)

SANDERS, A. (1994) 'The Silent Code' *New Law Journal* 8 July 946

——and YOUNG, R. (1998) *Criminal Justice* (2nd edn., London, Butterworths)

SARTRE, J-P. (1957) *Being and Nothingness: An Essay on Phenomenological Existence* (London, Methuen)

SCHEINGOLD, S. (1994) 'The Contradictions of Radical Law Practice' in M. Cain and C.B. Harrington (eds.) *Lawyers in a Postmodern World* (Buckingham, Open University Press)

SCHLESINGER, R.B., BAADE, H.W., DAMASKA, M.R., and HERZOG, P.E. (1989) *Comparative Law: Cases, Texts, Materials* (4th edn., Mineola, NY, Foundation Press)

SCHMITT, R. (1995) *Beyond Separateness* (Boulder, CO, Westview Press)

SCHNAPPER, E. (1978) 'The Myth of Legal Ethics' *American Bar Association Journal* 202

SCHNEEWIND, J.B. (1991) 'Modern moral philosophy' in Singer (ed.)

SCHNEYER, T. (1984) 'Moral Philosophy's Standard Misconception of Legal Ethics' *Wisconsin Law Review* 1529

——(1991) 'Some Sympathy for the Hired Gun' 41 *Journal of Legal Education* 11

——(1992) 'Professionalism as politics: the making of a modern legal ethics code' in Nelson, Trubek and Solomon (eds.)

SCHOLTZ, J.T. (1984) 'Cooperation, Deterrence and the Ecology of Regulatory Enforcement' 18 *Law & Society Review* 179

SCHRADER, D.E. (1988) *Ethics and the Practice of Law* (NJ, Prentice-Hall)

SCHWARTZ, D. (1983) 'The "New" Legal Ethics and the Administrative Law Bar' in Luban (ed.)

SCHWARTZ, M.L. (1978) 'The Professionalism and Accountability of Lawyers' 66 *California Law Review* 669

——(1983) 'The Zeal of the Civil Advocate' 3 *American Bar Foundation Research Journal* 543

——(1985) 'Comment' 37 *Stanford Law Review* 653

—— (1988) 'On Making the True Look False and the False Look True' 41 *Southwestern Law Journal* 1135

SCOCCIA, D. (1990) 'Paternalism and Respect for Autonomy' 100 *Ethics* 318

SCOTT, P. (1995) *The Meanings of Mass Higher Education* (Buckingham, SRHE/Open University Press)

SELDON, A. (1987) *Law and Lawyers in Perspective* (Harmondsworth, Penguin)

SELZNICK, P. (1985) 'Focusing Organization Research on Regulation' in R. Noll (ed.) *Regulatory Policy and the Social Sciences* (Berkeley, University of California Press)

—— (1987) 'The Idea of a Communitarian Morality' 75 *California Law Review* 445

—— (1993) *The Moral Commonwealth: Social Theory and the Promise of Community* (Chicago, Chicago University Press)

SENNETT, R. (1998) *The Corrosion of Character: The Personal Consequences of Work in the New Capitalism* (London, Norton)

SERON, C. and FERRIS, K. (1995) 'Negotiating Professionalism: The Gendered Social Capital of Flexible Time' 22 *Work & Occupations* 22

SHAFFER, T.L. (1988) 'The Unique, Novel, and Unsound Adversary Ethic' 41 *Vanderbilt Law Review* 697

SHAPIRO, S. (1990) 'Collaring the Crime, Not the Criminal: Reconsidering the Concept of White-Collar Crime' 55 *American Sociological Review* 346

SHAPLAND, J. and SORSBY, A. (1996) *Professional Bodies' Communications with Members and Clients, Vol. 2* (East Molesey, Office of Fair Trading)

SHAVELL, S. (1988) 'Legal Advice About Contemplated Acts: The Decision to Obtain Advice, Its Social Desirability, and Protection of Confidentiality' 17 *Journal of Legal Studies* 123

SHEINMAN, L. (1997) 'Looking for legal ethics' 4 *International Journal of the Legal Profession* 139

SHEPHERD, J.C. (1981) *The Law of Fiduciaries* (Toronto, Carswell)

SHERR, A. (1993) *Legal Practice Handbook: Advocacy* (London: Blackstone Press)

—— (1995) 'Of Super Heroes and Slaves: Images and Work of the Legal Profession' 48 *Current Legal Problems* 327

—— (1997) 'Editorial: Dinners, library seats, wigs and relatives' 4 *International Journal of the Legal Profession* 5

—— (1999a) *Client Care for Lawyers* (2nd edn., London, Sweet & Maxwell)

—— (1999b) 'Blanchement, Formation, Culture and Obedience: Teaching Money Laundering Ethics Across the EU' paper to the Third Theory in Legal Education Colloquium, London, January 1999

SHERR, A. and WEBB, J. (1989) 'Law Students, the Market and Socialisation: Do We Make Them Turn to the City?' *Journal of Law & Society* 225

SHERR, A. and WEBLEY, L. (1997) 'Legal Ethics in England and Wales' 4 *International Journal of the Legal Profession* 109

SHINER, M. (1997) *Entry into the Legal Professions: The Law Student Cohort Study—Year 4* (London, The Law Society)

—— and NEWBURN, T. (1995) *Entry into the Legal Professions: The Law Student Cohort Study—Year 3* (London, The Law Society)

SHUCHMAN, P. (1968) 'Ethics and Legal Ethics: The Propriety of the Canons as a Group Moral Code' 37 *George Washington Law Review* 244

SILVERMAN, F. (1989) *Handbook of Professional Conduct for Solicitors* (2nd edn., London, Butterworths)

—— (1997) 'Professional Conduct' in Bramley S. *et al*, LPC *Pervasive Topics* (Bristol, Jordans)

SIMMONDS, N.E. (1986) *Central Issues in Jurisprudence: Justice, Law and Rights* (London, Sweet & Maxwell)

SIMON, W.H. (1978) 'The Ideology of Advocacy: Procedural Justice and Professional Ethics' *Wisconsin Law Review* 29

—— (1988) 'Ethical Discretion in Lawyering' 101 *Harvard Law Review* 1083

—— (1990) 'Reply: Further Reflections on Libertarian Criminal Defense' 91 *Michigan Law Review* 1767

—— (1993) 'The Ethics of Criminal Defense' 91 *Michigan Law Review* 1703

—— (1998) *The Practice of Justice: A Theory of Lawyers' Ethics* (Cambridge, MA, Harvard University Press)

SINGER, P. (ed.) (1991) *A Companion to Ethics* (London, Blackwell)

SISAK, J. (1997) 'Confidentiality, Counseling and Care: when others need to know what clients need to disclose' 65 *Fordham Law Review* 2747

SKARLATOS, N.J. (1991) 'European Lawyers' Right to Transnational Legal Practice in the European Community' *Legal Issues of European Integration* 49

SLINN, J. (1984) *A History of Freshfields* (London, Freshfields)

—— (1987) *Linklaters and Paines: The First 150 Years* (London, Longman)

SMART, C. (1989) *Feminism and the Power of Law* (London, Routledge)

SMITH, M. (1991) 'Realism' in Singer (ed.)

SMITH, R. (1996) 'Legal Aid on an Ebbing Tide' 23 *Journal of Law & Society* 570

SOMMERLAD, H. (1994) 'The Myth of Feminisation: Women and Cultural Change in the Legal Profession' 1 *International Journal of the Legal Profession* 31

—— (1995) 'Managerialism and the Legal Profession: A New Professional Paradigm' 2 *International Journal of the Legal Profession* 159

SPIEGEL, M. (1979) 'Lawyering and Client Decisionmaking: Informed Consent and the Legal Profession' 128 *University of Pennsylvania Law Review* 41

STANLEY COMMISSION (1986) *In the Spirit of Public Service: A Blueprint for Rekindling Lawyer Professionalism* (Chicago, American Bar Association)

STANLEY, C. (1988) 'Training for the Hierarchy: Reflections on the British Experience of Legal Education' 22 *Law Teacher* 78

—— (1991) 'Enterprising Lawyers: Changes in the Market for Legal Services' 25 *Law Teacher* 44

STEELE, E.H. and NIMMER, R.T. (1976) 'Lawyers, Clients and Professional Regulation' *American Bar Foundation Research Journal* 936

STEPHEN, J.F. (1861) 'The Morality of Advocacy' 3 *Cornhill Magazine* 477

STEWART, S. and VAUGHAN, D. (1975) 'Does Legal Professional Privilege Exist in the EEC?' 72 *The Law Society's Gazette* 5 November 1111

STIER, S. (1991) 'Legal Ethics: The Integrity Thesis' 52 *Ohio State Law Journal* 551

STIVERS, R. (1994) *The Culture of Cynicism* (Oxford, Blackwell)

STOBBS, M. (1999) 'Discussion Forum: Should Lawyers Blow Whistles?' 2 *Legal Ethics* (forthcoming)

STRAUSS, M. (1987) 'Toward a Revised Model of Attorney-Client Relationships: The Argument for Autonomy' 65 *North Carolina Law Review* 315

STRETCH, C.K. (1995) 'Lawyer Regulation in the 1990s: Creating a system that is more open, accessible, responsive and responsible' *Bar Leader*, March/April p.21

SUBIN, H.I. (1985) 'The Lawyer as Superego: Disclosure of Client Confidences to Prevent Harm' 70 *Iowa Law Review* 1091

SUGARMAN, D. (1993) 'Simple Images and Complex Realities: English Lawyers and Their Relationship to Business and Politics, 1750–1950' 11 *Law & History Review* 257

—— (1996) 'Bourgeois collectivism, professional power and the boundaries of the state: The private and public life of the Law Society, 1825–1914' 3 *International Journal of the Legal Profession* 81

SUMMERS, R.S. (1982) 'The General Duty of Good Faith—Its Recognition and Conceptualization' 67 *Cornell Law Review* 810

SUSSKIND, R. (1996) *The Future of Law: Facing the Challenges of Information Technology* (Oxford, Clarendon Press)

SWEET, P. (1998) '*Pro Bono*—the Role of Trainee Solicitors' *The Trainee*, Autumn 1998, 11

SWIFT, D. (1996) *Proceedings Before the Solicitors' Disciplinary Tribunal* (London, The Law Society)

SZTOMPKA, P. (1998) 'Trust, Distrust and Two Paradoxes of Democracy' 1 *European Journal of Social Theory* 19

TAM, H. (1998) *Communitarianism: A New Agenda for Politics & Citizenship* (Basingstoke, Macmillan)

TAPPER, C. (1995) *Cross and Tapper on Evidence* (8th edn., London, Butterworths)

TEMKIN, J. (1993) 'Sexual History Evidence—The Ravishment of Section 2' *Criminal Law Review* 3

TESCHNER, P.A. (1970) 'Lawyer Morality' 38 *The George Washington Law Review* 789

THIBAUT, J. and WALKER, L. (1975) *Procedural Justice: A Psychological Analysis* (Hillsdale, NJ, Lawrence Erlbaum)

THOMAS, L. (1991) 'Morality and psychological development' in Singer (ed.)

THOMAS, P.A. (ed.) (1982) *Law in the Balance: Legal Services in the Eighties* (Oxford, Martin Robertson)

THOMAS, P.A. (1992) 'Thatcher's Will' in P.A. Thomas (ed.) *Tomorrow's Lawyers* (Oxford, Blackwell)

—— (1997) 'Introduction' in P.A. Thomas (ed.) *Socio-Legal Studies* (Aldershot, Dartmouth)

THOMASON, T. (1991) 'Are Attorneys Paid What They're Worth? Contingent Fees and the Settlement Process' XX *Journal of Legal Studies* 187

THOMPSON, E.P. (1975) *Whigs and Hunters: The Origins of the Black Act* (London, Allen Lane)

THORNBURG, E.G. (1993) 'Sanctifying Secrecy: The Mythology of the Corporate Attorney-Client Privilege' 69 *Notre Dame Law Review* 157

THORNTON, A. (1995) 'The Professional Responsibility and Ethics of the English Bar' in Cranston (ed.)

THORNTON, M. (1996) *Dissonance and Distrust* (Oxford, Oxford University Press)

—— (1998) 'Technocentrism in the Law School: Why the Gender and Colour of Law Remain the Same' 36 *Osgoode Hall Law Journal* 369

TMS CONSULTANTS (1992) *Without Prejudice? Sex Equality at the Bar and in the Judiciary* (Bournemouth, TMS)

TOMASIC, R. (1985) *The Sociology of Law* (London, Sage)

TOULMIN, J. (1991–92) 'A Worldwide Common Code of Professional Ethics' 15 *Fordham International Law Journal* 673

TRIBE, D. (1993) *Negotiation* (London, Cavendish Publishing)

TRONTO, J.C. (1993a) *Moral Boundaries: A Political Argument for an Ethic of Care* (London, Routledge)

—— (1993b) 'Beyond Gender Difference to a Theory of Care' in Larrabee (ed.)

TUR, R.H.S. (1992a) 'An Introduction to Lawyers' Ethics' 10 *Journal of Professional Legal Education* 217

—— (1992b) 'Confidentiality and Accountability' 1 *Griffith Law Review* 73

—— (1994) 'Accountability and Lawyers' in Chadwick (ed.)

—— (1995) 'Family Lawyering and Legal Ethics' in Parker and Sampford (eds.)

TWINING, W. (1988) 'Hot Air in the Redwoods: A Sequel to the Wind in the Willows' 86 *Michigan Law Review* 1523

—— (1994) *Blackstone's Tower: The English Law School* (London, Sweet & Maxwell)

UVILLER, R. (1973) 'The Virtuous Prosecutor in Quest of an Ethical Standard: Guidance from the ABA' 71 *Michigan Law Review* 1145

VAN HOY, J. (1997) *Franchise Law Firms and the Transformation of Personal Legal Services* (Westport, CT, Quorum Books)

VEATCH, R.M. (1972a) 'Medical Ethics: Professional or Universal?' 65 *Harvard Theological Review*

—— (1972b) 'Models for Ethical Medicine in a Revolutionary Age' *Hastings Center Report*, vol. 2, p.1, June 1972

VELJANOVSKI, C. (1991) 'The Regulation Game' in C. Veljanovski (ed.) *Regulators and the Market* (London, Institute of Economic Affairs)

WALKER, C. and STARMER, K. (1999) *Miscarriages of Justice* (London, Blackstones)

WALZER, M. (1973) 'Political Action: The Problem of Dirty Hands' 2 *Philosophy & Public Affairs* 160

—— (1987) *Interpretation and Social Criticism* (Cambridge, MA, Harvard University Press)

WANNER, C. (1975) 'The Public Ordering of Private Relations. Part Two: Winning Civil Court Cases' 9 *Law & Society Review* 293

WARD, A. (1985) 'Professional Responsibility when Dealing with Parental Irresponsibility' in Cranston (ed.)

WARNOCK, G.J. (1971) *The Object of Morality* (London, Methuen)

WARNOCK, M. (1970) *Existentialism* (Oxford: Oxford University Press)

WARREN, S. (1848) *The Moral, Social, and Professional Duties of Attornies and Solicitors* (Edinburgh and London, William Blackwood & Sons)

WASSERMAN, D. (1990) 'Should a Good Lawyer Do the Right Thing? David Luban on the Morality of Adversary Representation' 49 *Maryland Law Review* 392

WASSERSTROM, R. (1975) 'Lawyers as Professionals: Some Moral Issues' 5 *Human Rights* 1

—— (1983) 'Roles and Morality' in Luban (ed.)

WATERS, M. (1989) 'Collegiality, Bureaucratization and Professionalization: A Weberian Analysis' 94 *American Journal of Sociology* 945

—— (1995) *Globalization* (London, Routledge)

WATSON, A. 'The Lawyer as Counselor' (1965) 5 *Journal of Family Law* 7

WATKINS, J., DRURY, L., and PREDDY, D. (1993) *From Evolution to Revolution* (Bristol, University of Bristol)

WEBB, J. (1986) *Law Students and Legal Practice: The Socialization Effects of English Legal Education*, unpublished LLM thesis, University of Warwick

—— (1995) 'Where the action is: Developing artistry in legal education' 2 *International Journal of the Legal Profession* 187

—— (1996) 'Inventing the Good: A Prospectus for Clinical Education and the Teaching of Legal Ethics in England and Wales' 30 *Law Teacher* 270

—— (1998a) 'Ethics for Lawyers or Ethics for Citizens? New Directions for Legal Education' 25 *Journal of Law & Society* 134

—— (1998b) 'Conduct, Ethics and Experience in Vocational Legal Education: Opportunities Missed?' in Economides (ed.)

—— (1999) 'Post-Fordism and the Reformation of Liberal Legal Education' in F. Cownie (ed.) *The Law School: Global Issues, Local Questions* (Aldershot, Dartmouth)

WEBER, M. (1954) *Max Weber On Law and Economy*, M. Reinsten (ed.) (Cambridge, MA, Harvard University Press)

—— (1978) *Economy & Society* (Berkeley, University of California Press)

WEBLEY, L. (1998) *A Review of the Literature on Family Mediation* (London, Institute of Advanced Legal Studies)

—— (1999) *Trainee Solicitors' Group/Young Solicitors' Group Pro Bono Survey* (London, Institute of Advanced Legal Studies)

WEXLER, S. (1970) 'Practicing Law for Poor People' 79 *Yale Law Journal* 1049

WHEAT, K. (1998) 'Confidentiality and Public and Private Interests' 1 *Legal Ethics* 184

WHITE, D.R. and JENKS, P.R. (1991) *The Official Lawyer's Handbook* (London, Harriman House)

WHITE, J.J. (1980) 'Machiavelli and the Bar: Ethical Limitations on Lying in Negotiation' *American Bar Foundation Research Journal* 926

WIGMORE, J.H. (1961) *Evidence in Trials at Common Law* vol. 8 J.T. McNaughton (ed.) (Boston, Little Brown)

—— (1974) *Evidence in Trials at Common Law* vol. 5 J.H. Chadbourne (ed.) (Boston, Little Brown)

WILHELMSSON, T. (1993) 'Questions for A Critical Contract Law—and a Contradictory Answer: Contract as Social Cooperation' in T. Wilhelmsson (ed.) *Perspectives of Critical Contract Law* (Aldershot, Dartmouth)

WILKINS, D.B. (1990) 'Legal Realism for Lawyers' 104 *Harvard Law Review* 468

—— (1992) 'Who Should Regulate Lawyers?' 105 *Harvard Law Review* 799

WILLIAMS, B. (1972) *Morality: An Introduction to Ethics* (Cambridge, Cambridge University Press)

—— (1978) 'Politics and Moral Character' in S. Hampshire (ed.) *Public and Private Morality* (Cambridge, Cambridge University Press)

—— (1983) 'Professional Morality and its Dispositions' in Luban (ed.)

—— (1985) *Ethics and the Limits of Philosophy* (London, Fontana Press)

WILLIAMS, G. (1955) *The Proof of Guilt: A Study of the English Criminal Trial* Hamlyn Lectures, Seventh Series (London, Steven & Sons)

—— (1985) 'Letting off the Guilty and Prosecuting the Innocent' *Criminal Law Review* 115

WILLIAMS, T. (1996) *Dealing with Customer Complaints* (Aldershot, Gower)

WITZ, A. (1992) *Professions and Patriarchy* (London, Routledge)

WOLF, S. (1982) 'Moral Saints' 69 *Journal of Philosophy* 419

—— (1983) 'Ethics, Legal Ethics and the Ethics of Law' in Luban (ed.)

WOLFE, A. (1989) *Whose Keeper: Social Science and Moral Obligation* (Berkeley, University of California Press)

WOLFF, R.P. (1973) *The Autonomy of Reason* (New York, Harper & Row)

WOLFRAM, C.W. (1977) 'Client Perjury' 50 *Southern California Law Review* 811

—— (1978) 'Barriers to Effective Public Participation in Regulation of the Legal Profession' 62 *Minnesota Law Review* 619

—— (1983) 'A Lawyer's Duty to Represent Clients, Repugnant and Otherwise' in Luban (ed.)

—— (1986) *Modern Legal Ethics* (St Paul, MIN, West Publishing)

WONG, D. (1991) 'Relativism' in Singer (ed.)

WOOLF, LORD (1995) *Interim Report to the Lord Chancellor on the Reform of the Civil Justice System* (London, The Stationery Office)

—— (1996) *Access to Justice: Final Report* (London: The Stationery Office)

WOOLLEY, A. (1996) 'Integrity in Zealousness: Comparing the Standard Conceptions of the Canadian and American Lawyer' 1 *Canadian Journal of Law and Jurisprudence* 61

WORBOYS, P. (1985) 'Convicting the Right Person on the Right Evidence' *Criminal Law Review* 764

WORDEN, K.C. (1985) 'Overshooting the Target: A Feminist Deconstruction of Legal Education' 34 *American University Law Review* 1141.

WRIGHT, R.G. (1994–5) 'Cross-Examining Legal Ethics: The Roles of Intentions, Outcomes and Character' 83 *Kentucky Law Journal* 801

WYDICK, R.C. (1995) 'The Ethics of Witness Coaching' 17 *Cardozo Law Review* 1

YAMAGISHI, T. and YAMAGISHI, M. (1996) 'Trust and Commitment in the United States and Japan' 18 *Motivation & Emotion* 129

YARROW, S. (1997) *The Price of Success* (London, Policy Studies Institute)

ZACHARIAS, F.C. (1989) 'Rethinking Confidentiality' 74 *Iowa Law Review* 351

ZANDER, M. (1968) *Lawyers and the Public Interest* (London: Weidenfeld and Nicolson)

—— (1988) *A Matter of Justice: The Legal System in Ferment* (London, Tauris Publishing)

—— (1997) 'Rights of audience in the higher courts in England and Wales since the 1990 Act: what happened?' 4 *International Journal of the Legal Profession* 167

Index

Note: Where relevant, page references to the main discussion are indicated in **bold face**.